Modern Judaism

Modern Judaism

AN OXFORD GUIDE

Edited by

Nicholas de Lange
Miri Freud-Kandel

*This book has been printed digitally and produced in a standard specification
in order to ensure its continuing availability*

OXFORD
UNIVERSITY PRESS

Great Clarendon Street, Oxford OX2 6DP
Oxford University Press is a department of the University of Oxford.
It furthers the University's objective of excellence in research, scholarship,
and education by publishing worldwide in

Oxford New York

Auckland Cape Town Dar es Salaam Hong Kong Karachi
Kuala Lumpur Madrid Melbourne Mexico City Nairobi
New Delhi Shanghai Taipei Toronto
With offices in
Argentina Austria Brazil Chile Czech Republic France Greece
Guatemala Hungary Italy Japan South Korea Poland Portugal
Singapore Switzerland Thailand Turkey Ukraine Vietnam

Oxford is a registered trade mark of Oxford University Press
in the UK and in certain other countries

Published in the United States
by Oxford University Press Inc., New York

© Oxford University Press 2005

ISBN 978-0-19-926287-8

To my students past and present
N de L

To my teachers past and present, especially Jonathan
MF-K

Contents

Judaism and the other

List of contributors

Judith Baskin University of Oregon

Jonathan Cohen Hebrew Union College, Cincinnati

Eliezer Don-Yehiya Bar-Ilan University, Israel

Lois Dubin Smith College, Northampton, Massachusetts

Reuven Firestone Hebrew Union College, Los Angeles

Miri Freud-Kandel University of Oxford

Harvey Goldberg Indiana University

Susannah Heschel Dartmouth College, Hanover, New Hampshire

Elliot Horowitz Rutgers, The State University of New Jersey

Paula Hyman Yale University

Eran Kaplan University of Cincinnati

John Klier University College London

Ezra Kopelowitz The Jewish Agency, Jerusalem

Nicholas de Lange University of Cambridge

Ruth Langer Boston College

Yaakov Malkin Tel Aviv University

David Novak University College Toronto

Peter Ochs University of Virginia

Emanuele Ottolenghi University of Oxford

Robert Jan van Pelt University of Waterloo, Ontario

Uzi Rebhun Hebrew University of Jerusalem

Steven Resnicoff DePaul University College of Law, Chicago

Daniel Rynhold King's College London

Norbert Samuelson Arizona State University

Kenneth Seeskin Northwestern University, Illinois

Daniel Sinclair College of Management Academic Studies, Rishon Lezion, Tel Aviv

Mark Solomon Liberal Jewish Synagogue, London

Nurit Stadler Hebrew University of Jerusalem

Margie Tolstoy University of Cambridge

Jeremy Wanderer University of Cape Town

Chaim Waxman Rutgers, The State University of New Jersey

George R. Wilkes St Edmund's College, Cambridge

Michael Zank Boston University

General introduction

The editors

This book attempts to present the study of modern Judaism to students in its complexity and variety.

We have tried to be as complete as possible, within the constraints of space and of the development of study so far, and it is our hope that the book will not only serve as a helpful map of the subject but will widen students' horizons, indicating possible approaches to the study of Judaism of which they had not previously been aware.

Inevitably it has not proved possible to focus attention on every single aspect of the subject. We have been compelled to leave out certain areas to make room for others that we felt had greater claims to space. In general we have concentrated on approaches and subjects that have an established academic literature, although we have also tried to find room for some newer strands. On some levels our choices reflect the tendency in much modern scholarship and in particular in considerations of Judaism to prioritize certain voices that have achieved dominance. However we hope that, following trends in more recent scholarship, a growing acknowledgement of those voices that have been silenced has also been facilitated.

What is 'Judaism'?

We have not tried to define the term 'Judaism' too closely. Broadly, we understand it to be the religion of the Jewish people. But we recognize that this is not satisfactory as a definition. 'Religion' suggests a body of beliefs and practices. But beyond the most basic level of description, to limit our project in this way would have immediately raised problems. Who decides which beliefs and practices are authentically Jewish? The different religious movements of Judaism assume rival definitions and within each movement there is a great variety of individual practice: should individuals or movements dominate our approach? What kinds of beliefs and practices are eligible for inclusion? Does Zionism, for example, with its beliefs and its attendant public rituals, qualify as a form of Judaism? And in general, what place is there in a book on Judaism for the large sector of the Jewish public, perhaps the greater part, which rejects supernatural beliefs yet asserts a Jewish identity which may involve a strong sense of national purpose or continuity with the past? The nature of Jewish identity therefore becomes part of our story, as do the historic experiences of the Jewish people, and indeed the very concept of a Jewish people with its development of numerous opposing positions. It has been argued with some force that the idea of 'religion' cannot appropriately be applied to Judaism. (It is not an idea, for example, that can be easily expressed in pre-modern Hebrew.) So maybe the nature or natures of Judaism needs to be sought elsewhere.

We have tried to explore a diverse range of these issues within the chapters of the book, addressing such factors as the historical, sociological, theological, and gendered understandings of Judaism that have developed. These all contribute their own perspectives on the nature of Judaism which make it inappropriate, even if it were possible, to construct a single useful definition of the meaning of Judaism in the modern period.

What is 'modern Judaism'?

As for the term 'modern Judaism', this enfolds two main elements. The first is a temporal element. We accept the widespread use of the term 'modern' to indicate the period since the rise of the Enlightenment, an intellectual movement characterized by rationalism and a belief in human progress that gradually gained influence in Europe in the seventeenth and eighteenth centuries (in convenient Jewish terms, between Spinoza and Mendelssohn). For the Jews, Enlightenment is closely associated with two other developments, political emancipation and a social reintegration, which mark the emergence from the segregation of what we loosely call the ghetto, and a dramatically enhanced involvement in the currents of history, both political and intellectual. The second element in the term 'modern Judaism' indicates the encounter between the Jews and modernity in all its aspects.

Among the key issues in the study of modern Judaism are rationalism, social and political reform, and religious reform. Prominent figures include Moses Mendelssohn, Hermann Cohen, Franz Rosenzweig, and Martin Buber, all of whom wrote in German, and more recently English-language writers such as Mordecai Kaplan and Abraham Joshua Heschel. This is only a very partial list, of course, and many other names could be added in the area of religious thought. Some would also want to add writers from other domains, literary figures such as Franz Kafka or Isaac Bashevis Singer, historians of ideas such as Gershom Scholem or Leo Strauss, thinkers such as Walter Benjamin or Emmanuel Levinas, or indeed political writers such as Theodor Herzl and Ahad Ha'am.

Surveying this very partial list, we may be struck by certain common features (and even if the list were extended it would hardly alter this picture). All the distinguished and influential figures just enumerated were male, and with very few exceptions they were born in Central or Eastern Europe. This comment is not made in the interests of 'political correctness' alone. Writing about Judaism was for a long time in the hands of men of this type, and this had a determinative effect on the discourse of Judaism, on the world-view that shaped it, and on the directions in which it developed. Even if a few authors from outside the Ashkenazi milieu, such as the Italians Samuel David Luzzatto or Elia Benamozegh, with their greater attachment to tradition and reservations about the rationalist programme, were occasionally cited, the canon remained all-male.

In the past decades the picture has been gradually changing. A sexual revolution arising out of modernism has had its impact on Judaism, and feminism has changed the ethos of Jewish studies for ever. The presence of a small number of Jewish women thinkers and activists, such as Lily Montagu and Henrietta Szold, has been identified, even though their contributions have only recently attracted serious attention. The importance of women's roles in facilitating acculturation and assimilation (and indeed receiving the blame for failing to construct Jewish homes that nurtured Jewish identity) is also beginning to be acknowledged and examined for its implications. The need for a gendered critique of received understandings of Judaism has emerged. An analysis of Jewish history, received traditions, beliefs, and practices has made explicit what was always clear: women's voices have been marginalized and silenced throughout Judaism's development so that much of what is termed Judaism is in fact merely a male construct. As Judith Plaskow noted in her seminal work *Standing Again At Sinai*, Judaism presents history read as 'his story'. Following the impact of feminism, modern Judaism has experienced numerous changes affecting all those who identify with Judaism in manifold ways: from religious reform to the rewriting of feminist midrash; from Zionist constructions of female models to post-Zionist critiques of female suppression by Zionism; from Orthodox apologetics defending a Jewish tradition of women as 'equal but different' to re-imagings of Judaism that introduce goddess models. Both gender and sexuality provide new tools by which a multitude of received conceptions of Judaism are now being reassessed. The long-term effects on Judaism of these rereadings remain unclear, beyond the recognition that they are radically altering most Jewish preconceptions.

Whilst feminism has led to a critique of gendered understandings of Judaism, postmodernism and historiographical revisionism have also helped cultivate the sense that attempts to construct traditionalist readings of Judaism are often misplaced and problematic. On one level, modern Jewish historiography suggested that the received notions of Jewish history needed to be questioned and rewritten in the light of new insights, experiences, and self-perceptions brought about by modern developments such as Enlightenment and emancipation, or Zionist thought. An additional level of more recent historiographical work questions the agenda that drove the earlier modern historiographers. The very notion of objective historical truth has come to be questioned. The narratives produced by the earlier historiographers have now become subject to critique, as they are perceived to have been propelled by an array of domineering motifs current in modern thought which privileged certain voices whilst silencing others that were present. Consequently, far greater diversity has been introduced into the study of Judaism, and countless established orthodoxies have been challenged.

This turn to introspection, with its focus on those who appear underprivileged and its rejection of narratives focusing upon elites, is a product of a growing sense of the normalization of the Jewish experience. As Jewish scholars have come to feel more comfortable in their social, cultural, and intellectual milieus, they have demonstrated a greater willingness to be critical of Judaism. This process of normalization is a product of postmodernism, which questions old certainties and encourages a growing tolerance of difference.

Earlier accounts of Jewish history and ideas were dominated by a distinctly Eurocentric outlook: narratives focused exclusively on developments in eastern and western European Jewries and their offshoots in North America, the Land of Israel, and elsewhere. The influence of this slanted outlook can still be felt, but it is increasingly being realized that it is only a part of the story. While European Jewries were facing up to modernity in their own way, the Jewries of North Africa and the Middle East were undergoing an analogous process, but the results were markedly different. In particular, often there was far less of a radical break with Jewish tradition, and less willingness to throw religious values out of the window. In Muslim countries the underlying issues of emancipation were quite different from those operating in countries of Christian culture, and indeed the whole basis for relations between Jews and non-Jews was entirely different. In post-war France, Jews of North African origin have radically altered ways of writing about Judaism. In Israel too, where academic life has been dominated by Ashkenazim and where political factors intervened to buttress the Eurocentric narrative, signs are emerging of a greater openness to alternative versions of the Jewish historical experience and of Jewish responses to modernity.

The Nazi genocide (which mainly affected European, and specifically Ashkenazi, Jewry) was a trauma that encouraged postmodern approaches. It undermined accepted values and challenged widespread suppositions about the process of political emancipation and social reintegration. Gone were the old certainties, about religion as well as society. And with a rethinking of the Enlightenment programme, with its faith in universal values, came a re-evaluation of the particularistic elements in Judaism.

As the certainties of modernity have been threatened, those sectors of Judaism that rejected its values from the outset have been strengthened. One of the key features of contemporary Judaism has been the strengthening of Orthodox groups within Judaism, which had appeared most under threat in Jews' encounter with modernity. In this sense too, then, the presumed shape of modern Judaism can be questioned. However, in this sphere the celebration of certain dominant traditional narratives has been crucial in attempts to address the anomie engendered by modernism and inculcate new Orthodox responses that purport to be traditionalist.

Terminological precision

As any student will quickly have noted, the study of modern Judaism is beset by terminological difficulties. Such terms as Orthodoxy, Traditional, Reform, Liberal, Progressive, Sephardi, and Mizrahi have different connotations in different settings. In some cases these differences reflect local issues. They may also reflect theological issues, historiographical concerns, and sociological problems.

Orthodoxy, for example, is sometimes used as shorthand for Modern Orthodoxy and at other times it is used to embrace both Modern Orthodoxy and all other forms of traditionalist Judaism. The term Tradition may refer to an unselfconscious preservation of received values and practices, or it may refer to a more self-conscious pursuit of such elements, whether genuinely traditional or retrieved and applied with new vigour. Reform, Liberal, and Progressive are sometimes used interchangeably, but each can have a more specific meaning. For example, in Britain Reform and Liberal refer to two different religious movements, the latter more radical than the former, and historically the term Progressive has been adopted by some Liberal synagogues. In America, by contrast, at an institutional level only the label Reform is generally used, while in continental Europe the label Liberal is preferred. At the same time, it is common to refer to all non-Orthodox religious Judaism as 'progressive'. The term Sephardi has at least two meanings. The term properly refers to Jews whose origins are considered to be in the Iberian peninsula and identifies the prayer rite of these Jews. In Britain and America traditionally such Sephardi synagogues have also used the label Spanish and Portuguese. In Israel a different usage grew up in which the term Sephardi designated all non-Ashkenazi Jews, including such communities as the Georgian, Persian, or Adeni Jews, who historically have no Iberian roots. With the migration of Jews from Muslim countries to Europe and America, the original definition has somewhat broken down. The term Mizrahi (meaning 'oriental') is used in Israel interchangeably with Sephardi in the second sense. However, this term (in this sense usually written Mizrachi) is also used to refer to religious Zionists. In this book, while not imposing strict terminological precision on the various authors, we have generally tried to avoid ambiguity.

The structure of the book

The book begins with an exposition of the present state of the Jews in the world: their geographical distributions with its recent and present changes, as well as a demographic analysis and projections for the future. This section is placed first as it provides an introduction to the concrete subject-matter of the book, namely the Jewish people, and underlines the priority of people over ideas which is inherent in most definitions of Judaism.

Following on this essentially contemporary beginning, the next section engages with the impact of the past on the present. This is encompassed in four separate chapters focusing on very different areas. The first is the essentially intellectual impact of the Enlightenment, which has practical repercussions in terms of religious reforms and political emancipation, explored further in later chapters. Chapter 3 tackles the theme of the isolation and victimization of Jews in the modern world, focusing particularly but not exclusively on the Nazi genocide and its impact today. Chapter 4 looks at the consequences of the creation of a Jewish state. This narrative of intellectual awakening and integration—persecution and rejection—independence and homecoming, in which the State of Israel serves as the culmination of the Enlightenment and a counterpoint or even remedy to the pogroms and Shoah, under- lies many if not most presentations of contemporary Jewish history. It is now begin- ning to be challenged by some historians, both in its broad outlines and in its details. By way of example of this new trend, Chapter 5 looks at the Israeli 'revisionist historians' who have challenged the accepted story of the achievement of the Zionist dream.

The encounter between Judaism and modernity provoked a range of responses, from a reactionary traditionalism that turned its back on the modern world to a Jewish secularism that preserved a sense of Jewish particularism while rejecting all religious beliefs. (We are not concerned here with the most extreme forms of assimilation, that abandoned Jewish particularism in its entirety or favoured conversion to the dominant faith.) Chapters 6 to 9 focus on four classes of response. Chapter 6 surveys the middle ground, mapping a variety of formulae that attempted to combine the best values of Jewish tradition with the best the modern world had to offer. Chapter 7 looks at attempts to cling more closely to Jewish tradition, combined with a radically critical stance towards modernity and a willingness to forgo its opportunities. Chapter 8 considers efforts to build a Jewish identity free from what are seen as the irrational, outdated, and obscurantist elements of religious pietism and supernatural beliefs. Chapter 9 considers some more recent shifts that have emerged in Jewish attempts to construct a religious response to modernity and particularly postmodernity. This has introduced often innovative interpretative approaches in the attempt to invest Judaism with contemporary meaning.

One issue that emerges clearly from the section on Issues of Religion and Modernity is that of pluralism, which is such a marked characteristic of Judaism today. Whereas in the middle ages and the early modern period it was possible, indeed relatively common, to invoke the language of 'heresy', and the ban (*herem*) was pronounced on individuals and groups that refused to conform to the dominant mode of Jewish belief or practice, nowadays such language is rarely heard, and pluralism is not only something that is remarked on by sociologists but is accepted by most Jews as a fact of life. The label 'Jewish' is available for any person or group wishing to lay claim to it: there is no universally acknowledged way of 'being Jewish'. Ultimately, what counts is membership of the 'Jewish people', rather than fidelity to any particular creed or praxis. This extends to the recognition that a Jew does not need to believe anything in particular: the rejection of supernatural religious beliefs, a logical outcome of the Enlightenment, is seen by many not as an abandonment of Judaism but as a legitimate form of Jewish self-expression.

The next section, on Local Issues, examines a different kind of pluralism: the geographical, political, and cultural diversity that is a prominent feature of Judaism today. Five major regions of the Jewish world are examined separately, in terms of their recent history, social and political status, local problems, and religious and cultural issues. The five different areas selected differ enormously, not only in relative size (the United States and Israel between them account for some 80 per cent of world Jewry, as explained in Chapter 1), but also in terms of their history, political situation, and culture, including such factors as language and religious tendencies. Other countries and regions might have been included, had space allowed, and this would have permitted us to illustrate other varieties of Jewish experience, such as the religious traditionalism of some of the communities in North Africa and the Caucasus. Broadly speaking, however, most types of Jewish culture and most forms of engagement with the wider society are represented here.

American Jewry is most clearly characterized by religious pluralism: no one religious denomination is dominant, and there has been historically a high level of interaction and co-operation between the different groupings. Like many other Jewish communities of the Americas and the English-speaking world this is a largely immigrant community, not so much in consisting of recent immigrants as in preserving a strong consciousness of its immigrant roots. Few American Jews can trace their American roots back beyond the early 1880s, and hardly any beyond Independence into the colonial period. Yet this is not in itself something that marks Jews out from many other Americans. A strong level of attachment to religious communities is another factor that unites American Jews with American non-Jews. The origins of American Jewry lie in every part of the Jewish world, but Eastern and, to a lesser but significant extent, Central Europe predominate, both numerically and in every other way that counts; so much so that the most widespread image of American Judaism combines Polish and American elements in a distinctive way. To acknowledge a different origin (to be an Iraqi, Syrian, or Greek American Jew, for example) is to carry an additional label that indicates a minority of a minority. Religious freedom has been proudly enshrined in the American Constitution since the early days of the state, and theoretically every office of state could be held by a Jew, although reality lags behind theory in this respect. This experience of separation between religion and state has had a marked impact on the development of American Jewry in numerous ways. Amongst other factors, it has also influenced the manner in which, in a society deeply divided and stratified, the Jews have succeeded in integrating and have generally come to be considered to belong to the higher strata, so that active discrimination appears to be a thing of the past.

Israeli Jewry is unique in many ways, not least because Jews constitute a large majority of the population of the country and enjoy considerable advantages under the unwritten constitution. Although nominally a secular democratic state, Israel also identifies itself as a 'Jewish state'; Jewish observances are woven into the fabric of the life of the state, and rabbinic courts and religious councils are part of the administration. Israel is the only democracy today where Jewish political parties regularly win seats in the parliament. And although, like American Jewry, Israeli Jewry is predominantly an immigrant society, there has been an uninterrupted Jewish presence in the Land of Israel since ancient times, as archaeological discoveries are constantly reminding the public. At the same time, it is a society that is torn apart by rivalries and antagonisms of an ethnic and religious nature, in a way that cannot be paralleled anywhere else in the Jewish world. While religion is strong and visible in Israel, in few if any other Jewries does Jewish religion evince the same depth of public indifference and in some circles even loathing and contempt. For various reasons, Conservative and Reform Judaism have established themselves only slowly and against concerted opposition. Segregated schooling for Jews and non-Jews (at least de facto) in the public sector and the existence of a strong private religious educational sector contribute, along with exclusion of most non-Jews from the army, and the delegation of areas such as marriage and burial to the religious authorities, to the maintenance of a high degree of separation between the Jewish and non-Jewish populations, and even divide Jew from Jew. Such is the background to the study of Israeli Jewry.

In some respects American and Israeli Jewries are competing with one another for ultimate authority in determining the future shape of Judaism. As is highlighted in Chapter 16, Jews in both countries are subject to rather different influences and experiences that affect the positions adopted by individuals and movements in each locale. Beyond their demographic significance, both are central to Jewish development in their different ways in terms of their intellectual output.

France represents a totally different model: staunchly secular and republican, yet guaranteeing equal rights for all citizens. The Jewish community, like other religious groups, is formally regulated by the state, under a system set up in the early nineteenth century. But French Jewry is also deeply marked by the memory of the Second World War and the deportations, by the colonial past and the decolonization of the 1950s and 1960s, and by relatively high levels of anti-Jewish prejudice in some sectors of the population. Immigration from Algeria, Tunisia, and Morocco compensated somewhat, both numerically and in terms of the dynamism of the community, for the losses of the war, and changed the ethnic character of the community dramatically. Mainly Orthodox in character, the community has a visible Sephardi–Ashkenazi divide. Liberal Judaism is very small and divided. The assimilationism of French Jewry began to be challenged in the years following the 1967 war in the Middle East by more assertive attitudes, as described in Chapter 9.

Interest in the study of British Jewry has grown as its importance in providing an alternative model of Jewish accommodation to modernity has become apparent. More recent historiographical work has emphasized the value of examining the less theologically driven, more individual adaptations adopted by British Jews in their attempts to fit into their host society and shape their Judaism and Jewish identities to the new opportunities encountered. British Jewry, largely unscathed by the Second World War, exists within a state that recognizes established churches, and where the highest office is reserved for an Anglican. Nevertheless, the ethos of Britain is tolerant, and anti-Judaism rarely takes concrete form. Britain, like France, has an imperial past which has left its mark on the Jewish community, and one may come across Jews from Gibraltar, Aden, India, South Africa, or Jamaica; but by far the largest sector, as in the United States, consists of immigrants from Eastern and Central Europe. In terms of religion, British Jewry is among the most pluralistic in the world, although the ethos created by an established church leads to attempts to mask this pluralism in communal representation.

The countries of the former Soviet Union have emerged from a long period of totalitarian rule that was hostile to all religion and where antisemitism was not unknown. The institutions of Jewish communal life are being developed rapidly, and the picture is not entirely clear, with rival religious denominations competing for power and influence. Among the areas selected for study here, this is the one that has experienced the most emigration (a feature of life in very many countries of the Jewish world in the twentieth century). Politically, socially, and culturally the situation is still fluid, and it is not easy to foresee future developments.

The seven sections which follow revolve around the multitude of different academic approaches taken in the study of Judaism in its various shapes. They reveal the multi-disciplinary character of Jewish studies and the richness and diversity that result from it. In most cases the section begins with a survey explaining the distinctive features of the approach in question, with specific reference to recent advances and some comments on current and likely future developments. The subsequent chapters in each section address specific concerns at the heart of the issues under consideration.

Social studies have come to occupy an important place within Jewish studies, with good reason. Since Judaism is not exclusively the name of a religion, social scientists study not only those aspects that might be expected to fall within sociology or anthropology of religion, but a much wider range of aspects concerned with Jewish life as a whole. This is well illustrated in the chapter on Jewish demography that opens the book.

Social studies, by concentrating on individual practice, draw attention to the difficulties of overemphasizing a top-down approach to the study of modern Judaism. In practice, Jews construct particular methodologies that may often appear inconsistent, both internally, in terms of how choices are made between particular rituals, and externally, with regard to the norms laid down for different groups of Jews by certain religious movements. Chapter 16 highlights one aspect of the choices made by individual Jews in their attempts to construct a sustainable form of Jewish identity. Generally within sociological studies it is helpful to examine the theory through reference to particular groups or individuals. Jewish identity is certainly a topic that is difficult to consider in the abstract, so this chapter focuses on the contrasts that can be identified between Israeli and American forms of Jewish identity. The experiences of Jews in these two locales differ significantly, and generally highlight the impact of geography, with its associated national features, on the development of diverse senses of how to identify as a Jew.

The religious pluralism that has emerged as a feature of modern Judaism provides one motivating factor in the development of Jewish forms of fundamentalism, which seek to preserve a single definition of how to be a 'good' Jew. As a growing phenomenon of modern Judaism this topic provides the next area of focus in the section on Social Issues. It is considered in Chapter 17 through an examination of some of the most common forms of so-called Jewish fundamentalist groups that have emerged.

We have not included a general survey of the history of religions approaches to the study of Judaism, because so much of this material is addressed elsewhere in the book. Instead, we have taken three specific topics that could not be discussed in other sections. Prayer and worship are central to religious life, in Judaism as in other religions. Both the form and the content of Jewish worship have changed considerably since the early nineteenth century, when Enlightenment values and the emancipation movement began to impinge visibly on Jewish life. The different approaches taken to these changes reflect the plethora of concerns that have emerged in modern Judaism.

One aspect of changes to prayer and worship, a factor that has often influenced the scope of liturgical reform, has been the changing attitudes that have emerged regarding the authority of texts in Judaism. This topic is considered in Chapter 19. There is a certain overlap, as is often the case, given the multidisciplinary nature of Jewish studies, between the subjects covered in the section on Social Issues and those addressed in the section on Religious Issues. Amongst certain fundamentalist groups the new emphasis on texts—their study, and their strict interpretation—has underpinned the shift towards more sectarian religious positions, which seek to reject the scope for Jewish pluralism. The introduction of far more stringent textual interpretation has contributed to the growing schism within Judaism between certain Orthodox sectors and other Jews predicated on the assertion of the unquestioned divine authority of texts. More generally, it has been the turn to texts and a consideration of their authority to direct Jewish action that has driven the development of all sectors of modern Judaism. Indeed, a more recent broadening of the Jewish bookshelf points to the burgeoning of non-religious forms of Jewish identity.

To some extent the following chapter develops this theme, considering the manner in which Jewish practice is shifting to reflect changing sensibilities. Research in this field revolves around both a practical and theoretical perspective, but it is the latter which is emphasized in Chapter 20 to present more clearly the ideas that underpin differing approaches to Jewish practice.

One of the most striking developments in Judaism since the Enlightenment has been the renewal of Jewish theology. In large part this has flowed from two factors, the opening up of a debate with Christianity and the emergence of a range of modernist denominations. Theology is central to Christianity in a way it is not for Judaism, which is a less credally oriented religion. To be a Christian is to assent, however tacitly, to a creed or set of beliefs. Different Christian denominations have slightly different creeds; and the merest credal difference can give rise to enormous theological debates. It is hard for Jews, in discussing religion with Christians, to avoid engaging in theological debate. Equally, when different Jewish denominations confront each other, theological differences tend to come to the fore. Modern Orthodoxy, for example, developed a strong theology of revelation in the course of its self-definition vis-à-vis Progressive Judaism. Much of the debate between Judaism and Christianity, since the time of the Christian apostle (of Jewish birth) Paul, has revolved around the theology of covenant. But theology of covenant is also nourished by the emancipation movement, with its debates about Jewish particularism and universalism. These concerns have functioned on both an internal and external level: regarding relations between Jews, and relations between Jews and others. The rise of modern Jewish pluralism raises questions regarding how to define the members of a covenanted people. Various thinkers, approaching the topic from differing positions, have constructed conflicting responses to such questions. The experience of persecution, followed by a postmodernist consciousness, has introduced additional considerations. The attempt to identify suitable models for covenantal understandings has inspired alternative readings of a number of Jewish traditions. These have developed to address the concerns presented to Jews as individuals, as members of religious groups, and in response to a range of external experiences. As the issue of who is to be counted within definitions of the 'Jewish people' becomes ever more pressing, the development of ideas in this area has acquired greater relevance.

Beyond questions of covenant, the rationalism of the Enlightenment issues a radical challenge to classical conceptions of God, a challenge that is taken up in the non-supernaturalist thought of Mordecai Kaplan, the founder of Reconstructionism, and more radically in secular Jewish humanism. The denial of the very existence of God makes it increasingly difficult to speak of theology, and much of this debate is easier to categorize as philosophical. The greatest challenge to classical Jewish theology in recent times—one which subsumes the elements just mentioned—is raised by the Nazi genocide, and here too the categories of philosophy are often more relevant. Many discussions of 'Holocaust theology', for example, focus on theodicy, which is concerned with the philosophical question: 'How can a god by definition all-knowing and perfectly good permit evil to happen?'

A wide range of material has been produced by Jewish thinkers from diverse perspectives that attempts to address the questions raised for Judaism by the problem of evil encountered in the Shoah. A number of these are considered in Chapter 25. This field now represents a major area of modern Jewish thought, which some have suggested has come to over-dominate Jewish attention. The focus on Jewish oppression is seen to have implications that impose certain limitations on the development of Jewish thought. At times the positions that have been developed appear not to fit into either theological or philosophical categories, as strictly defined. They focus on methodologies that may enable Jews to continue identifying with their faith without overemphasizing the why. However, in other cases they emphasize both the philosophical and theological difficulties that arise from consideration of the problem of evil: questions about the nature of God inevitably throw up additional questions about the nature of the Jews' relationship with their God.

A strong vein of modern Jewish religious thought concentrates on interpersonal relationships. This is particularly true of Martin Buber, whose famous book *I and You* portrays an intense relation between two human beings, each wholly open to the other, and uses this as the jumping-off point for a theology of relation, in which God is the 'Eternal You'. It is a relatively short step from this to the standpoint of Emmanuel Levinas, for whom an unconditional sense of responsibility to the other is the ground of all ethical behaviour. For Levinas as for Buber, ethics has replaced law as the central category of Jewish life in society. Not all Jewish thinkers have accepted this move: the inherent debate is discussed, with other aspects of ethical theory, in Chapter 26.

The relationship between ethics and halakhah is only one of a plethora of issues that modern Judaism has raised for consideration in the area of halakhah. Other modern halakhic issues include questions that fall under the heading of gender studies, or relate to ethical concerns, such as business or medical ethics. In the light of religious pluralism and arguments in favour of greater or lesser adaptation of halakhah from different sectors within Judaism, approaches to halakhic innovation reflect a number of the diverse currents that function across Judaism. Some of these are considered in the section on Halakhic Issues, highlighting the innovations, the stonewalling to reject the scope for change, and the often complex manoeuvres that characterize this field. The question of the appropriate relationship between halakhah and the State of Israel is one central area of debate and study. The extent to which halakhah can or should function within a democracy has attracted a broad cross-section of opinions. As the very question of the desirability and feasibility of maintaining Israel as a Jewish state has come into question, the role of halakhic influence has become a matter of further scrutiny. As in many other sections of the volume, the issues which emerge in this area highlight the conflict that is thrown up by the encounter between Judaism and the values of new ages with different conceptions of authority, autonomy, and relativism.

Certain halakhic considerations are examined further in the subsequent section on Gender Issues. Halakhic adaptation has provided one focus for Jewish feminists attempting to redress gender imbalance in Judaism and to address concerns regarding sexuality. However, it is clear that an examination of modern Judaism under the terms of gender studies extends far beyond these boundaries. The work of Jewish feminists often began by concentrating on efforts to compensate for women's traditional marginalization within Judaism, seeking halakhic and other reforms that could enable women to participate in traditionally all-male domains. As gender studies have developed subsequent research has tended to be more generally critical, noting that the equalizing of male and female roles fails to tackle far more integral problems that can be identified in all the various stages of Judaism's development. A broad range of issues has therefore fallen under the scrutiny of scholars in this field as the implications of new research becomes clearer. Alongside a new awareness of the historical and social influences in the development of Judaism, which have often underpinned the feminists' calls for reform, new work on male constructions within Judaism is also emerging.

The final section of the book addresses the question of the 'religious other': how do Jews interact with Christians and Muslims? By way of introduction, Chapter 33 investigates the portrait of Jews that is found in the writings of English-language travellers. This survey illuminates the issue of the otherness of the Jew, but it also draws attention to some of the common ground that unites Christians and Jews, and exemplifies the sometimes exaggerated sympathy or attraction that the deeply alien figure of the Jew could sometimes arouse in Christian observers.

The plain fact is that Christians cannot be simply indifferent or neutral towards Jews, as they can be towards, say, Tibetans. Attitudes to the Jews are inscribed within the New Testament Scriptures, the writings of the Church Fathers, and the words of traditional Christian liturgies. These texts were forged in a time of competition and intense rivalry, and the attitudes they convey are generally far from favourable. Since the Enlightenment Jews and Christians have had to begin to learn to live side by side and tolerate, if not respect, one another. For a long time progress was slow, but the Nazi genocide delivered an electric shock to the system, and since the Second World War concerted efforts have been made to attenuate the harmful effects of centuries of Christian prejudice, and to build better relations. In the process, scholars have reconsidered the history of Jewish–Christian relations, and have begun to paint a more nuanced picture of the past.

The same is broadly true of Jewish–Muslim relations, but progress has been even slower. As Chapter 35 shows, a careful and historically contextualized reading of the Qur'an and traditional Muslim texts can dispel some of the commonly held misconceptions about Muslim attitudes to Jews and Judaism.

Where now?

While we have tried to be as inclusive as possible in covering different approaches to the study of Judaism, at the time of writing it was clear that new trends are emerging, which could not be treated adequately either because as yet too little work has been published or because they have not yet been sufficiently integrated into the academic study of Judaism.

Psychology of religion is one area to which we felt we could not do justice in the context of Judaism, but the foundations are being laid in this area for promising future work. Attempts to make generalizations about Jewish practice have also been avoided in recognition of the broad range of observances individual Jews adopt. Moreover, many handbooks are available detailing the diverse approaches taken to religious practice by different sectors of modern Judaism. Cultural studies are concerned both with questions of defining what is Jewish about various artistic manifestations (whether literary or visual), and with ways in which the Jewish communities are harnessing the arts in the service of aims such as proclaiming and perpetuating Jewish identity, or, at another level, commemorating the victims of the Holocaust. The problem here was not so much a paucity of material (rather the contrary), as a difficulty in mapping the new approaches on the established terrain of Jewish studies.

The idea that Jewish studies has a central core of material which all students must study has been eroded by new approaches. Dominant narratives have been questioned, and emphasis on gender-, culture-, or ethnicity-based approaches has highlighted the diversities of the subject. Within the space of twenty or thirty years the field has developed enormously to reflect changing currents within the academic world and amongst Jews. These new and often exciting approaches, which will no doubt transform Jewish studies in the years to come, have been prominent in our thoughts as we have prepared this volume. Although there may not be one simple definition of modern Judaism, our hope is that this book will help students to appreciate and bring together the many strands encompassed within this subject.

1 | Demographic issues

Uzi Rebhun

The conceptual framework

Jews are variously defined as a community, a religious or ethnic group, a nation, or a people. Each of these definitions reflects an important, but incomplete, aspect of Jewish historical existence. A more comprehensive approach might see the most appropriate way of understanding the maintenance of Jewish continuity, despite periods of devastation, exile, and return, and in the light of fundamental changes in lifestyles and religious orientations, in terms of 'civilization'.[1]

Jewish identity may be differently conceived by people from outside the group (objective identity) and by the consciousness of the members of the group from within (subjective identity). Jewish populations consist of people who can be identified by detailed criteria of inclusion or exclusion, reflecting various perceptions of group boundaries and identity and a recognizable social composition. In the middle ages both Jewish law (halakhah) and non-Jewish law provided clear and universally accepted limits. In the modern period these limits have broken down, and many different patterns of Jewish collective life have been developed. More than ever before, we witness today an abundance of frameworks and components of cultural identity which draw from local Jewish experience as well as the influence of the host environment. Globalization has strengthened, rather than weakened, ethnic identities and organizations. With the establishment of the State of Israel a new dimension has been added: that of a sovereign majority Jewish society. While there may be differences, often substantial, in the social and economic structures of the various Jewish sub-populations, there are still many behavioural characteristics and interests shared by most, if not all, Jewish communities.

Demography, or population studies, provides an array of concepts and techniques for measuring individual and collective behaviour related to population change, and the compilation and analysis of demographic data have been gaining importance in religious research. Demographic changes do not operate in a vacuum, but may be the cause or the outcome of historical processes and social and cultural experiences. Jews, like any other group, have unique demographic behavioural patterns which eventually determine the reproduction and continuity of the group.[2]

The demography of the Jews, or Jewish demography, is the specialized study of the characteristics and trends of Jewish populations. As part of the wider discipline, it employs accepted methods of data collection, analyses the same types of variables, and uses the same measures, but in relation to the Jewish population. Even when the study of Jewish population extends, as often happens, beyond the narrow definition of demography (size, distribution, composition, and development) and includes specific social and even ethnic, religious, and cultural affinities of group belonging, the data are analysed by methods common to the general scientific research.

The fundamental basis of Jewish demography, as of population in general, is the size and behaviour of the components of change. According to this method, which connects biological and social elements, the Jewish population in a given place and time is the same population at an earlier time, with the addition of socio-demographic events that have occurred during the time-interval in question, including the balance between the number of births and deaths (natural movement), and that between immigration to the area and emigration away from it (net migration). In the case of a sub-group such as the Jews, defined by certain normative criteria, an additional factor must be taken into account: the balance between accession (whether through formal conversion to Judaism or not) and secession. Of these three components of change, natural movement and identificational changes affect the size of the Jewish population at both the local and the worldwide level, while net migration in a given area does not affect the size of the total world Jewish population. Nevertheless, indirectly, insofar as migrants adapt their behaviour patterns to those of the host society, it will have an affect on the overall size of the Jewish population.

Each of these factors of change in turn affects the composition and characteristics of the Jewish population: age, gender, generational status, and length of residence in the locality. The composition of the population also includes social and economic characteristics such as family status, level of education, and occupation. Attention must also be paid to patterns of ethno-religious identification. Changes in the composition of the Jewish population in terms of socio-economic and cultural characteristics may influence the likelihood of demographic events eventually affecting the size of the Jewish population.

Development of research sources in the modern period

The earliest sources of demographic data on Jews in the modern period, on the institutional level, are closely connected to official governmental population studies.[3] Most Jews were living in countries, primarily in Eastern and Central Europe, in which vital statistics as well as data on migration were gathered, in addition to population censuses. These sources included a question on religious affiliation. In France, England, the United States, and other countries such as those of Latin America, in which official statistics were forbidden to inquire into matters of religion, Jewish researchers sometimes employed indirect methods, whose degree of accuracy was problematic, such as the number of children who were absent from school on Yom Kippur, mother tongue (Yiddish), or country of birth, in cases where Jews constituted the principal group of immigrants from a particular country. Jewish communities often maintained registers of demographic events, which later constituted the infrastructure for activity concerned exclusively with Jewish statistics.

An established framework of independent Jewish statistics began to develop at the beginning of the twentieth century, expressing an intellectual interest in the social and cultural world of the Jews. A not-inconsiderable stimulus to this was the desire of Jews to respond to negative images fashioned using terms from the social sciences. In 1902 Alfred Nossig in Berlin established the Verein für jüdische Statistik (Organization for Jewish Statistics), whose purpose was to gather information about the state of European Jewry. Two years later this became the Bureau für Demographie und Statistik der Juden (Bureau of Jewish Statistics), headed by Arthur Ruppin, which also published a periodical. During the next two decades bureaus and institutes of Jewish statistics were established in other places in Central and Eastern Europe, all having a strong connection with the bureau in Berlin.

Perhaps the most important of these was the Yiddish Scientific Institute (YIVO), whose main office was in Vilnius, but which had branches in other places, including New York. One of its four main sections of research was economics and statistics of the Jews (headed by Jacob Lestschinsky). In 1914, with the direct assistance of the bureau in Berlin, the American Jewish Committee established a statistical bureau, which later merged with the departments of research and statistics of other Jewish national groups, and was responsible for the publication of an annual report on the world's Jewish population in the *American Jewish Year Book*.

Study of the demographic situation of Palestinian Jewry during the second half of the nineteenth and the beginning of the twentieth centuries was made possible, with varying degrees of completeness, by five censuses of Jews conducted on the initiative of Moses Montefiore, two Ottoman population censuses, and one conducted by the Palestine Zionist Office of the World Zionist Organization during the First World War. During the period of the British Mandate the Jewish Agency for Palestine established a Department of Statistics that gathered annual data on the size of the Jewish population and conducted several censuses. More comprehensive was the statistical infrastructure of the mandatory government.

The bureau in Berlin, along with its periodical, ceased to exist in 1931. In the late 1930s and early 1940s all the Jewish social research institutes in continental Europe were closed. The Second World War destroyed the entire infrastructure for social science research of European Jewry.

The major development in Jewish social science research during the second half of the twentieth century took place with the establishment by the State of Israel of a governmental apparatus for the systematic collection of demographic data. In the United States many Jewish communities have conducted surveys of their populations, and the umbrella organization of Jewish federations has conducted three nationwide demographic surveys. Other Jewish communities across the globe also periodically collect demographic data; and some gather information on an ongoing basis. General population censuses conducted in a number of countries provide a basis for updating Jewish demographic characteristics.

Many Jewish communities sponsor the gathering of data. These surveys, based on a sample of the Jewish population, are of variable reliability and quality, in relation to the sampling techniques employed. For example, data based on lists of Jews who are members of synagogues or Jewish organizations are biased towards those who identify as Jews and have strong ties to organized Jewish activity. Another technique, based on searching telephone directories or other directories of inhabitants of a given place for family names which are usually Jewish, involves a danger of removing entire family units from the margins of Jewish identity because for one reason or another they do not have a Jewish surname. Random dialling of telephone numbers within a given research area, while it greatly increases the cost of the research, provides an unbiased and representative sample of different kinds of Jews, including those with both strong and weak group commitment, and thereby the reliability of the data is increased.

The boundaries of the collective

A preliminary task of Jewish demographic research is to determine who is a Jew. This task is made more difficult by the ambiguity of Jewishness, that is viewed as both religion and ethnicity, as well as by the distinctive geographical dispersion and social stratification of Jews. The successful acculturation and integration of Jews into the societies within which they live, frequently characterized by the voluntary and pluralistic nature of religious affiliation, not anchored by legal provision, allows for fluidity and informal transitions from one group to another. Changes in religious affiliation are reversible. There may also be multiple bases of identity. While in censuses or surveys conducted in the Diaspora the Jewish population is defined on the basis of the subjective declaration of the interviewee, a classification employed in demographic and social research distinguishes three broad groupings:[4]

- *Core Jewish population*: this group includes all those who identify themselves as Jews, whether they see their connection with Jewishness as religious, ethnic, or cultural, as well as those who are of Jewish origin but lack any kind of religious preference. A slightly more flexible approach would also include those who define themselves as Jewish and have an additional religion, and those who have a religious identity that is not monotheistic if they have at least one Jewish parent or were raised as Jews. The core group also includes Jews by choice, that is, those who have joined Judaism, whether they have formally converted or not. This definition does not depend upon any operative commitment involving faith, religious observance, or communal involvement.

- *Extended Jewish population*: this group includes the core group, together with individuals who were born Jewish but have adopted another religion, as well as the descendants of mixed couples who do not identify as Jews or children who are not identified by their parents as Jews.

- *Enlarged Jewish population*: this includes the two previous groups and those without any Jewish background who live in the same household as someone who is Jewish.

The differential in the sizes of these groups is greatly affected by the extent of mixed marriages. It is possible for the core Jewish population to remain stable, or even shrink, while the extended or enlarged Jewish population expands.

In Israel, the Law of Return defines as entitled to immigrate to, and receive citizenship in, the Jewish state any Jew, as well as their non-Jewish spouse, children, and grandchildren and their spouses, and thus includes an even larger population than that defined here as enlarged. This does not, however, change the definition of who is a Jew, which is based on objective halakhic criteria, subject to the authority of the Interior Ministry and the rabbinic establishment, according to which a Jew is defined as a person whose mother is Jewish, or who has been converted to Judaism according to the Orthodox law, although Conservative and Reform conversions conducted abroad are recognized.

The evolution of Jewish population: a historical overview

Up to the beginning of the eighteenth century the world Jewish population was relatively small and stable. It has been estimated at approximately 1 million people, with slight fluctuations.[5] Demographic growth was disrupted by wars, famine, and epidemics which counterbalanced the high birth rate. Occasional massacres, expulsions, and residential and economic constraints contributed to significant irregularity of the demographic processes.

During the eighteenth century these negative factors began to be attenuated and by 1800 world Jewry had increased to 2.5 million. In Europe, improved sanitary conditions and developments in medical science diminished mortality rates, and this, combined with the still-high levels of fertility, resulted in a fourfold increase of the world Jewish population to 10.6 million by 1900. This demographic transition began earlier and proceeded at a faster rate among the Jews than among non-Jews, owing to such factors as a high rate of marriage, young age at marriage, frequent remarriage after marriage disruption, widespread observance of religious laws encouraging high fertility levels, hygiene and good nutrition, and mutual care and assistance. Jews and non-Jews were prone to different diseases, and those diseases which were more widespread among non-Jews (such as smallpox, typhus, and tuberculosis) presented greater risk of death. The numerical increase of the Jews might have been even greater had it not been not for defections from the community.

The demographic evolutions of the modern era were unevenly distributed. Most affected were the Jewish communities in Eastern Europe where, as a result, the vast majority of world Jewry became concentrated. In 1880 about three-quarters of the world's Jews lived in Eastern Europe, 14 per cent in Western and Central Europe, 8 per cent in Asia and Africa (including Palestine), and only 3 per cent in the United States. The rapid demographic growth produced population excess, and large numbers of Jews immigrated overseas, mainly to the United States, and in much smaller numbers also to Canada, Argentina, South Africa, and Palestine. Between 1881 and 1914 international migration of approximately 2.5 million people significantly altered the geographic dispersion, the United States becoming the world's largest Jewish concentration.

Although Jewish growth now slowed, owing to intensive urbanization, attainment of higher education, increasing gender equality, and secularization, numbers continued to increase to 13.5 million in 1914 and to an all-time peak of 16.5 million on the eve of the Second World War. In the 1920s and 1930s access to the major countries which had absorbed Jews had become seriously limited—the United States legislated two quota acts, in 1921 and 1924, and other countries followed suit. Nevertheless, after the accession to power of the Nazi regime many Jews emigrated from Germany, and from territories which were annexed by the Reich. By the outbreak of the Second World War some 300,000 Jews had left Germany (or 60 per cent of its Jewish population). The two main destinations were Palestine and the United States (which for a few years moderated its immigration policy), with almost equal division between the two countries, while a third settled in Western European countries.

Contemporary demographic trends and characteristics

Jewish population size and distribution

In 1945, in the immediate wake of the Holocaust, during which about a third of the Jewish people was destroyed, the number of Jews in the world was estimated at about 11 million. The main damage was among European Jewry, especially that of the eastern part of the continent, and combined with the mass exodus of Jewish survivors, both its absolute size and its relative share among world Jewry was greatly reduced. In May 1948, when the State of Israel was established, Europe accounted for a third of all Jews; about half lived in the Americas (primarily the United States), and about 12 per cent in Asia and Africa. The Jewish population of Israel constituted less than 6 per cent of world Jewry, or 650,000 people.

Over time numbers began to recover, reaching 12.1 million in 1960, 12.8 million in 1980, and 12.95 million in 2003.[6] There was thus a rapid growth until the beginning of the 1960s, to a large extent as part of a general 'baby boom', while thereafter the annual rate of growth decreased, and is now approaching 'zero population growth'. While Israel regularly has a positive rate of growth, the Diaspora has a shrinking Jewish population. International migration is an important factor in these differentiated tendencies, but part of the explanation lies in negative natural movement among most Jewish communities in the Diaspora, exacerbated by losses through assimilation.

Today close to 40 per cent of Jews (5.1 million) live in Israel, and a slightly higher proportion (5.3 million) in the United States; together these two countries contain 80 per cent of world Jewry. In descending order, there are additional concentrations in France (498,000), Canada (370,000), Britain (300,000), Russia (252,000), Argentina (187,000), Germany (108,000), Australia (100,000), and Brazil (97,000). Together, these ten countries account for about 95 per cent of the world Jewish population; the rest being scattered over some eighty-five countries, each with a Jewish population of at least 100.[7]

International migration and local movements

Since the end of the Second World War nearly 5 million Jews, with their non-Jewish relatives, have migrated across international borders. This amounts to a very high average yearly migration rate of nearly 1 per cent of the total Jewish population over a period of more than half a century. The main places of origin are Arab countries and Eastern Europe, and the primary destinations Israel, North America, and the countries of the EU. There has also been some migration, in both directions, between the latter regions and Israel.

Jewish international migration displays a wavelike pattern. One great wave occurred immediately following the creation of the State of Israel. This was followed by smaller waves, primarily from the emerging Arab states, which by the early 1960s were almost completely emptied of Jews. Another, far smaller, wave was that from the Western countries to Israel during the years immediately following the 1967 war. The second half of the 1970s and the early 1980s were marked by a modest increase in Jewish migration when, for a brief period, the gates of the Soviet Union were opened to limited numbers of Jews. The great exodus took place only after Perestroika and the breakup of the Soviet Union: since 1990 more than a million Jews have emigrated from the former Soviet Union, mainly to Israel, with smaller numbers going to the United States and Germany.

Jews also display high rates of internal mobility. Local redistribution occurs simultaneously in various spheres, including urbanization and suburbanization, long-distance mobility, repeat movement, and dual residence. Most of these population movements attest to fundamental structural transformation and to successful integration into the general society. This results in a wider spread of the Jewish population, reinforcing small, isolated communities, and at the same time weakening Jewish residential segregation and enhancing opportunities for interaction and informal relations with non-Jews, since geographic mobility often involves out-migration from long-established Jewish centres with strong organizational and economic infrastructures to more open and culturally pluralistic areas.

Family patterns and reproduction

As part of widespread changes taking place in contemporary western society, including increased emphasis on individualism and personal mobility, the family is experiencing far-reaching transformations. These include postponement of marriage, a greater tendency to cohabitation, higher divorce rates, lower fertility, and larger numbers of single-parent families, births outside marriage, and inter-faith marriages. Jews have not been immune to these developments.

Pronounced differences are to be found, however, between the Jewish family in the Diaspora and that in Israel, where, despite processes of change that are sometimes quite marked, more conservative patterns towards marriage and family stability subsist. These are attributed to a higher level of religiosity, a higher proportion of Jewish families originating in Muslim countries, socio-economic characteristics, as well as more general environmental conditions.

The incidence of marriages between Jews and non-Jews has reached very high levels: around 70 per cent in Eastern European and some smaller Western European communities, about 50 per cent in the United States, and 30–40 per cent in France, the United Kingdom, Canada, and Australia, with significantly lower rates in Latin American countries. Mixed marriages do not have a direct or immediate impact on the size of the Jewish population, as each partner retains his or her religious identity; the small number of religious conversions in each direction balance each other numerically. Nevertheless, mixed marriages do have an indirect demographic effect, as the offspring are generally not raised or educated as Jews. This comes on top of the already low fertility rate (0.9–1.7 children per couple) among Diaspora Jews, which is below replacement level (2.1 children).

Low fertility reduces the size of the younger age-group, leading to large concentrations in the middle-aged and older groups. In most Diaspora communities today the percentage of Jews above 65 is higher than that of children in the age-bracket 0 to 14. The inevitable result of such age profiles is a larger number of deaths than births and eventually negative natural movement. In Israel, on the other hand, patterns of high fertility (partially associated with the religious sector) assure the demographic continuity of the Jewish population.

Socio-economic stratification

Jews are outstanding for their educational and economic qualifications: about 70 per cent of the younger generation have university degrees in most Diaspora Jewish communities. A direct consequence of this is a high concentration of Jews in the upper strata of the employment hierarchy in the white-collar professions. In the United States in 2000 more than 60 per cent of all employed Jews were in the three highest-status job categories as compared to 46 per cent of all Americans, and the percentage of Jewish households with an annual income over $75,000 was twice that of all American households. At the same time, however, there is a non-negligible proportion of Jews, mainly among the elderly and new immigrants, who live in households with an income below poverty level.[8] Some recent evidence has pointed to a slight turn of Jewish males to manual labour, presumably associated with transient values and lifestyles and with increasing demand in new areas.[9]

Despite a noticeable increase in the educational level of Jews in Israel, it is lower than that of Diaspora Jews. One explanation is rooted in the ethnic composition of the population, about half of which derives from Muslim countries, where the priority placed on secular education has traditionally been much less than in Europe and North America. Furthermore, the economic structure of Israel requires a large, albeit gradually decreasing, number of industrial, service, and agricultural workers, which limits the number of jobs available in those professions requiring academic education. While the recent large wave of immigration from the former Soviet Union has raised the overall educational profile of the Israeli population, it has not changed the occupational composition to the same degree.

Population projections

On the basis of the age and sex structure of the Jewish population in each country or larger geographical area, and applying various assumptions regarding the anticipated levels of factors affecting population size, we may suggest a possible scenario of the demographic development of the Jews in the foreseeable future. This mathematical exercise makes use of moderate assumptions regarding the linear continuation of the recently prevailing tendencies. Such a demographic forecast anticipates a moderate growth of world Jewish population to nearly 14 million at the end of the first quarter of the present century and 14.5 million by the middle of the century. Within a few years Israel is expected to have the largest Jewish concentration, and towards the end of the projection period this will become the absolute majority of the Jewish people.[10]

From research to policy

Changes in the size, distribution, and composition of the population carry implications for planning and communal policy. Demography provides data on the reservoir of potential consumers of different services and helps to determine the division of resources among sub-groups within the population. These include Jewish education, activities for single people, outreach programmes for mixed couples, absorption of new immigrants, help for the needy, and support of the elderly. Analytic demographic research, which seeks to explore connections among variables and the determinants of various kinds of behaviour, helps in identifying the means of developing the Jewish community in a particular direction.

Demographic data help in evaluating characteristics of Jewish communities in the Diaspora and comparing them with those of the majority society and other ethnic or religious sub-groups. We may trace processes of integration and convergence, or distinctiveness, of Jews with all the influences these have on their group cohesion and ethnic or religious commitment.

In Israel, with its majority Jewish society, conditions exist for a direct population policy. Governmental demographic policy aims to influence demographic behaviour regarding fertility, geographical dispersion, and migration to and from Israel. Non-governmental organizations, such as the Jewish Agency or the Joint Distribution Committee, also play important roles in the shaping and implementation of demographic policy.

Overall, the gathering of data and Jewish demographic research have enjoyed a discernible growth in recent years. Because it addresses some of the central questions regarding Jewish continuity, demographic research is translated into the development of strategies of policy planning that contribute to the making and execution of decisions.

FURTHER READING

Bachi, Roberto. 'Personal Recollections on the History of Research in Jewish Demography', in S. DellaPergola and J. Even (eds.), *Papers in Jewish Demography, 1993* (Jerusalem: The Hebrew University of Jerusalem, 1997), pp. 33–7. The founder of the Division of Jewish Demography and Statistics at the Hebrew University of Jerusalem, and the first Director of the Israel Bureau of Statistics, reviews the development of Jewish demographic research.

Cohen, Erik H. *Les Juifs de France 2002: valeurs et identité* (Paris: FSJU, 2002). A detailed report on the socio-demographic and identificational characteristics of the Jewish population in France.

Cohen, Steven M. *American Assimilation or Jewish Revival?* (Bloomington and Indianapolis: Indiana University Press, 1988). Addresses some of the fundamental issues concerning the Jewish family and Jewish identity in late twentieth-century America.

Davids, Leo. 'The Jewish Population of Canada, 1991', in S. DellaPergola and J. Even (eds.), *Papers in Jewish Demography, 1993* (Jerusalem: The Hebrew University of Jerusalem, 1997), pp. 311–23. Makes use of data from the 1991 Canadian Census of Population to analyse the demographic evolution of Canadian Jewry.

DellaPergola, Sergio. 'Major Demographic Trends of World Jewry: The Last Hundred Years', in B. Bonne-Tamir and A. Adam (eds.), *Genetic Diversity Among Jews: Diseases and Markers at the DNA Level* (New York and Oxford: Oxford University Press, 1992), pp. 3–30. An analysis of the main socio-demographic trends of world Jewry over the nineteenth and twentieth centuries.

DellaPergola, Sergio. 'World Jewish Population, 2003', in *American Jewish Year Book, 2003*, pp. 588–612. Yearly review updates of the Jewish population worldwide and that of major regions and countries.

DellaPergola, Sergio, Uzi Rebhun, and Mark Tolts. 'Prospecting the Jewish Future: Population Projections 2000–2080', in *American Jewish Year Book, 2000*, pp. 103–46. Presents alternative projections for world Jewry and for a few major geographic regions over the twenty-first century.

Goldscheider, Calvin. *Israel's Changing Society: Population, Ethnicity, and Development* (Boulder, Col.: Westview Press, 2002). An in-depth assessment of Israeli society directing attention to immigration to Israel, demographic transformation, and ethnic diversity.

Goldstein, Sidney, and Alice Goldstein. *Jews on the Move: Implications for Jewish Identity* (Albany: State University of New York Press, 1996). Makes use of data from the 1990 National Jewish Population Survey to examine patterns of geographic dispersion and mobility among American Jews, and how these affect group identification and cohesion.

Hart, Mitchell B. *Social Science and the Politics of Modern Jewish Identity* (Stanford, Calif.: Stanford University Press, 2000). Explores the emergence and development of organized Jewish social science in Central Europe and the importance of statistics and other social-science disciplines for Jewish elites in both Europe and the United States.

Preston, Samuel H., Patrick Heuveline, and Michel Guillot. *Demography: Measuring and Modeling Population Processes* (Oxford: Blackwell Publishers, 2001). Presents the basic methods and measurements for the study of demographic behaviours.

Ritterband, Paul, Barry A. Kosmin, and Jeffrey Scheckner. 'Counting Jewish Populations: Methods and Problems', in *American Jewish Year Book, 1988*, pp. 204–21. The authors discuss both census and non-census proxies for the size of Jewish population in the United States.

Tolts, Mark. 'Jewish Demography of the Former Soviet Union', in S. DellaPergola and J. Even (eds.) *Papers in Jewish Demography, 1997* (Jerusalem: The Hebrew University of Jerusalem, 2001), pp. 109–39. A study of the demography of Jews in the former Soviet Union.

United Jewish Communities, *The National Jewish Population Survey 2000–01: Strength, Challenge and Diversity in the American Jewish Population* (New York: United Jewish Communities, 2003). This is a comprehensive report of the findings from a recent nationwide socio-demographic study of American Jews. Topics include population size, age structure, marriage and fertility, geographic characteristics, social and economic stratification, Jewish connections, the elderly, and poverty.

Waxman, Chaim I. *Jewish Baby Boomers: A Communal Perspective* (Albany: State University of New York Press, 2001). Critically analyses American Jewish baby-boomers and their commitment to Jewish continuity in both the private and public spheres.

WEBSITES

<http://icj.huji.ac.il/demog/index.htm>. The site of the Division of Jewish Demography and Statistics of the A. Harman Institute of Contemporary Jewry at the Hebrew University of Jerusalem. It contains information on its documentation centre and library with over 8,000 items, a list of publications of its series Jewish Population Studies, and information on its research activities and conferences.

<http://isdc.huji.ac.il>. The site of the Israel Social Sciences Data Center which collects, preserves, and distributes data files on social and economic issues in Israel.

<http://www.statistics.gov.uk>. The site of the Office of National Statistics of the United Kingdom. Among other things, it offers on-line access to material from the 2001 Population Census including data according to religious belonging in general and on Jews in particular.

<www.cbs.gov.il>. The site of the Israel Central Bureau of Statistics with on-line access to the Statistical Abstract of Israel and other data and reports on Israeli population, geography, economy, and more.

<www.jewishdatabank.org>. The site of the North American Data Bank located at the University of Connecticut. This is a joint project of the United Jewish Communities, the Jewish Studies Program at the University of Connecticut, and Roper Center. It serves as a repository for demographic and other quantitative social scientific surveys about North American Jewry.

NOTES

1. S. N. Eisenstadt, *Jewish Civilization: The Jewish Historical Experience and Its Manifestation in Israeli Society in a Comparative Perspective* (Albany: State University of New York Press, 1992).
2. Sergio DellaPergola, 'Demography', in M. Goodman (ed.), *The Oxford Handbook of Jewish Studies* (Oxford: Oxford University Press, 2002), pp. 797–823.
3. Mitchell B. Hart, *Social Science and the Politics of Modern Jewish Identity* (Stanford, Cal.: Stanford University Press, 2000).
4. Sergio DellaPergola, 'World Jewish Population, 2003', *American Jewish Year Book, 2003*, pp. 588–612.
5. This and other figures presented in this section derive from Sergio DellaPergola, 'Major Demographic Trends of World Jewry: The Last Hundred Years', in B. Bonne-Tamir and A. Adam (eds.), *Genetic Diversity Among Jews: Diseases and Markers at the DNA Level* (New York and Oxford: Oxford University Press, 1992), pp. 3–30.
6. Sergio DellaPergola, Uzi Rebhun, and Mark Tolts, 'Prospecting the Jewish Future: Population Projections 2000–2080', *American Jewish Year Book, 2000*, pp. 103–46; DellaPergola, 'World Jewish Population, 2003'.
7. DellaPergola, 'World Jewish Population, 2003'.
8. United Jewish Communities, *The National Jewish Population Survey 2000–01: Strength, Challenge and Diversity in the American Jewish Population* (New York: United Jewish Communities, 2003).
9. Sidney Goldstein, 'Profile of American Jewry: Insights from the 1990 National Jewish Population Survey', *American Jewish Year Book, 1992*, pp. 77–173.
10. See DellaPergola, Rebhun, and Tolts, 'Prospecting the Jewish Future', pp. 103–46.

Historical issues

2 | Enlightenment and emancipation

Lois C. Dubin

Enlightenment and emancipation were two crucial forces that affected Jews and Judaism since the mid-eighteenth century: Judaism as the religion of citizens participating in modern states is inconceivable without them. With its promotion of secular definitions of civil society and the state as well as ideals of shared rationality, humanity, and tolerance, the Enlightenment opened up a potential cultural and political space for Jews as members of modern European societies. Long cast as the quintessential religious dissenters and ethnic outsiders in Christian Europe, Jews could now be seen in principle as fellow human beings and citizens. Emancipation meant the removal of many prior restrictions on residence and activities, and a new status of legal equality and citizenship in constitutional states that enacted uniform laws and consequently equal rights and duties for all citizens. How to negotiate these processes of far-reaching cultural and political change greatly preoccupied European Jews from the late eighteenth century through the First World War.

Enlightenment and emancipation entailed significant transformation of both Gentile–Jewish relations and Jewish self-consciousness. As Jews actively embraced the challenge of forging a modern European identity for themselves, they produced a rationale and strategies for engagement with the non-Jewish world; they also reinterpreted Judaism in accordance with new values now internalized as their own. At the same time, they were never free from the pressures of explaining and defending Jews and Judaism in the face of ignorance and prejudice, both old and new. They discovered that even ardent champions of inclusive universalism could find Jewish particularity troublesome.

Creative tension with the non-Jewish environment is a hallmark of modern Judaism. It is a legacy of the Enlightenment and emancipation, for they challenged Jews to live and think as engaged yet distinctive participants, as insiders and outsiders, in modern cultures and societies.

The European Enlightenment

Eighteenth-century Enlightenment thinkers in Western and Central Europe popularized the new science and philosophy of Bacon, Descartes, Newton, and Locke, and scrutinized every aspect of culture and society according to their rationalist, empiricist, and naturalist premises. Intellectuals forged a secular, critical discourse whose watchwords were reason, nature, experience, utility, humanity, toleration, and progress. They considered rationality as the common and defining property of the human species, and enlightenment as the process whereby human beings dare to think for themselves rather than rely upon tradition, authority, or prejudice. They believed that the human mind could come to understand reason, nature, and humanity, and that knowledge and education were powerful tools for analysing and reshaping human society. This secular intelligentsia, active in coffee-houses, reading clubs, academies, and Masonic lodges, saw themselves as an elite vanguard of intellectual and moral arbiters providing a legitimate alternative to the Church. With a practical, this-worldly orientation, they prized human concerns, responsibility, and ethics rather than theological dogmas or metaphysical subtleties.

Enlightenment views of religion ranged from rationalist belief in a particular religion, through scepticism and deism, to materialism and atheism. Common to all was the tendency to measure religious traditions and institutions against the yardsticks of reason, nature, and universality. Some Enlightenment thinkers aggressively criticized religion; most, however, proposed alternative versions: either enlightened reinterpretations of existing religions consonant with modern science and philosophy, or theoretical constructs of natural religion. For many, an acceptable enlightened religion would require little more than belief in God, appreciation of the natural world's order, and the practice of justice and toleration. It should be reasonable, moral, socially useful, politically powerless, and non-coercive.

The bitter experience of religious wars in early modern Europe led to the Enlightenment's secular definition of civil society and the state. John Locke's *A Letter on Toleration* (1689) presented the state as a secular institution, responsible for the temporal goods of life, liberty, health, and property, but not the eternal salvation of its members. A religious sin is not necessarily a crime, for crime in a secular state means violation of public order. Civil peace is better served by toleration of religious diversity than by intolerance.

The Enlightenment axioms of common rationality and humanity, a secular state, and toleration promoted the view of Jews as humans like everyone else and provided the intellectual framework for their potential inclusion as full-fledged members of the civil realm and state. However, rationalist and cosmopolitan principles did not always remove negative feelings or distrust of Jews. Many Enlightenment figures envisaged the Jews as fellow subject-citizens only in theory, while seeing them in actuality as superstitious, materialistic, antisocial, and clannish. Voltaire especially depicted Jews as inferior, irrational, and immoral, yet in a gesture of tolerance he counselled not to burn them. In contrast, the dramatist Gotthold Ephraim Lessing depicted moral and noble Jewish characters, most notably Nathan in *Nathan the Wise* (1779), modelled on his friend Moses Mendelssohn, the renowned philosopher in Berlin. Yet, even their most staunch advocates believed that Jews needed considerable transformation. Most called for twofold improvement: for states to remove oppressive laws, which they held partially responsible for Jewish defects, and for Jews to divest themselves of the spiritual, moral, and economic habits deemed undesirable by others. Thus, Jews would demonstrate their morality and worth, and their humanity would be regenerated. Many Gentiles and Jews optimistically considered these as realistic expectations, but most did not grasp how fraught the process might be. The Enlightenment beckoned Jews toward modern Europe, but it offered ambiguous terms that bore the burdensome weight of the past.

Enlightenment from above

The state was one important channel by which the Enlightenment affected Jews. Combining Enlightenment principles and absolutist practices, late eighteenth-century monarchs such as Joseph II (Habsburg Monarchy), Catherine II (Russia), Frederick II (Prussia), and Grand Duke Peter Leopold (Tuscany, later Habsburg Emperor Leopold II) embarked on ambitious reform programmes in order to centralize and modernize their realms. Toward the general goal of making all subjects more productive for the common good, some specified practical measures for improving the conditions in which Jews lived and for fostering their fitness as citizens.

This approach was most clearly expressed by the Prussian bureaucrat Christian Wilhelm von Dohm in his essay *Über die bürgerliche Verbesserung der Juden* (1781, On the Civil Improvement of the Jews), and in the Toleration edicts of the Habsburg Emperor Joseph II (1781–90). In their states the matter seemed particularly urgent, since the 1772 partition of Poland-Lithuania brought sizeable Jewish populations along with new territories. Appearing within a few months of each other in 1781, Dohm's work and Joseph's first edicts became decisive reference points for subsequent debate in Europe. Abbé Gregoire's prizewinning *Essai sur la régénération physique, morale et politique des Juifs* (1787, Essay Concerning the Physical, Moral, and Political Regeneration of the Jews), penned in response to the Metz Royal Academy question, 'Are there possibilities of making the Jews more useful and happier in France?', also helped forge the reforming absolutist discourse on Jewish improvement and regeneration.

Their basic assumptions were common humanity, and the linkage of improvement, utility, and felicity. Dohm argued that Jewish defects—most notably corruption, over-concentration in commerce, and clannishness—were due not to the innate character or religion of Jews, but rather to environmental factors such as oppressive laws or discrimination. Like other human beings, Jews were malleable: state action could mould Jewish character and behaviour by eliminating oppressive laws and granting Jews civil rights equal or nearly equal to those of other citizens. Jews would naturally respond with gratitude, hard work, and patriotic eagerness to fulfil their civic duties. Dohm explained: '[T]he Jew is even more man than Jew'; and Gregoire: 'We see talents and virtues shine forth in them wherever they begin to be treated as men.'

The preambles to Joseph II's Toleration edicts similarly announced the goal of making Jews more useful to the state. They declared that Jews were to be 'regarded like any other fellow human-beings' and placed 'on a virtually equal level' with members of other religious groups, so that 'all subjects without distinction of nationality and religion should share in the public prosperity . . . and enjoy freedom according to the law'. Consequently, these laws eliminated humiliating distinguishing signs and increased educational and occupational opportunities for Jews. In order to diminish Jewish cultural isolation and to inculcate civic virtue, they also mandated state-supervised Jewish schools and use of the state language, German, for non-religious purposes.

Ideally, the tutelary state would regenerate the Jews' core of humanity by removing oppressive laws, guiding Jews toward moral improvement, and educating Gentiles away from prejudice. Enhancing the civil status of the Jews would result in their civil improvement: they would provide greater utility and enjoy more felicity. Since utility, humanity, and morality were intertwined, to be useful was to demonstrate humanity and morality.

In defining utility, most observers decried as unproductive the common Jewish pursuits of retail commerce and moneylending; they prized artisanry and wholesale international trade (both practised by some Jews) and agriculture (hardly practised by any). Urging subjects to be more productive was the essence of the practical orientation of reforming absolutist regimes. The large Jewish populations in East-Central Europe generally experienced such economic and cultural prodding as heavy-handed encroachment upon traditional ways. Accordingly, many treatments of absolutist policies have focused on forced assimilation rather than on more positive aspects.

Joseph II's Toleration programme offered Jews civil inclusion as nearly equal subject-citizens in exchange for utility, productive service, and the inculcation of civic morality. Elsewhere some Jews gained rights that put them on a par with socially comparable Gentiles. For example, Jewish seats were reserved on various municipal councils and mercantile exchanges and courts in London, Livorno, and Mantua, and Jews were partially incorporated into urban merchant guilds in Russia. Enlightened absolutists heeded both utility and humanity as they centralized their states, enacted more general laws, and mobilized their populations. Their legacy entailed both civil inclusion of Jews as members and subject-citizens of their realms, and the accompanying expectation of cultural and economic adaptation by Jews themselves. Reforming Old Regime states, comprised of corporate bodies with distinctive legal statuses, could not grant anyone general equality, but they could offer Jews improved conditions and practical steps of civil inclusion. Civil inclusion through more general laws was a step toward emancipation.

Enlightenment and Haskalah among the Jews

Enlightenment among Jews is usually identified with the Haskalah, the ideological movement calling for modernization of Jewish culture and society that flourished first in Germany from the 1770s to the 1790s and then in Galicia and Russia from the 1820s to the 1880s. This movement decried the insularity, Talmudic focus, and kabbalistic orientation of early modern Ashkenazic Judaism, and it urged a twofold reform: (1) broadening and reorienting the curriculum for purposes of internal Jewish cultural renewal; and (2) training Jews with new skills for purposes of rapprochement and participation in the Gentile world. Haskalah was a variant of Enlightenment critical rationalism and the first modern ideology of Judaism. It vigorously criticized Jewish cultural and social patterns as it offered a strategy of engagement with the modernizing West. It also inaugurated the modern phases of both Hebrew literature and Jewish philosophy. So large has this movement and its Ashkenazic world loomed in modern Jewish history that it has been easy to overlook other ways by which Jews became familiar with and exemplified Enlightenment principles.

Haskalah was not the only channel by which European Jews encountered Enlightenment in the eighteenth century. There were individuals in England, France, Holland, Italy, Germany, and even in East-Central Europe—such as Abraham b. Naphtali Tang, Isaac de Pinto, Benedetto Frizzi, Zalkind Hourwitz, and Markus Herz—who became engaged with Enlightenment science, philosophy, and literature through their direct reading in vernacular and classical languages and through social contacts with Gentiles. Many attended university medical schools in Padua, Halle, or Frankfurt-an-der-Oder; some were autodidacts; others were merchants whose commercial need for languages developed into broader cultural pursuits. A few worked as secretaries or librarians for Gentiles, and several frequented local intellectual societies and Masonic lodges. Some translated Enlightenment works into Hebrew, while others interpreted Jewish texts in Enlightenment terms. Many addressed themes of general cultural, scientific, and political interest.

These doctors, intellectuals, and men of letters lived in creative tension with their respective environments, as they sought variously to align Judaism with modern thought, to enter non-Jewish circles, and, when necessary, to defend Jews and Judaism. They were not forged by a Jewish ideological movement or belong to one. Through other routes, these individual Jews were touched by the European Enlightenment and became exemplars of its ideals of reason and cosmopolitan sociability.

More work is needed on these individual Jewish adherents of Enlightenment and their non-ideological adoption of European languages, values, and mores. What roles did Sephardic or Italian-Jewish cultural traditions, the dynamics of mercantile milieus, distinctive local cultures and politics, and indeed personal inclination play in their formation? Will there emerge generalizable patterns of encounters with Enlightenment that were not mediated by Haskalah? Should these be seen as early or moderate variants of Haskalah, or rather as alternative currents of Enlightenment?

Other Jews whose cultural adaptation and sociability with Gentiles accorded with Enlightenment values, though they were not necessarily engaged with Enlightenment ideas as such, were wealthy Jewish merchants and entrepreneurs. These included prominent Berlin families, some descended from court Jews, as well as port Jews, that is, Jews engaged in international maritime commerce in thriving mercantile centres, such as Bordeaux, Trieste, and Odessa. Factors besides Haskalah or Enlightenment could lead to cultural and social adaptation.

The terms Haskalah, the name of the Jewish Enlightenment movement, and *maskilim*, indicating its advocates, come from the Hebrew root *sekhel*—reason or intellect. Maskilim urged the acquisition and transmission of knowledge through reason and its use for critical appraisal of Jewish culture and society. Important figures were Moses Mendelssohn, Naphtali Herz Wessely (Weisel), Isaac Euchel, and David Friedländer in Berlin and Königsberg; Menahem Mendel Lefin, Joseph Perl, and Isaac Erter in Galicia; and Isaac Baer Levinsohn and Judah Leib Gordon in Russia. Despite variations, these maskilim generally drew on earlier rationalist philosophical trends and Sephardic models as well as on the Enlightenment in their efforts to reinvigorate Judaism through Hebrew language, poetry and belles-lettres, Bible, science, and philosophy. Reading their times optimistically, they also sought to equip Jews with the requisite skills and outlook to take advantage of new opportunities to function alongside Gentiles. They founded schools; voluntary associations such as Hevrat dorshei leshon ever (Society of Friends of the Hebrew Language, Königsberg 1783) and Hevrat marbei haskalah be-yisrael be'erez rusyah (Society for the Promotion of Enlightenment among the Jews of Russia, St Petersburg 1863); and printing presses and periodicals, such as the first modern Hebrew periodical *Ha-Measef* (The Gatherer, 1783–97, and intermittently to 1811). They discussed culture and current affairs with Gentiles in cultural associations and other venues of Jewish–Christian sociability. They wrote tracts urging reforms of Jewish practices as well as more civil and political rights for Jews.

Some early projects well illustrate Haskalah cultural ideals. In 1778 Mendelssohn and a team of maskilim began to publish *Sefer Netivot ha-shalom* (The Book of the Paths of Peace) and *Biur*, a new German translation of the Pentateuch written in Hebrew characters along with a new Hebrew commentary that emphasized literal and rationalist exegesis. Its advance subscribers, who were spread from England to Poland-Lithuania, numbered over 500. Its interplay of Torah, Hebrew, and German demonstrated the complexities of the Haskalah's cultural endeavours.

In 1782 Wessely, an associate of Mendelssohn, sparked a culture war with his pamphlet *Divrei shalom ve-emet* (Words of Peace and Truth). Seeking to convince Jews of the value of Joseph II's educational policies, Wessely articulated a new vision of Jewish culture. He urged that *torat ha-adam*—'the torah of man' or 'human knowledge'—be taught to Jewish youth before the 'Torah of God'. He meant that the kinds of knowledge universally accessible through human reason and empirical observation, for example, mathematics, natural science, civility and ethics, should precede the sacred texts and laws pertaining to Jews alone. (Within Judaic studies, he emphasized Hebrew language and grammar, the Bible, literal exegesis, and morality.) The thrust of his new concept was to broaden the Ashkenazic curriculum and to present a new cultural ideal: a person who would know well both Hebrew and the vernacular, exemplify the broad horizons and Hebraic ideals of the medieval Sephardic rationalist tradition, and behave honourably among Gentiles as a civilized human being and loyal, productive subject. Wessely saw Sephardim, Italians, and port Jews as exemplars of these goals.

It was not so much the new cultural ideal as Wessely's impolitic words concerning Torah scholars and rabbinic culture that provoked a firestorm among traditionalist rabbis. To argue that Torah scholarship alone, no matter how great, should no longer suffice, he recast a Talmudic phrase to suggest 'a carcass is better than a Torah scholar who lacks human knowledge'. His later protestations notwithstanding, he did not merely draw on past precedents to legitimate the supplementing of Torah with other intellectual disciplines. He criticized a long-standing ideal, calling for Torah to yield pride of place to other, more practical and universal bodies of knowledge, and disparaging those whose mastery was solely of the traditional religious corpus. For maskilim, a restructuring of knowledge and a new function for knowledge itself were to extend beyond Judaism: as a bridge to the outside world, it was to facilitate worldly success rather than religious salvation.

With *torat ha-adam*, Wessely delineated a sphere of Jewish culture separable from the classic religious texts. He also transposed Enlightenment values of natural religion, universal morality, and love of humanity into a traditional Jewish idiom. He presented a religious-cultural-civic ideal that expressed confidence in the Enlightenment programmes of civil improvement and inclusion. A Jew should see himself religiously as a Jew, but otherwise as a cultured human being and subject, as expressed in Judah Leib Gordon's later poem *Hakitzah ami* (Awake My People!, 1862–3): 'Be a man in the streets and a Jew at home | A brother to your countryman and a servant to your king.'

Similar values were expressed in *Ha-Measef*. Launched in 1784 by the Society of Friends of the Hebrew Language, it quickly gained almost 300 subscribers from Amsterdam to Lithuania. Exhorting its readers to think critically ('Be Men!'), it invited contributions in natural science, ethics, physical education, Hebrew language and poetry, and biblical and Talmudic exegesis (though Talmud hardly appeared on its pages), biographies of great Jews, current affairs, translations of Gentile books into Hebrew, and announcements of new books.

Mendelssohn's *Jerusalem* (1783) presented Judaism as a rational religion, that is, an amalgam of natural religion and revealed Torah law, and he argued strenuously for freedom of conscience and genuine religious toleration. His use of the tools of Enlightenment philosophy to provide a modern interpretation of revealed religion can be seen as an example of religious enlightenment, that is, attempted syntheses of Enlightenment and religious thought by Protestants, Catholics, and Jews in Central Europe. Mendelssohn's effort to harmonize Judaism with contemporary intellectual currents became paradigmatic for many Jews, though not necessarily in all its details. Like his, many subsequent formulations of Judaism hewed to the Enlightenment emphasis on rationality and morality while maintaining faith in divine revelation.

For many maskilim, the goals of reconfiguring Jewish culture or of modernizing Judaism went hand in hand with social critique and transformation. To propose a new curriculum meant to attack the authority of traditional religious leaders, now often depicted as obscurantist and uncultured. Galician maskilim were especially scathing in their indictment of Hasidic rebbes. Indeed, maskilim presented themselves as an alternative elite of public intellectual-activists whose authority derived from secular sources of authority. They wanted rabbinical and communal power curbed and the practice of excommunication ended. They criticized the ways Jews spoke, appeared, and earned a living. They denigrated Yiddish as a garbled jargon and promoted the value of pure Hebrew and pure German (or any other vernacular) instead. They wanted no distinctive Jewish garb, beards, or hairstyles. They inserted subjects such as arithmetic, languages, and arts and sciences into the curriculum so that Jews would acquire vocational skills and Jewish society become more productive. They criticized popular customs such as early burial that they thought violated rational, scientific norms.

In sum, the Haskalah combined renewal, rationalist analysis, rapprochement with the Gentile world, and rebuttal of Gentile criticism. Scholars have debated which elements dominated: its efforts at intellectual renewal of Judaism, its creation of a modern Hebraic culture, or its drive for approaching the Gentile world and achieving civil-political rights. Viewed as a whole and through its various phases, the Haskalah was a complex amalgam that contained all these elements and more. As a variant of religious enlightenment, it did seek to reinvigorate Judaism through renewal of rationalist traditions together with the application of Enlightenment science and philosophy. Yet many maskilim went further: to apply Enlightenment rationalism in the critique of Jewish culture and society. And they did inaugurate a secular revolution: they weakened the public standing of religion and the rabbinate, and they promoted secular culture, values, and institutions. Indeed, this emergent non-clerical elite sought to draw boundaries around religion, to compartmentalize Torah so that a sphere of human culture could be separated from its embrace. They reconfigured Jewish culture by broadening its purview, shifting its emphases, and secularizing. This incipient secularization meant limitation of religion, though not its delegitimation.

However, the Haskalah involved not simply intellectual renewal, cultural reconfiguration, and secularization but also acerbic social critique and clear civil and political goals. Maskilim internalized and expressed Enlightenment values, but when necessary they also defended Jews, Judaism, and Jewish values and behaviour against Gentile charges.

The Haskalah offered modern Jews a complex religious and secular identity as Jews, humans, and subject-citizens. Its opponents failed to see its delicate balancing act. Religious critics charged maskilim with heresy, while later nationalist critics charged them with betrayal of the Jewish people. In fact, the Haskalah, though innovative and in some respects revolutionary, did promote a moderate course. In creating a strategy of engagement with the Gentile world, it sought to avoid two extremes: either abandonment of Judaism or insular parochialism. Jews could be both Jews and moderns, bearers of a Judaic-Hebrew culture even as members of non-Jewish society—that was its core message and its legacy.

Emancipation: Jews as citizens

What the Enlightenment, reforming absolutism, and Haskalah were doing gradually—opening up a space for Jews in European culture and society, and improving Jewish legal status—was accomplished more dramatically and decisively by the French Revolution in 1789–91. The old regime of hierarchical, corporate orders was dismantled, and a new kind of constitutional, democratic state—the political expression of an emerging bourgeois society—was inaugurated in which all citizens as individuals were to enjoy equality before the law and to exercise the same rights and duties. This new kind of state changed the expectations for improvement of Jewish status throughout Europe: once the French National Assembly applied the 1789 Declaration of the Rights of Man and of the Citizen to Jews and proffered Jews equal civil and political rights, it became expected that a modern constitutional state would make Jews citizens. Legal equality and citizenship quickly became the gold standard of Jewish status, although the term 'emancipation' was not used until the 1820s (borrowed from the campaign for English Catholics' political rights). Emancipation did not mean an end to servitude, but rather the removal of disabilities and the attainment of equal civil and political rights within a modern constitutional state. For Jews, securing, maintaining, and responding to emancipation was the great issue of the long nineteenth century: from its first enactment in France in 1790–1; through the repeated enactments and retractions of emancipation in Central Europe until its achievement in 1867–71 in the Austro-Hungarian Empire and in the newly unified Germany and Italy; up to its enactment in April 1917 during the first Russian Revolution.

Various factors distinguished the course of emancipation in different countries: (1) Was it imposed from without or developed from within? (2) Was it a one-time enactment or a protracted on-and-off again process? (3) Did law reflect social developments or precede them? (4) How rooted were liberal, constitutional principles within a political culture? (5) How great were the strains of the socio-economic changes wrought by industrialization and urbanization? (6) What were the size, status, and image of the Jewish community?

Despite these variations, the core of emancipation was similar everywhere: (1) for Jews as individuals, civil liberties such as freedom of religion, residence, movement, and occupation—the rights that mattered most to Jews—and no denial of either civil or political rights due to religion; (2) for Jewish communities, the loss of juridical and corporate autonomy; and (3) the expectation, regardless of whether or not articulated formally as a quid pro quo, that Jews would transform themselves into productive, committed citizens and in the process tone down their distinctiveness.

Events in France are illustrative. In January 1790 the acculturated Sephardic merchants of Bordeaux and Bayonne and the Jews of Avignon were granted citizenship through the extension of civil rights long granted them by royal letters of patent. Ashkenazim had to wait until after adoption of the new French Constitution in September 1791. Taking the civic oath was then said explicitly to involve renunciation of prior privileges, which meant specifically corporate autonomy. During the lengthy debates Count Clermont-Tonnerre pronounced what became the classic statement on Jewish emancipation: 'The Jews should be denied everything as a nation, but granted everything as individuals.' By nation, he understood 'a separate political formation or class in the country'. The advocates of Jewish emancipation believed that the Constitution itself required equal citizenship for all, Jews included, while opponents worried that the Jews were too strange and separate a tribe to become part of the new French nation.

The grateful Jews, eager to prove themselves as worthy citizens, were willing to 'divest . . . [them-]selves entirely of that narrow spirit, of Corporation and Congregation, in all civil and political matters not immediately connected with . . . [their] spiritual laws . . .' (Berr Isaac Berr, 1791). In 1806–7 the recently emancipated Jews faced a moment of truth at the two grand Jewish convocations convened by Emperor Napoleon, the Assembly of Notables and Sanhedrin. He posed several questions about Jewish values and identity, for example, concerning marriage and divorce, military service, usury, and police-jurisdiction. The core issue was this: 'In the eyes of Jews are Frenchmen considered as brethren or as strangers? . . . Do the Jews born in France, and treated by the law as French citizens, consider France as their country?' The rabbis and lay leaders answered unequivocally: they considered France as their country, French laws supreme in all civil and political matters, themselves as Frenchmen, and all Frenchmen as their brothers. They disavowed belonging to a separate Jewish people, and they called their incorporation with the 'Great [French] Nation . . . a kind of political redemption'. They thus enunciated what was to become the classic Jewish position on emancipation: Jews would henceforth distinguish between the civil and religious realms, being French (or German or whatever) in the civil sphere while confining Judaism to the religious sphere.

Reality proved messier than the formulae and rhetoric. The apparently neat distinction between the civil and the religious sometimes proved difficult to discern or maintain in practice. For example, in the regulation of marriage and divorce there were often discrepancies between Jewish law and state laws, and disagreements arose about whether these matters were to be seen as civil or religious. Dissatisfaction with Jewish moneylending led Napoleon to restrict the economic and residential rights of Ashkenazim in Alsace-Lorraine from 1808 to 1818, thus violating the principle of equality before the law. Despite the individualist rhetoric of emancipation, nationwide Jewish communal organizations existed in France and elsewhere after emancipation. Napoleon gave Judaism and even the Jewish community official standing when he instituted the Consistoire system of communal organization, and the debts of the former Jewish corporations were transferred to the new state-supervised Consistoire. Communities, now divested of corporate autonomy, served the Jews themselves and governments, who often saw them as means to monitor Jewish behaviour and spur integration.

Legal emancipation was the beginning of a multifaceted and gradual process. It did not suddenly change patterns of behaviour or perceptions; nor could it alone guarantee social, economic, and cultural integration. The course of emancipation in this broad sense depended on socio-economic conditions and on political traditions and dynamics.

Legacies of emancipation

With emancipation, the corporate community of Jews became a religious denomination, a religious-ethnic minority, a subculture, and to a large extent a voluntary association. Jewish community persisted, but in changed forms. Though many Jews left Judaism for the larger society and majority religion, Jews on the whole remained a recognizable group with a distinctive sense of identity.

Citizenship in European states certainly called for readjustments in Jewish thinking about collective identity and religion. Now actors in a new public arena, Jews became hyperconscious of their image in Gentile eyes. Gentile expectations and Jewish longings helped generate new formulations such as 'Frenchmen of the Mosaic persuasion' which carried new emphases. Judaism contracted from an all-encompassing halakhically ordered way of life to a religion that stressed creed and universal moral teaching ('ethical monotheism') rather than uniquely Jewish commandment and deed. The benefits of dispersion among the nations outshone the travails of exile. Perhaps paradoxically, while the more purely religious aspects of Judaism were highlighted, Judaism and religion were delimited and, to some degree, secularized.

That Jews in the throes of Enlightenment and emancipation recalibrated Judaism did not mean that they responded cravenly to external pressures, as the later nationalist critique of emancipation as 'slavery in freedom' charged. They tried to fashion a Judaism that allowed them to be Jews, humans, and citizens simultaneously. The challenge was: could they synthesize these elements creatively rather than be driven to destructive dichotomies? As Jews reached out for the more general and universal, how much particularity would be permitted them?

Enlightenment and emancipation helped Jews rise into the middle classes and become European citizens. Their new opportunities and strategies conditioned modern Jewish life and modern Judaism. Enlightenment and emancipation brought the promise and perplexities of life in a broader society.

FURTHER READING

Birnbaum P., and I. Katznelson (eds.). *Paths of Emancipation: Jews, States, and Citizenship* (Princeton: Princeton University Press, 1995). Essays by different authors that stress variations in political and social dynamics in several European countries, the Ottoman Empire, and the United States.

Dubin, Lois C. *The Port Jews of Habsburg Trieste: Absolutist Politics and Enlightenment Culture* (Stanford, Calif.: Stanford University Press, 1999). A political, cultural, and social history of an Italian Jewish mercantile community that addresses broader issues of Enlightenment and civil integration.

Eisen, Arnold M. *Rethinking Modern Judaism: Ritual, Commandment, Community* (Chicago and London: University of Chicago Press, 1998). Stresses the continuing role and reinterpretation of religious practice for modern Jews since Enlightenment and emancipation.

Feiner, Shmuel. *The Jewish Enlightenment*, trans. Chaya Naor (Philadelphia: University of Pennsylvania Press, 2003). A comprehensive intellectual and social history of the eighteenth-century Haskalah that presents it as a variant of the European Enlightenment and as a secular revolution within Judaism.

Feiner S., and D. Sorkin (eds.). *New Perspectives on the Haskalah* (London and Portland, Oreg.: Littman Library of Jewish Civilization, 2001). Essays by different authors that raise new issues in the cultural history of the Haskalah, ranging from England to Russia.

Frankel J., and S. J. Zipperstein (eds.). *Assimilation and Community: The Jews in Nineteenth-Century Europe* (Cambridge: Cambridge University Press, 1992). Essays by different authors that emphasize group cohesion and solidarity during the emancipation process in countries throughout Europe.

Hertzberg, Arthur. *The French Enlightenment and the Jews: Origins of Modern Antisemitism* (New York: Columbia University Press, 1990) [first published 1968]. A survey of Jewish communities and the Jewish Question in eighteenth-century France, and the first work to link modern antisemitism to the secular Enlightenment.

Hess, Jonathan. *Germans, Jews and the Claims of Modernity* (New Haven and London: Yale University Press, 2002). Re-examines late eighteenth- to early nineteenth-century debates in Germany, with emphasis on political modernization, secular antisemitism, and critical Jewish responses.

Katz, Jacob. *Out of the Ghetto: The Social Background of Jewish Emancipation, 1770–1870* (Cambridge, Mass.: Harvard University Press, 1973). Still-classic analysis of emancipation that surveys ideology, process, and institutions in Western and Central Europe.

Katz, Jacob (ed.). *Toward Modernity: The European Jewish Model* (New Brunswick and Oxford: Transaction Books, 1987). Essays by different authors on Enlightenment and emancipation in several European countries and the United States, with focus on comparison to the well-known German experience.

Malino, F., and D. Sorkin (eds.). *Profiles in Diversity: Jews in a Changing Europe 1750–1870* (Detroit: Wayne State University Press, 1988) [first published as *From East and West*, Blackwell, 1990]. Studies by different authors of Jewish men and women in several countries, with attention to family, social, and cultural history.

Meyer, Michael A. *The Origins of the Modern Jew: Jewish Identity and European Culture in Germany, 1749–1824* (Detroit: Wayne State University Press, 1967). Clear exposition of the thought and dilemmas of key German-Jewish figures.

Nathans, Benjamin. *Beyond the Pale: The Jewish Encounter with Late Imperial Russia* (Berkeley, Los Angeles, and London: University of California Press, 2002). A detailed political and social study of late nineteenth- to early twentieth-century Russia that shows significant integration before full legal emancipation.

Reinharz, J., and P. Mendes-Flohr (eds.). *The Jew in the Modern World: A Documentary History*, 2nd edn. (New York and Oxford: Oxford University Press, 1995). Indispensable, wide-ranging collection of primary sources from the seventeenth to the twentieth century, with annotations and introductions.

Ruderman, David B. *Jewish Enlightenment in an English Key: Anglo-Jewry's Construction of Modern Jewish Thought* (Princeton and Oxford: Princeton University Press, 2000). An analysis of eighteenth- to nineteenth-century Anglo-Jewish thought that raises broad questions about varieties of Jewish Enlightenment and the significance of English liberalism for modern Jewish culture.

Schechter, Ronald. *Obstinate Hebrews: Representations of Jews in France, 1715–1815* (Berkeley, Los Angeles, and London: University of California Press, 2003). Emphasizes the importance of Jewish questions for general French debates on culture and politics, and stresses self-assertive Jewish responses to the challenges of Enlightenment and emancipation.

Silber, Michael. 'From Tolerated Aliens to Citizen-Soldiers: Jewish Military Service in the Era of Joseph II', in Marsha Rozenblit and Pieter Judson (eds.), *Studies in Central European Nationalism* (Oxford and New York: Berghahn Books, 2004). A study that shows the distinctive path of civil integration of Jews in the late eighteenth-century Habsburg Monarchy.

Sorkin, David. *Moses Mendelssohn and the Religious Enlightenment* (Berkeley and Los Angeles: University of California Press, 1996). Analysis of Mendelssohn's work that integrates his Hebrew and German writings, and discusses the use of Enlightenment to reinvigorate traditional religion.

Stanislawski, Michael. *For Whom Do I Toil? Judah Leib Gordon and the Crisis of Russian Jewry* (New York and Oxford: Oxford University Press, 1988). A biography of a major Haskalah figure that discusses the crucial issues facing the Russian Jewish community in the nineteenth century.

Sutcliffe, Adam. *Judaism and Enlightenment* (Cambridge: Cambridge University Press, 2003). A study of seventeenth- to eighteenth-century European thought that emphasizes the continuing fascination with Spinoza and the challenges of Jews and Judaism for Enlightenment theories of abstract universalism.

3 | Persecution

Robert Jan van Pelt

Since the destruction of the Second Temple, the majority of the Jewish people has lived as an ethnic and religious minority, subject to sustained prejudice, debilitating social and economic constraints, spatial confinement, and episodes of more or less intense persecutions, ranging from riots and pogroms to massacres and expulsions. The motivations of the persecutors were varied. For the Romans, the Jews were a political and social challenge to some of the underlying principles of the Pax Romana: they were considered to hate non-Jews and display contempt for the gods. For the Christians, the Jews were the murderers of Christ, and the persistence of Judaism provided a challenge to the legitimacy of the New Covenant embodied in the Church. For Muslims, the Jews were, in the words ascribed to Muhammad, 'vendors of error'. Religious discrimination marked the Jews as outsiders in the majority Christian and Muslim cultures, making them into easy scapegoats for many conflicts that arose within those cultures. In the late middle ages, for example, anti-Jewish riots were often the result of the tension between ordinary folk and royal authority, in which the Jews, nominally under the protection of the king, served as convenient stand-ins for the inviolable monarch. Christians and Muslims did, however, recognize that Jews had a purpose in God's creation, and until the modern age persecution did not culminate in attempts to eradicate all Jews. Also the force of tradition in a customary society helped to preserve a place for the Jews: because the Jews had been granted a place within society in the past, they could claim one in the present, and the future.

Jews developed ways of dealing with the permanent restrictions and recurrent persecutions. First of all, inequality was the norm in the hierarchical societies of the pre-modern era. Jews learned to appease and bribe the persecutors, and, if this failed, to hide from them or flee elsewhere. They also knew that, if all these mechanisms failed, they could avert death by apostasy. On a metaphysical level, Jews could explain the meaning of their exile and their sufferings to themselves through reference to Adam and Eve's expulsion from Paradise and the consequent homelessness of all people. Yet at the same time Jews paid a tremendous price for their existence as pariahs. The restrictions and persecutions created a suspicious community for which nothing except death was certain. And while the ghettos occasionally produced great scholars, fine poets, and rich merchants, the great majority of Jews were demoralized paupers seeking to cajole others into giving charity. And while all Jews remembered a glorious past, most experienced the present as shameful humiliation. The result was a great psychological strain.

The promise of emancipation and the rise of antisemitism

In the eighteenth century the prospects for European Jews improved. The *philosophes* questioned the validity of social or religious tradition as a way of navigating the great questions of existence, and called for a new society structured by the dictates of reason alone. Reason dictated that all men were created equal, and that all deserved, therefore, an equal opportunity of self-realization within a unified nation-state. The Enlightenment project, which informed the ideals of the American and French revolutions, initiated the political emancipation of the Jews as citizens.

Yet the promise of emancipation was frustrated by the paradox that accompanied the development of the nation-state in the early nineteenth century: while Jews deserved full emancipation as citizens of the state, they did not really belong to the nation, increasingly defined as a community of people of a common descent—the English descended from the Anglo-Saxons, the French from the Gauls, the Germans from ancient Germanic tribes, and so on. At the same time, thinkers on the left identified a so-called 'Jewish Question', because the Jews were too obsessed with money to be fit for the socialist commune. And reactionary politicians blamed the Jews as the cause of an assumed social and moral degeneration that came with laissez-faire capitalism, urbanization, industrialization, secularization, democratization, social mobility, and cultural modernism. Combined with a new concept that the world was divided into various incompatible races, that the Jews were of a different—'Semitic'—race from the 'Aryan' Europeans, and that race mixing led to physical, mental, and moral degeneration (ideas advanced in his Essai sur l'inégalitié des races humaines (1853–5) by the comte de Gobineau), those on the right proclaimed the emancipation and consequent assimilation of the Jews as a dangerous precursor to a feared destruction of European supremacy. By the late nineteenth century an antisemitic ideology that preached a reversal of Jewish emancipation had become a shorthand for, and part and parcel of, opposition to various manifestations of the modern world. As such, it created a whole host of anti-Jewish sentiments, images, and tropes that proved to have great imaginative and political power.

In this climate of polite oppression, talented and ambitious Jews faced both the promise of opportunity and incessant obstacles to social and economic mobility. This led to weariness, despair, and resentment. Many responded by abandoning the Jewish communities and religion through conversion to Christianity, and then found that they had exchanged their pariah status for that of a parvenu—still excluded, still an outcast. Many redirected their anger towards their own Jewish identity, or those Jews—especially the traditional *shtetl* Jews—who refused to assimilate. Jews, especially the assimilated Jews, continued to internalize their own humiliation and persecution, and came to hate themselves. Indeed, some of bitterest antisemites were to be found amongst Jews themselves.

Riots, pogroms, and calls for a final solution to the Jewish problem

Violence followed antisemitic rhetoric. In Russia the assassination of Alexander II in 1881 by anarchists, three of whom were Jews, initiated a wave of persecution. The government's formula for solving the Jewish problem was 'one-third emigration, one-third conversion, and for one-third death'. Jewish life was forcefully restricted to the Pale of Settlement, the area of Russia that had been Polish once. At the same time the economic situation in the Pale declined, creating widespread social unrest. The government found it convenient to blame the Jews, and the result was various waves of pogroms, some instigated and others tolerated by the government. The Kishinev pogrom of 1903 left fifty-one Jews dead, ten times as many wounded, 700 houses burned, and 600 shops looted. Following age-old practice, the Jews of Kishinev had not resisted the massacres. Perhaps passivity had helped the bulk of the community to survive, but many believed that such an attitude was obscene. In his poem 'In the City of Slaughter', the poet Hayim Nahman Bialik lashed out in fury against the passivity of the Kishinev Jews.

More than 700 pogroms followed the Japanese destruction of Russia's fleet in the Far East and the Revolution of 1905. As far as right-wing political organizations were concerned, Jews were to blame for everything. Pamphlets described an alleged international Jewish conspiracy that aimed to ruin Russia and enslave its population. Extreme right-wing political organizations then seized on a longer expression of the conspiracy theory, the so-called *Protocols of the Elders of Zion*, a fabrication that claimed to be the leaked minutes of a secret meeting of senior Jewish leaders revealing their supposed machinations to control the world.

Many Jews, like those of Kishinev, remained passive in the face of atrocity. Others tried to get out. The pogroms triggered a mass movement of unheard-of proportions: facilitated by the lack of border controls, some 2 million Jews left Russia between the 1880s and 1914 for Western Europe and America. Many of these Jews remained in the rapidly growing metropolises of Berlin and Vienna, where Germans and Austrians, already nervous because of the enormous social and economic changes brought by industrialization, regarded the arrival of these destitute *Ostjuden* (eastern Jews) with anxiety and anger.

Finally there was a political response, which took two forms. Many Jews opted for revolutionary struggle within Russia. This led to a predominance of Jews in the revolutionary parties, which confirmed the reactionaries and the government in their belief that the antisemitic policies had been justified after all. Another choice was Zionism. Judging antisemitism to be both ubiquitous and eternal, and that no amount of correct Jewish behaviour or political change in Russia would cause it to disappear, Zionists believed that the eventual establishment of a Jewish state would eliminate antisemitism, both because the Jews would shed their abnormality and become a people like other people, and because the Diaspora would cease to exist as Jews left Europe and returned to their homeland. Without Jews in their midst, the peoples of Europe would cease to fear and hate them.

The Great War and the Russian Civil War

The outbreak of the Great War of 1914–18 led, in all belligerent countries, to a wave of nationalistic hysteria that triggered profound xenophobia, which in turn led to a rapid deterioration of the position of the Jews. In Central Europe the bulk of the fighting between Russia and the Central Powers took place in the heartland of European Jewry. The Russian government initiated massive deportations of 600,000 Jews who, as Yiddish speakers, were considered pro-German agents. In Germany Jews were seen as being insufficiently patriotic and accused of shirking their duties at the front. In other words, they failed the test of war, and therefore did not belong to the national community.

After the Bolshevik Revolution of 1917 a vicious civil war broke out that raged in the Pale of Settlement. The Whites considered Bolshevism as a movement inspired by the writings of one Jew (Marx) and dominated by other Jews (such as Trotsky, Zinovyev, Kamenev, and Litvinov). Presses in White-held territory printed cheap editions of the *Protocols*, with a lurid addendum blaming the Bolshevik Revolution on a worldwide Jewish conspiracy, and linking it to the reign of the Antichrist. White forces focused their rage on the Jews in the areas under their control. At least 120,000 Jews became victims of systematic massacres. When the White armies were defeated, their officers fled to Germany and France, taking their hatred with them. By 1919 reactionary Germans became obsessed about the danger posed by a worldwide Jewish conspiracy. They blamed the defeat of Germany on a Jewish 'stab in the back.' They found evidence for this wherever they cared to look: Jews were doing well in the new Weimar Republic. For one political activist, Adolf Hitler, all Gentiles faced annihilation, and he promised that when he came to power he would deal with the Jews appropriately.

Yet, as things worsened for Jews there was also a horizon of promise. With the Balfour Declaration of 1917, pledging the Jews a homeland in Palestine, and the British Mandate of 1922 for that territory, a solution to the problem of persecution seemed at hand. The Zionist project to create a universal refuge for all Jews now really got under way. It was clear, however, that it could not be an immediate solution for the hundreds of thousands of Jews suffering in post-war Central Europe. Palestine was an underdeveloped country with little infrastructure and few resources. A proposal to transport 600,000 Jews from the Ukraine to Palestine was rejected because it would have led to the death of at least half of them after arrival. The Zionist leadership and the British agreed that immigration of Jews should occur on the basis of the absorption capacity of the country, and following sound demographic principles. The combination of the right skills and the right ideological motivation, not the fact of persecution, was to determine who was to be allowed to settle. Palestine was not to be a haven for the millions of destitute *Schnorrers* and *Luftmenschen*, but a land for hardy pioneers. It was expected to take many decades before the country would be able to offer hope to the majority of European Jews.

The inter-war period

In the post-war rearrangement of Central Europe, a number of new nation-states (Poland, the Baltic States, Czechoslovakia, Yugoslavia) emerged from the ruins of multinational empires. One state (Romania) was dramatically enlarged. And then there were the losers: Germany reduced; German Austria forbidden to join the German Reich and forced into sullen independence; and Hungary stripped of two-thirds of its land. Many of these countries had large and mainly destitute Jewish minorities that, in a situation of endemic poverty framed by national policies shaped by ethnic chauvinism, did badly throughout the 1920s and worse in the 1930s. In Poland the situation of the Jews became catastrophic in 1935, when a clique of semi-fascist officers came to power. They identified a 'surplus' of 1 million Jews and proposed schemes to deport them to Madagascar. By 1937 Poland was waging an undeclared war against the Jews, replete with organized pogroms, random acts of street violence, economic boycotts of Jewish businesses, and the destruction of Jewish property. In Romania both liberal and fascist politicians openly discussed the expulsion of all the Jews, and restrictions were added to restrictions. In Hungary the Jews had to put up with systematic discrimination. Jews living in the Soviet Union faced a different challenge. The communists destroyed Jewish communal organizations and restructured the economy, pushing Jews out of trades and crafts and into industry. Thus the Soviets solved the tsar's 'Jewish Problem' through forced assimilation. Antisemitism was dead as a political issue, yet popular antisemitism, driven underground, did not diminish.

The 500,000 Jews in the German Reich ascended high in the Weimar Republic, and fell deep in the years that followed. Between 1919 and 1933 they seemed fully acculturated and assimilated into a German society which, at least officially, embraced democracy. Jews enjoyed full access to the highest political offices. Yet throughout this period antisemitism remained alive on the far right. In 1933 Hitler's violently antisemitic National Socialists came to power amidst a terrible economic depression. Ascribing all of Germany's troubles to Jewish machinations, the Nazis immediately embarked on a policy of excluding Jews from German economic, social, and political life. A boycott of Jewish businesses (April 1933) was quickly followed by the dismissal of Jewish civil servants and teachers, limits on Jewish lawyers, the denaturalization of Jews naturalized after 1918, the establishment of a quota on the number of Jewish schoolchildren and students, restrictions on owning property, and so on. In two years the Jews were largely removed from German social, economic, and cultural life. It was a generally popular policy, as many German businessmen and professionals profited from the elimination of their competition.

With the passage of the Nuremberg Laws (1935), Jews were stripped of their citizenship, and marriages between Jews and non-Jews were forbidden. Initially those Jews who had been targets because of their political views had left the country, but most German Jews still believed that they would be able to outlast the Nazi regime. They believed that it would either moderate its racial views or fall. After 1935 its racial policies became more violent, and it became clear that the Nazis were there to stay. As German Jews now began to scramble to find refuge abroad, those western nations that in 1933 had offered places of refuge began to close their borders, and the English effectively closed Palestine in response to Arab riots.

After the countrywide pogrom of November 1938, known as *Kristallnacht* (the 'night of broken glass'), the Nazi regime completed the process of disenfranchisement and expropriation, and so destroyed the illusion of a Jewish future in Germany. Only as forced labourers who were paid a pittance and enjoyed no benefits or pension were Jews allowed to participate in the economy. In a systematic, bureaucratized persecution, Jews were banned from theatres, cinemas, concerts, exhibitions, and parks, and all Jewish communal organizations were shut down. With a massive destruction of synagogues that had begun on *Kristallnacht*, and the banishment of the music of Jewish composers and books written by Jewish writers, all traces of Jewish contribution to German civilization were now erased. At the same time, the media were filled with antisemitic propaganda depicting Jews as the enemies of light. The German people stood by, in silence.

By November 1938 Germany also included Austria, annexed in March of that year, and the formerly Czechoslovak Sudeten areas, handed over in the Munich Accord of September. Territorial expansion not only brought millions of Germans into the Reich, but in the case of Austria also 200,000 Jews. In the paradoxical euphoria that accompanied Austria's liquidation, Austro-Germans found great delight in subjecting their Jewish neighbours to public abuse and random violence that shocked even the Nazi invaders. All discriminatory laws and decrees passed in over five years in the German Reich were immediately applied in the formerly Austrian territories. The combination of physical violence and instant humiliation and destitution led all of Austrian Jewry to try to emigrate. With most countries unwilling to admit Jewish refugees, individual efforts had become almost useless. In response, the Gestapo sent its specialist for Jewish affairs, Adolf Eichmann, to Vienna to take charge of the emigration procedures through the creation of a 'conveyer belt' operation financed by expropriated Jewish assets. A centralized process of expulsion stripped each Jew of all his possessions, and gave him in return a passport with an exit visa. In six months Eichmann's Central Office for Jewish Emigration forced 50,000 Jews over the borders.

Hitler's European War, 1939–1941

In March 1939 the German Reich annexed what remained of the Czech lands, so proving that Nazi policy went beyond reuniting Germans with the Reich. Britain and France now tried to save what could be saved, and guaranteed the security of Poland. When, in September 1939, Hitler invaded Poland, the western allies declared war on Germany. This did not bode well for the Jews, as Hitler had announced only eight months earlier that a new war, which by definition would be the result of the international Jewish conspiracy, would lead to the annihilation of the Jews.

With the conquest of western and central Poland (the Soviets had taken the eastern part), the Germans acquired control over 2.3 million Jews, most of them destitute, and all of them despised *Ostjuden*. Initially the Nazis planned to create a Jewish reservation in the eastern districts of occupied Poland and to deport all of German, Polish, and Czech Jewry there. The German army objected, and in the summer of 1940, after the conquest of France, the German foreign ministry began to develop plans to deport all of Europe's Jews to the French colony of Madagascar—the proposal originally suggested by the Polish government in the mid-1930s. As the foreign ministry weighed its options, the Nazis implemented a reign of terror over the Polish Jews. They marked Jews with yellow patches or Stars of David, looted Jewish homes and institutions, attacked and sometimes executed individual Jews at will, established curfews, forbade Jews access to civil society, forced most men into forced labour battalions, and denied Jewish children education. Jews from Polish areas formally annexed to Germany were dumped in occupied Poland.

Awaiting the deportation of Polish Jewry to Madagascar, the Nazis began to isolate the Jewish population in occupied Poland by establishing closed ghettos nominally ruled by Jewish councils, but practically under direct control of German administrators. Insufficiently supplied with food, medicine, and other resources, these murderously overcrowded ghettos full of totally destitute people and vermin became death-traps. Starvation led to contagious disease. Tuberculosis, dysentery, and typhus were rampant. In Warsaw 18 per cent of the Jewish population died in the three years between the fall of the city in September 1939 and the deportations to the death camps in August 1942. In total, 800,000 Jews died in the ghettos established in Poland and, after 1941, elsewhere in Eastern Europe.

No ghettos were established in Western Europe, which came under German occupation (Denmark, Norway, Holland, Belgium, Luxembourg, northern France) or influence (southern France, Italy) in the spring and summer of 1940. But it did not take the Germans, or their allies like the Vichy French government, long to initiate a process of political disenfranchisement, social isolation, and economic expropriation that repeated the pattern developed in Germany in the 1930s. If in the case of Holland and Belgium the initiative was wholly with the German occupiers, in France the Vichy government took its own initiatives, imprisoning German Jewish refugees in desolate internment camps or consigning them to slave labour in the Sahara Desert, stripping Jews who had been naturalized of their citizenship, excluding French Jews first from the civil service and many professions, and then from their businesses and property. Remarkably enough, compared to Vichy France, fascist Italy proved much less enthusiastic in persecuting its Jewish population. Few in number and well integrated in society, the Italian Jews were never seen by their Gentile neighbours as representatives of some great conspiracy, and whatever antisemitic legislation was passed was applied without much enthusiasm.

As the war spread, most of south-east Europe came under German occupation (Greece, Serbia) or influence (Romania, Hungary, Bulgaria, Croatia), and the Jews faced quickly worsening conditions. In Romania the dictator Marshal Antonescu announced his desire to expel the whole Jewish community of 300,000 people after the loss of substantial territories to Hungary and the Soviet Union (1940). Romanian troops, enraged by that loss of land, massacred hundreds of Jews in the countryside. A wave of antisemitic legislation expelled Jews from schools, universities, and the professions, removed them from commerce, and expropriated Jewish-owned property and businesses. In a large pogrom in Bucharest, fascist Iron Guardsmen butchered hundreds of Jews and destroyed the major synagogues. In Hungary, economic restrictions were passed, and in 1941 marriages between non-Jews and Jews were forbidden.

Jews responded to this in various ways. Some opportunists quickly acclimatized to the bewildering situation all Jews found themselves in, and became big operators in a small world. Others just withdrew from the present, longing for the past or dreaming about the future. At the same time, many inmates of the ghettos and Western European Jews who were confined to an ever-shrinking world tried almost heroically to maintain the semblance of normal life. To organize classes when education was forbidden, to study and keep religious observances, to treat the sick when no drugs were available, to shelter orphans when no one else cared: these simple deeds became acts of great charity.

The non-Jewish world ignored the problems of the Jews. If emigration had been very difficult in the late 1930s, after the outbreak of the war it had become practically impossible as countries at war with Germany now completely sealed their borders in fear of German spies, and Germany kept the borders closed in Europe. In German-ruled Europe few took notice of what happened to the Jews. The citizens of occupied countries were too much concerned with their own suffering to notice that their Jewish neighbours had an even worse deal, and many people profited from the removal of Jews from civic society. Indeed, even resistors articulated the view that, after the desired and anticipated German defeat, Jews should not be allowed to return to their old positions.

The Holocaust, 1941–1945

By the summer of 1941 European Jewry had reached the bottom. Its situation was worse than it had been during the time of greatest restrictions in the middle ages. Effectively, Europe's Jews faced political, social, cultural, economic, biological, religious, and moral genocide, and within a generation it would have died. But while killing of individual Jews had been frequent, and massacres of Jews had occurred, up until 1941 the Jews had not been subjected to systematic killing. Genocide had not yet turned into a Holocaust.

This changed with the German invasion of the Soviet Union in June 1941. First the Romanian army began to massacre Romanian Jews in the border districts with the Soviet Union, continued with the massacres in Romanian territory occupied by the Soviets in 1940 and quickly recovered in June of 1941, and then unleashed its rage on Jews in Soviet territories granted to Romania in compensation for the loss of northern Transylvania to Hungary. After the Romanians had set new standards for cruelty, the Germans were to show the blessings of Teutonic rationale and efficiency. In 1938 and 1939 the *Anschluss* with Austria, the annexation of Bohemia and Moravia, and the conquest of Poland had brought almost 3 million unwanted Jews into the Reich: the Germans did not now want to end up with millions more unwanted Jews as the reward for victory over Bolshevism. Mobile killing squads (*Einsatzgruppen*: 'special operations units') swiftly followed the advancing army into Russia to identify, concentrate, and execute all communist leaders and Jews in the conquered areas. Initially killing mainly male Jews, from August onwards the killing squads massacred all Jews they encountered, men, women, and children. In a streamlined operation, the Germans had initiated the annihilation of Russian Jewry. More than 1.3 million Jews were to be shot and machine-gunned by the killing squads.

Once the German leadership had decided that killing was the solution to the 'Jewish Problem' in Russia, it did not take long for this to become the 'Final Solution' to the 'Jewish Problem' in all of Europe. A drift towards what was to become the Holocaust was strengthened because a powerful reason not to kill the Jews—the idea that Europe's Jews served as useful hostages to prevent the allegedly Jewish-controlled United States from entering the war—had failed to work. By the middle of August 1941 the United States and Britain were effectively allies, and in a joint declaration Roosevelt and Churchill called for the 'final destruction of Nazi tyranny'. With the Madagascar option dead because of the continuing war in the West, deportation of Jews to a territory outside Europe had ceased to be an option. Thus, the German leadership slowly moved towards the decision to kill all European Jews. In the early Autumn of 1941 German

Jews were marked with yellow stars, emigration was officially forbidden, and deportations of German Jews to occupied areas in the Soviet Union began. By late Autumn German Jews were included in the massacres of Russian Jews. When, in December 1941, the United States formally entered the war on the side of Britain and the Soviet Union, Hitler passed a death sentence on all Jews. Goebbels noted in his diary that, in a speech to the Gauleiters on 12 December, Hitler announced 'a clean sweep' to solve the 'Jewish Question'. Hitler stated that 'the world war has arrived, and the destruction of Jewry must follow. This matter is to be considered without any sentimentality.'

The only question that remained was who was to be in charge, and how it was to be done. With the Wannsee Conference of 20 January 1942, Himmler's SS and Heydrich's RSHA achieved formal authority over what had now become a programme of systematic genocide. Various methods of mass killing were tried, but the establishment of specially built extermination camps, equipped with gas chambers, emerged as the most efficient solution. In early 1942 construction crews began the building of three extermination camps, equipped with gas chambers, near the Polish villages of Belzec, Sobibor, and Treblinka. Located on railway lines, these camps came into operation in the summer of 1942. At the same time an existing concentration camp near Auschwitz was given more sophisticated extermination installations in the form of four new crematoria equipped with gas chambers. The official incineration capacity of these crematoria was 4,416 people per day. The gas chambers with the incinerators, to be operated by Jewish slave labourers, provided a thoroughly modern and technologically sophisticated solution to the problem of mass murder: it introduced an anonymity of procedure in which the killing was invisible, and issues of personal responsibility became diffused to such an extent that the SS doctors conducting the selection of arriving deportees could convince themselves that they were not accomplices in an enormous crime, but saviours of those whom they assigned to slave labour.

These camps quickly become the goal of massive deportations from the ghettos in the East and the collection points and transit camps in the West. The programme was organized and co-ordinated by the same Adolf Eichmann who had established the conveyer-belt system of expropriation and emigration in post-*Anschluss* Vienna. By this time Eichmann's agents ran offices in every capital of German-controlled Europe, but now 'emigration' had become 'deportation'. Between July 1942 and October 1944, when Himmler officially closed the last remaining killing installations, between 2.7 and 3 million Jews were gassed in these extermination camps, and another 150,000 Jews were to be killed in other concentration camps where they were sent for slave labour.

Rumours about the camps circulated from late 1942, but the Germans were successful in keeping the details about their operation secret until the summer of 1944. Most people, Jews and non-Jews alike, were unwilling to believe the unbelievable, and judged the stories to be propaganda lies. With the refusal to accept the existence of the extermination camps, both the Jewish and the Allied response to this radically new development in the history of persecution remained wholly inadequate. The best policy the Jewish leadership in the ghettos offered was to make the Jews indispensable to the German war machine as slave labourers. Based on reasonable assumptions, this policy did not address the madness of it all. The Allies decided that the only real remedy was an Allied victory—one that most likely was to occur too late. And so the salvation of Jews depended on the heroism of those thousands of individual people who sheltered them in hiding-places. Not everyone stood by silently or participated in genocide. The many rescuers, still far too few to make a real difference to the statistics of death, showed that other forms of behaviour were possible.

After Auschwitz

When the Germans were defeated in 1945, some 900,000 European Jews, condemned to death by the Nazis in early 1942, survived because they were sheltered in neutral countries, or by the British or Soviet armies. Another 1.5 million had survived direct or indirect Nazi rule. But some 6 million Jews had been killed, and most communities in what had been for almost a thousand years the heartland of the Jewish people were wiped out.

Antisemitism in post-war Europe was still rife, and the survivors had great difficulties in re-establishing themselves in societies that only a few years earlier had either welcomed, or at least tolerated, their disenfranchisement, expropriation, isolation, and deportation. In this situation Zionism offered the only viable answer, and many survivors moved illegally to Palestine and, after 1948, legally to the State of Israel. Yet the defeat of Nazism and the establishment of a Jewish state did not end persecution. Jews in the Arab world faced increased harassment, pogroms, and sometimes direct persecution. As a result, most Middle Eastern and North African Jews left for Israel, and with that another historically important part of the Diaspora ceased to exist. In its place the Arab world gained the ubiquitous presence of the imaginary Jew of antisemitic propaganda created in tsarist Russia and perfected in Nazi Germany.

European antisemitism declined in the 1950s, and in the 1960s the destruction of Europe's Jews, which became known as 'the Holocaust' or 'the Shoah' (Hebrew for 'ruin' or 'catastrophe') became a focus for historical scholarship, literary activity, moral and theological reflection, and political and social action. First in North America, Western Europe, and Israel, and since 1989 in Eastern Europe also, the Holocaust has become seen as the central crisis in Western civilization, separating history into two epochs, 'Before' and 'After Auschwitz'. The rise in the West of multiethnic and multicultural societies suggests that the Shoah may serve as an important warning of what might happen when racism is allowed free range. The result has been a remarkable scholarly and intellectual engagement with the history of the persecution of the Jews in general and the Holocaust in particular, which makes this field of study both exciting and relevant. The popularity as travel destinations of major Holocaust-related sites such as the Auschwitz-Birkenau State Museum (Oświęcim), the establishment and growth of significant centres for the representation of the Holocaust, such as Yad Vashem (Jerusalem), the United States Holocaust Memorial Museum (Washington DC), or the Anne Frank House (Amsterdam), and the success of academic programmes such as the one offered by Clark University (Worcester, Massachusetts), testify to the unique place of the Holocaust in the collective memory of the West.

FURTHER READING

Arendt, Hannah. *Eichmann in Jerusalem* (New York: Viking, 1963). A very controversial account of Eichmann, the Eichmann trial, and the Holocaust by a great Jewish philosopher.

Bauman, Zygmunt. *Modernity and the Holocaust* (Ithaca, NY: Cornell University Press, 1989). The classical sociological analysis of the Holocaust.

Browning, Christopher R. *Ordinary Men* (New York: HarperCollins, 1992). A fascinating case-study of the way ordinary German policemen turned into mass killers.

Cohn, Norman. *Warrant for Genocide* (New York and Evanston: Harper & Row, 1967). The classic study on the *Protocols of the Elders of Zion*.

Dwork, Debórah. *Children With A Star* (New Haven and London: Yale University Press, 1991). The first comprehensive history of Jewish youth in Nazi Europe.

Dwork, Debórah, and Robert Jan van Pelt. *Holocaust: A History* (New York: W. W. Norton, 2002). This book provides a concise yet comprehensive history of the Holocaust within the broader context of European history and the history of the Second World War.

Hilberg, Raul. *The Destruction of the European Jews*, 3 vols. (New York and London: Holmes & Meier, 1985). A massive and magisterial account of the German machinery of destruction.

Katz, Jacob. *Exclusiveness and Tolerance* (London: Oxford University Press, 1961). A classic study on Jewish–Gentile relations in medieval and modern times.

Katz, Jacob. *From Prejudice to Destruction* (Cambridge, Mass.: Harvard University Press, 1980). The classical introduction to modern antisemitism.

Langer, Lawrence L. *The Holocaust and the Literary Imagination* (New Haven and London: Yale University Press, 1975). A solid introduction to Holocaust literature.

Marrus, Michael R. *The Holocaust in History* (Toronto: Lester and Orpen Dennys, 1987). An indispensable introduction to the historiography of the Holocaust.

Mosse, George L. *Toward the Final Solution* (New York: H. Ferrtig, 1978). An excellent introduction to the history of European racism.

Van Pelt, Robert Jan, and Debórah Dwork *Auschwitz: 1270 to the Present* (London: Yale University Press, 1996). A history of the most notorious German death-camp.

Wyman, David S. (ed.). *The World Reacts to the Holocaust* (Baltimore and London: Johns Hopkins University Press, 1996). A superb collection of twenty five essays on the way different post-war societies—those of the former Axis powers, those that had been occupied by the Germans, those of the former Allies, and Israeli society—responded to survivors, questions of guilt and restitution, and the larger cultural legacy of the Holocaust.

4 | A national home

Emanuele Ottolenghi

Zionism was born in the midst of a prolonged struggle for the reinterpretation of Jewish identity which the Enlightenment, emancipation, and the rise of modern antisemitism had triggered. Emerging as an alternative for Jews seeking cultural renewal and escape from antisemitism in nineteenth-century Europe, Zionism culminated in the establishment of the State of Israel in 1948. Essentially, Zionism has been defined as: 'An ideology pertaining to the idea of a return to Zion and its restoration as a homeland for the Jews that not only transcended the messianic idea but also produced extensive social results and a continuous social development.'[1]

Important differences existed within Zionism. Not all Zionists made return to Zion a non-negotiable condition. Territorial Zionism was prepared to settle for the acquisition of any territory made available to Jews; cultural Zionism merely advocated the creation of a Jewish centre in the Land of Israel that would become a source of regeneration for the Diaspora; Diaspora nationalism promoted cultural autonomy for Jews where they mainly resided; political Zionism supported the achievement of national goals in the Land of Israel through international diplomacy and the active support of international powers; and practical Zionism proposed settlement in the Land of Israel with or without international support, ultimately creating a fait accompli through immigration, purchase of land, and creation of communities.

Zionists differed also on goals: was the national home a safe haven for persecuted Jews, or, regardless of whether physical survival was at stake, should it strive to create a new Jewish identity and foster a national revival? Territorial Zionism emphasized the former, practical and cultural Zionism the latter. Other differences arose regarding the shape of the national home, ranging from a liberal secular state to a Jewish state embodying the spirit and cultural heritage of Judaism. Finally, even among those considering the Land of Israel the non-negotiable locus of Jewish statehood, disputes arose regarding which part of biblical Israel should become home for the modern Jewish nation. As aspirations clashed with the realities of world politics, colonial interests, and indigenous opposition, different answers arose reflecting different conceptions of Zionism.

The Jews as a modern nation

That for centuries Jews viewed themselves—and were viewed—as a people is a truism needing no proof. That return to Zion was integral to Jewish tradition is also beyond dispute. Until the nineteenth century both notions reflected a religious tradition which viewed return to the ancestral land as the culmination of a redemptive process initiated by divine intervention and coincident with the end of times. It was a messianic vision that, despite significant exceptions, expressed a passive acceptance of exile in the present.

Four elements, common to all streams of Zionism, constitute a departure from these religious assumptions: (1) Jews are a collective bestowed with the distinct features of a *nation* in the modern, secular sense; (2) the Diaspora condition—living as a minority in exile—is defective; (3) a national project leading to national autonomy and at best national sovereignty is therefore desirable; and (4) this project has a worldly goal—either physical survival or cultural revival and regeneration for the Jewish collective, or more often a combination of both—rather than the traditional religious messianic one. In simple terms, for those advocating the establishment of a national home exile was neither the result of divine will—as tradition postulated—nor a mission bestowed on the people of Israel to bring a message to the world—as Reform Judaism suggested. Exile was an accident of history that was neither morally compelling nor irreversible.

Therefore, Zionism was both revolutionary in advocating a break with the Jewish past of tradition and exile, and steeped in the Jewish past in its hope to foster a Jewish renaissance. It tried to address Jewish distress in Europe, resulting both from cultural alienation and threats of physical annihilation, and offered an alternative to assimilation, Reform Judaism, and tradition.

By suggesting that Jews were a modern nation, with the attributes and rights of other nations, Zionism sought to normalize the Jewish condition in the world—making the Jews masters of their destiny through self-determination. Toward this end, Zionism advocated collective Jewish efforts to return Jews to their ancestral land and the creation of a Jewish state to make Jews 'a people like all peoples'.

In doing so, Zionism did not artificially create a national identity, nor was it simply the response to prejudice, as some have suggested. While nationalism is a modern phenomenon, it builds on existing elements of identity, reflecting more than the urge to escape discrimination. Persecution long preceded the rise of Zionism, and the traditional response had been flight to more hospitable environments. To make persecution the only cause of the rise of Zionism fails to explain why, starting from the second half of the nineteenth century, many Jews consciously preferred the nationalist option over migration to the New World. While elites selectively tapped into Jewish tradition, attempts to re-elaborate a collective identity in national terms would fail in the absence of a pre-existing strong, collective ethnic allegiance. Jews eventually embraced Zionism because it reflected elements of identity pre-dating the reformulation of Jewishness in modern nationalist terms. If anything, the abrupt appearance of emancipation had diluted those elements. The convergence of pre-existing ethnic ties with modernizing trends, coupled with a sense of alienation from surrounding society caused by the loss of traditional identity, eventually produced Zionism as a nationalist synthesis of tradition and modernity.

Intellectually, the genesis of Zionism is located in trends that precede the outburst of modern antisemitism across Europe during the second part of the nineteenth century. Prior to Zionism's rise a cultural revival emphasized, rather than downplayed, ethnic and cultural allegiance to a Jewish collective, seeking common roots for a people even as modernizing trends were drawing Jews away from tradition.

Zionism's innovative force lay not in the argument that Jews were a nation; it was rather embodied in the notion that, as a modern nation endowed with the attributes of other nations, Jews should pursue a similarly nationalist option. Through self-help they could achieve self-determination in the shape of a secular political project, pertaining to the mundane rather than the messianic sphere.

Zionism's paradox

For centuries, the idea of return to the Land of Israel in Jewish tradition coexisted with a passive acceptance of exile. Longing for Zion was central to Judaism, yet no collective action was undertaken to actively pursue it. A Jewish community—albeit small—had always existed in the Holy Land. Individual Jews moved there. And the bond with the land remained paramount in Jewish self-image. Jews understood themselves not only as a minority, but as a minority in exile. Their intimate bond with the land, rather than merely distinct beliefs and practices, prevented their shift to being simply a religious community.

Yet, despite the longing for Zion and the sense of estrangement from host countries—nurtured over generations through persecutions and maintaining the dream of redemption—few moved to Zion. A paradox characterized Jewish Diaspora existence, entailing a tension between *Galut* (exile) and the future condition of *Geulah* (redemption). Both entailed a geographic, concrete dimension and a metaphysical, spiritual one. Exile was more than a condition inherent to Jewish existence, it was its essence. Only redemption would end it. Praying for redemption did not cancel the exile, but helped make sense of it. The land laid waste, emptied of its people, reflected exile. Ending exile would redeem both people and land: gathering exiles from the four corners of the earth and restoring the land to make it flow with milk and honey.

This paradox becomes more intriguing with the rise of Zionism. Tradition loosened its grip on Jewish identity. But Zionism, though openly revolting against tradition, made return central to the idea of Jewish continuity.

Zionism emerged at a time when Jewish identity was fracturing. Tempting as it was to join the surrounding societies as equals, the Jewish condition was both easy to leave behind and hard to erase completely.[2] The dilemmas posed by modernity and emancipation gave rise not only to Reform Judaism, neo-Orthodoxy, ultra-Orthodoxy, and assimilation, but also to a revival of Jewish identity in secular guise through the Haskalah, and eventually Zionism.

Zionism was a reaction to the need to reformulate Jewish identity in post-emancipation Europe, largely embraced by thoroughly assimilated and acculturated Jews. The growing tide of modern antisemitism undoubtedly influenced their rejection of reform, assimilation, emancipation, and integration, for it showed precisely to those who had done most to shed their Jewishness that their escape from Judaism had been futile. As many Jews rallied to embrace the principled universalism of liberalism, nationalism started carving out boundaries of exclusivity and exclusion, which, as the nineteenth century progressed, removed the Jew, whether traditional or assimilated, from the rising nations of Europe. Overlapping with the emergence of a Jewish nationalism, the failure of assimilation made the return to Zion appear the only possible path available to Jews.

The rise of Zionism coincided with a wave of pogroms and antisemitic events both in Eastern and Western Europe. Former supporters of assimilation, Jewish intellectuals like Leo Pinsker (1821–91), Peretz Smolenskin (1842–85), and Moshe Leib Lilienblum (1843–1910) now concluded that no matter how much Jews tried to assimilate, Gentile societies would still reject them. Pinsker's *Autoemancipation* was published in 1882, shortly after the 1881 pogroms in Russia. Theodor Herzl's (1860–1904) *Der Judenstaat* (1896) followed the Dreyfus Affair. Both saw the rise of modern antisemitism as evidence that efforts to assimilate and shed the vestiges of traditional Judaism had only exposed Jews to a new form of Gentile hatred, leaving them without the dignity of a tradition and sense of belonging as tools to bear the burden of discrimination. Neither saw a retreat into the past as a solution for a growing mass of emancipated Jews who had by then abandoned their Jewish roots. Both concluded that the way forward was a national project achieved through self-help.

However, it would be reductive to ascribe the ascendance of a movement advocating Jewish nationalism exclusively to antisemitism. While the quest for a national home undoubtedly reflected an existential threat, it was not only physical, but also spiritual and cultural. Its intellectual roots thus lie elsewhere.

The trajectory from the ghetto to integration had not been without cost, even where it briefly succeeded. In many cases (especially in Western Europe) the promise of emancipation had implied the renunciation of tradition, which over time held nothing but the promise of cultural alienation. In other cases, emancipation had produced, through the Haskalah, a Jewish cultural revival through the newly acquired access to secular education and professions. The acquisition of a cultural awareness steeped in modernity and emphasizing secular rather than traditional religious traits, contributed to the rise of a new sense of national pride, rooted in a cultural and spiritual sense of a distinct Jewish identity.

Transforming Hebrew into a modern vernacular was central to this revival, an effort spearheaded by Eliezer Ben-Yehuda (1858–1923). Many note that, though similar to other national movements in its conscious development of a 'national' language, Zionism is unique among nationalisms. Nationalists across Europe abandoned the high language of culture—German or Russian—in favour of the low spoken vernacular of the masses. Zionism, choosing Hebrew over Yiddish, did the opposite: it abandoned the language of the masses in favour of one not previously spoken, except in religious contexts or by the educated elites. However, by reviving this ancient tongue Zionists were not consciously selecting the lingua franca of empire or high culture over a spoken dialect; they were reasserting ethnic pride by adopting a language that represented the shared heritage of the nation, which, unlike Yiddish—a Germanic idiom developed in exile—represented the ideal link to a distant past of national independence. Until then a language largely confined to sacred matters, Hebrew was transformed into a vehicle for secular culture, thereby becoming a symbol of Hebrew revival in a national, secular, and modern sense. From an instrument of prayer and halakhic disputation it became a means to conduct a national existence in all its trivial manifestations. In open competition with Yiddish, representing exile, and European languages, reflecting the self-negation of assimilation, Hebrew was the embodiment of national and cultural revival.

Calls for a restoration of Zion were first heard within the framework of cultural revival and optimistic adherence to the liberal winds of 1848 Europe, notably in the writings of Heinrich Graetz (1817–91) and Moses Hess (1812–75). Though Hess in particular presciently saw the threat of a new antisemitism arising in the wake of emancipation that would nullify Jewish efforts to integrate, in his *Rome and Jerusalem* (1862) he still expressed full confidence in liberalism's ability to liberate the Jews from their predicament and restore them to independence. As for Graetz, though imbued with secular culture and dedicated, through his monumental work *The History of the Jews* (1853–76), to the process of Jewish secular acculturation, he readily rejected Reform Judaism's efforts to efface from Jewish identity the centrality of the Hebrew language, the Land of Israel, and the concomitant notion of return. He thus welcomed Hess's exposition of the Jewish condition, which rejected assimilation and articulated the need to reassert Jewish ethnic pride and identity within the confines of a modern world. Neither author was expressing the opening gambit of Zionism, which they preceded by a generation. Neither fully articulated a truly nationalist option, nor would that option have appealed to their Jewish contemporaries. Their contribution lies in their identification of the compelling strength of the primordial bond uniting Jews, that no process of emancipation, integration, and acculturation— let alone one entailing alienation and rejection—could completely cancel. Their rejection of total assimilation and their battle against Reform Judaism was not yet a full-fledged nationalism, but represented a proud assertion of Jewish distinctiveness along ethnic and cultural lines, both indispensable ingredients in the later development of Zionism.

In fact, the often humiliating act of self-negation that assimilation implied caused a backlash among not only religious traditionalists but also, crucially, among the enlightened and acculturated Jewish intelligentsia. The response was a concerted effort to reassert Jewish cultural and ethnic specificity, which eventually, before antisemitism became a catalyst, provided the foundations for Jewish nationalism.[3]

The rise of modern antisemitism, which targeted the assimilated and emancipated Jew no less—and perhaps even more—than the traditional religious Jew reinforced this trend of self-assertion, providing the final spark for the rise of a modern Jewish secular national project. Building on this growing ethnic pride, the national option became attractive once emancipation's failure became manifest, especially among those who had moved out of the traditional Jewish mould hoping that emancipation would offer a successful alternative to Jewish identity. In this sense, modern antisemitism was the catalyst for the rise of Jewish nationalism rather than its cause.

The challenge of tradition

Advocating a political project aimed at restoring Jewish sovereignty in the land of Israel, Zionists had to confront a number of cherished assumptions about Jewish self-image: associated with tradition, geography, the relation between Jews and Gentiles, political power, and—perhaps most troubling—the consequences of political power, namely, the use of force.[4]

Jewish tradition always had a passive attitude to exile: it was accepted as punishment for Jewish misdeeds, which divine intervention alone could reverse. Prayer, repentance, and passive acceptance of Jewish destiny functioned both as ways to cope with the harsh realities of exile and as instruments to hasten redemption. Active human endeavours promoting collective return were, by contrast, discouraged and viewed as counterproductive—prematurely forcing the hand of God would cause a backlash, bringing more tragedy. Although overcoming this impediment would prove easier to Jews who had at least partially abandoned tradition, the first challenge to this attitude emerged among traditional Jewish leaders, particularly rabbis Yehuda Alkalai (1798–1878) and Zvi Hirsch Kalisher (1795–1874). Both leaders, though steeped in the traditional Jewish world, were exposed to nineteenth-century European nationalist awakenings. Both, while essentially remaining within the traditionalist Jewish framework expectant of divine deliverance, called on the Jewish people to initiate redemption by returning to their ancestral land.

Neither saw any contradiction between messianic expectations and active human endeavours. Both believed redemption would be achieved gradually through a process of collective return and revival of Jewish observance which would prepare the ground.

This approach proposed 'a third strategy of response to the impact of modernity and the attendant threat of Reform Judaism: the exploitation of emancipationist modernity itself in order to quicken the messianic redemption. The resettlement of Eretz Israel was to be the means to that end.'[5] Both thinkers still thought in traditional, redemptive and messianic terms. But their authoritative work, which inspired the first efforts of Jewish settlement in the Land of Israel by the Hibbat Zion movement in the latter half of the nineteenth century, was instrumental in bridging the gap between tradition and secular Zionism.

A synthesis between Jewish tradition and modern nationalism was in time produced by religious Zionism. Rabbi Abraham Isaac Kook (1865–1935), perhaps its most influential thinker, overcame in the most compelling fashion the contradiction between present and future, exile and redemption. His understanding of exile was not predicated upon the notion of divine punishment. He held that Jews had been exiled to draw them away from power in order to be spared its evils. In an essay published during the First World War, he argued that: 'Forces from without compelled us to forsake the political arena of the world, but our withdrawal was also motivated by an inward assent, as if to say that we were awaiting the advent of a happier time, when government could be conducted without ruthlessness and barbarism. That is the day for which we hope.'[6]

Kook's faith relied on the imminent coming of a better world: 'The day has come—it is very near—when the world will grow gentler; we can begin to prepare ourselves, for it will soon be possible for us to conduct a state of our own founded on goodness, wisdom, justice, and the clear Light of God.' Kook's Zionism must be understood in the context of his messianic fervour. Convinced that his generation, intent on creating a Jewish society in the 1920s, would witness the advent of the Messiah and the dawn of a new age, he saw no difficulty in co-operation with secular Zionists and in encouraging religious Jews to take part in an eminently secular project.

The challenge of religious Zionism was then the most difficult from a theological point of view. Secular Zionists, who advocated a man-made secular state to address a historical, not metahistorical, problem, were fearful of the messianic ideas underlying the concept of redemption: 'In their minds, the religious concept of redemption was bound up with Jewish helplessness and passivity; hence only if religious aspirations were sharply demarcated and the heavy weight of absolute, metahistorical messianism set aside, could the field be freed from concrete activity in the here and now.'[7] The religious, for their part, tried to keep their messianism separate from the political project, preventing the former from overtaking the latter. Zionism represented a practical solution to the plight of Jews, not an instrument to 'force the end' and hasten the coming of the Messiah. In addition, gradualism allowed the state to be viewed as 'the dawn of redemption', which facilitated co-operation with secular Zionists and justified participation in a political enterprise short of full halakhic observance.

Aside from theological unease about 'forcing God's hand', the conflict over power and its manifestations remained central to religious and secular Zionists. The Holocaust made this dilemma, which Kook thought would be resolved through redemption, largely obsolete: the need for a Jewish state made its desirability from the perspective of Jewish morality a foregone conclusion for all but the most vehement religious critics of the idea. Even the ultra-Orthodox world, represented by the Agudat Israel,[8] traditionally opposed to Zionism, accepted Israel's establishment, which alone guaranteed a hope for the remnants of their by-then vanished world. They could not halakhically justify a Jewish state before the end of times. Yet conceptually, it was difficult to claim that God's hand should not be forced lest another curse should befall the Jews.

The challenge of geography

Confronting religious impediments to collective Jewish return to the Land of Israel before the end of times proved a major challenge, which was eventually overcome: with a few notable exceptions, even ultra-Orthodoxy and Reform Judaism have today by and large acquiesced to—if not openly endorsed—Israel's establishment. Competition with the advocates of assimilation and Jewish continuity in the Diaspora proved a harder task, as both positions still enjoy support among Jews: indeed, only a minority of Jews reside in Israel. Even among advocates of Jewish nationalism there existed disagreement over the location of the national project. Three positions can be identified: territorialism; Diaspora nationalism; and 'Zionism of Zion'.

Territorialism saw various efforts in the nineteenth century to create Jewish colonies in the New World, and peaked with the 'Uganda Controversy' of 1903, when the British government briefly offered the Zionist movement portions of East Africa—then under British colonial rule—for Jewish settlement. The proposal, presented to the Sixth Zionist Congress in August 1903, caused a major split, underscoring profoundly diverging views: a few who were ready to embrace the proposal viewed any territory as preferable to no territory, while most delegates saw the Land of Israel as the only possible option, regardless of its practicality. Herzl, who presented the proposal to an astonished congress, viewed the need to offer a haven to Jews escaping European antisemitism as paramount. Besides, his political vision—expressed in his two landmark Zionist texts, *Der Judenstaat and Altneuland* (1902)—envisioned a secular liberal state embodying liberal values and scientific progress, where Jewish heritage had little role. A thoroughly assimilated Jew, his main concern—predicated upon the failure of emancipation—was Jewish survival. For territorialists, a state for the Jews was more urgent, more compelling, than a Jewish state.

The failure of the Uganda proposal—not least because the British government soon withdrew its offer—shows the centrality of the Land even for those advocates of Jewish self-determination who had long since abandoned tradition as the main frame of reference for Jewish existence. Over time, only the Land of Israel proved compelling enough for Zionists.

Nevertheless, exclusive focus on the Land both by political and practical Zionists—the former advocating diplomacy, the latter active settlement—faced formidable challenges. One was the presence of indigenous populations living—albeit sparsely—within the areas that once formed biblical Israel. Another was the unlikely feasibility and sustainability of a project that strove to relocate most Jews within a short time-span. The Jewish historian Simon Dubnow (1860–1941) advocated seeking cultural autonomy for Jews in Eastern and Central Europe. Given the high concentration of Jews, cultural autonomy in the Diaspora seemed more realistic than mass migration to the Land of Israel. A middle position, championed by Asher Ginzberg (1856–1927)—commonly known by his pen-name Ahad Ha'am (one of the people)—saw the Land as the preferable centre of Jewish renaissance, but emphasized the need for a national revival in spiritual, cultural, and even physical terms before independence and mass migration. He envisioned Jewish return as the spearhead of national revival, and a Jewish organized presence in the Land as a means to this end, whose beneficial influence would reverberate through the Diaspora.

Ahad Ha'am's argument was both less and more compelling than Herzl's. Though his emphasis on spiritual and cultural rebirth did not offer solace to the persecuted masses, his disdain for a Zionism that emphasized territory and migration without focus on the substance of the national project underlined the need for a national identity built on more than the need to escape persecution. Besides, given the survival of an important Diaspora culture even after Israel's establishment, his argument was not without reason. His argument—like Dubnow's—failed because it did not take into account the main factor motivating both territorial and practical Zionism, namely, that Jews could not wait. The rising tide of antisemitism would wipe them out long before a national centre's influence would exert its beneficial influence. As for Dubnow, the lands which in his view offered a more realistic, if less ambitious, national project became within three generations a desolate graveyard. Thus, both cultural Zionism and Diaspora nationalism failed to provide a practical answer to tangible Jewish distress. Cultural Zionism had a stronger case, for a Jewish nationalism building national identity exclusively on the need to survive would arguably fail, in the long term, to outlive the causes of Jewish distress if those causes were eventually removed. Mere physical survival was not enough to guarantee the rebirth and survival of a national culture.

Other factors caused divisions among Zionists. Practical and political Zionists were divided over questions of strategy on the one hand, and the shape and size of the territory on the other.

Political Zionism advocated concentration of all efforts on diplomacy in order to obtain access to territory and the means to settle and transform it, over time, into a national home, by generous deliverance of international powers. Its main success was, aside from Herzl's flamboyant diplomacy which brought Zionism squarely into the world arena, the Balfour Declaration (1917), through which Britain—the greatest power of the day—recognized the legitimacy of Jewish national aspirations. The

Declaration, incorporated by the League of Nations into the British Mandate over Palestine in 1922, sanctioned Jewish national rights over portions of the Land of Israel.

However, dependency on the goodwill of others proved ephemeral. When their perceived national interests moved in different directions, Zionism had neither money nor friends to affect diplomacy in its favour. It was practical Zionism, emphasizing Jewish immigration and the creation of facts on the ground, that produced—neither solely through diplomacy nor by means of cultural influence alone—the critical mass of people needed to form a veritable Jewish society, bestowed with the attributes of a national community and the means of self-government.

Even among Zionists of Zion, territory proved divisive. Given the clash of territorial claims between Zionism and Arab nationalism, and the arbitrary drawing of boundaries which colonial powers imposed on the region after the First World War, many of Zionism's territorial hopes were frustrated. Zionists had to withdraw their initial demand for a territory 'from the Dan region to Beer-Sheva' formulated during the Versailles Peace Conference (1919). Though the original Mandate included most of what Zionism had claimed as its own, hopes were quickly dashed by British designs in the region and by the harsh realities of sharing a land with a competing national movement: by 1921 the British had separated the western and eastern areas of what was meant to become the Mandate of Palestine, artificially creating in most of its parts a state—Transjordan—meant to satisfy the territorial claims of one of Britain's Arab allies.

With the mounting tensions between Jews and Arabs and British pandering to Arab demands, the first proposal for partition of western Palestine emerged from the Peel Commission in 1937. The Commission, sent to inquire about the 1936 disturbances (later known as the Great Arab Revolt), concluded that only by dividing territory between Jews and Arabs could further violence be avoided. Partition eventually became the founding principle for future peace proposals in the long conflict between Jewish and Arab nationalisms. Acceptance or rejection of this principle underscored yet another division within Zionism, where maximalist claims over the entire land were consistently defeated but nevertheless showed extraordinary resilience. By the time the Mandate was established, the idea of Jewish immigration as the central means to achieve Zionist goals, making the national claim both compelling and unavoidable, had been established. Faced with mounting Arab opposition and a local Arab counter-claim to the same territory, the prevailing view within the Zionist movement was that demography was more important than geography—up to a point. Hence, Zionist leaders accepted partition in 1937 and again in 1947 when the UN revived the idea. However, the bitter disputes that preceded and followed each partition plan testified then, as they do today, that even on matters of boundaries and territorial extension Zionism was not unified. The pragmatism that dictated support for partition resolutions did not necessarily reflect the abandonment of claims over the entire land. The longing for Zion, far from expressing exclusively intransigent national claims, shows the resilience of primordial bonds in shaping and perpetuating national identities.

Conclusion

The Jewish quest for a national home reflected more than a conscious re-elaboration of religious symbols by self-serving intellectuals. As in the case of other national movements, the notion that Jews were bestowed with the right of self-determination in their ancestral land struck a deep chord across the Jewish world. Despite opposition, Zionism's astonishing success—the fulfilment of its goal within fifty-four years, its establishment achieved despite formidable challenges and the tragedies faced by world Jewry in the twentieth century—bears witness to the potency of the idea and the strength of its appeal. Zionism revolutionized Jewish self-image, Jewish identity, and the place of Jews in the world in unforeseen ways. It thereby achieved, despite trials and failures, a veritable success: it not only gave Jews a safe haven from persecutions, it fostered the revival of an original and modern national culture, and enabled the Jews, in thinking and acting like a collective bestowed with national attributes, to be masters of their own destiny and, for better or worse, to be again 'a people like all peoples'.

FURTHER READING

Almog, Shmuel. *Zionism and History: The Rise of a New Jewish Consciousness* (London: Palgrave MacMillan, 1987). General introductory book on Zionism.

Avineri, Shlomo. *The Making of Modern Zionism: The Intellectual Origins of the Jewish State* (London: Basic Books, 1981). Excellent background reading on Zionist authors, who are discussed separately chapter by chapter.

Gilbert, Martin. *Exile and Return: The Emergence of Jewish Statehood* (London: Weidenfeld & Nicolson, 1978). Classic text on the history of the Zionist movement.

Halpern, Ben, and Yehuda Reinharz. *Zionism and the Creation of a New Society* (Oxford: Oxford University Press, 1998). Analysis of Zionism as ideology.

Hertzberg, Arthur (ed.). *The Zionist Idea: A Historical Analysis and Reader* (Philadelphia: Jewish Publication Society, 1966). Selected primary sources, with a comprehensive introduction on Zionism.

Laqueur, Walter. *A History of Zionism* (New York: Schocken Books, 1976). Comprehensive history of the Zionist movement and its ideology.

Ravitzky, Aviezer. *Zionism, Messianism and Religious Radicalism* (Chicago: University of Chicago Press, 1996). A study of religious Zionism in its past and contemporary manifestations.

Reinharz, Yehuda, and Anita, Shapira (eds.). *Essential Papers on Zionism* (New York: Canel, 1996). A comprehensive collection of essays by different authors on various aspects of Zionist history and ideology.

Sachar, Howard. *A History of Israel* (New York: Alfred A. Knopf, 1996). A comprehensive textbook tracing the history of the State of Israel from its intellectual and ideological origins, including the Zionist movement.

Shapira, Anita. *Land and Power* (Oxford: Oxford University Press, 1992). In-depth study of Zionism and its various responses to the challenges of state-building in relation to the use of force.

Shimoni, Gideon. *The Zionist Ideology* (Hanover and, London: Brandeis University Press, 1995). The most comprehensive and up-to-date in-depth study of Zionism.

Vital, David. *The Origins of Zionism* (Oxford: Clarendon Press, 1975).

Vital, David. *Zionism: The Formative Years* (Oxford: Clarendon Press, 1988). Two classical studies of Zionism.

NOTES

1. Gideon Shimoni, *The Zionist Ideology* (Hanover and London: Brandeis University Press, 1995), p. 85.
2. Barry Rubin, *Assimilation and Its Discontents* (New York: Random House, 1995), p. 117.
3. Shimoni, *Zionist Ideology*, p. 8.
4. These are discussed further in Chap. 35.
5. Shimoni, *Zionist Ideology*, p. 75.
6. Rabbi Abraham Isaac Kook, 'War' (1930), in Arthur Hertzberg (ed.), *The Zionist Idea* (Philadelphia: Jewish Publication Society, 1997), p. 422.
7. Aviezer Ravitzky, *Messianism, Zionism and Religious Radicalism* (Chicago: University of Chicago Press, 1996), p. 35.
8. A coalition of Hasidim and Mitnagdim from Eastern and Central Europe. See Chap. 6 for further details.

5 | Post-Zionism

Emanuele Ottolenghi

Post-Zionism encompasses many disciplines, including history, sociology, cultural studies, literature, and even archaeology, to challenge Israel's Zionist foundations through scholarship and public advocacy. As a study of the field asserts, 'postzionism is a term applied to a current set of critical positions that problematize zionist discourse, and the historical narratives and social and cultural representations that it produced'.[1] Questioning what it considers a partisan view of the past, serving Zionist interests, post-Zionism seeks to challenge what it calls 'the Zionist narrative' regarding the study of Israel's past.

As a critique from within, post-Zionism differs from opposition to and rejection of Zionism. As post-Zionist historian Ilan Pappé argues, post-Zionism is 'a hybrid of anti-Zionist notions and a postmodern perception of reality' which 'has become a convenient term that groups together Zionist and anti-Zionist Jews in Israeli academia and politics'.[2] But unlike anti-Zionism, 'Post-Zionism stresses the dynamics of change which transformed a fundamentally legitimate concept and ambition into an evil and destructive phenomenon'.[3]

Post-Zionist scholarship seeks to recover a past which, according to its proponents, was concealed for the sake of ideology. This effort produces a normative claim: the evidence unearthed exposes Zionism as an immoral ideology with pernicious consequences, which must therefore be replaced. Borrowing from postmodern terminology, post-Zionism claims that alternative voices and narratives of the past have been excluded by a hegemonic culture. Borrowing from Marxist theory, it seeks to unearth the oppressed or local narratives in order to empower them. Scholarship becomes a vehicle for change.

Justification stems from the post-Zionist argument that much injustice was committed in the name of Zionism. Post-Zionist scholarship seeks an active role in reshaping Israel's collective memory and identity outside the boundaries of Zionism for the sake of justice.

In their critique of the Zionist narrative, which purportedly distorted Israel's history in the interests of the official Zionist establishment, post-Zionists accuse their scholarly rivals of sacrificing their professional integrity to serve the interests of power, silencing dissenting voices. Post-Zionism thus presents itself as a myth-shattering endeavour, intent on telling Israelis the truth about their past. Unearthing uncomfortable historical truths should awaken the national conscience and, through recognition of injustice, induce repentance and change. Post-Zionism therefore considers itself an effort to uncover the less noble aspects of Zionism, in order to achieve two goals: first, to 'set the record straight', and second, by exposing the 'Zionist narrative' as false, rectifying Israel's collective memory and identity so as to reflect the multiplicity of narratives which post-Zionism seeks to unearth.

Post-Zionism as an attempt to confront the truth

Central to post-Zionism is the claim that Zionist Israel has no inherent moral validity. For post-Zionist scholars, Zionism negated Jewish Diaspora identities, oppressed Palestinians, and discriminated against non-European Jews who did not embrace the secular, socialist dominant brand of Zionism which established the state. The self-image of Jews as a nation entitled to a right to self-determination in the ancestral land caused much injustice, to Jews and Arabs alike. The active support of academics in writing an official version of history was part of a conscious effort to hide the uncomfortable truths of an inherently flawed, morally objectionable enterprise—the Jewish state.

Changing the historical account serves not only the purpose of critical scholarship, but also the political goal of undermining the moral foundations of Zionism. Post-Zionism seeks to replace Zionist Israel with a morally more compelling alternative: a post-national state of all its citizens, devoid of Jewish connotation and reflective of multicultural, liberal values. 'Postzionism strives to free Israeli public discourse from the limits imposed by zionism and to clear space in which to talk about Israeli history, culture, and identity in new and exciting ways. In so doing, [post-Zionists] strive to participate in producing a society that is democratic, creative, and humane.'[4] The scholarly dimension of this project is geared toward recovering the lost narratives of disempowered groups—Palestinians, women, non-European Jews. Recognition of those narratives and the injustice Zionism inflicted upon them is a necessary step toward the reordering of Israel's collective identity and memory in a non-Zionist direction.

The scholarly endeavour to 'set the record straight' is the necessary premise on which the political platform of post-Zionism is built. According to post-Zionists, the Zionist narrative attempts to present Zionism as a legitimate national movement, acting on behalf of the Jewish people, in an effort to recover its ancestral land through morally justifiable actions. The Zionist narrative is portrayed as presenting the Jews as weak, the Arabs as uncompromising warmongers, the British as imperialists in cahoots with the Arabs, and the world as hostile. It presents Israel's predicament as existential, its recourse to force justified under threat of destruction by uncompromising enemies who refused even to acknowledge Israel, let alone recognize its legitimate claims. Israel had wanted peace and reluctantly waged war in 1948, against the united onslaught of seven Arab armies, only to win against all odds. The Arabs were responsible for the resulting Palestinian mass flight. Israel sought peace after the war but the Arabs rejected it. The British sided with the Arabs, but Israel overcame all the odds to emerge victorious and independent, albeit at a heavy price. After the war Israel relentlessly pursued peace while successfully absorbing millions of Jewish refugees and giving them a new lease of life through the Zionist melting-pot. Out of this picture emerged a blameless Israel, built on the success and compelling nature of the Zionist project.

Post-Zionism questions all of these assumptions. Its targets in the academic debate are those academics who, against what post-Zionists see as overwhelming evidence to the contrary, backed the Zionist narrative with their work. Following the opening of Israel's historical archives in the late 1970s, post-Zionist scholars claim that their research, supported by previously classified documents, exposes the fallacies of Zionist historiography.

Post-Zionist historiography, however, proceeds beyond challenging 'the Zionist narrative' on documentary grounds. By portraying Israel's birth as tainted, and the scholarship associated with it as equally tainted, post-Zionism turns scholarship into a political battleground whose focus is on the events surrounding Israel's founding and their implications for the present, including—crucially—the shape of Israel's national identity and its character as a Jewish state.

Building on this argument in the public domain, post-Zionism aims to show Israelis that the narrative on which the nation's identity, self-image, and collective memory are built is false, distorted, selective, and hiding uncomfortable truths. Confronting and coming to terms with them is a key component in the post-Zionist strategy to change Israel's self-image, and ultimately its nature as a Jewish state built on Zionist foundations.

Post-Zionism accuses Zionism of aggressive expansionism, depicting it as colonialism, intent on displacing helpless natives in the name of an aggressive European nationalist ideology that could not possibly include Arabs in its fabric. Prominent in this argument are a group of self-defined 'new historians', who present their work as revisionist and innovative. They interpret the existential threat Israel supposedly experienced in 1948 and after as a pretext for aggressive policies, rearmament, and internal mistreatment of minorities. The unavoidable consequence of pursuing a national project in a foreign land was the expulsion of its indigenous population, and the new historians suggest varying degrees of Jewish responsibility in the creation of the Palestinian refugee problem in 1948. Zionism is depicted as containing the ideological seeds of Arab expulsion. Accounts of the 1948 war focus on the refugee problem as central to the war—rather than its unintended consequence—trying to prove the existence of a concerted effort, devised at the political level and implemented by the military, to drive the Palestinians out. Jewish atrocities are emphasized; Arab responsibility is downplayed.

While in the Zionist account of 1948 Arab rejection of the UN partition plan has a central role, new historians blur its importance. They contend that Zionists colluded with the Hashemite Kingdom of Transjordan (present-day Jordan) and even with the British, thus thwarting the otherwise possible creation of an Arab state in Palestine. Jewish acceptance of partition, for post-Zionists, was a disingenuous cover for a conspiracy to frustrate Arab-Palestinian aspirations to statehood. The conspiracy theory relieves the Arab side of any responsibility in rejecting partition and precipitating the 1948 conflict. That the conflict would be won by the Jewish side is, for post-Zionists, a foregone conclusion: in their writings, Jewish military might, superior organization, and motivation are crucial factors. Furthermore, Arab divisiveness, lack of co-ordination, and conflicting policy goals among Arab states prove that Israel's superiority was never in question, and its victory unsurprising.

Finally, post-Zionists dispute Israel's willingness to seek peace in the aftermath of 1948. In their account it was the Arabs, rather than Israel, who were ready for compromise. Israel rejected Arab overtures which, had Israel conceded to territorial compromise and the return of the refugees, would have led to peace. It was Israel's aggressive posture, its arrogance following its victory, and Zionism's inherently expansionist nature—embodied in the much-vilified figure of Israel's first prime minister, David Ben-Gurion—that nullified all peace efforts before those Arab leaders willing to make peace with Israel left the scene.

The post-Zionist critique extends beyond the Arab–Israeli conflict. Zionism is viewed as an identity artificially created by intellectuals, which effaced the authentic essence of Jewish experience in history. Imposing a European secular identity, it erased all vestiges of traditional Jewish Diaspora identities, including those of Jews from the lands of Islam, who had little in common with the East European Zionist founders.

Post-Zionism exalts the Diaspora as the authentic dimension of Jewish experience. In the context of the Middle East, Zionism is accused of having forced Mizrahi Jews to forsake their Arab roots, driving a wedge between them and their Arab neighbours, wilfully causing the uprooting and destruction of ancient Jewish communities in places like Yemen, Iraq, and Morocco. Once evicted and stripped of their properties in their lands of origin (which some post-Zionist scholars blame on Zionism), Jews were deprived of their dignity and identity in Israel. In this context, many scholars present their effort to recover a lost authentic Arab-Jewish identity as a struggle for truth.

In summary, post-Zionism suggests that Zionism had much to hide. It accuses an entire generation of academics of having sacrificed their integrity in the name of ideology and in the service of power. It sees a duty to uncover the truth, to discredit what it perceives as tainted, and in the process to help the public confront and reassess its past. This process will eventually lead to the demise of Zionism and the adoption of an alternative model for the State of Israel, based on a political vision that rehabilitates the narrative of all those groups excluded by Zionism. Post-Zionism is thus not just a different school of scholarship: it is also an ideological argument whose central aim is not simply to critically reassess Israel's foundations, but to replace them.

Post-Zionism's normative and ideological foundations

In its attempt to uncover the essence of Zionism and Israel's history, post-Zionism, beyond seeking to provide a more accurate rendition of the past, also questions the morality of Zionism and offers ways to amend wrongs committed in its name. Indeed, there is a direct correlation between the effort to uncover the truth and the moral foundation for political action. Post-Zionists locate this foundation both in Jewish tradition and morality in order to present post-Zionism as authentic and disqualify Zionism as forgery:

In Pirkei Avot it is written: 'Rabbi Shimon Ben Gamliel was wont to say: On three things the world rests: On justice, truth and on peace' (1:18). And he would quote Zechariah: 'execute the judgment of truth and peace in your gates' (8:16). Telling the truth thus seems to be an injunction anchored in Jewish tradition, and the Scriptures apparently link truth to peace in some indeterminate manner.

The new history is one of the signs of a maturing Israel . . . What is now being written about Israel's past seems to offer us a more balanced and more 'truthful' view of that country's history than what has been offered hitherto. It may also in some obscure way serve the purposes of peace and reconciliation between the warring tribes of that land.[5]

The post-Zionist effort to reshape Israel's self-image is not just conducive to a more accurate understanding of the past, but is a necessary prerequisite to the success of a political project that deems Israel in its current format as flawed because undemocratic, deceitful, and hence unjust. It may thus be viewed as a new form of Jewish anti-Zionism, engaged in a full-fledged ideological and moral struggle for the reassessment of Israel's collective memory.

Before Israel's foundation, Zionism's most committed opponents were Jewish exponents of competing ideologies. Their antagonism was rooted either in religious positions or in a number of arguments about the practicality of Zionism, the cost involved in achieving its goals, and opposition to the Zionist view that Jews were a nation endowed with the same attributes and rights of other national groups. Pre-1948 Jewish opposition to Zionism rejected its premises, the perceived impracticality of its project, or the impossibility of surmounting the moral dilemmas posed by its implementation.

Post-Zionism differs from its intellectual precursors in form rather than substance. Instead of attacking Zionism for the wrongs it might cause if implemented, post-Zionism attacks Zionism for the wrongs it supposedly has caused as a result of its implementation. Whereas old Jewish anti-Zionism feared the worst, post-Zionism holds that the worst has indeed happened, and actively seeks to rectify it.

This contention explains the focus of post-Zionism. Its main proponents seek to rewrite the history of Israel's founding, hence the predominant concentration on 1948 and the war that led to Israel's independence, a radical reinterpretation of Zionism's early history, and a reassessment of the Zionist movement, its ideology, goals, implementation, and the cultural artefacts which it produced along the way.

That such a project should concentrate on a nation's founding events is not unusual: 'Moments of historical breakthrough become the founding myth of the society in question and quite naturally arouse interest and curiosity.'[6] What is unusual is the moral dimension that post-Zionism introduces. Post-Zionists' stated intention is to have an active role, not only as a study of reality, but as an attempt to influence reality. Post-Zionism wants to highlight 'the shortcomings of Zionism and Israel, the injustice inflicted on others, and the historical alternatives whose realization may have been thwarted by the actualization of Zionism'.[7]

Post-Zionism's underlying assumption is that Zionism and its political achievements involved a loss of innocence for the Jewish people. Though the nature of the injustice varies, only post-Zionism (and its political consequences) is portrayed as capable of restoring innocence. In the debate over new history, new historian Benny Morris describes the abrupt descent from heaven as an 'original sin', a term pervading post-Zionist writings:

How one perceives 1948 bears heavily on how one perceives the whole Zionist/Israeli experience. If Israel, the haven of a much-persecuted people, was born pure and innocent, then it is worthy of the grace, material assistance, and political support showered upon it by the West over the past forty years—and worthy of more of the same in years to come. If, on the other hand, Israel was born tarnished, besmirched by original sin, then it was no more deserving of that grace and assistance than were its neighbors.[8]

Though new historian Avi Shlaim downplays the concept of 'original sin', he proceeds to ridicule the notion that Israel's creation might have equally been 'an immaculate conception'.[9] Such use of Christological terms indicates how the process of transition from Zionism to post-Zionism is a necessary effort to restore the sense of lost innocence. The argument that a Jewish state (the goal and achievement of the Zionist enterprise) is a negation of democracy, along with the claim that Israel was born in sin, is central to this theologically charged notion. Post-Zionism thus seeks to achieve Israel's political and moral rehabilitation:

Postzionists generally agree that Israel should be a democratic state of all its citizens. They thus reject the Zionist principle, inscribed in Israel's declaration of Independence, that Israel is the state of the Jewish people, a Jewish state. In contrast to Zionists, postzionists wish Israel to become a state that belongs to all who live within it, including Palestinian Arab citizens.[10]

Though no programmatic platform exists on how to achieve this goal, in general post-Zionists want Israel to abandon both its Zionist past and current Jewish specificity. Giving up Israel's Jewish nature becomes both synonymous with democratization and a means to remove the 'original sin' associated with Israel's founding. The Palestinian refugee problem is not just the consequence or even the side-effect of war (as Morris originally argued), but the inevitable and logical consequence of Zionist thinking. In that sense, Israel was born in sin: it was inherent in Zionism that Israel would engage in 'ethnic cleansing', as post-Zionists charge, and it is part and parcel of Zionism as a colonialist and nationalist project.

The two elements of post-Zionism thus come together in the form of a politically engaged scholarship, which does not limit itself to revising history, but uses its findings to justify a radical call for change in the nature of the body politic.

Coping with the loss of innocence

In order to understand the post-Zionist argument that Zionism involved a loss of innocence, which only its demise can restore, the roots of Zionism as a revolution in Jewish history, which entailed a radical reassessment of Jewish self-image, must be investigated. Israel's establishment meant the return of Jews to political independence. Modern statehood and human agency imply a radical redefinition of Jewish self-image in relation to the exercise of power and the use of force, both eminently distinctive attributes of sovereignty, from which Jews were removed for nearly 2,000 years.

Following emancipation, acculturated Jews developed new ways to understand the concept of a 'chosen people'. Many supported the idea that Israel was blessed with a universal message of morality for the Gentiles, which would make the Jews 'a light unto the nations'. The curse of exile became, therefore, a blessing. As minorities scattered through the world, Jews could bring their message to the four corners of the earth. This vision transformed exile from a temporary, if necessary, phase of Jewish history into a morally privileged position that enabled Jews to become the conscience of the world.[11]

Even among nationalists, some saw the lofty appeal of a universal mission extending beyond the narrow confines of the national movement of a small minority at the margins of history.[12] Others dissented. Not only did this proposition potentially entail the renunciation of the concept of a Jewish people—a renunciation that emancipation should have facilitated but in practice made more difficult—but it sounded arrogant. Why were Jews somehow gifted with the role of the conscience of the world? Would the world listen, or would it try to silence the troubled calls to moral behaviour?

This clash reflects the unease felt within the Jewish world—and by post-Zionists—about the amorality of political power and the occasional difficulty in explaining, let alone justifying, Zionist deeds in moral terms. Was Jewish survival a purpose unto itself—as Zionism suggested—or was it instrumental to moral goals? For Zionism, Jewish survival through self-determination was compelling and legitimate enough in its own right. Jews should not feel indebted to the world for their own freedom and independence. Its opponents insisted that more is demanded of Jews if they are to exercise their national rights. The use of force had to be framed within morally acceptable boundaries, or rejected outright. Traditional Jewish misgivings about the resort to force clashed with the needs of a national movement to achieve its goals.[13]

Post-Zionism expresses the moral difficulty in coping with the less appealing aspects of political life. It is the latest expression of traditional Jewish repugnance towards power, the latest Diaspora exaltation of the Jews' once supposedly quintessential powerlessness, which made Jews always innocent in a world of brutality, though all too often its victims. In this sense Israel represents, in the transition from powerlessness to empowerment, the loss of innocence.

If powerlessness granted Jews the moral high ground as eternal victims, power was necessarily evil. The return of the Jews to power meant reassessing this understanding, at least to reinstate the duality of power as both evil and necessary—not an easy and foregone conclusion. Hence a variety of responses emerged, sometimes ambiguous and sometimes utterly opposed to Zionism, because the establishment of the state meant that Jews would have to face the moral dilemmas posed by power.

In the realities of settling Palestine, in the encounter with the indigenous population and the resulting challenges, there emerged slowly a new generation whose transition from Diaspora to the Land entailed a revolution in Jewish self-image. From being seekers of redemption through work, seen as an instrument of national revival restoring human dignity to the Jewish collective, Zionists slowly resigned themselves to recognizing the need and summoning the resolve to conquer the Land by force—if necessary. Even as Zionism slowly came to terms with the possible use of force to achieve its goals, it tried to frame the concept of use of force within moral parameters derived from Jewish tradition. It is thus hardly surprising that, to this day, debates surrounding the Jewish state and its uses of sovereign power always intersect with the legitimacy of its project, the desirability and extent of Jewish power, the limits to be imposed on it, and the consequences of its misuse. Post-Zionism represents the latest form of this ongoing debate, which expresses Jewish traditional discomfort with power and its sometimes evil manifestations. The assumption, that Zionism entailed a loss of innocence, is an effort to come to terms with the moral consequences of power. Through an extreme rejection of amoral behaviour, it expresses an unbearable sense of guilt which, beyond 'fact-finding' missions, seeks moral solace in the redemptive idea of repentance through the demise of Zionism.

A critique of post-Zionism

Post-Zionism portrays itself as a critique of Zionism and a tool for undermining the ideology it represents. Since it promotes different interpretations of the past as well as an alternative normative framework for Israeli society, it is open to two types of criticism. The first is similar to the one it mounts on Zionism, namely, the validity of interpretations about the past through the use (and misuse) of sources. The second is a rejection of the moral validity or even the viability of the post-Zionist normative argument.

The argument on sources and their interpretation is seemingly modernist—it supports an interpretation based on what it considers novel evidence. Many post-Zionist scholars adhere to a modernist approach based on sources and documents. Shlaim, for example, clearly keeps the discussion out of the boundaries of method-ology, insisting instead on the availability and validity of sources and their inter-pretation. Despite his attempt to present the debate as one about sources and their interpretation, he *uses* a postmodernist framework and its terminology, sliding into a moral argument: according to Shlaim, the 'Zionist' historical account is self-serving propaganda, which the victors, *because they were victors*, could propagate more effectively.[14]

Shlaim lists five Zionist 'myths' to describe the stark divide between old and new history. In fact, the historiography debate is much more nuanced and far from resolved. Setting up a straw man serves the purpose of discrediting those who hold different views by portraying their argument as self-serving, simplistic, and skewed. The presentation of the debate on 1948 as a clash between innocent myth and damning truth seeks to achieve the purpose of discrediting the opponents of historical revision-ism. Moving the debate outside the confines of academe as a clash between truth-tellers and discredited academics, post-Zionism thus poses as the new custodian of an unassailable truth, and though its opponents have so far responded in kind, their accusations have lost potency due to the successful campaign to discredit them in the first place.

Despite the virulence of the debate, a few weaknesses must be highlighted in the post-Zionist argument. Discussing the outcome of the 1948 war, new historians evince intentions from results, showing how the historian's benefit of hindsight is presumed to be at the decision-maker's disposal as well. Human error and the impossibility of knowing with certainty the consequences of decisions and the full weight of alterna-tives not chosen are not appreciated. Dubious intentions dictated by an ideology post-Zionists disapprove of are always presumed.

That in wars the stronger side invariably wins appears as an uncontested principle used to demonstrate that if the Jews won, they had to be stronger. This judgement ignores—aside from the point that strength is not only measured in armour and soldiers—the fact that war is an uncertain business. Besides, the post-Zionist account of the 1948 war forgets the high human cost paid by Israel and the unexpected collapse of Palestinian society. The Arab states' divisiveness was indeed a weakening factor for their side but, had it been overcome, it would have made the Arabs a formidable opponent. As for the Arab forces' stated desire to evict the Jews, not merely defeat them, that is also crucially overlooked: that this did not happen, except in the few areas Arab forces managed to overrun, derives more from Israel's victory than from the assumption, which evidence contradicts, that the Arab side did not intend to do so.

New historians also downplay the heavy price exacted from Israel in exchange for peace overtures by Arab leaders whose internal weakness—nearly all Arab leaders were ousted within four years of the 1948 war—could not provide a guarantee that agreements would hold. Besides, Israel was expected to pay dearly, in the form of territorial concessions and refugee resettlement, in exchange for meagre and tenuous promises—harsh conditions even for a vanquished nation. But Israel had won, not lost the war. That post-Zionists would expect Israel to pay such a price reflects their view of Israel as a robber state with no legitimacy. Its survival in the region and recognition by its neighbours—as this judgement shows—would be a generous concession on their part.

As for the injustice supposedly suffered by non-European Jews and Palestinians, post-Zionism appears to stand on shaky ground here too. While there were genuine grievances against Israel's handling of Mizrahi immigrants, the claim that Zionism destroyed an existing Jewish-Arab identity ignores the fact that, prior to 1948, Jewish communities living in Arab lands did not see themselves as Arab, nor did they have so much in common with their neighbours as to hold a shared identity. The post-Zionist effort to create one for 'Arab' Jews is as artificial as the effort to efface it.

As for Israel's Arab minority, proving (as post-Zionist scholarship purports to substantiate) that Israel unfairly treats its Palestinian ethnic minority does not auto-matically demonstrate that such injustice inevitably derives from Israel's insistence as a nation-state. All states face the problem of the tyranny of the majority. If a minority is mistreated and discriminated against, that reflects a disregard for liberal values, not a betrayal of the values ascribed to the ethnic composition or the religious tradition of the majority.[15] The fact that there may be discrimination does not necessarily stem from the normative foundations of Israel as a Jewish state, something which must be demonstrated rather than simply surmised.

Finally, a problem stems from the moral dimension of the idea of an original sin associated with Israel's birth, resulting from Israel's alleged responsibility in creating the Palestinian refugee problem. The use of terms borrowed from Christian theology indicates that the subtext of post-Zionist discourse is informed with a vision of Israel that finds echoes in the very theology from which it borrows its terminology.[16] The idea of original sin refers to a congenital flaw, inherent in the essence of a phenom-enon, which only a radical act of repentance, changing not just the behaviour but also the essence of the sinner, can rectify. In theological terms, that act is obtained through baptism and the acceptance of Jesus as the saviour. In political terms, the moral equivalent of that process is the renunciation of Israel's Jewish nature as the inherent flaw of Israel, which caused its loss of innocence, and the embracing of a salvation doctrine that endorses the moral universalism of the present age.[17]

Different historical evaluations produced by post-Zionism are thus not based on a more comprehensive assessment of previously unknown sources, but on a moral judgement as to the validity and legitimacy of the Zionist enterprise.

Conclusion

Through its diversified scholarly endeavours, post-Zionism escapes easy classification: its exponents share neither methodology nor discipline, neither research interests nor academic background. What they do share is a moral and ideological argument, which is neither new nor dissimilar from past Jewish criticism of Zionism. Their novelty stems from the attempt to present a highly charged ideological argument in neutral and impartial academic dress, and the effort to use the research tools at their disposal to change the reality of Israel's Jewish nature in the name of morality, not for the sake of academic accuracy.

The success of post-Zionism in seizing Israel's public agenda and mainstream academia is an indication that its narrative has become an important reference point in the struggle over Israel's identity.

FURTHER READING

Evron, Boas. *Jewish State or Israeli Nation?* (Bloomington: Indiana University Press, 1995). A presentation of the post-Zionist argument against Jewish nationalism in favour of a bi-national solution.

Karsh, Efraim. *Fabricating History: Israel's New Historians* (London: Frank Cass, 1998). An attempt to refute the new historians' scholarship by accusing them of misusing sources.

Kimmerling, Baruch. *Zionism and Territory: The Socio-Territorial Dimensions of Zionist Politics* (Berkeley: University of California Press, 1983). A classical study of Zionism from the perspective of post-Zionist critical sociology.

Morris, Benny. *The Birth of the Palestinian Refugee Problem 1947–1949* (Cambridge: Cambridge University Press, 1987). A study of the Palestinian refugee problem: the first scholarly contribution to New History and Post-Zionism. See also the new and revised edition: *The Birth of the Palestinian Refugee Problem Revisited* (Cambridge: Cambridge University Press, 2003). For a rebuttal of Morris's argument see Shabtai Teveth, 'The Palestine Arab Refugee Problem and Its Origins', *Middle Eastern Studies*, 26: 2 (Apr. 1990), pp. 214–49, and Yoav Gelber, *Palestine 1948: War, Escape and the Emergence of the Refugee Problem* (Brighton: Sussex Academic Press, 2000), a study of the 1948 war and the refugee problem by a military historian, highly critical of New History.

Shafir, Gershon. *Land, Labour and the Origins of the Israeli–Palestinian Conflict 1882–1914* (Cambridge: Cambridge University Press, 1989). A study of the origins of the Arab–Israeli conflict from a Marxist perspective.

Shafir, Gershon, and Yoav Peled. *Being Israeli, The Dynamics of Multiple Citizenship* (Cambridge: Cambridge University Press, 2002). A post-Zionist analysis of citizenship in Israel.

Shapira, Anita. *Land and Power.: The Zionist Resort to Force, 1881–1948* (Oxford: Oxford University Press, 1992). A historical study of Zionism's approach to the use of force.

Shimoni, Gideon. *The Zionist Ideology* (Hanover and London: Brandies University Press, 1995). A comprehensive study of Zionism.

Shlaim, Avi. *Collusion Across the Jordan: King Abdullah, the Zionist Movement, and the Partition of Palestine* (Oxford: Clarendon Press, 1988). A study of Hashemite–Zionist relations, trying to demonstrate a triangular conspiracy between Transjordan, Great Britain, and Israel; the second important scholarly contribution to New History and post-Zionism.

Shlaim, Avi. *The Politics of Partition, King Abdullah, the Zionists and Palestine 1921–1951* (Oxford: Oxford University Press, 1998). The official post-Zionist version of the collusion theory between Israel and the Hashemites revisited. See, for a rebuttal, Avraham Sela, 'Transjordan, Israel and the 1948 War: Myth, Historiography, and Reality', *Middle Eastern Studies*, 28: 4 (Oct. 1992), pp. 623–88, and Yoav Gelber, *Jewish–Transjordanian Relations, 1921–1948* (London: Frank Cass, 2000).

NOTES

1. Laurence Silberstein, *Postzionism Debates: Power and Knowledge in Modern Israel* (New York and London: Routledge, 1999), p. 2.
2. Ilan Pappé, 'Post-Zionist Critique on Israel and the Palestinians, Part I: The Academic Debate', *Journal of Palestine Studies*, 26: 2 (1997), pp. 29–41.
3. Ilan Pappé, *Leonard Stein Inaugural Lectures*, delivered in Oxford on 9–10 May 2001 (unpublished), p. 2.
4. Silberstein, *Postzionism Debates*, p. 14.
5. Benny Morris, 'The New Historiography: Israel Confronts its Past', *Tikkun* (Nov.–Dec. 1988), pp. 102b.
6. Anita Shapira, 'Politics and Collective Memory: The Debate over the "New Historians" in Israel', in Gulie Ne'eman Arad (ed.), *Israeli Historiography Revisited*, special issue, 'History and Memory', 7: 1 (Spring–Summer 1995), p. 9.
7. Ibid., p. 11.
8. Morris, 'The New Historiography'.
9. Avi Shlaim, 'The Debate About 1948', *International Journal of Middle East Studies*, 27 (1995), p. 292.
10. Silberstein, *Postzionism Debates*, p. 8.
11. Ehud Luz, 'Jewish Ethics As An Argument In the Public Debate Over the Israeli Reaction to Palestinian Terror', *Israel Studies*, 7: 3 (Fall 2002), p. 150.
12. Anita Shapira, *Land and Power: The Zionist Resort to Force, 1881–1948* (Oxford: Oxford University Press, 1992), p. 27.
13. Ibid., p. 40.
14. Shlaim, 'The Debate', pp. 287, 291.
15. Leon Wieseltier, 'What Is Not To Be Done: Israel, Palestine and the Return of the Bi-national Fantasy', *New Republic* (27 Oct. 2003), p. 22.
16. Emanuele Ottolenghi, 'Paradise Lost: A Review of Laurence Silberstein's *The Postzionism Debates: Knowledge and Power in Israeli Culture*', *Israel Studies*, 8: 2 (Summer 2003), pp. 139–50.
17. Ibid.

Issues of religion and modernity

6 | Modernist movements

Miri Freud-Kandel

The age of Enlightenment raised questions that undermined the central tenets of religion in general and created a particular crisis for Judaism and Jewish identity. Enlightenment thought was predicated on the perception that all human beings shared an innate capacity to engage in rational thought. Ultimately this led to emancipation, as the notion of discriminating against people for their religion came to appear inappropriate. This notion of rationalism also inculcated the principle of individual autonomy, the idea that every person was empowered to use their rational capacities to choose and determine how to act for themselves. Submission to religious authority, which encouraged individuals to act in accordance with a higher power rather than following their own ethical imperative, came to be viewed as an imposition on the freedom of individual consciences. Religion's power to dictate action, let alone belief, was thus diminished. An additional feature of Enlightenment thought was a focus on universalist principles: that which united humans, rather than that which made them distinctive. Since the particularistic national components of Judaism conflicted with the principle of universalism, Jews found themselves in conflict with contemporary values in this respect also.

In 1806 a number of questions which highlighted the major concerns that 'modern' society entertained regarding the Jews and their participation in the nation-state were directed at the Assembly of Jewish Notables, formed under Napoleon's instructions that year. Whilst unease regarding Jewish moneylending provided one focus of the questioning, the Jewish Notables were primarily asked to address concerns regarding Jewish particularism, primitivism, and the sources of authority by which Jews were bound.[1]

A number of different responses developed from within Judaism. These emerging positions revolved around questions of religious authority, individual autonomy, the value of tradition, and the nature of Jewish peoplehood. Some rabbinical authorities sought to retain at least the intellectual ghetto walls which separated Jews from the ideas developed in the modern world. The development of what came to be referred to as ultra-Orthodox forms of Judaism, discussed in the next chapter, resulted from this tendency. Religious responses that can more obviously be characterized as modernist in one sense or another, rather than traditional or wholly secular, gave rise to four main denominations: Reform, Modern Orthodox, Conservative, and Reconstructionist.[2]

Religious authority and individual autonomy

Three traditional sources of authority can be identified in Judaism: divine, textual, and rabbinic. All three of these were assaulted by the modernist consciousness on various levels of rationalist, universalist, and scholarly principles. As already noted, willingness to submit to divine authority was undermined under the influence of Enlightenment thought. The literal interpretation of divine revelation was weakened both by rationalist sensibilities and by scientific study of the Bible, which led to such theories as the 'documentary hypothesis'. As the divine origin of the Bible was undermined, the authority invested in the traditional core texts of Judaism was weakened. The rabbinic development of biblical ideas found in the Talmud came to be viewed by some as unnecessary additions that distorted the meaning of Judaism and shifted the focus of traditional interpretation onto irrelevant minutiae which inappropriately emphasized the letter over the spirit of the law. *Wissenschaft des Judentums*—scientific study of Judaism—provided scholarly underpinning for the anti-traditionalist argument that Judaism had been subject to evolutionary processes. Rabbinic authority, particularly when used to preclude new adaptations, was also undermined by changing attitudes to religious authority in general and, more particularly, by negative views of the rabbis' actual use of their traditional powers.

An examination of traditionalist teachings highlighted their focus on particularistic ideas and practices that appeared to be in conflict with contemporary sensibilities: they rested on hopes for the salvation of a particular people, associated with supernatural notions of how this redemption would occur, with the Jewish collective restored to a separate national homeland in which a reconstituted sacrificial cult would be instituted in a rebuilt temple.

Initially, on purely aesthetic grounds, these traditional teachings appeared to conflict with modernist sensibilities triggering the first stage in the development of Reform Judaism. In the early decades of the nineteenth century reformed services were introduced reflecting the new concerns, beginning in Napoleonic Prussia. The emphasis on public worship was influenced by the central role of religious worship in the surrounding Protestant society. Prominence was given to decorum, achieved through the shortening of religious services, and improvements in the aesthetics, through choral and musical accompaniment, as well as increased use of the vernacular, certain liturgical reforms, and sermons.[3] A more formal theological reform followed, particularly centred around three rabbinical conferences held in the years 1844–6 in Brunswick, Frankfurt, and Breslau respectively.

Many of the changes were symptomatic of more general shifts, away from performance of traditional religious practices as a means of serving God and fulfilling religious duties, towards a perception of practice as a means to an end. Stripped of the idea that traditional sources of religious authority could demand obedience, and increasingly required to impress the individual's rational and spiritual sensibilities, religion came to be called upon to serve a purpose.

This shift in attitude facilitated an emphasis on the central principles of Judaism, displacing observance of minutiae which could obfuscate the religion's teachings. Moses Mendelssohn (1729–86) can be seen to have set this process in motion, perhaps unintentionally. In his book *Jerusalem* (1783) he famously distinguished between Judaism's rationalist, universally discernible doctrines, and its particularist revealed legislation. As emphasis came to be placed on the moral, universal components of Judaism, observance of its prescribed practices was downplayed. The prophetic texts and the teachings contained therein were elevated in importance. The battle for social justice was identified as the central component of the Jewish mission. The principle of ethical monotheism was developed to encapsulate these ideas. Practices which fostered particularism were viewed as especially problematic.

On the whole, traditional Judaism responded by rejecting the validity of the changes and condemning those who introduced them as heretics. The reformers' authority to innovate was denied. Their motivations, characterized as a desire for convenience and adaptation to alien standards, were castigated. In 1819 a volume of responsa (rabbinic opinions) condemning the reforms of the Hamburg Temple and its prayer book, entitled *Eleh Divrei Ha'Brit* was issued by twenty-two leading European rabbis, under the auspices of the Hamburg Rabbinical Court. Following the 1844 Brunswick Assembly of Reform Rabbis, 116 signatories asserted their opposition to Reform in a text entitled *Shelomei Emunei Yisrael*. They insisted that 'Neither we nor anyone else has the authority to nullify even the least of the religious laws'. The changes introduced by reformers were ascribed to an 'unrestrained pursuit of fame, wealth, and pleasure'.

However, the possibility for some innovation and adaptation of traditional Judaism was identified by a small number of proponents of what came to be termed Orthodox Judaism. The scope for engagement in the wider society, both physically and also intellectually, was demonstrated by rabbis like Isaac Bernays (1792–1849) and Jacob Ettlinger (1798–1871). They, in turn, taught and influenced Samson Raphael Hirsch (1808–88), who is often identified as the father of a group within Orthodoxy that has been characterized as 'Modern Orthodox'. Adherents of Modern Orthodoxy seek to combine a strict observance of the tenets and practices of a traditional Judaism with engagement in the societies they inhabit, seeking to effect a synthesis between the two spheres of orthodoxy and modernity. This ideology is predicated on the belief that Jewish engagement in the host society is not precluded by any central Jewish teachings. Rather, segregation has only occurred when it has been imposed as a result of external circumstances.

Hirsch castigated Reform for its approach to interaction. In a famous essay he criticized Reform for seeking 'progress allied to religion' rather than the reverse process. Although he was willing to accept the principle of change, he insisted that Jewish teachings had to take primacy, yet this did not remove the scope for adapting those teachings to contemporary circumstances.

The theology of 'Torah im derekh eretz'—Torah combined with engagement in the surrounding society—which Hirsch developed to underpin Modern Orthodoxy revolved around an educational programme.[4] This was first designed to ensure that an appropriate understanding of Judaism was achieved. Such an understanding was to be built on Judaism's own sources and was intended to inculcate an appreciation of the divine authority on which its teachings were based. The principle of 'Torah min haShamayim'—the divine origin of Torah—was placed at the heart of this theology. A somewhat dogmatic interpretation of divine revelation secured a certainty for Judaism's teachings which could ensure that engagement would not undermine the central principles of the religion. In addition, the educational programme was intended to highlight how engagement in the ideas of the host society was not only permitted, but was capable of contributing to Judaism and Jewish understanding.

The principle of 'Torah im derekh eretz' works on various levels. First, building on the Mishnaic origins of the term (Avot 2: 2), the acquisition of secular knowledge was seen to provide the means of securing a livelihood. Second, certain areas of study could help expand knowledge of specific Jewish teachings. Third, influenced by the Enlightenment focus on universalism, 'Torah im derekh eretz' also functioned as a means of emphasizing Judaism's role as a 'light unto the nations'. Under these terms it represents a mission theory, whereby the correct performance of Jewish teachings within the context of the societies Jews inhabit facilitates the infusion of Torah teachings into the *derekh eretz*. Finally, the study of secular wisdom provides the possibility of extending the knowledge of truth that can be achieved through Torah study alone. As Hirsch explained in his seminal *Nineteen Letters* (1836): 'True speculation takes nature, man and history as facts, investigating them in order to arrive at knowledge. To these, Judaism adds the Torah.'

The scope for Judaism to engage in the host society was acknowledged in this construction of a Modern Orthodoxy. The potential to adapt Judaism to the host society in ways that did not threaten its central teachings was identified. Provided change was introduced by placing Judaism first and ensuring that nothing contrary to Jewish teachings was introduced, new ideas could be celebrated and synthesized into Judaism rather than feared. Modern Orthodox Judaism thus sought to find a means for Judaism to accommodate itself to its surroundings, engage with it physically and intellectually, and yet maintain the traditional beliefs and practices of Judaism derived from the traditional sources of authority. However, this emphasis on the traditions of Judaism, particularly in the dogmatic form it has taken, undermines the genuine modernism of Modern Orthodoxy, since it does not allow individual autonomy to displace religious authority.

It was precisely the principle of individual autonomy that was vigorously promoted and upheld as Reform developed into its so-called classical stage, encapsulated by the Pittsburgh Platform of 1885. As Reform took hold in America and encountered far greater freedom to develop, unconstrained by established Jewish communities, the theological principles that had emerged in the German context were able to reach their culmination.[5] For Classical Reform, religious practices had to address contemporary sensibilities if they were to remain compelling. They were called upon to serve the purpose of 'modern spiritual elevation' and 'be in accord with the postulates of reason'. All particularistic practices, indeed, even conceptions of Judaism as something beyond a mere religious community, were rejected. The sense of progressive evolution, in definitions of revelation alongside general definitions of history, made many traditional Jewish practices appear primitive. This justified their displacement by the higher conceptions that modernity was seen to have heralded. Emphasis was placed on the contribution Judaism could make to the universal achievement of 'the kingdom of truth, justice, and peace among all men'.

Neither Reform nor Modern Orthodoxy has maintained the positions they adopted in the late nineteenth century. The tension between attempts to facilitate intellectual engagement in the ideas of the wider society whilst simultaneously rejecting individual autonomy and developing dogmatic interpretations of divine revelation, to safeguard traditional Jewish teachings, led to Modern Orthodoxy being accused of inconsistency by those both to its religious right and left. Charges of intellectual dishonesty are levelled at it for its willingness to engage in secular studies outside the sphere of Judaism, but to close off Jewish teachings from scholarly inquiry, which threatens its notions of revelation. From a sociological perspective also, it seems almost impossible to maintain a position in which Modern Orthodoxy appears in thrall to two divergent worlds, seemingly incapable of doing justice to either one without compromising the other.[6]

Reform's emphasis of the values of modernity at the expense of Jewish traditions became less tenable with the growth of antisemitism, the experience of the Shoah, and the creation of the State of Israel. The optimism which characterized the Pittsburgh Platform has been eroded; the possibility of portraying Jews solely as a religious community was undermined. Shifts from a modernist consciousness to postmodernism eased Reform's transition from its emphasis on the universal towards a reclamation of the particular. The growing acceptance of multiculturalism, particularly after the 1960s, and the increased value ascribed to religious pluralism led Reform to implement a process of retrieval. To strengthen Reform Jewish identities within contemporary societies, particularistic practices came to be viewed in more positive terms. Changes in theology could be discerned in declarations issued by the Reform rabbinical body of America, the CCAR, from 1937 onwards. However, the decision to return to Pittsburgh in 1999 to issue a new 'Statement of Principles for Reform Judaism' represented a clear attempt to explicitly progress beyond the 1885 Pittsburgh Platform and the values it had represented. The principle of progressive revelation which had underpinned the earlier declarations facilitated the sometimes dramatic theological shifts which Reform came to introduce. The emphasis unequivocally remained on the principle of individual autonomy, yet the more recent statements champion the increasing sense of importance attributed to particularism and notions of *mitzvah*—the sense of being commanded to observe Jewish practices.

Eugene Borowitz (b.1924) has been one of the leading influences in the development of this postmodern Reform theology which seeks to address the tension between autonomy and commandment. Synthesizing the thought of Martin Buber and Franz Rosenzweig, Borowitz has been instrumental in attempts to encourage Reform Jews to feel compelled as individuals to hear God's commanding voice. He has focused on reinterpretations of the principle of covenant in Judaism in a manner which could allow individual autonomy to coexist with commitment to Jewish traditions. The 1975 publication of *Sha'are Tefilla*—'Gates of Prayer'—pointed to the shifts emerging within Reform. This more traditional prayer book introduced increased amounts of Hebrew into the liturgy, reinstated references to Zion, and included prayers for celebrations of *Yom Ha'atzmaut* (Israeli independence day). However it also offered ten alternative Sabbath services to maintain individual choice, and, responding to new 'revelations' apprehended in the later stages of the twentieth century, removed much gender-biased language from the liturgy. The growth of alternative services reflected a rise in the importance of spirituality and the accompanying Havurah movement, which exerted some influence on Reform as well as other sectors of Judaism and is considered further below. The publication in 1979 of *Sha'are Mitzvah—Gates of Mitzvah: A Guide to the Jewish Life Cycle*—further demonstrated the shifts which have incited the process of retrieval that Reform has experienced since the latter decades of the twentieth century.

Tradition and peoplehood

Conservative Judaism has always represented an intermediary position between Reform and Orthodox Judaism. The beginnings of the movement can be identified in Zachariah Frankel's (1801–75) development of positive historical Judaism and the establishment in 1854 of a Jewish Theological Seminary in Breslau over which he presided. The notion of Judaism as a 'positive' phenomenon acknowledges the importance of the religion's prescriptive practices which introduce 'posited' rather than merely rationally discernible 'natural' laws into its religious system. The association of this positivism with an identification of the historic nature of Judaism, as a religion that spanned the ages, demonstrates the lasting value of these practices, both within and beyond history. It also demonstrates Judaism's ability to adapt in response to changing historical circumstances. Influenced by the Romantic movement, Frankel identified a national spirit at the heart of Judaism which provided a living revelation: the *Volk* or *Klal Yisrael*. It was this national spirit that ultimately defined the scope for reform, since it represented the living religious consciousness of the Jewish people.

The Conservative Jewish theology which emerged from Frankel's teachings and its later development in America rejects Reform, with its emphasis on ethics over law. It also rejects Orthodoxy, whose literalistic emphasis on the principle of 'Torah min haShamayim' was perceived to have removed the historical sense of Judaism which facilitated religious adaptation. However, although the principles of modernity are taken further than in Modern Orthodoxy, conflict remains at the heart of this theology: whilst the scientific study of Judaism was accepted as valid and appropriate, a core of the religion was identified which was to remain untouched. The questions that could be raised by study and by contemporary experience were to be limited. Conservative Judaism was thus open to critical analysis but closed to far-reaching reform. It was precisely this conflict that was avoided, in their different ways, by both Reform and Orthodoxy.

Conservative Judaism developed into a fully fledged movement in America, where it became the quintessential movement of American Jewry.[7] It enabled Jews to identify with their faith whilst being integrated in American society. Solomon Schechter (1847–1915), brought to America from Britain in 1902 to head a reconstituted Jewish Theological Seminary (JTS) which was designed to train rabbis who could spread a more Americanized form of Judaism than that practised by Eastern European immigrants, helped to establish an institutional base for Conservative Judaism. The United Synagogue of America, formed under Schechter's influence in 1913, uniting sixteen ostensibly Conservative synagogues, sought to provide an alternative synagogal organization to represent Conservative interests.[8] However, by not requiring from its member synagogues any uniform acceptance of basic positions that would constitute 'Conservative Judaism', the United Synagogue embodied the inconsistencies at the heart of the movement.

It was not until 1988 that Conservative Judaism finally sought to define a statement of principles that could provide a cohesive theology for its members. *Emet ve-Emunah*—'Truth and Faith'—produced under the guidance of Robert Gordis (1908–92), encapsulated these principles. In some respects, the compulsion finally to attempt to produce a definition of Conservative Judaism was influenced by the growing convergence between Conservative and Reform Judaism, as Reform increasingly emphasized the value of tradition and Conservatism introduced more far-reaching changes. The growing divergence from Orthodoxy had also become clear, most notably in the 1983 decision of the JTS to admit women for rabbinical ordination, reducing the inclination in some quarters of the Conservative movement to downplay its differences from Orthodoxy. Through the statement Conservative Judaism maintained its acknowledgment of the importance of halakhah, in contrast to Reform's emphasis on mitzvah. However, it sought to blend tradition and change alongside its stress on Jewish peoplehood. Whilst Orthodoxy championed the *Shulhan Arukh* as its key text, and Reform emphasized the prophetic texts, Conservative Judaism adopted a broader less clearly defined focus on 'tradition'. The designation of Conservative Judaism in Israel and certain other countries as 'Masorti' (traditional) highlights this emphasis.

Reconstructionist Judaism emerged out of Conservative Judaism, and for many years retained its association with the movement. Indeed, initially there was no intention that Reconstructionism should develop into a distinct movement.[9] Developed by Mordecai Kaplan (1881–1983), its ideas were meant to influence all sectors of Judaism, and particularly to speak to Jews who were unaffiliated, unable to reconcile Judaism with modern thought. Reconstructionism built on the ideas developed by Kaplan in his ministry at New York's Society for the Advancement of Judaism, which he led from 1922, and in his major work, *Judaism as a Civilisation* (1934). Critiquing the existing religious movements, and influenced by sociological models of religion, Kaplan championed a Judaism that could retain validity amongst Jews who were no longer able to accept the supernatural elements of the religion. Perceiving a need in contemporary society for the formation of social groups that could be invested with meaning, Kaplan argued that the maintenance of rituals, once they were relieved of their references to such concepts as divine revelation, notions of choseneness, and belief in the miraculous, helped to construct groups in which individuals could feel at home. From the outset, since Kaplan viewed Judaism as encompassing far more than religion, emphasis was placed on the centrality of Jewish peoplehood and Jewish cultural identity in defining practice and fostering group attachments. Keen to respond to modern currents of thought, it also implemented gender equality far more quickly than other movements.[10]

Reconstructionism built on the concept of synagogue centres that had emerged, particularly under Kaplan's influence, within Conservative Judaism. Designed to offer a focus for communities, they provided resources for non-religious activities, such as sport, in addition to the conventional services expected of synagogues. These centres to some extent embodied Kaplan's conception of Judaism as a civilization.

Reconstructionism's development as a distinct religious movement in American Jewry can be seen as a shift away from Kaplan's own vision. The Havurah movement and its burgeoning influence across American Jewry also served to alter Reconstructionism, introducing more spiritual, neo-Hasidic interpretations into some sectors of the movement. The growth in the latter decades of the twentieth century of a turn to religion to answer the search for meaning incited new currents in Reconstructionism.[11]

The Havurah movement began to develop during the 1960s, emerging first in university campuses in response to demands for smaller, more intimate Jewish groups (*havurot*) which could bring together like-minded individuals. They provided a forum for engaging in Jewish study, more informal types of religious worship, and general social interaction amongst Jews who were seeking alternatives to formal religion. The Havurah movement also spread to synagogues, particularly of the Conservative and, to a lesser extent, the Reform movement, where the sense of a loss of intimacy in established communities led to the creation of alternative settings in which to practise more spiritual forms of Judaism. The havurot sought to retrieve Jews who felt alienated from their communities but nonetheless sought religious content in their lives. They provided an opportunity to attend retreats and celebrate Jewish festivals together in smaller more intimate settings. They also often helped to foster more gender-inclusive Jewish environments.

Religious movements

Significant changes in the makeup of religious movements in Judaism occurred in the latter stages of the twentieth century. The creation of havurot, the growth of a Jewish Renewal movement, and the emergence of Reconstructionism as a distinct movement, alongside theological shifts in Reform, Conservative, and Modern Orthodox Judaism, were all features of these changes.

Judaism's ability to embody religious pluralism within its own boundaries is a matter of dispute. For some sections within Judaism, the development of groups that propound alternative interpretations of key doctrines has led to seemingly irreparable schism. Denominationalism, the religious position that accepts the validity of alternative religious interpretations and acknowledges that its own views only represent one option among many, is rejected by groups seeking to assert the sole validity of their own teachings. Orthodox Judaism, even within the Modern Orthodox sector, rapidly developed a sectarian stance towards Reform. In addition to his theology of 'Torah im derekh eretz', Hirsch later developed the principle of secession, designed to separate Orthodox Jews from Reform institutions as part of attempts to delegitimize non-Orthodox theologies. Thus, whilst the scope for openness towards the surrounding society was acknowledged, Modern Orthodoxy developed a closed position internally.

Reform Judaism did not develop in sectarian form. If anything, it was influenced by the denominationalism it encountered in Christianity. Its emphasis on individual autonomy also facilitated an acceptance of internal religious pluralism. Conservative Judaism, with its intermediary position between Reform and Orthodoxy, found itself in a more problematic situation. The religious pluralism permitted within Conservative Judaism itself at times undermined its claim to represent more than a mere amalgamation of like-minded congregations. The emphasis on Jewish peoplehood, designed to control change, was intended to ensure that only appropriate adaptations were introduced, but the United Synagogue and the Rabbinical Assembly's Committee on Law and Standards accommodated halakhic pluralism. Its retention of the importance of halakhah required Conservatives to grant legitimacy to Orthodoxy, primarily critiquing its loss of flexibility rather than its inherent nature. Hence, in this sense too religious pluralism was permitted within Conservative Judaism. Divergence grew between Orthodoxy and Conservative Judaism as the latter implemented more far-reaching reforms which, as we have seen, brought it closer to Reform and severed lasting connections with Orthodoxy. Co-operation with Reform has since increased, with both movements united in fighting for recognition of Progressive Judaism, arguing that the principle of religious pluralism should be extended within Judaism.

The focus on delineating modern Judaism according to its movements and their theologies could be presented as a distortion. The idea that the development of modernist Jewish religious movements entirely followed the theological principles propounded by its leaders presents an image of modern Judaism that marginalizes the role of individuals and prioritizes the relevance of theory over practice. It is clear that differences are to be discerned between the ideas of so-called 'folk' and their 'elites'. The construction of theological principles to underpin modernist movements and create responses to the ideological problems posed by the theories of a new age does not necessarily in practice influence the actions of individuals and their performance of ritual. The theoretical may, in fact, not play as great a role as the theorists might hope. Indeed, in Judaism, as Mendelssohn pointed out, a clear distinction can be drawn between beliefs and observances. The relationship between modern Jewish practice, belief, and identity is considered further in Chapter 20, but it is important here to acknowledge that the development of modernist movements in Judaism and their construction of theologies does not necessarily influence or explain the actions of Jewish individuals. Moreover, it could be argued that practical shifts in individual observance of Jewish laws have driven the development of the religious movements as much as the reverse.

As Jews were offered opportunities to engage in the nation-state, their sense of a distinct identity came into conflict with the development of identities linking them to the surrounding society. Whether consciously, responding to the development of religious movements, or on the basis of individual ad hoc decision-making, a balancing act of dual, and later multiple, identities was demanded of them in which the sense of Jewish identity was forced to contract to make room for alternatives. This enabled Jews to become citizens who practised Judaism, rather than simply Jews. The emergence of an 'adjectival' Judaism indicated a shift in understandings of the nature of Jewish identity, as an individual's religiosity came to characterize only one aspect of their identity rather than being the characteristic by which they were defined. A by-product of this shift was the introduction of additional qualifiers to distinguish between the types of Jewish religiosity that people adopted; hence the emergence of Judaisms defined as Reform, Orthodox, Conservative, or Reconstructionist.

FURTHER READING

See the guide to further reading in Chapter 10, 'American Jewry', for additional suggestions of works on the development of the distinct religious movements.

Alpert, Rebecca T., and Jacob J. Staub. *Exploring Judaism: A Reconstructionist Approach* (expanded and updated) (New York: Jewish Reconstructionist Federation, 1985). An examination of the theological underpinnings of Reconstructionist Judaism.

Borowitz, Eugene. *Renewing the Covenant: A Theology for the Postmodern Jew* (Philadelphia: Jewish Publication Society, 1991). A thoughtful presentation of the various problems posed for Jews as a result of postmodernism, identifying various strategies that can be adopted. See also Peter Ochs, *Reviewing the Covenant: Eugene B. Borowitz and the Postmodern Renewal of Jewish Theology*, with Eugene B. Borowitz (Albany: State University of New York Press, 2000)

Borowitz, Eugene. *Liberal Judaism* (New York: UAHC, 1984). A comprehensive account of the theology of Reform Judaism.

Bulka, Reuven (ed.). *Dimensions of Orthodox Judaism* (New York: KTAV, 1983). A comprehensive selection of essays addressing the numerous positions adopted within the various sectors of Orthodoxy.

Davis, Moshe. *The Emergence of Conservative Judaism: The Historical School in 19th Century America* (Philadelphia: Jewish Publication Society, 1965). An account of the early development of Conservative Judaism, considering its origins as a movement primarily opposed to Reform.

Gillman, Neil. *Conservative Judaism: The New Century* (New York: Behrman House, 1993). An analysis of the development of Conservative Judaism.

Goldsmith, Emanuel S., and Mel Scult (eds.). *Dynamic Judaism: The Essential Writings of Mordecai M. Kaplan* (New York: Schocken Books, 1985). An analysis of Kaplan's theology and influence.

Hartman, D. *A Living Covenant* (Woodstock, Vt.: Jewish Lights, 1997). A thoughtful presentation of strategies for understanding Judaism in modern terms, from a forward-thinking Orthodox perspective.

Hartman, D. *A Heart of Many Rooms: Celebrating the Many Voices Within Judaism* (Woodstock, Vt.: Jewish Lights, 1999). An analysis of the variety of positions that can be accommodated within contemporary Judaism.

Hirsch, S. R. *The Nineteen Letters About Judaism*, trans. Bernard Drachman, new edn. by Jacob Breuer (New York: Feldheim, 1969). Hirsch's seminal work acknowledging the concerns of modern Jews, whilst presenting an outline of the theology which he believes can resolve the problems.

Kaplan, M. *Judaism As a Civilisation: Toward a Reconstruction of American-Jewish Life*, with a new introductory essay by Arnold Eisen (Philadelphia: Jewish Publication Society, 1994). Kaplan's seminal work laying the foundation for the development of Reconstructionist Judaism.

Lamm, Norman. *Torah Umadda: The Encounter of Religious Learning and Worldly Knowledge in the Jewish Tradition* (Northvale, NJ: Jason Aronson, 1990). A presentation of Modern Orthodox theology as developed in American Jewry.

Meyer, Michael A. *Response to Modernity: A History of the Reform Movement in Judaism* (Detroit Wayne State University Press, 1995). An excellent historical account of the development of Reform Judaism, beginning with its European origins before considering the various changes it has experienced in America.

Rudavsky, D. *Modern Religious Movements: A History of Emancipation and Adjustment*, 3rd edn. (New York: Behrman House, 1979) A general account of the development of the distinct religious movements in modern Judaism.

Soloveitchik, J.B. *Halakhic Man*, trans. L. Kaplan (Philadelphia: Jewish Publication Society, 1983). A classic exposition of Soloveitchik's understanding of how to maintain an Orthodox life of observance.

NOTES

1. See P. Mendes-Flohr and Y. Reinharz (eds.), *The Jew in the Modern World: A Documentary History* (Oxford: Oxford University Press, 1988), pp. 125 ff.
2. The encounter with modernity experienced by Jewish women differed in a variety of ways from that of their male counterparts. In one sense it was influenced by the different nature of their

engagement with Judaism and the Jewish community. In addition, it was affected by the expectations related to their gender that existed in the societies to which Jews became acculturated. A full understanding of the processes of Jewish acculturation and adaptation needs to include consideration of women's distinct experiences, but this lies outside the scope of the current chapter. See Chap. 30 for further discussion.

3. See Chap. 18 for further analysis of modern changes to religious worship.

4. The translation of 'Torah im derekh eretz' is complicated by the changing meanings of the term *derekh eretz*, which literally means 'ways of the land' but can also denote a notion of etiquette and much beyond.

5. See Chap. 10 for further consideration of the development of Reform Judaism in America.

6. See e.g. S. Heilman and S. M. Cohen, *Cosmopolitans and Parochials: Modern Orthodox Jews in America* (Chicago: University of Chicago Press, 1989).

7. See Chap. 10, and Marshall Sklare's *Conservative Judaism: An American Religious Movement*, augmented edn. (New York: Schocken Books, 1972).

8. It is interesting to reflect upon Schechter's choice of name for Conservative Judaism's synagogal institution. Influenced by his encounter with the United Synagogue in Anglo-Jewry (see Chap. 13 for more details on British Jewry), where he had resided between 1882 and 1902, he appeared to identify parallels between the ostensibly Orthodox but umbrella organization represented by the British version of the United Synagogue and the institution he sought to establish.

9. Indeed, the requirement that members of the Reconstructionist Federation of Congregations and Havurot also affiliate with the UAHC or United Synagogue of America was only rescinded in 1961.

10. Space precludes consideration of questions thrown up for modernist movements of Judaism by feminism, which has led to major changes and has the potential to incite further shifts across all the movements. See Chaps. 30 and 31 and their bibliographies.

11. As a specifically American religious movement, Reconstructionist Judaism is considered further in Chap. 10.

7 | Traditionalist strands

Eliezer Don-Yehiya

The adherents of traditionalist strands in modern Judaism are those Jews who maintain their allegiance to traditional Jewish religion, even in the face of far-reaching changes in the life of Jews, which have occurred since the beginning of the emancipation of European Jewry. These Jews came to be known, especially in Central and Western Europe and in the United States, as Orthodox, while in Eastern Europe and Israel they are commonly called Religious, or Observant.

Those Orthodox Jews who are most committed to the strict observance of halakhah and adopt segregationist attitudes toward the wider modern society and to Zionism, came to be known as 'ultra-Orthodox'. In contemporary usage, especially in Israel, they are most frequently called *Haredim*, meaning 'fearful' (of God), or 'anxious' (to observe the Commandments). During the nineteenth and early twentieth centuries Haredim was used as a Hebrew translation of 'Orthodox'. It was only after the establishment of the Zionist movement that the term Haredim was limited to the non-Zionist separatist Orthodox.

Like Reform and Conservative Judaism, Orthodoxy in its various forms is a modern phenomenon, distinguishable from pre-emancipation traditional Judaism in two main respects. First, Orthodoxy is a kind of counter-reaction to the processes of modernization and secularization that have penetrated European Jewish society since the beginning of the emancipation. Observance of Jewish law and commitment to Jewish religious tradition were perceived as the natural order of things within traditional Jewish society. Therefore, they were not regarded as a way of life that needed special protection. By contrast, the threat to the traditional way of life following emancipation encouraged those who remained faithful to traditional religion to indulge in systematic efforts to protect the integrity of their sacred way of life.

Secondly, Orthodoxy is a modern phenomenon in the sense that, even when it rejects the contents of modernity, it tends to adopt many of its means and techniques in order to protect itself against modern secular society and its culture. Thus, from the beginning of emancipation leaders of Orthodoxy began to use modern forms of organization and propaganda to defend traditional Jewry against the threats of modernity and secularism.

The main characteristics shared by ultra-Orthodox Haredim are: a strict observance of halakhah; opposition to or reservations about modern Zionism; and a segregationist approach toward secular society and/or modern culture. A salient manifestation of this approach is the tendency of Haredim to concentrate in distinct neighbourhoods, and to maintain their own communities with separate religious, educational, and welfare institutions.

The most significant division within ultra-Orthodoxy is between traditionalist or conservative Haredim on the one hand, and modernist Haredim (better known as 'neo-Orthodox') on the other. This division is rooted in two schools of thought, which form two different reactions to the emancipation and the waves of modernization and secularization that followed in its wake.

The conservative Haredi school of thought has its origins in the writings and activities of Rabbi Moses Sofer (1762–1839) from Pressburg (then Hungary), known as Hatam Sofer, after his most famous book. Hatam Sofer is considered the spiritual father of Orthodox Judaism in general and of its ultra-Orthodox conservative variant in particular. He led an uncompromising struggle against modernism, secularism, and especially Reform, and was firmly opposed to any innovation, not only in halakhah, but in all areas of behaviour. This attitude has been expressed in the firm opposition of Hatam Sofer and his followers to modern practices and customs, even when they do not stand in open contradiction to halakhah.

The modernist Haredi school of thought, which came to be known as 'neo-Orthodoxy', was based on the teachings of Rabbi Samson Raphael Hirsch (1808–88). Hirsch and his followers did not share Hatam Sofer's total rejection of modern culture. Thus, while the adherents of Hatam Sofer maintained the traditional dress and manners of pre-emancipation Ashkenazi Jewry, the disciples of Hirsch adopted the modern dress and behaviour common in Western and Central Europe.

The most significant difference between the two variants of Haredi Jewry was reflected in their attitude to secular studies. While the conservative ultra-Orthodox were opposed to these studies, or at least reserved and cautious about them, the neo-Orthodox introduced them into the curriculum of their educational institutions alongside traditional religious studies.

Despite their differing attitude to modern culture and education, the two strands of Haredi Jewry shared a strict observance of halakhah and also a segregationist and separatist approach to secular Jewish society and its institutions. This was manifested in the establishment of separate Orthodox congregations by Hirsch in Germany and by Hatam Sofer's disciples in Hungary. These congregations established comprehensive educational systems and other institutions that were designed to unite observant Jews, to encourage them to join forces against the secularists and reformers and instil loyalty and devotion to the Jewish religious tradition. This is the reason why not only the traditionalist adherents of Hatam Sofer but also the neo-Orthodox followers of Hirsch can be considered Haredim (some call the latter 'enlightened Haredim').

The neo-Orthodox were very influential within Central European Orthodox Jewry, especially in Germany. Later they played a leading role in the formation of worldwide Haredi organizations, the most significant of which was Agudat Israel. However, neo-Orthodoxy did not penetrate Eastern Europe, where the great bulk of Orthodox Jewry lived until the Second World War.

Unlike their brethren in Western and Central Europe, most Jews in Eastern Europe were only gradually exposed to the processes of emancipation, modernization, and secularization. Consequently, those Jews did not initially recognize the need to establish their own separate congregations to guard against threats to their sacred ways of life. As the traditional leaders of East European Jewry did not experience modernity at first hand, they also lacked the organizational and political skills to confront it.

The neo-Orthodox leaders from Central Europe, especially from Germany, were thus much better equipped to confront modernity and secularism than the Orthodox leaders from Eastern Europe. This explains why Westernized Jews from Central Europe played the leading role in efforts to unite Orthodoxy in a common battle for traditional Judaism, when East European Jewish society was also exposed to the threats of secularism.

Haredim and modernization

Since the First World War there has been a gradual decline in neo-Orthodoxy, which was weakened still further after the Second World War. One of the main factors behind this development is the fact that most of the Torah sages and leaders of the *yeshivot* (religious academies) were of East European origin and they educated their students in the spirit of traditionalist Orthodoxy. Nevertheless, the legacy of Hirsch continues to influence various circles of both Haredi and modern Orthodox Jewry, although most of them are not members of neo-Orthodox communities.

The overwhelming majority of contemporary Haredim tend to adopt segregationist attitudes toward modern society and culture, though they differ in the degree of their rejection of modernism. There are several interrelated factors behind this position. First, pre-emancipation Jewish society, like other traditional societies, used to grant a sacred, religious value to traditional customs and practices, even when they were not an integral part of the religious law.

Second, the ultra-Orthodox reject the basic premises of modernity, which is perceived as a world outlook that places the emphasis on humans as sovereign beings empowered to decide for themselves how to shape their own lives. To many ultra-Orthodox Jews this seems irreconcilable with the traditional belief that God alone is the ultimate sovereign in all human affairs, and that only divinely revealed laws should govern the life of the individual and society.

Third, many ultra-Orthodox fear that any innovation might become a stepping-stone for further changes that will result in the disintegration of traditional Jewish society. The adoption of new customs and practices, and even certain modern technologies, was perceived as a threat because of their potential secularizing influences. Thus, many

Haredim refrain from viewing television or reading non-Orthodox papers, in order to avoid exposure to the secular content of modern mass media. In this way, rejection of modernity is part of the general strategy of segregation and self-insulation, which is the distinguishing mark of most Haredim.

The ultra-Orthodox leaders were aware of the devastating impact of the emancipation, which exposed traditional Jewish society to the surrounding society and culture and thereby brought about its disintegration. As they realized that they could not bring back the larger Jewish population to the traditional fold, they were determined to build their own separate and autonomous communities that should serve as a refuge against the threats from outside.

The traditionalist approach and segregationist strategy of the Haredim have been manifested in various ways. One of them is their distinct dress. Most contemporary Haredim dress in long dark coats and wear large-rimmed black hats and this because of two main reasons. First, this was the traditional dress of Jews in Eastern Europe, and secondly, it is a symbol of a distinct identity, which serves to unite the Haredim and set them apart from their surroundings. Many Haredim are also distinct in their physical appearance, maintaining long beards and sidelocks. This is mainly grounded in tradition, which grants religious value to this custom, but it also serves as another symbol of a separate and distinctive identity.

The traumatic experience of the emancipation is also one of the factors behind the tendency of the Haredim to be strict and punctilious in the observance of religious law and to interpret it in the most rigorous way. To a large extent this is part of a religious approach that perceives any deviation from religious tradition, however small, as dangerous because it might eventually result in a departure from the traditional way of life.

This approach is also manifest in the Haredi insistence on a rigid separation between men and women. Separation of the two genders has its origins in halakhah, and to a certain extent is a common practice among all Orthodox groups, especially in religious rituals. Thus, men and women sit apart in religious services in all Orthodox synagogues. However, in Haredi communities they sit apart in all public gatherings, such as wedding parties.

Separation of the genders is related to the value that halakhah places on adopting 'modest' behaviour and dress, especially with regard to women. To a certain extent the wearing of modest dress is required of all Orthodox women, but the Haredim are very strict about this, and all their women always cover their heads and dress in long skirts and sleeves.

One of the most distinguishing marks of Haredim is the central role that the study of Torah plays in their life. Traditional religious Judaism attached a significant sacred value to the study of Torah, but it was the Haredim who turned this into a way of life for the entire community. Torah is studied mainly in the yeshiva, the religious academy, which constitutes the intellectual and social basis of Haredi Jewry. It is more than an educational institution; it is a comprehensive and total framework of intensive religious socialization. Yeshiva studies are not designed to achieve practical aims—there are no exams, marks, or certificates; the students are engaged in the exclusive study of the sacred sources of Jewish religious law.

The yeshiva is an old and venerable institution in Judaism. However, the vast growth and proliferation of yeshivot began only in the nineteenth century in Eastern Europe. Because of their nature as total institutions that tend to insulate their students from their surroundings, most of the yeshivot thus became fortresses of the segregationist strategy of the Haredim, although there are also non-Haredi yeshivot.

Aside from the yeshiva, during the nineteenth century many other Orthodox organizations and institutions were established on a local or national basis. Only in the early years of the twentieth century were efforts made to unite and organize Haredi Orthodox Jews on a worldwide level. A significant motivating factor in these efforts was the advent of Zionism in the second half of the nineteenth century.

Orthodoxy and Zionism

Among the Orthodox opponents of Zionism, some rejected it for theological reasons. They perceived it as an effort to hasten the Redemption by natural means, which they claimed was forbidden by Jewish tradition. Other Orthodox Jews opposed Zionism because it was dominated by secular Jews and adopted a nationalist, secular ideology. They regarded it as an attempt to replace the Judaism of Torah and Commandments with a secular modern nationalism based on language and culture or on territory and state. Some Haredi thinkers were especially harsh in their criticism. Rabbi Elhanan Bunim Wasserman (1875–1941), one of the leaders of twentieth-century Orthodoxy, claimed that Zionism is a modern form of *avodah zarah* (idolatry).

The most coherent and total rejection of Zionism was produced by the late leader of the Satmar Hasidic dynasty, Rabbi Joel Teitelbaum (1888–1981). Teitelbaum and his disciples attribute demonic significance to Zionism and to the State of Israel. In their view, even if Orthodox Jews were to have the leading role in the Zionist movement and the State, it should still be regarded as *maase satan* (act of the devil), as there is no way to allow the formation of a Jewish state before the coming of the Messiah.

Unlike Teitelbaum and his followers, most Haredi opponents of Zionism were antagonistic to the secular nature of its ideology and leadership, but not to practical efforts at *aliyah* (immigration to the Land of Israel) and settlement, or to the establishment of a Jewish state.

Agudat Israel

The negative attitude towards modern Zionism, as well as the struggle against religious reform and secular Haskalah (enlightenment), induced traditional leaders from Western and Eastern Europe to join forces in what they perceived as a crucial battle for the survival of traditional Judaism. The world organization of Orthodox Jews, *Agudat Israel* (the Union of Israel), was established in 1912 in Kattowitz (then in Germany). The organization set as its aim: 'to solve in the spirit of Torah and the Commandments the various every day issues that will rise in the life of the people of Israel.'

The establishment of Agudat Israel helped to demarcate a clear boundary between two wings of Orthodoxy: the non-Zionist Orthodox, who came to be known as Haredim, and the non-Haredi Orthodox, who came to be known as 'religious Zionists' in Israel and 'modern Orthodox' in the Diaspora.

What united the various Haredi adherents of Agudat Israel was their segregationist strategy in regard to organizations and institutions that were dominated by secular Jews or were identified with secular ideology. This position was the common source of their opposition to Zionism.

Another position shared by all Haredi supporters of Agudat Israel is their attitude to rabbinic authority. Since its establishment there has been general agreement on the principle that, for Agudat Israel, the ultimate and undisputable authority on all affairs are *gedolei hatorah* (Torah sages). This principle was given operative expression by the establishment of *Moetzet Gedolei Hatorah* (Council of the Torah Sages), recognized as the supreme authority for Agudat Israel in all matters, religious as well as political. It was meant to comprise all the greatest rabbis and heads of yeshivot. However, not all the known and great Torah sages did participate in the Council.

The common ideological principles that underpinned the formation of Agudat Israel did not blur the differences between the various groups within the party and Haredi society in general. Agudat Israel united under the same organizational roof traditionalists and modernists, extremists and moderates, Hasidic Jews of various sects and non-Hasidic *mitnagdim*—'opponents' (of Hasidism)—also known as Lithuanians.

These differences, especially those of an ideological nature, were sources of tension and controversy. The most heated debates were held on the issue of attitudes toward the Zionist movement and its enterprise in the Land of Israel. Although all Haredi groups were united in their reluctance to join the Zionist organization, they were divided on the issue of relations with this organization and its affiliated institutions. At first the isolationist tendency within Agudat Israel gained the upper hand. However, there was a gradual retreat from this position, manifested in a growing willingness to co-operate with the Zionist movement and the *Yishuv* (the pre-state official Jewish community in the Land of Israel). The most dramatic change was Agudat Israel's decision to support the establishment of the State of Israel.

These developments gained momentum due to events that stressed the necessity of a Zionist solution. These included positive developments, such as the Balfour Declaration, the growth of the Yishuv, and the establishment of the State of Israel; and negative ones, including the rise of antisemitism in Europe between the world wars, the increasing rate of assimilation among Jews of the Diaspora, the Nazis' ascent to power, and especially the Holocaust.

The great majority of Agudat Israel supporters came to recognize the vital importance of the Zionist enterprise and resultant state to the physical survival of the Jewish people. Agudat Israel is still not a member of the Zionist organization, but this is not an expression of opposition to the State of Israel; it is rather a continuation of the tradition of taking exception to the secular nature of the Zionist movement and ideology.

Agudat Israel's willingness to co-operate with the Yishuv and state institutions stirred fierce opposition within the radical anti-Zionist elements of Haredi society. In 1935 they seceded and established their own separatist, anti-Zionist organization in Jerusalem, later known as *Neturei Karta* (Aramaic: Guardians of the City).

Neturei Karta refused to co-operate in any way with Zionist or state institutions. To this day they do not recognize the State of Israel and refuse to take any financial support from it. In Israel they are concentrated mainly in the Haredi quarter of Meah Shearim and its surroundings in Jerusalem. Members of the *Edah Haredit* (the Haredi Congregation, in which Neturei Karta forms an influential radical group) have their own separate educational system, in which the language of instruction is Yiddish. They also have their own rabbis and rabbinical courts, and most of them do not participate in elections to the Knesset or municipalities.

Members of Neturei Karta and the Edah Haredit are but a small minority within Haredi society in Israel. They receive support from ultra-Orthodox separatist groups outside Israel, who are concentrated mainly in certain quarters of Brooklyn and towns in Upper State New York, or in Haredi quarters of London, such as Stamford Hill. Many of the radical separatists are adherents of the Hasidic dynasty of Satmar.

On the opposite side of Haredi society, Poalei Agudat Israel (the Workers of Agudat Israel) was formed in the 1930s. It was led by Isaac Breuer (1883–1946), grandson of Hirsch, who had played a significant role in the formation of Agudat Israel. PAI was established as a Haredi workers organization affiliated to Agudat Israel. However, it developed a distinct ideology that attributed great significance to settlement in the Land of Israel, and was engaged in the establishment of Haredi villages and Kibbutzim.

PAI was the most ardent Haredi supporter of co-operation with Zionist and state institutions, but most Agudat Israel adherents also adopted a positive attitude to the State of Israel. This attitude is based mainly on a pragmatic approach, which did not lead Agudat Israel to identify the state with the prophetic vision of Messianic redemption. This attitude is manifested to this day in the unwillingness of most Haredi congregations to say the prayers for the State of Israel and their refusal to take part in Israeli Independence Day celebrations.

Haredim in Israeli politics

Since the establishment of the State of Israel until the 1984 Knesset elections, Haredim were represented in the political field by Agudat Israel and PAI, which together used to gain five or six Knesset seats. The most dramatic recent change in this regard has been the appearance of a new type of Haredi party, Shas (Sephardi Torah observant), which first won seats in the Knesset in 1984. Until then almost all the leaders of Haredi parties and most of their members were of East European Ashkenazi origin. The formation of Shas reflected the emergence of a Sephardi Haredi community, whose spiritual and political leader is the revered rabbi Ovadia Yosef (b. 1920). Shas also differs from other Haredi parties by appealing not only to Haredi adherents, but also to non-Haredi and even non-Orthodox supporters and voters. As a result, there is a marked difference between the Haredi elite of Shas and the majority of its adherents.

This is related to the fact that the Haredi leaders of Shas do not share the segregationist attitude of the Ashkenazi Haredim, although the Haredi core of Shas shares with the Ashkenazi Haredim strict observance of halakhah and also a unique style of dress and behaviour. The common denominator of Shas and other Haredi parties is their reliance on Torah sages as undisputed authorities in all matters. They also share a political attitude that is centred on religious issues and concerns, relegating foreign and defence policies to a secondary position.

Changes also occurred in Agudat Israel when most of its non-Hasidic supporters, the Mitnagdim, seceded from the party before the 1988 elections to form a new Haredi party under the spiritual leadership of Rabbi Eliezer Menachem Shach (1898–2001), who was considered the greatest of the Ashkenazi Torah sages. The immediate cause of the split was the controversy between Shach and Habad Hasidim regarding the latter group's messianic campaign centred on its venerated leader, Rabbi Menachem Mendel Shneerson of Lubavitch (1900–92).[1]

Contemporary Haredi society in Israel and in the Diaspora

The two most important centres of contemporary Haredi Jewry are in Israel and the United States. Israel has the largest and most influential Haredi population. In the 1999 survey of the Guttman Institute for Social Research, 5 per cent of the respondents identified themselves as 'Haredim'.

There are indications that the percentage of Haredim in Israel is even higher than 5 per cent (that is, about 250,000 people), since the extremist Haredim refuse to respond to such surveys. There are also those who would be considered Haredim by their way of life, but who refuse to be identified in this way because in Israel the term 'Haredi' has been commonly related to opposition to Zionism and refusal to serve in the army.

Thus, in the Guttman survey 16 per cent of respondents defined themselves as 'strictly observant', while only 5 per cent identified as 'Haredim'. We can therefore estimate that there are about 300,000–400,000 Haredim in Israel.

It is extremely difficult to asses the number of Haredim outside Israel, because of the lack of adequate surveys. According to the 1991 National Jewish Population Survey, there are 5.2 million 'core Jews' in the United States, of whom 10 per cent (520,000), are Orthodox. According to expert estimates, about 40–50 per cent of the American Orthodox can be considered Haredim. Hence there are roughly 200,000–250,000 Haredim in the United States.

Alongside the two largest Haredi centres in Israel and the United States, there are considerable concentrations of Haredim in Canada and in Western Europe, especially in England, France, Belgium, and Switzerland. Most of the Haredim are concentrated in certain quarters of urban areas.

A number of differences exist between traditionalist circles in Israel and the Diaspora.[2] First, we have to differentiate between two sorts of Haredim: Hasidim and non-Hasidim—the Mitnagdim. There is not much difference between Hasidim in Israel and in the Diaspora. They all maintain distinct traditional dress and appearance, and most adopt a segregationist approach toward modern society and culture. A special case is that of the Lubavitch or Habad Hasidim who, whilst maintaining their distinct traditional dress, appearance, and lifestyle, nonetheless adopt a co-operative approach toward other Jews—observant or secularists.[3]

Unlike the Hasidim, there are quite marked differences between Mitnagdim in Israel and the Diaspora. In contemporary Israel the overwhelming majority of Haredim—Hasidim and non-Hasidim—are distinguished from the surrounding society not only by their attitude towards Zionist ideology, but also by attitudes towards modern culture and lifestyle. In this they differ from many non-Hasidic Haredim in the Diaspora, who are much more influenced by their surrounding societies. This is the main reason why Haredim tend to be more differentiated from other Orthodox Jews in Israel than in the Diaspora.

This is reflected in various ways. The most significant difference between Haredi society in Israel and the Diaspora is manifested in the position of these two communities on the issue of general or secular studies. One of the salient characteristics of Israeli Haredim is their vigorous opposition to the integration of 'secular studies' beyond the most elementary level of instruction. Virtually all study time is devoted to religious learning, and especially to the study of Talmud. By contrast, general studies are incorporated in most ultra-Orthodox educational institutions in the Diaspora, apart from upper-level yeshivot.

Notwithstanding the great value that Diaspora ultra-Orthodoxy places on yeshiva study, the yeshiva does not constitute a global and total way of life. It is not uncommon for some among the Haredim not to continue their studies in an upper-level yeshiva, or not to remain there after marriage or beyond a specified period of study. By contrast, in Israel a unique and unparalleled phenomenon of a community of scholars has developed—focused on the various ultra-Orthodox yeshivot—as a total way of life that is, in practice, obligatory for all men, both young and old.

Moreover, the degree and severity of the isolation imposed by the yeshiva is usually far greater in Israeli Haredi society. In principle, the ultra-Orthodox yeshivot of the Diaspora have reservations about general or secular studies—especially in regard to university education. In practice, however, they resign themselves to the prevalent tendency among yeshiva students to enrol for higher education in evening and summer courses. The traditional ultra-Orthodox yeshivot in Israel, by contrast, vigorously resist any enrolment of their students in university courses.

These differences are tied to the structural conditions of the two societies. Only in Israel do the yeshivot enjoy generous government aid that permits students to devote all their energies to study for long periods of time. Moreover, the exemption from military service of these yeshiva students is predicated on them not engaging in any work.

The fact that the great majority of Haredim avoid any form of military service, and as a result are not integrated in the labour market, is itself a significant factor that distinguishes them from other groups in Israeli society, including the religious Zionists. There are, however, signs of increasing engagement of Israeli Haredim with Israeli society. Although their involvement in Israeli politics is motivated mainly by pragmatic considerations, it tends to influence their attitude toward the state. Israeli Haredim tend to criticize Israel, but they feel themselves a part of it. The very fact that they are living in the Jewish state induces them to harbour a great deal of concern about its existence, peace, and welfare. In this respect too they differ from the Diaspora ultra-Orthodox, many of whom feel less attached to Israel.

Revival, crisis, and change in Haredi society

As has been noted, the Holocaust played a prominent role in inducing the changes that occurred in Haredi attitudes towards the State of Israel. The Holocaust played a crucial role in developments that caused the destruction of Haredi Jewry in Eastern Europe and then its resurrection in Israel, America, and certain Western European countries. Haredi Jewry suffered a severe blow in the Holocaust. The Nazis murdered most of its adherents, who were concentrated in Eastern Europe, and the great Torah centres that were the bastions of traditional Jewry were completely destroyed. However, some Haredi spiritual leaders survived or managed to leave Europe before the Second World War, taking refuge in Israel, North America, and Western Europe. After the war they invested great efforts in rebuilding Haredi society in these countries.

Contemporary Haredi society is to a large extent a success story. This society is growing in numbers and also in its share of the Jewish population. One of the main reasons for this growth is the high fertility rate among Haredim, but another important factor is its success in keeping most of its members, especially the younger generation, within its fold. This is related to the greatest achievement of Haredi society, which is the development of its vast and growing network of educational institutions, especially yeshivot, in which the great majority of the Haredi population has been integrated. Haredi society has also managed to induce many non-Haredi and even non-Orthodox Jews to join its ranks. To a large extent this is due to the 'outreach' activities of certain Haredi circles, especially those of the Habad Hasidim and the activists of Shas.

The success of Haredim in sustaining and enhancing their social and political power has been especially notable in Israel. However, the very success of Israeli Haredi society is also one of the main causes of the severe problems with which it has been confronted, mainly in recent years. The large and growing number of people who do not work for their living, and the need to maintain a vast network of non-profitable institutions, impose a heavy burden on the Haredi community, making it dependent on government aid. In Israel this induces Haredi parties to participate in govern-mental coalitions in order to ensure public finance for the community and its institutions.

In order to maintain its cohesion and integrity Haredi society must rely on its separate educational system, and if it is severely hurt by financial difficulties this might put it in grave danger. However, the crisis may serve as a motivating force for required changes in the structure of Israeli Haredi society.

There are already indications of such changes emerging. Economic difficulties have led to an unprecedented development in Israeli Haredi society: the opening of vocational and academic courses for Haredim. Another recent development is the formation of special army units for Haredim who are not studying in yeshivot.

The changes in Israeli Haredi society are only beginning to take place, but they have already stirred sharp controversy. Some rabbis have given a limited approval to academic courses for Haredim who are not able or willing to continue their studies in yeshiva, but others vehemently oppose it. Even more controversial are the special arrangements for military service of Haredim. It is not easy to predict how the crisis will affect Haredi society. We can nevertheless assume that this ultra-conservative society is about to undergo remarkable changes, especially in its most important centre—the State of Israel.

FURTHER READING

Bacon, Gershon C. *The Politics of Tradition: Agudat Yisrael in Poland, 1916–1939* (Jerusalem: Magnes Press, 1996). A historical study of Agudat Israel in Poland, where it was one of the most influential Jewish parties between the two world wars.

Don-Yehiya, Eliezer. 'Origins and Development of Agudah and Mafdal Parties', *Jerusalem Quarterly*, 20 (Summer 1981), pp. 49–64. A historical and sociological study of Israel's religious political parties.

Don-Yehiya, Eliezer. 'Jewish Orthodoxy, Zionism and the State of Israel', *Jerusalem Quarterly*, 31 (Spring 1984), pp. 10–30. A study of the ideological positions of noted Orthodox thinkers on Zionism and Israel.

Don-Yehiza, Eliezer. 'Does Place make a Difference?: Jewish Orthodoxy in Israel and the Diaspora', in Chaim Waxman (ed.), *Israel as a Religious Entity* (Northvale, NJ: Jason Aronson, 1994), pp. 43–74. A comparative study of Jewish Orthodoxy in Israel and the Diaspora.

Don-Yehiza, Eliezer. 'The Book and the Sword: The Nationalist Yeshivot in Israel', in Martin Marty and Scott Appleby (eds.), *Accounting for Fundamentalisms: The Dynamic Character of Movements* (Chicago: University of Chicago Press, 1994), pp. 262–300. A sociological study of the 'nationalist Yeshivot' in Israel, which presents them as the main source of the emergence of religious-political radicalism there.

Friedman, Menachem. 'Religious Zealotry in Israeli Society', in S. Poll and E. Krausz (eds.), *On Ethnic and Religious Diversity in Israel* (Ramat-Gan: Bar-Ilan University Press, 1975), pp. 91–111. A study of extremist Haredim, representing them as modern 'zealots'.

Friedman, Menachem. 'Life Tradition and Book Tradition in the Development of Ultra-Orthodox Judaism', in H. E. Goldberg (ed.), *Judaism Viewed from Within and From Without* (Albany: State University of New York Press, 1986). The main argument of the author is that in Haredi society the 'living tradition' of traditional Judaism is replaced by a total reliance on the written religious law.

Friedman, Menachem. 'Haredim Confront the Modern City', in Peter Medding (ed.), *Studies in Contemporary Society*, vol. 2 (Bloomington: University of Indiana Press, 1986). This article seeks to explain why Haredim are concentrated mainly in urban centres, and what their relationships are with their neighbourhood.

Heilman, Samuel C., and Menachem Friedman. 'Religious Fundamentalism and Religious Jews: The Case of the Haredim', in Martin Marty and Scot C. Appleby (eds.), *Fundamentalism Observed* (Chicago: University of Chicago Press, 1991), pp. 197–264. A study of Haredi ideology and way of life, presented as a special kind of religious fundamentalism.

Heilman, Samuel C. *Defenders of the Faith: Life Among the Ultra-Orthodox* (New York: Schocken Books, 1992). An anthropological study of Haredi society.

Helmreich, William. *The World of Yeshiva* (New York: Free Press, 1982). A sociological research of the American Yeshivot.

Katz, Jacob. *Out of the Ghetto: The Social Background of Jewish Emancipation, 1770–1870* (New York: Schocken Books, 1973). A historical study of the emancipation and its impact on Jewish society by one of the most renowned Jewish historians.

Liebman, Charles, and Eliezer Don-Yehiya. *Civil Religion in Israel: Traditional Judaism and Political Culture in the Jewish State* (Berkeley: University of California Press, 1983). A study that depicts Zionist ideology and enterprise as an attempt to provide a secular surrogate for Judaism, and investigates the reactions of Orthodox Jewry to this attempt.

Liebman, Charles S., and Steven M. Cohen. *Two Worlds of Judaism* (New Haven: Yale University Press, 1990). A comparative study of Israeli and American Judaism.

Ravitzky, Aviezer. 'Exile in the Holy Land: The Dilemma of Haredi Jewry', in Peter Medding (ed.), *Studies in Contemporary Jewry*, vol. 5 (New York: Oxford University Press, 1989), pp. 89–125. The author argues that the main distinguishing mark of the Haredim is their perception of Israel as yet another exile.

Waxman, Chaim I. 'Religion in the Israeli Public Square', in Uzi Rebhun and Chaim I. Waxman, *Jews in Israel: Contemporary Social and Cultural Patterns* (Lebanon, NH: University Press of New England and Brandies University Press, 2004), pp. 221–39. A study of the role of religion in Israeli public life.

NOTES

1. See Chap. 15.
2. See Chap. 14.
3. See Chap. 15.

8 | Humanistic and secular Judaisms

Yaakov Malkin

What is secular humanistic Judaism?

The concept 'secular Judaism' has two meanings. It refers to the section of the Jewish people who do not feel bound by any observance of religious commandments, and also to the extensive body of culture and creative work produced by secular Jews over the past 250 years.

In the early nineteenth century men such as Leopold Zunz and Heinrich Heine—members of the Verein für Kultur und Wissenschaft der Juden—saw Judaism as a culture, and not only a religion. This perception of Judaism as culture prevails today among secular Jews, who view the Bible (rather than the Talmud) as the foundation of Judaism, as represented in works of all streams of Judaism throughout the ages, including the Talmud, the works of Philo and Josephus, the Apocrypha and Pseudepigrapha, the New Testament, and Karaitic, Samaritan, and Hasidic literature, as well as contemporary Jewish art and literature.

Sigmund Freud, in the preface to the Hebrew edition of *Totem and Taboo* (1930), wrote that he was estranged from the Jewish religion, as from all religion, that he was ignorant of its ancient national language and culture, but that he had never repudiated his Jewishness, and if the question were put to him what is there left to him that is Jewish he would reply 'a very great deal, and probably its very essence', which he could not express clearly in words, but that would some day, no doubt, become accessible to the scientific mind.

Freud was one of the greatest modern Jewish thinkers. His Jewishness, like that of Heine, Mahler, Einstein, Pissarro, Modigliani, Proust, and Bergson, affected his life, thought, and work, although he himself was estranged from Judaism as a religion and from Jewish social and cultural life. His work is part of the culture created by Jews, just as the work of Van Gogh is a part of the culture created by the Dutch and that of Gauguin forms part of the culture created by the French.

Most Jews who live within Jewish society and culture in the Diaspora simultaneously live within the culture of the people and nation in which they reside; in Israel most Jews live only within Jewish Israeli society and culture, which, like all contemporary national culture, is influenced by the cultures of other peoples.

The Land of Israel in the twentieth century produced hundreds of secular Jewish cultural communities, primarily in the kibbutzim. In Europe and the Americas cultural communities created secular (Yiddish) schools, political parties, and trade unions. In the 1960s new secular cultural communities were established in the Diaspora, such as the Centre Communautaire Laïc Juif (Espace Yitzhak Rabin) in Brussels, the Centre Bernard Lazare in Paris, secular *havurot* (prayer and study groups) in the United States, and the dozens of secular synagogues associated with the Society for Humanistic Judaism founded by the first secular rabbi, Sherwin T. Wine, in the United States and Canada. Branches of the International Federation of Secular Humanistic Jews operate in Israel, Mexico, Australia, Italy, France, Uruguay, Argentina, and Russia. The International Institute for Secular Humanistic Judaism trains rabbis and teachers to serve as communal leaders, and to conduct ceremonies marking public and personal events.

Today very many secular Jews take part in Jewish cultural activities, such as celebrating Jewish holidays as historical and nature festivals, imbued with new content and form, or marking life-cycle events such as birth, bar/bat mitzvah, marriage, and mourning in a secular fashion. They come together to study topics pertaining to Jewish culture and its relation to other cultures, in havurot, cultural associations, and secular synagogues, and they participate in public and political action co-ordinated by secular Jewish movements, such as the former movement to free Soviet Jews, and movements to combat pogroms, discrimination, and religious coercion. Jewish secular humanistic education inculcates universal moral values through classic Jewish and world literature and through organizations for social change that aspire to ideals of justice and charity.

Secular Jewish culture embraces literary works that have stood the test of time as sources of aesthetic pleasure and ideas shared by Jews and non-Jews, works that live on beyond the immediate socio-cultural context within which they were created. They include the writings of such Jewish authors as Sholem Aleichem, Itzik Manger, Isaac Bashevis Singer, Philip Roth, Saul Bellow, S. Y. Agnon, Isaac Babel, Martin Buber, Isaiah Berlin, H. N. Bialik, Yehuda Amichai, Amos Oz, A. B. Yehoshua, and David Grossman. It boasts masterpieces that have had a considerable influence on all of western culture, Jewish culture included—works such as those of Heinrich Heine, Gustav Mahler, Leonard Bernstein, Marc Chagall, Jacob Epstein, Ben Shahn, Amadeo Modigliani, Marcel Proust, Franz Kafka, Max Reinhardt (Goldman), Ernst Lubitsch, and Woody Allen.

Secular Jewish culture in the modern age

Building on foundations laid by the pioneers of Jewish enlightenment (Haskalah) in the eighteenth century, such as Moses Mendelssohn and Naphtali Herz Wessely, ninetenth-century secularists sought to integrate humanistic culture and general education with Jewish culture free of rabbinical dictates. Belief in the veracity of the biblical narratives and in the existence of a personal God was shaken. The rapid development of the Jewish press in Hebrew and Yiddish disseminated the ideas of the Haskalah and the Jewish and European nationalist movements that aimed to liberate culture and the state from religion and the religious establishment.

Ahad Ha'am (Asher Ginzberg, 1856–1927) made a distinction between Jewish national identity, religion, and religious observance, and laid the foundations for systematic secular Jewish thought. He viewed the individual or national 'self' as a juncture between memory of the past and awareness of the future. Ahad Ha'am saw knowledge of Jewish religious cultural tradition as essential to the education of secular Jews, and 'Jewish morality' as the distinctive essence of Mosaic law and the Jewish people.

By the early twentieth century these conclusions had already become the subject of dispute within secular Judaism. Writers like J. H. Brenner (1881–1921) and M. J. Berdyczewski (1865–1921) denied the existence of a 'unique morality'. Jewish culture had, in their opinion, always been pluralistic, marked by conflicting trends in every era. Moral values are always universal, and although acquired through education in national culture, should not be perceived as being unique to Judaism. Education in Jewish culture today, as in all past eras, is integrated with the cultures of the peoples among which Jews live. Jewish cultural heritage thus includes Jewish works (religious and secular), as well as the classic works of other peoples. The poet H. N. Bialik (1873–1934) saw Jewish cultural heritage in the works produced by all streams of Judaism throughout history, especially works possessing the quality and power to evoke an emotional and poetic experience—like the books of the Bible—thereby creating a bond between the reader and Jewish culture.

Saul Tchernichowsky (1875–1943), in his poem 'Before the Statue of Apollo', expressed rebellion against the tradition of halakhic religion, which in the eyes of many secular Jews repressed love of nature and beauty as well as erotic love. Berdyczewski saw Judaism throughout the ages as a clash between a natural, sensual tendency and a tendency towards repression—reflected in prohibitions and restrictions, laws and 'fences' around the law. He saw the Hasidic movement—with its encouragement of celebration, joy, and ecstasy—as an expression of rebellion against halakhah and a rabbinical establishment that tried to impose it upon all of Jewish culture. Like the sociologist Émile Durkheim, Berdyczewski believed religion and God to be embodiments of tribal or popular unity, and, like Martin Buber and Gershom Scholem after him, he numbered Kabbalah, Hasidism, folklore, and art among Judaism's creations.

From 1870 to the time of the Nazi Holocaust, European secular Judaism produced 18,000 titles in Yiddish and thousands more in Hebrew and European languages, hundreds of plays and theatre productions, silent and talking films, cabarets and folksongs, works of scholarship and philosophy, art in all its forms, and educational institutions for children and adults. Culturally, no other period in Jewish history has been as varied and prolific.

The works of Kafka and Proust may be reckoned among the greatest of Jewish creations, becoming an integral part of western culture. They give intense expression to the alienation of the individual from the community, in all cultures that have experienced urbanization and secularization. The individual, as represented by the protagonists in these works, lives both within and beyond the society and culture to which he seeks to belong. Their works appealed to readers throughout the West, as the 'crisis of meaning'—to use the term coined by Viktor Frankel—spread. Jewish writers such as these came to represent universal literature, while never ceasing to be aware of their Jewishness.

The Jewish creations produced by secular Jewish culture played a role in the cultural development of the countries of Central and Western Europe, where, however, as in Eastern Europe, both leaders and ordinary people collaborated with the Nazis in the systematic murder of the Jewish population and the destruction of the centres of Jewish creativity and culture. Secular Jewish culture, along with other Jewish cultures in Europe, was virtually eradicated during the Holocaust.

The realization of the Zionist dream—the establishment of the State of Israel in 1948 and the rebirth of Hebrew as the living language and culture of most of the country's inhabitants—may be seen as secular Judaism's greatest achievement. In the 1970s the movement for Secular Humanistic Judaism, led by Yehuda Bauer, was founded in Israel, combating religious coercion. In its framework Yaakov Malkin established the College for Judaism as Culture in 1994 and the journal *Free Judaism* in 1995—later to become the Secular Jewish Library series, in co-operation with Keter Publishing.

In Israel, secular Jewish culture is the predominant culture, shared by a majority of the population. Most Israeli parents send their children to one of some 2,000 secular schools, at which they study Bible, Jewish history and literature, and celebrate Jewish holidays that have become national holidays, without prayer or religion. Every year secular Jewish culture in Israel produces some 4,000 new Hebrew books, hundreds of films and television programmes, dozens of theatre productions, and thousands of songs, as well as art and folklore exhibits in a thousand Jewish museums. During the second half of the twentieth century scores of institutions dedicated to the study of Judaism as culture and secular Jewish culture were founded—institutions such as Hamidrasha at Oranim College, Meitar—The College for Judaism as Culture in Jerusalem, Alma College in Tel Aviv, and Keren Kolot in the Negev. Courses in the new discipline of 'Judaism as Culture' are now offered at a number of colleges and universities in Israel and the United States. Scores of books have been published on the secularization of Judaism and twentieth-century non-religious Jewish culture, casting all forms of Judaism throughout history in a new light.

Israeli literature reflects the secular Jewish culture that has developed in the Land of Israel, contemporaneously with the unique Jewish culture that has developed in the United States. Israeli literature differs from the literature that characterized the secular-ization of Judaism in the late nineteenth and early twentieth centuries. Whereas the earlier works described the disintegration of religious communities and the spiritual crisis engendered by the passage from religious to secular culture and society, most works of Israeli fiction focus on the individual, particularly as s/he encounters a reality fraught with contradiction and conflict, and the historical memory that lies at the heart of a new and rapidly changing culture. Echoes of the past resound throughout a body of literature that deals primarily with the present in the works of writers such as S. Yizhar, Moshe Shamir, A. B. Yehoshua, Natan Alterman, Yehuda Amichai, David Grossman, and Meir Shalev. The writers and their protagonists address the dissonance between humanistic Zionist ideals and the reality of war and social upheaval in Jewish Israeli society. What most of these works have in common is their portrayal of life in a secular culture and society, in which religion and religious culture exist only in the realm of memory.

The beliefs of secular humanistic Judaism

Secular humanistic Judaism encompasses many non-religious beliefs. What they all have in common is a belief in human autonomy as the source and purpose of moral, humanistic laws. Human beings discover, through human wisdom and science, the correlation between seemingly unique occurrences, and describe the laws that apply to the universe and the animal kingdom. Secularists maintain that the scientific world-view refutes belief in the version of reality depicted in religious mythology and the books of the Bible. 'Refuting the Bible' played a central role in the ideological revolution that took place in Enlightenment circles throughout Europe and America, Jewish circles included, undermining belief in the biblical depiction of reality and in a world governed by a personal god. Non-religious beliefs, where God is perceived as indefinable or non-existent, in an infinite reality beyond which there can be nothing, run contrary to belief in the validity of commandments attributed to a personal god by those who purport to do this god's will.

Secular humanistic Jews believe in humanity's autonomy to shape moral principles and effect humanization within the family and society. These two institutions exist within the framework of what we call today a national culture, because people share a common language and consciousness of a common past, and often the duty to express solidarity with one's society.

Universal moral values internalized within the context of national culture are decisive factors in selecting or rejecting any law or precept, whether religious or civil. In Judaism, the great first-century rabbi Hillel concisely defined the essence of the Torah as the essence of morality: do not do unto your fellow that which is hateful to you. In German culture at the end of the eighteenth century Immanuel Kant put it as follows: treat humanity always as an end and never as a means only; and insisted that there is no moral law that is not universally valid. These maxims represent the essence of humanistic morality in western democracies today.

Ever since Baruch Spinoza (1632–77), the belief has gradually developed within secular Judaism that all moral laws are intended to serve, as well as possible, human welfare and wellbeing. The belief that the aim of morality and moral laws is the good of humanity distinguishes non-religious humanistic morality from morality that is based upon the belief that the objective of good deeds and observance of the commandments is to fulfil the will of a personal god, as interpreted by those who speak in his name. Belief in the universal validity of morality runs contrary to all self-centred ideologies—secular and religious alike—such as male chauvinism, racial or class discrimination, and religious fanaticism. Such ideologies encourage dehumanization through a culture of complete obedience to leaders who speak in the name of God or the nation, enabling us to do unto our fellows that which is hateful to us, to see them as means, and to restrict the application of justice to members of a particular race, class, or religious sect.

'Agnostic morality', taking the place of religious morality, develops the human sense of morality through education and family life, from early childhood, when one first becomes aware of the need to balance selfish desires and consideration for others. Pre-school children distinguish between 'fair' and 'unfair' as the point of departure for their moral consciousness. In the passage from infancy to maturity a sense of duty to be considerate to others develops, in constantly expanding human circles, as education and society instil an awareness that moral behaviour is essential to the quality of one's own life. Such an awareness is contingent upon the belief that it is better to do the right thing, to act in a humane fashion, in keeping with principles such as those expressed by Hillel and Kant, in order to ensure both one's own quality of life and that of one's fellow human beings. Behaviour in keeping with this kind of 'agnostic morality' does not depend upon religious belief in the existence, will, or precepts of a personal god. The French Positivist philosopher August Comte saw this belief in the ideal of 'humanity' as the spiritual source of morality for those who do not believe in God as the source and purpose of doing good.

Belief in moral values that guarantee human rights, equality, and personal freedom repudiates religious precepts that discriminate, for example, against the female part of the population, through rabbinical courts in which women can be judged but cannot serve as judges. At the root of the controversy between secular humanistic and Orthodox Jews lies a clash between opposing systems of belief: belief in the universality of moral values and their capacity to repudiate any religious precept or civil law on the one hand; and, on the other, belief in the supremacy of religious commandments which all Jews are required to observe, according to Orthodox rabbinical interpretation. In the Jewish state the secular majority's acceptance of discriminatory laws has been the result of political constraints, which serve to highlight the moral dilemma expressed in the Book of Exodus as the paradox 'thou shalt not follow a multitude to do evil'—implying that one must abide by the decision of the democratic majority, but one must not accept a decision that is morally wrong, even when supported by a majority.

Secular humanistic Jews generally share the following convictions:

- Only knowledge based on theories that can be either proved or disproved is worthy of belief, and no credence should be given to religious interpretations of reality that can neither be proved nor disproved.

- Belief as to what can and should be done must be based upon knowledge of reality and the changes to which it is subject.

- The purpose of morality is to improve human lives, and one must strive to uphold the rights of all people and all peoples.

- Human beings must be educated within the framework of family and national culture, while developing a sense of morality and acquiring values of social justice in both national and international society.

- The right to personal autonomy, equality, and freedom of opinion and choice can be realized only within a democratic society, and only when the individual fulfils all of her/his obligations to that society, obeying its laws and asserting her/his rights and those of others.

- Just as human beings should be educated to perceive reality in a scientific manner, they must also be taught to engage in dialogue with unique others, with artistic and philosophical creations, and with inherently unique natural phenomena.

- Secular Jews see themselves as committed to the struggle against discrimination— economic, social, or spiritual—within their own and in other cultures. Religious and secular humanists must struggle together against secular and religious ideologies that are selfish and promote dehumanization, antisemitism, racism, sexism, or chauvinism.

- Humanistic ideals are not contingent upon non-religious beliefs, but humanistic practice must be based upon majority decisions guided by moral values, even when they require the repudiation of religious precepts and traditions.

- The prevailing belief in secular Judaism is that the biblical God is a literary figure created and fashioned by human beings. Human beings thus bear exclusive responsibility for their actions, laws, and moral values. Such belief denies individuals the right to claim to speak for God.

- Judaism, throughout the ages, is perceived as a pluralistic culture. This pluralism is the principle that affords legitimacy to debate. The legitimacy of debate does not however, provide justification for the concept of relativism, as asserted by postmodernists, who see relativism as the only absolute, and the principles of universal morality as absolute anachronisms.

Weaknesses of secular Judaism

Most secular Jews are unaware of their beliefs or cannot articulate them as such, and thus accept the unflattering designation of 'non-believer'. A lack of awareness regarding the significance of secular humanism within secular Judaism leads to a lack of political involvement in defence of equality between the sexes and between the various streams of Judaism, and in the allocation of resources between religious and secular education.

This weakness in the secular majority of Israeli Jews is reflected in the political compromises they are willing to accept, such as the existence of a religious court system alongside the civil judiciary, or the extension of military service for secular conscripts as a result of the exemptions afforded to all of the students of the ultra-Orthodox religious colleges, the *Haredi yeshivot*.

Secular Judaism's lack of organized communities in Israel frequently stems from the secular aversion to any social organization that appears to restrict individual autonomy. The lack of secular communities and professionals trained to run them leads to disorganization, a lack of educational and cultural leadership, an inadequate presence within representative Jewish institutions in Israel and the Diaspora, and a lack of secular Jewish schools in the Diaspora.

FURTHER READING

Alter, Robert, and Kermode, Frank (eds.). *The Literary Guide To The Bible* (London: Fontana, 1987). Writings on the Bible as literature.

Biale, David (ed.). *The Cultures Of The Jews* (New York: Schocken Books, 2002). A collection of writings on the variety of Jewish cultures in each historical era.

Chadwick, Owen. *The Secularization of the European Mind in the Nineteenth Century* (Cambridge: Cambridge University Press, 1975). Discusses the social and intellectual problems in the process of secularization.

Kaplan, Mordechai. *Judaism As a Civilization* (Philadelphia: Jewish Publications Society, 1934). A new approach to Judaism as a culture, including but not identical to religion.

Kogel, Renee, and Katz, Zev (eds.). *Judaism In A Secular Age* (New York: KTAV, 1995). An anthology of secular humanistic Jewish thought.

Kurtz, Paul. *Embracing The Power Of Humanism* (Latiham, MD: Rowman and Littlefield, 2000). On ethical truth, humanism, and the independence of the individual.

Malkin, Yaakov. *What Do Secular Jews Believe?* (Jerusalem: Free Judaism Publishing, 1998). Presents secular Jews as believers in Judaism as culture and in ethical values.

Malkin, Yaakov, *Secular Judaism—Faith, Values and Spirituality* (London: Vallentine Mitchell, 2004). General account of secular Judaism.

Wine, Sherwin T. *Judaism Beyond God* (New York: KTAV, 1995). Describes the secular revolution and the ethical culture in Judaism.

Wine, Sherwin T. *Celebrations—A Ceremonial And Philosophical Guide For Humanistic Jews* (Amherst, NY: Prometheus Books, 1998).

9 | Jewish renewal

George R. Wilkes

Introduction

Though calls for renewal have inspired Jews since biblical times, concepts of 'Jewish renewal' only developed in the twentieth century. From the 1970s a variety of programmes and movements have used this concept, some more spiritual, some determinedly secular. This chapter examines where they differ, what they hold in common, and how they can be evaluated.

Programmes which appeal for Jewish renewal have received marginal attention in academic Jewish studies. The most interesting commentaries available are written by figures associated with one concept of Jewish renewal, and focus on movements in only one country. Today a wide range of attempts to revitalize Jewish communities also use the term without distinguishing it from concepts of Jewish continuity, return, and revival. By tracing the historic development of ideas of renewal and Jewish renewal in Judaism—a history in which Martin Buber's work stands out for its profundity—the first half of this chapter shows the impact of the encounter with the non-Jewish world on the concept of 'Jewish' renewal, sometimes associated with more secular understandings of the challenges facing the Jewish community, sometimes with programmes with a clearly spiritual focus. The second half of the chapter offers a comparison of some of the factors most commonly invoked by advocates of the different approaches to Jewish renewal, first in addressing the disaffection of individual Jews with Jewish communities, and secondly in pressing for new responses to the relationship between Jews and the societies in which they live.

The long history of renewal in Judaism

The concept of renewal (*hiddush* in Hebrew) is much invoked, indeed celebrated, in Jewish tradition. Before the eighteenth century, however, this renewal was not thought of as a 'Jewish' renewal, and the early sources of Jewish tradition contain no explicit reference to either a Jewish renewal or a renewed Jewish identity, religion, or outlook.

The richness of biblical precedent laid a number of foundations for later explorations of the concept of renewal. The Psalms invoke God's renewal of the face of the earth (Psalm 104) and renewal of the righteous spirit (Psalm 51: 10). Lamentations (3: 22–3; 5: 21) calls on God to renew 'our days as of old', and this prayer is recalled at every Torah service in Orthodox and non-Orthodox communities. The books of the prophets—notably Isaiah, Amos, and Jeremiah—envision the making of new worlds, societies, and covenants. Though they refer to the new rather than the renewed, a substantial element of Jewish interpretive tradition views the prophetic vision as a call to renew the relationship established between God and Israel in former days.

The Talmud provides further grounds for identifying traditional Jewish ideas of renewal. The Sages describe creation as constantly renewed by God, and regard the appearance of the new moon beginning each month (*hodesh*) in the Hebrew year as a symbol of renewal. From Talmudic discussions of the authenticity of original insights (*hiddushim*) in legal or midrashic interpretation of Scripture, medieval Jewish tradition developed a mandate for human creativity in imitation of God's renewal of creation. Finding a hiddush—being *mehadesh*—has been one of the ultimate achievements to which a student at a *yeshiva* (religious academy) can aspire. In the twentieth century the link between creativity and renewal has inspired a range of Jewish philosophers, from the Modern Orthodox rabbi Joseph B. Soloveitchik (1903–93) in the United States to Emmanuel Levinas (1906–95) in France.

Much contemporary discussion of Jewish renewal is inspired by the Hasidic revolution initiated by the teachings of Israel ben Eliezer, the Baal Shem Tov (1700–60). The Jewish Renewal movement in the United States—also referred to by many as 'Jewish renewal', denoting a movement or tendency less formalized than the older, self-contained streams or denominations within Judaism—has cast itself as a non-Orthodox revival of the earlier Hasidic movement, following Martin Buber (1878–1965) and Abraham Joshua Heschel (1907–72) in identifying key Hasidic figures for whom intention (*kavanah*) behind a religious action represented a higher value than its form (*keva*). However, renewal appears infrequently in Hasidic literature, and the easily related concepts of mending the world (*tikkun olam*) and return or repentance (*teshuvah*) were more central to the mystical cosmological belief system which the Hasidim adapted from the Kabbalah. The extent to which even the early Hasidim consciously sought renewal is therefore contested. The Orthodox writer Herbert Danzger, advocating a renewed Orthodox Jewish identity, argues that revival is a better description of Hasidism than renewal, since—as he sees it—these Hasidim were near to, not far from, Judaism.[1] The terms in which Judaism is understood are thus crucial in defining the nature and legitimacy of Jewish renewal.

With the growing influence in Western Europe of new concepts of historical progress and social order in the eighteenth and nineteenth centuries came a continuous stream of programmes aimed at the 'regeneration' and 'reform' of 'rigid' and 'lifeless' Judaism. Occasionally reformers also referred to renewal, a renewal which identified truth and progress with what was universal and rational, not with particularist or irrational traditions. The rationalists' idea of a transformation of the Jewish religion was not purely an abstract philosophical concept, but also applied to the relationships of Jews to wider society: reformers aimed to purge Jewry of its alleged anti-social characteristics, from ignorance of secular realities to isolationism and criminality.

Thus, in 1796 the Prussian Jewish educator Isaac Daniel Itzig (1723–99) published the *Erneuerten Gesetze für die Lehrlinge* (Renewed Regulations for Apprentices), designed to introduce the Jewish youth of Berlin to Enlightenment standards of regulated discipline and behaviour. The Enlightenment had inspired a new focus on the secular dimension of Jewish life, in which form was more important than it was for the Baal Shem. However, the renewal programmes inspired by the idea of Enlightenment were also heavily coloured by a moralistic or idealist conception of the need for spiritual improvement in society, and this focus on the spirit still inspired the new concepts of Jewish renewal forged a century later.

The birth of Jewish renewal

The idea of a Jewish renewal was born as reformers became convinced that particularistic national cultures were also important vehicles for progress. Particularly in the West, this Jewish renewal was still to take place through realigning Jewish culture to fit the modern age, purging Jewish national life of medieval folk superstition and practices. In this rationalistic spirit, the philosopher of culture and ethics Moritz Lazarus (1824–1903) wrote *Die Erneuerung des Judentums* (The Renewal of Judaism, 1909). Similarly, the neo-Kantian philosopher Hermann Cohen (1842–1919) sought to 'revitalize' Jewish ethical monotheism by repositioning it at the core of German liberal nationalism. By contrast, disciples of Ahad Ha'am (1856–1927) in Eastern Europe argued that the preconditions for a national 'renaissance' were the encouragement of Jewish cultural and spiritual life in Palestine and a new appreciation of the spirit and culture of the Jewish masses in Eastern Europe, of their folk-tales, and of their religiosity. In both East and West, advocates of renewal aspired to a new cultural Judaism based on a positive conception of Jewish values, not defensively geared to antisemitic definitions of 'the Jewish problem'.

Martin Buber's first contribution to the history of Jewish renewal was to elaborate this cultural programme in broader philosophical terms, relating his ideas of Judaism and Jewishness to a more universal humanistic vision. Initially, Buber was drawn to Ahad Ha'am's concept of a 'renaissance'. In the first years of the twentieth century he chose 'renewal' in response to contemporary philosophers, notably Friedrich Nietzsche (1844–1900), who suggested that a deeper sense of humanity and community would be created by the example set by heroic individuals endowed with a heightened awareness of the power of human personality. Buber's 'Jewish renewal',[2] Zionist and inspired by Hasidism, met with greatest support in the heart of the multinational Habsburg Empire, particularly in Prague, where the sympathy of Czech nationalists made Jewish nationalism more popular among young Jewish intellectuals than it was further to the West. In Western Europe the idea of Jewish nationhood held less power, and Buber's ideas were commonly seen as hopelessly romantic. Even Buber's closest collaborator, the influential religious philosopher Franz Rosenzweig (1886–1929), preferred a model of 'new thinking' and 'religious return' which was not national and which sought a basis for Jewish religious experience in Judaism's more intellectualist traditions.

Contemporary Jewish renewal movements

The distance between concepts of renewal focused on secular and spiritual dimensions of Jewish life has since widened further.

Buber's more spiritual programme has exercised its greatest influence in America, largely thanks to its compatibility with the work of Abraham Joshua Heschel. Heschel's Hasidic spirituality had initially been viewed sceptically at the Conservative Jewish Theological Seminary of America (JTSA) where he taught from the 1930s. At the time JTSA was engaged in an ongoing debate about the 'reconstruction' of Judaism advanced by his colleague, Mordecai Kaplan (1881–1983), a concept closer to the rationalistic cultural reform of Lazarus which already many Conservatives found too radical. Nevertheless, by the early 1960s Heschel's concept of renewal was echoed among leading younger Conservative Jewish thinkers, from Arthur Cohen (1928–86) to Robert Gordis (1908–92). In the 1970s still more self-consciously radical advocates of Jewish renewal sought to liberate Jewish communities from what they saw as establishment politics and institutionalized religion. The Havurah movement was one of the most developed communal attempts to create a living liturgy and politically engaged lifestyle responsive to the alienation of younger Jews from established synagogues—sometimes the groups (*havurot*) would be small communities in their own right, sometimes alternative prayer services within Reform, Reconstructionist, or Conservative synagogues. Jewish Renewal has been one of the most lasting and successful attempts to institutionalize the movement's spiritual engagement, though the most politically engaged leaders of Jewish Renewal now represent a minority trend within the movement.

Though the leading figures within Jewish Renewal have attempted to present the movement as non-denominational, key figures have ordained rabbis, established congregations, and created enough momentum to exist as an alternative to the other contemporary Jewish movements. The most widely recognized Renewal leader, Zalman Schachter-Shalomi, came to the movement from the Lubavitch Hasidim. His closest associate there, Shlomo Carlebach, was a musician whose compositions have inspired the liturgies of Jewish Renewal communities, as well as the spread of

'Carlebach services' in Orthodox synagogues in North America and Israel. Through the links between advocates of renewal in different denominations, the goal of spiritual renewal has spread widely in the Modern Orthodox and Reform movements in Israel, the United States, and elsewhere. It need not clash with more secular preoccupations, though prominent spiritual renewal programmes have cast themselves as alternatives to traditional attempts to stave off assimilation by strengthening the secular dimension of Jewish community life.

From the 1970s, more secular programmes for communal renewal have also been exported worldwide by Jewish organizations from the United States. One of the most successful is the American-sponsored Project Renewal, which supports the regeneration of financially impoverished communities in Israel. After the fall of communism in Eastern Europe, the Lauder Foundation spearheaded American attempts to renew Jewish communities in cities across the region, initially at least riding a wave of expectation that the liberated Jewish populations of Eastern Europe would reaffirm their attachment to traditional expressions of Jewish identity en masse.

Of the scores of secular Jewish renewal programmes in Europe, the most ideologically challenging has been Renouveau Juif in France, created in 1980–1 but with roots stretching back at least two decades. In the 1960s French Jewish intellectuals—Raymond Aron (1905–83) and André Neher (1914–88) prominent among them—had responded to the recrudescence of antisemitism and anti-Zionism with a renewed discussion of their distinctive identity as Jews. In the 1970s a younger generation of Jewish activists, led by Henri Hajdenberg, pressed for the Jewish community to give its frustration still more public and political expression. In 1981 Hajdenberg announced that Renouveau Juif would campaign against President Giscard d'Estaing in the coming elections if France persisted with a foreign policy that effectively undermined the State of Israel. The campaign brought tens of thousands of Jews onto the streets of Paris, and arguably constituted a tip-over factor in the election of President Mitterrand.[3] The leaders of Renouveau Juif subsequently took over the established French Jewish organizations they had once criticized, and used Renouveau Juif to foster debate over the future of deliberately secularist Jewish thought and identity in France.

Jewish renewal and the relationship between individual and community

Common to most conceptions of Jewish renewal is the assumption that a vibrant Jewish communal life is one in which an individual's Jewishness is not compartmentalized into a purely ritual or religious conception, nor into a purely private preoccupation.

The more radical spiritual forms of Jewish renewal have been the most attentive to the needs of the individual in the face of the fragmentary nature of contemporary society. For Buber, the whole of Europe at the turn of the twentieth century—'atomistic' and 'decadent'—was in need of spiritual healing, and this would come through the recovery of a sense of the majestic personality of the individual 'I'. Of all religions, Buber argued, Judaism had most successfully promoted periods of renewal, when heroic personalities—from Jesus to the Hasidim—revealed their essential task and nature through deliberately seeking a personal encounter with God. Jewish teaching, identity, and community might aid an individual to attain sufficient self-awareness for such encounters, but only an unconditioned spirituality, transcendent while also absolutely personal, was capable of overcoming the fetters of the material world.

Both Buber and Renewal advocates in America have been criticized for the centrality they give the individual's search for religious experience, allegedly at the expense of law and custom. By contrast, many self-consciously Orthodox renewal movements—from Modern Orthodox study programmes like Aish HaTorah to the outreach initiatives of the Lubavitch Hasidim—focus instead on the value of law and observance for individuals seeking to strengthen their Jewish identity and sense of history and community. Often these programmes teach the value of renewed adherence to conservative social values and traditional forms of religious observance, by characterizing the general western environment as unspiritual or decadent. From this perspective, Jewish Renewal is commonly derided as 'Judaism Lite'—Judaism without commitment to community or tradition. Such criticisms may be levelled at all the non-Orthodox denominations in the United States, but Jewish Renewal leaders have made an especial virtue of recognizing a sense of alienation from traditional justifications for religious obligation. Jewish Renewal has wholeheartedly sanctioned the transformation of Jewish liturgy, traditions, and texts to give voice to a renewed discourse of communal intimacy, and to express contemporary social and political challenges and the experiences of individual members of Renewal communities. A contentious interpretation of the weekly Torah reading or a political use of a Passover *Seder* which may be divisive elsewhere is far less likely to cause a stir in Jewish Renewal communities. From the 1970s, the immediate precursors of Jewish Renewal set out to rediscover a tradition that would counter the perspectives of the powerful, a 'counter-culture' that acknowledges that tradition can be abused and distorted by the drive for power over others. In *A Big Jewish Book* (1978), Jerome Rothenberg collected a large number of stories which he identified with this counter-cultural tradition. Similarly, the three *Jewish Catalogs* (by Michael Strassfeld, Schachter-Shalomi, Arthur Waskow, and others, 1973–80) provided examples of traditions 'brought alive' through personalized, contemporary, or politicized interpretation.

By contrast, the most self-consciously secular approaches to Jewish renewal treat the wellbeing of individual Jews as a product of their identification and engagement with the Jewish community and its concerns, not as a function of spiritual engagement. The construction of new Jewish community centres in the United States in the 1960s attempted to ensure that young Jews would have a place to socialize, whether or not they were interested in Judaism or Jewish affairs. The United Jewish Communities' well-funded Jewish Continuity programme prompted a renewed wave of international interest in communal renewal in the 1990s. In Britain, Chief Rabbi Jonathan Sacks announced that the Jewish community's response to the Protestant Churches' Decade of Evangelism (referred to as the Decade of Evangelization by the Catholic Church) would be a Jewish Decade of Renewal, and launched a national Jewish Continuity programme which followed much of the programme laid out by its American counterpart. For the adherents of the Jewish Renewal movement, these renewal programmes do not address the question at the core of the spiritual crisis faced by alienated modern Jews: they may temporarily cure some symptoms of the contemporary Jewish condition, but they may also alienate a further generation from organized Jewish life.

The differences between the competing renewal strategies are illuminated by their divergent responses to the role of women. A number of the leading figures in Jewish Renewal suggest that the second-wave feminism of the late 1960s was one of the most important formative influences on the Jewish Renewal movement—the oppressive nature of the Jewish establishment was made evident, the personal and the political became one. The gains women seek determine the type of community they 'return' to. According to Lynn Davidman, women who join Hasidic communities generally find themselves in supportive communal institutions which validate commitment over questioning; those who become Modern Orthodox may seek a similar degree of ideological certainty and social stability, but value the ability to question the appropriate expression of Jewish tradition in contemporary society.[4] In both cases, the communities they join are changed by the creation of educational programmes by or for such women, increasing the community's religious engagement and transforming gender relations in the process. By contrast, gender-sensitive renewal programmes have been surprisingly underdeveloped in the work of secular Jewish organizations.

Transforming the place of Jews in society

In 1996, in an essay on European Jewish identity (see Further Reading), Diana Pinto presented one of the most stimulating discussions of the relationship between Jewish renewal and public engagement. According to Pinto, a new Jewish identification with being European, celebrating the positive experiences of Jewish–non-Jewish relations in Europe as well as the contributions made by European Jews past and present, holds out the prospect of transforming the state of Jewish communities in Europe. The key to Pinto's analysis is the observation that, in the past, Jewish community leaders established national Jewish identities based on a direct loyalty to the state, a loyalty which, in turn, was expected to defend Jews against antisemitism within society. Instead, Pinto argues, Jews should cast their lot with the burgeoning civil societies of Europe, which are the key to a multicultural, tolerant life on the European continent. She builds upon and then reverses the arguments of the Jews in France and other Western European countries who, from the 1970s, promoted a new public self-assertion as a response to antisemitism. Pinto maintains that only a public identity associated more emphatically with inter-group harmony can provide European Jews with security and pave the way for a renewal of the dynamic cultural traditions of European Jewry.

Not all Jews would be content to identify more closely with a wider civil society. Pinto's civic Jewish identity does not directly respond to the identities of Jews who consider their Jewishness a private concern or purely a matter of family life and history. Moreover, Pinto herself argues that this new identity would not appeal to Jews living in the small traditionalist enclaves of Antwerp and other cities. Indeed, insofar as her programme would marginalize tradition as a feature of Jewish renewal, it breaks with the visions of most Jewish religious leaders in Europe today. This may be an advantage, for progressive and traditionalist communities across Europe are locked in combat over whether renewing tradition means going back to the faith of the majority of Jews in a given country before the Holocaust—when the majority traditions in Germany and the Czech Republic, for instance, were liberal—or to the prevalent conception of Judaism at the beginning of the eighteenth century when liberal Judaism was not yet born.

A serious complication to the European Jewish renewal project lies in the fact that public and political expressions of Jewish identity are received in starkly divergent ways in different national contexts. In France, the Jewish community took decades after the Holocaust before younger members began to assert their Jewishness in public, demonstrating against antisemitism in the streets and making clear demands for respect with a force which previous generations had not felt necessary or productive. Many French Jewish intellectuals have constructed European identities, often as a mark of their dissatisfaction with the policies advanced by the state. In post-communist Hungary, by contrast, prominent Jewish figures often express the choice they face as a product of the freedom to be Hungarian, European, and Jewish, each capable of signifying a new belonging to the democratic community. Public demands for Jewish rights are still controversial, not least because of the other religious and ethnic tensions which plague political life in Hungary. A positive European Jewish identity will inevitably reflect the differing discourses about Jewishness and Europeanness in each national context.

Among American Jews, discussion of the renewal of public expressions of ethnic or religious identity has responded to very different historic relationships between religion, ethnicity, and politics in society at large. American Jewish organizations have been at the forefront of public pressure to maintain the separation of religion and state. However, both liberal and conservative thinkers, from Steven Wise (1874–1949) to Will Herberg (1901–77), have been prominent in the promotion of concepts of a religious dimension within civil and even political discourse. The openly religious character of their political activism is increasingly paralleled by conservative Jewish organizations supporting the social and educational positions of the Christian right.[5]

The dynamism of ethnic and denominational politics in America makes it difficult to judge whether Pinto's close identification with civil society would be an appropriate measure of renewal programmes in the United States. Deliberately Jewish activism reflects a range of different approaches to the relationship between Jewish and non-Jewish Americans. The Havurah and Jewish Renewal movements drew inspiration for their political commitments from rabbis like Abraham Joshua Heschel, who famously marched with Martin Luther King against segregation. When a group of Heschel's colleagues wrote to express support for King, they made a point of acknowledging that their humanistic commitments were also an expression of their understanding of the interests of the Jewish community in America. Similarly, the Reform and Orthodox political lobbies which developed support for non-Jewish religious and ethnic campaigns in the 1990s have generally chosen issues with an eye to distinctive Jewish interests.

The cultural context framing American Jewish religious politics has also affected the most deliberately counter-cultural of Jewish Renewal advocates. Thus, from the 1970s, when many leading figures in Jewish Renewal applied the concept of radical political ethics afresh to Palestinians, they deliberately crossed two boundaries which had hitherto shaped American Jewish activism. Pro-Palestinian Renewal leaders—most notably Michael Lerner—created the first religious Jewish lobby promoting Palestinian rights that was and is deliberately anti-establishment, and the first, too, that was neither non-Zionist nor anti-Zionist. Overshadowing their focus on the plight of Palestinians, Lerner and others have concentrated on American Jewish settlers, representing the 'dark' and 'violent' attitudes embedded in traditional Judaism. While their form of Jewish renewal remains highly distinctive, it is more clearly oriented to the contemporary religious and political context of American Jewry than to the life of Israelis or Palestinians.

Despite evidence of expanding American Jewish political commitments, in practice these do not extend as far as Pinto's programme of renewal through close identification with civil society. Despite considerable mistrust of the Christian right in Orthodox circles, regular collaboration between the two communities is possible because American politics has a developed tradition of loose issue alliances, of a kind still far less common in Europe. European Jewish organizations, by contrast, have yet to broaden their political engagement beyond issues where Jews have distinctive interests or perspectives. To attempt a more political engagement in Europe will be seen by many as more likely to obstruct than facilitate a renewal of Jewish values and identity there.

In Israel, the difficulties of using religious politics to stimulate a renewal of religious values or a sense of community are further complicated by the tensions between religious and secular camps within the Jewish majority population. Proponents of religious renewal in Israel—from Emanuel Rackman to David Hartman and Mordecai Gafni—have held out great hopes for the reintegration of religion into all areas of Israeli politics and society. However, religious political parties have historically found that the political process subverts their original intentions. The National Religious

Party was founded to promote Modern Orthodox conceptions of morality and social concern in the young Israeli state, and was transformed into an extreme right-wing party whose social conservatism and outright opposition to reconciliation with the Palestinians its founders would barely have recognized. A moderate Orthodox party, Meimad, established in the 1990s, sought to promote religious–secular rapprochement by 'taking religion out of politics'. As with the secularist Shinui Party, established for the same reason, Meimad's greatest successes have had only an indirect bearing on the relationship between religion and society.

Similarly, the greater the efforts of *Haredi* (Orthodox non-Zionist) parties to focus on their own moral or social concerns, the greater the friction this has caused in their relations with ideologically secularist Israelis, frustrated that issues of peace and prosperity can be held to ransom by debate over budgets for religious schools or control of the Ministry for Religious Affairs. This social fragmentation dampens the renewal of public religion in Israeli life, as expressed in Holocaust memorials and services for fallen soldiers, in national festivals and in reflection on the religious dimension of Jewish history and culture.[6]

With battle-lines drawn between the secular and religious, many Israeli advocates of Jewish renewal—organized in the umbrella body Panim—have chosen to focus on individual communities, or on the spread of Eastern or New Age-style religious activities, from meditation to mysticism and communion with nature. The liberal thinker Dow Marmur has called on Israeli Jews to divorce their search for religious or spiritual experience from civil religion, which in his view is inherently stultifying.[7] The problems of creating a space for Jewish values in politics and society will, however, remain while public discourse about Jewishness is under the sway of pragmatic politicians and narrow and sometimes negative pressure groups.

Spiritual renewal programmes such as the American Jewish Renewal movement are, moreover, as prone to social pressures from the non-Jewish environment as are civil society or political movements. When Jews are absorbing Native American spiritual teachings and Eastern meditation, are they creating a 'New Age Judaism' or a 'Neshamah [Soul] Spirituality', or are they merely clothing essentially secular or non-Jewish beliefs in Hebrew terminology? Answers to such questions are meaningless unless they reflect a serious assessment of the social context in which Renewal communities attempt to assimilate non-Jewish approaches to their own ideas of spirituality. Jewish spirituality cannot be easily divorced from the identities—Jewish and other—of the Jews who practise it.

Conclusions

The examination of the different renewal movements given in this chapter suggests that such questions can be answered in two ways, and this applies as much to secular as to religious Jewish renewal programmes. The value and power of renewal may, on the one hand, be viewed in the light of fixed forms of belief or communal organization. A conservative position is then obvious—positive forms of renewal revitalize traditions without changing them. Even the more radical Jewish Renewal advocates like Schachter-Shalomi and Roger Kamenetz have argued that Jews need not fear the encounter with Eastern religions, because Judaism prepares its adherents with a framework within which to assimilate other religious teachings, and because a core element of human spirituality is shared between the world's established religious traditions, however different the terms used in these religions may be.

On the other hand, the strengths and weaknesses of renewal projects may be measured by how they respond to the challenges thrown up by the times and the societies around them. In this context, a conservative position may even involve more acceptance of change than a more liberal position might, justifying adaptation as a response to crisis designed to preserve or promote core values at the expense of second-ary features of Jewish tradition. Inter-religious encounter—a central feature of the Jewish Renewal programme in the United States—is, for example, often presented, positively or critically, as a relatively conservative response to the religious crisis faced by Jews and others in the world today. Similarly, Diana Pinto justifies her programme of engagement with more liberal elements within European civil society in terms of the acceptance Jews will find as central actors within a cultured elite. In sum, an adequate assessment must take account of the role of both content and context in shaping the direction advocated in any renewal project. If this is not attempted, notions of what is 'conservative' and what is 'liberal', what valuable and what misguided, can easily break down.

FURTHER READING

Aviad, Janet. *Return to Judaism: Religious Renewal in Israel* (Chicago: University of Chicago Press, 1983). Useful discussion of the *ba'al teshuvah* movements in Israel.

Birnbaum, Pierre (ed.). *Histoire politique des Juifs de France* (Paris: Presses de la Fondation Nationale des Sciences Politiques, 1990). Historical essays on the changing relationship between Jews and the French state, with discussion of ideologies of regeneration and renewal from the eighteenth century to the twentieth.

Buber, Martin. 'Renewal of Judaism', in Nahum N. Glatzer (ed.), *On Judaism by Martin Buber* (New York: Schocken Books, 1967), pp. 34–55. Classic essay distilling Buber's early thought on the subject.

Dosick, Wayne. *Dancing with God: Everyday Steps to Jewish Spiritual Renewal* (San Francisco: Harper, 1997). Stimulating discussion of the contemporary Jewish Renewal movement.

Lerner, Michael. *Jewish Renewal: A Path to Healing and Transformation* (New York: Putnam, 1994). A religio-political manifesto, with commentary on the history of Jewish Renewal, from a leading proponent of Renewal, founder of *Tikkun* magazine, and student of Abraham Joshua Heschel.

Pinto, Diana. *New Jewish Identity for Post-1989 Europe* (London: Institute for Jewish Policy Review, 1996). Brief booklet manifesto for a transformation of the position of Jews in the reunited Europe after the end of the Cold War.

Schachter-Shalomi, Zalman. *Paradigm Shift* (Northvale, NJ: Jason Aronson, 1991); *Spiritual Intimacy: A Study of Counseling in Hasidism* (Northvale, NJ: Jason Aronson, 1996). Key works of the most widely recognized spiritual teacher of the Jewish Renewal movement.

Trigano, Shmuel. 'From Individual to Collectivity: The Rebirth of the "Jewish Nation" in France', in Frances Malino and Bernard Wasserstein (eds.), *The Jews in Modern France* (Hanover, NH: Brandeis University Press, 1985), pp. 245–81. Stimulating essay on forms of renewed Jewish identification in France after 1945.

Waskow, Arthur. *Godwrestling* (New York: Schocken Books, 1978); *Godwrestling Round 2* (Woodstock, Vt.: Jewish Lights, 1996). Personal accounts of the political and spiritual dimensions to the life of one of the leading Jewish Renewal rabbis.

NOTES

1. *Returning to Tradition* (New Haven: Yale University Press, 1989), p. 16.
2. Buber, Martin, 'Jewish Renewal' (1911), in Nahum N. Glatzer (ed.), *On Judaism by Martin Buber* (New York: Schocken Books, 1967), pp. 34–55.
3. See further in Pierre Birnbaum (ed.), *Histoire Politique des Juifs de France* (Paris: Presses de la Fondation Nationale des Sciences politiques, 1990).
4. *Tradition in a Rootless World* (Berkeley: University of California Press, 1991).
5. See David Dalin and Irving Kristol (eds.), *American Jews and the Separationist Faith* (Washington, DC: Ethics and Public Policy Center, 1993).
6. Charles Liebman and Eliezer Don-Yehiya, *Civil Religion in Israel* (Berkeley: University of California Press, 1983).
7. *The Star of Return* (Westport, Conn.: Greenwood Press, 1991).

Local issues

10 | American Jewry

Chaim I. Waxman

The development of American Judaism reflects both the experiences of various groups of immigrants and the cultural patterns of American society. Indeed, the latter may be even more important because, in every society and especially an open one such as the United States, the culture of the society influences groups within the society.

The first Jewish communities in the United States were created by Sephardim, who arrived to escape the Spanish Inquisitions. The initial communities were in New York, Philadelphia, Newport, Charleston, and Savanna. During the eighteenth and nineteenth centuries the majority of immigrants were of German and Central European background, most of whom immigrated voluntarily, for economic reasons. Typically, they were among the least rooted in their native Jewish communities, and traditional Judaism did not control their lives significantly. During the second half of the nineteenth century, especially after 1881, and up until the mid-1920s there was a massive wave of Eastern European immigration, fleeing economic, social, and religious persecution.

An important feature of the first synagogue communities was the absence of rabbinic leadership. Rabbis did not begin to appear significantly on the American scene until well into the nineteenth century, and the rabbi-scholar elite did not arrive until the twentieth century. The synagogue reader (*hazzan*) was not ordained; he was invariably the most Jewishly educated male in the community. Matters relating to divorce and other issues requiring rabbinical involvement were referred to the rabbinate in Amsterdam and London.

The absence of rabbinic leadership, coupled with American culture, in which voluntary groups are of great importance and in which individual efforts are valued, make it unsurprising that the attempt to reform Judaism in the United States developed as a grassroots movement. As immigration increased there was a westward expansion of Jewish communities during the nineteenth century. Many Jewish immigrants from Central Europe arrived without traditional communal ties. Seeking economic advance, they spread around the country and established synagogues in accordance with their needs and desires, without co-ordination with previously established communities. Religious disorganization thus prevailed when Isaac Mayer Wise (1819–1900), who was born in Bohemia and studied in Austria, arrived in New York in 1846 to serve as rabbi of Congregation Beth El in Albany. Concerned by the prevailing religious chaos, between 1854 and his death in 1900 he devoted himself to organizing American Judaism, becoming the foremost institution-builder of Reform Judaism in America. Wise dreamt of organizing all the congregations in the country, but his deviations from religious tradition led the traditionalists to refuse to associate with him. In 1873, however, representatives of thirty-four Reform congregations convened in Cincinnati, officially organizing the Union of American Hebrew Congregations (UAHC). In 2003 the organization was renamed the Union for Reform Judaism (URJ). Until then its name identified it as American, not solely Reform, although it rapidly became the synagogue and temple organization of American Reform Judaism. Similarly, when Wise established a seminary for the training of American rabbis, Hebrew Union College, founded in Cincinnati in 1875, its name identified it simply as Hebrew, without the Reform designation. Hebrew Union College today has branches in New York, Los Angeles, and Jerusalem, and is the school of higher learning of American Reform. When Wise's dream of establishing a synod of American rabbis was finally realized in 1889, the Reform designation was again missing, although the Central Conference of American Rabbis (CCAR) was, and remains, the rabbinical body of American Reform. All of these organizations saw themselves as representing *American* Judaism as a whole, and not simply one branch of it. They were convinced that Judaism would develop in the United States only by conforming with the prevalent American culture. In religion, this reflected the patterns of the Protestant church, both in form—including types of building and 'proper' dress—and content—including 'decorous' services, the role of the clergy, liturgy in English, and so on. Implicitly or explicitly, the new organizations of 'American' Judaism also saw themselves as the most authentic representation of contemporary Judaism.

Traditionalists were not Wise's only opponents. He had many within the Reform rabbinate as well. He was the organizer and institution-builder, and therefore somewhat of a pragmatist. Hence he was scorned by radical Reformers who had neither respect nor patience for Wise's approach. In 1885 the radicals had their principles adopted in the Pittsburgh Platform of Reform Rabbis. These principles, which came to define Classical Reform, presented Judaism as rational, universalistic, and positivistic, and asserted that the traditional dietary laws, among others, were archaic and obstructive to contemporary moral elevation; that Jews today are solely a religious community and do not expect a return to Zion; and that traditional notions of resurrection, as well as Hell and Paradise, are to be rejected.

In accordance with rationalism and universalism, they eliminated the notion of a single temple in one specific Holy Land, designating each synagogue a temple. They correspondingly revamped the synagogue-temple service: eliminating 'obsolete' prayers; praying solely in English, accompanied by an organ; dispensing with archaic, particularistic temple dress, including *kipot* (skull caps) and *talitot* (prayer shawls) and, for the more radical, redesignating the Sabbath from Saturday to the more common, Christian, Sunday.

Reform Judaism is, by definition, a changing religion, and it underwent revolutionary change from the beginning to the end of the twentieth century. For example, at the onset of the century it was hostile to Zionism and the notion of Jewish peoplehood, and voiced opposition to the Balfour Declaration. Fifty years later, in June 1967, the CCAR declared its 'solidarity with the State and the people of Israel. Their triumphs are our triumphs. Their ordeal is our ordeal. Their fate is our fate.' By the 1980s the overwhelming majority of Reform Jews agreed with the statement that 'the existence of Israel is essential for the continuation of American Jewish life'.[1] These and other fundamental changes, however, were inconceivable at the end of the nineteenth and beginning of the twentieth centuries. The changes regarding Israel and Zionism are invariably products of socio-political change in the wider American society—which shifted from a melting-pot ideology to one of cultural pluralism during the second half of the twentieth century—as well as the establishment of the State of Israel and its growing ties with the West in general and the United States in particular. The reservations that adherents of Classical Reform had held about Zionism and Israel were no longer relevant in the United States, especially after the 1960s.

Traditionalist responses

In response to the successes of Reform, and especially what were considered its extreme and intolerable principles, Henry Pereira Mendes (1852–1937), rabbi of New York's Congregation Shearith Israel, and Sabato Morais (1823–97), successor to Isaac Leeser (1806–68), hazzan of Congregation Mikveh Israel in Philadelphia, decided that they too must institionalize. They organized a group of traditionalist rabbis, educators, and laymen to establish the Jewish Theological Seminary of America (JTS) in New York City, on 31 January 1886. Initially JTS was the seminary of American traditional Jews. In 1902 it was reorganized under the leadership of Solomon Schechter (1847–1915). This marked the beginning of the emergence of Conservative Judaism as a distinct branch of American Judaism, a process finalized in 1913, when its synagogues founded the United Synagogue of America, now United Synagogue of Conservative Judaism.

In the same year that JTS was originally founded, on 15 September 1886, a group of traditionalists of Eastern European background founded Yeshivat Etz Chaim to meet the Jewish educational needs of the newly arriving Eastern European Jews. Eleven years later, in 1897, the Rabbi Isaac Elchanan Theological Seminary (RIETS) was founded to train Orthodox rabbis. In 1915 RIETS and Etz Chaim merged to become Yeshiva College, later Yeshiva University.

Whereas in 1880 American Jewry numbered approximately 250,000 people, mostly of Central European background, between 1881 and 1923 about 2.5 million Jews arrived from Eastern Europe, primarily from towns and villages—shtetlach in Yiddish—in which they were the majority. Traditional Judaism was the religion of the shtetl and its culture as well. Jews living in the shtetl's traditional monoreligious culture would almost certainly have been confused by western distinctions between religious and ethnic groups. To them, there were only *Yidn*, Jews, and *Yiddishkeit*, the Jewish way of life. To be a 'good Jew' meant observing the norms of traditional Judaism as defined by the rabbis-scholars of the community.

Upon immigrating to the United States they founded synagogues, because these were the central institution in their native communities. Even when personally non-observant, they founded and joined Orthodox synagogues because these were the only synagogues with which they were familiar. However, as they and—especially—their children became established socio-economically, they invariably left immigrant neighbourhoods for newer, more affluent communities. As the melting-pot ideology prevailed, Orthodoxy was identified with the Old World and poverty. Moreover, Orthodoxy was viewed as too restricting in the open American society, which was perceived to offer unlimited opportunity for material success to anyone who worked hard enough.

Many more-established Jews and their children, therefore, left Orthodoxy for Conservative and, to a lesser extent, Reform Judaism. The plain, small synagogue of the immigrant neighbourhood was replaced by magnificent and imposing synagogue structures. Conservative Judaism, initially founded by moderate traditionalists as a bulwark against Reform, came to represent a uniquely American religious movement responding to the changing needs and values of American Jewry. Whilst rejecting Reform's denial of the authority of halakhah, it also rejected what it viewed as Orthodoxy's denial of halakhah's evolving nature. The leaders of Conservative Judaism argued that socio-historical circumstances have always influenced halakhah, hence some changes are legitimate and even mandated. For the masses of second-generation Jews, who found Orthodoxy too confining, inhibiting their socio-economic mobility, but who wished nevertheless to retain their Jewish ethnic and religious identity, Conservative Judaism became the ideal model. It also reflected the prevalent patterns of social stratification, situated between the upper-class Reform and the lower- or working-class Orthodox. For many, affiliation with Conservatism reflected social status more than religious ideology.

Even as traditional Jewish norms were shed, these Jews did not eliminate religion from their group self-definition to become solely an ethnic group. Nor did they seek to eliminate the ethnic component of Jewishness and define Judaism solely in religious terms, as Reform has done. Conservative Judaism provided a framework for behaving as Americans while espousing an ideological commitment to tradition which also maintained an emphasis on the ethnic character of Judaism. Conservative synagogues thus became the central institutions of new Jewish communities, providing a focus for religious and secular ethnic activities. The conception of the synagogue as such a centre was most clearly articulated by Mordecai M. Kaplan (1881–1983), one of the most influential thinkers of Conservative Judaism and the founder of Reconstructionism.

Reconstructionism

The Reconstructionist movement is a branch of Judaism which was founded in 1922. It is based on an ideology developed by Kaplan, who was reared in Orthodoxy and initially served an Orthodox congregation before affiliating with Conservative Judaism. Kaplan argued that Judaism is not a religion in the western sense, but a religious civilization. Rooted heavily in Émile Durkheim's sociology of religion, Kaplan viewed religion as a human creation and the symbolization of the group's ultimate values. The American philosopher John Dewey, an educational theorist with strong liberal-to-left socio-political convictions, and Ahad Ha'am, a leading thinker of the Jewish Enlightenment who espoused the value of Jewish peoplehood from a cultural, rather than religious, perspective, also influenced Kaplan's thinking. Although the ideology of Reconstructionism is, essentially, atheistic, Kaplan did not adopt the antipathy to tradition which characterized radical Reform Judaism. He urged Jews to appreciate Jewish history and culture, including its religious rituals, since these could enhance the sense of Jewish identity. Accordingly, Reconstructionism was always pro-Israel, though it never defined immigration to Israel as a value for all Jews.

Despite its appreciation of Jewish tradition, Reconstructionism has never opposed cultural change, perceiving it as necessary to prevent cultural stagnation. Moreover, Jewish culture must be innovative, Reconstructionism avers, if Jewish civilization is to have a positive influence on world civilization.

Reconstructionism formally became a denomination within American Judaism with the founding of its Reconstructionist Rabbinical College, in Philadelphia, in 1968. It is the smallest denomination, comprising only a small fraction—approximately 1.5 per cent—of American Jewish baby-boomers.[2] It is also not clear whether the movement is traditionalist or modernist. Theoretically it could be either. One 1996 survey of the movement found, with respect to ritual observances, that: 'In general, childhood observance was higher in the older (i.e. earlier) generation, than in later generations of current married adults.'[3] This lends support to the perception that the movement began as more traditional and is becoming increasingly modernist. Although it has a small percentage of affiliates, it is suggested that most American Jews are, de facto, Reconstructionists.

Mid-century—the decade of content

By mid-century American Jewry appeared to have successfully adapted Judaism to American culture. Despite acculturation, Jewish affiliations were maintained, especially in synagogue memberships, and religious rituals with a family and/or social orientation were retained. However, observance of rituals like *kashrut* and Sabbath regulations was declining, as was synagogue attendance. Moreover, celebrations of Hanukah and Passover were often retained because, as Marshall Sklare noted, the holidays came but once a year, the rituals were family-oriented, they were perceived as Jewish variations of widely celebrated Christian holidays of the same season, and they were reinterpreted to symbolize American values. Synagogue memberships were retained because of the prevalent emphasis on the value of religion in American life.

By mid-century a number of observers of American Judaism had begun to question the characteristic religious patterns of American Jewry. One prominent religious thinker, Will Herberg, argued that they were actually not manifestations of religion, but worship of the goals and values of American society. Alongside high rates of religious identification and affiliation and even increases in the percentage of those who attributed importance to religion, it was in fact secular American social and cultural values that were revered.

Some sociologists argued that the so-called religious patterns of American Jews were actually manifestations of ethnicity. For example, Herbert Gans's study of a major suburban Jewish community concluded that temples, synagogues, and Jewish schools were manifestations 'of the need and desire of Jewish parents to provide clearly visible institutions and symbols with which to maintain and reinforce the ethnic identification of the next generation'.[4]

Regardless of these claims, at mid-century optimism about the future prevailed in American Jewry. What most of American society failed to see was the growing alienation of increasing segments of the American population, and especially youth. This growing tension erupted in the 1960s into a widespread movement for greater equality, affecting all spheres of American society, including all denominations within American Judaism.

Intermarriage—the end of an illusion

By the early 1960s there was almost a consensus among social scientists of American Jewry that there was a steady decline in both the quality and quantity of American Jewish life. In 1964 a gloomy prognosis for American Jewry was provided in two widely read and discussed articles. One was a cover story in the popular *Look* magazine, entitled 'The Vanishing American Jew', which focused on declining American Jewish birth rates. The other was an article in *Commentary* by the leading sociologist of American Jewry, Marshall Sklare, entitled, 'Intermarriage and the Jewish Future', in which he warned that intermarriage is 'a matter more crucial to Jewish survival than any other', and projected a bleak outlook for the Jewish future. Empirical studies of American Jewish communities throughout the 1960s and 1970s confirmed the concerns of both articles. The American Jewish population as a percentage of the total American population had declined from 3.7 per cent in the 1930s to 2.67 per cent in

1979. Meanwhile intermarriage rates rose from about 15 per cent in the early 1960s to 29 per cent by the mid-1960s, and to 48 per cent by 1973. In 1977 a *Midstream* article argued that American Jewry could decline to 10,000 people by the year 2076. Although most social scientists viewed this as an exaggeration, few questioned the trend of decline.

Reform Judaism took the most explicit steps for dealing with intermarriage. First, it adopted a policy of outreach, encouraging the conversion of non-Jewish spouses among intermarried couples. While no such de jure policy has yet been adopted by Conservative or Orthodox Judaism, increasing numbers of Conservative and Modern Orthodox rabbis have urged traditional Judaism to change its stance so as to encourage conversion, and increasingly it is the de facto policy of most Conservative and Orthodox rabbis to encourage conversion in mixed-marriage couples.

Reform's second major initiative was the adoption of patrilineal descent, recognizing as a Jew the child of either a Jewish mother or father, providing the child wishes to be so recognized. This new policy was designed to keep the children of intermarried couples within the community. Although this policy was vigorously criticized by both Conservative and Orthodox rabbinic bodies, in addition to some dissent within the CCAR itself, there was no major joint effort to rescind it, and the whole issue vanished from the organizational agendas of the rabbinic organizations. But it was a central element in the 'Who is a Jew?' controversy which played a major role in the Israeli elections of 1988 and has polarized much of American Judaism since.[5]

Orthodoxy revitalizes

Initially Orthodox Jewry was ill-equipped to overcome the challenges of the open American society, and experienced both institutional and numerical decline. The Holocaust changed this, since although many Orthodox Jews had previously resisted coming to the United States, they now had no choice, and so were forced to transplant their religious culture in America. The available evidence suggests that Orthodox Jews were disproportionally represented among Holocaust refugees who immigrated to the United States.

The rabbinic-intellectual elite, who had been most resistant to migration, now sought refuge there as well. Their number included heads of advanced rabbinical seminaries (*yeshivot*) in Eastern Europe, and they almost immediately began reconstructing these on American soil. Such leaders as rabbis Aaron Kotler, Abraham Kalmanowitz, Eliyahu Meir Bloch, and Mordechai Katz re-established their yeshivas in Lakewood, Brooklyn, Cleveland, and elsewhere, helping to spawn a generation of knowledgeable, ideologically committed Orthodox Jews, many of whom subsequently established other advanced yeshivas elsewhere in America.

As a first step, the National Society for Hebrew Day Schools, Torah Umesorah, was formed to found Jewish day schools across the country. By 1975 there were a total of 425 day schools and 138 high schools, with an enrolment of 82,200 in thirty-three states. Although a number of day schools had been founded early in the twentieth century, their numbers, and hence their impact, had been relatively small. Since the mid-1970s day schools have become recognized as valued institutions within Conservative and Reform Judaism as well. Indeed, by the 1990s non-Orthodox day schools were the fastest-growing phenomenon in the American Jewish community.

Analysis of the 1990 National Jewish Population Survey (NJPS) data on baby-boomers indicates that day-school education correlates with almost all measures of Jewish identity and identification, and for many of those measures the correlation is much higher than it is with other types of Jewish education.

Also among the refugees were many members and some leaders of Hasidic sects. Determined to retain their traditional way of life even within the modern metropolis, they were largely successful, not least as a result of American cultural pluralism, which became dominant in the 1960s.

The new infusion of ideologically committed Orthodox provided the numerical strength for Orthodoxy's eventual renaissance. It influenced an intensification of religious belief and practice across Orthodoxy, as well as increasing rifts with the non-Orthodox. In the last quarter of the twentieth century Orthodox Judaism, and especially its ultra-Orthodox *Haredi* sectors, achieved levels of social status and organizational sophistication unanticipated in previous years. As Orthodox Haredism grew, it became increasingly self-confident and triumphalist.

Conservative tensions and struggles

In contrast to the dynamic growth and optimism of Conservative Judaism during the first six decades of the twentieth century, the latter decades were filled with tension and declining numbers. Much of the tension surrounded the movement's growing deviation from tradition. Perhaps the first major indication of that pattern was at mid-century when the Committee on Jewish Law and Standards (CJLS) of the Rabbinic Assembly, Conservative Judaism's rabbinic organization, permitted driving to synagogue on the Sabbath in special circumstances. Despite the ruling's explicit limitations, driving rapidly became the norm, not only for synagogue attendance but for any reason. In effect, the ruling erased religious restrictions on driving on the Sabbath. Increasingly, however, the Conservative was not attending synagogue even when they could drive, and the Sabbath was further secularized.

The 1960s was a tumultuous decade in the United States, and one of its characteristics was the emergence of a significant counter-culture. The Havurah movement was Conservative Judaism's counter-culture, initiating a move away from large, formal, and impersonal synagogues to smaller, intimate prayer-groups (*havurot*). Committed as some Havurah members may have been, their movement contributed to the decline of the institutionalized synagogue. As an in-depth study of one havurah, the Kelton Minyan, revealed, its members sought to synthesize Jewish religious tradition as they understood it with their own modern American norms and values, and the Minyan functioned as the place where prayer and study were meant to be experienced in an egalitarian manner. Things did not, however, always turn out as envisioned, and most defectors from formal synagogues did not join havurot; they simply ceased attending synagogue services.[6]

At the 1971 convention of the Rabbinic Assembly, a delegation of women belonging to a Jewish feminist organization, Ezrat Nashim, promoted a manifesto that demanded more complete participation of women in religious activities. The manifesto was widely supported by the Women's League for Conservative Judaism, the United Synagogue of America, the majority of the CJLS, and the faculty of JTS. In 1973 the CJLS ruled that women could be counted in the minyan (the prayer quorum), evoking a front-page story in the *New York Times*. However, the issue of ordination of women was fiercely debated for a number of years. Most lay bodies of the movement voted in its favour, but the majority of the rabbinic faculty at the JTS remained opposed. One major study argued that ordination of women would only accelerate defections from Conservative Judaism: the core group within Conservative synagogues, those who observed kashrut and provided intensive Jewish education for their children, were the sector most strongly opposed to the issue, indicating that they would leave and affiliate with Orthodoxy if the ordination of women was accepted. Conservative Judaism would thus lose its strongest link with the future. By the second half of the decade, however, the struggle was over and women were ordained by JTS.

The modernizing of Conservative Judaism is apparent in a number of more recent developments, including growing ambivalence regarding ordination of gays and lesbians, and over same-sex marriages. In contrast to previous statements, the United Synagogue and Rabbinical Assembly have called for civil rights for gays and lesbians.

The divergent trends in Conservative and Orthodox Judaism in America can be seen in their respective Torah translations and prayer books. The increasing religious modernism of Conservative Judaism was evident in the 2001 publication of an authorized Torah translation and commentary, *Etz Hayim*, which included essays explicitly questioning, if not rejecting, the historicity of various biblically recorded events. Although the movement has always permitted a less than literal interpretation of Scripture, it had also not explicitly rejected the literal reading.

By contrast, Orthodoxy appears to be becoming increasingly traditionalist in its religious outlooks. It is increasingly replacing the Torah translation and commentary, *The Pentateuch and Haftorahs*, by the late chief rabbi, Dr J. H. Hertz, used in many Orthodox synagogues, and introducing the ArtScroll translation. The Hertz edition is increasingly viewed as 'unkosher', because of its citation of non-traditional and even non-Jewish sources. The ArtScroll translation is more reflective of the Haredi perspective, and is increasingly becoming the unofficial Torah translation found in American

Orthodox synagogues. Likewise, the *ArtScroll Siddur*, with its strict traditionalist perspective, has become the most popular prayer book.

Traditional Judaism

A group of rabbis, some of whom taught at JTS, and laypeople who opposed changes spearheaded a new group, the Union for Traditional Conservative Judaism (UTCJ), which initially was to be a 'loyal opposition' within Conservative Judaism. Subsequently it viewed Conservative Judaism as deviating further from tradition. UTCJ objected to, amongst other issues, some of the textual revisions in the new Conservative prayer book, *Sim Shalom*, as well as the Conservative alliance with Reform in a struggle to have Israel accept non-halakhic conversions. UTCJ argued that Conservative Judaism was initiating reforms which even conflicted with its own halakhic authorities. Consequently the group formally broke with Conservative Judaism and was renamed the Union for Traditional Judaism (UTC). Its membership comes primarily from the Conservative right and the Orthodox left, and seeks to de-emphasize denominational labels. It has established a rabbinic seminary, the Institute of Traditional Judaism (Metivta), and a rabbinic organization, Morashah (Moetzet Rabbanim Shomrei Hahalakha), but is as yet a small organization whose impact and future remain to be seen.

Declining Conservative numbers

Conservative Judaism has experienced a significant decline in recent years. By 2001 only 26.5 per cent of America's Jews identified as Conservative. Demographic decline had been occurring for two generations, primarily as a result of intermarriage, with as many as three out of four Jews who were raised as Conservative becoming unaffiliated or affiliating with Reform.

Some observers argue that the movement suffers from leadership malaise as well as the lack of a clearly formulated and compelling ideology. Alternatively, it has been argued that Conservative Judaism is experiencing a winnowing, similar to that of Orthodoxy in the first half of the twentieth century, with younger Conservative Jews more committed than their elders. Formal education has experienced something of a renaissance, becoming more intensive, and there are now sixty-six Conservative Solomon Schechter lower schools and eight high schools in the United States, as well as a Conservative yeshiva in Jerusalem offering a variety of intensive study programmes for young adults.

Contemporary Reform Judaism

Like Conservative Judaism, Reform does not have a *coherent* ideology, but it has not experienced quite the same consequences. Indeed, Reform has been growing. The movement's numbers grew fivefold since 1937. The figures for all American Jewish adults, including the unaffiliated, show that 39 per cent identified with Reform in 1990. Amongst synagogue members, Reform affiliation has grown from 35 per cent in 1990 to 38 per cent in 2001. Despite this growth, Reform appears to be undergoing a process of self-evaluation and a search for meaning. Whilst Classical Reform all but excised spirituality from Judaism, contemporary Reform has reintroduced it with a passion. It has also reintroduced Hebrew into its most recent official prayer book, *Gates of Prayer*, and has re-emphasized the notion of *mitzvah* and the bar and bat mitzvah ceremonies, as well as a wide range of traditional rituals earlier defined as antithetical to modern sensibilities. The revolution in its position on Zionism and Israel was discussed above. It has also reversed attitudes to Jewish education, establishing a number of Reform day schools. Indeed, contemporary Reform sounds at times little different from Orthodoxy, although that is hardly the case. The essential difference remains that, for Orthodoxy, religious observances are viewed as *mitzvot*, in the literal sense—commandments of a Higher Authority. For Reform, such observances do not have the binding character of halakhah, they are not commanded, but are symbolic acts which derive from and appeal to personalism and voluntarism, a search for self-meaning. There is, therefore, no inconsistency between Reform's adaptation of traditional rituals while simultaneously sanctioning behaviour which is taboo in the tradition, such as intermarriage and same-sex partnerships, which in 2000 the CCAR declared as 'worthy of affirmation through appropriate Jewish ritual'. Thus, despite Reform's 'traditionalist' manifestations, the rift between it and the traditional Jewish community remains wide.

Until recently, 'triumphalism', the prediction by one denomination of the demise of another, was limited to the Conservative and Orthodox. Reform has now entered the fray and, in an article in a CCAR publication, one of its leaders predicted that the Conservative and Reconstructionist movements' congregational and rabbinic organizations will soon either join the Union for Reform Judaism or disappear. The prediction exacerbated relations between the Reform and Conservative movements. Ironically, it may also spark a reaction that could slow or even halt the Conservative decline.

Neo-Hasidism

The 1960s heralded a search for 'purpose' and 'meaning' in individual personal existence, a quest that has produced significant patterns of spiritualism in the United

States at the turn of the twenty-first century. In American Judaism, the 1960s produced patterns of neo-Hasidism both within the denominations and, perhaps even more significantly, outside them. Among traditionalists, Shlomo Carlebach, a Habad Hasidic rabbi, gave birth to an entire genre of spiritualism, including music and storytelling. He founded several open and inviting synagogues, sparking a movement for the infusion of music and spirituality into synagogue services. There are growing numbers of Carlebach *minyanim*, in which services are replete with song and dance and are much longer than those in institutionalized congregations. Increasing numbers of these congregations are non-denominational. Although most of their participants may identify as Orthodox, the congregations themselves do not identify denominationally and are open to all Jews.

Cultural identification

One final outgrowth of the 1960s has been a growing trend of religious non-identification among America's Jews. There has long been a significant population of American Jews who did not affiliate with synagogues, and many who did not identify with any specific denomination. They did, however, identify as Jews religiously. In recent years their increasing tendency is to identify as Jews culturally but not religiously. That is, when asked what their religion is, they reply 'None'. Whether these patterns of cultural identification and non-denominationalism will seriously challenge the prevalent denominational structure of American Judaism remains to be seen.

Conclusion

Jews and Judaism have always reflected the patterns of the society and culture in which they exist. It is, therefore, no surprise that American Judaism reflects many of the characteristics of broader American religious patterns. What may be surprising to some is that, despite those similarities, American Judaism, in its most conservative as well as its liberal manifestations, continuously seeks creative approaches for meeting the challenges which are presented by ever-changing social and cultural conditions.

FURTHER READING

Sociology of American religion

Wolfe, Alan. *The Transformation of American Religion: How We Actually Live Our Faith* (New York: Free Press, 2003).

Social History of America's Jews

Waxman, Chaim I. *America's Jews in Transition* (Philadelphia: Temple University Press, 1983).

Sociology of America's Jews

Farber, Roberta Rosenberg, and Chaim I. Waxman (eds.). *Jews in America: A Contemporary Reader* (Hanover, NH: Brandeis University Press/University Press of New England, 1999).

Waxman, Chaim I. *Jewish Baby Boomers: A Communal Perspective* (Albany State University of New York Press, 2001).

History of American Judaism

Raphael, Marc Lee. *Judaism in America* (New York: Columbia University Press, 2003).

Analyses of American Judaism

Liebman, Charles S. *Aspects of the Religious Behavior of American Jews* (New York: Ktav, 1974); and *Deceptive Images: Toward a Redefinition of American Judaism* (New Brunswick, NJ: Transaction Books, 1988).

Denominational studies

Elazar, Daniel J., and Rela Mintz Geffen. *The Conservative Movement in Judaism: Dilemmas and Opportunities* (Albany: State University of New York Press, 2000).

Kaplan, Dana Evan. *American Reform Judaism* (New Brunswick: Rutgers University Press, 2003).

Lazerwitz, Bernard, J. Alan Winter, Arnold Dashefsky, and Ephraim Tabory. *Jewish Choices: American Jewish Denominationalism* (Albany: State University of New York Press 1998).

Sklare, Marshall. *Conservative Judaism: An American Religious Movement*, augmented edn. (New York: Schocken Books, 1972).

Wertheimer, Jack (ed.). *Jews in the Center: Conservative Synagogues and Their Members* (New Brunswick: Rutgers University Press, 2000).

Hasidim in America

Fishkoff, Sue. *The Rebbe's Army: Inside the World of Chabad-Lubavitch* (New York: Schocken Books, 2003).

Mintz, Jerome. *Hasidic People: A Place in the New World* (Cambridge, Mass.: Harvard University Press, 1998).

Tensions of American Judaism

Freedman, Samuel G. *Jew vs. Jew: The Struggle for the Soul of American Jewry* (New York: Simon & Schuster, 2000).

Wertheimer, Jack. *A People Divided: Judaism in Contemporary America* (Hanover, NH: University Press of New England, 1997).

The Havura

Prell, Riv-Ellen. *Prayer and Community: The Havurah in American Judaism* (Detroit: Wayne State University Press, 1989).

Feminism and American Judaism

Fishman, Sylvia Barack. *A Breath of Life: Feminism in the American Jewish Community* (Hanover, NH: Brandeis University Press/University Press of New England, 1995).

WEBSITES

This is a listing of the major rabbinic organizations, seminaries, and synagogue organizations of American Judaism, and is intended as an introduction. It is not comprehensive; for example, there are many Orthodox institutions and organizations that do not have websites.

A. Rabbinic organizations

1. Reform: <www.ccarnet.org>—Central Conference of American Rabbis.
2. Conservative: <www.rabassembly.org>—Rabbinical Assembly.
3. Orthodox: <www.rabbis.org>—Rabbinical Council of America.
4. Reconstructionist: <www.theRRA.org>—Reconstructionist Rabbinical Association.
5. Traditional: <www.utj.org>—Union for Traditional Judaism.

B. Seminaries

1. Reform: <www.huc.edu>—Hebrew Union College—Jewish Institute of Religion.
2. Conservative: <www.jtsa.edu>—Jewish Theological Seminary.
   <www.uj.edu>—University of Judaism.
3. Orthodox: <www.yu.edu>—Yeshiva University.
4. Reconstructionist: <www.rrc.edu>—Reconstructionist Rabbinical College.

C. Synagogue organizations

1. Reform: <www.uahc.org>—Union for Reform Judaism (formerly Union of American Hebrew Congregations).
2. Conservative: <www.uscj.org>—United Synagogue.
3. Orthodox: <www.ou.org>—Orthodox Union.
   <www.youngisrael.org>—National Council of Young Israel.
4. Reconstructionist: <www.jrf.org>—Jewish Reconstructionist Federation.

NOTES

1. Gerald L. Showstack, *Suburban Communities: The Jewishness of American Reform Jews* (Atlanta, Ga.: Scholars Press, 1988), pp. 89–92.

2. Post-Second World War America witnessed a significant rise in the birth-rate, and the term 'baby-boomers' refers to those Americans who were born between 1946 and 1964. In 2000 they comprised one-third of the American population. The 2001 NJPS found that approximately 2 per cent of all Jews by religion identified as Reconstructionist.

3. Michael Rappeport, *1996 Demographic Study of the Reconstructionist Movement—Full Report*, Jewish Reconstructionist Federation (Nov. 1996), p. 11.

4. Herbert J. Gans, 'The Origin and Growth of a Jewish Community in the Suburbs: A Study of the Jews of Park Forest', in Marshall Sklare (ed.), *The Jews: Social Patterns of an American Group* (New York: Free Press, 1958), p. 247.

5. See Chap. 27.

6. Riv-Ellen Prell, *Prayer and Community: The Havurah in American Judaism* (Detroit: Wayne State University Press, 1989).

11 | Israeli Jewry

Eran Kaplan

Israel is home to diverse Jewish groups that, though united in a single political entity, are deeply divided in their attitudes to Jewish nationalism, religion, and Jewish history. The tenuous relations between state and religion, and between secular and religious Jews, grow out of the inherent contradictions of Zionism, which sought to be at the same time a modern national movement and the legitimate representative of an ancient religious tradition; and which sought to provide a home for all Jews, yet accepted Orthodox–Ashkenazi–Judaism as the only authentic representation of the Jewish tradition. This chapter first examines the complex and ambivalent relations between Zionism and its leaders and traditional Judaism, exploring the legal, political, and social mechanisms that developed in Israel to permit coexistence between the modern state and the Jewish religion. The chapter then looks at the two major religious groups in Israel: the ultra-Orthodox who reject the notion of Jewish nationalism and do not identify with the country's founding ideology, and the national-religious camp that attempted to create a viable synthesis between Jewish nationalism and the Jewish religion. The chapter examines the effects on Israeli Jewry of the immigration of Jews from Muslim countries in the early years of the state, and of Jews from Ethiopia and the former Soviet Union in the 1980s and 1990s. Lastly, the chapter explores the development of a distinctively Israeli Jewish model—kibbutz Judaism—and the growing popularity of alternative forms of Jewish spirituality in Israel in recent years.

Zionism and Judaism

In the crucial months before Israeli independence David Ben-Gurion, seeking support from all factions of the Jewish community in Palestine, assured the leaders of the ultra-Orthodox community that certain existing arrangements concerning religion and religious institutions—namely, the autonomy of religious education, the observance of Shabbat and *kashrut* by public institutions, and the full jurisdiction of religious courts over matrimonial matters—would be maintained by the Jewish state. These promises laid the foundations for the 'Status Quo' agreement, which would shape relations between religion and state in modern Israel.

Ben-Gurion was the leader of a national movement that was on the verge of realizing a goal which, only half a century before, had been the domain of ideological seers and utopian tracts. For the Zionists only the creation of a modern state, which would be the absolute negation of Jewish life in the Diaspora, would solve the Jewish problem; the role of the Jewish national movement was to transform the Jews into a sovereign nation rather than a landless religious entity. The Zionists imagined a modern secular society for which Judaism would be a national and cultural rather than a religious framework. Yet, despite their desire to negate the heritage of the *Galut* (exile), for both practical and ideological reasons Ben-Gurion and other Zionist leaders could not distance themselves entirely from the Jewish religion, and instead fostered an intricate relationship with traditional Judaism that was formalized by the Status Quo agreement.

The Zionist relationship with Orthodox Jewry was motivated by the fact that the Jewish nationalists saw themselves as the vanguard of the entire Jewish people, representing the interests of its different groups, including the Orthodox. Moreover, the old Yishuv (Jewish community) that existed in Palestine prior to the beginning of the Zionist settlement consisted mainly of observant Jews, and a substantial number of the Jewish immigrants who came during the major Zionist *Aliyot* (waves of immigration to Israel) were Orthodox. The Zionist leadership, which claimed that the only place where Jews could live freely was in their own land, had to accommodate the religious and spiritual needs of these Orthodox Jews. The Zionists could not replicate in the Holy Land the same atmosphere of anti-Judaism that was at the root of the Jewish experience in the Diaspora. Yet, beyond these and other practical considerations, the Zionist willingness to give the Jewish state certain traditional Jewish characteristics was also grounded in ideological reasons.

In their desire to negate the ethos of Galut, Zionists were not interested in a religious restructuring of Judaism; they did not seek to turn Judaism into a spiritual platform that would meet the demands of the modern world as, for example, the Reform movement in Judaism had done. The Zionists were materialists, and their preferred form of spirituality was the cult of labour and productivity, whose most eloquent advocate was A. D. Gordon. At the same time, however, the Zionists saw themselves as the leaders of an ancient people, seeking to return to their ancestral homeland. The Zionists needed to justify their call to lead the Jewish people from the different countries and communities in which they had lived, in some cases, for centuries to a distant and desolate land: the justification was the history and historicity of the Jewish people. For many Zionists, Orthodox Jewry, despite being a faint and somewhat misguided representation of the Jewish tradition, was nonetheless the closest thing to a living presence of historical Judaism. Therefore, by incorporating certain aspects of Orthodox Judaism into the fabric of Jewish life in Israel, the Zionists felt that they were maintaining their connection to a tradition that warranted their presence in the Land of Israel.

State and religion in modern Israel

The principles of the Status Quo were established well before the establishment of the State of Israel. Under Ottoman rule religious communities in the Land of Israel enjoyed great freedom in religious matters, including complete jurisdiction over personal status (marriage, divorce). Under British rule the religious communities in Palestine continued to enjoy this autonomous status. The British authorized the creation of a Rabbinical Council, which appointed two chief rabbis (Sephardi and Ashkenazi) as well as the members of the rabbinical courts that continued to enjoy full jurisdiction over matrimonial matters. Also, since 1920 the Yishuv had developed two educational systems: a general and a religious one, and since the mid-1930s it was agreed that Shabbat and kashrut would be observed by official institutions in the Yishuv.

In the early years of the State of Israel these arrangements became law. In 1951 the Knesset passed the law regulating days of rest, which compelled all Jewish employees to rest on Shabbat and the Jewish holidays; in 1953 the law that confirmed the authority of the religious courts over marriages and divorces was passed, and that same year two national school systems general and religious, were created.

These laws provided the basic structure for religion–state relations in Israel. Yet the constantly changing political and cultural currents in Israel made these relations rather elastic and often contentious, alternating between secular and traditional-Orthodox poles, and reflecting the fundamental Zionist tension between its modern, secular vision and its desire to represent the historical Jewish nation. For example, the enforcement of the law regulating days of rest was left up to municipal authorities, and over the years more and more cities allowed restaurants, theatres, and eventually stores and shopping malls to operate on Shabbat. At the same time, however, in 1982, succumbing to pressure from religious parties, El-Al, the Israeli national air carrier, which had previously operated flights on the Sabbath, was ordered by the government not to fly on the Jewish days of rest.

The issue that put the already fragile status quo between secular and religious Jews in Israel to its most serious test was the question that the Israeli legislator failed to address early on: who was a Jew, according to Israeli law? This issue was of importance with regard to two other laws that the Knesset passed during its first term: the Citizen's Registration Act of 1949 and the Law of Return in 1950. Under the Registration Act all citizens had to declare their religion and their ethnicity, and the Law of Return granted any Jew the right to Israeli citizenship; but the Israeli legislator did not specify who was legally a Jew, and left it to the Ministry of the Interior and its officials to make those determinations.

In 1958 the interior minister, Israel Bar-Yehudah of the Labor Party, sought to formalize the criteria for determining who is a Jew, creating guidelines which stipulated that any person who declared himself Jewish in good faith would be regarded as such by the state without having to prove it further. The representatives of the religious parties in the Knesset saw this as a violation of the Status Quo agreement and left the Labour-led government. When a new government was formed a year later, it was decided to abolish these official guidelines, yet the question of 'who is a Jew?' remained unresolved.

In 1970 the issue resurfaced in Israeli public discourse when an officer in the Israeli army, Benjamin Shalit, demanded that his children from a Christian mother be registered as Jewish according to their ethnicity. His case reached the Israeli Supreme Court that year, which ruled that his children were to be registered as 'members of the Jewish nation without a religion'. A political storm followed the court's decision, and the Knesset passed an amendment to the Law of Return stipulating that a Jew is a person born to a Jewish mother or who underwent a conversion and does not belong to any other religion. The amendment also said that the child or the grandchild of a Jew, the spouse of a Jew (regardless of his/her religion), and the spouses of a child or a grandchild of a Jew were eligible to become Israeli citizens under the Law of Return.

The 1970 amendment came as a result of political pressure by the religious parties, and it gave a legal definition to the question of who was a Jew under Israeli Law. The legislature, however, did not specify that the conversion had to be Orthodox, leading to further tensions between the religious and secular camps. Another outcome of this legislation was that in subsequent years, with massive immigration to Israel from the former Soviet Union, thousands of non-Jews became Israeli citizens under the new, more expansive parameters of the Law of Return, creating yet new animosities between religious and secular Israelis.[1]

Ultra-Orthodox

While the Israeli leadership tried to create a balance between secular and observant Jews, their ultimate goal was to create and to sustain a modern society and culture in which Judaism would become synonymous with Jewish nationalism. The ultra-Orthodox religious camp in Israel, the *Haredim*, has had an altogether different vision of Jewish life in Israel. To them the Jewish religion, in its traditional guise, was to be the core of the social, cultural, and political experience of Jews in Israel.

The Haredi camp in Israel consists of many groups and traditions. What unites the members of different Hasidic courts, the members of Lithuanian congregations, and many non-affiliated Jews that make up this diverse, and in many ways divided, camp is their basic opposition to Zionism and the modern State of Israel, which they regard, paradoxically perhaps, as yet another phase in the exile of the Jewish people from its promised land.

Within the ultra-Orthodox camp, the most radical critics of Zionism are *Neturei Karta* (the Guardians of the City). At the root of their radical anti-Zionist position is a belief that any human attempt to bring the Jews to Israel undermines the messianic process, and Jews must not hasten the end of days (*dehikat ha-ketz*). Only the very few of the most righteous believers could live in the Holy Land; whereas the Zionist ideal of the physical development of the land leads to cultural and moral decay. To Neturei Karta, Zionism is a form of *avodah zara* (foreign worship), and some in the anti-Zionist camp went so far as to explain the Holocaust as punishment for the Zionist attempt to hasten the end of days. Neturei Karta have sought complete isolation from the state and its institutions, treating it as a foreign entity. Its leaders have prevented their followers from voting for the Knesset and from participating in government or receiving any services or aid from the Jewish state. Some members, eager to see the elimination of the Jewish state, openly supported the PLO. Although in recent years the influence of Neturei Karta within the Haredi community in Israel has drastically diminished, they remain a very vocal group, and for many secular Israelis they represent the old suspicion with which the Haredim viewed the idea of a modern Jewish state.

The approach of most Haredim (outside of Neturei Karta) to Zionism and the state of Israel, while rooted in deep mistrust, is practical and at times even sympathetic. Most Haredim accept the Jewish state de facto, and they co-operate with its institutions. They regard the state as an administrative tool, which has no theological or teleological significance, and they do not identify with it ideologically.

The political body that represents the majority of the ultra-Orthodox community in Israel is Agudat Israel, which was founded in 1912 to counter the growing influence of the Zionist organization and to provide an alternative political body for observant Jews. In the elections for the first Knesset the Agudah ran jointly with other religious parties as part of a united religious party, and it even had a representative in the government. Agudah leaders saw co-operation with the Zionists as a necessary evil; however, the Agudah left the government in 1952 over its opposition to the mandatory conscription of women to the Israeli army. When Menachem Begin and the Likud (a bloc of right-wing political movements) defeated Labor in 1977, however, the Agudah again joined the ruling coalition. Though it did not have ministers in the cabinet, its representatives held some very important positions in Knesset committees and served as lieutenant ministers.

In recent years the Haredim in Israel have become increasingly involved in Israeli life, and their political representatives have exerted considerable influence over many issues facing Israeli society. At the same time, the ultra-Orthodox parties and their leaders are still seen as the representatives of a specific sector, putting the interests of their community before that of the nation as a whole, especially when it comes to the question of military service. In the early years of the state Ben-Gurion, bowing to pressures from ultra-Orthodox leaders, exempted Haredi yeshiva students from military service. At the time the exemption covered several hundred students, but with the rapid growth of this community it now applies to tens of thousands of young Haredi males (Israeli women are allowed not to serve if they declare that serving in the army infringes their religious beliefs). The fact that most Haredi Israelis do not serve in the army is a reminder to other Israelis that the Haredim do not accept the

Zionist world-view and still regard themselves as outside the mainstream of Israeli society.

Religious Zionism

Despite the overwhelming opposition to Zionism in Orthodox circles, some Orthodox Jews and rabbis were instrumental in the development of the early stages of Zionism and were active in *Hibbat Zion* (Lovers of Zion) and other pre-Herzlian Zionist groups. Mizrahi, the national (Zionist) religious faction, was created in 1902 in order to promote the role of the Torah and the Jewish tradition within the Zionist camp.

Mizrahi's Zionist vision combined the neo-Orthodox principle of 'Torah im derekh eretz' (combining traditional Judaism with civil life) with a realization that Zionism was the most practical and viable solution to the immediate problems (antisemitism) that Jews faced in Europe.

In 1921 the office of the Chief Rabbinate in Palestine was established and Rabbi A. I. Kook (1865–1935), a rebellious religious scholar who gave an ideological and theological basis to the connection between nationalism and Judaism, became the Ashkenazi chief rabbi of the Yishuv. This gave the national religious camp an import-ant position in the cultural and spiritual leadership of the Yishuv and helped establish its co-operation with the Zionist establishment in Israel. Kook was one of the first religious leaders to see in the activities of the *halutzim* (pioneers) a critical step in the Jewish national redemption, carrying out God's plans in preparing the physical road for the eventual spiritual redemption.

In the first Knesset, Mizrahi joined forces with the Agudah, but from the second Knesset on it ran as an independent party (it became the NRP—National Religious Party—in 1956). In the early years of the state Mizrahi's leaders believed in working from within the political consensus to advance the causes of Orthodox Zionists. Their main political activities in those days concentrated on securing the Status Quo and assuming control over most of the state's religious institutions. After the 1967 war, however, the NRP adopted a much more proactive political agenda initiated by a new generation of activists, taking an active part in the settlement movement.

In the pre-state period and the early years of the state, the institution that allowed young religious Zionists to combine their commitment to Orthodox Judaism and to the ideals of pioneering and the redemption of the land was the religious kibbutz, which combined the values of secular kibbutzim—working the land, communalism—with traditional Judaism. After 1967 it was primarily the settlements in the West Bank and Gaza that gave the younger members of the national religious camp an arena in which to carry out their ideological vision. The young NRP members took inspiration from the teachings of Kook and his son, Rabbi Zvi Yehuda Kook, who argued that redemption was not solely in the hands of God—people too must take concrete steps to advance the next phase in the redemptive process, and the redemption of the newly acquired land by Jews was a critical step in that direction.

When Mizrahi emerged it sought to allow Orthodox Jews a place within the Zionist movement alongside the secular majority; in recent years the leaders of the national-religious camp have presented themselves as the real representatives and inheritors of the pioneering spirit of Zionism, which they claim has been vanishing from Israeli national life.

Immigration and Jewish life in Israel

While the old Yishuv in the Land of Israel consisted of Jews from a variety of backgrounds and traditions, from the emergence of the Zionist settlement in Israel at the end of the nineteenth century until the 1950s the Jewish community in Israel was a rather homogenous group, comprised primarily of Eastern and Central European Jews. In the early years of the state, however, the ethnic composition of Israeli Jewry radically changed with the massive immigration of Jews from Muslim countries, known as Mizrahim (designating their Eastern—*mizrah*—origins).

Mizrahi Jews had a profoundly different historical experience from their Ashkenazi co-religionists. They did not experience the type of clash between tradition and modernity which, in the European case, brought about both processes of reform and liberalization, but also a radicalization of the Orthodox camp in reaction to the threat of modernity. In the East, tradition was never challenged in such an all-encompassing manner, and it did not have to defend itself; Judaism in the Muslim world did not encounter the secular–religious dichotomy that defined much of the Ashkenazi experience after the emergence of the Jewish Enlightenment (Haskalah). Jewish life in the East followed, by and large, well-established customs, maintaining patterns that thrived for generations. However, when they came to Israel in the 1950s and were called upon to undergo a rapid process of Israelization, the Mizrahi community did, rather forcefully, experience the conflict between modernity and tradition.

While the Zionist establishment regarded religious (Ashkenazi) Jews with a degree of deference, seeing them as the 'authentic' representatives of the Jewish past, they considered Mizrahi Jews to have been left behind by the forces of history. The moderate nature of the Jewish practices of Mizrahim, as opposed to the strictness that characterized Ashkenazi Orthodoxy, was regarded by many as inauthentic, the product of a primitive culture rather than a manifestation of true religious fervour. Consequently, most Mizrahim were perceived as essentially non-religious people, needing to undergo a process of modernization to rid them of their ancient habits. This was quite a traumatic experience for many, breeding a sense of resentment, deprivation, and injustice. It also led to the development of an approach to Jewish life that became typical of many Mizrahim in Israel: *masortiut* (traditionalism), which entailed living like a secular modern Israeli in public, but maintaining some Jewish traditions, mainly in the private realm.

Not all Mizrahim, however, abandoned their religion after arriving in Israel; but those who wanted to provide their children with religious education had to send them to Ashkenazi yeshivas. In the Ashkenazi religious institutions these young Mizrahim had to adopt Ashkenazi interpretations of Judaism (some even had to learn Yiddish), which also, ultimately, bred a growing resentment among Mizrahi religious scholars and activists. Sensing this growing dissatisfaction among Mizrahi yeshiva students, the leaders of the Lithuanian community (a substantial number of Mizrahim attended Lithuanian yeshivas), who wanted to strengthen their political power vis-à-vis the Hasidic elements within Agudat Israel, helped in the creation in 1984 of Shas (an acronym for observant Sephardim), a political party that represented Mizrahi, ultra-Orthodox Jews.

Initially, the spiritual and ideological leader of Shas was Rabbi Eliezer Shach, the leader of the Lithuanians in Israel, but as the movement grew it distanced itself from the Ashkenazi religious establishment and made Rabbi Obadiah Yoseph, the former chief Sephardi rabbi of Israel, its spiritual and ideological leader. As a religious party Shas pursued three main goals: it was an ultra-Orthodox party that sought to strengthen and protect the role of Judaism in Israeli life; it was a social movement that fought on behalf of Mizrahim in Israel; and it wanted to restore the glory of Sephardi Judaism. By the mid-1990s Shas emerged as the third-largest party in the Knesset, receiving votes not only from ultra-Orthodox Sephardim but also from many Mizrahim who saw in Shas a party that represented their social interests. Shas used its political power to develop an independent educational system, religious institutions, and a host of social programmes that were driven by its religious world-view.

The political rise of Shas has signalled the growing role of Mizrahim in Israeli public life, and has allowed different manifestations of their spiritual traditions to re-emerge. One Sephardi tradition that has increasingly re-established itself, especially among North African Jews in Israel, is the pilgrimage to tombs of saints. Perhaps the most popular destination is the tomb of the Baba Sali—Rabbi Abu-Hatzera, a celebrated Moroccan religious authority who settled in the southern Israeli town of Netivoth. After his death in 1984 his tomb became an important religious and spiritual centre. Every January tens of thousands of pilgrims converge on the town for a special celebration in honour of the late *Tzadik* (saint). Over the years the site has gained the reputation of a holy place where miracles are regularly performed—an Israeli Lourdes. The site has also become a multi-million-dollar industry, where posters and tapes of the late Tzadik are sold, as well as different talismans, including the popular Baba-Sali holy water. Shas has made considerable use of this sort of popular piety in its political campaigns. It employed, for example, the services of Rabbi Yitzhak Kedourie, an ageing mystic and kabbalistic sage, to attend political rallies and appear on television adverts, blessing Shas supporters and promising them health and prosperity.

Over the past two decades, with the arrival of nearly a million Jews from the former Soviet Union (FSU), immigration once again has had a profound effect on the character of Israeli Jewry. Unlike the Mizrahi Jews, who came from a background steeped in Jewish traditions, the immigrants from the FSU lived for decades under a communist regime that repressed most forms of religious expression. Moreover, many of these immigrants were not Jews according to halakhah (about half of the immigrants that came after 1998). These immigrants, while Israeli citizens by virtue of the Law of Return, were denied the services of the religious courts (marriages and divorces) and burial rights in Jewish cemeteries—soldiers who died in the service of the state were not allowed to be buried in military cemeteries—bringing the question of 'who is a Jew?' back to the Israeli public debate.

Another group of recent immigrants who have called into question the boundaries and definitions of Israeli Jewry are Ethiopian Jews. This community, which practised a form of pre-rabbinic Judaism, was 'discovered' by the established Jewish world in 1904. In the mid-1970s the Chief Rabbinate recognized this community as Jewish, making the Law of Return available to them. In the 1980s and 1990s, as a result of civil wars and severe famine, over 45,000 Ethiopian Jews were brought to Israel. There were questions about the Ethiopians' Judaism, especially their divorce and conversion practices, and initially they were all required to undergo a symbolic conversion. This demand, which enraged the community and its leaders, was later limited to those who were married by the Israeli religious courts. Another controversial issue regarding the Jews from Ethiopia had to do with the Falash Mura community, Ethiopian Jews whose forebears were forced to convert to Christianity in the nineteenth century, and who have sought, because of the situation in Ethiopia, to immigrate to Israel. The Falash Mura, which the Ethiopian Jews regard as part of their community, were not recognized as Jews by the Israeli religious establishment and were not covered by the Law of Return. However, a few thousand Falash Mura have been allowed to immigrate to Israel in recent years for humanitarian reasons.

New forms of Jewish spirituality in Israel

One outcome of the Status Quo agreement was the complete control of the Orthodox parties over religious institutions in Israel. This allowed them to exclude all other forms of Judaism (Reform, Conservative) from playing a role in Israeli public life. All religious services in Israel (marriages, divorces, burials) are conducted according to the Orthodox tradition, while alternative ceremonies are not recognized by the state and have no official status. Thus, alternative practices of Judaism in Israel are relatively marginal, operating without public assistance or recognition. This Orthodox stranglehold over the religious establishment has also created much antagonism between Orthodox and non-Orthodox Jews in Israel, and has led many Israeli Jews to view Judaism as a national category, leaving the practice of Judaism as a spiritual entity almost exclusively to Orthodox Jews. However, throughout the history of Israel, and especially in recent years, a growing number of 'secular' Israelis have searched for alternative and progressive forms of Jewish identity.

One of the first attempts to redefine spiritual aspects of Judaism and to adapt them to life in modern Israel took place in the kibbutzim, the vanguard of secular Zionism. The kibbutzim developed new ways of celebrating the Jewish holidays, especially Sukkoth, Pesah, and Shavuot, which are tied to the Israeli agricultural cycle. They transformed the biblical tradition of making a pilgrimage to the Temple in Jerusalem to offer the fruits of the harvest into a celebration of the kibbutz's harvest and of the renewed connection between the Jewish people and the Land of Israel. The kibbutzim developed new *Haggadot* for Pesah, transforming the Haggadah from a religious into a national text. They omitted many of the references to God in the traditional Haggadah as well as many of the midrashic and Talmudic elements, and replaced them with texts celebrating the Israeli landscape and the Zionist notion of working the land; the kibbutz Haggadah became an ode to nature and the Land of Israel.

More recently, with the rising sense among Israelis that the main goals of Zionism—the desire to create a Jewish national home and then to secure its existence—have been fulfilled, a void in the lives of many non-Orthodox Israelis has emerged. This has led to a growing search for alternative cultural and ideological frameworks that would provide meaning to the notion of Jewish life in the Land of Israel. This has produced a growing interest in Judaism and what is called a return to 'aron ha-sefarim ha-Yehudi' (the Jewish bookshelf). Different educational institutions have been established in Israel, such as Alma College in Tel Aviv and Beit ha-Midrash in Jerusalem, that teach Judaism in relation to other cultures and traditions while relying on traditional Jewish texts and educational frameworks, such as the *hevrutah*—a small group of students studying texts together.

In addition to these new institutions, there are a number of new communities in Israel, especially in the desert, such as Lotan and Ketura, which combine New Age sensitivities with classic Jewish themes. Unlike the older religious kibbutzim that adhered to an Orthodox interpretation of Judaism, these communities combine Reform and Progressive Jewish teachings that preach equality and pluralism with awareness of ecological and environmental issues. These groups provide a new meaning to the Zionist connection between Judaism and the Land of Israel. The land is no longer simply a territory that allows the Jews to define themselves as a national entity; instead of conquering the land on the way to political redemption, these communities seek to liberate the land from the abuses of modern technology as part of a spiritual experience.

Conclusion

Zionism set out to transform and modernize Jewish life in Israel, to negate the heritage of the exile and turn the Jewish people from a landless religious community into an independent nation. Zionism treated Judaism strictly from a national, political perspective, leaving the Orthodox community as the only recognized representative of the Jewish faith in Israel. Yet, as Zionism evolves into a movement that is concerned not only with political solutions, but also with providing cultural and spiritual answers to younger Israelis, new approaches to Judaism that are concerned with providing spiritual significance to the Jewish presence in Israel are gaining greater importance.

FURTHER READING

Bilu, Yoram, and Eyal Ben Ari. 'The Making of Modern Saints: Manufactured Charisma and the Abu-Hatseiras of Israel', *American Ethnologist* 19: 4 (1992), pp. 29–44. A sociological analysis of the role of saints in the religious culture of Moroccan Jews in Israel.

Cohen, Asher, and Bernard Susser. *Israel and the Politics of Jewish Identity: The Secular–Religious Impasse* (Baltimore: Johns Hopkins University Press, 2000). Two writers from opposite sides of the religious–secular divide in Israel assess the problems in fostering an Israeli Jewish identity.

Don-Yehiya, Eliezer, and Charles S. Liebman. *Civil Religion in Israel: Traditional Judaism and Political Culture in the Jewish State* (Berkeley: University of California Press, 1983). Presents a detailed study of the role of religion in modern Israel.

Hartman, David. 'Zionism and the Continuity of Judaism', in id., *A Heart of Many Rooms: Celebrating the Many Voices Within Judaism* (Woodstock, Vt.: Jewish Lights Publishing, 1999). An essay that places Zionism within the Jewish tradition.

Liebman, Charles S., and Elihu Katz (eds.). *The Jewishness of Israelis* (Albany: State University of New York Press, 1997). A series of articles that offer demographic and sociological analyses of the degree and importance of religious observance in modern Israel.

Lilker, Shalom. *Kibbutz Judaism: A New Tradition in the Making* (East Brunswick, NJ: Cornwall Books, 1982). A detailed study of the place of Judaism in kibbutz life.

Ravitzky, Aviezer. *Messianism, Zionism, and Jewish Religious Radicalism* (Chicago: University of Chicago Press, 1996). Provides a comprehensive analysis of different Jewish orthodox responses to Zionism and the State of Israel.

Segev, Tom. *1949: The First Israelis* (New York: Henry Holt & Co., 1998). The book's third part, 'Between the Orthodox and the Secular', provides an insightful look at the relations between the two communities in the early years of the state.

Sprinzak, Ehud. *The Ascendance of Israel's Radical Right* (New York: Oxford University Press, 1991). Offers a thorough analysis of the religious Zionist's shift to the right after the 1967 war.

Tabory, Ephraim. 'The Influence of Liberal Judaism on Israeli Religious Life', *Israel Studies*, 5: 1 (Spring 2000), pp. 183–203. Examines the history of liberal Judaism in Israel and the challenges it has faced.

NOTE

1. See Chap. 28 for further consideration of the clash between halakhah and the state.

12 | French Jewry

Paula E. Hyman

The history of France and its Jews is complex. On the one hand, France was the first nation in Europe to accord full civic equality to its Jewish population. On the other hand, with the Dreyfus Affair, France experienced the single most significant outbreak of antisemitism in nineteenth-century Europe. During the Second World War the Vichy regime decreed its own antisemitic laws and collaborated with the Nazis in the murder of more than 75,000 Jews. At the turn of the twenty-first century a new form of antisemitism has emerged in France.

Within the context of Jewish history on the European continent, however, France's commitment to the equality of its Jewish citizens has been unparalleled. The emancipation of the Jews during the French Revolution set the standard for the political aspirations of Jewish populations worldwide. There were only about 40,000 Jews in France on the eve of the Revolution. At least three-quarters of them were Ashkenazim, concentrated in the eastern provinces of Alsace and Lorraine. Living for the most part in villages, they supported themselves as pedlars and cattle-dealers, or commission agents, lending money on the side. The remainder included a small group of more acculturated and prosperous Sephardim, descendants of Spanish and Portuguese *conversos* (converts to Catholicism), who lived in the south-west, and the Jews who had lived for centuries under papal control in the cities of Avignon, Carpentras, and Cavaillon in the south-east.

Despite the small size of the Jewish population, the anomalous status of Jews had been a focus of French thinkers throughout the eighteenth century, because the existence of Jews raised questions about issues of fundamental importance at the time: primitive life versus civilization, especially the value of commerce as opposed to agriculture; the nature of tolerance; and how to construct the nation and how inclusive it should be. To be sure, Enlightenment thinkers generally agreed with conservative opponents of Jewish emancipation that the Jews were primitive and superstitious, and their economic pursuits detrimental to their peasant customers. However, they asserted that the 'faults' of the Jews were a result of their mistreatment and would disappear with the granting of civic rights. As a result of the logic of the slogan of 'liberté, fraternité, égalité', and the Revolution's putting an end to a society organized according to estates, the Jews were emancipated in two steps: Sephardim in January 1790 and Ashkenazim in September 1791. Political emancipation affected Jews differently depending on their place of residence and their socioeconomic status. Jews welcomed emancipation, primarily because they viewed it as an opportunity to free themselves from the economic restrictions of the *ancien régime*.

Emancipation conferred on Jews the same rights and responsibilities as other French citizens, but it did not recognize any claim of Jews to the retention of group rights. As the famous statement of Count Stanislas de Clermont-Tonnerre, who supported emancipation, put it: 'To the Jews as a nation, nothing; to the Jews as individuals, everything.' Emancipation *à la française* did not include the legitimation of cultural difference.

In fact, the Emperor Napoleon, who came to power in the wake of the Revolution, was openly suspicious of the ability of Jews to become good French citizens. His armies brought emancipation to Jews in Germany and Italy, but in France he convoked an Assembly of Jewish Notables in 1806, and a 'Sanhedrin' the following year, to make it clear that Jews were to declare publicly that their prime loyalty was to the French state and not to Jewish law; and in what Jews called the 'Infamous Decree' of 1808, he subjected Jews to restrictions on their economic activity. Through a system of consistories, which paralleled the structure of the organization of Protestants, he also gave governmental recognition to Jewish communities understood in religious terms, but thereby placed them under governmental control. Unlike Catholics and Protestants, until 1831 the Jews were responsible for the salaries of their clergy. The centralization of French political life was reflected in the organization of its religious communities. Local Jewish communities, for example, were supervised by departmental consistories, which in turn reported to the Central Consistory in Paris. A governmental minister of religions served as a conduit between Jewish leadership and the state. In 1818, after Napoleon's fall from power, the economic restrictions of the 'Infamous Decree' were allowed to lapse, and French Jews enjoyed legal equality through every change of regime in France until the fall of the Third Republic with the Nazi invasion of 1940.

Legal equality did not guarantee social acceptance and freedom from sporadic antisemitic outbreaks, particularly in Alsace and during times of revolutionary instability, as in 1830 and 1848. However, emancipation offered Jews the possibility to move freely within France and to take advantage of the economic opportunities of a capitalist economy. Moreover, Jews experienced few obstacles to a career in the army, in government service, and in the university.

French Jews migrated internally, drawn to urban centres and especially to Paris. Unlike other French migrants to the city, who tended to become factory workers, most Jews, who entered cities as impecunious petty merchants, stayed within commerce and experienced upward social mobility in that sphere. Although they did not achieve the financial success of members of the bourgeoisie until the last quarter of the century, they adopted bourgeois values earlier and aspired to become bourgeois in all matters.

By 1861 the Jewish population of Paris had reached 25,000, more than a quarter of the total French Jewish population of 96,000. It was in Paris that some Jews became major players in French economic life, particularly in banking and capitalist financing of railroads and large-scale wholesaling. The prosperous elite established showy residences along with their commercial houses. The Rothschilds, part of a family of international dimensions, became the symbol of capitalism in France. Just as France was governed by a coterie of notables, so too, the French Jewish community looked to its economic elites for its leadership.

Jews sought acculturation and integration into French life, but most also tried to retain some form of Jewish identification. In Alsace and Lorraine, where most Jews lived in villages and small towns, traditional Jewish observance continued into the latter part of the nineteenth century. Jews preserved the Alsatian form of Yiddish, much as their fellow Alsatians spoke their local Germanic dialect. Their acculturation to French language and culture was more gradual than in Paris or even Metz, a major urban centre in Lorraine.

Like most emancipated Jews in the modern period, French Jewish leaders articulated the consonance of Jewish and general culture. As Frenchmen, they saw a particular affinity between French and Jewish values. They also promoted the *régénération* of Jewish economic and social behaviour that the spokesmen of the Enlightenment had sought. To achieve their goals, beginning in 1817 they established governmentally recognized Jewish schools, which placed an emphasis on secular studies while including some religious instruction, with modern French textbooks. Boys' schools came first, but girls' schools were also established. In Alsace the Jewish consistories effectively eliminated traditional private Jewish schools by denying certification to schoolmasters ignorant of French, and by limiting charitable assistance to families that sent their children to certified schools.

The consistorial leadership also promoted the modernization of Judaism, but religious reform was moderated because the sensibilities of traditional Jews in Alsace had to be taken into account. Moreover, in contrast to Jews in Germany, emancipated French Jews did not feel that their political status depended on their form of religious expression; nor was there much social pressure to eliminate Hebrew from the liturgy when French Catholics also prayed in a language they did not understand, Latin. Official consistorial leadership, however, did support reforms that diminished the differentness of Judaism in the French imagination. Jewish elites who sought social approbation realized, for example, that modernizing the communal treatment of women signalled to the larger society that Jews had adopted French ways. They were aware, in particular, that the segregation of women in public Jewish rituals was a visible reminder of the oriental origin of Jews and Judaism. Beginning in the 1840s, the moderate reformists who dominated the consistories called for the enhancement of women's role in the synagogue and introduced confirmation for adolescent girls as well as boys.

As they learned French and acquired secular education, Jews in France experienced few obstacles to their integration into French political and professional life. Indeed, Jews saw no need to convert in order to participate in all sectors of French society. Pierre Birnbaum has documented the careers of French Jews who became army generals, high-level civil servants, and politicians. By the 1840s Jews held political office on the national as well as the local level. Three Jews, among them the lawyer and consistorial activist Adolphe Crémieux, even served as ministers in the first government established after the Revolution of 1848. Jews also regularly received professorships at French universities. In fact, Jews with doctorates from Germany immigrated to France because they could have illustrious careers there, at a time when conversion to Christianity was a virtual *sine qua non* for achieving a regular position in the German academic world.

Although Jews enjoyed the rights of citizenship and were well integrated into many French institutions, antisemitic prejudices did not entirely disappear. There were antisemitic riots in dozens of communities in Alsace in the early days of the Revolution of 1848. Catholic conservatives opposed Jews' teaching sensitive subjects in public schools, and in 1849 prevented Isidore Cahen from occupying the lycée position in philosophy to which he had been appointed. Lawyers and judges sometimes referred to the origins of Jewish litigants while not identifying others in court cases in a similar way. In many instances popular prejudice against Jews was used as a rationale to justify denying them the absolute equality to which they were entitled as citizens. In 1858 *L'Univers*, a Catholic newspaper, published a series of articles that vilified Jews and Judaism and renewed the charge of ritual murder. The consistories sometimes protested to the government, and sometimes maintained silence as their strategy of choice. Most French Jews viewed this antisemitism as an atavism, destined to disappear. The antisemitism they encountered disturbed them, but they considered it no real danger because of the government's commitment to protect all its citizens.

In international affairs, however, the French Jewish leadership opted for activism. In response to the Mortara affair of 1858, when the Vatican kidnapped a Jewish child from his home because a Catholic family servant had baptized him, two years later six young French Jews, intellectuals, professionals, and businessmen, including Isidore Cahen, established the Alliance Israélite Universelle. They were an intellectual elite alienated from the consistorial leadership. As a defence organization which defined itself as international in scope, the mission of the Alliance was to defend Jews abroad who were subject to persecution and discrimination. Critical of the consistories' quietism, it ultimately drew consistorial leaders, among them Crémieux, to its work, and was active both in international diplomacy and in colonialist efforts at cultural betterment, providing a modern education to Jews in North Africa and the Levant through a network of schools that it established. It earned governmental support because of its promotion of French language and culture in countries in which the French had interests. The leaders of the Alliance Israélite Universelle put French Jewry on the international map, and demonstrated that Jews could be more effective in their self-defence in a unified, indeed international, organization that would speak publicly in a collective voice for the Jews of many lands.

The Alliance did not involve itself in combating domestic antisemitism, sharing the general faith of Jews in the government. Yet antisemitism in France became more pervasive in the 1880s and 1890s. Jews were identified with modern developments that struck many Frenchmen as both economically harmful and culturally destructive. They were associated with the city, where they appeared to flourish, and with capitalism, which hurt both small shopkeepers and artisans. Moreover, they were seen as promoters of a modern, secular world-view that eroded the traditional Catholic culture that drew its strength from the countryside. *La France juive*, published by the journalist Édouard Drumont in 1886, widely disseminated these views, blaming Jews for all of France's problems. With more than 100,00 copies sold within a year, it became one of France's best-sellers. Although Drumont presented the Jews as foreigners on French soil, and referred to them in racial terms as polluters of French society, he never developed a systematic racism of the sort that characterized an important segment of German antisemites of the time. However, he was the key figure in transforming the arrest for high treason of a Jewish officer, Alfred Dreyfus, into the Dreyfus Affair, which lasted from 1894 until 1906.

When Alfred Dreyfus, the only Jew on the army's general staff, was arrested, Drumont used the pages of his antisemitic newspaper *La Libre Parole* to accuse the government of a cover-up. Drumont and his allies transformed a military case into an 'affair' that split French society, particularly in the cities. Despite the absence of evidence, Dreyfus was convicted and sent to Devil's Island. A small band of supporters kept the issue alive and recruited more and more intellectuals and politicians to their ranks. In January 1898 the famous novelist Émile Zola published his call for justice, 'J'Accuse', in the paper *L'Aurore*, further fuelling the debate. The drama played itself out in the courts, the press, and among French intellectuals and the political elite for several more years. Dreyfus was retried and convicted again, in a second court martial in 1900, and was finally exonerated in 1906 when the Court of Appeals annulled his second conviction. As a result of the Affair, France initiated the separation of church and state.

The Dreyfus Affair demonstrated that France was divided into two camps. The Dreyfusards supported the Revolution and an egalitarian modern state which defended the rights of the individual and conferred citizenship irrespective of origins. The anti-Dreyfusards envisaged a hierarchical France of peasantry, nobility, and church, rooted in the legacy of Joan of Arc.

Although historians have often downplayed the extent of antisemitism in the Dreyfus Affair, the latest scholarship has indicated that it played a key role. Moreover, through archival research Pierre Birnbaum and Stephen Wilson have uncovered widespread violence against Jews in many towns and cities after Zola's conviction in February 1898 following the publication of 'J'Accuse'. They have also documented that French Jews, far from being passive during the affair, demonstrated a variety of forms of resistance to antisemitism. Still, Jews were relieved when the Affair came to an end, and saw its favourable resolution as confirmation of their status as equal citizens.

At the end of the nineteenth century Jewish immigrants from Eastern Europe, most from Poland-Lithuania, became a substantial component of French Jewry. About 44,000 eastern Jews, one-third of them women, settled in France in the years

1881–1914, with most arriving after the failed Russian Revolution of 1905. They contributed to a total Jewish population of some 80,000 in 1900, growing to 150,000 two decades later. (With the loss of Alsace-Lorraine as a result of the Franco-Prussian War of 1870, the number of Jews in France had fallen significantly.) These Yiddish-speaking immigrant Jews, who concentrated in Paris and a few other cities, were primarily working-class, labouring in large numbers in various sectors of the garment industry and in other artisan trades.

The immigrant Jewish community, which flourished until the Second World War, was a vibrant one, both culturally and politically. It established its own institutions, and did not defer to the native French Jews who still sought to speak for all Jews in France. Its socialist (Bundist), communist, and Zionist organizations, which were largely independent of French and French Jewish organizations, aroused the greatest concern in the native Jewish establishment, because they differed so radically from its own moderate politics and anti-Zionist views and were perceived as tangible signs of the foreignness of the immigrants.

These political and social divisions were exacerbated during the inter-war years. During the 1930s, in particular, the arrival of thousands of Jewish refugees from Nazi Germany, growing antisemitism and xenophobic nationalism, economic depression, and the question of Zionism all elicited very different responses among native and immigrant Jews. When Léon Blum became France's first Jewish premier in 1936, at the head of a Popular Front government of socialists and communists, antisemitic rhetoric became widespread, even entering the Chamber of Deputies. Immigrant Jews wanted a militant response to antisemitism, while native French Jews preferred a quietist response. In any case, they feared that the foreignness of the immigrants, in political style as well as birth, would endanger the status of all Jews in France. The growing French hostility to German Jewish refugees in France in the latter part of the 1930s brought native and immigrant Jews together in a common opposition to a draconian governmental policy.

The surrender of the French to Nazi forces, which occupied the northern three-fifths of the country, and the establishment of the antisemitic Vichy regime in the south compelled the Jews of France for the first time since Napoleon to contend with hostile authorities, both foreign and indigenous, bent on their destruction. More than 75,000 of the estimated 300,000–350,000 Jews in France in 1940 were deported to death camps, and at most 2,500 of them survived. Thousands of Jews, most of them immigrants and refugees, were arrested and interned in camps on French soil under dire conditions. And all of France's Jews were subject to antisemitic legislation, some initiated in October 1940 by the Vichy regime and some decreed by the Nazi occupiers, which restricted their economic and political freedom.

The war years demonstrated that the long-standing faith of French Jews in the protection offered by the state was misplaced. It was French policemen who guarded the Jews in the camps and who rounded up Jews for deportation. In 1942 the situation of the Jews in the occupied zone (which was extended to include the whole country in

November) as well as under Vichy worsened, as the Nazis determined to deport French Jews to the death camps in the east. Ironically, the habit of obedience to the law of Jews in France only facilitated their deportation. They registered for the census of Jews that the Nazis decreed in the Autumn of 1940. The UGIF (Union Générale des Israélites de France), the central organization of Jews whose establishment was ordered by the Nazi and Vichy authorities, kept meticulous records of Jews who made use of their social welfare institutions.

Even as Jews were forced to wear the yellow star and were increasingly excluded from economic and social life, and then arrested and deported, most French citizens remained passive bystanders. To be sure, some non-Jewish relief organizations offered assistance to those interned in French camps. The Protestants were particularly active, and the small Protestant village of Le Chambon-sur-Lignon, located in a remote region, is credited with hiding and saving about 5,000 Jews.

The public round-up of Jews, conducted by French police, provoked growing outrage. Christian clergy protested to the Vichy government, and in August 1942 the archbishop of Toulouse even issued a pastoral letter, to be read publicly in all the churches of his diocese, that condemned the harsh measures to which Jews were being subjected, and called upon Christians to recognize their common humanity with Jews. No Christian clerics in the occupied zone, however, were willing to risk the consequences of openly opposing the Nazis. Still, Christian organizations that had provided relief now moved on to illegal activity and the rescue of Jews, including hiding Jews in convents and monasteries.

Jews themselves organized rescue activities and participated in the French Resistance, especially in communist-led resistance groups. Even the UGIF co-operated in illegal activity. Some Jews also insisted on establishing a Jewish branch of the Resistance that, by demonstrating Jewish heroism, would assert Jewish ethnic pride in the face of racism, and would also avenge the Jewish victims of the Nazis. Although armed resistance was a minority phenomenon among Jews as among non-Jews in France, and did not significantly disrupt Nazi control, its psychological impact was considerable.

The survival of three-quarters of France's Jewish population during the Holocaust was among the highest proportions in Europe. The willingness of some individuals and groups within French society to dissent from the antisemitism promoted by their own state as well as by the Nazis, and to engage in behaviour that prevented the deportation of Jews in their midst, was a significant factor in the high survival rate of Jews in France. Equally important, however, was the size of the country and its topography. There were many places for Jews to be hidden that were remote from Nazi and Vichy police surveillance, as compared with the Netherlands, for example, where 80 per cent of the Jewish population perished.

In the aftermath of the Second World War French Jews struggled to rebuild their community, traumatized and decimated by war and genocide. The fact that fully 85 per cent of all name-changes among French Jews between 1803 and 1957 occurred between 1945 and 1957 suggests that after the Holocaust many French Jews wanted to mask their Jewishness. Still, French Jews built new institutions to unite the community, the largest in non-communist continental Europe, although only 250,000 strong. Those institutions included the Conseil Représentatif des Juifs de France (CRIF), an umbrella organization founded in 1943 during the Holocaust; a unified philanthropic Fonds Social Juif Unifié (FSJU), founded in 1949 to centralize fund-raising and the distribution of grants for social needs; and Jewish primary schools and lycées.

The rebuilding of French Jewry was aided immeasurably by the immigration, beginning in the 1950s and continuing well into the 1960s, of thousands of Jews from Algeria, Morocco, and Tunisia who felt increasingly vulnerable in their home countries. Many of them—all of the Algerians—held French citizenship and felt culturally close to France because of their education under the auspices of the Alliance Israélite Universelle. In the 1950s alone 220,000 Jews from North Africa settled in France. By the 1970s French Jewry, numbering an estimated 535,000, became the largest European Jewish community after the Soviet Union. It is currently the largest Jewish community in Europe, with a population estimated at 600,000.

French Jewry has been transformed both demographically and culturally in the post-war decades. Settling in cities and their suburbs, the immigrants expanded the number of Jewish communities in France. Initially of a somewhat lower social stratum than native Jews or those of East European immigrant origin, many have experienced upward mobility into the bourgeoisie. Comfortable with a Jewish identity rooted in religious traditions and a culture that expressed itself in French as well as Arabic, North African Jewish immigrants have stimulated the multiplication of synagogues, community centres, and Jewish schools. They have inserted a more assertive style of Jewishness into the public culture of French Jewry.

That new cultural style was reinforced by the 1967 Six Day War, by developments in French politics and society, and by a number of antisemitic incidents of the 1980s and the reappearance of antisemitism in France in the early twenty-first century. Although French Jews manifest a diversity of identities, most were deeply affected by the Six Day War and by the pro-Arab tilt of France's Middle Eastern policy at the time and subsequently. Like other Jews throughout the world, they experienced the Arab threat to Israel in May 1967 as a potential second Holocaust. French Jews organized major demonstrations in support of Israel during the crisis days of May, and vigorously criticized President Charles de Gaulle for his policies and his overt resentment of Israel and of French Jewish support for Israel that was expressed in terms that many interpreted as antisemitic. The newly militant stance of the French Jewish community was reinforced by the politicization of many young French Jews during the 1968 student-led uprising. The 'events' offered broad strata of French Jewry a model of political activism.

As Israel and Zionism occupied an increasingly central place in French Jewish consciousness, French Jews organized themselves to support Israel more effectively. The Comité Juif d'Action (the Jewish Action Committee), established in 1973, held several massive demonstrations in 1976, 1977, and 1980 (under the new name Renouveau Juif, Jewish Renewal), that each involved 150,000 Jews. By 1987 a survey revealed that only 5 per cent of French Jews (as opposed to more than 50 per cent twenty years earlier) felt that the destruction of the State of Israel would have no consequence for the situation of the Jews of the world. In 1977 CRIF published a communal charter articulating the importance of Israel for France's Jews.

French Jews demonstrated their new cultural and political style in their response to antisemitic incidents of the late 1970s and 1980s. Although there had been some political antisemitism in France in the 1950s, reflecting the stresses that accompanied decolonialization and the election of Pierre Mendes-France as France's second Jewish premier, Jews had not expected its subsequent flare-up. Most frightening to French Jewry was a series of bombings of Jewish institutions in Paris that demonstrated both the vulnerability of Jews to terrorism on French soil and the inadequacy of governmental responses to it. The most significant was the bombing in 1980 of the Liberal synagogue in the Rue Copernic, in which six people were killed. The horror of the incident was deepened for Jews when Premier Raymond Barre differentiated between the Jews going to synagogue, for whom the bomb was intended, and the 'innocent Frenchmen' crossing the street who were struck by it. The message that Barre sent, probably inadvertently, was that the intended Jewish victims were neither innocent nor French. The incident elicited public demonstrations of solidarity with Jews and strengthened the activism of French Jewish youth.

Since the 1970s French Jews have experienced a cultural renaissance of sorts. The reappropriation of Jewishness among the masses, as manifested in popular demonstrations, has been accompanied by the proliferation of Jewish schools and study groups as well as by the engagement of French Jewish intellectuals with the meaning of Jewishness after the Holocaust. Figures like Alain Finkelkraut, Richard Marienstras, Bernard-Henri Lévy, and Shmuel Trigano have all explored new ways to combine Jewish distinctiveness with French citizenship and identity. They have contributed to the popularization of the slogan 'the right to be different' within French cultural and political life. Moreover, Jews have continued to play a significant role in French universities.

Despite the impressive successes of Jews within French society, the beginning of the new century has brought a spate of unexpected antisemitic incidents. Cemeteries have been desecrated, Jewish institutions bombed, and individual Jews targeted for attack. In contrast to the past, the perpetrators of the violence appear to be young Arab Muslims, children of immigrants whose opportunities for social mobility in France are limited. By attacking Jews in France they seem to see themselves as combatants in the great war between 'the Zionists' and the Arab nation. Young neo-Nazis have also been implicated in the incidents. The fact that the French government reacted slowly to the violent acts directed at Jews and their institutions, refraining for at least two years from labelling them hate crimes and from vigorously pursuing their perpetrators, has contributed to a sense of malaise amongst French Jewry.

Governmental spokesmen have belatedly responded, and the situation of Jews in France does not seem precarious. French Jews are prepared to mobilize support for the protection of their rights and to continue to negotiate the balance between equality and particularism that has defined the shifting contours of Jewish life in France since the Revolution. If France remains committed to the equality, and protection, of all its citizens, as well as to the right to be different, French Jewry will continue to constitute a vibrant Jewish community.

FURTHER READING

Benbassa, Esther. *Jews of France: A History from Antiquity to the Present*, trans. M. B. DeBevoire (Princeton: Princeton University Press, 1999). A good general introduction.

Berkowitz, Jay. *The Shaping of Jewish Identity in Nineteenth-Century France* (Detroit: Wayne State University Press, 1989). Analyses the ways in which Jews transformed their identity and institutions in the context of post-emancipation France.

Birnbaum, Pierre. *Jews of the Republic: A Political History of State Jews in France from Gambetta to Vichy*, trans. Jane Marie Todd (Stanford: Stanford University Press, 1996). An innovative study of the integration of French Jews into civil and political positions in France during the Third Republic.

Birnbaum, Pierre. *Jewish Destinies: Citizenship, State, and Community in Modern France*, trans. Arthur Goldhammer (New York: Hill & Wang, 2000). Reflections on the French Jewish experience by a prominent scholar and intellectual.

Bredin, Jean-Denis. *The Affair: The Case of Alfred Dreyfus*, trans. Jeffrey Mehlman (New York: G. Braziller, 1986). The best comprehensive study of the Dreyfus Affair.

Friedlander, Judith. *Vilna on the Seine: Jewish Intellectuals in France Since 1968* (New Haven: Yale University Press, 1990). An examination of the revival of Jewish culture among Paris intellectuals in the post-'68 generation.

Hyman, Paula E. *The Jews of Modern France* (Berkeley and Los Angeles: University of California Press, 1998). A synthesis of the modern French Jewish experience.

Malino, Frances. *A Jew in the French Revolution: The Life of Zalkind Hourwitz* (Cambridge, Mass., and Oxford: Blackwell, 1996). Explores the French Revolution and the Jews through the experience of an immigrant Jewish man of the Enlightenment.

Poznanski, Renée. *Jews in France during World War II*, trans. Nathan Bracher (Hanover, NH: University Press of New England, 2001). An exhaustive study of the Holocaust in France.

Schechter, Ronald. *Obstinate Hebrews: Representations of Jews in France, 1715–1815* (Berkeley and Los Angeles: University of California Press, 2003). Offers a new interpretation of the 'Jewish Question' in French thought and politics, as well as an account of Jewish self-presentation.

Schnapper, Dominique. *Jewish Identities in France: An Analysis of Contemporary French Jewry*, trans. Arthur Goldhammer (Chicago: University of Chicago Press, 1984). A sociological analysis of the varieties of French Jewish identities in the post-war years.

13 | **British Jewry**

Miri Freud-Kandel

The modern history of Jews in Britain, their experiences of tolerance, persecution, and emancipation, differs markedly from that of Jews in continental Europe, although continental European Jewry itself was not subject to uniform processes of emancipation. Anglo-Jewry, as the predominantly London-based community is popularly known despite small contingents from elsewhere in the United Kingdom, was influenced by a number of crucial factors.

Upon resettling in Britain in 1656 the developing Jewish community was greatly affected by the presence of an established church. This served to influence both the discrimination directed against Jews and Anglo-Jewry's construction of communal and specifically religious institutions.

With some exceptions, the discriminatory legislation which Anglo-Jewry faced was not directed specifically at Jews but was aimed at all dissenters from the Church of England. These formed part of a variety of state mechanisms designed to secure the authority of the established church. Amongst other restrictions, non-Anglicans were prevented from holding public office, entering certain professions, or becoming freemen of the City of London. The 1829 Catholic Emancipation Act and subsequent reforms ameliorating the status of Christian nonconformists provided an impetus to attempts to secure full emancipation for Jews so that they could enjoy the same privileges as other non-Anglicans. The focus of Jewish efforts fell on the right for Jews to take up a seat in Parliament, from which they were precluded until 1858 by the requirement that all MPs make statutory oaths 'upon the true faith of a Christian'.

The absence of significant legislation directed specifically against Jews created an entirely voluntary Jewish community in Britain. Jews suffered from no legal requirement to associate with their religious group, hence those counted within the Jewish community were all self-identifying. However, a feature of this voluntary community was the absence of enforceable means through which Anglo-Jewry's leaders could secure the funds to finance religious provisions: synagogues, welfare organizations, or facilities such as *shechitah* (ritual slaughter of animals). With no authority to collect taxes from their members, they were reliant on voluntary contributions. Aside from charitable donations, synagogue membership fees thus became a primary method for raising the funds required to sustain the community's institutions. The importance of synagogue membership was consequently heightened, and emphasis was placed on the centralization of communal resources.

An additional feature of the voluntary community was the absence of legal sanctions which communal leaders could access to impose uniformity in religious practice within Anglo-Jewry. Although synagogue membership provided the principal means of identifying with the community, a gap developed between synagogal affiliation and religious practice. Hence, membership of an Orthodox synagogue was not necessarily concomitant with strict religious observance.

Another factor in the emergence of a gap between Jewish identity and practice in Anglo-Jewry resulted from the liberal political tradition that Jews encountered in Britain, which exerted considerable influence over the community's development. In continental Europe emancipation often appeared to take the form of a contract requiring Jews to respond appropriately to concerns regarding Jewish nationalism, particularism, and vocational propensities. In Britain, no legal mechanisms detailing the limits of the Jewish presence were outlined. This removed conditionality from Jews' experience. Anglo-Jewry's encounter with 'modernity' was thereby markedly different. They were largely freed from any burden to construct a religious identity that would enable them to view themselves as 'Englishmen and women of the Jewish persuasion'. Consequently, the theological debates that characterized the encounter with modernity of Jews, most notably in the German states, were generally missing.[1]

With few barriers in the host society encouraging Jews to discard their Jewish identity, there was an absence of any well-thought-through understanding of the theology that underpinned Jewish identity, which could have encouraged strict observance of Judaism's teachings. Allied with the low priority Anglo-Jewry traditionally placed on the provision of Jewish education, an unthinking Judaism was fostered: emphasis was placed, both at an institutional and individual level, on religious affiliation rather than the theology and practice upon which that affiliation was built. The distinction between religious identity and religious observance was thereby strengthened. Anglo-Jewry accommodated to its host society through minor, largely external, aesthetic-driven reforms. No need was perceived to address Judaism's nationalist components, and since exacting standards of religious practice were not required, reform of Jewish rituals seemed unnecessary.

This liberal idealism encountered by Jews in Britain fostered a tolerance that extended to the social, political, and economic spheres, thereby facilitating integration into the host society. However, such tolerance was subtly qualified. English society, though steadfastly genteel, was inhospitable to diversity and conceived of only one paradigm of genuine Englishness. Subsequently, although Anglo-Jewry's experience of antisemitism was more limited than in other areas of Jewish settlement, British Jews were deeply influenced by the sensibilities and institutions encountered in the English society against which they were judged. This in turn would affect their construction of Jewish identities and their attitudes towards religious practices.

Notwithstanding the particular experiences of Anglo-Jewry, it might be expected that theological ideas developed in other centres of Jewish life would have been disseminated into the Anglo-Jewish community. In fact, although certain religious leaders were able to introduce and spread foreign influences, the unthinking nature of mainstream Anglo-Jewry was such that only large-scale immigration, particularly in the 1880s and 1930s, which involved large numbers of people championing alternative ideas, forced changes upon the theology of the community.

These various factors combined to create a peculiarly British form of Judaism and Jewish identity, deeply influenced by the host culture. The experience of antisemitism, the growth of Zionism, and relations with world Jewry also took distinctive British forms. Yet the impact of various stages of immigration, and the changing role of the host society, has led to sometimes far-reaching adaptations to Anglo-Jewish norms.

Following a brief historical sketch of Anglo-Jewry's development, this chapter will focus on an examination of the community's religious make-up, considering why it has altered in the manner it has, and the impact this exerts on individuals, institutions, and the overall ideology of the community.

Historical background

After the expulsion in 1290, the earliest Jewish settlers in Britain were Sephardi Jews residing in London as New Christians. Following the outbreak of war between Britain and Spain in 1655, as self-identifying Spanish Catholics these Jews were threatened with the confiscation of their property. Perhaps emboldened by Menasseh Ben Israel's (1604–57) petitions to Cromwell to permit Jewish resettlement (1655–6), some of these Jews sought to avert their plight by revealing their Jewish identities. No official act was ever issued formally permitting the readmission of Jews to Britain, yet by the end of 1656 a number of London-based Jews had evidently received sufficient governmental assurances to worship openly as Jews. The restoration of the Stuart monarchy in 1660 did not alter the status quo, leaving Jews without any legal act guaranteeing their rights, but also enabling them to settle without restrictions.

By 1690 the steadily growing number of Ashkenazi immigrants, mostly from Central Europe, decided that they were sufficiently established to create their own synagogue, subsequently known as the Great Synagogue. By 1750, of approximately 8,000 Jews in Britain, only 2,000 were Sephardim. For a time, although the Ashkenazim had more members, the more established Sephardi community maintained its dominant position in Anglo-Jewry. However, as the size of the Sephardi community continued to remain static and its more acculturated members assimilated, severing their connections with the community, the Ashkenazim began to develop their own hierarchies that eventually enabled them to dominate Anglo-Jewry.

As the community became more established and engaged in institution-building, it formed what later became known as the Board of Deputies of British Jews, designed to improve communal representation. Like much else in Anglo-Jewry, this institution mirrored a model in the wider English society, the London Board of Dissenting Deputies, established in 1723 by nonconformist Christian groups. Formed in 1760, the Jewish Board only truly gained impetus under the presidency of Moses Montefiore (1784–1885, president 1838–74), when it was transformed into a central institution of Anglo-Jewry representing the 'Jewish position' on various issues and becoming involved in securing the final elements of emancipation.

As Anglo-Jewry became established in British society, both the community and its Board came to be perceived as capable of exerting an influence in world affairs of the Jews. Montefiore's well-publicized efforts to alleviate the plight of Jews in Damascus in 1840, following the accusations of a blood libel, and the Board's efforts to encourage the British government to intervene on behalf of many other persecuted Jews, conformed to this pattern.

By 1880 the Board represented fourteen London congregations and an additional thirteen provincial communities. Its constitution strengthened synagogue member-ship as the key determinant of affiliation to the Jewish community, since initially the only Jewish bodies that could elect deputies were synagogues. Jews identifying with Anglo-Jewry through alternative means have remained under-represented.

The radical transformation of Anglo-Jewry that occurred as a result of mass immigration from Eastern Europe between 1881 and 1914 increased the Board's activities, but also highlighted its inability to represent the entire community, which became split between its so-called native and immigrant elements. By the mid-nineteenth century Jews from Eastern Europe had already created a number of their own *chevrot*—societies—which were small, independent, places of worship, free from the Anglicized forms of religious service that characterized established synagogues. The explosion in Eastern European immigration from 1881 strengthened this sector of the community and irrevocably altered Anglo-Jewry.

By the time the First World War brought immigration to a halt, the Jewish community in Britain had quadrupled in size, from approximately 60,000 to more than 250,000. The London Jewish community, estimated to number 46,000 in 1880, grew to 135,000 in 1900, of whom 120,000 were resident in the East End. By 1914, notwithstanding the impact of the 1905 Aliens Act, it had further expanded to 180,000. A survey of London Jewry in 1883 calculated that more than half of the community was native-born and could be classified as middle-class or above.[2] By 1904 an analysis of weddings registered in Anglo-Jewish synagogues found that 71 per cent of the participants were now immigrants.[3]

This mass immigration incited a wave of popular anti-alien feeling, associated with the immigrant Jews' foreignness, unsanitary living conditions, and concerns over their employment, perceived to contribute to sweating industries and crime. The associated antisemitic undertones further contributed to the sense of qualified tolerance which Jews experienced in British society.

The immigrants also contributed to the development of Zionism in Britain. When the British government obtained the Mandate over Palestine and issued the Balfour Declaration in 1917 (addressed to Lord Rothschild, as presumed representative of World Jewry), Anglo-Jewry split into a number of camps. In 1917 leading notables of the community, following typical anti-Zionist models, formed the League of British Jews to oppose the creation of a Jewish state which could undermine the Jews' status in Britain. In contrast, certain sections of Anglo-Jewry influenced by Britain's mandatory role and the image of liberal imperialism advocated a distinct form of British Zionism, favouring the creation of a Jewish settlement functioning with limited autonomy under the oversight of the British Empire. This represented a significant shift away from mainstream Zionist goals championed by the World Zionist Organization and British Zionists, who did not identify with the ideals of the established Anglo-Jewish community.

The established community's inclination to present a single view as '*the* Anglo-Jewish position' discouraged them from allowing alternative views to surface. Commenting on Chaim Weizmann's assertion that Zionist ideals were supported by a majority of Anglo-Jewry, a member of the established community asked with incredulity: 'Was Anglo-Jewry now to be re-defined as the numerical majority of Jews living in Britain, of foreign origins . . .?'[4] The established model of Anglo-Jewish identity was under threat.

The immigration of some 55,000 refugees from Nazi Europe, primarily German, but also Austrian and Czech, did not have the same demographic impact on Anglo-Jewry as the earlier Eastern European immigration. However, it further contributed to changes in the religious contours of the community which the Eastern European immigration had set in motion. Ultimately this would influence the fragmentation of Anglo-Jewry.

The post-Second World War expansion of communist Europe brought a number of Hasidic immigrants to Britain, bolstering the development of right-wing Orthodox secessionist communities who developed strongholds around Stamford Hill, Gateshead, and Manchester. The Hasidim have slowly increased their influence over right-wing Orthodox institutions in Anglo-Jewry, superseding the German-style Orthodoxy that had dominated previously. Generally these communities have maintained separatist institutions which keep them apart from mainstream Anglo-Jewry. The growth of Habad-Lubavitch communities represents something of an exception. Engaging in 'outreach', to encourage Jews to adopt a strict Orthodoxy, they have infiltrated mainstream Anglo-Jewry, establishing Habad houses on a number of university campuses and supporting the appointment of Habad rabbis in numerous United Synagogue pulpits.[5]

In the aftermath of the Second World War, Anglo-Jewry was influenced by Britain's changing role in Europe, the break-up of the British Empire, and the creation of the Commonwealth. The latter development has enabled Anglo-Jewry to maintain its strong ties with Jewish communities in Australia, New Zealand, Canada, and South Africa. However, the traditional links, which were established as these communities had developed in the nineteenth century and relied on the British chief rabbi for religious decisions, and indeed for the authorization of new congregations, are fading.

Attempts at enhancing relations with European Jewish communities have included the creation of the European Conference of Rabbis in 1957, which Israel Brodie (1895–1979), the incumbent chief rabbi, took the initiative in establishing. Leo Baeck College's training of rabbis for Progressive communities across Europe achieves a similar effect. Britain's entry into the European Union has also provided opportunities to develop this link, although they have yet to be fully realized.

In religious terms Anglo-Jewry has differed markedly from Jewish communities elsewhere, developing peculiarly English forms of traditional and progressive Judaism. At the turn of the twenty-first century these models have come under threat, as Victorian-era institutions have sought to deal with a changing community subject to different influences.

Religious identities

Reform and Liberal Judaism

The prime motivation in the establishment of the first Reform synagogue in Britain, the West London Synagogue of British Jews, created in 1842, was the desire to create a synagogue in the West End of London, to cater for Jews who had moved out of the original area of settlement in the East End. The members of this new synagogue came from both the Sephardi and Ashkenazi communities, frustrated by both communities' failure to serve the needs of sections of their membership. The founders rebelled against restrictions on the establishment of new synagogues, which might poach members from pre-existing congregations. However, the absence of a principled public debate on Jewish emancipation in Britain removed the compulsion to develop a theological debate along the lines of the Reform thought that was contemporaneously emerging in the German states. Hence, the only significant religious reform introduced initially was the abolition of observance of the second day of festivals. Nonetheless, efforts were made to improve the aesthetic nature of religious services, enhance religious instruction, primarily through the introduction of sermons, and implement certain limited reforms

Reform synagogues were subsequently formed in Manchester (1856) and Bradford (1873), but it was not until the arrival of Reform Jews as refugees from Nazi Europe that Reform in Britain developed a more comprehensive theology. The immigrants included thirty-five trained rabbis, who initiated a Reform *bet din* (court of law) and a seminary to train English and European rabbis (Leo Baeck College). The cultivation of fledgling communities was also facilitated by the presence of rabbis willing to assist and serve nascent Reform communities.

Prior to these changes, the inherent conservatism of British Reform encouraged the creation of an independent Liberal form of Judaism in Britain. Emerging out of the Jewish Religious Union (JRU), formed in 1902, Liberal Judaism was created by Lily Montagu (1873–1963) and Claude Goldsmid Montefiore (1858–1938). The JRU sought to provide a more universalist, less ritualistic interpretation of Judaism. Theologically closer to Classical Reform, the JRU was also influenced by the liberal theology of Unitarianism. It focused on individual autonomy, and emphasized the prophetic message of the Hebrew Scriptures whilst rejecting their divine authority or authorship. The reforms went too far for members of the West London Synagogue, who refused to allow services to be held on their premises, leading to the eventual creation of an independent Movement For the Advancement of Liberal Judaism in 1909. Although its co-operation with Reform increased through the twentieth century, the two movements remain distinct entities striving for recognition and influence in a community that continues to be dominated by Orthodoxy.

The gradual strengthening of Progressive Judaism empowered it to seek to assert its voice more forcefully, including agitation for better representation on the Board of Deputies, which it had struggled to achieve from the outset when Moses Montefiore prevented the West London Synagogue from appointing deputies. In 1971 the Board approved a constitutional change facilitating consultation with non-Orthodox religious authorities. Sections of the Orthodox community walked out in protest, undermining the Board's attempt to be fully representative and illustrating the difficulties involved. The 1971 ruling was later undermined by a 1984 ruling guaranteeing that consultation with Progressives would not lead to the promulgation of positions which conflicted with the chief rabbi. The struggle between Orthodoxy and Progressives thus continues.

Anglo-Jewish Orthodoxy

The presumptive dominance of Orthodox Judaism in Anglo-Jewry has been influenced by the nature of British Jews' emancipation, the model of an established church, and the inclusiveness fostered in a voluntary community. The major institutions of Anglo-Jewry were intended to cultivate a unified community, with highly developed lay and religious hierarchies which sought to impose control but were also open to all who wished to affiliate and contribute synagogue membership fees. Although there were always divisions—between Sephardim and Ashkenazim, between native and immigrant groups, and between reformers and traditionalists—the attempt to project a single Anglo-Jewish voice represented an important principle of the community.

The office of chief rabbi ostensibly evolved in the religious sphere to represent the religious views of the community. However, instead of appointing the most prestigious halakhic authority, the lay leadership of Anglo-Jewry, influenced by Anglican church models rather than traditional Jewish practice, sought to create a representative figurehead who could provide a suitable image for the community and share a platform with church leaders. The actual authority vested in the Chief Rabbinate was limited, as the *Jewish Chronicle*, the weekly newspaper of the community created in 1841, noted: 'It did not derive any of its real authority and grandeur from man-made laws of the State or from official authority and sanction. Its power and influence depended entirely upon the character and achievements of the incumbent of the office, which means, in effect, that its authority was personal and intimate.'[6]

The first formally elected chief rabbi, Nathan Marcus Adler (1803–91), born in Hanover, was appointed in 1845 by a committee of delegates from the major London Ashkenazi synagogues and twenty-one representatives of provincial congregations. Following his appointment, assessing the nature of the community he had been elected to lead, he published a detailed outline for religious governance in Anglo-Jewry. His regulations sought to centralize and concentrate all religious authority in his own office, sensing that Anglo-Jewry lacked the religious substance to maintain independent communities in the various port cities and industrial centres where Jews outside London settled. The *dayanim* (judges) of the Bet Din were explicitly relegated to a position subservient to the authority of Adler's office. The appointment of new religious functionaries by synagogues under the chief rabbi's control also fell under his supervision. In 1855 Adler secured funding for the creation of Jews' College, an educational institute designed to produce Jewish ministers for the community. Designated by the title 'reverend', they oversaw the daily pastoral needs of their communities but were entirely subordinate in religious matters to the chief rabbi, lacking the halakhic training to obtain the *semikhah* (rabbinic ordination) that would have qualified them to make halakhic judgements.

When Adler was succeeded by his son, Hermann (1839–1911), in 1891, the pattern of dominance from the centre was reinforced and the influence of Anglican church models was heightened. The chief rabbi and his ministers adopted the religious dress of their Christian counterparts, adorning themselves with clerical collars, and Adler came to view Anglo-Jewry, and in fact all Jewish communities in the Empire, as a single communion over which he stood as prelate.

The formal amalgamation in 1870 of the major Ashkenazi London communities into a single synagogal movement, the United Synagogue, enhanced the image of a community in harmony with its host society. The formation of the United Synagogue was driven by the concerns of a voluntary community, conscious of the importance of unity to secure survival, influenced by the role of the established church, and designed to function as an umbrella organization in which all Jews who were willing to affiliate, regardless of their levels of personal observance, could be included.

In the 1880s the immigrants arriving in Britain encountered a Jewish community characterized by Anglicized forms of Jewish worship, in cathedral synagogues, ministered over by reverends attired in clerical robes, overseen by a single chief rabbi in whom all religious authority was vested. The low levels of observance permitted in ostensibly Orthodox institutions, which prioritized religious affiliation over theology and practice, led some immigrants to question the religious leadership that had enabled this situation to develop. In particular, the standards of *kashrut* maintained under the supervision of the chief rabbi were questioned. The immigrants thus began a process that would undermine the centrist Orthodox hegemony that had traditionally dominated the community's umbrella institutions, changing the shape of Anglo-Jewry.

The Federation of Synagogues, established in 1887, sought to maintain the immigrants' more intimate, traditional, and less Anglicized forms of worship whilst pooling resources to improve the conditions in which services were held. Although independent of the United Synagogue and only sometimes accepting the authority of the chief rabbi, this immigrant-oriented institution generally remained aligned with Anglo-Jewry's centrist Orthodoxy. The emergence of other immigrant bodies, disinclined to foster the traditional Anglo-Jewish values of unity and inclusiveness, would have greater impact in inculcating religious polarization.

The Machzike Hadath, an immigrant body formed in 1891, through the merging of two chevrot, was established to question the religious authority of the chief rabbi, criticizing his superintendence of shechitah. Central control over shechitah provided an important source of communal revenue, making this a major issue. The secessionist Adath Yisroel congregation emerged out of this group and later formed the Union of Orthodox Hebrew Congregations (UOHC). Created in 1926 as an independent synagogal movement determinedly on the right wing of Anglo-Jewish Orthodoxy, UOHC provided further impetus to attempts to displace the image of Anglo-Jewry as a unified body, represented in the religious sphere by the chief rabbi. This group was spurred into action by the disparity it encountered in mainstream Anglo-Jewry between superficial Orthodox dominance and the reality of lax observance. Its position was strengthened by the arrival of refugees from Nazi Europe who had been members of the Austrittsgemeinde (secessionist communities) of Germany and Austria on which UOHC was modelled.

Following the Shoah's destruction of the traditional European centres of Jewish life and learning, these Orthodox sectors in Anglo-Jewry came to view their activities as having heightened significance. Perceiving themselves as amongst the last bastions of European Orthodoxy, the self-importance with which they conducted their activities increased, which has also influenced the stringency of their religious decision-making. The development of independent communities, questioning both the validity and also the long-term viability of the centrist, umbrella-oriented stance preserved in mainstream Anglo-Jewish Orthodoxy, therefore flourished.

The influence of these right-wing groups has extended across a broader spectrum of the community as a result of the traditional unthinking nature of the community. With little value ascribed to religious learning and the rabbinate, centrist Orthodox institutions have often relied on external appointments of rabbis and dayanim. This has facilitated the growing influence of ideas which are unrepresentative of traditional Anglo-Jewry over the community. The traditional inclusive, centrist principles of Anglo-Jewish Orthodoxy's umbrella institutions have thus been undermined.

A similar process of strengthening, which has nonetheless introduced significant change in the traditional makeup of sectors of Anglo-Jewish Orthodoxy, has occurred amongst the Sephardim. In the 1950s the Sephardi community was reinforced, but also reshaped, as Jews from Arab countries and outposts of the Empire emigrated to Britain and came to outnumber those who practised the Spanish and Portuguese *minhag*. By the turn of the twenty-first century Sephardi synagogues and many other communal provisions have burgeoned. The proud Spanish and Portuguese community, which had been the first to resettle in Britain, was revitalized by this immigration. However, its attempts to maintain its established traditions are now reliant on the beneficence of Sephardi Jews with very different traditions to those which initially dominated this highly Anglicized community.

Masorti

A Conservative form of Judaism was only introduced into Britain in the 1960s, created by members of the United Synagogue who chose to secede to establish the New London Synagogue, the forerunner of Masorti Judaism in Britain, under the leadership of Louis Jacobs (b. 1920). This development was precipitated by the so-called 'Jacobs Affair', which revolved, at least in theory, around the correct interpretation of the Jewish principle of revelation, 'Torah min hashamayim'. Jacobs argued, in a book entitled *We Have Reason To Believe*, that Orthodoxy was wrongly caught up in a genetic fallacy (a misplaced focus on origins rather than content) in its insistence on a literal interpretation of divine revelation. Acknowledging the findings of critical scholarship, Jacobs asserted that a reinterpretation of 'Torah min hashamayim' need not undermine traditional Jewish practice, or even traditional conceptions of God.

These views were deemed to place Jacobs outside the fold of Orthodox Judaism, preventing his appointment as principal of Jews' College and his return to the pulpit of a United Synagogue congregation, which created a public furore. Yet in some respects what was really at stake during the Jacobs Affair was not theology but the question of who would define Orthodox Judaism for the Anglo-Jewish community. Although Jacobs's views pushed the boundaries of Orthodox Judaism to their limits, through his actions he was attempting to address genuine issues faced by modern Jews as they sought to balance their engagement in both Jewish and non-Jewish spheres of thought. As in earlier periods, the community as a whole invested no energy in constructing theological responses to the perplexities created by encouraging Jewish participation in British society. Such interaction could lead to a questioning of the fundamental religious principles on which Jewish identities were built, and Jacobs sought to tackle these issues and thereby address a core constituency of Anglo-Jewry. However, rather than discussing the ideas Jacobs developed, the Affair appeared to be driven by a battle between the constituent elements of Anglo-Jewish Orthodoxy: the representatives of the old values of an inclusive, centrist Orthodoxy, and those who aligned themselves with a more right-wing Orthodox position, who viewed the laxity permitted under the 'umbrella' of Anglo-Jewry as inappropriate and incapable of sustaining Orthodox Judaism.

Initially Masorti portrayed itself as the true inheritor of Anglo-Jewish values which Anglo-Jewish Orthodoxy had spurned. It has since experienced modest growth, leading in 1984 to the formation of the Masorti Assembly of Synagogues and in 2002 to the publication of *Darkenu—The Masorti Vision*, seeking to encapsulate the movement's developing theology.

A community in decline?

The centrist Orthodoxy of Anglo-Jewry has continued to lose ground. Although there has been a religious revival in some spheres, this has been accompanied by an overall diminution of the community. The centre is shrinking fastest, but Anglo-Jewry as a whole is diminishing. From a peak population after the Second World War of approximately 400,000, Anglo-Jewry has contracted to around 250,000, and dissension is growing.

Between 1900 and 1940 97 per cent of Anglo-Jewish marriages occurring in synagogues were held under the auspices of 'Central Orthodoxy', incorporating the United Synagogue and Federation. By 1975 this figure had fallen to 70 per cent. The number of marriages carried out under Liberal and Reform auspices had risen to 22 per cent; and 6 per cent were carried out by 'right-wing Orthodoxy'.[7] In 2002 centrist Orthodoxy's share had fallen to 53 per cent, UOHC had ballooned to account for 24 per cent, and Reform and Liberals performed 17 per cent.[8] The once-dominant centre is thus en route to becoming a minority position.

In 1992 a review of the United Synagogue found that the institution was facing a financial crisis, largely caused by a significant decline in membership. In 2002 it was the turn of Jews' College to face financial difficulties, which forced it to end its rabbinical training programme. Throughout this period the Chief Rabbinate stumbled from one calamity to another, in controversies over women's rights in Orthodox Judaism, relations with Progressive Jews, relations with the religious right, and even charges of heresy.

These communal disputes have undermined the Chief Rabbinate's already dwindling ability to function as representative of the many voices now emerging in the community. In a New Year address to the Board of Deputies in 2003, Chief Rabbi Jonathan Sacks (b. 1948) sought to defend the right of the Board, advised on religious matters by the Chief Rabbinate, to speak on behalf of all Anglo-Jewry and present a united view as representative of all sections of the community. He argued that the promulgation of multiple Jewish views would serve only to drown each other out. However, it is highly doubtful that a single view can be presented. In the continued absence of Anglo-Jewish support for public debate on theological matters, the community is uncertain where it stands. Subject to diverse influences from within the community and also from Israel and America, the distinctive values of Anglo-Jewry are disintegrating.

Whilst these changes could be seen to point to a community in decline, whose shift from its traditional values has undermined individuals, institutions, and overall ideology, there are signs of positive developments. The growth of a cultural Jewish identity has strengthened amongst British Jews, unrelated to the traditional Anglo-Jewish focus on synagogue membership. Limmud, an annual conference for all sections of the Anglo-Jewish community, promotes a diverse range of educational and cultural activities, attracting increasing numbers of British Jews interested in exploring varied aspects of their Jewish identities. Alternative adult-educational programmes are flourishing. An annual cycle of Jewish cultural festivals has evolved from Jewish Book Week, celebrating Jewish contributions to the arts, literature, and film. As Britain has begun to celebrate its multiculturalism, British Jews are developing proud, secure Jewish identities. There are greater numbers of Jewish children in more Jewish schools than ever before, and Jewish studies programmes in universities have multiplied. These developments are often causes of dissension though, rather than being celebrated as evidence of a flourishing community.

Diverse elements within the community are thriving in their individual domains as Jews in Britain reassess the nature of their Jewish identities and the character of Anglo-Jewry as a whole. As a unit Anglo-Jewry is in decline, but within its individual constituencies it shows signs of strengthening, developing new, sustainable Jewish identities.

FURTHER READING

For general overviews of the Jewish community in Britain, see G. Alderman, *Modern British Jewry* (Oxford: Clarendon Press, 1992); and T. M. Endelman, *The Jews of Britain 1656–2000* (London: University of California Press, 2002). Endelman provides more detailed analysis of Anglo-Jewry in his *Radical Assimilation in English Jewish History: 1656–1945* (Bloomington: Indiana University Press, 1990), and *The Jews of Georgian England: Tradition and Change in a Liberal Society, 1714–1830* (Ann Arbor: University of Michigan Press, 1999). A number of interesting essays are collected in a selection of books treating Anglo-Jewry. These include D. Cesarani (ed.), *The Making of Modern Anglo-Jewry* (Oxford: Basil Blackwell, 1990) S. S. Levin (ed.), *A Century of Anglo-Jewish Life 1870–1970* (London: United Synagogue, 1971).

Endelman, T. M., and A. Kushner (eds.). *Disraeli's Englishness* (London: Vallentine Mitchell, 2002). An interesting examination of the construction of Anglo-Jewish identities and the influence of the host society's attitudes. See also David B. Ruderman, *Jewish Enlightenment in an English Key: Anglo-Jewry's Construction of Modern Jewish Thought* (Princeton and Oxford: Princeton University Press, 2000). A critique of many standard historiographical accounts of Anglo-Jewry's intellectual development and its relation to the development of modern Jewish thought in Europe.

Freud-Kandel, M. J. *An Ideology Forsaken: Theological Shifts in Anglo-Jewish Orthodoxy* (London: Vallentine Mitchell, 2005). An in-depth analysis of the twentieth-century development of the Orthodox community in Britain and the role of the Chief Rabbinate.

Homa, Bernard. *A Fortress in Anglo-Jewry: The Story of the Machzike Adath* (London: Shapiro, Valentine & Co., 1953). One of a number of works by this author detailing the development of the right-wing Orthodoxy in Britain.

Jacobs, L. *We Have Reason To Believe* (London: Vallentine Mitchell [1957], 2004). The book which set off the 'Jacobs Affair'; later editions contain a summary of the events which made up the affair.

Kershen, A. J., and J. A. Romain. *Tradition and Change: A History of Reform Judaism in Britain 1840–1995* (London: Vallentine Mitchell, 1995). A good history of the development of Reform in Britain.

Mosse, Werner E. *et al.* (eds.). *Second Chance: Two Centuries of German-Speaking Jews in the United Kingdom* (Tubingen: J. C. B. Mohr, 1991). A selection of interesting essays on the influence of German Jews in Anglo-Jewry.

Roth, C. *History of the Jews of England*, 1st edn. (Oxford: Oxford University Press, 1941). This represents the classic account of Anglo-Jewish history, albeit with little consideration of the community following the impact of immigration after the 1880s. It has subsequently been subjected to a historiographical critique for the apologetic tone it adopts.

Williams, B. *The Making of Manchester Jewry: 1740–1875* (Manchester: Manchester University Press, 1976). An account of the development of one of Anglo-Jewry's major provincial communities.

NOTES

1. David Ruderman's study of a number of Jewish thinkers in Britain who addressed a variety of issues that emerged in the eighteenth and nineteenth centuries suggests that some attempts were made by Anglo-Jewry to construct modern Jewish thought. Nonetheless, as Ruderman himself acknowledges, the activities of these individuals never coalesced to form an intellectual movement in Anglo-Jewry. See in particular his *Jewish Enlightenment in an English Key: Anglo-Jewry's Construction of Modern Jewish Thought* (Princeton and Oxford: Princeton University Press, 2000).

2. Cited by T. M. Endelman, *Radical Assimilation in English Jewish History: 1656–1945* (Bloomington: Indiana University Press, 1990), p. 74.

3. S. J. Prais and M. Schmool, 'Statistics of Jewish Marriages in Great Britain: 1901–1965', *Jewish Journal of Sociology*, 9: 2 (Dec. 1967).

4. Robert Henriques, *Sir Robert Waley Cohen 1877–1952: A Biography* (London: Secker & Warburg, 1966), p. 263.

5. See Chap. 17 for further consideration of Habad activities.

6. *Jewish Chronicle*, 18 Jan. 1946.

7. S. J. Prais, 'Polarisation or Decline? A Discussion of Some Statistical Findings on the Community' in Lipman and Lipman (eds.), *Jewish Life in Britain 1962–77* (New York: K. G. Saur, 1981).

8. Report on Community Vital Statistics for 2002, Board of Deputies, p. 3. These figures include the figures for Masorti marriages within Central Orthodoxy.

14 | Jewry in the former Soviet Union

John Klier

The Jews in Tsarist Russia

The depiction of the Russian Empire as a uniquely antisemitic state was the creation of Jewish historians writing early in the twentieth century, who spoke of 'traditional Russian religious antisemitism'. Russian tsars sought to convert the Jews to Christianity by coercion (military recruitment and legal discrimination, especially the Pale of Settlement regulations that barred most Jews from residing in the Russian interior), and monetary rewards. Only at the end of the nineteenth century was religious Jew-hatred secularized, and given a political colouration. Equating Jewry with revolution, Russian state officials incited deadly anti-Jewish riots, the pogroms, seeking 'to drown the Russian revolution in Jewish blood'. Educated Russian society was receptive to the lure of ideological antisemitism. The 'dark masses', sunk in poverty, ignorance, and superstition, were easy prey for instigators of anti-Jewish outrages.

Contemporary historians have challenged this narrative. They argue that, following the partitions of Poland when Russia acquired a Jewish population at the end of the eighteenth century, Russian policy shared Enlightenment-era assumptions about the Jews. Jews were to be pitied as victims of centuries of religious persecution, even while it was recognized that this persecution had corrupted them. Jews were a 'people apart', hostile to their non-Jewish neighbours. They were 'religious fanatics', whose Talmud taught them to hate the Gentiles. The Jews disdained physical labour, and were content to live as parasites—petty traders, usurers, tavern-keepers—at the expense of their Christian neighbours. The keys to resolving the 'Jewish Question' lay in weaning the Jews away from 'talmudic fanaticism', and directing them into 'productive work', especially agriculture. Russian state policy, therefore, promoted Jewish integration and assimilation, albeit in a heavy-handed manner. Efforts to block 'Jewish economic exploitation' led to the relaxation of restrictions on categories of Jews judged to be useful or productive, and the promotion of secular education among Jews. 'Unproductive' Jews were the targets of restrictive laws, such as the Pale.

The outbreak of the pogroms led the authorities to reconsider their efforts to encourage Jewish integration. The pogroms were widely interpreted as a response of the peasantry to Jewish 'exploitation', a convenient explanation for the unsettled social and economic conditions following the emancipation of the serfs in 1861.

Segregation, rather than integration, appeared to be the best defence against popular violence.

Educated Jews were also targeted. The Jews in the Russian borderlands had long been considered politically unreliable because of their close economic ties with the notoriously disloyal and restive Polish noble landowning class. In the last decades of the nineteenth century Jews joined the growing Russian revolutionary movement. Home-grown ideological hostility to the Jews easily assimilated European antisemitic stereotypes, especially from Germany. However, Russian antisemitism remained largely political and social, not racial. The perceived disloyalty of Jews made their increased use of educational opportunities, and their movement into the professions, especially law, appear to be highly undesirable. Abandoning the policies of integration, the government sought to move Jews out of the countryside, deny them ownership or lease-holding of land, strengthen the restraints of the Pale of Settlement, and limit the number allowed into secondary and higher education. Restrictions on the Jews endured even after the creation of constitutional government, with its promise of equality before the law, following the Revolution of 1905.

The Jews fared no better with the outbreak of the First World War in 1914. The war briefly united the country, but military defeat spread discord and a search for scapegoats. Much of the eastern front ran through the Pale of Settlement, exposing the Jews not only to military depredations, but also to the mistrust of the Russian military command. They were quick to accuse the Jews of spying, and prone to expel whole communities from the vicinity of the front lines. This wholesale expulsion effectively dismantled the Pale of Settlement, but it also engendered a refugee crisis.

The February Revolution of 1917, which created a short-lived democratic republic, was welcomed by many Jews. Indeed, one of the first acts of the Provisional Government was to abolish all restrictive legislation against the Jews. Although individuals of Jewish origin, most notably Leon Trotsky, played a major role in the October Revolution that brought Lenin's Bolsheviks to power, most Jewish political activists opposed the Bolshevik coup.

The political pace quickened dramatically after the Bolshevik takeover. Russia withdrew from the war and signed a punitive peace treaty with the Central Powers. National minorities, such as the Finns and Ukrainians, declared national independence. Foreign armies intervened in Russia. The former Russian Empire deteriorated into a brutal civil war (1919–21), accompanied by a brief war with Poland. Jews became targets for all the warring factions, and the civil war in the south-west was marked by numerous pogroms of unprecedented ferocity. Understandably, many Jews welcomed the victory of the Red Army since it brought peace and a semblance of order.

The Jews in the Soviet Union

Soviet power, especially in its early years, may be characterized as 'bad for the Jews, and good for the Jew'. For Jews as a religious community, with a culture based on ancient traditions, the communist regime was a disaster. Judaism, lacking a strong central religious authority, while placing great emphasis upon personal study and the performance of set rituals, was ill-equipped to defend itself against the new government's anti-religious policies, or the rapid social and economic changes the government implemented. Synagogues were closed or transformed into workers' clubs. Rabbis and religious functionaries were branded as 'parasites', and persecuted. Campaigns were directed against religious practices, such as circumcision, and educational institutions, such as the *cheder*. The use of Hebrew, while not banned, was officially discouraged. Ritual observance and the sanctity of the Sabbath were crowded out by the new rhythms of Soviet life.

For the individual Jew, in contrast, the dawn of the Soviet period offered unparalleled opportunities. Jews were denied civil-service or military careers in Tsarist Russia. The new Soviet state was in desperate need of reliable individuals to staff all levels of the state apparatus, especially if they were literate, as many Jews were. Jews flooded into party, military, and security positions. The vast majority of Soviet Jews remained poor and under-employed, and their opportunity came only with the great transformation unleashed by the first Five Year Plan at the end of the 1920s. Jewish tailors and market traders were transformed into proletarians, office workers, and administrators. Jews became the most urbanized ethnic minority in the USSR.

One can speak of Soviet Jews as an ethnic minority because they were thus defined by the state. 'Jew' (*Evrei*), became one of the ethnic categories that were included in the domestic passport. Soviet Jews, it was declared, had no links with European Jews, and still less with 'world Jewry'. They were a Soviet ethnic group bound by a common language (Yiddish), a common culture (from which the religious elements had been stripped), and a common historical fate in Eastern Europe. State-sponsored Yiddish culture reflected the Soviet dictum that it be 'national in form, Soviet in content', that is, national languages were to serve as the conduit for the transmission of communist ideals and policies. Cheders were replaced by state schools operating in Yiddish, although many Jewish parents sent their children to Russian-language schools, which provided better career opportunities. The state also created a Jewish 'national homeland' in Birobidzhan, on the Soviet–Chinese border, but it never attracted significant numbers of Jewish settlers.

Efforts to 'ethnicize' Soviet Jewry highlighted the differences between the Ashkenazim and other groups. Collectively, the latter were more rural, religious, and traditionalist, in ways resembling their non-Jewish neighbours. The Jews of Georgia, for example, spoke the local dialects. Daghestan and Azerbaidzhan were home to the 'Mountain Jews', who spoke an Iranian dialect, Judeo-Tat, and were famed for their martial traditions. The so-called 'Bukharan Jews' lived in Uzbekistan, and spoke a Tajiki-Jewish dialect of Persian. A small community of 'Krimchaks' had survived the Holocaust in the Crimean peninsula.

The Soviet Union boasted that it was the first state in the world to make antisemitism a criminal offence, but if individual Jews could seek legal redress after being called a 'dirty Yid', in other respects ethnic Jews suffered all the vicissitudes of Soviet nationality policies, especially at the start of the 1930s when national consciousness became ideologically suspect. During the Great Purges in the second half of the 1930s, Jews suffered alongside non-Jews when state repression cut a swathe through the Communist Party, the Red Army, and the security organs, as well as through the general population.

The Soviet phase of the Second World War, the so-called Great Patriotic War (1941–5), marked by the German invasion and occupation, witnessed unimaginable horrors for the entire Soviet population. An estimated 24 million Soviet citizens were killed, and many more maimed and disabled. These figures hid a special subcategory of suffering: the Nazi Holocaust carried out on Soviet soil. Approximately one-third of the 6 million Jewish victims of the Holocaust were Soviet citizens. Occupied Soviet territory became the site of Jewish ghettos and mass murder actions, such as the notorious liquidation of the Jewish population of Kiev at Babi Yar.

In an effort to generate support for the Soviet war effort among its wartime allies, the Soviets rediscovered 'world Jewry'. Soviet propaganda officials created a Jewish Anti-Fascist Committee (JAFC), headed by the well-known actor Solomon Mikhoels. The JAFC was charged with publicizing Nazi atrocities (although not necessarily those of their local collaborators), in order to strengthen support for the Soviet war effort among Jews in the Allied countries. JAFC efforts were intended to be purely propagandistic, but the JAFC unexpectedly evolved into the sole 'Jewish address' in the USSR. Jews approached the JAFC with appeals for help in locating lost relatives, to seek material assistance, or to complain about local incidents of antisemitism. The JAFC actively responded to these appeals. It published a Yiddish-language newspaper, *Eynigkayt* (Unity). The JAFC floated a proposal to designate the Crimean peninsula for settlement of Soviet Jewish survivors of the Holocaust.

In the course of the war, the Soviet people had been promised a relaxation of the ideological and material constraints that had dominated the 1930s. Instead, as the USSR and its wartime allies drifted into the Cold War, ideological reindoctrination was given priority, and the concerns of daily life were subordinated to military needs. In this climate of growing repression, foreign links were especially dangerous, as was any suspicion of 'bourgeois nationalism' among the peoples of the USSR. These conditions left the leaders of the JAFC terribly exposed. In 1948 Mikhoels died in a 'road accident' organized by the secret police. The JAFC was closed, and before the end of the year most of its members were arrested. They were secretly tried in 1952, and thirteen defendants were executed on 12 August 1952. This 'Night of the Murdered Poets', an act of cultural genocide, eliminated the Soviet Yiddish cultural leadership at a stroke. Worse was to come: on 13 January 1953 the Party newspaper *Pravda* announced that nine doctors in the Kremlin medical clinic had been arrested, charged with attempting to murder members of the ruling Politburo. Most of these 'assassins in white aprons' were Jews, prompting widespread panic that a national pogrom was in the making, to be followed by the deportation of the Jewish population to camps in Siberia or Soviet Central Asia. Within a month Stalin died, and the 'Doctors' Plot' was repudiated.

The motives underlying these events remain disputed. The repression has been linked to Soviet-Jewish support for the USSR's pro-Israel stance in 1948. Recent scholarship suggests that the cause lay in charges against the JAFC of 'bourgeois nationalism', associated with the Crimean proposal. The more serious charge of links to foreign espionage services was possibly connected to internal rivalries within the security services. New studies have failed to locate any evidence for a pogrom or forced resettlement of Soviet Jews en masse, but it has revealed a wider incidence of antisemitic incidents and repression. But whatever Stalin's long-term plans, Jews emerged from this period still well represented in Soviet academic and economic life.

The immediate post-Stalin era had to deal with the dictator's legacy of centralized control buttressed by terror. While the Doctors' Plot was formally repudiated, Stalin's successors did little to remedy the climate of antisemitism created during this period. Growing Soviet hostility to the State of Israel was exacerbated by the sweeping Israeli victory in the Six Day War of 1967 over Arab states armed and supported by the USSR. Soviet propaganda attributed this victory to the support Israel had received from the USSR's capitalist enemies. 'Zionism' was identified as an especially dangerous ideological foe. Distinctions made between 'Zionists' and 'Jews' were lost on Soviet Jews, just as they were on the Soviet population as a whole. Ironically, Soviet emphasis on the might and power of Israel made it a source of pride for many Soviet Jews. A combination of fear and pride motivated a small number of Soviet Jews to demand the right to emigrate to Israel.

The Soviet Union, pressed by world opinion on issues of human rights, made the fateful decision in 1966 to permit emigration, justifying this as 'the reunification of families'. Having conceded the principle of emigration, the Soviet leadership found it impossible to control when a growing number of Soviet Jews sought to leave. The emigration of Soviet Jews to Israel threatened a 'brain drain' of skilled personnel, and outraged the USSR's Arab allies. A massive outflow undermined the USSR's self-proclaimed status as 'the workers' paradise'. The various ruses that the Soviets adopted to discourage emigration—excessive bureaucratic demands, a hefty 'education tax', the dismissal of would-be emigrants from employment—served only to produce a body of victims, the so-called 'Refuseniks', whose plight became a cause célèbre abroad. Foreign Jewish groups mobilized world opinion under the slogans 'Let my people go!' and 'Save Soviet Jewry'. The campaign's greatest success occurred in 1972–4, when the United States Congress attached an amendment to a Soviet–American trade treaty which required the USSR to permit greater emigration (and scuppered the treaty).

The emigration movement reinforced the identity of many Soviet Jews. It also produced an ongoing debate as to the nature and implications of this identity. Should Jews seek only to emigrate to Israel, or should they work to create a Jewish space in the USSR? To what extent should Jews aim to revive religious and cultural traditions? Was it legitimate for fully assimilated Jews to use their imposed ethnic identity as a passport to a better material life in the West? Soviet Jews faced the central query of modern Jewish identity: 'what does it mean to be a Jew?'

Decline and fall of the Soviet Union

The emergence of the policies of *glasnost* (openness) and *perestroika* (reform) sponsored by Mikhail Gorbachev from 1987 had serious repercussions for Soviet Jews. In an effort to improve Soviet–American relations, the regime relaxed emigration restrictions. Committed Zionists, as well as those who sought a better economic life and greater political or personal freedom, left in large numbers. For the millions of Soviet Jews who chose to remain, Gorbachev's efforts to create a new civil society, less constrained by rigid orthodoxy and centralized control, offered new opportunities to shape a specifically Jewish life, whether based on religious, ethnic, or communal principles. There was no shortage of advice and assistance from foreign Jewish groups. Synagogues began to reopen in the guise of both houses of worship and community centres. Following on from local initiatives, primarily in the Baltic States, Soviet Jews began to create national bodies, exemplified by the Association of Jewish Organizations and Communities of the Soviet Union (the Vaad of the USSR) founded in 1989, and by 1991 numbering 250 institutional members. A special role in the reassertion of a Jewish consciousness was played by a burgeoning Jewish press, primarily published in Russian. Some of these newspapers, such as the *Evreiskaia gazeta* (Jewish Newspaper) in Moscow and *Ami/Narod moi* (My People) in Leningrad, sought to play national leadership roles.

The emergence of the national movements that portended the break-up of the Soviet Union created special problems. Soviet Jews were among the most 'soviet' of Soviet citizens. Lacking a territorial homeland, they were scattered all over the USSR, especially in the capital cities of the union's republics. They were firmly embedded in the Soviet economy, and they had assimilated Russian culture. There were differences between the Jewish populations of the pre-1940 Soviet republics and those added after 1940, such as the Baltic republics of Estonia, Latvia, and Lithuania. Lithuania in particular had once had a large and dynamic Jewish population, much of which had been exterminated by Nazi genocide. Lithuania's post-war Jewish population comprised a surviving core of Yiddish- and Lithuanian-speaking 'natives', and a community of Russian-speaking Jews who were part of the post-war Soviet colonization of the Baltic States. Significant 'native' Jewish populations had survived the war in Belorussia and

Ukraine; they could declare Yiddish, Ukrainian, Belorussian, or Russian as their native language. A wide range of identities was clearly on offer. In Ukraine, for example, one might be either a 'Soviet Jew', a 'Ukrainian Jew', a 'Soviet-Ukrainian Jew', or a fully assimilated Russian or Ukrainian. This situation was not unique to Jews, but was especially pertinent given their status as a diaspora nationality even within the internal ethnic borders of the USSR.

As the existence of the USSR drew to a close, most citizens of the pre-1940 Soviet Union expressed support for its continuation in some form, as evidenced by the Gorbachev-sponsored referendum in 1991. In contrast, the citizens of the Baltic States and the western Ukraine were much more nationalistic and anti-Soviet. The anti-Gorbachev coup of 1991 allowed the president of the Russian Federation, Boris Yeltsin, to expedite the formal break-up of the USSR into independent states and autonomous regions at the end of 1991. The situation of Jews outside the Russian Federation became straightforward: those who wished to maintain a Jewish identity were obliged to do so in the context of their new national states. Those who rejected a Jewish identity either assimilated entirely into the 'native' ethnic population or became 'Russians in the Near Abroad'.

Jews in the former Soviet Union

The demise of East European Jewry has often been predicted by observers who point to the demographic profile of an ageing population, widespread assimilation, and mass out-migration. Whatever the apparent long-term trends, however, the Former Soviet Union (FSU) will continue for some time to have one of the world's largest Jewish populations. For statistical purposes, demographers define 'Jews' by arbitrary categories, such as the halakhic definition, synagogue or association affiliation, or Soviet-era ethnic categories. The FSU Jewish population itself, however, tends to be very inclusive. In practical terms, the most useful category may be 'Jews by choice', identifying those who, for whatever reason, claim a Jewish identity. It is these self-defined individuals who will ultimately decide the survival or disappearance of a significant Jewish community in Eastern Europe.

The phenomenon of emigration, especially to Israel, has proved to be more problematical than predicted. Many of the almost 1 million Jewish immigrants to Israel from the Soviet Union and the FSU have been highly educated, imbued with the values of a sophisticated culture, and accompanied by numerous family members who cannot be considered Jews by any of the usual criteria. These realities have ensured that the process of absorption into Israeli society has not followed the patters of earlier *aliyot*. The *olim* (immigrants) from the FSU have created a distinct cultural community in Israel, with its own infrastructure (press and electronic media, internet sites, shops and restaurants) and a growing political influence. Moreover, the post-Soviet situation has enabled many olim to maintain or develop family, cultural, and financial links to the FSU. These mutual influences will have a continuing impact on Jews in Israel and in the FSU.

While the question of a possible Jewish revival in the FSU is best explored on a regional basis, a number of factors are at work in all the Soviet successor states, exemplified by the efforts of three ubiquitous institutions: the Sokhnut, the Joint, and Habad-Lubavitch.

The Jewish Agency for Israel (Sokhnut) is a Zionist organization whose ultimate goal is the emigration of Jews to Israel, an agenda it pursued energetically as the Soviet Union was collapsing. Aware that many Jews at present intend to remain in the FSU, the Jewish Agency has received certification from the Russian government, and devotes more attention to educational initiatives, especially the creation and maintenance of Jewish primary schools.

The American Jewish Joint Distribution Committee (the Joint) was the principal twentieth-century Jewish welfare institution in Eastern Europe, despite post-Second World War bans in the USSR and Eastern Europe. With the collapse of communism, the Joint became the chief source for humanitarian assistance to Jews in the region. It financed community centres, Hesed welfare centres for the provision of food and clothing to elderly Jews, and a wide series of educational initiatives, ranging from financing Jewish kindergartens to support for Sefer, the Moscow-based umbrella group promoting the spread and professionalization of Jewish studies in higher education in the FSU.

The branch of the Hasidic movement known as Habad-Lubavitch has adopted as a special mission the revival of Jewish religious life in Eastern Europe. Habad possesses a great advantage over other branches of Judaism, including both the Orthodox and Progressive traditions, because of its ability to supply rabbis on a long-term basis for congregations throughout the FSU. In 1994 the movement withdrew from the Orthodox-dominated Congress of Religious Organisations and Congregations in Russia, and created the Federation of Jewish Communities of Russia (FJCR). In 2000 the FJCR precipitated the 'rabbi wars', when it named Berl Lazar as the chief rabbi of Russia although there was already an Orthodox holder of the post, Abraham Shaevich, a veteran of the Soviet era. A similar dispute occurred in Ukraine in 2003, when the Habad-dominated Congress of Ukrainian Rabbis sought to replace the serving chief rabbi of Ukraine, Yaakov Dov Bleich, with the Habad rabbi Azrael Haikin. As these disputes reveal, the office of chief rabbi in Eastern Europe holds no real power, but is a highly symbolic and prestigious post.

The Russian Federation

Post-Soviet Russian Jewry spawned a plethora of organizations, whose creation represented the emergence of a new generation of communal leaders, 'the Vaad generation', replacing the former Refusenik leaders and the 'Official Jews' of Soviet times. In the wider society, individuals of Jewish descent (whose origins always became widely known) played very prominent roles in the political and economic changes that marked life in the new Russia. Especially noteworthy was the emergence of the so-called 'Oligarchs', many of whom were of Jewish origin. The Oligarchs made vast fortunes out of the skilful manipulation of the privatization of Soviet-era industries, especially in the gas and oil sector. Some Oligarchs sought to translate their economic power into political power. Two of them, Boris Berezovskii and Vladimir Gusinskii, built substantial media empires.

The Soviet-era umbrella group, the Vaad, broke up into national bodies, the largest of which was the Association of Jewish Organizations and Communities of the Russian Federation (the Russian Vaad). Initially, the Russian Vaad concentrated on issues of emigration, and documentation of and resistance to manifestations of antisemitism. (It might be noted here that successive Russian governments have made little effort to repress minor but widespread antisemitic incidents in Russia, such as the vandalizing of synagogues and cemeteries, antisemitic graffiti, and occasional hooliganism. No action was taken against antisemitic publications or rhetoric. On the other hand, no post-Soviet political movement has been able to use antisemitism as a effective means of political mobilization.) Jewish religious life produced its own umbrella organizations, the Orthodox Congress of Jewish Religious Organizations and Communities of Russia (1993), the Progressive Congress of Jewish Religious Organizations and Communities of Russia (1995), and the Habad-dominated Federation of Jewish Communities in Russia (1999).

Most Russian Jews supported President Boris Yeltsin both in his confrontation with the Russian parliament (Duma) in 1993, and in his electoral struggles with the Communist Party in 1996. They saw Yeltsin as the best guarantor of democratic ideals that would protect Russian Jewry. The Oligarchs, led by Berezovskii, supported Yeltsin because his system allowed them wealth, power, and influence. Although only a few of the Oligarchs, chiefly Gusinskii, took an interest in Jewish affairs, Jewish communal institutions were drawn into political infighting. Incidents such as the 'rabbi wars' of 2000 were as much political as religious. In the post-Yeltsin era, the FJCR became the Jewish communal organization favoured by the government of President Vladimir Putin.

In 1996 the 'Vaad generation' was joined by another group claiming communal leadership. These were those Oligarchs, like Gusinskii, who offered resources to the Russian-Jewish community. Gusinskii and other Russian-Jewish businessmen founded the Russian Jewish Congress (RJC) in 1996, with a range of charitable and representational objectives. The creation of the RJC was highly symbolic, because it represented a domestic initiative, not dependent upon the resources of foreign organizations. In its first seven years the RJC announced that it had raised and dispensed over 63 million dollars. The RJC managed to survive the fall and exile of Gusinskii. He was replaced as president in 2001 by the Jewish businessman and activist Evgeny Satanovskii. Gusinskii's rise and fall was repeated in 2003 when another Jewish

Oligarch, the oil magnate Mikhail Khodokovskii, who financed the liberal political opposition as well as many Jewish organizations and institutions, was arrested by the Putin government.

Another development with much potential for Jewish communal life in Russia was the passage of a law in the Duma on 'National-Cultural Autonomy', which promised support and resources for 'diaspora groups' within the Russian Federation, such as Ukrainians, Armenians, or Tatars. Jews, as the archetypal 'diaspora nationality', were an obvious candidate. A number of provincial Jewish communities, as in Sverdlovsk Region, began the process of registering as a 'national autonomy', and in 1999 a group of activists formed the Federal Jewish National-Cultural Autonomy. It remains to be seen if the various 'national autonomies' will received the promised governmental support and resources, specifically for the support of schools organized by the various nationalities.

The Euro-Asian Jewish Congress, formed in 2002 and headed by the leaders of the Ukrainian and Russian Vaads (Joseph Zissels and Mikhail Chlenov), seeks to function as a transnational body that will represent the interests of all Jewish communities in the region. A successful EAJK could establish East European Jewry as a substantial force among international Jewish organizations.

It should be stressed that none of the central institutions of Russian Jewry has ever possessed substantial political power, since they themselves were often dependent upon the will of external donors. This situation encouraged the development of Jewish communities in the regions, often receiving support from abroad without any over-sight from Moscow. There are roughly seventy such communities, scattered across the Russian Federation, which oversee the dispensation of welfare and the organization of primary education. The religious community typically has a rabbi provided by Habad, while charitable assistance comes from the Joint. Jewish community centres sponsor musical, choral, and dance groups. A number have published histories of the community. Many sponsor museums. Regional communities are well situated to apply for the status of 'national-cultural autonomy', which gives them a formal legal identity within the state. One such body, the Jewish National Autonomy of Sverdlovsk Region, served as the conduit for a complaint to the regional public prosecutor against the Sverdlovsk Russian Orthodox diocese for disseminating the antisemitic forgery *The Protocols of the Elders of Zion*.

As home-grown Jewish organizations appeared, tensions with foreign donors, especially the Joint, emerged. A particular focus of dispute was the wish of the Joint to seek more efficient ways of providing aid, such as by relocating all Jewish communal activities and bodies to a central site. Controversies flared over plans for such centres in Moscow, St Petersburg, and Kiev (see below).

One of the most notable successes of Moscow and St Petersburg has been in the development of academic Jewish studies. The Moscow-based Sefer holds a broad variety of conferences, workshops, and seminars for students and academic staff in the field of Jewish studies. Both cities have adult-education programmes organized in 'independent' (that is, non-degree-granting) Jewish universities. Both cities are developing Jewish museums. Moscow boasts two publishing houses that specialize in the publication of Judaica in the Russian language.

Outside the Russian Federation

Ukraine, which has the second-largest Jewish population in Eastern Europe, most resembles the Russian model. The newly independent Ukrainian state quickly established good relations with the State of Israel. A Ukrainian Vaad was chartered, headed by a veteran dissident, Joseph Zissels. The same institutions that assist Jews in the Russian Federation are active in Ukraine. As noted above, Ukraine has had its own 'rabbi war'. While there are far fewer Ukrainian Jewish Oligarchs, at least one, Vadim Rabinovich, has played an active role in the community while also generating enormous controversy. Rabinovich's international business dealings have been controversial, and he has become a significant media magnate in Ukraine and abroad. He has made substantial donations to Jewish organizations in Ukraine. In 1997 he created the Ukrainian Jewish Congress, and organized a merger between the Vaad and the Union of Jewish Religious Organizations of Ukraine. The merger broke up at the end of 1998. The split was in part occasioned by a bitter controversy that illustrates the limits of foreign assistance to Jewish communities in the FSU. The Joint proposed to finance construction of a Jewish community centre at the site of the Nazi mass-murder of Kiev Jews, Babi Yar. The complex would serve as a distribution point for welfare services, as a community centre, and as a memorial museum to commemorate the mass murder. The proposal has engendered an ongoing debate between supporters and those who saw it as a desecration of the site. The Vaad subsequently helped to create a new body, the Jewish Confederation of Ukraine, in 1999.

Ongoing political instability and corruption in Ukraine have worked against the evolution of a civil society in which Jewish communities might be securely entrenched. Like Russia, the Ukrainian authorities do little to combat occasional antisemitic incidents, but antisemitism in Ukraine lacks any meaningful political base.

Jewish communities are to be found in all the other post-Soviet states in the region. Virtually all the governments recognize the utility of good relations with Israel and international Jewish organizations, but it is impossible to make generalizations, especially about politically unstable states such as Belarus, where Christian Orthodox clerical influence has sought to undermine initiatives to promote Jewish studies at Minsk State University. Some communities, as in Moldova, are well organized, and maintain very close ties to Israel. Almost all are losing their Jewish population through mortality or out-migration to Russia, Israel, and the West.

The impact of war, Holocaust, and totalitarianism cost East European Jewry its status as the demographic and cultural centre of world Jewry. The remnants of this shattered civilization will endure, in shrunken form, for some time to come. Efforts inside and outside the region are attempting to rebuild a Jewish life there. Whatever its ultimate prospects, it will be far different from the East European Jewish community that existed at the dawn of the twentieth century.

FURTHER READING

The Jews in Tsarist Russia

Dubnow, S. M. *History of the Jews in Poland and Russia*, 3 vols. (Philadelphia: Jewish Publication Society of America, 1914–16). The classic study: Dubnow created the field of Russian-Jewish history, and his cultural and political views colour his work. Dubnow took a 'lachrymose' view of the history of the Jews in Eastern Europe, equating it with continual persecution.

Frankel, Jonathan. *Prophecy and Politics: Socialism, Nationalism, and the Russian Jews, 1862–1917* (Cambridge: Cambridge University Press, 1981). An instant classic by a contemporary master of the history of Jewish politics. In a dense, wide-ranging work which demands and rewards a careful reading, Frankel explores the rise of modern Jewish politics in Eastern Europe. Essential reading.

Freeze, ChaeRan Y. *Jewish Marriage and Divorce in Imperial Russia* (Hanover and London: University Press of New England, 2002). An outstanding and pioneering work of Jewish social history. Freeze explores the changing demography of Jews in the Russian Empire, and the impact of modernity upon the traditional Jewish family.

Klier, John D. *Russia Gathers Her Jews: The Origins of the Jewish Question in Russia, 1772–1825* (DeKalb, Ill.: Northern Illinois University Press, 1986). Seeks to place the treatment of Jews in the Russian Empire in the context of the political and economic concerns of early modern Russia.

Klier, John D. *Imperial Russia's Jewish Question, 1855–1881* (Cambridge: Cambridge University Press, 1995). As the title implies, this work seeks to see the Jewish Question in an imperial context, especially in connection with the treatment of other national groups, such as the Poles and Ukrainians. The work explores the shifts in public opinion towards the Jews, and the responses of acculturated Russian Jews.

Klier, John D., and Shlomo Lambroza (eds.). *Pogroms: Anti-Jewish Violence in Modern Russian History* (Cambridge: Cambridge University Press, 1991). The only work available that tries to place the pogrom phenomenon in the wider contexts of Russian and world history. Greatest emphasis on the 1881–2 and 1903–6 pogroms. Rogger's summary chapter is an important work in itself.

Lederhendler, Eli. *The Road to Modern Jewish Politics: Political Tradition and Political Reconstruction in the Jewish Community of Tsarist Russia* (New York and Oxford: Oxford University Press, 1989). Important for demonstrating the political sophistication and political flexibility of segments of Russian Jewry under Tsarist rule.

Miron, Dan. *A Traveller Disguised: A Study of the Rise of Modern Yiddish Fiction in the Nineteenth Century* (New York: Schocken Books, 1973). Miron demonstrates the importance of the debates surrounding Yiddish literature for the emergence of a modern Jewish identity in Eastern Europe.

Stanislawski, Michael. *Tsar Nicholas I and the Jews* (Philadelphia: Jewish Publication Society of America, 1983). Stanislawski argues that the treatment of the Jews in Russia was not anomalous, while showing how Russian Jewry was transformed by the social engineering pursued in Nicholas's reign.

The Jews in the Soviet Union and Successor States

Gitelman, Zvi. *Jewish Nationality and Soviet Politics: The Jewish Sections of the CPSU* (Princeton: Princeton University Press, 1972). A classic study of efforts of the Soviet regime to 'bring the revolution to the Jewish street'.

Gitelman, Zvi. *A Century of Ambivalence: The Jews of Russia and the Soviet Union, 1881 to the Present,* 2nd expanded edn. (Bloomington: Indiana University Press, 2001). A broad survey of Russian-Jewish history, particularly useful for chapters on post-Soviet Jewry.

Kostyrchenko, Gennadi V. *Out of Red Shadows: Antisemitism in Stalin's Russia* (Amherst, NY: Prometheus Books, 1995). An important study of the Jewish politics of late Stalinism.

Pinkus, Benjamin. *The Soviet Government and the Jews, 1948–1967: A Documented Study* (Cambridge: Cambridge University Press, 1984). A judicious selection of original texts plus a fine explication makes this an outstanding study of post-war Soviet Jewry.

Redlich, Shimon. *Propaganda and Nationalism in Wartime Russia: The Jewish Anti-Fascist Committee in the USSR, 1941–1948* (Boulder, Col.: Eastern European Monographs, 1982). An important study of how Soviet Jews responded to the Nazi threat.

Social issues

15 | Social issues: survey

Harvey E. Goldberg

Beginnings

The academic study of Judaism and systematic research into social issues both took initial shape early in the nineteenth century. Leopold Zunz (1794–1886), a leader of the *Wissenschaft des Judentums* movement, included a Jewish sociology or *Statistik* in his view of a Jewish science. Then, 'statistic' referred to qualitative assessment as well as to quantitative investigations. Productive interaction between social thought and questions of contemporary Jewish life and Jewish history emerged only toward the end of the century.

One reason for the delay was that nineteenth-century thought was evolutionist, picturing society as moving through stages. Social analysts attending to Jews, or to the Hebrew Bible, viewed Jewish life as representing an 'early' stage of development. Thus, William Robertson Smith (1846–94), analysing social dimensions of 'Old Testament' religion, saw it as a step on the ladder leading to Christianity, as did his student James George Frazer (1854–1941) in *Folklore in the Old Testament* (1918). Jews therefore usually resisted a sociological or anthropological 'gaze'. Jewish scholars stressed the high points of Jewish cultural and literary creativity, demonstrating their rightful place among the nations of Europe. In addition, the dominant orientation of Jews at the time was integrationist, envisioning a future within the emerging nation-states of Europe. A sociology focused only on Jews ran counter to this desired outcome.

The resistance to becoming a separate sociological object notwithstanding, Jewish organizations laid the groundwork for an eventual sociology of Jewish life. Statistics were assembled on demographic trends and associated socio-economic problems in various parts of Europe, and Jews in Western and Central Europe also gathered information on Jewish communities in North Africa and the Middle East as part of their philanthropic and educational programmes there. Some countries in Europe included a special category for Jews in their censuses. In these ways, data accumulated yielding a broad view of social trends among Jews.

Zionism provided the specific thrust creating a sociology of the Jews. The argument for a future national existence required that data similar to those available to nation-states be available to the Jewish people. At the World Zionist Congress in 1901 Max Nordau (1849–1923) asserted, 'we must know with greater precision the national material (*Volksmaterial*) with which we have to work', and mentioned anthropological, biological, economic, and intellectual statistics. The following year a Bureau of Jewish Statistics was established in Berlin. It was directed by Arthur Ruppin (1876–1943), who from 1907 headed the Palestine office of the World Zionist Organization. There, Ruppin engaged in purchasing land for the Jewish National Fund, but also continued economic and demographic research. He was appointed to the Institute of Jewish Studies of the new Hebrew University in 1925, and in 1930–1 published his integrative work *Die Soziologie der Juden* (The Sociology of the Jews).

A link between Zionism and sociology also appears in the work of Martin Buber (1878–1965). In promoting national revival, Buber used the concept of *rasse*—race—as a kind of vital wellspring in the collective past and consciousness of Jews. Later he denied parallels drawn between his ideas and the way Nazism used race to demean and oppress groups which they viewed as biologically inferior. This example shows, however, that in the early twentieth century many scholars took it for granted that biological-like forces affected social and cultural developments. Notions of individual health and national 'vigour' interpenetrated one another. Studies of Jewish demography typically were concerned with matters of 'social hygiene', and there emerged an anthropology of the Jews which sought to combat the results of racial research that demonstrated the 'inferiority' or 'weakness' of Jews. The social situation of Jews concerned many Jewish groups, not only Zionists. In 1925 YIVO—the Jewish Institute of Social Research—was established in Vilna, and its director, Max Weinreich (1894–1969), advocated a philosophy of continued Jewish collective existence in the Diaspora. Weinreich developed ties to American anthropology, in particular with the linguist-anthropologist Edward Sapir (1884–1939).

Research carried out by Jewish institutions and individual scholars in Europe studied factors that shaped the character of Jewish communities in the first decades of the twentieth century: migration, age-structure, occupational distribution, intermarriage, indications of poverty or other social problems, and the prevalence of diseases. Jewish organizations in the United States also tracked demographic and related trends. From the beginning of the twentieth century the American Jewish Committee put out the *American Jewish Yearbook* and documented demographic and social developments. This sociological activity, however, was not tied to conceptual or theoretical developments within the discipline.

Jews and social thought

Some major sociologists discussed Jews in attempts to forge concepts and modes of analysis. Émile Durkheim (1858–1917) compared rates of suicide among Catholics, Protestants, and Jews in a study that formulated the concept of 'anomie' and sought to establish the importance of a social level of analysis, in contrast to a psychological level. Max Weber (1854–1920) authored *Ancient Judaism* (1920) in his project of understanding world religions in terms of their social settings and economic activities. One outstanding study of Jewish life in America was published in 1928: Louis Wirth's (1897–1952) *The Ghetto* placed the new American Jewish experience against the background of ghetto existence over the centuries in Europe. Wirth became a well-known sociologist at the University of Chicago, but did not further follow Jewish topics.

In addition to Durkheim and Wirth, there were other central figures in the social sciences who were Jewish. One was the anthropologist Franz Boas (1858–1942), who was born in Germany and shaped academic anthropology in the United States from the turn of the twentieth century. Boas argued for the importance of culture, rather than race, in determining the characteristics of societies. He focused on the cultures and languages of Amerindian groups, but was also a physical anthropologist. His criticisms of racial theories attracted much attention, and some of his studies dealt with Jewish immigrants to the United States. He showed that various so-called Jewish 'racial characteristics', as they were then measured by anthropologists, changed among the children of immigrants to the country, so that they could not be attributed to 'biological inheritance'. Boas paid no attention, however, to Jewish culture. His long-range expectation for Jews, Afro-Americans, and other immigrant groups was that they would assimilate into American society.

The Nazi period in Germany and its atrocities during the Second World War placed all social science perspectives linked to notions of race under a cloud. It is often forgotten that these ideas had been taken seriously by many, including researchers with liberal orientations. In broad overview, it is now clear that intellectual positions which challenged the relevance of race for understanding society and history represented the avenue of advancement. But to eliminate biological explanations completely from social science required a theoretical formulation of other factors that accounted for group definitions and continuity in behaviour. Advance in this direction took place around the turn of the twentieth century in several disciplines, often with important contributions made by researchers and thinkers of Jewish backgrounds. In addition to Durkheim's stress on 'society' and Boas's emphasis on 'culture', there was Sigmund Freud's (1856–1939) elaboration of the symbolic side of human thought in *The Interpretation of Dreams* (1900), or the philosophical work of Ernst Cassirer (1874–1945) that influenced Sapir (who was a student of Boas). The shared implication of these different perspectives is that all of human culture is potentially available to all members of the human species. No group is 'essentially' barred from participating in any form of cultural behaviour or creativity. This claim was not universally accepted when it first emerged, but the aftermath of the Second World War and the Holocaust set the stage for its becoming basic in contemporary social science.

One large-scale research project organized in the United States in the post-war period dealt with the 'the authoritarian personality'. It wanted to explain why some people were attracted to antisemitic or fascist ideologies. The research explored a combination of social and psychological factors leading to modes of thought and behaviour that excluded and demeaned 'outsider' ethnic groups. The inspiration for this research came from the writings of the 'Frankfurt School' that had been active in Germany in the 1920s, in particular the work of Theodor W. Adorno (1903–69). Adorno and some other members of that group were Jewish, but they denied the relevance of their background for their research. However one may interpret the link between background and scientific motivation, it is notable that this post-war research in the United States was funded by the American Jewish Committee.

Sociology and anthropology in Jewish history

Sociological thought also began to influence some historians dealing with the Jewish past. In the mid-nineteenth century many *Wissenschaft des Judentums* scholars wrote history in a manner that stressed the development of religious ideas. They wanted to show how the religion of Judaism deserved a respectable place when one examined the unfolding of world history. Later in the century Heinrich Graetz (1817–91) expounded a national (but not yet Zionist) perspective on Jewish history, stressing the specific historical circumstances affecting groups of Jews in different periods and places. After that, Simon Dubnow (1860–1941) introduced a more systematic consideration of social conditions. His work stressed autonomous Jewish communal existence in the Diaspora by analysing political and social structures supporting that existence. Salo Baron (1895–1989), perhaps the last generalist among Jewish historians, also moved in this direction in his multi-volume oeuvre *The Social and Religious History of the Jews* (1957–83). Some scholars were directly influenced by the work of Weber. Louis Finkelstein (1895–1991) provided a study of the Mishnaic period and the sage Rabbi Akiba, interpreting the tension between the Pharisees and Sadducees in terms akin to social class. Other historians and textual scholars were critical of these attempts. Perhaps the first widely recognized attempt to merge Jewish historiography with social analysis was the work of Jacob Katz (1904–98), who adopted the notion of an 'ideal type' in describing Central European Jewry on the eve of the emancipation is his *Tradition and Crisis* (1961; original Hebrew edition 1958). He pointed to the interaction between religious developments and a variety of economic, institutional, and political trends. S. D. Goitein (1900–85) also incorporated socio-economic and socio-cultural perspectives in his multi-volume study of Jews in the Muslim world during the tenth–thirteenth centuries, *A Mediterranean Society* (1967–88). He called his approach 'sociography', claiming that he made the people of that period 'speak for themselves' through the documents they produced. Goitein had earlier studied the spoken language of Yemenite Jews who had moved to Mandate Palestine, and in this setting was influenced by anthropology as well.

Anthropology too began to be incorporated into the work of Judaic scholars. Early in the twentieth century Talmudist Louis Ginzberg (1873–1953) began his seven-volume

Legends of the Jews (1909–38). Ginzberg was also a student of folklore, and was partially inspired by Frazer. Several volumes of *Legends of the Jews* were translated from German by Paul Radin (1883–1959), an anthropologist who had studied with Boas. At that time many people distinguished folklore from anthropology, seeing the former as dealing with the 'simple people' of 'advanced civilizations' and the latter focusing on 'primitive societies'. Ginzberg was thus able to discuss aspects of Talmudic literature in terms of folklore. This approach appeared in Mandate Palestine as well, in the work of Raphael Patai (1910–96). Patai and his colleagues also began the ethnographic study of extant Jewish communities, in particular Jews originating from Middle Eastern countries. This work incorporated older anthropological assumptions that the main task of anthropology was to 'salvage'—through documentation—ways of life that would soon disappear. A similar motive ran through an earlier study of Ashkenazi Jews. Solomon Rappoport, author of the play *The Dybbuk* and more widely known by his pen-name Ansky, conducted ethnographic research in eastern Galicia from 1912 to 1916. The ideology animating that work was not only that this way of life would not survive, but that there were features of the 'spirit' of the 'folk' that had value for future Jewish existence.

Trends in America after the Second World War

The Second World War changed the face of Jewish demography and social existence. North America became the major population centre of world Jewry. Little was known in the West about the Jews in the Soviet Union, who remained behind the Iron Curtain. The State of Israel was established in 1948, and in three-and-a-half years more than doubled its Jewish population, reaching 1.4 million. Jewish life in America and in Israel provided different challenges for social research.

In the United States, there was a major move to the suburbs of the big cities. Many Jews by then were third-generation Americans. There was a considerable growth in Conservative and Reform synagogues. It became clear that Jewish life had taken on new organizational forms and cultural content. Many wondered whether these developments would last over the generations. Oscar Handlin, historian of American immigration, documented how Jews maintained a sense of collective existence, while the content of their lives differed little from that of other middle-class Americans. Sociologist Marshall Sklare supplied a portrait of Conservative Judaism, subtitling his book *An American Religious Movement* (1955). He showed that Jews followed their traditions while feeling part of America, but also highlighted the compromises that their religious leaders had to make. Other sociologists distinguished various phases of acculturation and assimilation, indicating how Jews adopted many American patterns but did not disappear as a separate group. Essayist Will Herberg called his work *Protestant—Catholic—Jew* (1955) religious sociology; he claimed that in America it was important to have a religion, and that now all three faiths were acceptable expressions of American life. These social analyses had an impact well beyond academia. They were discussed by rabbis in pulpits, who condemned Handlin's 'agnosticism' concerning an American Jewish future and celebrated Herberg's formulation. Another oft-quoted statement in those years came from a general study of immigration to America by M. Hansen that created the aphorism: 'What the second generation wants to forget, the third generation wants to remember.' This generalization was not necessarily confirmed by data, but became a 'sociological truth' repeated by a leadership committed to Jewish continuity.

Cultural anthropology also became a way of understanding Jewish life. At first it focused on the past. *Life is With People*, by Mark Zborowski and Elizabeth Herzog, was based on interviews of people who had grown up in *shtetls* (small rural towns of Yiddish-speakers) in Poland, portraying a way of life that had been eroded by social change since the late nineteenth century and then destroyed by the Holocaust. There was also ethnographic study of ultra-Orthodox communities in America, reflecting the soon-to-be-questioned assumption that anthropological work is mainly appropriate for 'exotic' groups which somehow carry the past into the present.

A second phase of ethnographic work focused on old people of East European background who had by then lived most of their lives in America. It showed how, as these people became elderly, their memories of a past culture were mobilized creatively in new contexts. This set the stage for field research dealing with contemporary America, a trend that was abetted by the way Jews living there reacted to the events of the 1960s.

During that decade the growing political consciousness and activities of American blacks brought the issue of ethnicity to the foreground. Simultaneously, the Vietnam War underlined United States interference in the affairs of other regions. The resulting perception of US foreign policy as a form of imperialism created a basis for sympathy with Palestinian Arabs who came under Israeli military occupation after the 1967 Six Day War. Many young Jews shared a critical view of US policy with other middle-class Americans of their age, but were sensitive about having Israel cast in the role of an oppressor. Within these ideological and ethnic cross-currents, heightened by the new technology of videotapes and colour television, young Jews forged viable personal and ethnic identities.

These developments were reflected in social research. One ethnographic study focused on the Jewish Defense League (JDL), an organization that advocated 'Jewish Power' vis-à-vis other ethnic groups, challenging the liberal ethos that had characterized the more economically established Jewish community over the previous generation. Other studies documented the rise of the Havura movement. This was spearheaded by young people from Conservative and Reform backgrounds who were looking for intense and intimate ways of expressing and deepening Jewish knowledge and commitments. They organized themselves in small groups (*havurot*), devoted to prayer and study, that engaged all members of the group as equals. This involved 'going back' to forms of *davening* (prayer) that prevailed in Eastern Europe, but in other ways havurot were bold innovations. Women assumed ritual roles within them that in the past were only assigned to men. Havurot thus reflected current trends in the wider society, such as the rise of feminism, but were also predicated on critical analyses of extant Jewish life. In a manner different from the JDL, they were also sceptical about Jewish life in large, well-to-do suburban synagogues. They sought to break the pattern in which a rabbi was 'the expert', distant from the congregation in style of dress and his place on an elevated dais. Some also insisted that Jewish leadership and education show more sensitivity to broader social problems. Researchers of the havurot were typically sympathetic to the movement or even members of a havura themselves. This was a new use of ethnography in which studying a group was linked to a sense of advocacy and empowerment.

Similar trends appeared in the study of Orthodoxy. Researchers no longer found Orthodox life of interest only as a vestige of the past, but documented the way synagogues, Talmud study groups, and *yeshivot* functioned in the context of American society. One of the results of the 1960s in the United States was fuller acceptance of the public expression of ethnic differences, and many Orthodox Jewish men began to feel comfortable wearing skullcaps in public. Survey data reflected these changes. Up to that period there had been a steady decline in the number of people identifying themselves as Orthodox. Typical findings were that they constituted well under 10 per cent of American Jews. From this period, however, the decline in Orthodox identification was arrested, and the percentages even rose a little. There also appeared various forms of *hazara bi-teshuvah*—Orthodox 'outreach' seeking to bring other Jews 'back to' strictly observant Judaism—and this too became the subject of ethnographic study.

Dilemmas of survey research in America in the late twentieth century

The organized Jewish community in the United States continued to support survey research in order to document trends within it. Studies dealt with a variety of topics, such as demographic developments, observance of Jewish practices and affiliation with traditional Jewish groups, and a topic intersecting both of these concerns: marriage and intermarriage.

Recent decades have seen trends among Jews that parallel demographic shifts among middle-class Americans generally. This involves demographic movement to the south and to the west. The big cities of the eastern seaboard and Chicago are still the major centres of Jewish life, but their dominance has been lessened by the growth of communities in Los Angeles and in other large cities. Jews continued to be socially mobile in terms of level of education and socio-economic status. There were also significant trends within Jewish families. The average age of marriage rose, and the birth rate declined. Divorce and remarriage became more common. There was also a growing percentage of older people in the Jewish population, implying that a serious proportion of communal resources should be devoted to planning for and assisting with problems of old age. The field of Jewish communal work emerged in the form of degree programmes in some universities that featured Jewish studies, or within the seminaries that were initially established to train rabbis and teachers.

Surveys documented the degree to which Jews still followed 'traditional' patterns, both in terms of religious observance and their extent of affiliation with other Jews and Jewish institutions. It became clear that what was once viewed as 'standard' observance declined over the years, but questions concerning lighting candles on the Sabbath or celebrating a Passover *seder* continued to be recognized by many Jews, and they often reported maintaining some form of these practices. Many sociologists consider issues of 'structure' to be more basic than those of cultural content, and studies also examined the degree to which Jews lived in neighbourhoods with other Jews, provided Jewish education for their children, and affiliated themselves with synagogue or ethnic organizations. Very often these patterns were maintained even as the observance of religious practices weakened. Another trend growing out of patterns of affiliation which has direct implication for the content of daily life is the degree to which Jews marry one another. This issue came into the spotlight of sociological self-reflection among American Jews in the 1990s.

Immediately after the Second World War the rate of Jews marrying Gentiles (intermarriage) was less than 10 per cent. By the mid–1980s it constituted about one-third of Jewish marriages. Research carried out in 1990 by the National Jewish Populations Survey was an extensive and carefully organized attempt at assessing many social and cultural trends among American Jews (and parallel efforts were made in other countries the same year). It reported an intermarriage rate among younger people of over 50 per cent. Many leaders of the Jewish community viewed this with alarm, but there were a variety of reactions to and interpretations of the figure. Some saw it as a normal continuation of the assimilatory process by which Jews had entered American life since the mass immigration at the end of the nineteenth century. Among some economically mobile groups, such as Japanese Americans, the rate was even higher. An interesting finding of the study was that intermarriage was in fact slightly lower among Jews who were higher on the socio-economic scale than among those whose mobility was limited. A significant number of Jews with a range of life choices were still making an effort to select Jewish spouses.

In the years prior to the study there had been much discussion of intermarriage in relation to conversion to Judaism. Some claimed that intermarriage had the possibility of increasing the Jewish population, if it were followed by the conversion of the non-Jewish partner, but the opposite possibility existed as well. The 1990 study undermined the notion that conversion after intermarriage might significantly augment the number of Jews. It did help focus the debate on the relation between these trends and the content of Jewish life. One notion emerging in the debates over conversions was the term 'Jews by choice'. It was becoming clear that all Jews were now 'Jews by choice', whether born into Jewish families or not, in that they chose how important Jewishness was to them and how they expressed it. Some argued that the growing intermarriage rate was less of a threat than it seemed because those who were 'lost' were marginal to begin with, while those who remained connected to Judaism were more committed than many in earlier generations. It also became obvious that American Jews were taking their own initiatives regarding what being Jewish meant to them and what patterns of behaviour they maintained and cultivated. It was no longer possible to measure adherence to Judaism by a simple accounting of forms of behaviour that had marked Jewish life in the past.

From this time on there has been a gradual penetration of methods of 'qualitative' research, derived from ethnography, life-history interviewing, and narrative analysis, into the quantitative survey research on American Jewry. Researchers now assume that they should begin with the understandings and forms of behaviour of the population they are studying. Thus, some interviews inquire whether or not respondents meditate. This is paralleled by a growing interest, on the part of the Jewish community and of researchers, in the whole lifespan of Jewish experience and socialization. Some Jewish organizations encourage students to take courses in Jewish studies at college, and much energy and money have been invested into sending teenagers and college students on educational—but also 'fun'—trips to Israel. Social research now tracks these developments. In order to assess them it is imperative to see how individuals and families integrate these experiences into the ongoing trajectory of their Jewish and general life stories.

While North America and Israel are the demographic centres of Jewish life, important communities are found in some European countries. The French community underwent demographic change by incorporating Jews from North Africa who now constitute the majority of French Jewry. Jewish life, particularly among the young, was stimulated by the 1968 student revolt, demanding the appreciation of 'difference' within French society. Along with social survey studies of the community, ethnography has shown how North African Jewish cultural patterns were both preserved and changed to fit into new situations. Studies also have documented how some North Africans have been attracted to the Habad Hasidic movement. Another central topic, that of collective memory, has been explored with regard to Jews in France with East European, Balkan, and North African origins.

Sociology and Israeli society

When Israel was established in 1948 the social sciences were encouraged in order to serve the needs of the new state. Sociology was viewed as a theoretical discipline built on an empirical base, with little interest in the Jewish sociology earlier encouraged by Arthur Ruppin. The first generation of sociologists were students of the philosopher Martin Buber, but did not pursue research continuing his concern with Jewish nationalism and culture. Buber's influence was reflected in two ways. One was that sociology at the Hebrew University was highly theoretical and placed questions concerning Israeli society into a comparative context. This tendency was reinforced by study in England, where the founding sociologists were exposed to both sociology and social anthropology, sometimes defined as comparative sociology. The second Buberian influence was an interest in the kibbutz. That new collective way of life had been both practically and symbolically important in linking the 'return to Zion' to notions of a new way of being Jewish that rebelled against the Judaism of the Diaspora. The developing social sciences mostly ignored the Jewish past.

This was also apparent in the way sociology related to the main challenge of the post-independence decades: immigration from Europe and the Middle East that, in a few years, outnumbered the Jews present when Israel was established. The emergent sociology paradigm insisted that the success of immigration depended upon immigrants' distancing themselves from their origins and past cultures and fitting into the developing Israeli society and culture. It also distinguished among types of backgrounds of immigrant groups, defining a scale running from 'traditional' to 'modern'. One pole was typified by Jews from rural areas of the Middle East such as Kurdistan or Yemen, and the other end by European immigrants with western education and occupational skills. Sociologists also discouraged anthropological research which focused on the culture and history of each particular group. The sociological typology of backgrounds pointed to some non-obvious findings. Successful integration into the society took place among both 'traditional' and 'modern' populations, while frustration and social problems were often concentrated in 'transitional' groups from the Middle East. These immigrants had had some contact with the West, expected that moving to Israel would bring them social mobility, and were disappointed when their aspirations for advancement did not materialize. The typology also meshed with the growing societal tendency to view Israel as being composed of two segments, Westerners and Easterners.

In the 1970s there emerged opposing views of the original paradigm of Israeli sociology, in parallel with worldwide developments in the field. The earlier school of thought assumed that society was based on consensus, and that new immigrants would eventually share the values and behaviours of the old-timers, while the new approaches emphasized conflict. They argued that the socioeconomic growth of the country entailed veterans of European origin advancing through the exploitation and even downward mobility of Middle Eastern newcomers. Moreover, they claimed, initial Israeli sociology did not maintain a critical perspective, but its ideas reinforced the social structure characterized by a growing ethnic gap. These approaches highlighted important aspects of Israel's development, but focused on areas of tension and did not illuminate the mechanisms of widespread social mobility that took place as well. Both earlier and later approaches downplayed the specific histories of the immigrants, and the role of Jewish culture and religion in their lives.

Religious patterns among Middle Eastern Jews were initially subsumed under the rubric of 'traditionality'. Some studies examined the political and legal accommodation between a purportedly secular democratic state and the way religion was institutionalized in it, such as in laws restricting Sabbath travel, or the relegation of realms like marriage and burial to the bureaucratic control of the rabbinate. Israeli sociologists paid more attention to religious content when it became linked to political issues, like the claims that Israel must remain in the West Bank after the 1967 war, or the emergence of the Shas party which combined Middle Eastern symbols with European-style ultra-Orthodoxy. Recently anthropologists have studied pilgrimages to graves of sainted rabbis spread throughout the country, in which Middle Eastern Jews preserved traditions from abroad and reworked them to express attachment to and seek empowerment in their new home. These practices are thus understood in terms of their present significance, not just as relics of the past.

The sociological study of religion in Israel typically entails public and political dimensions quite distinct from the personalized approaches to Judaism characterizing many Diaspora communities. At the same time, certain issues now link the concerns of Jews in Israel and abroad, such as women's roles in religious life, or the control of the Orthodox rabbinate over matters of personal status. These topics, and other 'global' Jewish issues, are now coming under comparative sociological scrutiny. An overarching challenge for Jewish social science is to identify cultural themes and practices which inform Jewish life both in Israel and in Diaspora communities, and to analyse their expression in diverse social circumstances.

FURTHER READING

Aran, Gideon. 'Jewish-Zionist Fundamentalism', in M. Marty and S. Appleby (eds.), *Fundamentalisms Observed* (Chicago: University of Chicago Press, 1991), pp. 265–345. A sociological analysis of the merging of religion and nationalism in the Gush Emunim movement in Israel.

Bahloul, Joëlle. *The Architecture of Memory: A Jewish-Muslim Household in Colonial Algeria, 1937–1962* (Cambridge: Cambridge University Press, 1996). A study of collective memory among Jews from Algeria in France as it related to their past and present situation.

DellaPergola, Sergio. 'Arthur Ruppin Revisited: The Jews of Today, 1904–1994', in Steven M. Cohen and Gabriel Horencyzk (eds.) *National Variations in Jewish Identity: Implications for Jewish Education* (Albany: State University of New York Press, 1999), pp. 53–84. An overview of the contribution of one of the creators of the sociological study of Jewry, and a discussion of the relevance of his work today.

Deshen, Shlomo, and Moshe Shokeid. *The Predicament of Homecoming: Cultural and Social Life of North African Immigrants in Israel* (Ithaca, NY: Cornell University Press, 1974). A series of social-anthropological discussions of North African Jewish immigrants in Israel and how they became part of Israeli society.

Dolgin, Janet. *Jewish Identity and the JDL* (Princeton: Princeton University Press, 1977). An anthropological analysis showing how the militant Jewish Defense League arose against the background of events in the United States in the 1960s.

Goldberg, Harvey E. (ed.). *The Life of Judaism* (Berkeley: University of California Press, 2000). A collection of ethnographic and autobiographical essays portraying Jewish life over the last century in Europe, North Africa, the United States, and Israel.

Hansen, Marcus L. 'The Third Generation in America', *Commentary*, 14 (Nov. 1952), pp. 492–500. An essay by a historian of immigration which was widely cited by Jewish communal and religious leaders.

Kugelmass, Jack. *The Miracle of Intervale Avenue: The Story of a Jewish Congregation in the South Bronx* (New York: Columbia University Press, 1996). An ethnographic account of a congregation of old and very diverse members and the way it handled the social and demographic changes that transformed its neighbourhood.

Liebman, Charles S., and Steven M. Cohen. *The Two Worlds of Judaism: The Israeli and American Experiences* (New Haven: Yale University Press, 1990). A comparative study by a political scientist and sociologist of the differences and similarities in the way Judaism has developed in the American and Israeli settings

Myerhoff, Barbara. *Number Our Days* (New York: Simon & Schuster, 1978). A study of the way elderly Jews in California who had been born in Eastern Europe drew upon their childhood culture in dealing with the challenges of old age.

Shafir, Gershon, and Yoav Peled. *Being Israeli: The Dynamics of Multiple Citizenship* (Cambridge: Cambridge University Press, 2002). An overview of Israeli society reflecting the most recent sociological trends and analyses.

Sharot, Stephen. *Judaism: A Sociology* (London: David & Charles, 1976). An attempt to create an inclusive sociological framework for studying Judaism throughout history and in diverse settings.

Sklare, Marshall. *Conservative Judaism: An American Religious Movement* (New York: Schocken Books, 1972). One of the major sociological studies examining Jewish life in America as it emerged in the post-Second World War period.

Soloveitchik, Haym. 'Rupture and Reconstruction: The Transformation of Contemporary Orthodoxy', *Tradition*, 28 (1994), pp. 64–130. A view of the revival of orthodox life in the United States in the period after the 1960s and the dilemmas entailed by that development.

Wertheimer, Jack. *A People Divided: Judaism in Contemporary America* (New York: Basic Books, 1993). A view of the historical and social developments explaining the present diversity of Jewish life in the United States.

16 | Jewish identities

Ezra Kopelowitz

In 2000 there were approximately 13 million Jews living in the world, with the vast majority in Israel (approximately 5 million) and the United States (approximately 5.5 million).[1] My goal in this chapter is to compare the ways that Jews in these two major centres of world Jewry construct their Jewish identities.

I begin by describing three distinct models of Jewish identity, based on: (1) the manner in which people maintain inconsistent or consistent patterns of Jewish behaviour as they move between the various social spaces of everyday life; and (2) the answer that people give to the question: Who has authority to determine authentic Jewish behaviour? After presenting the three models, I will then look at how each gains expression in contemporary American and Israeli life.

Moving between social spaces in Jewish ways

Jewish identity can be distinguished amongst types of Jews based upon the way they move between social spaces—from home, to synagogue, to school, to the bus, to the office, and so on.

At one end of the Jewish identity spectrum are Jews who attempt to maintain high levels of religious observance as they move between social spaces. Important examples include attempts to maintain gender separation, the laws of *kashrut*, and prayer throughout the spaces of everyday life. Among the ultra-Orthodox (Haredim) there is an aspiration to maintain gender separation to the greatest extent possible throughout the spaces of everyday life. For example, we immediately recognize a synagogue as Orthodox when we see men and women sitting separately. Likewise, there are health clubs that offer separate hours for men and women; and in both Israel and the United States there are private bus lines which seat men and woman separately. In Israel the Haredim have been pushing for many years for public transportation with separate seating for men and woman.

Gender separation is an expression of Orthodox Jewish identity precisely because it is not limited to a single social space such as the synagogue, but spills over into other social spaces. The same is true of the desire to maintain kashrut and pray at regular intervals. It is not enough to observe kashrut or pray in the home; a Jew is expected to maintain these rituals no matter where they are located at any given moment.

At the other end of the Jewish identity spectrum we find individuals who do not move between social spaces in a consistent Jewish manner. The 'liberal Jew' sees no value in attempting to draw a connection between the Jewish things done at home, at the synagogue, or elsewhere. For example, liberal Jews will go to the synagogue to pray, but have no expectation that they must then pray at home. Likewise, a person might maintain some of the laws of kashrut at home, but will not expect these rules to be followed elsewhere, even in the synagogue. If the rules of kashrut are followed, then the person would not dream of demanding that others observe them in exactly the same way.

It is important to note that, from a sociological perspective, the terms 'consistent' and 'inconsistent' do not denote positive or negative ways of being Jewish. Rather, the terms simply describe patterns of behaviour. There are many liberal Jews who devote large amounts of time to constructing a meaningful Jewish identity—by reading Jewish books, learning about Jewish cooking, attending prayer services, or involving themselves in the running of a synagogue, community centre, or school, and so on. However, in comparison to the consistent Jew, this person will insist that Jewish identity should be built in liberal ways, allowing each individual to create a meaningful Jewish experience by choosing how best to draw the connections between the spaces of everyday life.

Towards the middle of the identity spectrum we find people with relatively strong notions of 'authentic Jewish behaviour', that tend to rest on the idea that a 'good Jew' should maintain traditional forms of religious practice in as consistent a manner as possible in the various spaces of everyday life. However, these types of Jews will only partially maintain what they consider authentic Jewish behaviour. For example, whilst wanting kosher food in the synagogue and observing some of the kashrut laws at home, major elements of kashrut are disregarded elsewhere.

Like the consistent Jew, Jews in the middle will agree that consistent religious observance is a goal. However, like the inconsistent Jew, they will argue that individuals have the right to decide for themselves the extent to which they will observe the religious tradition. Yet, unlike the liberal Jew, autonomy is not seen as an ideal unto itself, but rather as a means of balancing the demands of living in a secular society with the need to maintain a meaningful Jewish life. The classic situation is the desire of a businessperson to eat in a non-kosher restaurant with colleagues. The consistent Jew will not enter the restaurant; the inconsistent Jew sees no contradiction between eating in the non-kosher restaurant and Jewish identity. In contrast, the Jew of the middle lives in what Merton and Barber describe as a state of 'sociological ambivalence'—attempting to balance two or more conflicting social roles simultaneously.[2] In the case of the business lunch, the Jew of the middle attempts to balance acceptance of the principle that 'a Jew *should* eat kosher food' with the imperative that 'to succeed in business you need to eat lunch with your colleagues and clients'. Consequently, along the middle of the identity spectrum Jews do eat in non-kosher restaurants, but will engage in different types of practices, like not eating pork or refraining from mixing milk and meat, in order to maintain a sense of continuity between what is done at home, in the synagogue, and the restaurant.

Who has authority to determine 'correct' Jewish behaviour?

The behavioural differences that appear when we compare Jews who stand at the 'consistent', 'middle', and 'inconsistent' points of the Jewish identity spectrum tend to correspond with the ways people answer the question: 'Who has authority to determine "correct" Jewish behaviour within a given social space?'[3]

The consistent Jew will consult the rulings of a respected rabbinical figure to help determine legitimate from illegitimate Jewish behaviour. In contrast, at the liberal end of the identity spectrum, the authenticity of a particular pattern of Jewish behaviour is determined by the people who are members or inhabitants of the social space in question. For example, in most Reform synagogues the religious standards of the institution are determined by a vote of the membership. Moreover, the members of the synagogue do not expect people to demand that the synagogue be run according to the way they act at home and vice versa. Likewise, in the liberal world-view it is family members, and not a rabbinic authority, who determine the Jewish content of the household. Each space of everyday life gains autonomy from others; hence the ability to move between social spaces without the expectation that what a person does in one social space needs to be done elsewhere in order to identify as a Jew.

Jews of the middle tend to judge the legitimacy of a particular type of behaviour by looking at its effect on others with whom they interact in a given social situation, while at the same time attempting to maintain traditional forms of religious practice. For example, many Jewish parents increase their religious observance as their children get older in order to influence them positively. Here we see that contextual issues related to the household coexist with the assumption that 'influencing my children positively requires adoption of authentic forms of Jewish behaviour as defined by traditional religious practices'. Likewise, these same Jews might observe kashrut at home or other customs that might not be understood or agreed with in order that more traditional friends can eat with them. Demands of social context balance the expectation of adherence to the strict letter of the law as defined by rabbinical authorities.

In summary, each point on the identity spectrum represents both a distinct way of moving between social spaces, as well as a unique ideological position vis-à-vis the interaction of the individual with social context and rabbinical authority in determining 'authentic' Jewish behaviour.

The Jewish identity spectrum in Israel and the United States

American and Israeli Jews tend to use identity labels that primarily focus upon religious practices. The American terms 'Reform', 'Conservative', 'Orthodox', or 'unaffiliated Jew' all revolve around belonging to, or identifying with, a religious denomination. Likewise, Israeli identity labels such as 'Secular', 'Traditional', or 'Religious' also focus on religion, but without reference to a religious denomination. 'Secular' is equated with those who do not practise religious commandments; 'Traditional' means some-one who practises some religion but does so inconsistently; and 'Religious' refers to a person who practises religious commandments in a comprehensive and consistent fashion.[4]

Although Jews in both countries use identity labels orientated towards religion, some important differences exist. What the Israeli Jew calls 'Religious', the American Jew calls 'Orthodox'. In fact, American Jews who are active in a particular synagogue or religious movement will consider themselves 'religious' regardless of how many *mitzvot* they do on a particular day. In contrast, for an Israeli the term 'religious' is only applied to those people who maintain a high and consistent level of traditional religious observance. Another important difference is seen in the use of non-Orthodox identity labels. For an American the term 'secular' is a negative label, associated with those who reject their Jewish identity altogether. In contrast, Israeli Jews use the term 'secular' in a normative fashion, while the term 'Reform' is often used in a negative sense to connote someone who is not serious about religion or poses a danger to the religious tradition.

These differences between American and Israeli identity labels are influenced by the ways Jews in each country move between different types of social spaces in order to build their Jewish identities. The crux of the national differences is captured by the answer an American and Israeli parent might give to the question: 'What do you need to do in order that your child will identify as a Jew?' The Israeli, as opposed to the American, has the luxury of responding: 'I really don't need to do anything! By the fact that I live in Israel my children will identify as Jews.' By this the Israeli parents signal that their children will participate in the public life of the Jewish state, dance at Israeli Independence Day celebrations, mourn for fallen soldiers on Remembrance Day, and participate in Holocaust commemoration ceremonies at their school, as well as live by a public calendar that includes many public holidays that are religious holidays. More-over, issues touching on the Jewish character of the Israeli state are central to public discourse in Israel, and by law Israeli Jews must conduct life-cycle events such as divorce, marriage, and burial through the religious establishment. In short, it is hard for Israelis to forget that they are Jewish, and even if someone wishes to forget, the nature of public life in Israel means that it is virtually impossible.

In contrast, a Jew in the United States cannot depend on interacting with other Jews in everyday life, or for the American government to provide a framework for Jewish living. An American Jew, or any Diaspora Jew, must take private initiatives to inculcate Jewish identity. These private initiatives can include small decisions, like buying Jewish books or art for the home, or attending Jewish cultural events with the family; or big commitments, like paying large sums of money to send one's children to a Jewish day school or taking membership in a synagogue. Regardless of the financial scale and commitment of time, all of these actions occur in the private sphere in that they are the result of an active decision by an individual to choose to identify *and* behave as a Jew at the level of everyday life.

Comparing the 'Secular Israeli' to the 'American Reform' Jew

The American Reform and Israeli Secular Jews are similar in that they: (1) move as Jews between the spaces of everyday life with relatively little expectation of creating consistent Jewish connections; and (2) locate the authority to determine authentic Jewish behaviour in the hands of those who are co-present in a given social environment. Nonetheless, the Secular Israeli can assume the existence of a larger Jewish public sphere, while the American Reform Jew cannot. A consequence of this difference is seen in the very different approach of each to religion.

American Reform identity rests on the assumption that innovations to religious tradition are not only desirable but also necessary to create a meaningful Jewish identity in contemporary society: 'if the religious tradition is not meaningful then I must change it, or one of the most important resources that I have for transmitting a Jewish identity to my children is lost.'

In contrast, the Secular Israeli tends to be very conservative on matters of religion. One is likely hear the following statement from many Secular Israeli Jews: 'I am not interested in maintaining the religious commandments, so why would I want to change in them in order to make religion more meaningful? In fact when I get married, my extended family is going to demand that we get married according to the religious tradition and not in a Reform ceremony.' A well-known statement that Secular Israelis make is that 'the synagogue I don't go to is an Orthodox one'.[5]

The comparison between the American Reform and Israeli Secular Jew demonstrates how the lack of a public Jewish environment increases the need for individuals to make the religious tradition meaningful to their private lives. The Israeli public sphere facilitates the lack of interest of Secular Israeli Jews in religious reform—they simply do not need to practise religious ritual at the level of private, everyday life in order to build Jewish identities. The Secular Israeli Jew literally empties out everyday life of Jewish content, reserving moments of Jewish identity to larger events such as the celebration of national and religious holidays. The result is a Jewish identity based on the idea that in my private life 'I am not religious'.

The reliance of Secular Israeli Jews exclusively on the public environment in Israel for creating their Jewish identities creates a conflation between being Israeli and being Jewish: 'to be Israeli is to be Jewish.' In this Secular (Jewish) world-view 'religion in the private sphere' becomes associated with being 'Jewish', while 'public Jewishness' is simply associated with 'Israeliness'. Thus, in the minds of many Secular Israelis the concept of 'Jewish identity' is one and the same as 'religious identity', and the national or ethnic component is simply seen as 'Israeli'. Hence, the rather convoluted twist that leads Secular Israelis to end up using religion as the benchmark for determining Jewish identity.

Orthodox Americans v. Religious Israelis

The marked difference between the Orthodox/Religious and Reform/Secular identities is the fact that the former strive to connect the social spaces of everyday life in as consistent a manner as possible. As such, both the American Orthodox and Israeli Religious pay considerable attention to their behaviour in the private sphere, and in terms of the 'quantity' of religious behaviour in everyday life there is little difference between them. The goal is to be consistently religious according to standards determined by respected rabbinical authorities.

However, once again the presence or absence of a Jewish public sphere comes into play. Like the Israeli Secular, the Israeli Religious cannot forget that they are part of a larger public sphere. For Secular Jews this means dealing with aspects of religious law and the religious calendar whether they want it or not. In the case of the Religious they are forced to interact with Secular Jews, secular law, and 'secular Jewish spaces' whether they like it or not.

We can take the mess hall in the Israeli army as an example of a public Jewish space that provides challenges for both the Secular and Religious soldier. The food in the mess hall is kosher and the soldiers, by order, must respect the separation of milk and meat utensils. Thus, for example, one can witness a Secular sergeant getting red in the face and yelling because the milk dishes are being mixed with the meat dishes. At the same moment the Religious soldier needs to be willing to trust the fact that Secular soldiers in the kitchen are indeed observing the rules of kashrut when they prepare the food. Likewise the Religious soldier has to interact with Secular female soldiers who have different conceptions of modesty, and on Shabbat the Religious soldier continually has to grapple with the extent to which he can break Sabbath laws in order to fulfil the law of *pikuah nefesh* (saving souls) which has been interpreted to allow the Religious soldier to perform his military duties on Shabbat.

Segments of the Israeli Religious population, who are known as the National Religious, are willing to deal with the ambiguity of leaving their homes and spending time in social spaces such as the army in which their degree of control over religious practice is greatly reduced. In contrast, Haredim are not willing to make this compromise and most of them dodge conscription.[6] Either way, the Religious Jew has to make an explicit decision about the approach towards interaction with Secular Jews. In other areas of life, such as public transportation, even the Haredi Jew is unable to avoid contact with Secular Jews. Thus, for example, one often sees confrontations between Haredi men and Secular women over the right of the latter to sit where she pleases on the public bus. The male Haredi does not want to sit next to a woman other than his wife.

The ability of the individual to control consistent religious behaviour across the social spaces of everyday life is affected in Israel by the existence of public spaces which have Jewish content, such as kosher food, that might not be in exact accordance with a person's religious ideology. In contrast, American Orthodox Jews have the ability to maintain greater control over their religious observance, as they can choose to avoid contact with non-Orthodox Jews. The American Orthodox thus more easily avoid situations that force them to compromise religious consistency.

While there has recently been a marked shift towards more extreme forms of religious practice among both the American Orthodox and Israeli Religious (see below), this shift has been stronger among the Israelis. Because the Israeli Religious are forced to interact with Secular Jews, they work harder to develop lines of 'defence'. For this reason, most of the major liberalizing innovations among Orthodox Jews come out of American Orthodoxy—recent examples include greater participation of women in the prayer service and the attempt to add changes to the marriage document in order to protect women.

Conservative Americans v. Traditionalist Israelis

As discussed above, for Jews in the middle the question of social context is paramount for determining the level and type of religious behaviour in which they engage. In the United States 'Conservative Jews' are normally located in the middle of the Jewish identity spectrum, while in Israel Jews in the middle are often described as 'Traditionalists'.

Traditionalist Israelis have not built religious or educational institutions that cater specifically to their world-view, and instead make use of schools and synagogues provided by the state, which are controlled by Religious Jews. In this sense the Traditionalist Israeli is in most ways a person who simply does less than the Religious Jew, but views the more stringent lifestyle of the Religious Jew as truly authentic Judaism.

This description was once apt for the average member of the Conservative movement in the United States. However, over time the middle of the American Jewish spectrum has changed. Here, once again, the presence of a public sphere, or the lack of one, comes into play. Prior to the Second World War most Jews in the middle of the American Jewish spectrum, like the contemporary Traditionalist Israeli Jew, did not have their own religious and educational institutions. Rather, they lived in an ethnic neighbourhood that provided 'a public Jewish environment'. As people moved between social spaces within the neighbourhood they could assume that they would meet other Jews and generally be immersed within an ethnically Jewish environment.

Following the Second World War the vast majority of American Jews moved out of the urban ethnic neighbourhoods into suburbia. In the suburbs public spaces lacked the 'Jewishness' of the ethnic neighbourhood, and Jews who wanted to socialize with other Jews had to actively seek one another out. For most, the local synagogue became the primary space outside the home in which one could socialize with other Jews.[7] The 1950s and 1960s witnessed a major expansion in the number of synagogues built by American Jews, as well as the increasingly larger building space occupied by an average synagogue. If previously most of the physical space of the synagogue was dedicated to prayer, in contrast, the suburban 'Synagogue Centre' added space for classrooms, entertainment, and sport, often reducing the area dedicated to prayer to no more than 10–20 per cent of the entire building.

In other words, the suburban synagogue replaced the ethnic neighbourhood as a primary space for Jews to socialize with one another outside the home. The primary social contexts of American Jewish life today are found in the synagogue and institutions of the religious movements with which a person's synagogue associates (that is, the youth movement, the day school, and summer camp). Thus, Conservative Jews tend to spend most of their time interacting with other Conservative Jews, meaning that Orthodox Jews are not in the primary field of social reference when decisions are made about introducing change into tradition. Consequently, since the Second World War significant changes, most notably the promotion of full participation of women from the 1970s onwards, have been introduced.[8] Those Conservative Jews who reject the liberal innovations of their movement will often assert that it is not the legal issues that bother them but the rupture they cause in relations between Conservative and Orthodox Jews. The liberal Conservative Jew answers that Orthodoxy does not consider Conservative needs when making religious laws more stringent, hence Conservatives need not consider the Orthodox when introducing more liberal practices. Both answers are characteristic of the middle of the Jewish identity spectrum, in that they are concerned with the social rather than the legal consequences of religious innovation.

Conclusion

This chapter introduces the reader to the practice of analysing Jewish identity from the perspective of the everyday strategies individuals use when they move between social spaces. In most cases the concept of 'social space' is associated with a particular institution, such as the home, the community centre, the school, the synagogue, and so on.

From a sociological perspective, the assumption is that identity labels such as Reform, Conservative, Secular, and Orthodox all describe distinct strategies that individuals use at the level of everyday life as they move from one institution to the next. Which institutions do Jews use to build their Jewish identities? How do different types of Jews move between the institutions of everyday life in a recognizably Jewish manner? How do they determine 'authentic Jewish behaviour' within a particular institutional (social) context?

The preceding analysis operated on two levels. One is the level of the individual in everyday life, and the other is the level of the individual who lives in Israel or the United States. It is important to note that all of the identity labels used by Jews capture a broad diversity of behaviour.

Due to space limitation, I have not considered the effect of 'ethnicity' on the way people are placed on the Jewish identity spectrum. For example, there is a marked difference between the ways Jews of European ancestry (Ashkenazim) build Jewish identity vis-à-vis those of North African and Asian ancestry. In most countries Ashkenazi Jews have a greater tendency to seek strong ideological models of consistent or liberal behaviour, whilst Sephardim tend to adopt strategies associated with the middle of the Jewish identity spectrum. Why this is the case, and the extent to which it plays out in different countries and among different populations, is beyond the scope of this chapter.

When considering the effect of country on the building of Jewish identity in everyday life, I broached in an introductory fashion one of the biggest issues in the study of contemporary Jewish identity—namely, the nature of the relation between the institutions of private, communal, and public life. The primary difference between the experience of living as a Jew in Israel and in the United States is the presence or absence of a Jewish public sphere—mandatory public institutions in which all individuals have to participate 'as Jews'.

Many of the central questions for the sociological study of Jewish identity touch on the nature of the relationship of Jews to public institutions, whether at the level of the state in Israel, or the level of civil society and community in the Diaspora. We may ask how do Jews pick and choose between existing institutions? When do they attempt to build new types of institutions? And, what is the level of an individual's commitment to a particular institution or set of institutions? In its most basic sense, the sociological study of Jewish identity requires an understanding of the institutions which exist beyond the family, which individuals can or cannot use in their attempts to construct a connection to the Jewish collective.

FURTHER READING

General readings

Cohen, Steven Martin, and Gabriel Horenczyk. *National Variations in Jewish Identity: Implications for Jewish Education* (Albany: State University of New York Press, 1999). A collection of articles whose aim is to enable the reader to understand the diversity of Jewish identities as they have developed worldwide. Some of the articles offer comparative overviews of issues touching on Jewish identity and education in different countries; others focus on particular countries.

Kopelowitz, Ezra. 'Ethno-Religious vs. Religious Ritual: A Look at a Learning Ritual That Brings Together American and Israeli, Orthodox and Non-Orthodox Jews', *Research in the Social Scientific Study of Religion*, 13 (2002), pp. 1–22. Shows how the differences between American and Israeli Jews appear in one specific type of activity—reading biblical texts.

Liebman, Charles S., and Steven M. Cohen. *Two Worlds of Judaism: The Israeli and American Experiences* (New Haven: Yale University Press, 1990). A detailed discussion of the similarities and differences in the development of Jewish identity in the United States and Israel. The authors take key issues relating to Jewish identity and draw on survey data to examine how the issues play out in each country.

American Jewish identity

Alba, Richard D. *Ethnic Identity: The Transformation of White America* (New Haven and London: Yale University Press, 1990). An overview of the historical and social trends that are producing a steep decline in ethnic identification among 'white ethnic groups' in the United States. While Jews have retained a relatively large degree of ethnic particularism, they too are influenced by broader trends in American society.

Cohen, Steven M. 'Religiosity and Ethnicity: Jewish Identity Trends in the United States', in *Who Owns Judaism? Public Religion and Private Faith in American and Israel* (New York: Oxford University Press, 2001), pp. 101–30. Like Alba, Cohen notes the decline of ethnic identification among American Jews; however, Cohen argues that while American Jews are less ethnic, they are actually becoming more religious. Jews are more likely to perform religious ritual, but are less likely to do it with other Jews outside of the family home.

Cohen, Steven M., and Arnold M. Eisen. *The Jew Within: Self, Family, and Community in America* (Bloomington, Ind.: Indiana University Press, 2000). An authoritative statement about the manner in which 'marginally affiliated' American Jews understand their connection to Jewish communal life. Based on survey data and in-depth interviews, the reader receives a rich description of the influence of American culture and individualism on Jewish identity and belonging.

Sklare, Marshall. *Jewish Identity on the Suburban Frontier: A Study of Group Survival in the Open Society*, 2nd edn. (Chicago: University of Chicago Press, 1979). The classic statement of the influence of suburban life on Jewish identity by the founding father of the sociology of American Judaism.

Wertheimer, Jack, *A People Divided: Judaism in Contemporary America* (New York: Basic Books, 1993). A historical account of the development of Jewish religious 'denominations' and their role in fanning the culture wars between the various ideological streams of American Jewry.

Israeli Jewish identity

Deshen, Shlomo. 'The Social Foundation of Israeli Judaism', in Calvin Goldscheider and Jacob Neusner (eds.), *Social Foundations of Judaism* (New Jersey: Prentice Hall, 1990), pp. 212–39. A classic statement of the different streams within the Israeli Jewish population.

Deshen, Shlomo, Charles S. Liebman, and Moshe Shokeid (eds.). *Israeli Judaism: The Sociology of Religion in Israel* (New Brunswick, NJ: Transaction Publishers, 1995).

Liebman, Charles S., and Elihu Katz (eds.). *The Jewishness of Israelis: Responses to the Guttman Report* (Albany: State University of New York Press, 1997). In 1990 the first major survey of Israeli Jewish identity was undertaken. This book includes a collection of essays written by prominent Israeli academics, all of whom offer their opinion about the significance of the survey results.

Shokeid, Moshe. 'The Religiosity of Middle Eastern Jews', in Shlomo Deshen, Charles S. Liebman, and Moshe Shokeid (eds.), *Israeli Judaism: The Sociology of Religion in Israel* (New Brunswick, NJ: Transaction Publishers, 1995), pp. 213–38. A useful overview of some of the central differences between the two forms of ethnic Jewish identity to be identified amongst Askkenazi Jews and Jews from Middle Eastern backgrounds.

Sobel, Zvi, and Benjamin Beit-Hallahmi (eds.). *Tradition, Innovation, Conflict: Jewishness and Judaism in Contemporary Israel* (Albany: State University of New York Press, 1991). Two collections that consider most of the important issues on the topic of Israeli Jewish identity.

NOTES

I would like to thank Steven M. Cohen and Samuel Heilman for the feedback they gave during the writing of this chapter.

1. See Sergio DellaPergola, 'World Jewish Population, 2001', in *American Jewish Yearbook*, vol. 101 (New York: American Jewish Committee, 2001).

2. Robert K. Merton and Elinor Barber, 'Sociological Ambivalence', in Edward A. Tiryakian (ed.), *Sociological Theory, Values, and Sociocultural Change: Essays in Honor of Pitrim Sorokin* (Glencoe: Free Press, 1963). This idea has been elaborated in the Jewish context by Samuel C. Heilman, 'Inner and Outer Identities: Sociological Ambivalence Among Orthodox Jews', *Jewish Social Studies*, 39 (1977).

3. The idea that a connection exists between the boundaries of social territories and the nature of authority that determines normative behaviour within that territory is discussed in Stanford M. Lyman and Marvin B. Scott, 'Territoriality: A Neglected Sociological Dimension', *Social Problems*, 15: 1–4 (1967).

4. One should note that the dominance of religious identity labels is relatively recent. As late as the first half of the twentieth century many Jews also used identity labels that referred to belief in secular Jewish economic and Zionist ideologies. There were 'Jewish Socialists', 'Bundists', 'Labor Zionists', and 'Revisionists'. There were also Jewish identities that were tied to geography. For example, *Litvak* Jews looked down upon *Galiciana* Jews, and vice versa. Almost all of the secular ideological and geographical identity labels have fallen out of use amongst American and Israeli Jews.

5. Steve Bruce, 'The Supply-Side Model of Religion: The Nordic and Baltic States', *Journal for the Scientific Study of Religion*, 39: 1 (2000), describes a similar phenomenon of conservative Secularism on matters of religion in European countries where there is a strong connection between religion and state.

6. On the relations between Religious and Secular Israelis and the implications for Jewish identity, see Charles S. Liebman, *Religious and Secular: Conflict and Accommodation Between Jews in Israel* (Jerusalem: Keter, 1990).

7. For the classic statement of the challenges for Jewish identity posed by the move out of urban neighbourhoods and into suburbs, see Marshall Sklare, *Jewish Identity on the Suburban Frontier: A Study of Group Survival in the Open Society*, 2nd edn. (Chicago: University of Chicago Press, 1979).

8. Neil Gillman, *Conservative Judaism: The New Century* (West Orange, NJ: Behrman House, 1993).

17 | Fundamentalism

Nurit Stadler

Since its penetration into popular modern discourse, the term 'fundamentalism' has given new meaning to concepts such as religious zealotry, martyrdom, suicide-bomber, and holy war. In common parlance, the term conjures up a type of behaviour associated with violence justified on religious grounds. Even though it has a significant impact in the political sphere, the term continues to be misused and has thus been subject to endless reinterpretation. In contrast, the vast academic literature has emphasized the need to define the term and has developed various theoretical frameworks to analyse and discuss fundamentalist issues, several of which are Jewish. Nonetheless, this literature has also produced confusion, since it has been applied to a wide range of phenomena. It is against this background that this chapter examines some of the arguments relating to definitions of the term in the contemporary Jewish world.

The specific origin of the word fundamentalism dates to an early twentieth-century American religious movement. The movement took its name from a compendium of twelve volumes published between 1901 and 1915 by a group of Protestant laymen entitled: *The Fundamentals: A Testimony of the Truth*. This movement was part of the evangelical revivalism tradition that had inspired the Great Awakening of the early nineteenth century. Though the term was originally applied only to Christianity, its utilization has expanded to other religious traditions and is currently used to describe a variety of modern religious expressions. The transfer of this term to other religious contexts, especially Judaism, appears problematic, since features peculiar to specific Protestant infrastructures differ in many respects from other religious traditions.

Moreover, as noted, since it is extensively used in both popular discourse and the media, it can be employed pejoratively and with a sense of stigma, which in turn can prove misleading. Nonetheless, the main assumption as to the usefulness of the term is that it has not only historical but also generic characteristics, and therefore it is assumed to apply to a multiplicity of religious phenomena that are not uniquely Christian. Furthermore, the context and features of modernity, such as secular education, the mass media, and technology, seem to contain various triggers of religious fundamentalism that are distinctive. As such, religious fundamentalism is a product of contradictory pressures on the religious mind. Utilizing fundamentalism as a theoretical-comparative tool is therefore considered a helpful means of explaining a variety of religious experiences, including Evangelical Christianity in the United States, Iranian revolutionaries, Egyptian Islamic radicalists, militant Sikhs, and Buddhist resistance fighters, under the same analytical framework. A comparative analysis of these trends allows an in-depth look into particular traits, similarities, and differences within distinct radical religious platforms and expressions that appear to share distinctive models of reaction to the values of modernity. By using the term in the modern Jewish context, a better understanding of the uniqueness, exclusiveness (historically as well as culturally), and differences of various present-day Jewish movements may be offered.

To comprehend the contribution of the term to the analysis of distinct contemporary Jewish movements, we will begin with general definitions, followed by an illustration of its central features through a short analysis of three Jewish cases.

General definitions

In what is the dominant framework for the study of fundamentalist movements, such groups are seen primarily through their active character of protest against the established order, especially what devotees describe as the elements of modernity, such as secularization, individualism, and hedonism. Nevertheless (and perhaps paradoxically), these movements inevitably participate in modern political life, benefit from it, and are actively involved in the common discourse about modernization, political structure, and economic planning. In this context how can we distinguish and define these movements? In what ways can definitions of the term contribute to characterizing different modern Jewish movements?

Fundamentalism can be defined as a set of strategies by which devotees explain and express exclusive religious identities in the modern cultural market. The religious authorities of these groups develop a clear theoretical scheme to explain and deal with present issues, such as economic matters, political affairs, or the various relations with the modern state. Within this process, devotees believe the world will be saved from the profligacy and destruction manifested by modernity and secularization. Accordingly, they use religious reasoning to explicate history and tradition as well as contemporary reality. Fundamentalists perceive their faith as part of a glorious unbroken tradition, beginning with the earliest prophets and practitioners of the faith and continuing into the present. Therefore fundamentalists regard themselves as the true heirs of the ancient: the sole authentic performers of faith today and the guardians of sacred manifestations. Within this framework, religious authorities (such as preachers, gurus, imams, or rabbis) reconstruct sacred texts, re-create the group's collective memory, and are thereby engaged in the construction of new religious identities and practices. This kind of definition characterizes two major groups within current Jewish so-called fundamentalism, that will be discussed below: the *Haredim* and *Gush Emunim* (the bloc of the faithful). These groups can be distinguished from conservative and reformist trends within Judaism, the Haredi Mizrahi (Sephardi) segment, or the New Age, as well as from Haredi communities in other historical periods.[1]

This renewed fundamentalist religious identity is constructed through the utilization and careful selective retrieval of doctrines, religious symbols, beliefs, and practices—a process known as scripturalism. These symbols and meanings are selected from a sacred imaginary past and utilized as a subjective act in response to what are perceived as the consequences of modernity. Thus, religious fundamentalists are actively involved in the selective process of choosing and picking specific elements from their traditional sacred texts while implementing them in their future plans, visions, and fantasies: for example, the emphasis on the time of the great Jihad in the Islamic imagination, the period of the Talmudic Sages in the Jewish utopia, and the days of biblical miraculous manifestations in Christian memory. By selecting particular elements of tradition, fundamentalist groups seek to remake the world according to their unique goals and desires. By doing so, devotees believe that the road to salvation and redemption is shortened and reaffirmed.

The construction of the fundamentalist conscience also entails religious radicalism and extremism. While fundamentalists claim to reinforce tradition, they also transcend and employ it as a vehicle for radical environmental and political alterations. Therefore, this religiosity becomes the exclusive basis and rationale for re-creating the new political and social order. Yearning for the new order is invigorated with messianic, apocalyptic, or spiritual concepts. One example is the importance of the Land of Israel, which for various Jewish Orthodox groups, as well as Christian evangelists, is perceived to be a sacred element of the divine plan that therefore must be inhabited by Jewish people and kept as an eternal Jewish treasure.

However, even though it is inspired by the past, the fundamentalist imagination is oriented towards the future and this-worldliness. To develop the above example, the sacredness of the Land of Israel, in the fundamentalist imagination, is also used as a political device in many levels of their religious existence. Therefore, although fundamentalists seem to be traditionalists, their focus is on the future, not the past. Consequently, they are strongly involved in attempts to implement their future plans in light of what they see as their sacred past, and as the absolute truth.[2] This quest requires consistent answers, rituals, and practices that will arrange reality according to past piety. Consequently, a continuous tension evolves between the religious-inspired behavioural models of the past and the radical political ideology oriented towards the future. These unresolved tensions reinforce radicalism, violence, and dissent. For example, the vision of the Islamization of the modern state entails the reinterpretation of the Sharia (Islamic law) and its implementation in different fields, such as the economic, educational, and political. If we focus on the modern banking system, implementing the Islamic law about interest prohibitions might prevent all economic activities and growth in the future. Although this tension is acknowledged by the religious fundamentalist authorities, it is usually left unresolved.

Scripturalism[3] reinforces the importance of social institutions such as religious seminars, yeshivot, madrasas, churches, theological schools, bible schools and other religious institutions. As mentioned earlier, the fundamentalist imagination looks upon prior ages as the time of true piety. Accordingly, the generations of their fathers and forefathers are not perceived to have been adequately religious. Consequently, the mimetic aspect of socialization in these communities (a feature often found in traditional communities) is reduced. Hence the family is not considered as the sole significant institution for socialization and education. As in the example of the Habad movement (examined further below), special nursery schools and after-school children's group activities are dedicated to the implementation of the Rebbe's creed and the Habad style of life. Members of the groups are obliged to participate in these institutions, that function as central devices for the intensification of religion and the construction of the fundamentalist consciousness, and which tend to become total institutions, meaning that they encompass and are responsible for all fields of members' everyday lives.

Finally, religious fundamentalists possess a dual concept of an enemy. On the one hand, the group objectifies an external 'other' and identifies it as an oppressor, while advocating active resistance against that oppressor.[4] For example, this struggle can involve aggression and violent actions toward the state which represents modern agencies. The battle against state laws stems largely from the fear that secularization and modernization would brutally detract from the authority of the sacred, as well as from the tension between religious fantasies of past devotion and corporeal reality. Christian protests against abortion in the United States and violent Haredi demonstrations against the Israeli courts offer two examples. On the other hand, these movements fortify and construct a battle of an inner personal devil perceived as embedded in all devotees. Evil inclinations stress the need to control the religious body according to specific codes and regulations. This realization results in the subjectivization of the religious experience manifested through the creation of various bodily and spiritual training programmes established to invigorate the character of those who wish to participate in the restoration of a divine plan. These practices vary from group to group, and include prayer, extreme meditation, an emphasis on zealot ascetic practices, and military and physical training. In this context, aspects of asceticism and individual martyrdom are emphasized and become powerful models of behaviour in fundamentalist groups (suicide-bombers are the most extreme example of this inclination).

Jewish fundamentalisms: explanations and examples

In light of the features described above, we can now examine three Jewish examples described in the literature as fundamentalist: the Haredim, and more specifically the 'world of the yeshivas'; the Lubavitch-Hasidic or Habad movement; and the 'bloc of the faithful'—Gush Emunim. These cases were analysed as part of the Chicago project.[5]

The world of the yeshiva scholars—*b'nei torah* in Israel

For *b'nei torah* (sons of the Torah), the study of the sacred text is considered the most central act of God's devotion and the only way to preserve Judaism and the continuity of the Jewish entity. Yeshiva Jews are those who claim to be following the traditions and practices of the Eastern European yeshiva academies of Lithuania. *Torah lishma*—study for 'its own sake'—is considered a central theological doctrine of yeshiva religiosity. It is acquired by the lifelong exposure to sacred texts and an ongoing dialogue with them. The yeshiva is not only an educational tool but also serves to distinguish devotees from the surrounding secular society, in which they authenticate themselves by worship, language, food, and law. A Haredi-style devotee is one who fulfils the world of the Torah through every detail of his life in order to realize the perfect religious models of the past.

Haredi members consider themselves a direct offshoot of the European Orthodox Jewish legacy and their only continuation in the present day. As such, they stress an ideology that tends to reject modern culture (through the interpretation of the sacred texts) and the western lifestyle and profoundly condemns every expression of it. Most scholars have viewed the Haredi community as embodying what is often referred to as a 'culture of the enclave', stressing punctiliousness and stringency in the observance of halakhic rules and an isolated lifestyle.

The commandment in Deuteronomy 6: 7, to study Torah 'when you sit at home and when you walk abroad', has been accorded absolute centrality in Haredi interpretation nowadays. According to current Haredi interpretations, this commandment obliges all male members to join the yeshiva as a part of belonging to the community and its legacy. This obligation is stressed by the use of central symbols drawn from their imaginary-invented cultural and traditional past, especially the school of the Gaon of Vilna, Rabbi Elijah ben Solomon, and his disciple Rabbi Hayyim of Volozhin. This utilization of tradition to legitimize participation stands in sharp contrast with the historical account of the European tradition. In Lithuania, among Eastern European Jewish communities, only a handful of prodigies, members of a select elite, dedicated their life to studious activities, while in the present day most adult male Israeli Haredim are obliged to devote most of their lives to the yeshiva. Accordingly, Haredi members regard anyone who accepts the legitimacy of modern culture as embracing an essentially anti-Jewish attitude, and therefore as a potentially contaminating influence. For example, television is perceived as a vicious tool to penetrate and desecrate Haredi consciousness.

In contemporary Haredi communities behaviour is constructed and transmitted through popular interpretations of sacred texts. Traditionally, all Jewish religious communities were constituted as 'text-centred', meaning a community based on male literacy and interpretations of sacred texts. However, the difference between past communities and contemporary Haredim is significant. In the past, social behaviour was transmitted mainly by socialization through the imitation of behavioural models of the family and the community. Nowadays the interpretation of everyday life is based on the interpretation of male experts, virtuosi of sacred texts, who are given the power to translate textual knowledge into everyday practices. The reliance on Scripture and rabbinical interpretations to justify behaviour represents a non-traditional reading of traditional texts, which is selective by nature: it focuses upon certain parts of the Scripture while ignoring others, which usually contains variations, gaps, and contradictions. The parts selected, often marginal and non-representative, are presented as a comprehensive explanation of reality and behaviour.

Moreover, text centralism requires full dedication to yeshiva life and activities. Accordingly, b'nei torah are obliged to be distanced from this-worldly activities and excluded from responsibilities of earning a livelihood or central state duties (such as army service in Israel). This dynamic is illustrated by one example of the Haredi interpretation of the work/body relationship reflected in their view of the biblical Adam. In this view, the biblical image of Adam corresponds to bodily images of the Haredi scholar: a perfected, ascetic body striving to avoid shame or sin which threatens to contaminate his life. Therefore, this body is not expected to work, toil, engage in the labour market, or make any physical effort in order to survive; he acts only in order to worship and honour God. Actions are thus designed and dedicated solely towards the divine. Reshaping the narrative of the first man highlights the unresolved tension between images of past piety and everyday behaviour. The world is polluted, therefore the active man who labours in the temporal world (a view of man that was dominant in the canonical texts) is viewed as pretentious and as a sinner. This interpretation presents all aspects of corporeal work as an obstacle to salvation, and stresses worship of God and man's withdrawal from the temporal world.

Habad/Hasidic Lubavitch

The Habad Hasidic movement, known also as the Lubavitch Hasidic, is another example of the manifestation of scripturalism and yeshiva religiosity. Yet, in contrast to the religiosity of b'nei torah, Habad devotees spread the teaching of the text through missionary activity, while struggling and adjusting to the modern world. Habad—the name derives from an acronym of three Hebrew words that distinguish and characterize the movement: *hokhma* (wisdom), *bina* (intelligence), *da'at* (knowledge)—originally appeared in Russia, but today is based mainly in the United States and Israel, and is also represented in France, England, Argentina, Australia, and numerous other countries. The movement combines a fervent conviction in absolute scriptural truth with an equally enthusiastic belief in the imminent coming of the Messiah, who will establish his kingdom on earth. Through the years Habad has developed a messianic theology which concentrates on the charismatic leadership of Rabbi Menachem Mendel Schneerson (since 1950, the seventh leader in the Habad dynasty). The Rebbe enjoyed a special status in the community, immense admiration, and authority until his death in 1994. During his leadership Habad enjoyed a great increase in popularity and spiritual authority that was related to the resurgence of Haredi communities worldwide (especially during the 1950s). In light of this resurgence, Habad devotees see themselves as guardians of rabbinic law and the Jewish legacy, and therefore as fighters against secularization and its influence upon Jewish adherents. A Habad devotee is a Jewish warrior and a zealot proselytizer. In contrast to many Haredi movements (such as b'nei torah, or other Hasidic segments) that oppose modernity and see it as threatening, Habad adopts a different approach. Habad is not blind to the influences of modernity and the threats it poses to Judaism and the accompanying issues of assimilation, yet it seeks a close dialogue and mutual relations with the surrounding society. Therefore, its relation towards the world is complex; Habad devotees wish to reshape reality through the traditional Jewish symbols and values, while not employing segregationist strategies. On the contrary, forming a close dialogue and relations with modernity is believed to be the foundation of their effort to bring young Jews to the Orthodox way of life and therefore prevent assimilation and ignorance in Jewish matters. This view is related to a central religious objective: to bring about the coming of the Messiah. In this view the concept of the external devil, mainly secularization, is reduced; however, since devotees work through the corporeal realm, the inner battle with 'evil inclinations' is accentuated.

Accordingly, Habad devotees make use of all modern media and direct personal contacts for evangelist promulgation. In this respect they are like all other modern missionary movements (such as American Evangelists or Pentecostals), utilizing technical and advanced resources in order to restore as many Jews as possible, in every part of the world, to the true faith, and to expand their community boundaries. For example, from its inception in the United States the movement's aim was to reinforce the Habad Jewish identity in the American multicultural context. In that respect, they have invested in fund-raising campaigns to maintain their court and yeshivas. As such, in sharp contrast to the b'nei torah religiosity, Habad is a transnational organization, working globally on the intensification of what its followers see as the struggle for the strengthening of Jewish identity worldwide.

Theologically Habad has developed a messianic interpretation of worldly events. In its view, all events are part of a redemptive process of preparing the world for the coming of the Messiah. For example, in 1991 the Rebbe declared that it was the time for redemption and that all Jews should prepare for the coming of the Messiah and should endeavour to urge his arrival. This view served also to explain why the Rebbe stayed in the United States and not Israel, on the premise that until the Messiah's arrival one may live a full Jewish life only in the Diaspora. Messianic explanations are also given to world events, such as the first Gulf War (1991), that was explained as the struggle and victory of God over all Jewish enemies. This messianic idea is also believed to explain why the Rebbe was such an extraordinary individual and his leadership considered a miracle. Following the Rebbe's death in 1994 the movement has experienced an internal schism, splitting into two different sects: those who view the Rebbe as the coming Messiah, and therefore reject the idea of his death; and the rationalistic sect, who have denied such concepts and have sought reform.

The Habad messianic mission is distributed through the 'Habad House' and the campaigns of emissaries. Habad work is organized mainly through the House, which is a free and open residence that encompasses all mission activities and religious information. Accordingly, the House is a central institution and provides information on Jewish religion, customs, and rituals according to the Habad interpretation. For example, it offers the products and instructions for Jewish holidays, such as matzot for Pesah, the four species for Sukkot, kiddush wine and instruction pamphlets on holy fasts and feasts. In the House one will find written information and open lectures on many Jewish topics as well as free internet access for Jewish tourists all over the world. In these respects the House serves as a mechanism to spread Habad ideas worldwide in an attractive and friendly manner.

The second missionary strategy is the campaign run by young devotees. These messengers leave their homes and yeshivas to do their work on the streets of the modern secular city. They attempt to encounter non-committed Jews and persuade them to engage in a specific ritual, partake in Sabbath meals, and read some of the movement's popular literature. The best-known campaign of Habad on the streets is the tefillin ritual, in which a person is invited to put on phylacteries in the midst of secular surroundings. According to Menachem Friedman, although traditionally the tefillin ritual requires sacredness and purification, which cannot be achieved in the middle of the street, Habad devotees openly desecrate the sacred, as they believe that by doing so a person declares his Jewish identity in public and the process therefore promotes an important goal.[6] According to the Habad view, the tefillin ritual might ultimately help another Jewish soul join the Habad group. Thus they integrate Jewish rituals into the public sphere, fight the Jewish foes with the ritual of the tefillin, and thereby bring Judaism inside the modern secular city. Violating the sacred in public emphasises the fundamentalist tension between the aspiration to live according to past piety and the obligation to be strongly involved in this-worldly activities, especially through missionary activities.

Gush Emunim—the Bloc of the Faithful

The case of the Gush Emunim underscores different aspects of Jewish fundamentalism. Strong scripturalism and a yeshiva orientation are expressed alongside radical interpretations of the sacredness of the Land of Israel and its centrality to the redemption of the Jewish people.

While Haredi participation in the political game can be explained in pragmatic terms (that is, in order to maintain their unique interests), members of Gush Emunim, mainly settlers in the West Bank and Gaza, are involved in all aspects of the state and civil society (economics, civil duties, culture, and education). However, they are ready to violate the state's laws and sacrifice themselves in order to uphold their particular reading of the Jewish faith. Thus, in the name of sacred laws members of this group have used violence to thwart any action endangering the holiness of the land. The secular reality, as a historical stage, provides the tools that help to advance the purpose of the return of the holy land to the Jewish people and the unfolding of the divine plan for messianic redemption. Accordingly, members of Gush Emunim may be viewed as activists preoccupied with the Israeli political agenda, especially regarding territories.

In contrast to b'nei torah and Habad, the movement has been embedded in Israeli existence and politics from its inception. The rise of the movement itself, in 1974, however, was triggered by the 1967 Six Day War, that was given a profound theological meaning. The movement interpreted the Israeli victory, and especially the return to the Temple Mount, as a sign that the God of Israel did not desert his people, but had saved them from a vicious enemy and extended their territories. This triumph was interpreted as a miracle, and therefore accepted as a sign of heavenly redemption.

Not unlike the construction of b'nei torah religiosity, the creed of Gush Emunim was elaborated and transmitted through the reinforcement of the yeshiva institution, emphasizing the centrality of sacred texts. Yet, in contrast to the Lithuanian yeshiva style that underscored traditionalism, 'Merkaz Harav' (Rabbi Kook's Universal Yeshiva) declared its goals as a disruption and possible transformation of the previous order, accordingly encouraging radical political activism. Therefore its missions were to be practically involved in the struggle for control of 'the whole land of Israel' and in promoting the idea of bringing under Israeli control the historical heart of biblical Palestine (that is, Judea and Samaria).

The spirit of Merkaz Harav was shaped and guided by the authoritative teaching of Rabbi Avraham Yitzhak Hacohen Kook (1866–1935), the first chief rabbi of Palestine and the movement's spiritual leader. It was later augmented by Rabbi Zvi Yehuda Kook, his son and later the mentor of Gush Emunim. According to Kook the elder, the secular Zionist movement was considered sacred and its rise indicated the commencement of the process of redemption. Therefore, all events related to the Zionist movement and return of the Jews to Palestine gained theological interpretations and were explained in messianic terms. Accordingly, Merkaz Harav yeshiva represents a new type of response to Zionism and modernity, aspiring to expand its religious influence to all aspects of social life and provide sacred meaning to the process of modernization and the creation of the State of Israel. The group of Merkaz Harav headed by Rabbi Kook the younger saw its gospel becoming attractive to the sector of religious Zionism, and especially to its activist youth movement, Bnei Akiva. This served as a sort of ready-made cadre, assuming the form of a religious sect striving to fulfil transcendental concepts with a strong reliance on rabbinical authorities. This radical group saw the settlement of Judea and Samaria as a way of preserving the divine gift, locking it in, so to speak, and hence hastening the redemption. This was the religious gloss on the old (secularist) Zionist belief that nurturing the Land of Israel is the only way towards a true return to Zion. The 1973 war urged the movement into intensive settlement activity as part of the realization that redemption should be actively accelerated rather then anticipated passively, as in other Jewish Orthodox movements. This era can be explained as the charismatic stage of the movement, when it crystallized and shaped its unique methods and ideas, particularly the ideology of the settlements. During this time, loyal to the Kookist doctrine of the sacredness of the land, Gush Emunim used methods of non-violent demonstrations. Yet, by the end of the 1970s their methods changed and the movement adopted more militaristic strategies against Arabs. Their motivation is part of a conviction that the state has failed to enforce the law or to establish order. Therefore, acting through the law of the land and God, and as guardians of the true Judaism, they have the right to defend themselves from the enemies of the Jewish people. While doing so they believe they protect the Land of Israel, and in this way contribute to the process of redemption. Through this religiosity the fundamentalist tension between the aspiration to realize past piety and modern reality increases. If the existence of the Jewish people could only be kept through the redemption of the land, more specifically the biblical land, behaviour in the world should be devoted exclusively to this task. In the circumstances of Israel today, this tension is connected to violence and aggression.

Concluding remarks

Whilst acknowledging the difficulties of importing ideas related to fundamentalist studies into the account of Judaism, it appears useful to analyse specific Jewish groups within the generally accepted parameters. Features such as scripturalism, political radicalism and activism, a dual concept of the enemy, and a continuous tension between the religious inspired models and the current radical political ideology can all be identified in the examples considered. The utilization of these features can aid our understanding about group diversity within contemporary Judaism, in contrast to other Jewish models from the past, and in comparison with other religious movements in diverse religious settings. As demonstrated in the Haredi case study, ideally men are obliged to engage and devote themselves to the yeshiva, to study and be expert in Talmudic doctrines, and be able to translate these ideas into an everyday reality. Accordingly, meanings and activities are shaped and practices are justified through the yeshiva, while reinforcing commitment and authority. The Habad movement integrates scripturalism and yeshiva-based centralism with a strong emphasis on charismatic leadership and missionary activities. As demonstrated, the Habad House is utilized as a primary agent to promote activities, knowledge, and rituals. Finally, Gush Emunim's scripturalism focuses on the radical interpretations of the sacredness of the Land of Israel and the centrality of the redemption of the Jewish people.

These three cases highlight different Jewish fundamentalist orientations and strategies: the emphasis on different texts, diverse orientations towards the world, and distinctive relationships with modernity (otherworldliness, integration, and so on). These strategies are distinct from other current trends in Judaism, such as the charismatic tendencies popular in Israeli Mizrahi Haredi groups like Shas, which focus on the religious experience and adapt some mystical practices, or the New Age Jewish groups that combine various sources or techniques of Jewish mysticism with dance, magic, astrology, or new interpretations of Oriental philosophies.

FURTHER READING

Almond, G. A., E. Sivan, and S. R. Appleby. 'Examining the Cases', in M. E. Marty and R. S. Appleby (eds.), *Fundamentalisms Comprehended* (Chicago: University of Chicago Press, 1995), pp. 445–82. Provides examples and an introduction for the study of fundamentalism.

Ammerman, N. T. *Bible Believers: Fundamentalism in the Modern World* (New Brunswick and London: Rutgers University Press, 1987). Provides a general introduction to the study of fundamentalism.

Aran, G. 'Return to the Scriptures in Modern Israel', *Bibliotheque de l'école des Hautes Etudes Sciences Religieuses*, 99 (1993), pp. 101–31. Explains in detail the return to the Scriptures in Jewish modern movements.

Beeman, William O. 'Fighting the Good Fight: Fundamentalism and Religious Revival', in Jeremy MacClancy (ed.), *Exotic No More: Anthropology on the Front Lines* (Chicago: Chicago University Press, 2001). Describes the anthropological aspects of fundamentalism.

Friedman, M. 'The Haredim and the Israeli Society', in J. Peters and K. Kyle (eds.), *Whither Israel: The Domestic Challenges* (London: Chatham House and I. B. Tauris, 1993). Provides an introduction to Haredi culture in Israel.

Marty, E. M., and R. Scott Appleby (eds.). *Fundamentalisms Observed* (Chicago: University of Chicago Press, 1991) and *Accounting for Fundamentalisms: The Dynamic Character of Movements* (Chicago: Chicago University Press, 1994). These two books contain chapters including general analysis of Jewish fundamentalist movements; Zionist fundamentalism; Habad history and religiosity; the messianic features of modern Habad; yeshiva fundamentalism in Israel; and the centrality of the text in Haredi communities.

Stadler, N. 'Is Profane Work an Obstacle to Salvation? The Case of Ultra-Orthodox (Haredi) Jews in Contemporary Israel', *Sociology of Religion*, 63: 4 (2002), pp. 455–74. Provides an understanding of the ways texts are translated into conduct in a fundamentalist surrounding.

NOTES

1. For further consideration of these phenomena see Chaps. 6, 7, and 11.
2. S. N. Eisenstadt, *Fundamentalism, Sectarianism and Revolution* (Cambridge: Cambridge University Press, 1999).

3. Haym Soloveitchik, 'Migration, Acculturation, and the New Role of Texts in the Haredi World', in Martin E. Marty and R. Scott Appleby (eds.), *Accounting for Fundamentalisms* (Chicago: Chicago University Press, 1994), pp. 197–235.

4. G. A. Almond, E. Sivan, and S. R. Appleby, 'Examining the Cases', in Martin E. Marty and R. Scott Appleby (eds.), *Fundamentalisms Comprehended* (Chicago: Chicago University Press, 1995), pp. 445–82.

5. The Chicago project is a five-volume work on the question of fundamentalism. It deals with theoretical issues of religious extremism through varied examples from Christianity, Islam, Judaism, Buddhism, and Hinduism.

6. Menachem Friedman, 'Habad as Messianic Fundamentalism: From Local Particularism to Universal Jewish Mission', in Marty and Appleby (eds.), *Accounting for Fundamentalism*, pp. 328–57.

Religious issues

| **Prayer and worship**

Ruth Langer

Introduction

Traditional Judaism integrates the holy into every aspect of life. Consequently, prayer and the synagogue represent only one, not particularly privileged, subset of Jewish sacred activities and locations. Other activities, like Torah study, being charitable, or even eating, and other places, like the study hall or the home, are also sacred. However, the Christian world's stricter separation of sacred and secular spaces and activities meant that the synagogue took a leading role in Judaism's move into modernity. If Jews and Judaism were to be accepted as legitimate parts of western society, then public Jewish religious life, to which Christians would first look in characterizing Judaism, needed to be 'presentable' in Christian eyes. Beginning in some places as early as the eighteenth century, this concern resulted in a far-reaching set of revolutions in public and private Jewish ritual life, the impact of which still reverberates today. Affecting mostly Western Europe (and its colonies), the New World, the large cities of Eastern Europe and the Arab world, and Israel, these changes neither occurred in all places nor did they occur uniformly in any one place or at any one time. In many cases, the transformations in more traditional settings were responses to the challenges raised by liberal reforms. The analysis that follows characterizes mostly the experiences of pre-Holocaust Western Europe and America, and contemporary America and Israel. It needs to be understood within the larger history of the modern movements of Judaism.

The aesthetics of the synagogue

Christian visitors to a typical pre-modern Jewish synagogue would not have compre-hended most of what they encountered. Although local architectural and decorative norms often influenced the building's style, its iconography was distinctively Jewish. That the liturgy was entirely in Hebrew would not have been so strange to Catholics accustomed to the Latin Mass, but Protestants would have noticed the absence of vernacular worship. A member of the congregation, not clergy, led the services, generally with minimal musical sophistication, especially on weekdays. For most parts of the service this man stood directly before and below the ark containing the Torah scrolls, in a deliberately humble position. Like the Catholic priest before the twentieth-century liturgical reforms, he stood with his back to the congregation, but he did so for the entire liturgy, acting as the congregation's representative before God rather than its spiritual leader. The synagogue's seating also spoke to his relative unimportance. Rather than the forward-facing formal pews characteristic of western churches, many synagogues oriented their seating towards the raised platform located in the middle of the synagogue floor, from which the Torah was read. Most striking to the visitor, particularly in an Ashkenazi synagogue, would have been the lack of decorum. Many worshipers arrived after the service started, prayed at their own pace, and studied or wandered around visiting friends during the service. Although the congregation would join the prayer-leader for certain prayers, particularly for special holiday rituals, this would not have overridden the outsider's general impression of strangeness, cacophony, controlled confusion, and lack of reverence.

In many communities, first steps towards modernization of the synagogue addressed these perceptions. To do so required only superficial alterations that did not contradict—and often were supported by—the laws (halakhah) governing the conduct of the liturgy. A trained cantor could lead the prayers, improving their general performance as well as their musical aesthetics. A men's choir could accompany him, often enhanced by the addition of pre-adolescent boy sopranos. Congregations insisted on greater personal decorum, quieting the gossipers, limiting their wandering, and encouraging greater focus on the prayers. Reconfiguration of the synagogue space to conform more closely to public religious spaces in the greater community encouraged this enhanced decorum. Congregants could sit in rows, facing the front of the building, often even in pews as in a church. Some synagogues placed increased visual emphasis on those leading the prayers, moving more activities to the front of the synagogue and creating elaborate elevated lecterns, often still situated below and before an ornate and even more elevated ark. Once granted rights of residence in leading European cities, Jews built grand synagogues that accommodated and even demanded such changes. The newly emancipated Jews rejoiced in their citizenship in European societies and sought to lessen those factors that marked them as different.

Other changes challenged not just customs of Jewish prayer, but the actual laws governing it. No matter how good a cantor and choir, the musical expression of a traditional synagogue could not rival that of a church, where instrumental music and mixed-gender choirs provided a richer variety and sophistication. Among the earliest issues of synagogue reform was the introduction of an organ and of women singers— and the styles of music appropriate to them. Various aspects of instrumental music, permitted during the week, violate the traditional laws of Sabbaths and holidays, the occasions of the most elaborate liturgies. The strict separation of the sexes in traditional Judaism includes a prohibition on men's listening to women's singing. While some communities tried to answer these halakhic concerns and make changes—sometimes by employing only Gentiles to provide music—for others this became a locus for public rejection of tradition and definition of themselves as modern and open to reforms. As musical tastes changed, some congregations, particularly in America, broadened this musical repertoire to include other instruments, including, in recent decades, the guitar. All Reform congregations permit both musical instruments and female vocalists. No Orthodox congregations allow either. Between these extremes exists a spectrum of practices. Increasingly, Conservative congregations do not use musical instruments on the Sabbath, but do not differentiate between male and female vocalists. In all cases, the shifting musical norms of the surrounding cultures have penetrated, to greater and lesser degrees, the melodies of the synagogue.

The location of people in the synagogue created some other issues. Traditionally, men and women sit separately, with a barrier separating them physically and visually. Generally, women were in a balcony or on the periphery of the main floor. While in Europe this differed little from Gentile customs, American churches had developed the concept of family pews. American Reform Jews adopted mixed seating, first as a matter of convenience when, in 1851, an Albany congregation purchased a church equipped with pews, but this quickly became a matter of ideology. Mixed seating spread as far as some left-wing Orthodox congregations in the United States (these congregations usually designated three sections, only one of which was mixed), but by the close of the twentieth century separate seating had become one of the defining factors of an Orthodox service. Few synagogues continue compromise seating today.

Building a grand synagogue created another practical challenge: making the liturgy audible. One solution was for the prayer-leader to turn around and face the community. However, traditionally, certain key prayers must be physically directed to the Jewish world's center of holiness in Jerusalem, and synagogue architectural norms dictated that the Torah ark be placed on the Jerusalem-facing wall. A prayer-leader facing the congregation would have his back to both the ark and Jerusalem. Nineteenth-century Reformers found theological justifications for this change. They rejected the messianic hope for an ingathering of the exiles and the reconstitution of the Jewish state. They also rejected the ongoing holiness of the site of the Jerusalem Temple. Instead, they understood themselves to be loyal citizens of their countries of residence; true holiness was present in all synagogues. Confining God to a particular locale made little philosophical sense. Consequently, if the available synagogue site made orienting the sanctuary to Jerusalem awkward, some communities abandoned the traditional geographical direction of prayer altogether. Eventually, the invention of the microphone and then the rise of Zionism made this theological shift less necessary. However, because microphones generate an electrical current, considered by most traditional Jews to be a form of fire and hence prohibited on the Sabbath, this too became a dividing line between Orthodox and more liberal congregations. In liberal communities some prayer-leaders do pray facing the ark for at least part of the service today.

The aggregate of these changes radically transformed the aesthetics of the synagogue service. From a participatory community of individuals, each with primary responsibility for fulfilling his or her own prayer obligations, loosely led by the prayer-leader, the congregation became more of an audience sitting politely and passively through a ritual performed by professionals. To answer the need for congregational participation, liberal Jews crafted responsive readings. Unlike the litanies of the church, where the congregation responds fervently with the same response (or set of responses) to each line, most Jewish responsive readings divided translations of traditional prayers into sentences recited alternately by the reader and the congregation. Such readings became a standard part of Reform liturgies and a frequent phenomenon for English prayers in Conservative synagogues as well. Israeli liberal liturgies also adopted this mode of congregational prayer. Deeper education in Hebrew and encouragement of communal recitation of English prayers is now increasing participation in many synagogues.

Reaction to these changes—other than their rejection outright by the most traditional Jews—emerged in the latter decades of the twentieth century, particularly in the Havurah movement, that strove to recapture much of the atmosphere of the traditional synagogue without necessarily sacrificing other liberal ideals. These deliberately smaller prayer communities (*havurot*) encourage universal participation, congregational rather than performed singing, and informal seating, often in the round. In imitation, many liberal synagogues built in recent decades feature flexible seating, smaller and less hierarchical worship spaces for more intimate services, congregant-led services, and less formal music. Decorum persists, but it is decidedly more ethnically Jewish. The explosion of Jewish folk music, inspired by Israeli and neo-Hasidic culture, has affected most parts of the Jewish world, including many Orthodox synagogues. Most contemporary Jews seek spiritual engagement, not Teutonic awe and reverence.

Evolving ritual roles

These aesthetic changes caused alterations in the roles of the various players in the synagogue service. Mixed seating moved women from the physical periphery into the centre of activity. As women gained access to education, and as suffragism grew into modern feminism, women gradually became less accepting of peripheral ritual roles. Traditional separation of the sexes meant that women were never called to the Torah, never served as a prayer-leader, never became rabbis, and exceedingly rarely became synagogue presidents. By the early twentieth century liberal Jews had accepted, in principle, that nothing excluded women from these roles, but only with the general calls of the 1960s for equal rights and roles in the greater society did this begin to penetrate the synagogue reality. Today, in liberal settings, women assume all ritual roles. In the Orthodox world public segregation of the sexes in worship remains an absolute legal norm. However, some communities address the challenges raised by feminism by reconfiguring the synagogue space so that the women's section is not peripherally located; by developing separate women's services at which women lead prayers and read Torah; by encouraging women to engage in serious study and teaching of traditionally men's texts; and by welcoming women's lay leadership in non-ritual matters. In all these settings, the traditional prayer that God bless 'this holy congregation . . . them, their wives, sons and daughters and all that is theirs' no longer describes the reality: the congregants now have husbands too. In all but the Orthodox world, since 1972 women have become rabbis and cantors.

These changes helped reshape the roles of synagogue professionals. Rabbis and cantors existed in pre-modern communities, although their presence was not a prerequisite for public prayer. The cantor (*hazzan*) functions as a professional prayer-leader, expected to be an expert in the intricacies of the liturgy and its musical presentation. Thus, communities preserving the traditional Hebrew liturgy but lacking Jewishly educated men often hired a cantor before a rabbi, giving the cantor a ministerial title. The aesthetic changes discussed above also led to a professionalization of the cantorate. Competition with Christian liturgical music required the cantor to have musical sophistication. This, together with grander synagogues, required operatic-quality voices. Decorum meant that congregants paid attention to the cantorial performance. The aesthetics of the musical performance of the prayers and the aesthetics of the synagogue structure were deeply entwined. However, this change also led to the diminishment of the cantor in some liberal settings. There, organs and choirs took over the musical responsibilities. With the turn to spoken rather than chanted vernacular prayers, the cantor's expertise became dispensable. Thus, by the turn of the twentieth century, while some synagogues adopted elaborate cantorial musical styles, others eliminated the cantor entirely, handing non-musical ritual tasks to the rabbi. While in more traditional settings cantors or lay prayer-leaders retain responsibility for the performance of the liturgy, in more liberal settings the interface between the liturgical roles of cantor and rabbi remains rather fluid, differing greatly from one synagogue to another. Although cantors traditionally learned their craft by apprenticeship, a need to professionalize and revitalize the cantorate has resulted in the American movements' post-Holocaust turn to investiture of cantors by schools associated with their seminaries.

Modernity transformed the rabbi's ritual role even more dramatically. The pre-modern rabbi was a teacher and a legal decisor for his community. If he led prayers, it was simply as a member of the community. Most preached only twice a year, on the Sabbaths before Passover and the Day of Atonement. Frequently his primary appointment was by the community rather than a specific synagogue within that community. Along with the modernization of the synagogue arose a demand that rabbis take on roles more similar to that of Christian clergy. They became pastors to their flock, expected to minister in times of joy and sadness, and, most importantly, to preach frequently and well. In liberal synagogues the rabbi became the chief liturgical officiant, leading the performance of spoken prayers, vernacular and Hebrew, and reading Torah. More so than the cantor, many rabbis came to see themselves and be seen as embodiments of holiness, set apart from the rest of the community in priestly manner. Although Orthodox rabbis did not take over the leading of services, and legal leadership of their community remained a significant part of their roles, they too found themselves now ministering and preaching, at least in the Diaspora. While Orthodox women may not become rabbis, they do share in these new pastoral and educational roles.

The prayers themselves: vernacular language, changing theologies

The Christian visitor to the pre-modern European synagogue could perhaps comment on its aesthetics, but could not comprehend the statements of its liturgy, not only because then it was entirely in Hebrew with a smattering of Aramaic, but also because its theological assumptions and structure bore little resemblance to that with which he was familiar. The formal structure and basic theological content of that liturgy dated to early rabbinic times, around the end of the first century CE. The precise wording of the prayer book, encoded by law and tradition, had evolved more gradually, but had changed little from the end of the first millennium. It had become mandatory to recite a virtual torrent of words, lasting for about two hours on an ordinary Sabbath and much longer on holidays. Daily prayers were shorter, but primarily because they were recited even faster.

However, the aesthetic changes that modernity introduced into the synagogue included calls for shorter services and vernacular prayer. Challenged by the need to construct a liturgical experience that would attract assimilating Jews and prevent their conversion to Christianity (a significant problem in early nineteenth-century Germany), reform-minded leaders complied. The result, though, was much more far-reaching.

Some have described the Jewish prayer book as anthological. Throughout history, Jews had addressed new liturgical needs by adding to the prayers. As Jakob J. Petuchowski observed, though, one generation's spontaneous prayer became the next generation's fixed required prayer. Shortening the service meant a revolutionary upset of this dynamic, an elimination of 'required' prayers. To do this in a meaningful fashion meant establishing criteria by which to judge the contents of the received prayer book. Ideally, on the model of the Protestant Reformation, Reformers could retrieve some 'original' form of the prayers. However, modern Jewish liturgical scholarship and its search to reconstruct early liturgy was, at best, in its infancy. The Talmudic-era library preserves only occasional discussions of prayer texts; our earliest liturgical manuscripts date only from the end of the first millennium, and these were only discovered at the very close of the nineteenth century. To the extent that early Reformers used this method, they discerned which prayers were more essential and preserved them before others.

The call for vernacular prayer generated another mode of liturgical reform. The evolved Jewish liturgical texts are highly poetic, constructed of a Hebrew in which almost every word alludes to a biblical verse or a rabbinic concept. They are open to multiple interpretations. The sheer volume of words forces the worshipper to privilege some words and concepts over others, unpacking some poetry and letting some slip by. This is fundamentally untranslatable. A translator, no matter how adept, must choose a particular single meaning, ignoring most poetic valencies. Consequently, there were few translations of the prayer book before this period, and most of these were more commentaries to aid less educated traditional Jews participate in the Hebrew prayers.

In contrast, translations meant to be used as the synagogue's primary prayer texts must be theologically appropriate and aesthetically pleasing. Nuances culturally specific to their Hebrew context can become embarrassments in a modern European language. Once the prayer is in the vernacular, its content must convey the right impressions, both to the non-Jew and the assimilated Jew. Consequently, on a number of levels, vernacular prayer raised a new set of challenges, ultimately leading to much more radical changes in liberal liturgies. Translation effectively moved Jewish liturgy from a Jewish cultural context into a western cultural context, with its consequent demands.

Early nineteenth-century German Reformers were very conscious of living in new times. The first forays into aesthetic changes in the synagogue had pre-dated Jewish emancipation. This new situation demanded more coherent, theologically grounded moves to fit into western society. Reformers therefore rejected increasingly explicitly anything that contradicted their understanding of the 'truths of religion', especially any allusion to Jews' being in exile from the Land of Israel. They eliminated prayers for a messianic return there, for the rebuilding of the Jerusalem Temple, and the creation of a Jewish state under messianic Davidic rule. They also eliminated most references to Jewish particularism and any negative references to Gentiles. If Jews truly believed that they were at home in Europe, and if they wanted Christians to accept this unhesitatingly, they could not in good conscious even want to pray for a change in circumstance. Theological changes of this sort, which introduced new meanings and language for canonized prayer texts, received an added boost from the burgeoning scientific study of Judaism, especially from Leopold Zunz's attempt to reconstruct original prayer texts in his book on Jewish preaching (*Die gottesdienstliche Vorträge der Juden*, 1832). This suggested that the apparent stability of Jewish liturgy was illusory, and that there had been significant change since the original compositions of the prayers. If so, contemporary Jews could justifiably adapt the texts to suit their changed circumstances.

Literally hundreds of liberal liturgies have been published in the past two centuries, both by national movements and by individual rabbis and congregations. These represent a vast spectrum: from minimal changes in the earliest years of reform; to prayer books with no or almost no Hebrew, that barely preserve recognizably any structures of the traditional liturgy; to retrieval of traditional structures and prayers; and, most recently, to transliterated Hebrew texts, encouraging congregational participation. Prayer books also reflect the intellectual currents and historical experiences of their times. During the peak of nineteenth-century rationalism, Reformers eliminated hints of the supernatural. Prayer books published in the 1960s and 1970s added reflections on the Holocaust and began to celebrate the State of Israel. Feminism and egalitarian language, first about humans and then about God, appeared in the 1980s. These more recent prayer books also admit to a search for spirituality and to non-rational approaches to God. Even humanism, a Judaism without God, finds its place in the 1975 American Reform prayer book *Gates of Prayer*, but alongside nine other services, each representing a distinct theology. Typical of the America of that time, this prayer book represents an 'anything goes' approach to Judaism and Jewish worship. Revised editions of it, its successor in the works, and liberal prayer books published in England and Israel, have reduced the numbers of options. In general, they point to a selective retrieval of tradition and a greater comfort with Jewish particularism, reflecting the development of a truly modern Jewish, Hebrew-speaking culture in Israel, and the Holocaust's message that Jews cannot escape antisemitism by blending in.

Reform Judaism's destabilization of the liturgy challenged its neighbours to respond. Modern Orthodoxy continues to teach that the received prayers are legally non-negotiable. However, this does not apply to the poetic embellishments to these prayers. Accepting a late medieval Sephardi legal argument that liturgical poetry interrupts and hence invalidates required prayers, the nineteenth-century Orthodox Ashkenazi Jewish communities also shortened their liturgies. Today most traditional Jews only retain this poetry on the High Holy Days. Many also added weekly sermons to enhance the intellectual quality of the services. Although many Orthodox prayer books include vernacular translations, these are often too infelicitous for actual public prayer.

Conservative Judaism did not produce many identifiable liturgical changes until, with the growth of the movement, it began in 1927 to publish its own liturgies in the United States. The 1946 *Sabbath and Festival Prayer Book* presents a very traditional liturgy, but designed many translations and new English prayers for actual use, sometimes as responsive readings. More significantly, the editors, especially where they could find precedents in older liturgies, retrieved versions of prayers that they found theologically more appropriate. Therefore, some prayers ask for peace for all the world, not just for Israel; the additional service, instead of praying for the restoration of sacrifices, simply recalls their offering in the past. The movement's current prayer book, *Sim Shalom*, perpetuates these changes, makes more allowances for English prayer, and makes the prayers for peace all pray for universal peace. In addition, its most recent 1998 version adds egalitarian language in English and an optional reference to matriarchs along with the patriarchs in the *avot*, a key paragraph of the prayers.

A full survey of the liturgical variants of the past two centuries, even in Germany and America, let alone in Israel, England, and other western communities, is impossible in this space. All make liturgical decisions according to the theological, historical, and aesthetic challenges discussed here, placing themselves along the spectra of tradition versus innovation, Jewish versus western cultural identity, and theological particularism versus universalism.

Rationalism and mysticism

Translation of Hebrew prayer into the vernacular presupposed a rationally accessible text in which the words, in their simple, obvious meanings, transmitted the ideas of the prayer. These ideas, then, could readily transfer from Hebrew to a modern European language without significant loss of content. However, in the history of Jewish liturgy this had not, for centuries, been an obvious assumption. Jewish mystics, beginning at least in the traditions of the Rhineland Hasidei Ashkenaz recorded and preserved in the twelfth and thirteenth centuries, continued by the various schools of kabbalist mystics, and reshaped yet again by the modern Hasidic masters beginning in the eighteenth century, had understood the prayers to operate on other levels too. Prayers recited properly, that is, with the correct words, in Hebrew, and with correct intention, had positive impact on the divine realms. The true meaning of the prayers lay not in the dictionary meaning of their words, but in their cosmic impact. While for centuries this approach to prayer was esoteric knowledge confined to the mystic adept, by the sixteenth and seventeenth centuries parts of this system were increasingly common practice, shaping the communal perception of the meaning of prayer. Indeed, the fixed prayer texts of Jewish liturgy retained their vitality precisely because of the communities' abilities to infuse them with new and timely meanings. Particularly important in the early modern period was the sense that, through prayer (and proper performance of the commandments in general), Jews might be able to affect the course of history and bring the Messiah. This understanding was and is characteristic of much of modern Hasidism and ultra-Orthodox Judaism, and thus remains a piece of our portrait of Jewish worship in the modern period. Because the effectiveness of mystical meditation on prayer requires that the prayer texts be precisely correct in all respects, this also contributes to the resistance to liturgical modernization in these circles.

Prayer book commentaries give us a glimpse into this dynamic. From the medieval world we have inherited three genres of commentary: those providing halakhic commentary on correct performance of the prayers; those focusing on the literal meaning and derivations of the language of the prayer book; and those providing mystical insights. By the early modern period we find a preponderance of two genres: those providing philological and grammatical commentary, attempting to correct 'printers' errors', and kabbalistic commentaries. This suggests that the *meaning* of the prayer, for large numbers of Jews, resided in its mystical import. By the nineteenth century a new dynamic arises, beginning in Germany: historical and rational commentary that utterly ignores and even rejects the mystical teachings. Even among Orthodox Jews the spirit of rationalism prevailed, replacing the commentaries of the mystically oriented Isaiah Horowitz and Jacob Emden with those of Wolf Heidenheim, Samson Raphael Hirsch, and Seligman Baer.

In recent decades many modernized Jews have come to find rational approaches to prayer to be spiritually barren. While most have no desire or ability to re-access authentic kabbalistic approaches, various trends speak to a search for and a validation of less intellectual approaches to worship. Ironically, one expression of this desire to delve more deeply into the prayer book is the recent publication of many prayer books with significant commentary, much of which points the reader to the spiritual potential of the text. Notable on this account is the new prayer book series from the American Reconstructionist movement, entitled *Kol Haneshamah*. Another expression of this trend is the movement towards more participatory services with the inclusion of Hasidic-inspired music. The melodies of Shlomo Carlebach, a neo-Hasid, shape Orthodox and Reform liturgies alike. Crowded Carlebach *minyanim* (prayer quorums) are widespread, with Sabbath services significantly extended by meditative communal singing. Particularly in liberal contexts, Jews are also experimenting with the use of meditation within worship contexts.

Non-liturgical prayer

To this point we have discussed exclusively the scripted, halakhically mandated worship of God that constitutes the liturgy of the synagogue. The Jewish tendency to fixed liturgy was such that even those places in the liturgy initially designated for private supplication had been scripted by the high middle ages. Personal incidental prayer penetrated the formal liturgy only on its margins, if at all, and it is only starting to be part of the normative discourse of Jewish liturgical scholars. Some of the interest in private prayer arises from the interest in the history of women's spirituality. Because women were largely marginalized in the synagogue, they frequently developed other loci of spiritual expression deserving of our attention.

Where Christians, especially Protestants, expect that one should be able to generate an extemporaneous prayer to fit any occasion, this model never penetrated deeply into the Jewish world. Even where Reform liturgies imitated Protestant models and deviated far from traditional forms, rabbis scripted and published the new texts. While Judaism certainly never discourages private prayerfulness, it does not particularly encourage it either. Where even minimally literate women developed their own times for prayer, they too scripted these prayers. Unlike official synagogue prayers, though, when times changed these prayers could be jettisoned or rescripted.

The nature of traditional women's prayerful expression varied greatly. In some communities women learned Hebrew and recited the traditional liturgy. In others, women's education focused on Yiddish or a European language; although women attended the synagogue, at least on important days, they could not follow the service. Elsewhere, especially among Jews from Muslim countries, women were totally illiterate and took no role in synagogue life. Particularly in this last group, a non-scripted, action-oriented women's spirituality developed, centred around rituals like candle-lighting, visiting tombs, and food preparation. In Europe women developed their own verbal prayer texts that were, at least eventually, recorded and published. These prayers accompany rituals specific to women, especially candle-lighting and fertility-related rites, but also include many prayers for recitation in the synagogue in parallel to, but quite distinct from, the official liturgy of the institution.

With modernization, these prayers largely lost their force. Fanny Neuda's German 'translation' in the mid-nineteenth century, *Stunden der Andacht* (Hours of Devotion), translates not the words but rather the entire world-view, from a rich, folksy Yiddish spirituality to a German rationalism. This genre remains a rich source of creativity. In many corners of today's Jewish world new collections of liturgical suggestions for 'women's' moments emerge frequently. These collections include not only parallels to established men's life-cycle rituals, but they also celebrate previously ignored moments unique to women's lives, like weaning and menopause.

Conclusion

The contemporary synagogue continues to address the evolving challenges of modernity. Thus, contemporary Jewish communities do not answer precisely the same questions as their ancestors two centuries ago. Feminism, the search for spirituality, or negotiation with Israeli culture were unimaginable then, but shape Jewish religious life today. However, the fundamental question remains: how can Jewish religious life be a harmonious piece in the larger cultural quilt of the civilized world without giving up its authenticity? In seeking to answer this question, Jews have evolved a diverse richness of answers that shape the shifting textures of their public and private religious lives.

FURTHER READING

Caplan, Eric. *From Ideology to Liturgy: Reconstructionist Worship and American Liberal Judaism* (Cincinnati: Hebrew Union College Press, 2002). The only comprehensive history of Reconstructionist liturgies.

Cardin, Nina Beth (ed. and trans.). *Out of the Depths I Call to You: A Book of Prayers for the Married Jewish Woman* (Northvale, NJ: J. Aronson, 1995). Cardin presents the texts of an Italian Jewish tradition of women's prayers.

Friedland, Eric L. *'Were Our Mouths Filled With Song': Studies in Liberal Jewish Liturgy* (Cincinnati: Hebrew Union College Press, 1997). Collects Friedland's studies, mostly on American Reform liturgies.

Krinsky, Carol Herselle. *Synagogues of Europe: Architecture, History, Meaning* (New York: Architectural History Foundation, and Cambridge, Mass.: MIT Press, 1985). This richly illustrated volume presents the history of European synagogue architecture through the modern period.

Meyer, Michael A. *Response to Modernity: A History of the Reform Movement in Judaism* (New York: Oxford University Press, 1988). This is the definitive study of Reform Judaism, containing an extensive discussion of Reform liturgy and its dynamics.

Petuchowski, Jakob J. *Prayerbook Reform in Europe: The Liturgy of European Liberal and Reform Judaism* (New York: World Union for Progressive Judaism, 1968). Petuchowski bases his masterful analysis on an exhaustive study of 171 European prayer books, including close readings of their introductions and texts.

Reif, Stefan C. *Judaism and Hebrew Prayer: New Perspectives on Jewish Liturgical History* (Cambridge: Cambridge University Press, 1993). The later chapters of this volume provide the finest extant global survey of the dynamics of modern liturgical history.

Sered, Susan Starr. *Women as Ritual Experts: The Religious Lives of Elderly Jewish Women in Jerusalem* (New York: Oxford University Press, 1992). Sered's anthropological analysis of the spiritual expression of illiterate Jewish women from Kurdistan and Yemen provides unique insights into Jewish worship outside the synagogue.

Slobin, Mark. *Chosen Voices: The Story of the American Cantorate* (Urbana and Chicago: University of Illinois Press, 1989). In addition to analysing the development of the cantorate in America, provides an overview of the history of the cantorate since its inception.

Weissler, Chava. *Voices of the Matriarchs: Listening to the Prayers of Early Modern Jewish Women* (Boston: Beacon Press, 1998). Weissler's ground-breaking work analyses Yiddish women's prayers, discussing the history of the genre, and uncovering elements of women's spirituality.

19 | The authority of texts

Nicholas de Lange

Judaism has always been a text-based religion. Literacy has traditionally been highly valued, and the written word has enjoyed a status that is all the stronger for want of a well-developed continuous tradition of musical or visual art. In the past the book was accorded a status little short of magical. At the heart of Jewish worship is the display, reading, and exposition of a written text, the Torah. Public education has been accorded a high priority in Jewish society down the ages, and the possession of books has been a feature of Jewish homes even when it was rare in the surrounding culture. Scholarship has been valued as a profession, and those who earned their livelihood by other means have made time in their lives to pursue it, often to a high standard. Scholars have been the custodians and transmitters of Jewish culture throughout the centuries. Respect for the book as an object is enjoined in the codes of Jewish practice, and this applies not only to sacred texts but to books of all kinds, which must not be used for inappropriate purposes, or defaced, or even left lying open or fallen on the ground. When a religious book is no longer fit for use it is not thrown out but buried with due honours in the cemetery. A great rabbi of the fifteenth century banned from attending his lectures a student who had refused to lend another student a book. With the invention of printing Jewish books were among the first to be printed in large numbers, and in many places Hebrew presses were the first printing-presses to be set up. Even today, when the publishing and reading of books is widespread, Jews are prominent among writers, publishers, and readers. But whereas in earlier times general literacy distinguished Jews from the Christian environment, in our age of universal education Jews are exposed to a much wider array of written materials, and the Jewish writings have to struggle to make their voices heard, while the respect formerly accorded to learning has become diminished in most Jewish circles.

In the specific context of Jewish religion, arguments that in other circles might hinge on an appeal to common sense or rational proof are liable to turn on an appeal to texts. This tendency can be discerned everywhere, from rabbinic discussions in the Talmud to current debates on medical ethics or politics. But since the Enlightenment the supernatural authority formerly accorded to certain texts has been undermined in various ways, and widely differing accounts have emerged of the nature of authority in Judaism. What we call 'Jewish pluralism' often boils down to fundamental disagreements about the authority of texts.

This weakening of the authority of texts, which is a key element in the development of Judaism over the past 200 years, has provoked a strong reaction in Orthodoxy, which began as a modernizing movement but now feels called to defend what are seen as authoritative Jewish beliefs and practices. This defence is now anchored in a radical assertion of the unquestionable authority of certain texts, as interpreted by certain figures who have, in turn, been invested with a very strong authority. The appeal to sacred texts, severely limiting the autonomy of the individual, has come to be a defining feature of Jewish Orthodoxy. Yet, in one way or another all branches of Judaism, including those that have rejected belief in a personal god, have a strong tendency to attribute authority to texts.

A Jewish home contains books. It is a commandment to study Torah 'when you sit at home and when you walk abroad' (Deuteronomy 6: 7). 'The Jewish book is the great instrument which helps to shape our life according to this commandment. The Jewish book belongs to the Jewish home. Without it the Jewish people cannot continue to exist.'[1] The hierarchy of books on the Jewish bookshelf is not the same for everybody. Jewish pluralism can also be studied in terms of which books are important to particular groups or individuals.

The Bible

The authority of the books of the Bible, or *Tanakh*, is enormous. However, the different books enjoy different kinds and levels of authority, and different sectors of Jewry have different understandings of the claims the books exert on Jews today. At the heart of the matter is a theological question: whether the books are believed to emanate directly, so to speak, from the 'mouth of God'. For the whole of the Jewish tradition down to the beginning of the nineteenth century, and for all traditionalist and Orthodox authorities today, the five books of the Torah at least are believed to be a direct revelation from God given to Moses and the people of Israel at Mount Sinai. This tenet has been challenged in the past two centuries from a number of angles, historical and philological, philosophical and theological, but despite all the challenges the authority of the Torah has remained strong, and is invoked even by Jews who reject any supernatural belief. Also in the modern period the appeal to the prophets has become stronger, particularly among Reform and socialist Jews, who admire the loud and confident cry for justice and compassion for the less privileged members of society.

The reading of the biblical books is inseparable from their interpretation, and the Jewish tradition of interpretation is embodied in the classical sources of the Targum (Aramaic translations and paraphrases), midrash (rabbinic elaborations and explanations), and commentary (*perush*). The main classical commentaries are those of Rashi (1040–1105), who lived and wrote in Troyes in Champagne, and Abraham Ibn Ezra (1089–1164) and David Kimhi (*c.*1160–1235), who represents the Spanish tradition characterized by an interest in the study of grammar and a rationalist philosophical orientation. Many other commentaries survive from the middle ages.

A new era in Jewish Bible commentary was inaugurated by Moses Mendelssohn, the towering figure of the German Jewish Enlightenment movement of the eighteenth century. Mendelssohn published in the 1780s his own translation of the Torah into German, accompanied by a commentary in Hebrew (known as the *Biur*) composed by a group of scholars under his direction, combining traditional comments with the ideas of the Enlightenment. Subsequent Hebrew commentaries have tended to follow this pattern, combining traditional and modern insights.

Since the time of Mendelssohn various different factors have combined to undermine the authority of the Bible. The prevailing rationalism was inimical to a narrative studded with miraculous events, while the ethical outlook was uncomfortable with a legal and social system founded on slavery and the subordination of women to their fathers and husbands. Philological and historical researches, while they confirmed some aspects of the biblical text, cast doubt on others. Science undermined the biblical account of the origin of the world. Different sources were identified within the Torah and the Book of Isaiah, and the dating of some Scriptures was revised by scholars, some being placed as late as the Hellenistic period. In addition, theological developments called into question the very idea of a text uttered or delivered by a deity to human beings. These changes did not all take place at once, and their impact was not uniform, but their cumulative effect was very damaging to the traditional authority of the Bible.

In the nineteenth century the theological doubts about revelation and the quest for different documentary sources within the Torah and the re-dating of some other parts of the Bible (including, for example, a very late date for some of the Psalms, traditionally attributed to King David) threatened to undermine completely the traditional rabbinic view of the integrity and authorship of the biblical books. Several of the leading figures in the nascent Orthodox movement were quick at first to realize the possibilities of modern biblical criticism, but as the confrontation between Orthodox and Reform rabbis became more outspoken, a dogmatic rejection of modern approaches to biblical criticism became more pronounced on the Orthodox side. The new attitude is best encapsulated in the public questions addressed in 1853 by Samson Raphael Hirsch, rabbi at Frankfurt am Main and a leading opponent of Reform, to the founders of a new-style rabbinic seminary at Breslau. Hirsch was actually a firm believer in bringing Judaism out of the ghetto and in taking advantage of modern methods of education and research, while Zacharias Frankel, who had been invited to be the principal of the new seminary, was a rather traditional modernist. But as the spokesman of the new Orthodoxy, Hirsch evidently felt called on to make a strong statement on this occasion. His opening questions were:

What will revelation mean in the proposed seminary? For Orthodox Judaism it is the direct word of the one, personal God to man, and 'God spoke to Moses' is a simple, supernatural fact, just as one man speaks to another. Do the leaders of the seminary acknowledge this Orthodox belief?

What will the Bible mean in the proposed seminary? Orthodox Judaism believes in the divine authenticity of the Bible, and knows nothing of the various authors of the Pentateuch, nor of Pseudo-Isaiah, nor of Maccabean songs under the name of David, nor of Solomon's Ecclesiastes from the time of the Second Temple, and so forth. What do the leaders of the seminary say about the authenticity of the Bible?

This outspoken challenge to modern approaches to the Bible is important because it has continued to influence Orthodox Judaism to this day. Whereas the other streams in modernist Judaism, both radical Reform and the more conservative stance of which Frankel was a pioneer, have been willing to accept modern research on its own terms, even if they have resisted some of its more extreme trends, Orthodoxy has always inclined to put forward the rejection of radical biblical criticism as a fundamental issue of faith.

Meanwhile the Reform movement, which embraced biblical scholarship and drew attention to aspects of the biblical teachings that seemed to be primitive and untenable in a modern society, stressed the moral grandeur of the Bible and its honoured place as the foundation document of Jewish peoplehood. The 'Pittsburgh Platform' of 1885 contrived to put forward an apparently positive statement about the Bible coupled with outspoken rejection of some of its teachings:

We recognize in the Bible the record of the consecration of the Jewish people to its mission as priest of the One God, and value it as the most potent instrument of religious and moral instruction. We hold that the modern discoveries of scientific researches in the domain of nature and history are not antagonistic to the doctrines of Judaism, the Bible reflecting the primitive ideas of its own age and at times clothing its conception of divine providence and justice dealing with man in miraculous narratives.

We recognize in the Mosaic legislation a system of training the Jewish people for its mission during its national life in Palestine, and to-day we accept as binding only the moral laws and maintain only such ceremonies as elevate and sanctify our lives, but reject all such as are not adapted to the views and habits of modern civilization.

We hold that all such Mosaic and Rabbinic laws as regulate diet, priestly purity and dress originated in ages and under the influence of ideas altogether foreign to our present mental and spiritual state. They fail to impress the modern Jews with a spirit of priestly holiness; their observance in our days is apt rather to obstruct than to further modern spiritual elevation.

The effect of such declarations went far beyond the status of the Bible, and touched every aspect of Jewish life and thought. Subsequent generations of Reform thinkers have been faced with the task of simultaneously maintaining in general terms the immense role and standing of the Bible for Jews (all the greater because of the common ground it represents in the encounter with Christianity) while rejecting its divine character as taught in traditional Judaism, and particularly the divine sanction it conferred (together with the Oral Torah) on the rabbinic legal system, the halakhah.

In the twentieth century, in the wake of such developments, and in the ambit of the feminist movement, Jewish feminists began to question the Bible from their own particular standpoint. They challenged the authority of a narrative which enshrined the subordination of women to men, and protested against granting divine sanction to an inherently sexist legislation. The outcome, however, has not been a rejection of the Bible so much as a rereading. Feminist commentaries are being written, and in this way the old text is given a new lease of life.

Curiously, the mainly atheist Zionist movement, too, attributed a positive value to the Bible, as the foundation document of the people of Israel and its claim to the Land of Israel. The Zionists explored the Land with Bible in hand, and made Bible study a key element in the school syllabus. In the biblical prophets they found support for their key belief in the return to the Land, and for the principles of social justice that they embraced. One of the leading socialist Zionists, David Ben-Gurion, devoted himself to biblical studies, and the Israeli Declaration of Independence, although framed in secular terms, speaks of 'the Ingathering of Exiles' and proclaims that 'the State of Israel will be . . . based on freedom, justice and peace as envisaged by the prophets of Israel'.

In some ways the status of the Bible is as strong today as it has ever been, even among those Jews, the majority, who reject its divine origin.

The prayer book

After the Bible the best-known Jewish book is the prayer book. The Hebrew prayers were first codified in the ninth century, but considerable variation between different rites continued, and today, with the burgeoning of different religious tendencies and synagogal organizations, the diversity of prayer books has become even more marked. Recent prayer books of the liberal wing of Judaism tend to incorporate not only vernacular translations (first introduced in the late eighteenth century) but additional materials of a meditative, instructional, or explanatory character. In Britain an important milestone in the standardization of worship was the publication in 1890 of the *Authorised Daily Prayer Book of the United Hebrew Congregations of the British Empire*, commonly known as 'Singer's Prayer Book' after its editor, Simeon Singer. Singer's Prayer Book has been issued in a succession of revised editions, and is still very widely used in British Orthodox synagogues and is found in many homes, although the American 'ArtScroll' editions, that adopt a traditionalist approach to the service, and are equipped with notes and explanations aimed at inculcating a traditionalist praxis, are becoming increasingly popular.[2] Meanwhile the various synagogue organizations in Britain and America have issued their own prayer books.

The prayer book has two faces: it is a repository of religious beliefs that have accumulated down the ages, and it is an important textbook: in the absence of definitive creeds or catechetical education, it constitutes the only induction many Jews ever receive in the theological beliefs of their faith. This is a largely unconscious process, and prayer books are not usually cited to settle disputes about matters of doctrine, but their influence is considerable, and the various modernist movements have not been slow to realize this and revise the books in line with the message they wish to put across.

But what are the theological beliefs of the liturgy? Here it is necessary to draw a distinction between traditional liturgies, which evolved over a long period by a kind of sedimentary process without the active intervention of an editor, and modern liturgies, edited by individuals or more often by panels of rabbis, concerned to purge the text of theological ideas that have been discarded and to incorporate others that have been adopted.

Among the distinctive features of modern liturgies are the abandonment of many passages deemed too obscure or antiquated for contemporary worshippers (especially when translated into the vernacular), the introduction of some modern prayers and meditations, and in some books anthologies of passages for study or discussion. Gender-inclusive language has been adopted, some formulae that could be deemed offensive to non-Jews have been removed, and contentious religious beliefs, such as bodily resurrection, have been amended. In such ways the liturgy has been brought up to date, and made more suitable for worship in the modern age.[3]

The Talmud

The foundation text of rabbinic Judaism is the Talmud. Although its authority in traditional rabbinic Judaism is enormous, even outstripping that of the Bible in some respects, its claim to authority has not gone unchallenged. In the middle ages the Karaite movement denied its authority, and demanded a return to Scripture alone, and in the early nineteenth century the reformer Abraham Geiger declared that it was an 'ungainly colossus' that must be toppled if there was to be any true religious or political progress for the Jews. His contemporary Samuel Holdheim wrote boldly: 'The Talmud spoke with the ideology of its own time, and for that time it was right. I speak for the higher ideology of my own time, and for this age I am right.'[4] The Reform movement has accepted that the Talmud—like the Bible, if not more so—is not a divine text but a human creation.

Study of the Talmud does, however, figure on the syllabuses of contemporary Reform rabbinical colleges, even if the laws and regulations which make up a large part of its subject-matter, and have a great influence on Orthodox practice, are not considered binding. It is seen as an important historical document, and a source of many inspiring teachings. Equally, in many respects the criticisms to which the Talmud has been subject in the modern period have increased the authority which has been invested in it by Orthodoxy.

The *Shulhan Arukh*

Although the Torah and the Talmud are major sources of halakhah, their prescriptions cannot be applied today without recourse to the enormous subsequent tradition that has refined and adjusted them to changing conditions. Much of this tradition is embodied in a succession of codes produced throughout the course of the middle ages, and in collections of responsa, authoritative rabbinic replies to questions, usually of a practical nature. The codes resolved contradictions and uncertainties, while the responsa, in applying the old laws to actual situations in ever-changing circumstances, constantly renewed and extended the halakhah.

Observant Jews today seeking the answer to a halakhic question are likely to refer to the *Shulhan Arukh* (Spread Table), compiled by Joseph Caro (1488–1575), and first published in 1565, or to one of the various abridgements of it that have been made for popular use.

Although it is now more than 400 years old, and in the intervening period many changes have taken place in Jewish life and many developments have been introduced in halakhah, the *Shulhan Arukh* has never been superseded as a basic reference work. It is available in abridged and translated form, and new commentaries continue to be written. Elijah, the Vilna Gaon (1720–97), wrote one important commentary (*Biur ha-GRA*), tracing the sources of every law in the Talmud and medieval commentators, thus investing it clearly with the authority of the Oral Torah. The authority which Orthodoxy continues to attribute to the *Shulhan Arukh* highlights the distinctive approach it adopts to textual authority, in some respects as a backlash against Reform.

The most important and influential of the modern commentaries are the *Mishnah Berurah* of Israel Meir Ha-Kohen, known as the Hafets Hayyim (1838–1933), and the *Hazon Ish* of Abraham Isaiah Karelitz (1878–1953), generally known by the title of his enormously popular book, who significantly undermined the authority of received tradition and insisted on that of the text itself.[5] Each of these authors was among the great leaders of traditional Judaism in his own day, and both alike succeeded, by focusing on the exhortation to moral and spiritual perfection, in breathing life into the dry bones of the halakhah, and making the code into a guide to religious living instead of merely a list of dos and don'ts.[6]

Mystical works

Even though relatively few Jews today describe themselves as kabbalists, the *Zohar* (Radiance), the classical text of Kabbalah (Jewish mysticism), still enjoys a following, seven centuries after its appearance in late thirteenth-century Spain.[7] Written in an artificial Aramaic, the book has the form of a commentary on the Torah, outwardly resembling the midrash and purporting to go back to the time of the ancient rabbis. The work is a vehicle for the theosophical ideas of the Kabbalah, centring on the doctrine of the *sefirot*, ten powers within the godhead produced by emanation from the ultimate and unknowable *En Sof* (Infinite).

The Zohar spread from Spain around the Mediterranean, and became enormously influential in Hasidism. The opponents of the Hasidim, led by the Vilna Gaon, also accepted the sanctity of the Zohar. However, this sanctity never became a matter of dogma, and Jewish rationalism was strongly opposed both to Kabbalah as a whole and to the exaggerated respect paid to the Zohar. The great Prague Talmudist Ezekiel Landau (1713–93), for example, was deeply suspicious of Kabbalah, and it was partly under his influence that the Austrian emperors Joseph II and Franz Joseph II forbade the importation of kabbalistic literature into the empire. Jewish scholars, religious modernists, and *maskilim* (supporters of the Haskalah) shared an antipathy to the mystical tradition, in keeping with the anti-obscurantist spirit of the Enlightenment.

The modern study of the subject was pioneered by Gershom Scholem,[8] who laboured untiringly on kabbalistic and other mystical texts, analysing the ideas they contain and tracing their history and their relationship with traditions outside Judaism. Scholem was not a kabbalist himself; on the contrary, he was a product and an adherent of German-Jewish rationalism. But his scholarly work had the effect of encouraging a renewed interest in the kabbalistic tradition. Unfortunately, genuine interest in recovering an authentic Jewish heritage has become confused with a modern quest for esoteric exotica and a spiritual 'quick fix'. Study of the Jewish mystical tradition requires linguistic skills and painstaking work, as well as a sympathy with the aims of the earlier kabbalists. A large number of the publications about the *Zohar* and Kabbalah available now are compiled by people lacking these resources, and in extreme cases have little or nothing to do with Judaism. Kabbalah is penetrating mainstream Judaism, but it is also becoming a fashionable rallying cry for individuals and groups, both Jewish and non-Jewish.

Other Jewish books

There is another class of books that have never enjoyed a sacred or canonical status, yet represent an important stream in Jewish thought and have exerted a great influence at various times, namely, works of religious philosophy. Among these, Moses Maimonides' *Guide of the Perplexed* has been widely regarded as the masterwork of medieval Jewish religious thought, and indeed it was received and cited with approbation by medieval Muslim and Christian thinkers.[9]

In the nineteenth century the Lithuanian Musar movement, founded by Israel Salanter (1810–83), was responsible for a remarkable renewal of the medieval spiritual and ethical tradition, from which it takes its name (*musar* being the Hebrew for 'ethics'). Unlike Hasidism, of which it was in some sense a rival, the Musar movement did not discourage the academic study of the Talmud, but urged that it should be complemented by deep personal piety and by meditation on ethical texts, many of which were revived and republished as a result of this renewed interest. Study of these texts was a feature of the 'Musar houses', where both professional scholars and members of the wider public would retire for a period of self-scrutiny every day, and in the academies which came under the influence of the movement they were chanted aloud to special tunes.

Meanwhile Jewish philosophy of religion has been pursued in German and other European languages. The landmarks of German Jewish thought include Hermann Cohen's *Religion of Reason Out of the Sources of Judaism* (published posthumously in 1919), Franz Rosenzweig's *Star of Redemption*, and Martin Buber's *I and You*.[10] Notable authors in English are Mordecai Kaplan, A. J. Heschel, and Milton Steinberg, and among French Jewish philosophers Emmanuel Levinas stands out.

All of these philosophical writings have attracted a following among thoughtful Jewish readers, but none of them can be said to command authority comparable to the key texts mentioned earlier. Others do indeed exert authority, but only among a limited readership. An example is the *Tanya* of Shneur Zalman of Lyady (1747–1812), the fundamental text of Habad Hasidism.

It would be a very remarkable Jewish home that contained all the aforementioned works. With the notable exception of the Bible and prayer book, they represent distinct streams within Judaism. An Orthodox Jew who possesses well-thumbed copies of the Talmud and *Shulhan Arukh* and related halakhic works may never have opened the *Zohar* or Maimonides' *Guide*, while the latter works would appeal to very different types of readers, with an inclination to mysticism and rationalism respectively.

Moreover, mention of these classic Jewish works does not begin to exhaust the other, very different, types of book we might find in a Jewish home. Novels, books of poetry, cookery books, and history books all have their place on the Jewish bookshelf. Grammars and dictionaries of Hebrew, too, both the biblical and the modern language. There is a burgeoning Hebrew literature from Israel which, even if it is inherently secular, has a great deal to say on Jewish subjects. There is also a literature in Yiddish which has come to be appreciated for its own sake and not only out of folksy nostalgia.

The earlier literature such as the Talmud covered every conceivable subject: no topic or genre was ruled out because it was not 'serious' or 'religious' enough. To the modern literature, in all its diversity, Ignaz Maybaum applies the term 'European Talmud':

It covers the literature in which European Jewry discussed Jewish problems, wrestled with the spirit of its environment, succumbed to it, escaped it and finally assimilated it to the Jewish spirit and thus renewed the old legacy. This new literature is Jewish literature. Are Herzl's writings and diaries 'profane' literature? They are not as far as we Jews are concerned. Is Samson Raphael Hirsch's Bible commentary less Jewish than that of Rashi because the former was written in the nineteenth century? Hermann Cohen, Franz Rosenzweig, Mendele Mocher Seforim and Bialik,

Ahad Ha'am and Solomon Schechter, these and numerous others are the rabbis of the European Talmud.[11]

These words were written in 1945. Time has moved on, and Jewish literature today is no longer only a European literature; it is American and Israeli as well. This is an open-ended 'Talmud' that grows and grows. Like the original Talmud, it does not seek final answers to perennial questions, but revels in a debate which respects the arguments of the other side, and finds as much value in analysing a problem as in solving it.

FURTHER READING

Helpful suggestions may also be found in the chapters in this book on 'Fundamentalism', 'Prayer and worship', 'Philosophical issues: survey', 'Theological issues: survey', and 'Contemporary issues in halakhah'.

Appel, Gersion. *The Concise Code of Jewish Law: Compiled from Kitzur Shulhan Aruch and Traditional Sources: A New Translation With Introduction and Halachic Annotations Based on Contemporary Responsa* (Hoboken, NJ: Ktav, 1977). Exploits traditional legal texts to form a guide to Jewish practice today.

Berlin, Adele, and Marc Zvi Brettler (eds.). *The Jewish Study Bible* (New York: Oxford University Press, 2004). A study resource drawing on a wide range of interpretative sources.

Donin, Hayim Halevy. *To Be a Jew: A Guide to Jewish Observance in Contemporary Life: Selected and Compiled from the Shulhan Arukh and Responsa literature, and providing a rationale for the laws and the traditions* (New York: Basic Books [1972], 1991). Gives a good sense of how the legal sources can undergird actual practice.

Fishbane, Simcha. *The Method and Meaning of the Mishnah Berurah* (Hoboken, NJ: Ktav, 1991). A guide to one of the most popular modern commentaries on the *Shulhan Arukh*.

Kellner, Menachem. *Must a Jew Believe Anything?* (London: Littman Library, 1999). Philosophical discussion of the authority of creeds in Judaism.

Shapiro, Marc B. *The Limits of Orthodox Theology: Maimonides' Thirteen Principles Reappraised* (London: Littman Library, 2004). Re-examines the authority of Maimonides' famous 'creed'.

Soloveitchik, Haym. 'Rupture and Reconstruction: The Transformation of Contemporary Orthodoxy', *Tradition*, 28: 4 (1994), pp. 64–130. Masterly account of contemporary Orthodoxy, including the new authority of sacred texts.

NOTES

1. Ignaz Maybaum, *The Jewish Home* (London [1945]), p. 148.
2. See Chap. 10, which notes the growing popularity of ArtScroll prayer books in American Orthodoxy. Generally, the growing popularity of ArtScroll publications points to shifts within Orthodoxy towards a more traditional, more rigorously defined interpretation of Jewish practice which is built on a heightened sense of the authority of texts.
3. See Chap. 18 on 'Prayer and worship'.
4. Abraham Geiger, letter dated 1831, tr. in M. Wiener, *Abraham Geiger and Liberal Judaism*, tr. E. J. Schlochauer (Philadelphia: Jewish Publication Society, 1962), p. 100; Samuel Holdheim,

Das Ceremonialgesetz im Messiasrecht (Schwerin, 1845), tr. in D. Philipson, *Reform Movement in Judaism* (Hoboken, NJ: Ktav [1907], 1967), p. 43 n. 1.

5. See Mosheh M. Yashar, *Saint and Sage: Hafetz Hayim* (New York: Bloch Publishing Co., 1937); Shimon Finkelman, *The Chazon Ish: The Life and Ideals of Rabbi Yeshayah Karelitz* (New York: Mesorah, 1989).

6. See Chap. 17 for further consideration of the newly popular emphasis on texts rather than mimetic tradition within Orthodoxy.

7. Anyone wishing to approach this key text and its ideas today would be advised to make use of the excellent annotated compilation originally published in Hebrew by Fischel Lachower and Isaiah Tishby and now available in an excellent English translation: *The Wisdom of the Zohar: An Anthology of Texts*, arranged by Fischel Lachower and Isaiah Tishby, tr. David Goldstein (Oxford 1989). A new scholarly translation of the whole *Zohar* by Daniel C. Matt is being published by Stanford University Press (2004–).

8. See David Biale, *Gershom Scholem: Kabbalah and Counter History* (Cambridge, Mass.: Harvard University Press, 1982).

9. Moses Maimonides, *The Guide of the Perplexed*, tr. with an introduction and notes by Shlomo Pines (Chicago and London: University of Chicago Press, 1963). See also Oliver Leaman, *Moses Maimonides* (London: Routledge, 1989).

10. Hermann Cohen, *Religion of Reason Out of the Sources of Judaism*, tr. Simon Kaplan (New York: F. Ungar, 1972); Franz Rosenzweig, *The Star of Redemption*, tr. William W. Hallo (London and New York: Routledge & Kegan Paul, 1971); Martin Buber, *I and Thou*, tr. W. Kaufmann, 3rd edn. (Edinburgh: T. & T. Clark, 1970).

11. Maybaum, *The Jewish Home*, p. 149.

20 | The future of Jewish practice

Jeremy Wanderer

Two ways of approaching Jewish practice

A visitor to a small village approaches the local rabbi in the hope of finding somewhere to stay. The rabbi thinks for a moment before saying: 'Unfortunately the only available place would be at the home of Yechiel.' 'Why is that a problem?' 'Well,' says the rabbi, 'Yechiel is notorious in these parts for being somewhat of an *apikorus* (heretic).' Desperate, the visitor contacts Yechiel and settles down for the night, curious to witness the behaviour of this heretic. Next morning he awakes to discover Yechiel, wrapped in a prayer shawl and phylacteries, fervently reciting the morning prayers. Puzzled, the visitor challenges Yechiel to explain his meticulous practice despite his notoriety. 'Look,' responds Yechiel, '*Apikorus* I may be, *goy* (Gentile) I am not!'

Old (in many senses) it may be, but the joke captures an important insight into thinking about Jewish practice, namely, that there are two distinct conceptual frameworks within which such practice tends to be considered. The first could be called a *theory-based framework*, which considers the rationality of Jewish practice in light of the beliefs held by the practitioner. In such a framework, a heretic, broadly conceived to include anyone who lacks the relevant beliefs that would rationalize the particular practice, ought not to perform the action in question. The second could be called an *identity-based framework*, and considers practices in terms of the Jewish identity of the practitioner, with particular practices understood as an expression of that person's Jewish identity. In our case, it is not as a believer that Yechiel donned phylacteries and prayed, but as a Jew. Here, within an identity-based framework, heresy is not a bar to practice.

Noting two fundamentally different frameworks for thinking about Jewish practice need not imply that these two frameworks are contradictory. First, it is possible for the same practice to be understood both in light of a theory held by the practitioner and as an expression of identity. Secondly, although both purport to be accounts of Jewish practice, the range of practices under consideration differ depending on the framework employed. It is not just that the scope of such practices differs between the frameworks, but that the very notion of a Jewish practice differs. Within the identity-based framework, more or less any type of practice could become a Jewish one, provided it is an expression of one's Jewish identity. The focus, therefore, is not on the type of practice per se, but on the practitioner. Within the theory-based framework, the focus tends to be on the particular type of practice. Certain types of practices are seen as Jewish by virtue of a relationship between practices of that type and some notion of Jewish tradition, in the widest sense of the term.[1]

Even if the two frameworks are not contradictory, they are sometimes portrayed in competition with each other. In one widespread caricature, the two frameworks are taken to represent different sides of a supposed divide between secular and religious conceptions of Judaism. As should become clear, I find this characterization to be thoroughly misconceived. Even accepting this characterization however, what is at issue is not whether one can think of Jewish practice through these two frameworks, but a debate as to which conception should be taken as central. Since neither side denies the role of either identity or theory per se, one can explore either without taking a stand on the relative importance of one over the other.

What emerges then are two different, though not contradictory, ways of conceiving a set of more or less overlapping observances that could be called Jewish practices. Historically, the theory-based framework dominated discussion of Jewish practice, whilst more recent discussion tends to focus on matters of identity.[2] Interestingly, although talk of practice features prominently in these more recent discussions on Jewish identity, its role is often secondary to that of identity itself. In contrast, the focus here is primarily on the relationship between identity and practice. After placing the topic in a broader context in the following section, I will consider two different models for understanding the relationship between identity and practice, before considering some implications of these for the future of Jewish practice.

From theory to identity

One way to highlight the difference between these two frameworks is to consider the question of the future of Jewish practice. To make things more concrete, let us focus on the example of *kashrut*—Jewish dietary practices.

Discussions of the future of Jewish practice a century ago were dominated by the accusation of anachronism and irrelevance. In American Reform Judaism's Pittsburgh Platform of 1885, practices such as kashrut were said to have originated under various influences in earlier times that were no longer relevant. Similarly, it was common to hear claims such as: 'dietary laws are irrelevant now that there are strict health laws.'[3] Both those seeking to defend such practices by demonstrating their contemporary relevance, *and* those who level the accusation, share a common assumption: that a successful charge of anachronism ought to lead to a practice's abandonment. This assumption is only relevant within a theory-based framework, where the practice is rationalized by a particular theory that has the potential to become anachronistic.

When considering practices within an identity-based framework, however, debates regarding anachronism hardly feature. Indeed, through powerful motivating notions such as nostalgia, anachronism is almost celebrated rather than seen as a threat. Instead, recent debate over the future of practices such as kashrut has focused on the role it plays in maintaining Jewish identity. In recent years, for example, American Jewish organizations have spent much effort in conducting socio-demographic surveys, such as the National Jewish Population Survey (NJPS), the most recent being in 2000–1. Respondents are asked questions about their patterns of Jewish practice, including whether they observe kashrut in the home, because these practices are seen as important indicators of Jewish identity.

Whilst this turn to matters of identity in answering the question: 'What ought I to do?' is not limited to Jewish studies alone, there is a specific Jewish context for this move.[4] The context is a crisis of continuity; decreases in traditional beliefs and practices, combined with low or negative demographic growth and assimilation have led people to ask: 'Will we have Jewish grandchildren?'[5] Understanding the complexities of identity is seen as the first stage in developing strategies for future Jewish survival, on the assumption that the factors traditionally seen as having ensured survival, especially practice, are unlikely to continue playing such a role.

Given this contrast between practice and identity, it is not surprising that discussions of Jewish identity typically relegate practice to a secondary role, either ignoring it entirely or seeing it as little more than a measure of identity.[6] This failure to take practice seriously when thinking about identity is unfortunate, as doing so sheds important light on both concepts.

Identity and reasons

The identity-based framework itself incorporates disparate approaches to Jewish practice. In what follows I will focus on one particular approach within this framework, a conception of identity and practice implicit in the comments of Yechiel cited earlier. This particular conception is one in which (a) the agent has a relatively strong sense of identity and self, and (b) the agent sees this identity as providing a normative reason for action. A preliminary characterization can be achieved by contrasting this with two other ways of conceiving identity: the first sees identity (read: 'identities') as plural and shifting, whilst the second places identity outside the space of reasons.

The first alternative would simply not find Yechiel to be of much contemporary interest. The joke is set in a different age, in which geographical and social boundaries were more rigid and fixed. Nowadays, few have such a strong and singular identity. We now live in 'a third space', 'an imaginary homeland', where the boundaries between self and other are so fluid and shifting that a case such as Yechiel's, who stridently asserts a clear identity as rationalizing a particular action, fails to capture the complex and hybrid notion of identity and self that lies at the heart of the postmodern condition.[7]

As will become clear, I have no wish to deny the phenomenon of multiple identities and shifting boundaries. I am also prepared to admit that 'more and more people in general, not only . . . marginalized people, are beginning to think of themselves, of their identities . . . in terms of movement and hybridity', for whom comments such as Yechiel's will appear strange.[8] Nonetheless, for many people, certain of these multiple identities play a central role in particular periods of their lives, and for these people Yechiel's comments are neither alien nor dated. Whilst such identities may not feature as the fascinating subject of novels or films, they still remain sufficiently widespread and interesting to merit study.

According to the second alternative, one's identity may be said to cause but not rationalize certain behaviours. When Yechiel says that he prays and dons phylacteries as a Jew, he is not rationalizing his actions but citing some social or cultural circumstance that explains them. In contrast, the approach pursued here explores the way in which identity provides normative reasons for action. Normative reasons for action are considerations to which we appeal in constructing a rational justification of the agent's conduct. If the agent were sensitive to such reasons, the agent would be immune from rational blame.

When Yechiel cites his identity as an explanation of his actions, he provides a normative reason for his past actions. Identity commitments project into the future too. They place demands on the agent regarding future courses of action, so that if the agent failed to perform certain actions without providing reasons (to themselves or others) it would provide strong grounds for questioning whether this was indeed a genuine part of that person's identity. In rejecting the second alternative above, the key is to see such future projections not as predictive but as normative. When Yechiel tells us how he will act in light of his identity, he is not making a prediction based on psychological profiling and socio-demographic data, but is expressing what he sees as the normative demands of his identity commitment. It is this latter interpretation of Yechiel's comments that will concern us for the remainder of this discussion.

Jewish identity and external reasons

What, then, would it mean to say that identity provides a normative reason for a particular action? It is possible to distinguish between two different senses of the term 'identity', in which each sense links identity to action in a different way. The first sense of identity, to be explored in this section, could be called an *external sense of identity*, and this sense provides an *external reason for action*. The second sense of identity, to be explored in the next section, could be called an *internal sense of identity*, which provides an *internal reason for action*.[9]

Yechiel has numerous different traits that we could use to characterize him. He could, for example, be male, white, a father, a Jew, a Polish citizen, and a heretic. Under different social or historical circumstances some of these characteristics could become more salient than others. Further, from this list of characteristics we could distinguish two groups: a narrower group that includes only those characteristics that Yechiel has and identifies with, and a wider group that includes those characteristics with which he does not necessarily identify. The distinction is not between characteristics of which Yechiel is aware or not, but of those with which he identifies, which involves, at minimum, valuing those characteristics. The narrower group will form part of Yechiel's own self-conception, henceforth referred to as his *internal identity*. The wider group separates the notion of identity from self-conception, and could be called that person's *external identity*.

The terms 'internal' and 'external' are not used here to refer to the individual's conscious awareness, but refer to what could be called 'moral psychology', the rational perspective of the agent assessing what ought to be done in light of other beliefs, desires, and values. An internal conception of identity places it firmly within the moral psychology of the agent, allowing identity to play a role in rational deliberations regarding actions. As such, it allows for identity to provide an *internal reason* for action, a reason for the agent to perform an act that appeals to some evaluative aspect of that agent's rational perspective. In contrast, an external identity places identity outside the realm of the agent's moral psychology and, whilst an external identity could provide a reason for action, it is an *external reason* in the sense that it need not appeal to other evaluative factors that are within that agent's rational perspective.

For many, Jewish identity is conceived in external terms. Hence the *Encyclopaedia Judaica*'s entry on Jewish identity begins: 'Through the ages, Jewish identity has been determined by two forces: the consensus of thinking or feeling within the existing Jewish community in each age and the force of outside, often anti-Jewish, pressure which continued to define and to treat as Jewish even such groups which had in their own consciousness and in that of the Jews already severed all ties with Jewry.'[10] The question that the accounts of identity surveyed in the entry try to answer is: 'what is it for an individual person to be considered a token of the social type "Jew"?' As the remainder of the entry makes clear, the nature of the answer provided by the two forces identified in the quotation varies depending on the motivation of the questioner. Nonetheless, this survey of historical attempts to answer this question of Jewish identity makes no essential reference to characteristics of an individual with which they identify. In this sense, the notion of identity under discussion is clearly an external one.

The entry continues by noting that 'the most enduring definition of Jewish identity has been the *halakha*', the traditional Jewish legal system, according to which one of the following two conditions is sufficient for one to be a Jew: either one is the child of a Jewish mother, or one converts to Judaism. This identity does not depend in any way upon factors within a particular individual's perspective. Indeed, even an explicit denial of one's identity is not relevant on this conception, a point poignantly captured by the statement in the Talmud: 'even though he has sinned [in the sense of becoming an apostate], he remains a Jew.'

Further, such a notion of identity could be seen as prescribing just what it is that a Jew ought to do, in terms of practices themselves captured by halakhah. Here, Jewish identity provides an external reason for practice. This should not be seen as simply an idiosyncrasy of halakhah. Consider the popular practice of what Susan Glenn has termed 'Jewhooing', the widespread activity of claiming people, especially public personalities, as Jewish.[11] People freely use external criteria in identifying people as 'one of us', and seem to expect that certain behavioural practices ought to follow from such an external identity.

It is common to hear critiques of such conceptions of identity and practice using the term 'essentialism', a term supposed to be one of abuse. Essentialism, however, is not negative per se. There may be certain circumstances where, for pragmatic reasons, articulation of an external Jewish identity could be seen as desirable. To use a controversial example, it could be argued that if a country is going to have a Law of Return granting automatic citizenship and benefits to Jews, then that country ought to specify clear, external criteria for Jewish identity. Provided that one understands the pragmatic reasons for asserting such an identity, and does not see this version of identity in exclusionary terms, an external notion of identity need not be dismissed outright.

Nonetheless, since external identity easily lends itself to exclusionary practices, it is hard to think of external identity without thinking of the dangers of the abuse of power. Indeed, it is likely that the externalist conception of identity will strike the contemporary reader as politically incorrect, quite literally! The grim history of the past century has thankfully ensured a general reluctance towards attempts, in political theory and practice, at imposing identity and resultant practice on individuals against their will. External identity can easily lead to such tyranny, where the tyranny need not just take the more dramatic form of state or political intervention. More subtle exclusionary practices could also easily emerge from such an external conception of identity, where members of a particular externally identified constituency feel coerced into thinking that there is a specific or correct way to express or conceive of that specific identity at the expense of others, or into highlighting this aspect of themselves at the expense of other things they may value more. Given these all-too-real dangers of external identity, it is difficult to embrace such an understanding wholeheartedly.

Can we then understand Yechiel's assertion of his Jewish identity in defence of his practices as invoking an external Jewish identity to provide an external reason for his practice? Possibly, although the reservations about external identity make this proposal unappealing. Luckily there is an alternative, and to my mind far more interesting, way to understand Yechiel's comments: namely, as an expression of his internal identity.

Identity and internal reasons

An internal conception of identity focuses on those characteristics people see themselves as having and with which they strongly identify. For example, Yechiel sees himself as a Jew, and strongly values this characteristic. When Yechiel says that he prays and dons phylacteries as a Jew, therefore, he is expressing a certain way in which he thinks about himself that makes donning phylacteries and reciting prayers the action that he ought to do.

There is, however, more to identity than just valuing something. Whilst Yechiel may, for example, also be a parent and value parenting, this may not be part of his internal identity. In addition, there is an intransigence to our identities; they somehow are deeper, and more reluctant to change, than our commitments to other values. This is not to say that our identities do not change over time; they do, as with many of the things we value. The way we hold them in the present, however, is to value them as intransigent. Akeel Bilgrami tries to capture an aspect of this strength by suggesting that, in the case of identity, one values something such that 'one wants it fulfilled even if one were not to have the desire'.[12] For Bilgrami, identities are not immutable, but fundamentally involve a desire for something that is immutable.

On this account, having a Jewish identity means, in part, valuing this characteristic of yourself in a manner which you hope will not change or disappear over time.[13] Alan Dershowitz provides a typically outspoken account of his own identity: 'I am a deeply committed Jew. Though I am also an American, a civil libertarian, an academic and many other things, my primary identification is as a Jew. I believe that I will always be an American . . . a civil libertarian, an academic and all those other things that now characterise me. But I *know* I will always be a Jew.'[14] In characterizing his Jewishness, Dershowitz looks ahead. He values his Jewish identity in such a way that included in the holding of the identity itself is the strong sense in which he *knows* it will not disappear over time. Part of one's present identity, then, is a tacit disapproval of oneself if one would not have this characteristic value at any other stage. This is acutely felt when a person is forced to do something that conflicts with such a fundamentally held value: one does not just feel bad about the action, but is left feeling different about themselves, a distinct sense of loss.

This notion of identity normatively rationalizes certain behavioural practices in the present: behaviours that *reflect* those values or characteristics in the present, and behaviours designed to ensure that the same individual continues to value these in the future. The idea of reflection lies at the heart of the identity-based framework. The practice acts as a mirror of the self-identity of the practitioner; it reflects those values that are held in that stronger sense that thereby forms one's self-conception. Identity and practice are not things to be considered independently, but are two sides of the same coin; identity makes the behaviour into the practice it is, whilst the practice represents the identity itself. Contrast this with the theory-based framework for thinking about Jewish practice. Consider, for example, someone who says that she maintains Jewish dietary practices because they provide a healthy way of living, be it in this world or the next! Here, the relationship between reason and practice is not a reflective one; the reason transmits justification to the type of practice, whilst both reason and practice could be considered independently from one another.

Identities may involve a desire for something immutable, but even strongly held identities do change over time. By this I mean both that the identity-involving commitment to a value itself and/or the content of the conception of the identity may change. In terms of the commitment itself, particular identities become especially prominent or questionable at certain periods, often due to external factors and influences. For example, in the case of Jewish identity a perceived rise in antisemitism may lead to an increased commitment to Jewishness by way of defence.

Alternatively, even when the fundamental commitment to a value does not alter, the content of the identity, especially in terms of the behaviours reflecting that identity, may alter. Practice itself may lead the way in this, whereby accidental or forced participation in certain practices—say, as the result of political changes effecting Jews in a certain area—could lead to gradual reconceptions of strongly held Jewish identity from within. In this sense, the relationship between identity and practice is more dynamic and less formalized than the relationship between theory and practice, and the process of change and development is one of internal dialogue and feedback loops, rather than formal analytic categorization and debate.

Admittedly, this account of identity leaves many issues open. Nonetheless, enough has been said to suggest that this could be a plausible and revealing understanding of sentiments such as those demonstrated by Yechiel. A strongly held Jewish identity, in which one desires to live by these values even when one no longer has that desire, provides normative reasons for engaging in certain Jewish practices that are seen as reflecting that identity. Practices are rationalized, although not by invoking some generalized theory that rationalizes the type of practice in question.

Some implications for future practice

Rather than attempting to provide a sweeping survey of current trends in Jewish practice, or trying to engage in risky prophecies regarding the likely or desirable patterns of future practice, the discussion here has focused on one way of thinking about such practice: namely, from within an identity-based framework. Within that framework, one particular conception of Jewish practice was selected for discussion, one that sees such practices as rationalized by the Jewish identity of the practitioner. It has been suggested that, in certain cases, we should understand the relationship between identity and practice such that the former, thought of as internal identity, provides internal reason for the latter.

By way of conclusion, it is worth spelling out briefly the patterns of future Jewish practice associated with this particular understanding of identity. The pattern will combine a strong sense of commitment to a set of practices together with a diversity of such practices, both between people and over time. The personal commitment stems from the fact that these practices are seen as reflective of the personal identity of the agent, and thus intimately tied to self-conceptions. People could not just give up on these practices without giving up on a conception of themselves. This does not mean that the practices never change. They alter over time, since both the commitment to the identity itself and the content of the identity may change as the result of both internal negotiation and external pressures.

In addition, there will be a great deal of variation in the details of practice between people, since the relationship between identity and practice is linked to the internal values of the individual in question. This is particularly the case in light of the fact that Jewish identity itself may be further divided to include other adjectival forms of Jewish affiliation, in which the term 'Jew' is accompanied by prefixes such as Orthodox, Secular, Sephardi, Hasidic, and suchlike. Even in the case of a strong generalized Jewish identity, multiple identities ensure that other values of the agent are likely to be held in a similar identity-conferring manner, and the practices that emerge will be the product of internal deliberation and negotiation between the various identity commitments. So someone identifying as, say, a Feminist, a Jew, and a Liberal will have a distinctive set of practices that reflect this multiple identity, achieved as the result of internal dialogue between them.

The key to all this is not hybridity and a dissolution of identity, nor essentialism and conformity to the group, but a process of rationalization over time from within the evaluative perspective of the agent involved, leading to an array of novel practices. Identities such as Yechiel's are of particular interest in that they are, under certain conditions, able to combine a strong and intransigent sense of Jewish identity with a wide array of changing and novel practices, practices that are Jewish in that they rationally reflect, amongst other identities, the Jewish identity of the practitioner. Understanding both the process and the conditions involved is a central task in future thinking about Jewish identity and Jewish practice.

FURTHER READING

Charme, S. 'The Varieties of Modern and Postmodern Jewish Identity', *Religious Studies Review*, 22 (1996), pp. 215–22. Provides an extended review of nine books published in the early 1990s on the theme of Jewish identity. Serves as a useful entry into the literature.

Cohen, S., and A. Eisen. *The Jew Within: Self, Family, and Community in America* (Bloomington: Indiana University Press, 2000). A sociological study of contemporary American Jewish attitudes, based on in-depth interviews with 'moderately affiliated' Jews. Chapter 4 explores attitudes to observance.

Donin, Hayim Halevy. *To Be a Jew: A Guide to Jewish Observance in Contemporary Life: Selected and compiled from the Shulhan Arukh and Responsa literature, and providing a rationale for the laws and the traditions* (New York: Basic Books, 1972). A survey of the traditional Orthodox understanding of Jewish ritual.

Eisen, A. M. *Rethinking Modern Judaism: Ritual, Commandment, Community* (Chicago: University of Chicago Press, 1998). A subtle and theoretically sophisticated exploration of the central role that observance plays in Judaism's encounter with modernity.

Rothschild, Sylvia, and Sybil Sheridan (eds.). *Taking Up the Timbrel: The Challenge of Creating Ritual for Jewish Women Today* (London: SCM, 2000). A survey of recent feminist attempts to construct new rituals, that provides a useful example of the bidirectional, internal dialogue between identity and practice.

Rynhold, Daniel. *Justifying One's Practices: Two Models of Jewish Philosophy* (Oxford: Oxford University Press, 2005). A sustained philosophical reflection on the theory-based framework for thinking about Jewish practices.

Silberstein, L. J. (ed.). *Mapping Jewish Identities* (New York: New York University Press, 2000). A collection of essays critical of the essentialist underpinnings of earlier theorizing on Jewish identity. The editor's introductory essay provides a particularly clear outline of the alternative.

Soloveitchik, H. 'Rupture and Reconstruction: The Transformation of Contemporary Orthodoxy', *Tradition*, 28 (1994). Brilliant analysis of the meaning of recent changes in patterns of observance within Ultra-Orthodoxy. Rich in detail and a fascinating case-study for discussing issues of tradition, culture, and authenticity with regards Jewish practice.

NOTES

1. Admittedly, the focus on types of action alone is not sufficient here: for example, someone can observe Shabbat by resting in some sense, but doing so unintentionally; or by intentionally having a day of rest without knowledge of the concept 'Sabbath'. As such, even if one could spell out the vexed notion of tradition, additional conditions may be required to rule out such cases.

2. The theory-based approach will not be explored here. A detailed exploration is D. Rynhold, *Justifying One's Practices: Two Models of Jewish Philosophy* (Oxford: Oxford University Press, 2005). See also A. M. Eisen, *Rethinking Modern Judaism: Ritual, Commandment, Community* (Chicago: Chicago University Press, 1998), pp. 135–55. It is important to note that the difference between identity-based and theory-based frameworks will be lost if identity is seen as 'just more theory', such that someone's belief in their Jewish identity can be used to explain a particular practice. As will emerge below, the relation between identity and practice is quite different from this. G. A. Cohen captures an aspect of this well in the following comments about his own identity: 'Being Jewish plays a role in my practical identity, as does being a Fellow of All Souls College. But neither of those features signifies an attachment for me because I believe some principle that says: cleave to the ethnic group to which you belong, or to the College that was sufficiently gracious to receive you.' In C. M. Korsgaard, *The Sources of Normativity* (Cambridge: Cambridge University Press, 1996), p. 175. Further aspects of this will be developed later.

3. Cited in an interview conducted as part of a study of contemporary American Jewish attitudes to, amongst other things, practice. Reflecting on the comment, the authors of the study note that the observation is 'notable because a generation ago such rejection of ritual practice, on the grounds that it affirms or requires beliefs that are no longer relevant, was far more common'. S. Cohen and A. Eisen, *The Jew Within: Self, Family, and Community in America* (Bloomington: Indiana University Press 2000), p. 86.

4. In terms of a wider context, the recent popularity of what is called 'identity politics' in social theory and of communitarian alternatives in ethical theory should be noted, both of which stress

the central role played by identity in thinking about practice. For a plausible narrative explaining this turn to identity, see Keith Graham, *Practical Reasoning in a Social World* (Cambridge: Cambridge University Press, 2002), pp. 11–16.

5. Jonathan Sacks, *Will We Have Jewish Grandchildren?* (London: Vallentine Mitchell, 1994).

6. The contrast between practice and identity is explicit in D. M. Gordis and Y. Ben Horin, *Jewish Identity in America* (Los Angeles: Wilstien Institute, 1991), p. xiv. This secondary status of practice is a feature of the NJPS, in which questions of practice are explored merely as indicators of Jewish identity. This can be traced back to Sklare's seminal work, M. Sklare and J. Greenblum, *Jewish Identity in the Suburban Frontier*, 2nd edn. (Chicago: University of Chicago Press, 1979), which explicitly claims that one can measure identity (a term surprisingly ill-defined in the book) through a consideration of peoples' ritual practice (p. 51). Although the list of practices has changed over the years, the assumption appears to be repeated in a number of related studies.

7. The quoted terms are, in order, from Homi K. Bhabha, *The Location of Culture* (London: Routledge, 1994), p. 15, and Salman Rushdie, *Imaginary Homelands: Essays and Criticism 1981–1991* (Harmondsworth: Penguin, 1991), p. 15.

8. L. Silberstein (ed.), *Mapping Jewish Identities* (New York: New York University Press, 2000), p. 4.

9. A similar distinction is found in Akeel Bilgrami, 'Identity and Identification', in *The International Encyclopaedia of the Social and Behavioural Sciences* (New York: Elsevier, 2003), drawing in turn on an idiosyncratic reading of Bernard Williams, 'Internal and External Reasons', in his *Moral Luck: Philosophical Papers 1973–1980* (Cambridge: Cambridge University Press, 1981). My thinking about identity is profoundly indebted to Bilgrami's work in this area; for example, his 'What is a Muslim?' reprinted in K. A. Appiah and H. L. Gates (eds.), *Identities* (Chicago: University of Chicago Press, 1995). Readers familiar with the Williams-inspired literature on 'internal and external reasons' will be aware that, although I help myself to these terms in this article, their usage here differs considerably from the way they are typically used in that literature

10. Hertzberg, 'Jewish Identity', in C. Roth (ed.), *Encyclopaedia Judaica* (Jerusalem: Keter, 1971), vol. 10, p. 54.

11. S. A. Glenn, 'In the Blood?: Consent, Descent, and the Ironies of Jewish Identity', *Jewish Social Studies*, 8 (2002), pp. 139–52.

12. Bilgrami, 'Secularism and the Moral Psychology of Identity', in R. Bhargava (ed.), *Multiculturalism, Liberalism and Democracy* (New Dehli: Oxford University Press, 1999), p. 172.

13. In the case of an internal Jewish identity, two criterion have been identified: (1) a self-perception of having fulfilled certain criteria that give one group membership; and (2) strongly valuing this membership. This differs from some other instances of internal identity, such as people seeing themselves as liberal in a way that becomes part of identity. Here, all there is to having such an identity involves valuing something in the strong way already indicated. There is much to say about this important distinction, but in this context it will suffice to highlight the fact that *both* of these are examples of internal identity, and the key in our case is the self-perception of having fulfilled the criterion of membership, even if the agent's conception of these criterion may involve external factors.

14. A. M. Dershowitz, *The Vanishing American Jew* (Boston: Little, Brown & Co., 1997), p. 179.

Theological issues

Theological issues: survey

Norbert M. Samuelson

What is Jewish theology?

Aristotle named the book that comes after (*meta-*) his book on physics (*physica*) 'theology' because its subject-matter was a systematic and logical study (-logy) of God (theo-). His *Physics* deals with the general causal principles by which what we call the 'natural' world must be understood, principles whose ultimate foundation rests logically and causally on a first and final cause of everything. He (and other natural philosophers of the ancient Greek world) called such a principle 'deity' (*theos*), and he devoted an entire book solely to that principle. Hence, as the term 'theology' was introduced into western philosophical discourse, the term referred to any philosophic study whose object was God (or gods) and to any study in natural philosophy (or, what we today would call the physical sciences) of 'metaphysics', which are the ultimate principles of all that is.

In modern times the term 'theology' refers to more than philosophy and to more than the topic of deity. There are modern Jewish theologians whose focus is barely on God at all. Rather, what they reflect on in their writings is the nature of the Jewish people and its right to exist as an autonomous collective. Perhaps the clearest example of such a theologian is Mordecai Kaplan. But this classification would also fit many contemporary theologians who write less about God and more about what they call 'spirituality'. A notable example of a contemporary Jewish spiritualist theologian is Arthur Green. Similarly, theologians may converse about God and/or Judaism from any number of disciplines besides philosophy. These disciplines include, among others, sociology and intellectual history. Two notable examples of contemporary Jewish theologians whose discipline of discourse is history are Leo Strauss and Gershom Scholem. Two notable examples of contemporary Jewish theologians whose discipline of discourse is sociology are Richard Rubenstein in the middle of the twentieth century and Arnold Eisen.

Because of this extension of the term 'theology' in contemporary discourse, we can distinguish between thinkers who write about the 'philosophy of religion' and others who are 'theologians'. Many Jewish thinkers (as well as many Christian thinkers) are both. We can call them Jewish philosophers as well as Jewish theologians. I have already mentioned some Jewish theologians who were not Jewish philosophers. Restricting ourselves solely to twentieth-century Jewish thinkers, the most important names are Richard Rubenstein, Leo Strauss, and Gershom Scholem. Some would also include Mordecai Kaplan and others would also include Abraham J. Heschel, but their classification this way is a bit murkier. Kaplan had some training in philosophy, but it was not at a professional level. However, the content of his theology was philosophical even if his discussion of it was not professionally disciplined. With Heschel there is an opposite problem of classification. Heschel was a professionally trained philosopher who purposely omitted technical philosophy from his theological writings. The same can be said of Leo Baeck.

Baeck simultaneously studied to become a liberal rabbi under Jacob Freudenthal and worked on his Ph.D. in philosophy under Wilhelm Dilthey. The two interests were brought together in Baeck's studies, also in Berlin, with Hermann Cohen. However, the importance of Leo Baeck does not lie in his philosophy. In part, Baeck's importance is as an apologist for Judaism against contemporary attacks by German Christian theologians. Notable in this respect is his *Essence of Judaism*, which he both modelled on and wrote in response to Adolf von Harnack's *Essence of Christianity*. However, more important was the way Baeck lived his life. Like Abraham J. Heschel in the United States, it was the theologian's life that provided the paradigm for how to live as a Jew in the modern world, far more than the content of his writings. (Similar claims can be made about the theologians Martin Buber and Franz Rosenzweig.) Baeck rose to a position of national leadership of the Jewish community in Germany through the strength of his intellect as well as through his leadership of Germany's most prestigious liberal synagogue in Berlin. In 1933 he was elected the president of the Reichvertretung, the representative governing body of all German Jewry; he stayed in that position until he was arrested in 1943. Baeck had many opportunities to leave Germany after the rise of Hitler, but he refused to abandon his flock to the forces of darkness that engulfed his people. He was an inmate in the Theresienstadt concentration camp from 1943 until the Allies liberated Germany in 1945. Afterwards he moved to London, where he was the chair of the World Union of Progressive Judaism until 1948, and then to Cincinnati, Ohio, in the United States to become, until his death in 1956, Professor of Religion at the Hebrew Union College.

The clearest examples of contemporary Jewish theologians who were also Jewish philosophers were Baeck's teacher, Hermann Cohen, as well as Cohen's younger associate, Martin Buber, and Cohen's other notable student, Franz Rosenzweig. Cohen was a philosopher of mathematics and science who used his specific interpretation of the scientific method to interpret the philosophy of Immanuel Kant and to reconstruct the classical philosophy of Moses Maimonides into a contemporary idealist rationalist Jewish philosophy, which he further used to interpret rabbinic classics such as the Babylonian Talmud. Cohen's student Franz Rosenzweig was deeply influenced, at least in his early writings, by Cohen's philosophical method. While Rosenzweig was personally committed to the anti-rationalist, German, so-called 'Romantic' tradition of philosophy, all of his writings about philosophy and theology were based on Cohen's rationalist method of textual interpretation.

For now the focus of our attention is solely on defining what Jewish theology is, particularly as a discipline distinct from Jewish philosophy, and for that purpose no clearer statement can be given than the one formulated by Franz Rosenzweig. Rosenzweig identifies philosophy with a tradition of texts that begins with the writings of Plato and ends with Hegel. The topics discussed in these texts fall under three general headings—God, the world, and the human. Rosenzweig identified the references for these headings with the main elements of reality, but not with reality itself. Rather, reality is to be understood as a series of interrelated processes whose asymptotic ends are the elements. While philosophy did succeed in identifying these elements, it failed to do anything more. What we know about each is that we can know nothing about them until we comprehend them in dynamic interrelationship, and the comprehension of those relations lies beyond the domain of the knowable. Rather, these relations are at best something about which we may have reasonable beliefs, but nothing more.

The source of these beliefs is a reality external to what our human reason on its own can grasp. Science and philosophy can only form judgements based on what our intellects, armed solely with the data of sense experience, comprehend through the rational tools of logic. Beyond philosophy, however, there is the revealed presence of the divine whose manifestation is recorded in books of revelation. For Jews this source is the Hebrew Scriptures.

Understanding the Scriptures does not yield knowledge. Knowledge can be gained only through empirically rooted reasoning. Rather, what understanding the Scriptures yields is belief, which, while lacking the certainly of knowledge, enables us as humans to comprehend more or less adequately in some fashion all of reality.

Rosenzweig's analysis of human comprehension involves three steps. The first is natural philosophy—the study of nature and texts about the study of nature from Plato to Hegel. Here there are three identified branches of philosophy—positive theology (whose object of study is God), positive physics (whose object is the world), and positive ethics and psychology (whose object is the human). The second step is metaphilosophy—the realization of radical doubt about the positive claims of philosophy through logical extension from philosophy itself. These negative branches of metaphilosophy are metaphysics, metalogic, and metaethics. Metaethics is the realization of radical doubt about our knowledge of what is distinctly human; metalogic is the same negative realization about the world; and similarly, metaphysics is the realization of radical doubt about our knowledge of God. The third step is to reflect further on the elements of philosophy in the light of the negative philosophies in terms of the professed revealed word of God. In this case the reflection moves beyond the elements to contemplate the relations between them—creation (divine action on the passive world of being), revelation (divine action on the receptive human intellect), and redemption (human action in response to revelation on the moralization of the ethically neutral actuality of the divinely created universe). This entire activity—the study of creation, revelation, and redemption out of the interpretation of Scriptures—is called 'theology'.

Note that Rosenzweig takes over the full range of earlier uses of the term 'theology', synthesizes them, and moves beyond his own unity to define in a distinctive way what should be the methods and concerns of the theologian. The theologian studies two kinds of texts—the inherited Scriptures and the liturgy of the worship community. The words of these texts, as they are understood in a worship community, function as the premises for reasoning about the three major movements beyond the elements in the course of reality towards its end. It is the associated communities that determine the major subdivisions of theology. For Rosenzweig there are only two primary sub-divisions—Jewish and Christian. What defines Jewish theology as 'Jewish' is that it is reflection exclusively on the claimed Scriptures and liturgies of the Jewish people.

My use of the expression 'Jewish theology' in the remainder of this essay is not identical with, but closely follows, Rosenzweig's use of the terms. I define Jewish theology as any study of who or what God is and what God does, where to 'study' means to think reflectively and critically about what the Hebrew Scriptures say as their words are interpreted in a 2000-year tradition of reflections and textual commentaries by rabbis, as well as how those conceptions were translated into forms of communal worship in rabbinic liturgies. By 'modern' Jewish theology I mean Jewish theology written by Jews since their political emancipation in the nation-states of western civil-ization. In this case I will briefly survey how modern Jewish thinkers have interpreted biblical and rabbinic traditional texts in the light of modern academic disciplines to interpret the fundamental beliefs of Judaism.

Issues in modern Jewish theology, from the seventeenth to the early twentieth centuries

The cornerstones of Jewish religious belief have two interrelated formulations. One is in terms of the conceptions of three entities—God, the Torah, and the Jewish people. Pre-modern committed Jews affirmed all three. However, there are many kinds of mod-ern Jews who affirm their identity as Jews even though they reject one or two of these foundational conceptions. Notably, there are many Jews throughout the world who affirm their identity with the Jewish people but reject the existence of God. We call them 'secular' Jews. Conversely, there are other Jews who affirm the existence of God, but reject the notion that the Torah is a divinely revealed text and that the Jewish people are God's elect or chosen. They do not entirely reject the claim that there is something special about the Torah for the Jewish people, or that there is significant value in remaining identified as part of the Jewish people, but they interpret this identity in ways that most pre-modern learned and committed Jews would find objec-tionable. In the pre-modern Jewish world these three conceptions were seen to be equally fundamental. In the modern Jewish world they are prioritized. Zionists, for example, may affirm all three, but insofar as they are Zionists the commitment to the Jewish people has a special priority. Conversely, Reform Jews have tended to give priority to the affirmation of God and emphasize his role as a guarantor of universal ethics over whatever relationship God may have as God to the Jewish people as a particular people, as well as to the more particularistic commandments in the rabbinic tradition of Torah.

An alternative way to state the cornerstones of Jewish belief is in terms of three sets of relations between God and his creatures—God as the creator, the revealer, and the redeemer. 'God as creator' deals with the conception of creation as an expression of the relationship between God and the world, often in relationship to conceptions of the origin of the universe in the physical sciences. 'God as revealer' deals with the concept of revelation as an expression of the relationship between God and humanity, often in relationship to the life sciences and the critical-historical study of the Hebrew Scriptures. Of special importance in this connection are interpretations of the subordinate concept of 'covenant'. Finally, 'God as revealer' deals with the concept of redemption as an expression of the relationship between humanity and the world, usually in relationship to philosophical and social scientific conceptions of both individual and collective ethics, and sometimes in relationship to conceptions of the end of the universe in the physical sciences.

Let us integrate these two lists of basic Jewish beliefs and briefly outline what modern Jewish theologians have said about each in terms of the following topics: (1) Creation and the creator; (2) Revelation, covenant, and the Torah; and (3) Humanity, redemption and the Jewish people.

Creation and the creator

Maimonides and other pre-modern Jewish philosophers had argued that the creation of the world is an event that transcends human comprehension. In contrast, contemporary astrophysics, which affirms creation no less than Judaism, claims that it is in principle an intelligible event from which the universe originated. However, the difference here is not as great as it might seem, since physicists claim that the origin is something called a 'singularity', which, as such, lies beyond what our language is capable of explaining.

What remains the critical difference between modern scientific and biblically rooted Jewish theological accounts of creation has to do with purpose. For modern science the tools for explanation are mathematical and mechanical, whereas Jewish theology explains creation in terms of moral purpose for the universe as a whole and for everything in it. Some scientists and some religious Jews believe that these two modes of explanation are incompatible. However, most Jewish theologians, pre-modern as well as modern, argue for the compatibility of the two accounts. Minimally the two explanations are independent of each other. Maximally, one enlightens the other.

Revelation, covenant, and the Torah

To be a Jew is understood to mean participating in a people who are defined by a covenant relationship between Israel and God. The Torah is generally viewed as the text that defines the nature of that covenant. A Jew who is born into a Jewish family is a Jew no matter what he or she believes or practises. Nonetheless, it is the Torah that is the foundation of the collective identity.

In modern Judaism there is a central political disagreement over how to define a Jew. For example, is it sufficient to be Jewish to have a Jewish birth mother or a Jewish birth father? Similarly, can someone who is born of Jewish parents and converts to a different religion be Jewish? Underlying these political questions are issues about the source of authority for determining the nature of the covenant between God and Israel. At this level there is a critical issue dividing traditional and liberal Jewish religious theologians. Is 'Israel' the national collective, so that God's covenant is primarily with the collective, and individual Jews participate in it secondarily through their membership in the nation? Or is 'Israel' simply a general term for Jews, so that God's covenant is with each and every individual? Reform Jews in particular have assumed an individualistic understanding of the character of the relationship of the Jewish people to God, while traditionalist Jews have assumed a collectivist understanding,

This dispute mirrors the historic theological conflict between Protestants and Catholics in the early modern period of Western European history. However, in recent decades it seems that the argument about who is the ultimate source of authority—the rabbinate, the formal representative of the community, or each autonomous individual—has faded, primarily because the liberal movements have increasingly become people/nation-oriented in their understanding of Jewish religious or spiritual life. The change, at least in part, reflects a trend in liberal Jewish thinking, away from German philosophy, where the doctrine of autonomy played a central role, to an emphasis on American sociology and anthropology, where conceptions of communal norms are central.

Despite the increased emphasis in Jewish popular thinking on sociology over philosophy in Jewish theology, there remains no doctrine more central to defining Judaism than revelation. From its very origins it was the belief that God gave the Torah to Moses at Sinai that defined Judaism, and throughout most of the pre-modern period almost all people in the western world accepted this claim. The critical issue between Jews and Muslims was whether the Torah as the rabbis transmitted it contained deviations from the original, and the critical issue with the Christians was whether or not the Torah was superseded in authority by the Gospels, but no one doubted that the Torah was a gift from God to Israel through Moses.

In the modern period all people, including the majority of modern Jews, have by no means universally accepted belief in the revealed nature of the Torah. Hence, this belief required justification and interpretation at a level that is uniquely characteristic of modernity.

Traditional forms of Judaism, especially Orthodoxy, continue to assert that the Torah, which they call the 'written law', is something given by God, and that the way that the rabbis have interpreted the text, which they call the 'oral law', has its source as well in the word of God. Liberal forms of Judaism, especially Reform, do not share all of these beliefs. A radical separation is made in authority between the written law (Torah) and the oral law (rabbinic tradition). The latter is seen to be entirely a human work, which, as such, is subject to error. All people, no matter how gifted intellectually and spiritually, are products of a particular time and place, and because of this limitation they will make judgements that fall short of the truth, so that subsequent generations of human beings can improve on these judgements, even though they are neither more intelligent nor more spiritual than their ancestors.

The written Torah is in some sense more authoritative than the oral law, even though it too is subject to human imperfection. The classical liberal Jewish way of expressing the balance between viewing the Scriptures as divine (in which case they are authoritative and beyond human fallibility) or human (in which case they are fallible and not authoritative) is through the doctrine of divine inspiration. It is claimed that God uniquely inspired the Torah, but that it nevertheless remains human. God may have in some sense dictated what the Torah says, but what we possess is not God's word. Rather, the Torah is the way that the children of Israel understood that word. Therefore, since the Scriptures are in part a human product, they may be reinterpreted in each generation.

In the early modern period liberal religious Jews tended to maintain that where the Scriptures are reasonable they should be followed, but otherwise not. At the present time this understanding, while essentially unchanged, has been made less narrowly rationalist. Now the position of liberal Jews on the texts of the Torah is that where they are unreasonable they should not be followed, but otherwise what they say is compelling to guide both belief and practice. The result of this shift in theological emphasis is a narrowing of differences between liberal and traditional Jews in their observance of traditional religious practices.

Humanity, redemption, and the Jewish people

Pre-modern Jewish theology was particularistic, in the sense that it claimed that the Torah was given specifically to the Jewish people and not to any other nation in the world. However, the theology was also universalistic, in the sense that the Torah was understood to design a programme by which the Jewish people could bring redemption to the entire world. Maimonides in particular understood the Torah to be the constitution of a political state through which all of humanity would be progressively transformed into a higher, angelic nature, where all people would be able to attain the ultimate goal of existence, which is conjunction with God.

The traditional Jewish ideal for the end of days was affirmed and explained in early twentieth-century theology in the language of German, neo-Kantian philosophy. The goal of human life is knowledge; the ultimate object of knowledge is God; and Torah, properly understood, is a critical guide in bringing all of humanity to this universal, human realization.

By the end of the twentieth century this messianic vision of the purpose of the existence of the Jewish people was de-emphasized by most Jewish theologians in favour of a less grandiose goal of securing the survival of the Jewish people as a people in what is basically a hostile world. The most obvious reason for this change in collective objectives is the experience of antisemitism through most of the century. But there are also other reasons, intellectual as well as political. Most importantly, at the beginning of the century the belief in the future of Judaism was tied to a belief in the messianic power of rational philosophy and science, whereas by the end of the century all people were increasingly conscious of the severe limitations of what reason can accomplish.

To be sure, the powers of reason are impressive. There are some Jews who, in the second half of the century, have adopted a form of anti-rationalism more characteristic of early Christian thought than of any period in pre-modern Judaism, but these modern non-rationalists continue to be a minority voice in Jewish thought. However, the achievement of the messianic age is no closer to realization today than it was in the past.

Still, messianism remains a central belief in most modern Jewish theology. It remains something to be hoped for, even when it is affirmed that its realization is not (perhaps cannot be) imminent. While the world cannot be made good, it certainly can be made better than it is, and this more modest goal continues to be central to all Jewish theology.

New issues for Jewish theology in the late twentieth and early twenty-first centuries

What may prove to be the most original form of new Jewish theology for the twenty-first century is feminist Jewish theology. What feminism does is, at least potentially, both to open new ways to think about old questions and to think about new questions that have eluded reflection because of the limitations of Jewish thinking to a single perspective. However, what these new ways and new topics of thinking will be remains at the present moment (which is only the beginning of Jewish feminist theology) an open question. Some theologians have argued that feminism will alter the competitive models of Jewish thinking in which classifications are usually bipolar, in favour of a more unified form of thinking about both life and the world. However, monistic thought is not new to Jewish (or non-Jewish) thinking by men. The clearest example in Jewish theology is the Kabbalah, especially as it is contained in the *Zohar*, which seems successfully and uniquely to transcend gender distinctions in its images of God. However, some scholars of Kabbalah, notably Elliot Wolfson, have argued that this particular Jewish feminist motive for interest in Kabbalah is not justified by the texts themselves. While the impact of feminism and gender studies on Jewish theology is still an open question, there is no doubt that this new sensitivity has deeply changed Jewish life for the near future.

Beyond the issue of gender consciousness, without doubt the two most important historical events in Jewish life in the twentieth century have been the Holocaust and the creation of the State of Israel. A great deal need not be said here about these topics because there are separate essays in this book devoted to each (Chapters 3 and 4). Let me only note that it is not necessarily the case that an event that has major historical and political importance for a people need also have theological importance. There are Jewish theologians who argue that the Holocaust raises no new issues that were not already there, and that it is too soon to tell what is the theological significance, if any, of the creation of a pre-messianic Jewish nation-state. However, there are many who do argue the deep theological significance of both, and both the Holocaust and Zionism have been major topics of Jewish theology throughout at least the second half of the twentieth century. Among the earliest and most seminal Jewish theologians in this respect have been Richard Rubenstein and Emil Fackenheim. The writings of Fackenheim in particular have also contributed to the rise of two other directions in Jewish theology in the late twentieth and early twenty-first centuries. One is Jewish spirituality and the other is postmodernism.

Fackenheim argued that because of the impotence of philosophy to resist the Holocaust, philosophy itself is discredited. This negative judgement by the most influential post-war Jewish philosopher in North America contributed to a popular decline in belief, among late twentieth-century Jewish intellectuals, both in the value of the modernist enterprise in society and in the value of rationalist thinking in philosophy. These denials have contributed to the growth of what is popularly called Jewish 'spirituality' as well as Jewish 'postmodernism'.

'Postmodernism' is a term that comes to our society from contemporary literary criticism, whose sources are primarily French. However, the term has been extended in its use by contemporary Jewish theologians such as Peter Ochs to include all post-Holocaust critiques of the modernist values that had spread throughout western civilization by the time of the French Revolution. These theologians see all of the modern forms of Judaism—be they liberal or traditionalist, or more generally, religious or secular—as adaptations of traditional rabbinic Jewish life and thought to accommodate the assumed values of western Christian civilization. These postmodernist Jewish theologians call those new forms of Judaism into question—first in terms of their coherence with the values of traditional Judaism, and second in terms of their truth in the light of the Holocaust.

Part of the critical stance towards the post-emancipation reinterpretation of

Judaism is a rethinking of the application to Judaism of the distinction—Protestant in origin—between the secular and the religious. The rejection of that distinction has given rise to an emphasis in Jewish theology on 'spirituality' rather than religion. The term 'religion' is taken to refer primarily, to public, institutions with formalized structures of communal worship. 'Spirituality', in contrast, refers to mental states of individuals in relationship to their human and physical environments. A spiritualist Judaism shares with Jewish religion a rejection of the tendency in western rationalist thought to reduce all non-material phenomena to what is material and quantitative. At the same time, it shares with Jewish secularism a scepticism about the purported spiritual values of organized religious institutions. In its claim to transcend both, contemporary Jewish spirituality draws heavily for its grounds of authenticity as a Jewish cultural movement on the classical texts of Jewish mysticism, especially those of the pre-modern Hasidim, as well as on the theological influence of Abraham J. Heschel. Today the two most influential voices (at least at the academic level) are Zalman Shachter-Shalomi and his former student Arthur Green.

It should be noted that not all contemporary Jewish theology is anti-rationalist and anti-modern. At a more popular level, the influence of Heschel's colleague at the Jewish Theological Seminary, Mordecai Kaplan, continues to be influential in the religious life and thought of many Jewish intellectuals. Kaplan's theology, like that of Peter Ochs, is grounded in a form of process theology whose early twentieth-century source was the writings of the philosopher Alfred North Whitehead. Among the contemporary Jewish thinkers who continue to follow in this process tradition of interpreting Jewish faith is one of the most influential congregational rabbis in the United States, Harold Schulweis.

In the case of Christian theology, process thought has been the dominant foundation used to evaluate the interrelationship between modern science and religious belief. This is certainly the case with the writings of Ian Barbour, who has been the seminal figure in contemporary Christian studies, in both England and North America, in the development of a growing academic discipline of the study of science and religion. Jewish thinkers are just beginning to enter this discipline as well, although process theology seems to be less influential with Jewish theologians than for their Christian counterparts. Still, what will emerge as the dominant form of Jewish theology and philosophy, developing out of a serious confrontation with the implications of modern science, remains to be seen.

FURTHER READING

Because of the space limitations in this volume I was forced to list only a single example of each kind of theology mention in this essay. A more comprehensive bibliography is available in Norbert M. Samuelson, *Jewish Philosophy: A Historical Introduction* (London and New York: Continuum, 2003).

Hartman, David. *A Living Covenant* (Glencoe: Free Press, 1985). For traditional Jewish theology.

Borowitz, Eugene B. *Renewing the Covenant* (Philadelphia: Jewish Publication Society, 1991). For liberal Jewish theology.

Baker, Leonard. *Days of Sorrow and Pain: Leo Baeck and the Berlin Jews* (New York: Oxford University Press, 1980). For Baeck.

Friedman, Maurice S. *Martin Buber's Life and Work* (New York: Dutton, 1983). For Buber.

Kaplan, Edward K. *Holiness in Words: Abraham Joshua Heschel's Poetics of Piety* (Albany: State University Press of New York, 1996). For Heschel.

Goldsmith, Emanuel S., Mel Scult, and Robert M. Seltzer (eds.). *The American Judaism of Mordecai Kaplan* (New York: New York University Press, 1990). For Kaplan.

Samuelson, Norbert M. *A User's Guide to Franz Rosenzweig's Star of Redemption* (Richmond: Curzon Press, 1999). For Rosenzweig.

Waskow, Arthur. *Torah of the Earth: Exploring 4,000 Years of Ecology in Jewish Thought* (Woodstock, Vt.: Jewish Lights Publishing, 2000). For ecology and Judaism.

Tirosh-Samuelson, Hava (ed.). *Women and Gender in Jewish Philosophy*, Jewish Literature and Culture (Bloomington: Indiana University Press, 2004). For feminist Jewish theology.

Fackenheim, Emil L. *To Mend the World* (New York: Schocken Books, 1989). For Holocaust theology.

Boyarin, Daniel. *Intertextuality and the Reading of the Midrash* (Bloomington: Indiana University Press, 1990). For postmodernist Jewish theology.

Samuelson, Norbert M. *Revelation and the God of Israel* (Cambridge: Cambridge University Press, 2002). For science and Judaism.

Eisen, Arnold M. *The Chosen People in America: A Study in Jewish Religious Ideology* (Bloomington: Indiana University Press, 1983). For sociology of Judaism.

Green, Arthur. *See My Face, Speak My Name: A Contemporary Jewish Theology* (Northvale, NJ: Jason Aronson, 1991). For spiritualist Jewish theology.

22 | Revelation

David Novak

Introduction

No doctrine is more important in Jewish theology than revelation. Jewish theology is a Jewish enterprise because it is primarily an analysis of the meaning of Torah. Torah presents itself as God's word to humans. Hence the fundamental meaning of the Torah, over and above that of its specific teachings, is to be discovered in the doctrine of revelation: the way the Torah is given to its human recipients (*mattan torah*). This doctrine teaches that real contact between God and humans takes place in this world.

Jewish theology which has been exposed to philosophy has asked basic philosophical questions of the doctrine of revelation. At the level of metaphysics, Jewish theologians have asked: *Why does God speak to humans?* A God who cannot or will not communicate with humans is hardly the God Jews have traditionally obeyed and worshipped. At the level of epistemology (theory of knowledge), Jewish theologians have asked this question: *How do humans know what God says to them?* A God whom humans cannot know at all is hardly the God Jews have traditionally obeyed and worshipped. And at the level of ethics Jewish theologians have asked this question: *What are humans obligated to do in response to God's word?* A God whose communication with humans involves no practical demands is hardly the God Jews have traditionally obeyed and worshipped.

I shall explore how these three philosophical questions about verbal revelation were asked by three of the most important modern Jewish theologians: Martin Buber (1878–1965), Franz Rosenzweig (1886–1929), and Abraham Joshua Heschel (1907–72). A 'Jewish theologian' is someone who is concerned with 'God-talk' (the original meaning of 'theology') and is concerned with it in the context of the Judaism to which he or she is personally committed. The God-talk of revelation is what God somehow or other communicates to humans with whom God is in contact. Each of these theologians is concerned with the metaphysics, the epistemology, and the ethics of revelation in the context of *his* Judaism.

Martin Buber

I–You consciousness

We shall begin with Martin Buber, who made interpersonal communication the central issue of all the twentieth-century Jewish thinkers who took revelation to be *the* question for modern Jewish theology.

Buber posits the dualistic structure of consciousness: there is always an 'I' and a 'not-I'. But human consciousness does not create its own objects out of itself. For most modern philosophers, the 'I' is a *subject* who first discovers *objects* already there for its *use*. Only through this process of human discovery of the non-human world do human discoverers encounter other human discoverers, that is, fellow humans to whom one can say 'you' in a way one cannot say 'you' to impersonal objects. For Buber, however, the order of consciousness is the reverse of this. That is, one first encounters others *to whom* one's primary mode of speech is 'you'. Only thereafter does one relate to the non-personal world *about which* one's primary speech is 'it'. I–you speech is speech with those for whom we are directly concerned as the unique persons we ourselves are. I–it speech, conversely, is speech to those persons who appear 'thing-like' to us because our relation to them is essentially connected to our relation to things, which is one that is essentially *useful*, even if only useful for our thought. Furthermore, whereas all human persons have the capacity for an I–you relationship, there are no human persons with whom we only relate on the I–you level. Even with those nearest and dearest to us, we inevitably fall from the pristine level of 'I–you' *dialogue* to the level of more mundane, more *objective*, 'I–it' speech. Thus what is a 'you' can and does become an 'it', which makes it like all those other objects that are incapable of ever being addressed as 'you'. One has *experiences* of an it; one has a *relationship* with a you: that is, I *encounter* 'my' you ('my' being a term of relation, not of possession).

With descriptive gifts unequalled in modern religious writing, Buber shows that our whole personal project from infancy to the moment of death is to seek more of an I–you relationship with other persons. The perversion of that personal project is to avoid that interpersonal quest and seek a false security in one's control of things which, more often than not—even when that treatment is honest and benevolent, not deceptive and malicious—turns out to be our being controlled by things and by persons who treat us like things.

At the metaphysical level, where we reach the limits of human consciousness, even consciousness of other persons, Buber's revelational theology begins. Whereas a human can be both a you and an it, God can only be a you. Buber calls God 'the eternal You'.[1] The only relationship possible with God is the I–You relationship. Once that relationship ceases to be at the I–You level, the human person is not relating to the same God at all. One can only speak *to* God; once we attempt to speak *about* God, we are already attempting to reduce the relationship with God to the I–it level, but that is a level of relation to which God, as it were, refuses to subordinate Godself. Buber even suggests at times that there is no difference between relating to God as an it and idolatry, which is the worship of what is not-God.

The phenomenon of revelation

Revelation, then, is God's self-presentation to humans so that they can address God as You. Revelation, which in Buber's native German means 'opening oneself up' (*Offenbarung*), is the only way it makes sense to speak of the God–human relationship. There is no other way either to or from God. As God opens Godself up to humans, so humans open themselves up to God. Revelation, then, is the highest form of consciousness possible for humans, and it is anything but self-consciousness. Moreover, whatever other relationships God has with what is not-God are simply beyond our knowledge and beneath our concern. As Buber writes in his 1923 masterwork *I and Thou* ('thou' being the original English translation of his use of the second-person familiar form of address in German, *du*): 'This is the eternal revelation which is present in the here and now. I neither know of nor believe in any revelation that is not the same in its primal phenomenon . . . That which reveals is that which reveals . . . nothing more.'[2]

Buber emphasizes that this revelation has no 'content', that it is only 'a presence'.[3] But if it has no content, is it like some sort of mystical vision, which cannot represent or depict (that is, describe) or even evoke? Without content, how can the recipient of revelation actively respond to the One who has so revealed Oneself to him or her? Without content, can revelation be anything more than our passive experience of Nothing, as indeed it is for many mystics? If this revelation is so contentless, how can it have any practical significance? Haven't previous Jewish theologians who dealt with revelation emphasized that revelation is supposed to result in the recipient of this revelation actually doing something tangible in the human world? When God reveals commandments to humans, isn't this revelation meant to motivate them to do something they wouldn't otherwise have known to do or how to do it? Finally, if Buber explicitly says that, in revelation, 'whoever steps before the countenance has soared beyond duty and obligation', how does he avoid charges that he is an antinomian, someone who, in his own words, has 'left behind forever ethical judgments'?[4]

But can one be antinomian and still be part of the Jewish tradition, however liberally conceived? And if one is a religious antinomian, doesn't this imply that one is probably a political anarchist, who is opposed to law altogether? But how can one be an anarchist and a contributing member of any human society? Yet we know that Buber situated himself within the Jewish community (religiously conceived), and that he clearly situated himself politically in the three states in which he lived: the Austro-Hungarian Empire into which he was born (in 1878); Germany, where he lived most of his adult life (until 1938); and finally and most importantly, Israel, where he spent his later years and where he died (in 1965) and is buried.

Buber was well aware of the antinomian and anarchistic implications of both his metaphysics and epistemology of revelation, and he knew quite well how to counter them in his thought. He is not antinomian, religiously speaking, since the encounters with God of which he speaks do result in a commandment from God. The very presence of God encountered in revelation definitely has authority, but it is not what we would normally call 'authoritative'. The God of revelation does make demands on us. Even our love of this God is not meant to be an experience of self-satisfied enjoyment. Revelation has immediate ethical import, but it does not give us anything like a system of law or ethics. What Buber vigorously rejects is the ordering of the I–You relationship with God (which for him can only be *present*) by the structure of law—which for him can only be *from the past*.

To make revelation 'legal' is to attempt to capture a past event in the present, by means of the same type of thinking that we regularly employ in our mundane I–it relations. Revelation ought to be an unanticipated present encounter that leads into an indefinite future. Buber criticizes classical Christian theology in much the same way he criticizes rabbinic Judaism. Where rabbinic Judaism attempted to capture the event of revelation in I–it-like law, classic Christian theology, beginning with Paul, attempted to capture the event of revelation in I–it-like dogma. Fidelity to authentic revelation is neither following a system of rules nor is it assenting to a dogmatic system.

For Buber, such 'legislation' is necessary and desirable in the I–it realm in which most of our time is spent. The anarchist does not realize that the very spontaneity of the I–you encounter is confused and endangered without the I–it realm and its ordered regularity to which the I–You encounter may be contrasted and thus made into something especially unique. What is spontaneous presupposes what is regular and normal. Thus Buber denied neither commandment nor law. Indeed, the German term he uses for 'commandment' is *Gebot*, literally meaning 'what we are *bidden* to do'. It is very much like *Gebet* (which is the German word for 'prayer'), when we *bid* or 'beseech' God to do something for us. Conversely, the German term he uses for 'law,' *Gesetz*, means 'what has been set down'.

Buber can certainly make a connection between the Jewish past and the Jewish present (and its thrust into the Jewish future) in the case of Jewish law. If Jewish law is the way Jews have governed themselves throughout their history, then there is a need for Jews to maintain this political continuity in a structured, lawlike way. One can see Buber's lifelong Zionism to be his commitment to Jewish political continuity. But Buber does not think this necessity of law (broadly conceived) is a religious necessity. It has no essential connection to revelation except, perhaps, as its necessary antithesis. For that reason, Buber fundamentally rejects traditional Jewish religious law (halakhah). Law has a place for him, to be sure, but that place is neither in the ethical relationship with other persons (every other 'you') nor in the religious relationship with God (the One You that cannot become an 'it' and remain the same). Not only does halakhah not follow from revelation in any kind of logical necessity, but it seems to be contrary to the true commandment, which can only be experienced in a way that precludes, even excludes, all structure and limit either before it or after it. Love, which is the essence of revelation, cannot be legislated; it can only be directly elicited, directly bidden by one lover to another. In other words, love is the only real commandment that cannot be legislated without being destroyed thereby. It is obvious why Buber's theology was repugnant to almost all Orthodox Jews, but attractive to many Liberal Jews, and to some Protestant Christians as well.

Revelation and ethics

Taking ethics to be the way we interact with other humans, one could say that, for Buber, even though I–you encounters with other humans cannot be set up at will, their spontaneity ought not be haphazard. In a certain sense, one needs to regard the very possibility of such encounters as *destined* in order to take them with utmost serious-ness. At this point, the ethical meaning of the I–You encounter with God emerges as the essential meaning of this encounter. This should be carefully distinguished from the 'ritual' or halakhic meaning that the I–You encounter does not, and indeed cannot, have for Buber. To appreciate fully the ethical significance of interhuman I–you relation-ships one needs to appreciate how the I–You relationship with God gives them their fullest and deepest character.

God's love, which must be taken as absolutely prior, *elicits* love from me, not for the sake of some sort of reciprocity, but in order to direct it to others. I am to love my neighbour—I can only love my neighbour—because I am loved by God's commanding love. Furthermore, even in the legally structured rabbinic tradition (which Buber usually dislikes), how one puts the commandment of neighbour-love into practice is something so personal that each individual largely decides for himself or herself just what to do in any particular personal encounter with an other. And that largely depends on one's intimately personal knowledge of the existential needs of the other for whom God has elicited our responsive love of God.

Buber skilfully used much material from the Jewish tradition (especially biblical and Hasidic texts) to illustrate his philosophical theology and the centrality of revelation in it. Nevertheless, many Jews have been troubled by the fact that he seems to have too little consideration of the communal aspects of Jewish existence, which have always had considerable religious significance for Jews (and even for non-Jews, like Christians, who have a strong historical affinity to Judaism). Is Buber's treatment of revelation the thought of a philosopher using Judaism more as illustration than inspiration?

At this point we first need to turn to Franz Rosenzweig and then to Abraham Joshua Heschel, who were Jewish theologians greatly influenced by Buber, but who were also much more identifiably Jewish in both their thought and their personal action. Both Rosenzweig and Heschel were personally close to Buber and worked closely with him in some important theological projects, yet each of them attempted to take the Jewish tradition, including the doctrine of revelation, in a more comprehensive way than Buber, who seems to limit it to ethics alone.

Franz Rosenzweig

Commandment and law

Franz Rosenzweig worked out his theory of revelation in his masterwork, *The Star of Redemption* (first published in 1921, but mostly thought out when he was a soldier in the German army in the First World War), but his theological collaboration with Buber in Frankfurt in the 1920s enabled him to clarify his theory and make it speak more directly to the Jewish intellectual and spiritual concerns of his time and place. Buber, being the better-known thinker, had set the theological agenda, especially on the question of revelation, even though Rosenzweig had already developed his own theory of revelation before he became Buber's friend and colleague.

In response to the antithesis Buber had set up between commandment and law, Rosenzweig wrote back to him in 1925: 'Thus revelation is certainly not Law-giving. It is only this: revelation. The primary content of revelation is itself . . . "He spoke" is the beginning of interpretation, and certainly "I am". But where does this "interpretation" stop being legitimate? . . . Or could it be that revelation must never become legislation? . . . I believe in the right of the Law to prove its character . . . against all other types of law.'[5] By the time he wrote these words Rosenzweig seems to have become a fully observant Jew, no doubt out of theological conviction (and despite the progressive paralysis that would eventually kill him a few years later). This is a powerful practical confirmation of Rosenzweig's theory, just as the fact that Buber observed very little of the Jewish tradition is a powerful practical confirmation of his theory. Both thinkers practised what they preached.

This emphasis on revelation as a communal event gives Rosenzweig's theory of revelation its more cogent ethical thrust, since communal ethics inevitably involves law. One can understand why Rosenzweig argues against Buber that practising God's commandments in the form of law enhances them by giving them structure and duration. It is only when the observance of the commandments becomes 'legalistic', in the sense that one observing the commandment does not intend God as the commanding presence behind and within the commandment, that Rosenzweig would agree with Buber's dichotomy between commandment and law. Yet even here it seems that Rosenzweig might well counsel one to observe the law anyway and strive to regain or attain its commanded character.

In 1924, in a letter to some of his disciples, Rosenzweig made a distinction between what can be communicated about revelation, which is its human interpretation, and what cannot be communicated, which is revelation as an event of direct confrontation between God and humans. But this distinction is more formal than substantial, since one cannot really divide biblical revelation into those words spoken by God and those words spoken by human authors. The idea that revelation contains both divine address and human interpretation as response is consistent with the text of the Hebrew Bible (which Rosenzweig and Buber were then translating together into a radically new German vocabulary). The biblical text frequently has God speaking in the second person (in the form 'I–you') *and* God being spoken about in the third person (as 'He' or 'Him'). Thus Rosenzweig's view of revelation has much more of a connection to the primary Jewish text of revelation than did Buber's.

A new metaphysics

In *The Star of Redemption* Rosenzweig developed an elaborate system of thought, which he ambitiously called 'the New Thinking'. This new thinking was meant to be a radical departure from the 'old' metaphysics, and at its core lies Rosenzweig's new theory of revelation (for which he later found considerable precedent in the work of the eleventh-century Spanish-Jewish theologian Judah Halevi).

In the medieval Jewish, Christian, and Islamic theology that had been heavily influenced by the philosophy of Aristotle, 'metaphysics' designates human concern with the realm of being beyond and above (one of the chief meanings of the Greek word *meta*) the physical and temporal world where birth and death occur. At the apex of this world stands God, with whom all intelligent beings are concerned and to whom they are intelligently attracted, but who is not concerned with them, let alone attracted to them. Moreover, it is assumed that God's concern with Godself alone is eternal: without beginning and without end and without any change. Such a God is clearly unresponsive to the temporal events in the lives of humans, even when it is assumed that God is the creator of the world and is directly related to God's human creatures. In this view, 'metaphysics' means the way in which the transcendent concerns of truly intellectual humans enable them to transcend their earthly limitations in the world at least partially, in order to become like the eternal God.

In Rosenzweig's radical reversal of meaning, metaphysics is not what humans do in order to come out of their mortal finitude, but rather God's coming out of Godself— out of God's eternal self-satisfaction—in order to become related to humans in the temporal world in which humans are born, live, and die. In the old metaphysical theology though, revelation is seen as an event in human experience where, as it were, the human subject glimpses at a temporal point in his or her life what has been eternally in the life of God. The fact that this human subject experiences this eternal reality *now* in no way affects the divine reality which is the object of his or her experience. For the old metaphysical theology, revelation is a totally subjective event, just as walking into a theatre during the showing of a film in no way affects the story being told in the film. That story will remain totally the same even if all the viewers of the film enter the theatre after the film has begun to be shown and leave while the film is still running.

For Rosenzweig, however, revelation is an event simultaneously present both in the life of God, who reveals Godself like an act of new creation in time, and in the life of the human subject to whom God reveals Godself and elicits a response which is as innovative as what God has revealed to him or her. Being an event both subjective and objective, revelation, in which God and humans confront each other, is thoroughly historical for both partners. It is like a play in which the spectators are actors themselves, so that their experience of the play and the play's story are identical. In fact, for Rosenzweig the play's elements are given in past creation, the play's content is shared in present revelation, and the play is concluded in future redemption. Rosenzweig speaks of the beloved human recipient of God's revelation responding by hoping and working for 'the coming of the kingdom . . . for the future repetition of the miracle'.[6] Rosenzweig sees Judaism and Christianity as being the only two religions of revelation as he understands it (unlike his medieval predecessors, he explicitly leaves out Islam): they take separate historical paths in the time between revelation and redemption, but will ultimately become reconciled at the redeemed end-time of all history.

God's love

But what is it that God reveals in an event that puts Godself into worldly time as much as humans are already created in worldly time? Rosenzweig's answer to this question comes in his magnificent meditation on the biblical Song of Songs, which forms the heart of *The Star of Redemption*. That most erotic of biblical books ostensibly speaks of male–female sexual attraction and consummation, yet it is interpreted by the ancient rabbis as a phenomenology (that is, a 'showing' or 'revelation') of the love between God and God's people, a love in which both partners are both active and passive, in which both partners give love to each other and receive love from each other simultaneously within the very same event in both of their lives.

Abraham Joshua Heschel

The divine ego

Abraham Joshua Heschel was in a significant sense Buber's pupil, even though he arrived in Germany in the late 1920s with a considerable background in the Jewish mystical tradition of the Hasidic community in which he was born and raised in Poland. While retaining much of Buber's theological vocabulary, Heschel's theory of revelation developed it in a very different direction conceptually, in which the influence of Kabbalah and Hasidism is very much evident.

For Buber, it should be recalled, the 'I' is the human person who addresses himself or herself to the divine 'You'. Judaism's most essential prayer constantly addresses God with the words 'Blessed are *You* O Lord our God'. Buber's main theological point is that God can only be addressed as 'You', unlike humans, who more often than not are really spoken about as 'it'. However, in the Jewish tradition prayer is subsequent in importance to the reading of the Torah, which is God's revelation to us. And the prime revelation for Judaism, the revelation of the Torah at Mount Sinai (beginning but not ending with the Ten Commandments), opens with the words: 'I am (*anokhi*) the Lord your God' (Exodus 20: 2). Heschel insists in his 1951 book *Man Is Not Alone* (written after he arrived in the United States in 1940) that in the I–You relationship it is primarily God who is addressing humans, and only then are humans prepared to address the God they *now* know is *there* for them. Heschel spoke of the Bible as 'not man's theology but God's anthropology', and as teaching 'our being known to God'.[7]

Like Rosenzweig, Heschel sees revelation to be the divine awakening of the human rather than the human awakening of the divine. But what does God communicate to humans in this revelation, how do humans receive this revelation, and what are the ethical directives that come out of this revelation?

Revelation experienced and spoken

In what many consider his central theological work, *God in Search of Man* (1955), Heschel makes this striking statement: 'As a report about revelation the Bible itself is a midrash.'[8] The rabbinic term midrash usually means the method for discovering the deeper meaning of a biblical passage and the actual meaning so discovered and enunciated. But Heschel means something different. Seen in the light of his thought as a whole, what he seems to be saying is that the words of the Torah are an exposition, a revelation, of something deeper than these words themselves, which are already interpreting rather than merely repeating what happened in the divine–human encounter we call revelation. In fact, Heschel seems to be implying that all language is essentially responsive and never truly original per se. Language, for him, seems to presuppose a form of thought that is metalinguistic, that transcends language while still making language possible.

On this point especially, Heschel's view of revelation is a serious departure from the views of Buber and Rosenzweig, both of whom seem to affirm the absolute priority of language in human experience, even in the experience of revelation. This may well be due to Heschel's greater reliance on the Jewish mystical tradition he knew so intimately, and to the fact that he was an accomplished poet. Poets, like prophets, know that they intend much more than they can actually say. For Heschel, 'in the beginning was *not* the word', a point he took from Maimonides' negative theology. (Unlike almost every other Jewish theologian, Heschel was able to blend elements from the medieval rationalist and mystical traditions.)

Heschel is convinced that the original content of revelation is wordless. His first work, published in 1937, was a study of the phenomenon of prophecy. (Phenomenology was the school of modern philosophy that influenced Heschel most.) Prophets, of course, do speak: the Bible records what some of them actually said. Yet before being concerned with what came out of the prophetic encounter with God, Heschel is concerned with *how* the prophet actually experienced that encounter. Heschel speaks of 'the nature of revelation' as 'being an event of the ineffable . . . something which words cannot spell, which human language will never be able to portray'.[9] But even if this event cannot be comprehended in speech, that does not mean that one cannot allude to its pre-verbal or meta-verbal originality. Otherwise how could one even mention revelation?

What sort of event, though, is Heschel alluding to? It is not verbal in the way an idea speaks to one. And it does not seem to be visual, since Heschel regards any depiction of revelation (even if only in one's mind) as equivalent to the error of conceiving of God's body (another point taken from Maimonides). The language coming forth from revelation is not the language of philosophers or of visual artists; it could only be the language of poets, since only poets primarily speak in a voice that evokes rather than describes or depicts the reality it is experiencing. Religious poets 'evoke', that is, they 'call forth' from us our participation in their experience of God; they bring us *into* God's revelation to them. Thus poets stand at the very frontier of language, not at its back door; they are anything but overly emotional would-be philosophers. Indeed, a poet participates in the very creation of the word. A religious poet who has apprehended the creation of the word as a truly divine act becomes almost like a prophet, a *navi*, meaning God's spokesperson (see Exodus 7: 1).

That the prophets experience God's thoughts about the human person created in God's image. These seem to be pure feeling, but directed feeling nonetheless. Heschel speaks of the prophet's 'knowledge of God' as being 'fellowship with Him',[10] which seems to be an emotional bond beyond words and images.

The ethical import of Heschel's view of revelation follows from his view of divine pathos. The one who experiences revelation closely identifies not only with the feeling God but also with those for whom God feels. Heschel sees divine pathos and human sympathy therewith to be at the heart of the concern of the biblical prophets for the poor, downtrodden, and forsaken in the human world. Feelings that do not inspire action would be a psychological indulgence offensive to the God with whom one is feeling so intimately. Heschel put his mystical theology of revelation into ethical action by his involvement in the anti-Vietnam War movement, the movement to attain equal justice for African-Americans, and his activist concern for the plight of the Jews trapped in religious and cultural annihilation in the Soviet Union.

In the fully religious life, halakhah supplies the content necessary for our regular co-operation with God in the sanctification of the essentially temporal world. It provides the means for our being directly related to God. Here we are with others in the celebration of the covenanted community's sacred times, whereas in ethics we go out from God to others in the larger world. This is consistent with Heschel's lifelong Jewish piety.

Subsequent Influence

It is hard to actually measure the influence of the thought of Buber, Rosenzweig, and Heschel on contemporary Jewish theology since it is ubiquitous. Until recently, when Jewish theology was still concerned with what might be termed their 'existential agenda', it would seem that Rosenzweig was most influential inasmuch as his phenomenology of biblical revelation (even though Rosenzweig himself would have probably disowned the appellation of phenomenologist) spoke most deeply to a generation of Jewish thinkers who largely, like himself, were 'returnees' to Judaism. No one is better than Rosenzweig in showing what it means for someone to be seized by the love of God and become an authentic Jew existentially in this event and its aftermath. In the aftermath of revelation, Rosenzweig offered a path into traditional Jewish observance that did not require one to adopt a literalist, authoritarian reading of the sources of Jewish law and observance. Nevertheless, when it comes to the actual inner experience of Jewish religious observance and its intention of the God to whom it is a response, no one is better than Heschel (who, I can say from personal experience, was happy to call himself a phenomenologist) in evocative description, probably because he knew it from the inside so much better than did Rosenzweig (who only came to it in adulthood) and certainly Buber (who had left it in adolescence).

However, with the recent turn in Jewish theology to ethics and political theory, Buber, whose social philosophy (indeed, he was Professor of Social Philosophy at the Hebrew University of Jerusalem from 1938 until his death in 1965) was more developed than that of Rosenzweig or Heschel, is becoming more and more the major influence.

That is due to his profound influence on the French Jewish philosopher, Emmanuel Levinas (1906–95), whose ethically grounded philosophy is most intensely discussed by younger Jewish thinkers today (even though Levinas himself claimed Rosenzweig as his major influence: a very debatable point). And, in fact, the theologian most discussed today by Orthodox Jewish thinkers, the American rabbi Joseph B. Soloveitchik (1903–93), can be seen within the type of ethical thinking that leads from Buber (whom Soloveitchik had definitely read) to Levinas (whom there is no evidence Soloveitchik had ever read or even heard of). This is especially so since Levinas, unlike Buber, lends himself to the type of theoretical law (halakhah) Soloveitchik spent his life explicating.

FURTHER READING

Buber, Martin. *I and Thou*, tr. Walter Kaufmann (New York: Scribners, 1970). This is Buber's main work, which set the stage for all subsequent discussions of revelation as interpersonal communication.

Buber, Martin. *The Prophetic Faith*, tr. Carlyle Witton-Davies (New York: Harper & Bros., 1960). A major work in which Buber applied his overall theory of interpersonal communication to biblical interpretation.

Cohen, Hermann. *Religion of Reason Out of the Sources of Judaism*, tr. Simon Kaplan (New York: Frederick Ungar, 1972). The most important nineteenth- /early twentieth-century idealist treatment of revelation. It inspired the existentialist reactions of Buber and Rosenzweig.

Friedman, Maurice S. *Martin Buber: The Life of Dialogue* (New York: Harper & Row, 1960). Still the most important treatment of Buber's religious thought.

Glatzer, Nahum N. *Franz Rosenzweig: His Life and Thought*, 2nd edn. (New York: Schocken Books, 1961). Still the best treatment of the relation of Rosenzweig's life and religious thought.

Heschel, Abraham Joshua. *God in Search of Man* (New York: Farrar, Straus, & Cudahy, 1955). Still the most profound theology of revelation written by any Jewish thinker in English.

Heschel, Abraham Joshua. *Man Is Not Alone* (Philadelphia: Jewish Publication Society, 1951). Heschel's theological debut in English.

Heschel, Abraham Joshua. *The Prophets* (Philadelphia: Jewish Publication Society, 1962). An English elaboration of Heschel's 1937 German book, which is a phenomenology of prophetic revelation.

Heschel, Abraham Joshua. *The Sabbath*, 2nd edn. (New York: Farrar, Straus & Co., 1952). Heschel's most important phenomenological meditation on Jewish religious life.

Kaplan, Edward K., and Samuel H. Dresner. *Abraham Joshua Heschel: Prophetic Witness* (New Haven: Yale University Press, 1998). Shows how Heschel's theology and his early life were interrelated.

Rosenzweig, Franz. *On Jewish Learning*, ed. N. N. Glatzer (New York: Schocken Books, 1955).

Rosenzweig, Franz. *The Star of Redemption*, tr. William W. Hallo (New York: Holt, Rinehart, & Winston, 1970). According to many, this is the most profound philosophical reflection on revelation by a twentieth-century Jewish thinker.

NOTES

1. Martin Buber, *I and Thou*, tr. Walter Kaufmann (New York: Scribners, 1970), p. 123.
2. Ibid., p. 160.
3. Ibid., p. 161.
4. Ibid., pp. 156–7.
5. Franz Rosenzweig, *On Jewish Learning*, ed. N. N. Glatzer (New York: Schocken Books, 1955), p. 118.
6. Rosenzweig, *The Star of Redemption*, tr. William W. Hallo (New York: Holt, Rinehart, & Winston, 1970), p. 185.
7. Abraham Joshua Heschel, *Man Is Not Alone* (Philadelphia: Jewish Publication Society, 1951), p. 129.
8. Heschel, *God in Search of Man* (New York: Farrar, Straus & Cudahy, 1955), p. 185.
9. Ibid., pp. 184–5.
10. Heschel, *The Prophets*, (Philadelphia: Jewish Publication Society, 1962), p. 223.

23 | Covenant

Peter Ochs

YHVH our God made a covenant with us in Horeb. YHVH did not make this covenant with our fathers, but with us, who are all of us here alive this day.

(Deuteronomy 5: 2–3)

Jewish sages, scholars, and thinkers have redescribed Judaism after each period of catastrophe in Jewish civilization. Still traumatized by the memory of Shoah, the Jewish people lives in such a period now, which means that this is an appropriate time to redescribe the Jewish religion. It is, therefore, an appropriate time to redescribe what Jews mean by covenant, since covenant—*brit*—refers to the bond that links all members of the Jewish people to each other and that ties the Jewish people as a whole to God. After times of catastrophe, Jews tend to ask what has happened to the covenant that forms them as a people: is it still intact? Are they still bound to their God and to one another? If so, why has God not protected them from this catastrophe? What have they done to merit this suffering? Responding to such questions after times of great loss, Jewish sages, scholars, and leaders tend to redescribe their religion by redescribing their covenant: what it means, what it promised, what went wrong, and what they might do now both to re-form and reaffirm it.

The Exodus narrative often serves as a prototype for such redescriptions. The family of Israel suffers (enslavement); Israel prays for help; God declares that His very name is 'I-am-with-you' (*ehyeh imakh*); a portion of Israel survives, to renew and re-form themselves through a covenant ceremony (receiving the Torah at Sinai). As retold in the Deuteronomic narrative, the covenant ceremony is marked by Moses's declaring that the covenant is made with 'all of us who are alive here this day'. This declaration introduces a rule for all subsequent efforts to renew the covenant after destruction: retell the story of Israel's covenant as your *own* story; know, thereby, that God is with you now in the work of renewing the covenant within the specific context of your suffering. In these terms, classical rabbinic Judaism may itself be redescribed as a comprehensive renewal and reformation of the covenant after the destruction of the Second Temple.

On one level, this chapter offers brief descriptions of how the biblical and rabbinic literatures reformulate Israel's covenant in the very act of retelling its history. On another level, the chapter also delivers a specific thesis: that to describe Israel's covenant *in this time after Destruction* is also to share in its reaffirmation and reformulation. In this spirit, the chapter redescribes the biblical and rabbinic accounts as a way of identifying resources for renewing the covenant today. The chapter concludes by introducing the work of some recent theologians as resources for responding to some of the issues that challenge Israel's covenant today.

The biblical prototypes

Read as a whole, the Hebrew Bible, or *Tanakh*,[1] presents Israel's covenant with God as both a love relationship and a legal document that binds both parties to certain obligations and rights. The biblical historians Mendenhall and Baltzer first noted that Israel's covenants appear to be variants of the 'suzerainty treaties' that ancient Hittite rulers offered their vassals. These treaties tended to have six features: a preamble; a historical prologue; a set of stipulations; an account of how the treaty would be read publicly and stored; a list of witnesses; a set of curses (for those who break the treaty) and blessings (for those who keep it). Historians suggest that the biblical covenants adopt most of these features, while replacing any human suzerain with God and displaying the new consequences such divine rule would have for human political behaviour. As portrayed in the Book of Genesis, for example, Abraham's covenant stipulated that God would give the land of Canaan to Abraham and his descendants and that they would circumcise their men. According to the Book of Exodus, the Mosaic covenant came with the Ten Commandments (or 'ten words') as stipulations, and it designated the 'Ark of the Covenant' as the place to deposit the text of these commandments. According to the Book of Deuteronomy, the Mosaic covenant also came with a list of curses and blessings (Deuteronomy 27–8). The most telling covenant narrative is provided in Joshua 24, which describes the treaty that bound all the tribes of Israel into a political pact with each other and with God. Here there are a detailed preamble and historical prologue; lists of stipulations, curses-and-blessings, and witnesses; and an account of how the treaty was read and deposited.

While the suzerainty format may account for the political-legal dimension of Israel's covenant, the biblical accounts display several other dimensions as well. For the prophet Hosea, for example, Israel's covenant with God is portrayed as a love relation and marital union (see Hosea 2: 16, 18, 21–2). For Amos, the covenant is a societal code within all nations (see Amos 1: 9). For Second Isaiah, the covenant is an ethical bond (see Isaiah 42: 6–7). And, in the Genesis narrative of Noah, the covenant is a cosmic bond between God and all living things (see Genesis 9: 8–11).

To understand the enormity of what it means to share in such a covenant, we must note all these portrayals and not reduce the covenant to any one model. The covenant is political, legal, social, spiritual, emotional, theological, metaphysical, and more. As the Bible portrays it, moreover, the covenant is not formed, once and for all, into some single set of clearly defined rules or principles. There is a sense in which it may not change—the way a lover's 'undying love' never wavers—but there is also a sense in which it continually changes. Writing in the shadow of the Shoah, my particular interest in this chapter is the continuity and change that accompanies Israel's efforts to renew the covenant after times of terrible destruction. At such a time one asks if Israel ever achieved such a renewal after previous destructions; and, if so, if there is some primordial covenant that remains through such renewals; and, if so, if that covenant is also reshaped in response to a particular catastrophe. My brief study will examine answers to those questions.

Yes, the Bible narrates terrible destructions that Israel has suffered

One prototype is Israel's enslavement under the Pharaohs of ancient Egypt. As portrayed in the Exodus narrative, the Children of Israel (Jacob) went to Egypt in time of famine, lingered, were enslaved, and, through generations of enslavement, suffered the loss of their familial, social, and religious order (see Exodus 2 ff.). A second prototype is the destruction of the First Temple in 586 BCE, and with it, the destruction of the Israelite monarchy and the exile of the priestly and prophetic classes to Babylonia (see, for example, Isaiah 1 and Lamentations 1).

But, yes, the Bible also narrates the renewal of Israel's covenant, reaffirming the covenants of Abraham, Isaac, and Jacob, and of Sinai

As portrayed in the Exodus narrative, our first prototype of destruction gives rise to a first prototype of repair: God remembers the covenant of Abraham and sends Moses to rescue the Children of Israel from slavery (see Exodus 3 ff.). After the rescue, the covenant is reaffirmed through the Torah that God reveals to Moses on Sinai. As portrayed in the Prophetic books of the Bible, our second prototype of destruction gives rise to a second prototype of repair: God inspires the kings of Persia, Cyrus and then Darius, to return the priestly and prophetic leaders from Exile to Jerusalem, restoring Israel to her land and cult. In the words of Second Isaiah, God declares to Israel, 'You are my friend and my servant', and 'I am (still) with you' (Isaiah 41–3).

But the renewed covenant also displays new features that transform Israel's social and religious order

Delivering instructions for the Exodus, the God of Israel also reveals a new name: previously known as 'the God of Abraham, Isaac, and Jacob', now God is to be known by the proper name represented by the four Hebrew letters YHVH (see Exodus 3).[2] Through the Exodus, furthermore, God's covenant partner is transformed, from an extended family to a 'kingdom of priests and a holy nation' (Exodus 19: 6); or, as depicted in the historical narratives of Deuteronomy, Joshua, and Judges, a federation of tribes served by elders, priests, and, when needed, charismatic warlords, who are eventually transformed into kings.

More transformations follow. Renewing the Sinaitic covenant after Israel's return from Babylonian exile, the scribal priest Ezra also introduces a new covenantal practice: a public reading of the entire Torah, accompanied by priestly teachers who translate it into the local language of the people (Aramaic) and interpret it in ways the people can understand (see Nehemiah 8: 5–8). This means that a class of scribal priests will now not only copy and preserve the words of the covenant, but also reinterpret them in ways that may anticipate the rabbinic sages' Oral Torah. At the same time, the polity of Israel changes as well. Israel is no longer a monarchy, but a nation ruled by priests and a governor in service to a foreign sponsor (Persia).

The rabbinic prototypes

A pair of images dominates the history of rabbinic Judaism even more than a text: the Burnt Temple (70–1 CE) and Jerusalem razed and salted (135 CE). How could the religion of Israel survive the loss of its Temple and priesthood, whose daily sacrifices atoned for Israel's sins and thus maintained Israel's covenantal obligations? How could the Jews continue to trust in God's promise to maintain the divine covenantal obligations? And how could they trust the words of Torah that delivered the terms of the covenant? The following midrash, or biblical interpretation, displays the dominant rabbinic understanding: that rabbinic Judaism itself was the answer. After the destruction of the Temple, Rabban Yochanah ben Zakkai once walked near Jerusalem with his disciple Rabbi Yehoshuah. Looking at the Temple in ruins, Rabbi Yehoshuah said: 'Woe for us; the place that atoned for Israel's sins has been destroyed!' Rabban Yochanah ben Zakkai replied: 'Do not fear, my son. We have another way of gaining such atonement: enacting deeds of loving kindness, as it is written, "I desire loving kindness, not sacrifices" (Hosea 6: 6).'[3] While this midrash comes from late in the rabbinic period, it reflects generations of meditation on how the covenant of Israel would survive this second destruction of Israel's Temple. In its plain sense the Torah says that Israel must worship God through sacrifices offered in the Temple, but Israel's prophets had already extended the covenantal meaning of sacrifice to include acts of loving kindness. Through midrashim like this one, the rabbis claimed only to further extend the prophets' meaning. Taking on the mantle of Ezra, they retaught the Written Torah and reinterpreted its commandments in the context of their own day. In the process, they also transformed the meaning of a scribal priesthood. In the Second Temple period the scribes remained a minority among Temple priests, whose primary concern was with Temple sacrifices. After the fall of the Second Temple, however, rabbinic practice eventually replaced all forms of priestly behaviour, replacing scribal work with Torah study and interpretation, and sacrificial work with the works of prayer and loving kindness through which Israel's covenant would be renewed and maintained.

Codified in the second century after the destruction, the Mishnah represents what we might call the rabbinic Book of the Covenant: an authoritative sampling of how the biblical covenant was reformulated by the first generations of rabbinic sages. Redacted as a book of reinterpreted commandments (*halakhot*), the Mishnah also includes what we might call ethical statements, as well as other forms of religious wisdom. One small tractate, *Avot* (Sayings of the Fathers), is of particular interest, since it collects ethical statements that would be useful for guiding the transformation of one set of covenantal rules into another. Since just after the Talmudic period, *Avot* has been inserted into traditional prayer books as a set of special readings for afternoon Shabbat services between Pesach and Rosh Hashanah. Each reading customarily begins with this midrash:

All Israel have a portion in the world to come, as it is written, 'Your people shall all be righteous; they shall possess the land forever; they are a shoot of My own planting, the work of My hands in which I shall be glorified' (Isaiah 60: 21).

(*Sanhedrin* 10: 1)

The midrash dramatizes the paradoxical setting of rabbinic Judaism. Imagine one of the sages reading Isaiah as he gazes, like Rabbi Yehoshuah, on the ruins of the Temple. 'We are all righteous?!' he might ask, 'We will possess this land?!' 'We are God's own work!?' The realities of Exile and Destruction seem clearly to contradict the prophecy and, thus, the terms of the covenant. But the midrash offers a simple no to the apparent contradiction: no, the Torah does not mislead; it is referring to the world to come, when all Israel shall be righteous, shall inherit this land, shall glorify God. This one line of interpretation displays a complex argument. The Torah speaks for every time in the past and not just one; each time displays different aspects of covenantal life, whose full meaning appears only through the series of *all* such eras, from the beginning to the end of days; glimpses of that end time enable the sages to read the Torah of their time out of the Torah of a past time; and midrash exemplifies this type of reading. But when is a midrashic rereading legitimate and authoritative? As if to answer this question, each weekly reading from *Avot* highlights a set of ethical sayings that could also serve as a set of rabbinic guidelines for reinterpreting the covenant in one's own day.

The first reading, from the beginning of *Avot*, sets the stage for all the rest: Moses received the Torah at Sinai and handed it down to Joshua, Joshua transmitted it to the elders, the elders handed it to the prophets, and the prophets handed it down to the men of the Great Assembly (the Sanhedrin, or Legislature, of the early Second Temple period) (*Avot* 1: 1). This genealogy establishes the priestly and prophetic authority of the rabbis. The transmission of Torah that begins with Moses—and that omits the line of priests, who maintained the scrolls of Torah in the Temple—ends with the men of the Great Assembly. It then extends, through the rest of *Avot*, to all the founding generations of rabbinic sages. This means that the genealogy also establishes the authority of the rabbinic teachings that follow. The second text of *Avot*, for example, delivers a teaching of Simon the Just, one of the last survivors of the Great Assembly, that the world stands on three things: Torah, worship, and loving kindness (*Avot* 1: 2). This teaching suggests not only that prayer and charitable acts are as important as studying words of Torah, but also that the words of the Written Torah that was maintained by the priests also contain something new: the Oral Torah that displays the meanings of the Written Torah to the sages of each generation.

The destruction of the Second Temple did not, therefore, break the chain that links all Israel to the prophecies of Isaiah and Moses. It did, however, mark the end of one formulation of the covenant and the beginning of another. For the rabbis, Simon the Just already displayed the rules of this new formulation in the middle of the Second Temple period. The new world of rabbinic Judaism will stand, like the world of the Mosaic covenant, on Torah, but this is the Oral Torah of the rabbis, as well as the Written Torah of the prophets. It stands on worship, but this is the 'service of the heart', or prayer (Babylonian Talmud, *Taanit* 2a), rather than the service of Temple sacrifice. And it stands on 'acts of loving kindness', which are commandments of Torah, but as the sages of each generation interpret them rather than as they appear only in the explicit words of the Bible.

Loosening and tightening the covenant in modernity

The Jewish theologian Eugene Borowitz offers a narrative of Judaism's move into and out of modernity. The emancipation drew European Jews into modernity:

After more than a millennium of ostracism and persecution, European Jews were astounded when the French Revolution signaled a turn to political equality in Europe, including even Jews ... Emancipation revolutionized Jewish spirituality, for whenever Jews were permitted to modernize, they did so avidly, and uncomplainingly accepted its accompanying secularization ... The startling effects of this fundamental shift of cultural context cannot be overemphasized. Freedom from segregated existence brought on a transition from a life oriented by revelation, tradition, and a sense of the holy to one in which religion became privatized if not irrelevant or obsolete ... Jews began to ask, 'What does it mean to be a Jew today? Why should one undertake its special responsibilities?'[4]

By what criteria would modern Jews choose which aspects of their Jewishness to retain and which to discard? On the whole, they chose criteria offered by Enlightenment sources, from which they learned to separate their lives into private and public spheres, relegating religion to the private sphere and adopting, for the public sphere, the ideals of scientific reason, modern statehood, individual rights, and universal ethics.[5] One consequence was a sharp divide between the beliefs of traditional Jews, for whom life was centred in Israel's covenant, and most modern Jews, for whom the covenant took on a broad range of new meanings. For fully secular Jews, whatever 'truth' the Torah had to offer would be identical to the truths of reason, which, they believed, were universal to all human beings. If it excluded non-Jews, then the covenant would be judged either untrue, or else simply an exaggerated name for the local customs of the Jews as an ethnic, rather than religious, group. For religiously liberal Jews—those who sought various degrees of accommodation between Judaism and Enlightenment—each religious group enacted the universal truths of humankind in different, but ultimately compatible ways. The Torah would therefore represent Israel's way of identifying universal truths, and the covenant its particular way of living them in society.

Traditional Jews adopted many strategies to deal with the threats and attractions of these modern approaches. For ultra-Orthodox Jews, modernity offered material and technological instruments of use in Jewish life, but the values of Enlightenment had to be shunned altogether. In fact, to guard Judaism from the threat of modernity, the boundary line between covenantal Israel and the rest of the world had to be defined as strictly as possible; the covenant was reconceived as an unchanging set of laws and doctrines. For modern Orthodox Jews, like Samson Raphael Hirsch, the strategy had two sides: to define Judaism's boundaries more carefully, while also identifying areas of significant accommodation to modernity. Jews should, for example, master the sciences, technologies, and politics of modernity, while being sure to draw their religious laws and ethical values only from traditional rabbinic sources. For Conservative Jews, finally—or others we might classify as 'in-between' Liberal and Orthodox Judaism—modern civilization represented just another historical context for covenantal life. Conservative thinkers argued that classical rabbinic Judaism was itself a model of the covenant's capacity to absorb new civilizational forms. Its pivotal practices of midrashic reading, for example, draw on Hellenistic methods of allegorical interpretation as well as on indigenous forms of intra-biblical exegesis. Torah is lived in the world, and to remain 'Torah true', modern Jews would have to be students of the sciences of modernity as well as of the evolving history of covenantal life.

For 200 to 300 years Jews have thus tended to pursue divided paths of covenantal life: tending either to the modern pole of non-covenantal belief or the traditionalist pole of an enclosed covenantal community. For many Jews in the late twentieth century, however, Enlightenment secularism lost its lure. In the face of decades of modern antisemitism and totalitarianism, many Jews lost their faith in 'the certainties about mind and self and human nature that once powered' the modern project.[6] As Borowitz observes, the Shoah was not the reason most Jews lost their faith in God. They had lost that faith long before, when they accepted the religion of modern humanism. What they lost in the Shoah was their faith in humanity.[7] One consequence has been a resurgence of Jewish religiosity. Along with the Reform movement's renewed interest in rabbinic tradition, there has also been a resurgence of interest in Orthodoxy and ultra-Orthodoxy. While less conspicuous, the most widespread change has, however, been toward the centre. Moving away from the polarities of Jewish life in modernity, contemporary Jews display increasing caution about both radical secularism and fundamentalism.[8] At the same time, they do not tend, as yet, to display any clear conviction about what a new centre would mean for Jewish observance, belief, and politics.

All we can observe, clearly, is that Judaism after modernity will transform at least three features of Israel's covenant. One feature is the status of women. After three to four decades of Jewish feminism, women have achieved positions of leadership in every denomination, and the covenant is being reshaped, even in modern Orthodoxy, by attention to narratives about women's experiences. Since women's voices have, for three thousand years, been only indirectly heard among 'all of us [who are] here alive this day [at Horeb]' (Deuteronomy 5: 3), re-hearing those voices will add new narratives not only to present-day Judaism, but also to what we hear within each of Israel's previous efforts to renew the covenant. A second feature to be transformed is the place of land and politics in the covenant. Six decades after the declaration of Israel's independence, the language, law, land, culture, and political controversies of Israel have once again become inseparable elements of Judaism's covenant. However embattled, Jerusalem is again at the centre of Jewish religious and intellectual life; the earth of Israel at the centre of Jewish legal debate, and Hebrew once again the living language of covenant. But how will rabbinic Judaism reapply its laws and ethics to the realities and responsibilities of a contested land and heterogeneous population? Scholars and leaders of this generation have only begun to respond to that question. A third feature is the topic of this chapter as a whole: how any covenant at all can be renewed after the fires of Auschwitz.

The renewal of covenant after the Shoah and after modernity

We have space to highlight three approaches that may signal the beginning of Judaism's path to renewal after Israel's most recent Destruction.

To cite the title of Eugene Borowitz's most important recent book, a *Theology For the Postmodern Jew* should centre on *Renewing the Covenant*. According to this liberal Jewish theologian, modern Jews will overcome the divisions of modernity only by reuniting the individuated modern Jewish self into the covenant of Israel. Echoing, in his own way, the rabbinic principles of *Avot*, Borowitz recommends several principles to guide this reunion. Modern Jewish life must again be God-centred, but—respecting the modern achievements of individual rights and dignity—the individual Jew must now play an active role in relation to God. This relation should bind together 'selfhood and ethnicity, with its multiple ties of land, language, history, traditions, fate, and faith'. 'The Covenant [should] render the Jewish self radically historical', displaying its relations both to previous epochs of Judaism and to the characteristics of our own time. The covenant should be oriented, moreover, to the future, anticipating Israel's and the creation's final redemption.[9]

The modern Orthodox thinker Irving Greenberg also characterizes Judaism after modernity as both a renewal and transformation of Israel's covenant.

The very quality of faithfulness to the covenant resists acceptance of new revelation—as it should . . . But no one said the Holocaust should be simply assimilable. For traditional Jews to . . . deny all significance to this event would be to repudiate the fundamental belief and affirmations of the Sinai covenant: that history is meaningful . . . There is an alternative for those whose faith can pass through the demonic, consuming flames of a crematorium: it is the willingness and ability to hear further revelation and reorient themselves.[10]

Introducing his essay with survivors' testimonies about children being thrown, alive, into the crematoria, Greenberg urges this working principle for reorientation: 'No statement, theological or otherwise, should be made that would not be credible in the presence of the burning children.'[11] Noting, furthermore, that religious and secularized Christians alike were complicitous in the evils of Nazi genocide, Greenberg argues that the covenant cannot be renewed in a vacuum: Jews have demands to make of others as well as of themselves. Noting that secular universalism weakened the ability of Jews to recognize and respond to the evil around them, Greenberg argues that Jewish secularism is a discredited alternative to covenantal life. Noting that traditional Jewish accounts of sin and repentance fail to account for both God's and humanity's role in these horrible events, Greenberg adds, however, that rigid Orthodoxy also fails to provide an adequate resource for renewing the covenant.

For the noted talmudist and Holocaust survivor David Weiss Halivni, Judaism's primary work after Shoah is *tikkun*—repair: mending the world by way of repairing our received readings and interpretations of the Torah. The primary engine of repair is a new practice of rabbinic midrash. Halivni introduces his Holocaust memoir with his own 'anonymous' midrash: 'The sword and the book came down from heaven tied to each other. Said the Almighty, "If you keep what is written in this book, you will be spared this sword; if not, you will be consumed by it" (Midrash Rabbah Deuteronomy 4: 2). We clung to the book, yet we were consumed by the sword.'[12] Reinterpreting a classic rabbinic midrash the way the rabbinic sages reinterpreted the written Torah, Halivni has already signalled a central lesson of his memoir: even after the Holocaust, he will renew the rabbis' covenant with God, but this renewal will bring transformation as well: 'We clung yet were consumed.' The rabbis' Oral Torah remains, but its received form is contested: just as the sages retained the words of the Written Torah ('Your people shall all be righteous . . .' Isaiah 60: 21) while also reinterpreting them ('All Israel have a portion in the world to come', Sanhedrin 10: 1).

Halivni's magnum opus, *Sources and Traditions*, is a life's work of critically reconstructing—and repairing—the Talmud's editorial form. As suggested in his recent writings on theology, this work also illustrates how to repair the covenant more generally. It is to give witness to the Shoah as a sign of rupture in every aspect of covenantal life, and to respond by rereading every aspect as if it were a 'maculated' word of written Torah. This is a word that displays, at once, the holiness of divine speech and the uncertainties that accompany all human efforts to comprehend that speech on earth. To devote one's scholarly energies to studying this word *at this time after Shoah* is to participate in Israel's ancient tradition of renewing and transforming the covenant after Destruction. This is, at once, to 'seek the divine voice'[13] that is the source of renewal *and* to draw on the scholarly sciences of one's day as instruments of that seeking. Unlike ultra-Orthodox critics of the academy, Halivni thereby endorses scientific study of the Talmud. As the Mishnah spoke of its time after Destruction, this too is a time 'to act for the sake of heaven' (Berakhot 9: 5): to take the extraordinary measures that will be needed to renew the covenant, such as Halivni's efforts to annotate the marks of human fallibility within the layers of Talmudic redaction. Unlike academic critics of Orthodoxy, however, Halivni offers his academic studies as a contribution, as well, to Israel's covenantal renewal. To attend more closely to the marks of humanity in the rabbinic tradition is also to reorient where and how the contemporary reader will hear the divine voice within the tradition. To reaffirm Israel's covenant after Shoah is to claim to hear that voice, again, within Israel's received tradition of Written-and-Oral Torah. To hear that voice after this Destruction is to read the words of that tradition in ways they could not have been read before the Destruction.

FURTHER READING

Baltzer, Klaus. *The Covenant Formulary in Old Testament, Jewish, and Early Christian Writings*, tr. D. Green (Philadelphia: Fortress Press, 1971). A classic study of the ancient covenants.

Borowitz, Eugene. *Renewing the Covenant: A Theology for the Postmodern Jew* (Philadelphia: Jewish Publication Society, 1991). A classic statement of Liberal Jewish renewal.

Feld, Edward. *The Spirit of Renewal: Finding Faith After the Holocaust* (Woodstock, Vt.: Jewish Lights, 1994). A brief and highly readable introduction to renewing Jewish faith by rereading the history of previous Jewish responses to destruction.

Greenberg, Irving. 'Cloud of Smoke, Pillar of Fire: Judaism, Christianity, and Modernity after the Holocaust', in E. Fleischner (ed.), *Auschwitz: Beginning of a New Era?* (New York: Ktav, 1977), pp. 7–56. *The* classic statement for Jewish theological renewal after the Shoah.

Halivni, David. *Mekorot U'mesorot* (*Sources and Traditions: A Source Critical Commentary on the Talmud*) (Tel Aviv: 1968; Jerusalem: Jewish Theological Seminary, 1975, 1982). In Hebrew, the major work of contemporary Talmudic reconstruction.

Halivni, David. *The Book and the Sword: A Life of Learning in the Shadow of Destruction* (New York: Farrar, Straus, & Giroux, 1996). Holocaust memoirs that show the setting for a life of renewing Israel's covenant after destruction.

Halivni, David. *Revelation Restored, Divine Writ and Critical Responses* (Boulder, Col.: Westview Press, 1997). A hermeneutics for renewal and repairing the covenant after modernity and after the Shoah.

Hartman, David. *Joy and Responsibility: Israel, Modernity and the Renewal of Judaism* (Jerusalem: Ben-Zvi-Posner, 1978). The Shalom Hartman Institute in Jerusalem offers the single most important voice for including the realities of Israel in a renewed covenant. This is an early and significant expression of the Institute's work.

Mendenhall, George. *Law and Covenant in Israel and the Ancient Near East* (Pittsburgh: Biblical Colloquium, 1955). The classic study of Hittite treaties as a model for biblical covenants.

Novak, David. *Covenantal Rights: A Study in Jewish Political Theory* (Princeton: Princeton University Press, 2000). The most important new theory of rights and duties in the renewed Jewish covenant.

Ochs, Peter, with E. Borowitz (eds.). *Reviewing the Covenant: Eugene B. Borowitz and the Postmodern Renewal of Jewish Theology* (Albany: State University of New York, 2000). Recent postmodern Jewish philosophers evaluate Borowitz's vision of covenantal renewal.

Orenstein, D., and J. Litman (eds.). *Lifecycles: Jewish Women on Biblical Themes in Contemporary Life*, 2 vols. (Woodstock, Vt.: Jewish Lights, 1997). Most of the major voices on the effort to re-narrate the woman's place in Jewish covenantal history.

Plaskow, Judith. *Standing Again At Sinai: Judaism From a Feminist Perspective* (San Francisco: Harper & Row, 1990). The now-classic call for re-narrating women's voices in the covenant.

Ravitzky, Aviezer. *Religion and State in Jewish Philosophy*, tr. R. Yarden (Jerusalem: Israel Democracy Institute, 2002). A more recent powerful voice out of the Shalom Hartman Institute.

NOTES

1. The traditional acronym stands for the three sections of the Bible: Torah, or the 'Teaching' of the Five Books of Moses; Nevi'im, or writings of the 'Prophets'; and Khetuvim, or 'Writings' of the Second Temple period. We will use the term Bible.

2. In Second Temple times this name was spoken aloud only by the High Priest on the Day of Atonement. After the Temple was destroyed the rabbinic sages no longer uttered this name at all; in prayers and formal readings it was replaced orally by the Hebrew word *adonai*—My Lord.

3. From *Avot d'Rabbi Natan* (11a); the translation is adapted from Jules Harlow (ed.) *Siddur Sim Shalom* (New York: United Synagogue of Conservative Judaism, 1985), p. 15.

4. Eugene Borowitz, *Renewing the Covenant: A Theology for the Postmodern Jew* (Philadelphia: Jewish Publication Society, 1991), pp. 3–4.

5. Eugene Borowitz, *Exploring Jewish Ethics* (Detroit: Wayne State University Press, 1990), pp. 26 ff.

6. Eugene Borowitz, *Choices in Modern Jewish Thought: A Partisan Guide* (West Orange, NJ: Behrman House, 1995), p. 283.

7. Ibid., pp. 215–16.

8. However, see Chap. 15 on the growth of fundamentalism within Orthodox sectors of Judaism.

9. Borowitz, *Choices*, pp. 288–93.

10. Irving Greenberg, 'Cloud of Smoke, Pillar of Fire: Judaism, Christianity, and Modernity after the Holocaust', in Eva Fleischner (ed.), *Auschwitz: Beginning of a New Era?* (New York: Ktav, 1977), p. 24.

11. Ibid., p. 23.

12. David Weiss Halivni, *The Book and the Sword: A Life of Learning in the Shadow of Destruction* (New York: Farrar, Straus, & Giroux, 1996).

13. In biblical terms, 'to seek God', as in 2 Chronicles. 22: 9, 'Yehoshafat, who sought the Lord with all his heart'; and Psalm 14: 2, 'The Lord looked down from heaven . . . to see if there were any who understand and seek God'.

Philosophical issues

24 | Philosophical issues: survey

Kenneth Seeskin

The best way to understand modern Jewish philosophy is to look at the medieval background from which it arose. According to Maimonides (1138–1204), the heart and soul of Judaism can be summed up in the first two commandments, which mandate worship of the true God and rejection of idolatry. By the 'true' God he means a God who is simple, immaterial, and radically unlike anything in the created order. In keeping with the standard medieval view, Maimonides argues that we can know that God exists but will never be in a position to know what God is. What we can know are the consequences or effects of divine activity, by which he means the structure of the world God created. Only by studying what God has made or done can we fulfil the commandment to love God.

To understand this structure, we must start with physics, proceed to metaphysics, and recognize that beyond the reach of any science is a God of awesome majesty and infinite power. The purpose of Judaism is to get us to this point. For Maimonides, Judaism is a world-view that stands or falls on its claim to truth. Though it might seem that this world-view owes more to Aristotle than it does to Moses, Maimonides maintains the opposite. Granted that if we read the Torah in a literal fashion we will wind up with a simplistic conception of God that any rational person would reject. But that is not the only option. We can also read the Torah in a way that looks for a deeper and more challenging level of meaning.

Behind Maimonides' view is the conviction that the Torah is the product of divine revelation and cannot contain anything that reason regards as abhorrent. Thus, any contradiction between the sacred literature of Judaism and the truths of science and philosophy must be resolved so that reason and revelation are in harmony. Not surprisingly, he went to great length to find philosophic messages in Scripture. For him there is *a* true picture of the world, and salvation depends on our ability to understand and accept it. The purpose of the commandments dealing with behaviour is to create the kind of environment in which the requisite forms of study and understanding can take place.

Considering the period in which he lived, Maimonides' views were not uncommon. The question is: What happens if science changes? Suppose we interpret Scripture in order to bring it in line with Theory A; then Theory A is shown to be wrong and gets replaced by Theory B? Though scientific disputes arose in the middle ages, no one experienced, or even imagined, upheavals of the sort we associate with the discoveries of Copernicus, Newton, or Einstein. So while Maimonides allows for the possibility of scientific change, he did not think those changes would be significant. If, however, one asked him what he would do if a genuine revolution did occur, he would have no option except to say that when the evidence for the new theory was firmly established, he would reread Scripture to make the two cohere.

The modern age began with a theory unlike anything Maimonides anticipated: the heliocentric solar system of Copernicus. Could one really say that, despite appearances to the contrary, Scripture was committed to this all along? The obvious answer is no, and with that answer came the recognition that significant portions of medieval philosophy could no longer stand.

Baruch Spinoza

The first prominent thinker to propose a new way of looking at these issues was Baruch Spinoza (1632–77). On a metaphysical level, Spinoza argued that the medieval conception of God made no sense. How could a God who is simple and immaterial produce a world that is material and complex? More importantly, how can a God whose essence is beyond comprehension serve as an explanatory principle for the existence of the world? These questions were motivated by Spinoza's understanding of cause and effect. Since an effect depends on, and is understood through, its cause, it is impossible for the cause, that is, God, to be radically unlike its effect.

Consider the attribute of extension. Maimonides thought it was heresy to suggest that God is a body or a force in a body. But, Spinoza objects, if we attribute some degree of reality to extended things, we must ask ourselves where they got it from. To suggest that extension is created by something that is unextended is absurd. How can something mental be the cause of something material? For Spinoza it cannot be. If God is infinite, the world must be infinite as well—both temporally and spatially. If the world contains extension, God must be extended too, at least in one aspect of his perfection. If the world contains minds, thought must be a way in which divine perfection manifests itself as well. In fact, Spinoza claims that divine perfection manifests itself in an infinite number of ways, thought and extension being only two.

For Spinoza, the tendency to insist on a radical separation between God and the world is simply wrong. This does not mean that he conceived of God as an aggregate of everything that is, but rather that he thought all of nature could be understood as a single, self-caused, self-sustaining whole, manifesting infinite perfection and existing forever. Insofar as everything is a part of nature, it is determined to exist by God. To traditional ears this sounds like naturalism or, worse, pantheism. To Spinoza it is the only sensible way to view God. So far from being the height of rationality, the view according to which an unknowable thing creates a world with which it has nothing in common is an admission of ignorance.

Spinoza's hermeneutics are just as radical. Why should we assume that Scripture contains philosophic and scientific truths, if those truths are beyond the reach of the audience for whom it was originally intended? In a nutshell, Spinoza was the first to maintain that the meaning of Scripture is distinct from the question of its truth. Though Scripture may contain doctrines we regard as false, the interpreter should not ask what we believe but what the original audience believed. This implies that Scripture can be wrong about science, and thereby challenges its claim to be the word of God. If the evidence shows that Scripture is committed to a geocentric view of the world, we have no choice but to interpret it this way. The opposite approach—to reinterpret it every time science comes up with a new theory—is to project our views onto a text that is innocent of them.

From Spinoza's standpoint, the whole suggestion that Scripture deals with physics and metaphysics is misguided. No one should turn to Scripture for a description of the solar system or an explanation of divine causality. Rather, we should turn to it for an account of how to live. It follows that the significance of revelation is practical rather than theoretical: instead of informing us about planets, elements, or the nature of God, it offers guidance on how to treat people with dignity and respect. While the practical dimension of Spinoza's thought would have appealed to Jewish audiences, it is clear that other aspects of his thought would not. It remained for someone within the sphere of Orthodoxy to take up the idea that revelation should be seen as a guide to behaviour rather than the presentation of dogma.

Moses Mendelssohn

On the issue of revelation, Moses Mendelssohn (1729–86) argues that there is a basic difference between Judaism and Christianity. While it is true that Judaism believes in a supernatural revelation, in Mendelssohn's view it does not contain any doctrine unique to Judaism. Behind this claim is the assumption that if there were doctrines necessary for human salvation—doctrines such as the existence, providence, and unity of God—it would be unjust for God to reveal them to one people and keep them hidden from others. For these doctrines reason alone is sufficient; we do not need revelation.

Where revelation is needed is in the area of legislation. Thus, no commandment says 'Thou shalt believe . . .', but rather 'Thou shalt do or not do . . .'. Although Mendelssohn is often taken to mean that Judaism has no doctrinal content at all, that is not his position. Rather, it is that Judaism has no doctrinal content over and above that which has been given to other people. So while Judaism has dogmas or principles, it has no *revealed* dogmas. Even so, he steadfastly resists the idea that any dogma can be forced on someone or that salvation depends on how much of that dogma one accepts.

Like Maimonides, Mendelssohn believes that the ritual component of Jewish law serves a purpose: it encourages people to reflect on God and the teachings of morality, to search out the truth, and seek instruction from people of learning. Since these commandments cannot be known by reason alone, and were given to Israel in a supernatural revelation, they are binding on all Jews until God rescinds them in a supernatural revelation. This does not mean that the synagogue has the right to coerce obedience. The only institution that can use coercion is the state, and then only to enforce civil as opposed to religious law. It means instead that, if a person living in civil society should ask: 'Why remain a Jew?', the answer is that God's plan for the world involves diversity and that Jews have been chosen by God to carry out a particular mission.

Since Judaism contains no revealed dogmas, it poses no threat to Christianity. Moreover, since the only thing that concerns the secular state is civil law, there is no reason why Jews cannot remain true to their heritage and still be loyal Germans, Frenchmen, or Englishmen. In this way, Mendelssohn was the first Jewish thinker to take up the problem posed by emancipation. The difficulty with Mendelssohn's theory is that it raises the very question it set out to answer. If Jews need rituals to study and reflect on God and morality, why do other people not need them as well? Why did God single out Jews by telling them not to eat pork or work on the Sabbath? Conversely, if other people can achieve salvation without these laws, why should Jews continue to obey them? Mendelssohn has no answer, except to fall back on the miraculous nature of revelation and the need for religious diversity.

Hermann Cohen

Hermann Cohen's (1842–1918) thought is best approached by starting with Immanuel Kant, whose influence on modern Jewish philosophy is matched only by Aristotle's influence on medieval. Though Kant is often seen as the philosopher who destroyed traditional metaphysics, it would be more accurate to say that he transformed metaphysics from a theoretical to a practical subject. Rather than a first cause or unmoved mover, God should be understood as a defender of morality. Morality, in turn, is defined by the categorical imperative, a law that asks us to treat all of humanity as an end in itself and never as a means only.

Cohen never doubts that the moral law is valid and that any religion worthy of being called rational must uphold it. The problem with the moral law is not its validity but its generality: it treats all people as instances of a single idea—humanity. Although the moral law is expressed as an imperative, there is a sense in which it is indifferent to its realization. Since it is valid a priori, the moral law is valid even if no one lives up to it.

That is where religion comes in. Something is needed that looks at people not as instances of a general rule but as individuals seeking, and in most instances failing, to do what the moral law requires. The moral law tells me I must not lie; but suppose I do, and begin to feel guilty? It does not help to point out that what I did was wrong, because I already know that. What I need is a way of admitting my mistake, asking to be forgiven, and resetting my goals. It is here that religion goes beyond and, in a sense, perfects morality, for without religion I would be consumed by guilt and reduced to despair.

Beyond the issue of self-esteem is the issue of my dealings with others. I can treat you as an instance of humanity and give you all the rights that go with it, but I can also go beyond the question of rights and treat you as a friend or comrade. It is in the transition from man (*Nebenmensch*) to fellow-man (*Mitmensch*) that I recognize you as a real person and, by implication, begin to act like a person myself. According to Cohen, this transition can only be completed when I take account of your suffering and devote myself to correcting it. Here he stresses how much the philosophic tradition, which is influenced by Stoicism, differs from the prophetic, which is concerned with the plight of the stranger, the widow, and the orphan.

For Cohen, the self is not something that exists in a moral vacuum and understands itself by introspection. I can realize the full nature of myself only by entering into relation with others, only by entering what Cohen calls correlation with our fellow-man and eventually with God. If God loves the stranger, we must love the stranger; if God heals the sick, sets free the captive, and clothes the naked, we must do likewise. When we fail to do so, we must come to God seeking forgiveness and striving not to repeat our mistakes. Rather than being an unmoved mover who sets the world in motion, Cohen's God shows his greatness by hearing our pleas for forgiveness and granting atonement.

Although Cohen's masterpiece is entitled *Religion of Reason Out Of the Sources of Judaism*, his claim is not that Judaism is *the* religion of reason but that it is *a* religion of reason. To the degree that other religions foster human dignity, the values of fellowship, and the need for atonement, they too have a share in reason. By the same token, he is aware that his view of Judaism is idealized, which means that he overlooks the mythical or particularistic aspects of Jewish tradition and focuses on its contribution to world culture. At its best, Judaism gave to world culture a vision in which all people are viewed as being made in the image of God and deserve to be treated as such.

In fact idealization is the central theme of Cohen's philosophy. I can view myself as a person trying to get along in a cold and competitive world or as a person trying to live up to the demands of the moral law. I can view my neighbour as just another person or as a friend and fellow. I can view God as an omnipotent being or as a being who is gracious, merciful, and slow to anger. For Cohen, the true nature of the self, the other, and God is found in the latter, which means that none can be understood in isolation. In seeking God, I will find my fellow-man and learn to treat him with tenderness and compassion; by finding my fellow-man, I will in the end find God as well. By finding God, I will complete the task of sanctifying myself.

From this point on, the dominant theme in Jewish philosophy becomes correlation. The standard criticism of Cohen is that while he introduced this theme, he did not go far enough. For Cohen, correlation is a relation between one ideal and another: not God and Moses as individuals, but the ideal of divinity and the ideal of humanity; not John and Jane, but the ideal of a self and the ideal of a fellow. As Cohen once remarked, love cannot be for anything but the ideal. Later thinkers challenged this claim, arguing that if we are to move beyond humanity as a generalization, we have to consider encounters between real people and not just idealizations. How can I be forgiven unless there is an actual person to say: 'I forgive you?' How can I love someone unless there is a person who returns my love?

Franz Rosenzweig

The best way to approach the thought of Franz Rosenzweig (1886–1929) is to take up the issue of love. Before creation God is concealed and self-sufficient. Creation is a way for God to become manifest. But even after creation, God remains hidden to some extent. An infinite power has spread out the universe before us, but has still not established a true relationship. Something more is needed, and it is here that we get revelation, which expresses itself in the command to love God (Deuteronomy 6: 5). How can love be commanded? You can command someone to do or not do something, but how can you command someone to love you? If the person loves you, a command is unnecessary; if the person does not love you, it will not accomplish anything.

Rosenzweig's answer is that what might seem bizarre coming from a human being or a third party makes perfect sense coming from God. The words 'Love me!' reach us at a level more fundamental than theory, even the moral theory of Kant and Cohen. Rosenzweig insists that, like love itself, the command is immediate and ever in the moment. It awakens the soul and calls it to action. Once heard and understood it changes everything, for the soul can never be lonely again. It is as if God has traversed the infinite distance that separates heaven and earth, broken through the systems of thought that philosophers have constructed, and compressed all of revelation into one simple request. So it is best not to view God's love in the traditional way—as an attribute of God—but as something that expresses itself in words and is communicated to a real person.

A demand for love is different from a declaration of it. The former is the voice of love, the latter ('I love you') a statement that occurs after the fact and is not constitutive of the fact. For the recipient, the beloved, it is otherwise. Here the appropriate response is a declaration that implies faithfulness and continuity. In that declaration Rosenzweig sees an admission of shame. The soul is ashamed of its former self, ashamed of being confined within itself and of requiring the shock of God's revelation to bring it into relation with God. In this way the command 'Love me!' is met with the confession 'I have sinned'.

With the confession of sin comes the recognition that God forgives sin. In short, the beloved comes to see that she does not love as much as she is loved. It is at this point, and no earlier, that the question of God's existence arises: in the experience of being loved, we recognize that the lover, God, truly is. Once again, experience is more fundamental than theory. We come to the existence of God not by reflecting on the cause of motion or the limitations of the moral law, but by responding to a commandment.

Though it is awakened, the soul still faces a problem: it is so wrapped up in the love of God that it becomes secluded. Like God, it must reach out and establish a relationship. This occurs when the soul realizes that to love God one must also love one's neighbour. Unlike Kantian moral theory, where love of (or respect for) one's neighbour is a consequence of a law whose validity can be seen by reason alone, Rosenzweig views love of one's neighbour as a consequence of God's love for us. By its very nature, the moral law is formal and open to a variety of interpretations; but, Rosenzweig contends, the command to love one's neighbour is clear and unambiguous.

In Rosenzweig we see the triumph of the personal over the universal. For some, including Rosenzweig himself, Cohen anticipated this move by suggesting that we must go beyond the point where we look at every person as an instance of humanity. We saw, however, that Cohen did not doubt the validity of the moral law, just its completeness. His point is that to realize it we have to come to grips with the suffering of our fellow-man and seek the forgiveness of God. By contrast, Rosenzweig rejects the validity of any abstract formula and tries to ground morality on an immediate encounter with God. The next two thinkers, Buber and Levinas, are closely allied with Rosenzweig.

Martin Buber

The idea of correlation is taken up and expanded by Martin Buber (1878–1965) into the relation between I and Thou. Though Cohen also used these terms, he understood them as ideals rather than concrete individuals who encounter one another directly. According to Buber, there are two primary ways of relating to something: I–you and I–it. In the latter, we relate to something as a means to an end, or else as an object over which we exercise control. In the former, the other person is an end in herself: we open ourselves to her and allow ourselves to be transformed by her presence, just as she allows herself to be transformed by us.

The essence of the I–you relation is reciprocity. It is not that two substances come into contact, like two ships signalling to each other in the night, but that each establishes its own identity by saying 'you' to the other. As Buber expresses it, the reality of each is in the space 'between'. We should not think of this as mystical union—that too would destroy reciprocity—but as a dialogical relation that confers on each partner a status it would not have in isolation. It follows that the I that is a partner to I–you is not the same as the I that is a partner to I–it. One is open, spontaneous, and respectful; the other regimented and controlling.

The danger of modern civilization is that too much of our experience is of the I/It variety, especially when it comes to God. A God who causes motion in the universe but is not open to encounters of this sort is an It. So too is a God who can be explained by universal principles and does not confront us in our individuality. One can accept or reject a universal principle, but not open oneself to it as one would to a person. By contrast, God loves as a personality and wants to be loved like a personality. God, then, is the eternal You. If so, the idea of a fixed way of relating to God is an illusion. Every I–you relationship is unique and in the moment. No account of what it is like to encounter God can guarantee what will happen in future encounters.

What, then, do we say about Jewish law? Moses encountered God in one of the paradigm cases of I–You. According to Buber, the record we have of that encounter is not the product of dictation from God to Moses but the product of their mutual inter-action. In that respect, it is as much human as it is divine. Buber's fear is that the record of Moses's encounter with God will be seen as a fixed set of rules robbing any future encounter of the element of spontaneity. Commandments serve a purpose by introducing us to the sphere of the sacred. But ultimately we must get beyond commandments to the One who commands.

As to how an infinite being can confront us as a personality, Buber has no systematic reply except to say that the combination of infinity with personality is a paradox with which the religious person must always deal. Like Rosenzweig, he holds open the possibility that God can break through the systems of thought we have constructed and stand to us as one person to another. Unless that is true, we run the risk of trivializing religion by finding things to take the place of God.

Emmanuel Levinas

In some respects, the thought of Emmanuel Levinas (1906–95) can be seen as a continuation of Buber's. The self is not a substance but something that exists in rela-tion to others. The other is not an idea I constitute but a person I confront. But Levinas goes further. The meeting between the self and another person should not be under-stood as a formal relation that takes place under ideal circumstances, but as the immediate experience of looking into the other's face. For Levinas, that face appears to me as naked and vulnerable, as something that summons me to care for it—even to give my life for it. Where Buber sees reciprocity, Levinas sees the opposite: I owe more to the other than the other owes to me. Indeed, I owe everything to the other, while the other owes nothing to me.

In this way, the experience of the other is as shocking or disruptive as the command 'Love me!' was for Rosenzweig. Before it, I am an ego who sees the world from my own point of view; after it, I am a moral agent who puts care for the other above everything else. The danger is that we will see the other as a being like ourselves, so that, in the last analysis, the other will not really be other but an extension of the self. The desire to make everything an extension of the self, which is to say, an idea constituted by the self, characterizes much of western philosophy. It was the certainty of the self on which Descartes tried to ground all of knowledge, including knowledge of God.

In opposition to an ego-based philosophy, Levinas stresses that the other is infinite, incomprehensible, and completely resistant to becoming an idea in a conceptual scheme. To treat the other like an idea is to do violence to him, to take what is different and try to assimilate it. There is, then, no category under which the other and the self both fall. It is only by letting the other be other that we are able to live with him in peace. With otherness comes authority. It is in the infinite height from which the other calls me that I experience the transcendence of God. The problem with much of western philosophy is that it tries to eliminate transcendence by subsuming everything under a single set of categories. When this happens we have neither God, nor the other, nor, for Levinas, the ethical self.

Conclusion

The thinkers discussed in this chapter were chosen not only because of their prominence, but because all tried to address the issue of modernity. Spinoza saw that the scientific revolution destroyed much of the medieval world-view and that the relation between science and religion had to be rethought. Mendelssohn saw that, with the walls of the ghetto coming down, one had to consider the place of Judaism in a secular society. For Cohen and his critics, the central question involves rationality. Is the primary fact of our existence that we are rational agents trying to fulfil our obligations or that we have opened ourselves to experiences that call our way of life into question? Is the meaning of life to be found in the ideal of moral purity or in an encounter that is in the moment?

Although generalization is always dangerous, certain themes have appeared throughout this discussion. First is a move from the theoretical to the practical. Rather than a theory about the structure of the world, Judaism is understood as a guide to behaviour. Ethics, as Levinas put it, is first philosophy. Second is a recognition that the self is a being in relation. From Cohen onwards, the goal of Jewish philosophy is to explain what one must do to become a self in the true sense of the term. Third is an attempt to retain and justify some notion of transcendence. Since the question of transcendence in Spinoza is controversial, we can put it aside. But there is no question that for the other thinkers the idea of a unique being, experience, or commandment is crucial. All of these trends are in keeping with a God who has no visible likeness (Exodus 20: 3–4) and commands the people to pursue justice above all else (Deuteronomy 16: 20).

At present Jewish philosophy is divided into several areas, most of which are continuations of the themes mentioned above. If one stresses the need to understand Maimonides and Spinoza, one will see historical study as the essence of Jewish philosophy and try to carry on the tradition of close textual analysis. If one stresses the practical dimension of Jewish thought, one will see Jewish philosophy as a commentary on Jewish law. If one stresses the freedom of the moral subject, one will emphasize the centrality of the covenant to which God and Israel have pledged themselves. If one stresses the critique of rationality, one will take Jewish philosophy in the direction of postmodernism, eschewing any claim to a theoretical foundation or total vision. If one stresses the devastating nature of the Holocaust, one will reject rationality as a paradigm and ask what sense it makes to remain Jewish in a world where people were led to gas chambers. If one sees feminism as a new paradigm, one will ask how Jewish tradition needs to be restructured to be more inclusive.

All of these trends are alive, and all are asking important questions. Rather than a symptom of weakness, the fact that there is no single trend that speaks for all of Jewish philosophy is a sign of vitality.

FURTHER READING

Borowitz, Eugene. *Choices in Modern Jewish Thought : A Partisan Guide* (New York: Behrman House, 1983). A roadmap to modern Jewish theology.

Buber, Martin. *I and Thou*, tr. Walter Kaufmann (New York: Scriber, 1970). Buber's masterpiece still inspires people of all faiths.

Buber, Martin. *Eclipse of God* (New York: Harper, 1953). Buber's essays still seem fresh and offer a powerful statement of his position.

Cohen, Hermann. *Religion of Reason Out Of the Sources of Judaism*, tr. Simon Kaplan (Atlanta: Scholars Press, 1995). Cohen's masterpiece is crucial for all subsequent Jewish thought.

Cohen, Hermann. *Reason and Hope*, tr. Eva Jospe (Cincinnati: Hebrew Union College Press, 1993). Cohen's views presented in a readable form for the non-specialist.

Frank, Daniel, and Oliver Leaman (eds.). *History of Jewish Philosophy* (London: Routledge, 1997). The best one-volume history of Jewish philosophy available.

Heschel, Susannah. *On Being a Jewish Feminist* (New York: Schocken Books, 1983). An anthology covering various aspects of Jewish feminism.

Levinas, Emannuel. *The Levinas Reader*, ed. Sean Hand (New York: B. Blackwell, 1989). Selections from Levinas's writings provide a good overview of his thought.

Levinas, Emmanuel. *Totality and Infinity*, tr. Alphonso Lingis (Pittsburgh: Duquesne University Press, 1969). A classic statement of the sanctity of the 'other'.

Maimonides. *A Maimonides Reader*, ed. Isadore Twersky (West Orange, NJ: Behrman House, 1972). A good single-volume guide to Maimonides' work.

Maimonides. *The Guide of the Perplexed*, tr. Shlomo Pines (Chicago: University of Chicago Press, 1963). Maimonides' masterpiece deals with the relation between philosophy and the revealed religion of the prophets.

Mendelssohn, Moses. *Jerusalem*, tr. Allan Arkush (Hanover, NH: University Press of New England, 1983). An extended treatment of the place of the Jew in a modern secular state.

Morgan, Michael. *A Holocaust Reader* (New York: Oxford University Press, 2001). Selections dealing with all aspects of the nightmare of the Holocaust.

Rosenzweig, Franz. *The Star of Redemption*, tr. William W. Halo (Notre Dame: Notre Dame University Press, 1985). A revolutionary book that had a profound impact on Jewish existentialism.

Samuelson, Norbert. *An Introduction to Modern Jewish Philosophy* (Albany: State University of New York Press, 1989). A good one-volume introduction to the entire subject.

Seeskin, Kenneth. *Autonomy in Jewish Philosophy* (Cambridge: Cambridge University Press, 2001). The development of the concept of freedom from the Bible to Spinoza, Mendelssohn, Cohen, Buber, and Levinas.

Spinoza, Baruch. *Theological-Political Treatise*, tr. Samuel Shirley (Indianapolis: Hackett, 2002). The book in which Spinoza proposes religious tolerance, a historical approach to Bible interpretation, and the need to keep science and religion separate.

Spinoza, Baruch. *The Ethics and Selected Letters*, tr. Samuel Shirley (Indianapolis: Hackett, 1982). Spinoza's treatment of God, human knowledge, the emotions, and the intellectual love of God will live forever.

25 | The problems of evil

Daniel Rynhold

At some point in their lives many people formulate, in however inarticulate a fashion, the problem of evil. But at least since the author of Job grappled with the apparently undeserved fate of his central character, this issue in ever more refined form has been a particular focus for philosophers of religion. The twentieth century inevitably stirred up renewed interest in this most ancient of conundrums as a consequence of the radical moral evil embodied in the Holocaust, which elicited responses from across the religious divide. Amongst Jewish thinkers, though, the question often takes on added poignancy for those who accept traditional covenantal notions such as that the Jews were chosen by God for a particular mission. As Elie Wiesel put it, 'when God gave us a mission, that was alright. But God failed to tell us that it was a suicide mission.'[1]

It has become de rigueur in analytic philosophy to distinguish between two forms of the problem. The logical problem of evil formulates the question as one of logical consistency. The claim that evil exists, it is argued, cannot be consistent with the claim that God exists and is omnipotent, omniscient, and perfectly good. To illustrate this version of the problem by taking just one of the attributes as our starting point (you can run analogous arguments for the other two), an all-powerful God presumably had the power to prevent the Holocaust. Since God did not do so, we can only conclude that either He did not care enough to want to (and is thus not perfectly good) or was unaware that it was happening (and is thus not, in the most straightforward sense, omniscient). Essentially, the existence of evil means that one of these attributes must be jettisoned.

This logical presentation of the problem often elicits similarly logical responses involving ever more subtle attempts to make consistent the traditional theistic view of God and the existence of evil. While medieval Jewish thinkers were in many cases all too familiar with persecution, one nonetheless gets the impression that to them the problem was indeed primarily an abstract puzzle that could be solved by a measure of intellectual ingenuity.

There is, however, a further formulation of the problem that focuses less on logical consistency and more on the evidential relation between the existence of evil on the one hand and that of God on the other. In this evidential problem of evil, the apparent pointlessness of actual evil is presented as decisive evidence against God's existence. Whilst few Jewish thinkers explicitly distinguish between the different versions, it is this formulation that seems closer to the visceral nature of the problem with which post-Holocaust Jewish thinkers have grappled.

After briefly sketching some traditional medieval responses to the problem of evil, in this chapter my focus will be on a necessarily limited selection of post-Holocaust theologians and philosophers, some of the most significant of whom, I will argue, appear to be converging around a particular approach to the problem.

The problem of evil in medieval Jewish philosophy

It was not until the medieval period that Jewish philosophers first reflected systematically on the problem of evil. I cannot here give an exhaustive analysis of their responses, but will rather outline two positions that emerged during the period for general comparison with those we find in post-Holocaust writings.

According to the broadly rabbinic approach of Saadia Gaon (882–942), God's acts conform to an objective standard of justice that human beings are able to understand up to a point. Saadia's commentary on the Book of Job, *The Book of Theodicy*, is therefore concerned to reconcile the evils that befall Job with some such account of divine justice.

For Saadia suffering has a purpose. It either serves to educate, punish, or test. After explicitly rejecting the idea that Job's travails are down to his own failings, Saadia subsumes Job's fate under the third category. His sufferings were a trial, the purpose of which, for a righteous person 'whose Lord knows that he will bear sufferings loosed upon him and hold steadfast in his uprightness, is . . . so that when he steadfastly bears them, his Lord may reward him and bless him'.[2]

Saadia here develops the classical rabbinic idea of *yissurin shel ahavah* (afflictions of love), the most developed discussion of which is found at Babylonian Talmud, *Berakhot* 5a–b, according to which suffering is to be understood as a gift from God. According to his 'no pain no gain' theology, the good achieved through effort or struggle is said by Saadia to be twice as good as one received effortlessly as a result of God's kindness. Thus, we are in fact better off for suffering when we take the long-term view, for, having passed this test of faith, our recompense in an eventual afterlife will be immeasurably greater. A traditional notion of the afterlife therefore plays a palliative role in Saadia's response.

In marked contrast, Moses Maimonides (1138–1204) gives us a more abstract philosophical perspective. For Maimonides, God does not produce evil 'in an essential act' (*Guide*, III: 10, 440),[3] since all divine acts are absolutely good. Evil instead is a 'privation', the absence of something rather than a positive existent, much as darkness is an absence of light rather than an existent thing. Ultimately, evil is just a side-effect of the creation of matter.

In Maimonides' Arabic Aristotelianism, independently existing entities (substances) are composed of the physically inseparable but conceptually distinct elements of matter and form. Form is 'the notion in virtue of which a thing is constituted as a substance and becomes what it is' (*Guide*, I: 1, 22). The form of human beings, for example, is rationality, which is what makes humans members of the species of humanity as opposed to anything else. Matter, in contrast, is the basic 'stuff' that individuates these forms so that there exist human individuals within that species. The form determines the true nature of any individual thing, with matter denigrated as the source of deficiency and ultimately, therefore, as the source of all evil. This obviously raises the question of why God should have created matter, Maimonides' treatment of which is beyond the scope of this chapter. The question, though, gives some indication of how answers to the problem often suppress it, only for it to reappear elsewhere.

Whilst one can understand how matter might be at the root of natural disasters and disease, for Maimonides, moral evil also traces back to our material constitution. When not fully under the control of our intellects (our form), the material aspect of our nature can lead to such things as greed and unreason, that in turn lead us to commit moral evils. Moral evil, therefore, is a result of ignorance, or at least of not giving the intellect its due.

Yet whilst knowledge can therefore prevent our committing moral evil, how can it prevent the suffering that occurs as a result of factors beyond our control? Losing one's child to a congenital disease, for example, can hardly be a result of one's ignorance. Here, though, it is a matter of having the correct understanding of what is truly valuable. Job's mistake, according to Maimonides, was to give too much emphasis to the material. With his knowledge of God, however, Job attains true happiness and the realization that 'a human being cannot be troubled in it by any of all the misfortunes in question' (*Guide*, III: 23, 492–3). The solution to the problem of evil is thus to transcend our material natures. Though Maimonides does acknowledge the necessity of physical health and political stability for the ultimate goal of intellectual perfection, he nonetheless concludes that if one apprehends God 'in the right way and rejoices in what he apprehends, that individual can never be afflicted with evil of any kind' (*Guide*, III: 51, 625). Thus, in a sense it is our material nature that is responsible for our even posing the problem of evil. One can avoid the question altogether if one has the correct system of values in place, that allows one to transcend physical suffering through the experience of eternity through intellectual contemplation. With such a world-view, the delights of the intellect can overcome any material travails.

Traditional responses to the Holocaust

Though they differ quite radically over the nature of eternity and how to achieve it, both Saadia and Maimonides share the idea that this true reward is the key to solving the problem of evil. For Saadia, suffering is in a sense justified by that reward as a means to a post-mortem end. For Maimonides, suffering is not justified by his approach to the problem of evil. Rather, it becomes insignificant.

Problems inherent in both approaches, however, are brought out particularly starkly by the Holocaust. Our less rarefied current world-views make it very difficult to be so enamoured as Maimonides is of the delights of the intellect, so as to ignore the physical and mental horrors of the Holocaust. There is a sense in which the Holocaust stands as the ultimate 'affirmation' of the importance of personhood and the undeniable reality of the evils we face as complete human beings.

Approaches that, like Saadia's, would find a theologically sufficient reason for evil and suffering do persist in the post-Holocaust world, with, for example, Rabbi Yo'el Moshe Teitelbaum, the Satmarer Rebbe, arguing that the Holocaust was a divine punishment. Teitelbaum claims that the particular sin the Jews had committed was that of 'forcing the end', in breach of the oaths listed at Babylonian Talmud, *Ketubot* 111a. The exilic existence of the Jews was understood to be an expression of divine will, to be ended at God's behest. The activism of Zionism was seen as a rebellion against God of the most severe kind that, according to Teitelbaum, merited a collective punishment as devastating as the Holocaust.

Whilst it is undeniable that the reward-and-punishment approach to suffering has plenty of textual antecedents in the Jewish tradition, it is far from necessary to adopt it. Indeed, God is portrayed as reprimanding Job's companions for suggesting such an approach to Job. Moreover, from a philosophical perspective, the contemporary thinker D. Z. Phillips has written, with reference to a child dying from cancer: 'If this has been *done* to anyone, it is bad enough, but to be done for a purpose, to be planned from eternity—that is the deepest evil. If God is this kind of agent, He cannot justify His actions, and His evil nature is revealed.'[4]

It was just such an approach, though this time presented by Dean Heinrich Grueber of the Evangelical Church of Berlin, that led Richard Rubenstein to the conclusion that indeed God could not be that kind of agent. Grueber, a German who had vigorously opposed Nazism, ending up in Dachau as a result, and the only German to testify against Eichmann at his trial, believed that the Holocaust was but another instance of God using certain people, whether Nebuchadnezzar or Hitler, to carry out the divine will. Rubenstein interpreted Grueber as offering another example of the retributive approach of Teitelbaum, though this time the implied sin, in Rubenstein's opinion, could only have been the classic Christian accusation of deicide. Rubenstein's response, in *After Auschwitz*, was the proclamation of the 'death of God' following the school of radical theology that had become popular amongst certain American Protestant theologians during the 1960s.

Though he now has some empathy with traditional believers, in the first edition of *After Auschwitz* Rubenstein asserted that theologies which cast the Holocaust as an intentional and purposeful act of God were obscene. Regardless of the changes time has wrought, the Holocaust remains for Rubenstein the final nail in the coffin of the traditional theistic conception of God, hence his proclamation that we are living in the time of the death of God. Rubenstein, however, denies that he is an atheist, speaking of God variously as 'the Holy Nothingness' or 'the source and life of nature',[5] as immanent rather than transcendent. Nonetheless, this immanentist approach leaves us in a meaningless universe cut off from any contact with a God who acts in history. Interestingly this very absence increases the significance of Jewish ritual for Rubenstein, albeit as a radically revised 'nature religion',[6] that answers some of our fundamental psychological needs. Not least of these is the notion that a meaningless world without a providential God 'calls forth our strongest need for religious community'.[7] It is precisely that link to a community, both present and past, that Judaism generates. Judaism becomes the way in which Jews create meaning in a universe that is ultimately meaningless. Nonetheless, Rubenstein's position seems paradoxical to many, since without the commanding presence of God, why would one choose to answer one's psychological needs through adherence to one specific religion, or indeed to any religion at all?

Of course, the either/or presented by the Teitelbaums and Rubensteins of this world are not the only possible responses to the Holocaust. Eliezer Berkovits criticizes both 'pious submission to it as a manifestation of the divine will, and . . . outright rebellion against the very idea of a beneficent providence' as desecrating 'the holy disbelief of those whose faith was murdered . . . [and] the holy faith of the believers'[8] respectively. It is worth noting, though, that Berkovits's own approach does reject the 'holy disbelief', persisting as he does with a belief in the existence of a personal God and presenting the classic free-will defence.

The free-will defence sees freedom and the responsibility that comes with it as the definitive characteristics of human beings. It is only if I freely choose to do good that I am worthy of praise. And it is only if I freely choose to do evil that I am deserving of blame. For God to intervene to prevent the occurrence of evil would necessitate the removal of this freedom of choice, putting paid to our concepts of morality and goodness and thus to life as we know it. God must therefore withdraw from history to an extent, an idea that Berkovits clothes in the traditional rabbinic terminology of God's hiding His face—*hester panim*. God is 'hiding himself mysteriously from the cry of the innocent',[9] in order to allow for history.

A number of philosophers have disputed the effectiveness of the free-will defence. For example, since it is not logically impossible for God to have created humans such that they always freely chose to do good, why did God not do so? The idea of always freely choosing to do good appears at first sight like a contradiction in terms, and to do justice to the argument would take us too far afield. For an indication, however, that there is more to it than first impressions might allow, we need only note a related side argument regarding the manner in which many religious thinkers, Berkovits amongst them, look forward to a messianic age in which this possible world becomes a reality— all human beings freely acknowledging God's existence and acting morally. If such a world forms part of one's theological outlook, it becomes a little more difficult to argue for its impossibility. It is to his credit, therefore, that Berkovits is suitably modest about his achievements. Berkovits states that he has simply changed the question from 'Why evil?' to 'Why a world? Why creation?', and concludes that rather than solving the problem he is revealing it to us 'in its true dimension [which] makes it easier for us to make peace with the circumstances from which it arises'.[10]

For all of their differences, what the views summarized in this section have in common is the attempt to subsume the Holocaust within accepted philosophical and/ or Jewish schemes of thought, all of which beg various moral or theoretical questions. However, there is a genuine issue regarding whether the Holocaust can be seen as just another in the catalogue of evils to which such traditional responses can be given.

The Holocaust as rupture: Emil Fackenheim

A significant number of thinkers have begun refusing to play the traditional game, claiming that the Holocaust has irreversibly changed the very way in which we must both pose the question and deal with it. Medieval and modern attempts at theoretical gymnastics, it is argued, simply do not take seriously the reality of the suffering endured. As Joseph B. Soloveitchik argues: 'It is impossible to overcome the hideousness of evil through philosophico-speculative thought.'[11] Emil Fackenheim goes further in terming any attempt to impute a purpose to the Holocaust blasphemous.

Most significant here for Fackenheim is the Holocaust's uniqueness. Berkovits states explicitly that the Holocaust is not unique but 'just' another of the many devastating events in Jewish history. As such, we can plunder the Jewish tradition in order to find a response to it. Fackenheim, in contrast, has argued at great length for the uniqueness of the Holocaust, drawing the implication from this that it cannot be treated with traditional philosophical or theological categories. Fackenheim is at pains to point out that he is not saying that a Jewish death is worse than that of a non-Jew. Rather, he emphasizes the importance of treating the Holocaust in all its particularity so as not to dilute it through comparison. More than its particularity must be at stake, however, for all evils can be argued to be particular in the sense of needing to be confronted in their own right—something that Fackenheim himself admits. Yet not every evil paralyses thought in the way that Fackenheim argues the Holocaust did. It must, therefore, be unprecedented in a more substantive sense if it is to have such an effect, so it seems that one must look for this sense in the radical nature of the evil of the perpetrators, rather than that of the tragedy for the victims. The unique 'antiworld' of Auschwitz, in which evil was pursued for its own sake with no ulterior motive, was more radical than any before it. In the face of that, one cannot sit comfortably with the old orthodoxies. Indeed, the Holocaust proved to Fackenheim that philosophy could not be immune to history. We have here a historical event that ruptured the history of philosophy and theology, both Jewish and otherwise.

What, therefore, is Fackenheim's response to the Holocaust? Response in fact is the key term here. Rejecting all attempts to explain, we can but respond, and Fackenheim's famous response is the 614th commandment: 'Jews are forbidden to hand Hitler post-humous victories.' According to Fackenheim, a commanding voice is heard out of Auschwitz that forbids Jews to despair of man or God. One must neither allow Judaism to perish nor allow victory to the forces of Auschwitz. In sum: 'A Jew may not respond to Hitler's attempt to destroy Judaism by himself co-operating in its destruction. In ancient times, the unthinkable Jewish sin was idolatry. Today, it is to respond to Hitler by doing his work.'[12] Fackenheim intentionally ignores the question of why the Holocaust happened, and is more concerned with our practical response. What do we do now? And for Fackenheim the answer is that we continue to affirm our Jewish identity and in so doing we perform a *mitzvah*.

Fackenheim has been variously criticized for arrogating divinity to himself in adding an extra commandment to the traditional 613, or for not in fact saying anything at all, since one implicitly indicates a commitment to Jewish survival through the observation of the other 613. The arrogation of divinity loses some, though not all, of its bite when we understand that Fackenheim follows Martin Buber in his understanding of revelation, and therefore understands commandments as human responses to the encounter with God. Thus, it is besides the point to ask if God really came down to deliver the 614th commandment as he did at Sinai, since that is not how such Jewish existentialists understand the idea of revelation, even at Sinai. Fackenheim is not, therefore, putting himself in place of God to deliver this commandment. At the same time, however, the commandment is one that appears to yield an absolute sense of obligation for Fackenheim, who does therefore seem to impose this mitzvah upon the contemporary Jew, meaning that he cannot get away from this criticism altogether.

Moreover, his subsuming our action under that religious category is not simply a figure of speech for Fackenheim, since he draws a number of important implications from it, not least that in the post-Holocaust world the distinction between religious and secular Jews is erased. The mere decision to identify as a Jew, even if not by adherence to one of the religious interpretations of Judaism, is to perform a mitzvah and hence to perform a religious duty. Thus, secular Jews become religious Jews by default. The 614th commandment is not, therefore, contentless, certainly not in its implications for the secular Jew. Moreover, the decision of the religious Jew to cling to the religion is, in a post-Holocaust world, utterly inexplicable. One could argue, therefore, that the very decision to make the commitment stands as a miraculous foundation for the continuation of religious life through the other 613, rather than a cumulative effect of them.

Fackenheim's 'commandment' terminology does not seem to me, therefore, to be accidental. The Holocaust has ruptured the world, Jewish and general, and thus this 'epoch-making event' necessitates a radical response that is both continuous with and yet radically different from the Jewish past. The terminology of the 614th commandment provides us with precisely this tension between tradition and radicalism.

A further criticism, however, is that survival for survival's sake is devoid of meaning and content. It is interesting, therefore, that Fackenheim in his later writing does seem to infuse it with content, not least in his Zionism. In *To Mend the World*, Fackenheim argues that where thought, whether of the philosophers or rabbis, was paralysed by the Holocaust, the survival of the Jews, the 'resisting thought' that yields existential survival, not the academic theories, overcomes the Holocaust. For Fackenheim the heroism of the survivors themselves points the way to the only 'philosophical' response that is appropriate. But this turns out to be a practical response rather than a philosophical one, if philosophy is defined as a theoretical enterprise, and the modern state of Israel 'has become collectively what the survivor is individually'.[13] A commitment to Zionism appears, therefore, to become an obligation for the contemporary Jew.

The problem of evil in modern Jewish philosophy: the practical turn

Has Fackenheim simply avoided the crucial question that we began with concerning God and evil? Whilst the short answer is obviously yes, it is notable that we find a number of other examples of this approach to the Holocaust, that ask 'How are we to respond?' rather than 'Why did this happen?' Thus, over a decade before Fackenheim presented his 614th commandment, Soloveitchik, having eschewed metaphysical speculation, wrote that the correct Jewish response is 'concerned about evil from a halakhic standpoint, like a person who wishes to know the deed which he shall do; I ask one simple question: What must the sufferer do so that he may live through his suffering?'[14] While Soloveitchik's approach is far more traditional in tone, and at times comes uncomfortably close to traditional explanations in referring to the need to utilize suffering for self-improvement, it ultimately also asks for a response, not an explanation. And Soloveitchik also goes on to emphasize the central role Israel has to play in the post-Holocaust world. The formal similarities to Fackenheim are notable.

Irving Greenberg similarly believes explanatory categories do not produce 'the proper response of resistance and horror at the Holocaust',[15] and in terms that recall Fackenheim's notion of rupture, argues that the Holocaust is such a devastating event that it has succeeded in shattering the traditional covenant between God and the Jews. God has no moral right to *enforce* a covenant if it exposes one to the agony of the Holocaust. Yet, in the face of the Holocaust, Jews have chosen voluntarily to reaffirm this now *voluntary* covenant, with the State of Israel again playing a central role as 'the greatest Biblical symbol validating the covenant'.[16]

For Greenberg, the Holocaust issues the most 'drastic call for total Jewish responsibility for the covenant'.[17] A covenant that we had previously been obligated to keep but that God also had to honour with eventual redemption, becomes a covenant in which both the keeping and redeeming are now in human hands. Notably,

Greenberg writes that the taking on of full responsibility was always the implicit aim of the covenant. It is just that the Holocaust brought this level of covenantal responsibility to the fore sooner than might have been expected. Yet again, though, this does not justify the Holocaust. The Holocaust acts as a catalyst for this response; it is not justified by it. Again, we find a theology that refuses to explain or justify the Holocaust, deciding instead to focus on the correct response, or rather responses, since Greenberg draws pluralistic implications from his theory akin to Fackenheim's breaking down of barriers between religious and secular.

Thus a pattern emerges: response over explanation, the significance of Israel within that response, and for Fackenheim and Greenberg at least, pluralism. All these formal convergences are fascinating in themselves, but perhaps also suggest the need for a rather more considered response to the question of whether or not Fackenheim, and now additionally Soloveitchik and Greenberg, are ignoring the really important questions. For now we can ask whether the original question was really the crucial one after all.

On the one hand, we might ask this for the Maimonidean reason that God is beyond our human discursive categories, and thus we are unable to deal conceptually with a problem that requires some understanding of how God works. According to Maimonides, we must not model our understanding of God on our self-understanding. God is not to be seen as a quasi-person whose job it is to dispense justice as we understand it. But this appears to reduce our conception of God to a vanishing point, and ultimately makes all God-talk impossible.

On the other hand, though, it does seem as if the very attempt to treat God as a 'being', immeasurably greater than us, but still a finite object of philosophical speculation, is one of the root causes of the whole problem. Thus, Howard Wettstein has asked whether the philosophical problem of evil is simply a creation of philosophers. As he points out, the definition of God that gives rise to the problem is one that appeals to specific attributes taken for granted nowadays in both philosophical and popular discourse, but that certainly does not answer to the portrayal of God in the *Tanakh* and the Talmud. Now, one might fear that a return to the biblical picture will lead us back to a reward-and-punishment explanation of evil and suffering. But the short shrift given to this idea in the biblical Book of Job seems to show that it was seen as inadequate even when the biblical picture was dominant. Wettstein's own suggestion is that we approach 'God-talk' wearing poetic rather than philosophical glasses, which is not to reduce its power or importance, but is to suggest that different tools are appropriate for engaging with God-talk. Ultimately, as Emmanuel Levinas has written, God 'expresses a notion religiously of utmost clarity but philosophically most obscure'.[18]

Nonetheless, as we see from the Book of Job, even without the philosophically constructed God, the problem of evil exercised the ancient mind. How, then, are we to respond to it? Kenneth Seeskin, developing the views of Steven Schwarzschild, writes that in Jewish philosophy 'the central philosophic category is that of conduct, what ought to be done. Logic, metaphysics, and epistemology are legitimate to the degree that they help us clarify the duties and aspirations we face as moral agents.'[19] Whether or not this constitutes some sort of 'essence' of Jewish philosophy, this practical turn, it seems, comes to the fore in a number of treatments of the problem of evil in modern Jewish thought. Whether that is to ignore the crucial questions depends on the wider issue of whether the crucial questions are ultimately metaphysical or practical.

FURTHER READING

Berkovits, Eliezer. *Faith After the Holocaust* (New York: Ktav, 1973). Berkovits's free-will defence.

Greenberg, Irving. 'Voluntary Covenant', *Perspectives* (New York: National Jewish Resource Center, 1982) pp. 2–36. A succinct expression of Greenberg's post-Holocaust theology.

Leaman, Oliver. *Evil and Suffering in Jewish Philosophy* (Cambridge: Cambridge University Press, 1997). Discusses a wide range of approaches to the problem of evil from the entire history of Jewish philosophy.

Morgan, Michael (ed.), *The Jewish Thought of Emil Fackenheim: A Reader* (Detroit: Wayne State University Press, 1987). An anthology of Fackenheim's writings authorized by Fackenheim himself, giving the most important statements of his post-Holocaust theology within the context of his thought as a whole. Also contains useful introductions to the main phases of his thought.

Rubenstein, Richard. *After Auschwitz: History, Theology, Radical Theology and Contemporary Judaism* (Baltimore: Johns Hopkins University Press, 1992). A substantially revised second edition that further develops his original death-of-God theology.

Soloveitchik, Joseph B. *Fate and Destiny: From Holocaust to the State of Israel* (Hoboken, NJ: Ktav, 2000). Soloveitchik's 'halakhic response' to the problem of evil.

NOTES

1. Quoted by Irving Greenberg in 'The Voluntary Covenant', in *Perspectives* (New York: National Jewish Resource Center, 1982), p. 15.

2. Saadia Gaon, *The Book of Theodicy: Translation and Commentary on the Book of Job*, tr. L. Goodman (New Haven: Yale University Press, 1988), pp. 125–6.

3. References are to *The Guide of the Perplexed*, tr. Shlomo Pines, 2 vols. (Chicago: University of Chicago Press, 1963), and take the form: (*Guide*, part: chapter, page no.).

4. D. Z. Phillips, *The Concept of Prayer* (London: Routledge, 1965), p. 93.

5. Richard Rubenstein, *After Auschwitz: History, Theology, and Contemporary Judaism* (Baltimore: Johns Hopkins University Press, 1992), pp. 298, 207.

6. Ibid., p. xiii.

7. Ibid., p. 238.

8. Eliezer Berkovits, *Faith After the Holocaust* (New York: Ktav, 1973), pp. 3 and 5.

9. Ibid., p. 96.

10. Ibid., p. 105.

11. Joseph B. Soloveitchik, *Fate and Destiny: From Holocaust to the State of Israel* (Hoboken, NJ: Ktav, 2000), p. 4.

12. Emil Fackenheim, *God's Presence in History* (New York: Harper & Row, 1970), p. 84.

13. Emil Fackenheim, *Encounters Between Judaism and Modern Philosophy: A Preface to Future Jewish Thought* (New York: Schocken Books, 1980), p. 167.

14. Soloveitchik, *Fate and Destiny*, p. 7.

15. Irving Greenberg, 'Cloud of Smoke, Pillar of Fire: Judaism, Christianity and Modernity after the Holocaust', in Eva Fleischner (ed.), *Auschwitz: Beginning of an Era* (New York: Ktav, 1977), p. 22.

16. Greenberg, 'The Voluntary Covenant', p. 16.

17. Ibid., p.17.

18. Emmanuel Levinas, *Nine Talmudic Readings*, tr. A. Aronowicz. (Bloomington and Indianapolis: Indiana University Press, 1990), p. 32. See Howard Wettstein, 'Doctrine', in *Faith and Philosophy*, 14: 4 (1997), pp. 423–43.

19. Kenneth Seeskin, *Jewish Philosophy in a Secular Age* (Albany: State University of New York Press, 1990), p. 4.

Jewish ethics in a modern world

Michael Zank

Jewish ethics: a conceptual hybrid or irreconcilable opposites?

Judaism is traditionally understood as a way of life founded on the Mosaic law and its rabbinic interpretations, whereas ethics—in the sense of moral philosophy—is a discourse on human perfection grounded in reason. Notwithstanding this difference, many modern Jewish theologians and philosophers have argued that the world-view of the biblical prophets is deeply moral and that their ethic—in the sense of a set of rules of conduct implicit or explicit in their oracles—is the inner principle of the entire development of the Jewish religion. From this point of view, the moral standards of the prophets became essential to Judaism, and Judaism is essentially a religion of heightened responsibility for the other, the fellow-man. The ideal of moral perfection is embodied by the God of the prophets, who is merciful and just. Morality is the meaning of the holiness commanded by this God. For Jews to imitate the ways of God means to be dedicated to acting justly and in accordance with moral reasoning.

Arguing that this identification of Judaism with prophetic morality is a construct of nineteenth-century apologetics, some more recent critics, such as Leo Strauss and Yeshayahu Leibowitz, have questioned the very possibility of a Jewish ethics.[1] Pointing to the heterogeneity of their respective origins and nature, they considered Judaism and philosophical ethics to be irreconcilable, much like revelation and reason, belief and unbelief, obedience to God and belief in the sufficiency of reason. This fundamental opposition must be resolved before we can try to give meaning to Jewish ethics in the modern world.

Judaism and ethics: divergences on principle

Let us begin by looking at arguments for an opposition between ethics and Judaism. If we think of ethics as the study of judgements on the good, as a discourse on what should be rather than what is, then arguments for or against a reconciliation of Judaism and philosophical ethics cannot be arrived at by looking empirically at the behaviour of any particular Jewish community or individual, past or present. The 'cultures of the Jews'[2] may be an indication of their ethics in the sense of a set of rules or standards adopted by a particular historical community, but they are not an indication of a normative moral philosophy that is intrinsically connected with the Jewish tradition. Philosophical ethics implies the pursuit of an ideal. If there is an opposition between ethics and Judaism, it must be a matter of principle. Differences emerge if one looks at the respective sources of Judaism and ethics (revelation as opposed to reason); they also emerge when one looks at their respective ends. Judaism aims at holiness attained by following the commandments, whereas the philosophical discourse on ethics aims at ordering our personal, social, and political affairs in a manner conducive to happiness. These goals are not necessarily contradictory, but there is a basic difference between philosophical notions of happiness and rabbinic assumptions about the goal of life. For the ancient rabbis, this life is an 'entry hall' where one prepares oneself for life in the world to come. This doctrine allows one to reconcile the existence of seemingly unjust suffering with the doctrine of divine justice. If the goal of life is to earn reward in the world to come, then suffering in this life may be considered 'chastisements of love' afflicting the righteous. On the other hand, for philosophical ethics happiness entails the overcoming of avoidable suffering or resignation in the face of it. This difference between the two world-views cannot be argued away by pointing to philosophical doctrines of immortality that resemble the rabbinic doctrine of the afterlife. Philosophical doctrines of immortality, from Plato to modern deists (for example, Moses Mendelssohn), are speculative assertions about the nature of the soul, whereas the religious doctrine of the resurrection of the dead involves not just the soul but also the body. Resurrection of the body expresses belief in divine justice and human accounting in the hereafter, whereas Plato's philosophical doctrine of immortality articulates the condition of the possibility for humans to attain true knowledge and intellectual perfection.

Are Judaism and philosophical ethics then indeed irreconcilable opposites—Judaism being a divinely ordained way of life and ethics a form of idolatry and atheism (Leibowitz)—and is Jewish ethics not just a conceptual hybrid but a contradictory concept? Since the critique of Jewish ethics voiced by Leibowitz, Strauss, and others is directed at a specifically modern configuration of ethics and Judaism, we need to consider the principal difference between modern Jewish ethical theory and its ancient and medieval predecessors.

Convergence of Judaism and ethics, or: from metaphysics to critical idealism

In the context of pre-modern rationalism, ethics is a discipline of practical reason, concerned with the question of how to live one's life, rather than a discipline devoted to theoretical knowledge. The most widely accepted philosophical approach to ethics was that of Aristotle, who criticized the Platonic idea of a 'good beyond being' as an unclear term and taught that, rather than an abstract value, moral virtue was the middle between extreme modes of behaviour. Taking their lead from their Muslim contemporaries, medieval Jewish rationalists interpreted the Torah as in fundamental agreement with Aristotle's doctrine. The classical treatise of medieval Jewish ethics, Maimonides' *Eight Chapters*, is an exposition of Aristotle's doctrine of the mean. From this perspective there is no contradiction between Judaism and Aristotelian ethics: both the Mosaic law and the practical art of distinguishing (relatively) good from (relatively) bad behaviour aim at imposing good habits and virtue on the individual and order on society. The deeper meanings of the law, however, are of no moral consequence and hence must not be divulged other than in private, one-on-one communication.

Ancient and medieval variants of Jewish rationalism and its concomitant esotericism, such as the above, came under fire in the age of the European Enlightenment and its critique of religion, which aimed at establishing a purely rational and universally valid, secular political order, free of religious coercion. Modern Jewish philosophy developed in response to the challenges to medieval Jewish rationalism posed by Spinoza, who argued that the Mosaic tradition contained no knowledge of scientific or esoteric value whatsoever, that the Jews had no exclusive claim to prophecy, and that the moral content of Scripture was of a universal kind. To meet this challenge, modern philosophers had to find a way of arguing for the indispensability of the Torah. The major discourse that allowed them to make this argument was the modern philosophical discourse on ethics which saw itself as the foundation of a rational advancement of social harmony and political well-being. The condition for the meteoric rise of ethics from a practical form of knowledge to the systematic core of all theoretical and practical sciences was the shift from an Aristotelian to a Platonic paradigm, where the good is the ultimate 'un-ground' of being. This shift transformed ethics into a system of reflections on first causes. In keeping with this modern philosophic turn to Plato, accomplished in the philosophy of German idealism (Fichte, Schelling, Hegel), modern Jewish thinkers attempted to explicate the idea of God in terms of a Platonic relation between God and the good as the transcendent ground of being.

With few exceptions, modern Jewish philosophers from Moses Mendelssohn to Franz Rosenzweig accepted that the Torah teaches nothing of theoretical value that could compete, or be in conflict with, modern science. In contrast to their ancient and medieval predecessors, however, modern Jewish rationalists could make this claim without having to bend the literal meaning of the Torah to conform with new scientific insights. Instead, following Spinoza, they relinquished the territory of natural philosophy to the sciences, while arguing, against Spinoza, for the ethical and/or aesthetic (that is, formative, educational) value of revelation. After the French Revolution and its horrors, Kantian ethics and humanistic aesthetics became important elements in European rhetorics of non-revolutionary civic amelioration, aiming to improve society gradually through reform, education, and the fostering of a unified national culture. Individual responsibility and solidarity with one's fellow-citizen became widely popularized values central to discourses on political legitimacy and national cohesion. In this cultural and political atmosphere, Jewish theologians, historians, poets, politicians, and philosophers invoked prophetic ethics and rabbinic moral teachings as the essential values of Judaism. By arguing for a moral core of the Jewish tradition, a core that could be located not only in the prophetic sources but also in medieval and early modern texts, they were able to pursue two related goals, namely, liturgical reform (fostering aesthetic acceptibility) and a moral congeniality with the Kantian consciousness of the duty-bound citizen of the modern state, an argument in support of Jewish demands for civic equality. Judaism was thus thoroughly reinterpreted as 'ethical monotheism', a religion that had nothing less than 'the love of the neighbour' (cf. Leviticus 19: 18) as its essential value. The 'mission' of Judaism—that is, its own mission and that of its ethically oriented daughter-religions, Christianity and Islam—was to bring this highest ethical normativity to all nations. Judaism could thus be celebrated as a religion with an elective affinity for Kantian ethics, and one could idealize Germanic culture as finally having raised the Christian religion to the level of a philosophical ethics that had long been anticipated by the prophets and their medieval successors, the Jewish rationalists. Judaism and Protestant Christianity converged on a level of cultural development where ethics and religion were mutually constitutive, where religious doctrine no longer interfered negatively with good citizenship or tolerance, and where the essence of religion was neighbourly love. Judaism was a religion that not only imbued its members with moral habits and a philanthropic attitude, but cared about purity of the heart more than about the fulfilment of ritual commandments. Devoid of irrational doctrines, and hence superior to the Christian religion, Judaism was the 'religion of reason' par excellence, precisely because of its radically ethical orientation.

Critique of the ideology of progress

Why, despite all the evidence to the contrary amassed by Jewish authors from Moses Mendelssohn to Mordecai Kaplan, did Strauss and Leibowitz decide to argue that Judaism has essentially nothing to do with ethics? Their argument is grounded in the realization that ethical theory had moved from the margins to the centre of Jewish thought when the metaphysical, mystical, and political aspects of the law were no longer acceptable as the basis for claims to the veracity and authority of the Mosaic legislation. Under the conditions of modernity, Judaism had to be reinvented to function as a particular religion in a pluralistic society, a function it could obtain only when it was possible to describe it as a persuasive source of the modern notion of moral autonomy.[3] The recent critics of the possibility of a Jewish philosophical ethics emphasize the dependence of this hybrid on an accommodation to modern political necessities, and thus deny its fundamental validity. To claim that the essence of Judaism lies in its morality or in the ethical sublimeness of its idea of God amounted, in the critics' view, to holding Judaism to standards that are alien to its sources, that estrange Judaism from itself, and that deliver a time-honoured religious system of symbols to culture-bound ideologies.

This intuition seems confirmed by the fact that the centrality of ethics to Judaism that characterized Jewish reform and conservative theologies in the nineteenth and the early twentieth centuries no longer characterizes what most Jews expect from their tradition. What one expects of Judaism today is that it act as a source of identity and spirituality. Identity was the driving force of the Zionist movement, and spirituality has been on the rise as the core value of American Judaism at least since the 1970s. This shift in the vital interests of the major Jewish communities has brought about a marginalization of ethics. This explains why virtually no major treatise on Jewish ethics of any further-reaching philosophical value has been written since Hermann Cohen's *Religion of Reason Out Of the Sources of Judaism* (1919). It should be obvious from the aforementioned, however, that Strauss's and Leibowitz's critical verdicts on ethics also apply to any other qualifier, such as identity or spirituality, that is used to displace the simple obedience to the commandments as the essential quality of Judaism. In any case, ethics no longer functions as the main criterion of what Judaism is all about, nor does it supply the master narrative for students of Jewish intellectual history.

At the root of the criticism is the observation that social and political progress is anything but rationally necessary or irreversible. Strauss's work is dedicated to recovering the original Platonic philosophy that the medieval Jewish philosophers and their Islamic teachers had still understood correctly, but that the moderns had distorted in order for it to conform with their optimistic, progressivist assumptions. Similarly, Leibowitz argued for a return to classical rationalism because he considered any admixture to halakhic Judaism, be it of a moralistic, emotional, or spiritual nature, to be a compromise that endangers its integrity and thus permits the Jews to embrace any kind of popular ideology. He argued that whenever this occurred, Judaism lost its ability to protect the Jews from error and idolatry. To thinkers like Strauss and Leibowitz, ethics and Judaism are irreconcilable opposites not because they believe that Judaism is devoid of morality or that Jews should be exempt from universal moral obligations, but because they react to the, perhaps exaggerated, expectation that ethical theory can serve as a rational path to the collective salvation of the Jews from the condition of exile and exclusion.

No matter where one comes down in this debate, it is obvious that to speak of Jewish ethics on the theoretical level is to make a statement about the essence of Judaism, a question that gave rise to a variety of Jewish movements, ranging from radical secular Jewish socialism to exclusivist forms of Jewish orthodoxy.

An alternative approach: identifying elective affinities between certain Judaisms and certain types of ethics

In order to move the question of Jewish ethics beyond the interminable discussion on the essence of Judaism, it is helpful to distinguish between certain kinds of Judaism (or 'Judaisms') and certain ethical theories, and examine whether there exist any elective affinities between them.

Ethical theories

Ways of ascertaining the good differ from one another on principle. There are eudaemonistic ethics whose goal it is to achieve individual happiness. Definitions of 'happiness' range from an absence of fear (Epicureanism) to an achievement of the highest level of intellectual perfection (Aristotle). Happiness is also the aim of utilitarianism (Bentham, Mill), but utilitarians think of it as the well-being of the greatest possible number of people rather than the individual. Radically opposed to any such consequentialism (that is, ethics as aiming at happiness or, more generally, at an empirical good achieved as the result of one's actions), Immanuel Kant equated the good with the rational lawfulness that determines one's intention: only such intentions may be considered purely good as are directed by maxims that conform with rules that meet all the criteria of a universal law (deontological ethics). While the natural-law and moral-sense theories of the Enlightenment period argued that knowledge of the good is innate in each and every individual, making us ultimately independent of both the conventions of positive law and the supernatural aid of revealed legislation, Kant's transcendental ethics locates the good in rational judgements whose presupposition, the autonomy of the self, lies beyond all possible experience. Among the successors of both the natural-law tradition and Kantian transcendental ethics are certain theories of value that invoke the ability to distinguish between higher and lesser values, and that postulate the ability to act upon such knowledge (Max Weber, Nicolai Hartmann). In opposition to all of these theories, legal positivism rejects any kind of unwritten law or extra-legal source of knowledge for the good that may be called upon to suspend the authority of specific laws or entire legal systems. The ethical universalism postulated by sensualists and transcendentalists is also called into question by moral relativism which considers value judgements as cultural constructs (Nietzsche). The most powerful argument against relativism may yet arise from the context of psycho-genetic research, if it can be shown that human sociability is anchored in evolutionary biology. This idea has its predecessor in the thought of Spinoza, for whom the desire for self-preservation may be the ultimate and sufficient reason for social organization. Delegating moral judgement to science, however, tends to turn into a powerful tool of oppression, as is obvious from the history of twentieth-century social experimentation, where fascist, totalitarian, and Stalinist regimes assigned the freedom and power to act upon the insights of social scientists to cadres of trained individuals, destroying all individual rights in the process. Ethical theories thus differ on principle, and there is no universal agreement on which theory is the right one, or the best.

Varieties of Judaism

Just as there are different schools of ethical theory, so too there are different Judaisms that display different attitudes toward law and ethics and invoke different strands of the tradition to justify their stance. Some of these Judaisms are particularistic, others are universalistic. There are mystical and anti-mystical, romantic and rational, modernist and anti-modernist, exclusivist and ecumenical types of Judaism. Some Judaisms are collectively self-centred, in that they emphasize the superiority and fundamental otherness of the Jewish people from everyone else. Other Judaisms are eager to emphasize commonalities and areas of agreement between different kinds of Jews, and/or between Jews and non-Jews. Some believe that the difference between Jews and non-Jews concerns ritual and historical matters alone, that is, the ceremonial law and the particular historical memory that has shaped Jewish identity. In this case, theoretical and applied ethics may be considered a bridge between Jews and non-Jews, in that one's moral obligation includes one's solidarity with, and responsibility for, the stranger. Others believe that ethics are marginal to Jewish life and constitute an accommodation to existence in exile. In this case, one will be inclined to consider all commonality of interest between Jews and non-Jews to be, at best, of a utilitarian nature. While it is possible to speak of a 'normative' Judaism in historical terms, it is not possible to determine which of the existing Judaisms is true.

Commonalities and congeniality: a pragmatic analysis

Setting the question of truth aside, some of the theoretical and practical approaches to ethics are more congenial to certain aspects of the Jewish tradition than others. Because of such affinities, even the most exclusivist Jewish groups may be able to determine areas of compromise and commonality between themselves and their respective Jewish or non-Jewish others. Depending on one's situation and assumptions, one will or will not work out differences between the indigenous legal and moral traditions and the sense of the good regnant in general society or in relevant segments of such a society. The ability to search for compromises between one's own tradition and what is acceptable to a relevant other community is a matter of prudence, but it may also be justified and enhanced by certain commonly invoked principles of Jewish moral and political reasoning.

For example, a well-known rabbinic dictum permits the bending of certain rules 'for the sake of peace'. In the Diaspora situation, the principle of *dina de-malkhuta dina* ('the law of the land is the law') made it possible to yield considerable power to Gentile authorities, especially in matters pertaining to criminal law or civil conflicts between Jews and non-Jews. In the contexts of debates on emancipation, when Jews were confronted with a shift from corporate constitution to individual citizenship, their claim to be able to abide by laws determined by a non-Jewish majority was supported by this very dictum. Rabbinic tradition has thus shown a remarkable ability to maintain fluid boundaries between the demands of Torah law and the demands of maintaining a successful communal existence in exile. This ability is rooted in the realization that very few acts are grave enough to warrant ultimate resistance, a differentiation that would be impossible without a strong sense of ethical fundamentals. While the laws generally maintain life in dignity and holiness, very few transgressions are so serious as to call for a choice of death over life. Only when forced to commit acts of murder, incest, or idolatry is one required to let oneself be killed rather than transgress the law.

Furthermore, the law as a whole functions in a discourse on wisdom that involves not only the Jews but also their neighbours, the nations of the world. Thus, according to Deuteronomy 4: 5–8, the 'statutes and judgements' commanded by God are 'your wisdom and your understanding in the sight of the nations, who shall hear all these statutes, and say, Surely this great nation is a wise and understanding people'. This implies that Jewish law must meet the standards of 'wisdom and understanding' that are the common property of all nations, a principle that makes it imperative to pay attention to how Jewish law is received among the nations. This principle may also be derived from the frequent mention in Deuteronomy, Isaiah, and Jeremiah of the nations as witnesses to the righteousness of God, or from the oracles of the prophet Isaiah, who refers to the Torah as an instruction that originates in Jerusalem but extends beyond the boundaries of the Jewish nation.

Jews, Christians, and Muslims share the sense that the respective revelation entrusted to them has elevated them above the status of other communities. Yet the biblical tradition distinguishes between the moral quality of the divine mandate and the empirical morality of the Hebrews. Simply put, God and his laws are standards of justice and models of goodness, whereas the Hebrews are not. In contrast to the saintly figure of Jesus in the Christian tradition, and in contrast also to the exemplary function of the conduct of the Prophet and his companions in Islam, the conduct of the cultural heroes of ancient Israel is often morally problematic, at least in the pre-exilic layers of the tradition. The lack of idealization and the realism in the depiction of the behaviour of the forefathers and foremothers may be a way of articulating the commonality of the human situation before God who alone is holy, that is, good.

While rabbinic thought may occasionally adopt a sceptical stance toward the theoretical question of human freedom ('everything is determined except for the fear of heaven'), the good remains a fundamental human possibility, attained through habituation rather than through philosophical knowledge. In the context of the Jewish tradition, this habituation is attained through diligent observance of the *mitzvot* that are Israel's 'wisdom and understanding'. Furthermore, Judaism may be said to show an elective affinity with Kantian deontological ethics, in that it regards the pursuit of the good for its own sake more highly than service of God for the sake of reward or out of fear of punishment.[4] Imitation of God, that is, the striving for divine perfection, is also central to Jewish ethical reasoning. Here too, the point is to encourage the pursuit of the highest possible standards of morality, especially with respect to social ethics, where the divine attributes of justice, mercy, compassion, and so on have their precise correspondence on the human plane.

Utilitarianism, the furtherance of mutual benefit for the greatest possible number of people, also has an important place in Jewish tradition. The recommendation 'to seek the well-being of the city' (Jeremiah 29: 7) has given the ethics of compromise between Jews and Gentiles a firm grounding in Jewish sources, and has justfied the adoption of a utilitarian attitude toward non-Jewish authorities and majorities.

Universalist humanism seems to be implicit in the very notion of the creation of all human beings in the image of God. Jewish ethics is predicated on a fundamentally universalistic notion of human nature. By making solidarity with the stranger a basic commandment (Leviticus 19: 18 and 34), biblical law entails considerations of mutuality that transcend ethnic boundaries.

Every text is open to interpretation, and many texts can be countered by other texts whose meaning may suggest the opposite. Textual references alone are therefore insufficient to determine an elective affinity between all Judaisms and a particular type of ethics or ethical theory. The Judaic tradition is deeply divided and diversified with respect to its preference for one type of ethics or another. Still, the preceding observations may serve as evidence that certain aspects of Judaism function in ways that are compatible with a number of widely accepted ethical traditions, such as Aristotelian virtue ethics, utilitarianism, and Kantian deontological ethics, and that Jewish law itself demands an articulation of its own excellence in terms comprehensible to universally acceptable norms. The only possible approach to ethics that is explicitly excluded is the mere pursuit of personal happiness for its own sake.

Judaism and applied ethics: modern challenges to Jewish law and morality

Even if one is inclined to reject ethical theory as irrelevant to the foundations of Judaism, and turns instead to halakhah as the unique and authentic ground of Jewish life and thought, one soon discovers the indispensability of ethical reasoning to the functioning of the halakhah itself. As a legal system, halakhah cannot be maintained and developed without being applied to unforeseen situations. One needs to use judgement when deciding unprecedented halakhic questions, and frequently there are moral, rather than legal, reasons that are the only possible ground for making such a decision, especially when the sources are ambiguous. This should not come as a surprise: on the fringes of every legal system there arise problems that cannot be satisfactorily resolved within the legal framework itself.

The relation between ethics and halakhah is discussed on a general theoretical level and on the level of what one may call *applied ethics*. On the general level, the introduction of ethics into the context of legal reasoning is usually framed in terms of the traditional distinction between halakhah and aggadah, whereby ethics would come under the latter heading. When framed in these terms, the legitimacy of applying ethical reasoning to legal matters appears problematic not only because of the heterogeneity, in principle, between atheistic moral philosophy and the Mosaic law, but also because arguments from aggadic sources are not usually accepted when deciding halakhic questions. There are many cases where such arguments were accepted, and it comes down to whether or not one considers this a legitimate procedure.

The association of ethics with aggadah, and thus in most cases with midrashic readings of classical texts, has two consequences that are no longer controllable by the halakhic process itself. One is reliance on texts that are inherently ambiguous, which puts the burden of spelling out the ethical implications of a text on the interpreter. The rabbis wished to exclude this kind of aggadic proof because they recognized its arbitrariness. The second consequence is the shifting of the weight from legal to theological concerns, which may be powerful homiletical tools but hardly serve as a reliable basis for establishing an ethical consensus or a legal rule. Those who favour a grounding of extensions to existing law in midrash and theology defend their position by arguing that halakhah itself is often at a loss without some kind of attention to the needs of the community. Such needs arise from a change in the overall conventions of what a society regards as just or acceptable, and from advances in technology that pose unprecedented challenges to all existing legal traditions. An example of needs arising from a change in what society regards as just is the problem of *agunot*, that is, women abandoned by their husbands without a writ of divorce or whose husbands have disappeared without trace. This phenomenon has troubled the rabbis for a long time, but it is only recently that some rabbinic courts have taken it upon themselves to determine new ways of legally dissolving these marriages. These decisions have not been universally accepted.

Examples of challenges arising from changes in what society regards as acceptable behaviour concern life-style choices (including sexual preference and family planning) and the desire to end one's life in dignity (euthanasia). Unprecedented challenges to legal systems, including halakhah, have arisen and continue to arise from advances in medical technology, such as increasing means of control of the beginning of life (cloning, reproductive medicine, stem-cell research, manipulating health, gender, and other genetic markers of an embryo, and so on). Similarly unprecedented are the widening range of human responsibility for ecological balance (sustainable growth) and the use of animals in pharmaceutical research, where traditional laws against cruelty toward animals no longer seem sufficient. In addition, in the context of the State of Israel Jewish law has been confronted with the challenge of ruling on questions of participation in government, warfare, and the control of another people.

In *Matters of Life and Death* (1998), one of the leading American Jewish ethicists sketches what he calls a 'Jewish approach' to the pressing issues arising from the advances in the modern medical sciences. The moral issues explored in this volume arise from technologies that have exponentially increased our control of the beginning and ending of life. Dorff's approach (sketched in Part I, on 'Matters of Method and Belief') is theological/midrashic rather than halakhic, which means that he derives his judgements from biblical and rabbinic notions concerning the value of life such as bodily health, the desire for genetically related offspring, and the mandate to heal. Part II ('Moral Issues at the Beginning of Life') covers issues of fertility and infertility treatments, ways of using one's own genetic material and ways of using donated genetic material (issues considered here include the value of matrimony, the potential for racism, legal and psychological implications of sperm donations and surrogate motherhood, as well as adoption and single parenthood), the prevention of pregnancy (masturbation, contraception, etc.), and the social context of sexuality (including genetic screening, sex education, and homosexuality). Part III ('Matters at the End of Life') deals with the preparation for death, the process of dying (including the options of suicide, assisted suicide, and euthanasia), and the treatment of the corpse after death (including the religiously fraught issue of donating one's body to medical research). In addition—and this is particularly interesting—Dorff inquires into the wider contexts of bioethical decision-making, such as having to confront the costs of medical care, having to deal with changes in our relations to our bodies (cosmetic surgery, body-piercing, mental health, diminution of exposure to people suffering illness, attitudes toward disabilities), and having to take personal and communal responsibility for health and the avoidance of hazards, and so on. In an epilogue to this impressive model of contemporary Jewish ethical reasoning, Dorff articulates an 'imperative to choose life', and an appendix offers reflections on the philosophical foundations of the author's approach to ethical decision-making in light of Jewish tradition.

It would lead too far to list and discuss the solutions to these new challenges that have been debated over the last few decades, but it is clear that the emerging fields of relevance for Jewish ethicists—bioethics, business ethics, social justice, gender equality, and our individual and collective responsibilities for sustainable growth, to name a few—are identical to those relevant for society in general.

FURTHER READING

Breslauer, S. Daniel. *Toward a Jewish (M)orality: Speaking of a Postmodern Jewish Ethics,* Contributions to the Study of Religion, No. 53 (Westport, Conn. and London: Greenwood Press, 1998). Breslauer locates his postmodern approach to Jewish ethics in a space between the historic shattering of conventional liberalism in the hyper-modernity of twentieth-century genocides and the indeterminacy of Jewish textual traditions. Rather than serving as a path to legal or ethical decision, postmodern Jewish ethics signals the impossibility of finding unambiguous guidance toward the good and turns instead into a source of Jewish identity after the Shoah.

Dorff, Elliot N. *Matters of Life and Death: A Jewish Approach to Modern Medical Ethics* (Philadelphia: Jewish Publication Society, 1998).

Dorff, Elliot N., and Louis E. Newman (eds.). *Contemporary Jewish Ethics and Morality: A Reader* (Oxford: Oxford University Press, 1997). A collection of essays from authors representing a wide range of recent American academic approaches to Jewish ethics. The volume is divided into Part I, on Jewish ethics, and Part II, on Jewish morality, a distinction which corresponds, by and large, to the more common distinction between ethical theory and applied ethics. Part I includes, among others, essays on the 'The Structure of Jewish Ethics' (Menachem Kellner), reflections on natural law (David Novak), on the relation between law, ethics, and religion (Louis Newman), on Jewish ethics in the modern age (Eugene Borowitz *et al.*), and on methodology (David Ellenson, Louis Newman). Part II includes, among others, essays on the virtue of 'humility' (Sol Roth), on sexual and family ethics (David Novak, Arthur Waskow, Blu Greenberg *et al.*), on matters of social justice and ecological responsibility (Robert Gordis, Seymour Siegel, Elie Spitz), on euthanasia (Fred Rosner, Byron Sherwin) and abortion (David M. Feldman, Sandra B. Lubarsky), and on politics and power in the State of Israel (Irving Greenberg, Judith Plaskow, David Hartman, and Einat Ramon).

Marvin Fox (ed.). *Modern Jewish Ethics: Theory and Practice* (Columbus, Ohio: Ohio State University Press, 1975). Covering the legal and the philosophical basis, this volume includes classic essays by Ernst Simon, Aharon Lichtenstein, Emmanuel Levinas, and the editor himself. The contemporary situation it explores in one of its chapters refers to the period following the Israeli victory in the Six Day War of 1967.

Newman, Louis E. *Past Imperatives: Studies in the History and Theory of Jewish Ethics* (Albany: State University of New York Press, 1998). A comprehensive critical introduction to the problem of Jewish ethics from a contemporary academic perspective, dealing with the relation between ethics and law, ethics and theology, and methodological issues in contemporary Jewish ethics. The book also includes an excellent bibliography on Jewish ethics.

Sherwin, Byron L. *Jewish Ethics for the Twenty-First Century: Living in the Image of God* (Syracuse, NY: Syracuse University Press, 2000). Sherwin covers a range of problems of applied ethics in the areas of health and healing, euthanasia, parent–child relations, and so on. The guiding idea is not halakhic but an ethics derived from the theological notion that man is created in God's image. Sherwin articulates what he believes to be the implications of this notion for individual and social ethics.

Steinberg, Paul. *Study Guide to Jewish Ethics: A Companion to 'Matters of Life and Death', 'To Do the Right and the Good', and 'Love your Neighbor and Yourself'* (Philadelphia: Jewish Publication Society, 2003). This textbook includes chapters on general concepts and theories of moral philosophy, on Judaism's methodology and moral course of action, on our bodies ('What Are We Responsible For?'), on sexual morality, abortion, infertility, parents and children, family violence, poverty, war, dying (suicide and euthanasia), and forgiveness ('an interpersonal process'). This is a companion to Elliot Dorff's three books on Jewish ethics, *Matters of Life and Death* (1998), *To Do the Right and the Good* (2002), and *To Love Your Neighbor and Yourself* (2003).

NOTES

1. For Leibowitz on ethics, see e.g. Yeshayahu Leibowitz, 'The Religious and Moral Significance of the Redemption of Israel' (1977), in Eliezer Goldman (ed.), *Judaism, Human Values, and the Jewish State*, (Cambridge and London: Harvard University Press, 1992), pp. 114 f. For Leo Strauss on the

difference between Greek and biblical morality, see e.g. 'Progress or Return?', in Kenneth Hart Green (ed.), *Jewish Philosophy and the Crisis of Modernity: Essays and Lectures in Modern Jewish Thought* (Albany: State University of New York Press, 1997), pp. 87–136, esp. pp. 105–16.

2. Cf. David Biale (ed.), *Cultures of the Jews: A New History* (New York: Schocken Books, 2002).

3. This is, indeed, exactly what the most widely read modern Jewish ethics, Moritz Lazarus's *Ethik des Judentums* (Frankfurt: J. Kauffmann, 1901), argued.

4. Cf. Shalom Rosenberg, 'Ethics', in Arthur A. Cohen and Paul Mendes Flohr (eds.), *Contemporary Jewish Religious Thought* (New York: Free Press, and London: Collier Macmillan Publishers, 1988), pp. 195–7.

Halakhic issues

27 | Halakhic issues: survey

Jonathan Cohen

Any survey of halakhic issues in the modern period requires an appreciation of the challenges that modernity presents to practitioners of halakhah. Modernity, launched with the French and American revolutions, has altered the living conditions as well as the status and identity of Jews throughout the world. It has also transformed the quality and extent of their interaction with non-Jews and non-Jewish institutions. Two principal expressions of modernity have affected Jewish life most significantly: political emancipation and the Enlightenment.

The political emancipation of the Jews of Western Europe began towards the end of the eighteenth century, and its implications are still unfolding in a number of areas. The essence of the transformation in the personal and communal status of the Jews was the recognition of the political rights of individual Jews, and the removal of recognition of the political rights of Jewish communities and their institutions. Through much of the pre-modern period Judaism was deemed a nationality or collective ethnic identity, and Jewish communities were recognized as political entities that regulated the lives of their members. The leadership of the Jewish community was authorized to make decisions that altered the personal, professional, and social lives of its members, and its decisions were to a great extent enforceable. In other words, positions of Jewish leadership entailed a certain degree of political and administrative force, and the decisions and rulings of communal institutions and rabbis bore legal, normative authority. The rules (of halakhah) that regulated Jewish life reflected the political and legal structures in which Jews lived and functioned in the pre-modern age. In fact, these structures were often legitimized and reinforced by rabbis who formulated the rules of Jewish law.

The political emancipation of the Jews is the process through which the state assumed much of the authority that had resided in the Jewish community and its organs. While individual Jews were promised equal treatment under the law, their institutions and leaders were stripped of political power, and of their ability to regulate most Jewish affairs. In this way, the pre-modern conditions that allowed for the enforcement and development of halakhah, and that were incorporated into it, were largely removed. While emancipation originated in Western Europe and North America, the weakening of Jewish institutions spread in varying degrees to other parts of the world. Today the overwhelming majority of Jews live in countries that afford them individual rights. Yet their communities lack the political authority to regulate themselves to the extent that they had done in the pre-modern period. The challenge that emancipation presents to the practitioner of halakhah may be understood in a number of ways: for some, the loss of rabbinic and communal authority entails new constraints on the development of Jewish law, and necessitates the preservation of pre-modern norms. Others suggest that rabbinic authority remains unaffected by changing conditions. Some argue that the changing conditions of Jewish life require more vigorous halakhic development and innovation. Yet others claim that the removal of rabbinic and communal authority has rendered halakhah entirely inapplicable and inappropriate to modern conditions.

Reason and its advancement are fundamental aspects of modernity and liberalism. The Enlightenment and the development of liberal thought have presented numerous challenges to halakhah, and have generated the need for halakhic responses to scientific, legal, economic, and other developments. During the late eighteenth and nineteenth centuries 'religious superstition' and 'outdated ritual' were suspiciously regarded by growing numbers of people, and religion was increasingly subjected to academic and scientific scrutiny and analysis. As biblical scholarship, Ancient Near Eastern studies, and archaeology developed, evidence suggesting that humans authored and edited the biblical text accumulated. Among many, this evidence and the scholarship that it fuelled undermined the notion of divine revelation, and previously accepted claims of rabbinic authority. At the same time, developments in the natural sciences raised questions relating to the Genesis narrative and to traditional approaches to the natural environment. In other words, while the emancipation profoundly altered the environment within which halakhah flourished, the Enlightenment gave rise to challenges of halakhah itself. The Enlightenment did not immediately undercut the enforceability or applicability of halakhic rules. Rather, it triggered a contest over the 'truth' and 'validity' of halakhah as a system of norms and rules. Debates over the validity and authority of halakhah have occupied scholars since the late eighteenth century and have divided the Jewish world.

Advances and innovations that emerge out of modern science often require halakhic consideration to determine how and to what extent they may be incorporated into Jewish life. Inventions ranging from electrical appliances to new treatments to enhance fertility demand a constant assessment of halakhic norms, and entail the regulation of interaction between practitioners of Jewish law and their environments. Developments that have revolutionized various aspects of daily life have led some Jews to question the adequacy of halakhic categories, while challenging others to find new halakhic methods to address and regulate them. One of the challenges experienced by Jews is the sense that halakhah is reactive to modern developments that are thrust upon it by its environment. While many Jews are at the forefront of scientific and social innovation, halakhah is sometimes deemed passive or reactionary.

While it is difficult to categorize Jewish reactions to modernity, a number of trends have given rise to the formation of movements within Judaism. The different movements have historically reflected various approaches to modernity. The most prominent movements are ultra-Orthodox Judaism (sometimes called *haredi* Judaism), modern Orthodox Judaism, Conservative Judaism, and Reform Judaism. Haredi Jews often distinguish themselves through their opposition to many of the effects of modernity on the Jewish community and its institutions. While they do not reject modern innovations, they seek to maintain pre-modern communal structures and institutions, and espouse pre-modern claims of rabbinic authority. Modern Orthodox Jews do not consider modernity and halakhah to be incompatible. Rather, they argue that halakhah as it has evolved through the pre-modern period is capable of addressing modern innovations and conditions. The Conservative movement also promotes adherence to halakhah. However, Conservative leaders have argued that the halakhic process itself must develop to make the best use of modern (scientific, and other) developments. Finally, Reform Judaism endorses the observance of various aspects of halakhah, but maintains that Jewish law is no longer communally enforceable. It also embraces modern scholarship and rejects traditional claims of divine revelation and authority that underpin pre-modern and orthodox halakhah.

This chapter outlines some of the major halakhic issues that have arisen during this period. These touch on four aspects of Jewish life: ritual practice, conversion, family relations and procreation, and medical care towards the end of life.

Ritual practice

Questions concerning ritual practice have attracted much attention and generated bitter debate from the late eighteenth century onwards. Yet the exchanges of the modern period do not occur against a background of uniform practice or consensus before the onset of modernity. The difference between modern debates and those of earlier periods relates to the influence of the emancipation and Enlightenment. The modern halakhic discussion is both ideologically motivated and prompted by the immediate need to address the situation of partisans and beneficiaries of the emancipation. It reveals a drive for acculturation, and for rendering religious services more meaningful and attractive to their participants. Thus, arguments advanced by David Friedlander (1750–1834) in Berlin in 1812 called for discarding kabbalistic (mystical) elements from the liturgy. They also sought to reflect the aspiration for a new age wherein Jews no longer wished to return to their ancestral land, but rather to realize their potential as citizens of the European states they now inhabited. Responsa (rabbinic rulings) published as early as 1818 promoted the use of the vernacular in prayer in order to enhance the understanding of congregants who were not conversant with Hebrew. They also permitted the use of organ music to accompany prayer, even on the Sabbath, and called for other changes in the service. Following the establishment of a new reformist temple in Hamburg towards the end of 1818, opponents of changes to religious services published a collection of responsa called *Eleh Divrei ha-Brit* (These are the Words of the Covenant). These responsa prohibited the changes proposed by reformers and demanded that the service be preserved in its traditional form. Many asserted that the changes were not authorized by halakhah, and undermined Jewish tradition and identity. These early stages of the contest established its hallmarks: members of the Jewish community advancing a modernist, reform, agenda clash with others who seek to preserve pre-modern traditions. The opposing positions do not lend themselves to compromise, and from the mid-nineteenth century onwards result in the formation of separate, ideologically defined, congregations.

Modernity has also altered the lives of modern Orthodox and Haredi Jews throughout the world. The growing role of the state in regulating intra-Jewish dealings has resulted in significant changes. A large proportion of pre-modern halakhic writing addressed economic regulation, communal administration, family law, and personal status. With modernity, the focus of the halakhic enterprise shifted. From the middle of the twentieth century onwards, halakhic teachings and publications on personal observance and ritual practice increased. These addressed issues such as dietary laws, dress, and prayer. While rabbinic authorities lacked the power to enforce most aspects of Jewish law, members of modern Orthodox and ultra-Orthodox communities have voluntarily subjected themselves to standards of halakhic observance that distinguish them from non-Jews as well as other Jews. Thus, the halakhic shift that has taken place is not only substantive, it is also structural. Halakhah has not only lodged itself in the personal practices and homes of the Orthodox, it has also become largely self-regulating. In the pre-modern period, Jews would be identified principally as a national or ethnic group; today they would identify themselves on the basis of personal observance and ritual practice.

Conversion

The halakhic discussion on conversion is inseparable from the debates over Jewish identity and the unity of the Jewish people. Since Israel was established as a Jewish state, the subject also touches on the identity of the state, and on the lives of its citizens and immigrants. The difficulties surrounding conversion are not new. Talmudic and medieval authorities debated the standards of Jewish education and expressions of commitment to Judaism that conversion requires. Yet by the late middle ages it was generally recognized that converts to Judaism must fulfil two central requirements: they must be sincere in their wish to join their fates to that of the Jewish people, even if this entails hardship and suffering; and they must accept the burden of the commandments.

In fact, according to one Talmudic ruling, a proselyte who agrees to follow all the commandments except for one should not be converted (Babylonian Talmud, *Bekhorot*

30b). The implication of these two requirements was that the motivations of proselytes should not be tainted by ulterior motives. Commonly cited ulterior motives included financial considerations, fear, and the wish to marry a Jew. One concern was that proselytes who wished to convert for such motives might not be entirely sincere and loyal to Judaism and other Jews, nor be truly willing to embrace the requirements of Jewish law. Therefore, Jewish law courts (*batei din*) were instructed to examine proselytes and ascertain their commitment to convert 'for the sake of heaven'. At the same time, generally accepted sources of Jewish law asserted that conversions were deemed valid once the ritual requirements had been fulfilled, even in cases of conversion known to be inappropriately motivated (*Shulhan Arukh (S.A.), Yoreh De'ah*, 268: 12).

The changes brought about by emancipation complicated the issue of conversion. Two main difficulties arose. First, since the rabbis were no longer empowered to enforce the precepts of Jewish law upon members of their own congregations, they could not guarantee the observance of commandments (*mitzvot*) by converts, nor punish lapses. The situation was further complicated by the perception that members of many communities had become lax in their observance of the commandments, and some had abandoned them completely. Under such circumstances, the concern was that converts would be tempted not to perform the requirements of halakhah. They would experience the discrepancy between the warnings of the rabbi and the practice among lay Jews, and effectively be doomed to transgress and fail. Secondly, as Jews interacted with non-Jews to a much greater extent since the emancipation and the erosion of socio-economic barriers, the potential for interest in conversion for inappropriate reasons had increased. The main concern was that conversions might be motivated by the wish to marry a Jew. These are the concerns expressed by numerous Orthodox rabbis. Some imposed or called for bans on conversion to Judaism in a number of countries, including Argentina and Switzerland.

At the same time, a number of Orthodox rabbis called for greater leniency and acceptance of conversion because of the special conditions that characterized modern Jewry. Prominent examples include rabbis David Zvi Hoffman (1843–1921) and Ben-Zion Uziel (1880–1954), Sephardi chief rabbi in Palestine. Their reasons for leniency addressed the wish to maintain and strengthen the Jewish affiliation of those who marry non-Jews, to enable committed spouses to join the Jewish faith, and to facilitate the raising of Jewish children. A number of rabbis and scholars pointed to distinctions between potential converts who sought to join Judaism for the sake of marriage, and non-Jewish spouses who would gain no such benefit through conversion. In this view, the conversion of non-Jewish spouses could constitute a 'lesser evil' than the refusal to convert.

Opposing views among Orthodox rabbis often reflected the tendency to attribute greater weight to one of two aspects of Jewish law: on the one hand, the rabbinic responsibility to maintain the integrity of conversion; and on the other, the rabbinic mandate to preserve and strengthen Jewish identity through appropriate accommodation. Yet, the core difficulty was the modern rabbi's inability to regulate the lives of

Jews who were exposed to changing family structures and evolving social norms. Reform rabbi Solomon Freehof (1892–1990) addressed this issue in a responsum that guides rabbis in exercising their discretion to accept or reject candidates for conversion.[1]

Recognition of the profound changes in the lives of Jews, coupled with persistent variation in rabbinic positions, has catalysed two important developments. Orthodox rabbis have recently demonstrated their willingness to resort to the annulment of Orthodox conversions. A number of prominent twentieth-century authorities hold that the failure to observe commandments following conversion reflects insincerity at the time of conversion. According to this view, such insincerity may invalidate the conversion *ab initio*. Additionally, halakhic disagreement has caused signs of fragmentation to appear, undermining the universal recognition of Orthodox conversion. The implication is that a person who is converted in one Orthodox community may not be accepted in other Orthodox communities. While, in principle, non-Orthodox conversions are not accepted by Orthodox rabbis, the compromised status of certain Orthodox converts further undermines the act of conversion as acceptance of an ethno-national identity. Throughout the past century conversion has become an increasingly communal, ideologically defined, rite.

Conversion to Judaism is a subject that has exposed deep divisions among Jews, as well as emotional debate over Jewish identity. In Israel the topic has become increasingly prominent following the recent arrival of hundreds of thousands of immigrants from the Former Soviet Union, many of whom are not Jewish. It has also been vigorously discussed in relation to the absorption of Ethiopian immigrants to Israel. Among liberal rabbis, attitudes towards conversion for the sake of marriage vary. Most would not officiate in intermarriage ceremonies (that is, marriages between Jews and non-Jews), and encourage some participation of non-Jewish spouses in Jewish ritual. On the whole, liberal Judaism is characterized by greater leniency towards conversion, even when it is motivated by prospects of marriage.

Family relations: marriage and divorce; fertility and procreation

As we have seen, emancipation had a profound impact on various aspects of Jewish life. Yet, while changing conditions create divisions and disagreements regarding conversion, the decision whether or not to convert newcomers to Judaism remains a matter of rabbinic discretion. In contrast, the issue of marriage and divorce among Jews, once regulated by halakhah and administered by rabbis, has been comprehensively 'nationalized' throughout the world. Even in Israel, where Jewish law courts regulate matters of personal status among Jews, they do so on the basis of the authority vested in them by its elected parliament in the Rabbinical Courts Jurisdiction (Marriage and

Divorce) Law, 5713-1953. The transfer of authority over this area from the jurisdiction of the rabbis to that of the state has touched all Jewish communities, and prompted a number of developments in modern halakhah. At the same time, mass migration, war, the Holocaust, and various social and medical innovations have generated further challenges that require halakhic consideration.

Marriage and divorce

The halakhic regulation of family relations is founded on the presumption of extensive authority over this area of law. It is designed primarily to restrict sexual relations among Jews, regulate the relationship between spouses, encourage procreation, protect the family structure from numerous challenges (such as prohibited extramarital relations), oversee the termination of the marital relationship, and direct the relationships among parents and children. The end of rabbinic jurisdiction in these matters has both rendered the observance of Jewish law requirements voluntary, and created the necessity for halakhic structures to interact with non-Jewish legal institutions to an unprecedented extent. Large numbers of Jews no longer follow pre-modern halakhic rules relating to marriage and divorce. One manifestation of this trend is the rising rate of intermarriage over the past fifty years (to nearly 50 per cent in the United States, according to recent estimates). On the other hand, those wishing to marry under the auspices of halakhah must satisfy both civil and halakhic requirements.

One of the problems exacerbated by this new reality relates to the termination of marriage. In Jewish law, the termination of marriage by divorce entails the execution of a *get*, a short document that releases the woman from the marital relationship and is given to her by her husband. Without this get, a civilly divorced woman is unable to remarry according to halakhah. One of the requirements associated with this document is that it cannot be executed under compulsion (although some pressure can be applied).

State regulation of marriage and divorce in France dates back to the early nineteenth century. However, following the passage of provisions for civil divorce in France in 1884, a debate erupted regarding the validity of civil divorce documents in the eyes of halakhah. One of the propositions advanced in France was that rabbinic courts should annul marriages that were terminated by the secular authorities. The core of this suggestion was that all Jewish marriages be contracted conditionally, so that they might be annulled as they were terminated by the secular authorities. Yet another initiative would empower Jewish lawcourts to annul marriages only if a husband refused to grant his wife a get. However, these suggestions, like a number of later ones, were rejected by leading Orthodox rabbis in Europe. Their reactions to these proposals were documented in a volume called *Ein Tnay be-Nissuin* (There is No Conditional Marriage) published in Vilnius in 1930. The unfortunate consequence of this impasse is that women who are divorced in civil law and whose husbands refuse to grant them a get are *agunot*, chained women, anchored to their husbands and unable to remarry according to Jewish law. For although they are divorced by civil authorities, in the eyes of halakhah they remain married.

Fertility and procreation

Some difficulties surrounding marriage and divorce reflect the incompatibility of civil and Jewish institutions, and the problems associated with the need to satisfy both in the context of the modern state. However, other challenges to the halakhic conception of the family arise from the increasing availability of scientific and medical innovations. Among these innovations, various responses to infertility stand out in their potential to both benefit many and, at the same time, undermine traditional notions of parenthood, procreation, and the social relations associated with them.

Over the past few decades various methods for overcoming infertility have become available. They include drug therapy, surgery, procedures for the artificial insemination of sperm, the insemination of embryos in the uterus, the placement of ova and sperm into the fallopian tube, and the transfer of an embryo to the fallopian tube (as opposed to the uterus). While procedures involving insemination are not free of halakhic difficulty, the notion of non-sexual insemination is already present in the Talmud (Babylonian Talmud, *Hagigah* 14b), and halakhic authorities tend to consider such intervention permissible. Greater difficulties arise when either the sperm or the ova are donated, and when another woman bears the child. In these cases, difficulties relate to the identity of the parents and the very definition of the family.

For example, the insemination of a married woman with donated sperm (that is not her husband's) is deemed adulterous by some halakhic authorities. Further, if the identity of the donor is not known, successful procedures may result in incest in future generations. In other words, they entail a risk that a person who was conceived using his mother's ovum and the sperm of an anonymous donor (who is not his mother's husband) might engage in sexual relations and procreate with a half sibling. Such intercourse would fall under the halakhic category of incest. Rabbi Moshe Feinstein (1895–1986) has ruled that such a donation would not give rise to this issue if the donor were not Jewish, because halakhah does not recognize non-Jewish family lineage on the father's side (*Iggrot Moshe, Even ha-Ezer*, no. 71). In another responsum he suggested that the donor may be *presumed* a Gentile even if the physician intimates that he is Jewish, since he notes that most donors in the Unites States are Gentiles, and the physician may try to misinform his Jewish patient intending to comfort her (*Iggrot Moshe, Even ha-Ezer*, no. 10).

While the donation of sperm entails some difficulties, the donation of ova and surrogacy arrangements are particularly problematic from the halakhic perspective, which requires the identification of the mother. This is not an easy task where there is a strong genetic association between the donor of the ovum and the newborn, while another woman carries the child and delivers it. In contrast, arrangements wherein a woman donates both an ovum and her uterus to carry the child to term are sometimes described in terms of surrogacy, but since the birth-mother is also the donor of the ovum, most scholars of halakhah would undoubtedly recognize her as the child's mother. The possible separation of the ovum donor from the surrogate (the woman who carries the child to term) has given rise to a discussion on the nature of motherhood in halakhah. One question is whether motherhood is defined on the basis of parturition, or on the strength of her genetic relationship to her offspring. Other aspects of surrogacy have also generated debate. Some object to the introduction of third parties into procreation in the context of marriage. Rabbi Immanuel Jakobovits (1921–99) has condemned the practice of surrogacy as an affront to human dignity, because it entails payment for the use of a woman's uterus as an incubator. A number of American rabbis and scholars also disapprove of the commodification of reproductive abilities. In the United States the cost entailed in surrogacy arrangements is high. Also, the potential gap in incomes between couples seeking surrogates and the surrogate may be high.

The introduction and increasing availability of procedures to overcome infertility have fuelled halakhic debate about both the social and biological aspects of procreation and parenthood. They have also undermined traditional conceptions of the family unit. Among liberal Jews, they have also contributed to the debate on the value and appropriateness of traditional halakhic analysis on the basis of sources that were composed before these revolutionary procedures became available. Thus, these innovations have contributed to both halakhic and meta-halakhic debates, and have undermined the commitment to the application of traditional halakhic arguments and categories to situations that defy pre-modern understandings of the world. In this respect, these and other scientific developments (such as the development of cloning techniques) are particularly significant.

Medical care towards the end of life

As medical advances have transformed our understanding of the creation of life, so they have altered our experience of the end of life. The ever-increasing ability to extend life, as well as the growing variety of treatment options, have changed the lives of patients throughout the developed world. While the benefits of scientific progress are evident, they also entail additional opportunities for patient (and family) participation in the medical decision-making process. This greater potential for direction and control is often juxtaposed with the need to make decisions regarding complex and uncertain procedures that affect both patients and their loved ones. These decisions tend to be particularly difficult and painful in end-of-life situations that are often characterized by advanced terminal illness, degenerative conditions, or multiple organ failure.

The halakhic requirement to heal and preserve life is categorical to the degree that it overrides other requirements of Jewish law (for example, Babylonian Talmud, *Yoma* 85b). Medieval authorities argue that one must break the Sabbath in order to treat a 'dying' man in spite of the likelihood of impending death (*Tos. Niddah* 44a–b), and a later ruling clarifies that one is bound to break the Sabbath to prolong life even for an hour (Resp. *Shvut Ya'acov* 1: 13). In fact, the duty to save a life is so central that in cases where patients decline treatment in order to observe other commandments (such as to celebrate the Sabbath), halakhah requires that they may be coerced to act so that their lives may be saved (Resp. *Radbaz* 4: 1139). The principle that informs these rulings is that the body belongs to God. Thus, the patient may not exercise complete control over his or her own body. For the same reason, Jews may neither injure themselves nor commit suicide (*Mishnah Bava Kamma* 8: 6, and *S.A. Yoreh De'ah* 345: 1).

On the other hand, following a number of Talmudic precedents that express the principle of God's ultimate sovereignty over human life, Rabbi Moses Isserles (1530–72) asserted that one should not do anything to impede the exit of the soul. On the contrary, one should act to remove such an impediment. The reason offered is that the removal of an impediment to death promotes the natural process, and does not constitute (undue) intervention (*Rema* on *S.A. Yoreh De'ah* 339: 1). Further, the requirement of coercion to save a life applies to those cases where medical treatment would achieve the desired effect. A number of rulings suggest that in cases of high risk or uncertainty coercion is not warranted by halakhah. In effect, much of modern Jewish law seeks to balance the duty to save a life with the notion of human dignity that allows for unimpeded death while insisting on a certain degree of patient autonomy.

Feinstein's rulings reflect the attempt to reognize the patient's autonomy clearly. In one ruling he explains that an adult patient's refusal to accept beneficial treatment should not lead to an automatic response. If the refusal reflects a momentary lapse, or lack of willingness on his part to subject himself to discomfort or pain in spite of his overall confidence in the course of treatment, then coercion is an appropriate option. However, should the refusal reflect lack of confidence in the course of treatment or in the physician, then coercion should generally be avoided. This remains the case even when the physician is certain of the need for the prescribed treatment, and when others concur. Feinstein also stresses that coercion should not result in trauma, since trauma may be counter-productive and render the treatments ineffective. Thus, Feinstein affords the patient a degree of autonomy that extends beyond medical uncertainty, and accounts for the psychological damage that may be caused by coercion (*Iggrot Moshe, Hoshen Mishpat* 2: 73d). Similarly, Feinstein rules that an adult patient should not be coerced to eat or receive nutrition. Every effort should be made to persuade the patient, but the actions of the physician must ensure that he is not harmed physically or psychologically (*Iggrot Moshe, Hoshen Mishpat* 2: 74c). These modern responses reflect halakhic determination to address difficult medical situations and promote the psychological well-being of the patient, rather than either to reject modern developments or use all available means to extend life.

Conclusion

Modernity presents a number of unprecedented challenges to scholars and practitioners of halakhah. Principally, it removed the conditions that fostered its development during the pre-modern period. In effect, halakhah underwent a forced transformation. While in the pre-modern period it was for the most part a recognized, state-sanctioned system that administered Jewish life, halakhah has now become a largely voluntary framework that survives and develops through the determination of its practitioners, and coexists with secular institutions. Its expression in the modern world reflects an ongoing struggle to maintain, develop, or respond to modern conditions using predominantly pre-modern sources. Many Jews would argue that halakhah is incompatible with modernity. Among them, some prefer it to modernity. Others are committed to the modern enterprise. Yet a large number of Jews hold that halakhah is compatible with modern life, and wish to continue to adapt and develop it. Thus, modernity has framed the halakhic discussion, and defines its parameters.

FURTHER READING

Elon, M. *Jewish Law: History, Sources, Principles* (Philadelphia and Jerusalem: Jewish Publication Society, 1994), vol. 4, pp. 1576–91. Contains a useful survey of the impact of modernity on halakhic observance.

Meyer, M. A. *Response to Modernity* (Oxford: Oxford University Press, 1988). Presents a full account of the emergence of Reform Judaism and the halakhic debates that accompanied it.

Siegel, Seymour, with E. Gertel (eds.). *Conservative Judaism and Jewish Law* (New York: Rabbinical Assembly, 1977). Contains articles that constitute a fine introduction to Conservative halakhah.

Soloveitchik, H. 'Rupture and Reconstruction: The Transformation of Contemporary Orthodoxy', *Tradition*, 28: 4 (1994), pp. 64–130. Offers an account of the transformation of Orthodoxy following the Second World War and the Holocaust.

Washofsky, M. *Jewish Living* (New York: UAHC Press, 2000). Presents a statement of contemporary Reform practice, and addresses the links between current practices and the sources of halakhah.

NOTE

1. Solomon B. Freehof, *Reform Responsa For Our Times* (Cincinnati: The Hebrew Union College Press, 1977), pp. 66–71, at pp. 68–9.

28 | Halakhah and Israel

Daniel Sinclair

The 3,000-year history of the halakhah continues in the modern State of Israel. Traditional sources are studied, new commentaries are compiled, and rabbinic authorities continue to seek solutions to halakhic problems in much the same way as they did in the past. There are, however, a number of halakhic topics which are unique to modern Israel. Some are related to the special halakhic status of the Land of Israel, others have arisen as a result of the fact that in Israel the halakhic community is an active participant in the life of a secular state. Included amongst these topics are the development of acceptable technologies for the running of hospitals and other vital services on Sabbaths and festivals; the search for legitimate ways to overcome the economically unacceptable biblical prohibition on agricultural work in the Land of Israel every seventh year (*shemittah*); the need to define the practical ramifications of the sanctity of holy Jewish sites in Israel; and the challenge of maintaining the dietary laws at a national level. Halakhic development has occurred in these and other areas, and the result is a highly dynamic and creative Israeli halakhah. The fact that Hebrew is the national language contributes to this development by making access to the sources of Jewish law linguistically easier. Consequently, the observant section of Israeli society, at both its lay and rabbinic levels, is often more halakhically literate than its Diaspora counterpart.

In methodological terms, however, there is no significant difference between traditional halakhic activity in relation to the above-mentioned topics and halakhic activity in the past. Contemporary Israeli halakhists use the same traditional sources as their Diaspora forbears, and they extrapolate from them using the same type of reasoning as that employed by rabbinic authorities throughout the ages.

There is, nonetheless, a genuinely unique aspect of halakhah in Israel: the interface of halakhah and secular law. An outline of this interface provides the focus of this chapter. The State of Israel is not a theocracy; its ethos is primarily secular and liberal in nature. There are, however, certain areas in which halakhah does play an official role in the state. Marriages and divorces of Jewish citizens of Israel fall within the sole jurisdiction of the Rabbinical Courts. The determination of Jewish identity is an important factor in Israel's secular citizenship law. The Sabbath and festivals are the official rest days, and there are certain areas in Israel where there is no public transport on these days in deference to the dictates of halakhah and the sensibilities of the religious population. The army is required by law to make provision for observant soldiers, and the maintenance of the dietary laws at a national level requires the co-operation of numerous secular institutions, both political and economic. Halakhah and liberal democracy, however, do not always coincide, and secular Israeli courts are often called upon to balance these two fundamental values in Israeli society. In this context, it is important to note that in 1992 the Knesset passed the Basic Law: Human Freedom and Dignity Act, section 8 of which states explicitly that 'the underlying values of the State of Israel are Judaism and democracy'. The courts have dealt with issues such as the legitimacy of closing off certain roads to traffic on Sabbaths and festivals, the release of rabbinical students from military conscription, the rights of women to participate in urban religious councils, and the proper jurisdiction of the rabbinical authorities in granting licences attesting to compliance with the traditional dietary laws.

The following two sections of this chapter deal with some of the principles forged by Israel's secular courts in the process of dealing with the intersection of halakhah and democracy in the areas of family law and civil Jewish identity. In each section, an attempt has been made to describe both the doctrinal and social forces which have shaped these principles.

The final section deals with another uniquely Israeli aspect of halakhah: its role in secular Israeli law in general. From a halakhic point of view, one of the most exciting aspects of the Israeli legal system is the application of halakhic principles both to legislation enacted by the Knesset, and to some of the difficult and complex cases coming before the country's secular courts. This enterprise is known as *Mishpat Ivri* (Jewish Law), and its significance for both legislation and case law in Israel is outlined below.

As is evident, the focus of this chapter is the role played by the halakhah in secular Israeli law. This is undoubtedly the most challenging aspect of the application of halakhah in Israel, since it also addresses what may be the major question for the future of the halakhah in the modern age: is it possible to be faithful to both halakhah and the principles of modern liberal democracy at a principled, and not merely at a pragmatic, level? The Israeli experience is an important resource for attempting to provide an answer to this question.

Family law in Israel

Judicial autonomy in matters of personal status, that is, marriage, divorce, and related matters, was granted under Ottoman law to the different religious communities living in what is today the State of Israel, and this arrangement was maintained by the British Mandatory government. The Rabbinical Courts charged with administering family law for Jews in both the Ottoman and the Mandatory periods were staffed by traditional rabbinical scholars, and applied pure halakhah. The Chief Rabbinate, which was established by the British Mandatory government and consisted solely of traditional scholars and rabbinical judges, passed a number of enactments in this area including the fixing of a minimum sum for the *ketubah* (marriage contract), the obligation to maintain children over the age of 6 years, the legal age for marriage, and rules of procedure for the Rabbinical Courts. Jurisdiction in matters other than personal status was in the hands of the secular courts system, and was not linked to religious-communal affiliation.

The legal system created at the time of the establishment of the State of Israel in 1948 was that of the British Mandate; consequently, matters of personal status affecting Jewish citizens of Israel remained in the hands of the Rabbinical Courts. Under the Rabbinical Courts Jurisdiction (Marriage and Divorce) Act, 5713-1953, 'matters relating to the marriage and divorce of Jewish citizens or residents of the State of Israel shall be within the sole jurisdiction of the Rabbinical Courts', and the law to be applied in these matters is 'the law of the Torah'. This Act also states that a recalcitrant husband who refuses to give his wife a *get* (bill of divorce) when ordered to do so by a Rabbinical Court may be imprisoned. The sole jurisdiction of the Rabbinical Courts in family law is well entrenched in the Israeli legal system, and the Women's Equal Rights Law, 5711-1951, specifically excludes matters of marriage and divorce from the principle of equality between the sexes enshrined in this law.

Judicial review of Rabbinical Court decisions in the area of family law by secular Israeli courts is limited to jurisdictional disputes, and breaches of natural justice. In *Nagar* v. *Nagar*, S.C. 1/81, P.D. 38(1) 365, it was held that Rabbinical Courts did possess jurisdiction in relation to a dispute between divorced spouses concerning their children's education, although it is arguable that education does not, strictly, fall within the rubric of marriage and divorce. During their marriage, the couple, both of whom were then secular Jews, sent their children to a secular school. After their divorce, Mr Nagar became an observant Jew, and petitioned the Rabbinical Court for an order directing Mrs Nagar to transfer the children, who were living with her, to a religious school. Her lawyer petitioned the secular district court for an order overriding the Rabbinical Court, on the grounds that the latter had overstepped its jurisdiction. It is noteworthy that the divorce agreement also contained a clause directing any future dispute regarding the agreement to be submitted to a Rabbinical Court. A Special Court, consisting of two Supreme Court judges and one Rabbinical Court judge, held that the education of the children of divorced parents is an issue relating to marriage and divorce, and does, therefore, fall within the binding jurisdiction of the Rabbinical Courts. However, the Special Court also directed the Rabbinical Court to apply the criterion of the welfare of the child in deciding this case, and not simply to follow the traditional halakhic view that education falls solely within the purview of the father. Times have changed, and contemporary halakhah recognizes the increasing role of women in Torah study, and in the education of their children.

In *Levi* v. *District Rabbinical Court of Tel-Aviv-Jaffa*, H.C. 10/59, P.D. 13, 1182, the Supreme Court, in its role as High Court of Justice, held that a Rabbinical Court decision to change a maintenance order in favour of the husband had been made in defiance of the principles of natural justice. The order was, therefore, null and void. In this case the Rabbinical Court had been persuaded by the husband to change the order on the grounds that his estranged wife had voluntarily moved out of the matrimonial home. She had not been advised of the hearing, and did not, therefore, attend. Her lawyer, arguing that the move was, in fact, a result of constant beatings by the husband, requested another hearing in which the wife could explain her reasons for the move. This request was denied, and the maintenance was fixed in accordance with the husband's account of the separation. The wife petitioned the Supreme Court for relief on the grounds that she had been unjustly denied the natural right to make her case before the tribunal passing judgement upon her. The court found in her favour and annulled the order. It also criticized the Rabbinical Court on the basis of halakhah, according to which absolute impartiality is a vital prerequisite in all judicial proceedings (Maimonides, *Laws of the Sanhedrin*, 21: 1–3).

Under Jewish law, the only way a woman may be divorced from her husband is by receiving a get from him. Rabbinical Courts may pressure the husband, and recent legislation permits the withholding of licences, passports, and credit from recalcitrant husbands, in addition to the imprisonment option referred to above. Ultimately, however, if the husband refuses to grant his wife a get, she remains legally married to him. Since the wife is dependent upon her husband for the divorce, it is not difficult for him to use his superior legal position to gain a more favourable settlement than he deserves. In some cases husbands resist all types of pressure to divorce, and cause their wives years of anguish before the get is finally granted. A woman who is unable to remarry because of her husband's refusal to give her a get, or lack of certainty regarding his death, is referred to as an *agunah*, and the failure of the halakhic authorities to provide an effective solution for these women is, undoubtedly, a major problem in contemporary Israeli family law.

Other problematic areas of Jewish family law, at least from the perspective of the secular community, are the prohibition on marriages between Jews of priestly descent (*kohanim*) and divorcees (or converts), and the ban on marriages between the progeny of incest or maternal adultery—known as *mamzerim*—and other Jews. Mamzerim are only allowed to marry amongst themselves. Secular Israeli couples who are unable to marry as a result of these prohibitions often marry abroad. Upon their return to Israel their married status is recognized, for all non-religious purposes, by secular Israeli law. Their children, however, suffer the same impediments in Jewish marriage inside Israel, and need a foreign marriage certificate in order to obtain the practical advantages of marital status under Israeli law.

Both the agunah issue and the impediments to marriage arising from the laws applying to kohanim and mamzerim are important items in the ongoing discussions in contemporary Israel between religious and secular Jews. Amongst the solutions suggested for solving the agunah problem is the Talmudic principle that, in certain cases, the rabbis are empowered to annul marriages (*hafka'at kiddushin*). As far as the other problems are concerned, the introduction of civil marriage is often viewed as a possible solution.

Jewish identity

Under the Law of Return, 5710-1950, 'every Jew has the right to come into Israel as an immigrant'. This law was passed shortly after the establishment of the State of Israel and in the aftermath of the European Holocaust. The intention was to provide all Jews with automatic Israeli citizenship, so that no Jews would again be forced to wander the world as stateless persons. In the leading case of *Rufeisen v. Minister of the Interior*, H.C. 72/62, P.D. 16, 2442, the Supreme Court ruled that the petitioner, although born to a Jewish mother and hence halakhically Jewish, would not be granted citizenship under the Law of Return, on the grounds that he had converted to Catholicism during the Second World War, and stood before the court in the garb of a Carmelite monk with the name of Brother Daniel. The court held that the Law of Return is a secular law, hence the definition of 'Jew' is not a halakhic one. It is, in fact, to be defined by secular criteria, that is, empathy with the history of the Jewish people, and affinity with its religion. On this basis Brother Daniel could not be recognized as a Jew for purposes of automatic citizenship. The outcome of the case, which occurred not long after the end of the Second World War, was undoubtedly influenced by the negative view of Israeli society at the time towards both Holocaust apostates and the Catholic Church. The Catholic Church was particularly resented because of its attitude towards the Jews during the Holocaust.

A few years later the Supreme Court applied its secular approach to Jewish identity in a case involving an Israeli naval officer who had married a non-Jew, and wished to register his children in the Population Registry as 'Israelis without any religious affili-ation' (*Shalit v. Minister of the Interior*, H.C. 58/68, P.D. 23, 477). Since the children were not born to a Jewish mother, they were not halakhically Jewish. The court, however, following the Brother Daniel precedent, held that in principle there would be no legal bar to this type of secular registration. Nevertheless, it was unable to order the minister to register the Shalit children as secular Israelis, since there was no such category in the Population Registry Law; any change in the law would require new legislation by the Knesset. This decision incited a heated public debate between religious and secular Israelis over the issue of Jewish identity in Israeli law, and in its wake the Law of Return was amended: a Jew, for the purposes of this law, was defined as someone 'born to a Jewish mother, or converted to Judaism, and who is not the member of another faith' (sec. 4B). The amendment also provided that the right of a Jew, as defined under section 4B, to automatic citizenship 'was to be vested in a child and grandchild of a Jew, the spouse of a Jew, the spouse of a child of a Jew, and the spouse of a grandchild of a Jew, except for a person who has been a Jew, and has voluntarily changed his religion' (sec. 4A). This legislation incorporated both the halakhic definition of Jewish identity and the precedent established in the Brother Daniel case into the enacted law. It also gave expression to the secular belief that the right to automatic citizenship should not be withheld from close family members who are not halakhically Jewish for at least three generations.

The amended Law of Return has given rise to a number of issues. In *Beresford* v. *Minister of the Interior*, H.C. 265/87, P.D. 43 (4) 793, the Supreme Court was faced with the question of whether messianic Jews, that is, those born to Jewish mothers but committed to the belief that Jesus is the Messiah, are 'members of another faith' for purposes of the Law of Return. The court held that belief in Jesus is incompatible with the secular definition of Jew formulated in the *Rufeisen* and *Shalit* cases, and the messianic Jews, therefore, failed in their bid to become citizens under the Law of Return.

The issue of non-Orthodox conversion to Judaism has been considered by the Supreme Court on a number of occasions. In *Association of Torah Observant Sefardim-Tenuat Shas* v. *Director of the Population Registry*, H.C. 264/87, P.D. 40(4) 436, the court held that a declaration on the part of an immigrant that they had been converted to Judaism in the Diaspora, together with an official certificate attesting to that fact, would suffice for the purposes of citizenship under the Law of Return, and registration in the Population Registry. Once again, the court followed the secular approach to Jewish identity for citizenship purposes established in its earlier decisions. It also followed the principle of international law according to which certificates in matters of personal status issued by other countries, including certificates of conversion to Judaism, must be accepted at their face value unless patently false. In his minority judgment, Justice Elon, an Orthodox judge, argued that just as the legislator had adopted the halakhic criterion for establishing the Jewish identity of a born individual, that is, the matrilineal principle, the status of a converted Jew also ought to be determined by halakhah. In his view, only Orthodox Diaspora conversions should be recognized by Israeli law for purposes of the Law of Return and the Population Registry.

Until recently, the underlying assumption in Israeli law was that conversions carried out inside Israel would only be valid if they were approved by the Chief Rabbinate, which is, of course, an Orthodox institution. The legal basis for this assumption lay in a Mandatory Ordinance dating from 1925 which required the authorization of any conversion by the head of the religious community which the convert was seeking to join. Since the legal heads of the Jewish community are the Orthodox chief rabbis of Israel, it was evident that non-Orthodox conversions inside Israel would not possess any legal validity. This changed, however, with the decision of the Supreme Court in *Pessaro (Goldstein)* v. *Minister of the Interior*, H.C. 1031/93, P.D. 49(4) 661. In this case, the majority held that the 1925 Ordinance only applied to matters of family law, it did not affect citizenship; hence, the validity of a Reform conversion carried out inside Israel did not turn on the 1925 Ordinance. The court justified its ruling in terms of statutory interpretation, and the argument that the democratic rights of non-Orthodox Jews would be adversely affected by any other interpretation of the Ordinance, both in relation to their freedom of religion, and in the light of the principle of equal protection before the law. It is worthwhile emphasizing, however, that the court limited its decision to the scope of the 1925 Ordinance; it did not directly address the question of whether Reform conversions would be recognized by Israeli law in relation to citizenship and registration. The president of the Supreme Court, Justice Barak, stated:

We have decided that in order to recognize a conversion pursuant to the *Law of Return* and the *Population Registry Law*, it need not comply with the requirements of the 1925 Ordinance. We are not taking this matter any further. We are not deciding which conversion is valid under these two laws. We are also not deciding whether a Reform conversion is valid pursuant to the *Law of Return* ... Hence we have not ordered that the petitioner be recognized as Jewish under the *Law of Return*, and we have not ordered that she should be registered as Jewish in the Population Registry.

The strength of this caveat and its repetition attest to the tension generated by the debate over the definition of Jewish identity for the purposes of Israeli citizenship and registration. The issue of Jewish identity is fraught with symbolism, and is one of the main flashpoints in the ongoing conflict between the religious and secular populations in Israel. The Supreme Court has often been required to act as an arbiter with regard to the determination of Jewish identity in Israel, and it has never been very comfortable in this role. Clearly, the court in the *Pessaro* case did not want to make a definitive pronouncement to the effect that Jewish identity for citizenship purposes is a totally secular matter, and chose, therefore, to limit its decision to the clarification of the scope of the 1925 Ordinance.

In his minority decision, Justice Tal, an Orthodox judge, differed from his colleagues. In his view, the 1925 Ordinance granted sole jurisdiction over conversion to Judaism to the Chief Rabbinate in civil as well as family law. Furthermore, he did not accept that it was undemocratic to refuse citizenship to certain individuals on purely religious grounds. He could not find any principled distinction between refusing citizenship on grounds of poor education or low income, and doing so for religious reasons.

The Supreme Court's decision was strongly criticized by the religious parties in the Knesset, and the Ne'eman Committee was established by the Israeli government in 1990 to attempt to resolve the conversion issue in relation to citizenship and registration. In its report the Committee recommended the establishment of an educational institution for the training of candidates for conversion from all the streams of contemporary Judaism. The actual conversion ritual, however, would be performed by a Rabbinical Court consisting of Orthodox rabbis only, and the conversions would be recognized as valid by the Chief Rabbinate. There is halakhic precedent for setting up such special Rabbinical Courts for the purpose of converting candidates of dubious motivation in order to maintain Jewish unity, and stem the tide of assimilation.

However, the Ne'eman Committee's proposals were not accepted by the Chief Rabbinate, and consequently the national initiative collapsed—although one such conversion institute was established on a private basis in Jerusalem. The struggle for a formula which will accommodate both liberal democracy and fidelity to the halakhah in the area of conversion to Judaism is one of the focal issues in the contemporary dialogue between Orthodox and non-Orthodox Jews in Israel.

Mishpat Ivri

The dream of a number of nineteenth- and early-twentieth century Zionist jurists that the legal system of the Jewish state would be based upon the halakhah did not come to pass, for both practical and ideological reasons. However, the study of halakhah from the perspective of modern legal analysis (Mishpat Ivri) did become a popular and dynamic field of study for academic jurists, and courses in Mishpat Ivri are taught at all Israeli law schools. Furthermore, the selective application of halakhic rules and principles by the secular courts to a diverse range of legal problems has always been a feature of Israeli jurisprudence.

Mishpat Ivri has also underpinned a number of Israeli laws, including the Bailees Law, 5727-1967, and the Do Not Stand Idly by the Blood Of Your Neighbour Law, 5758-1998. Mention should also be made of the Foundations of Law Act, 5740-1980, which states that: 'Where a court finds that a question requiring a decision cannot be answered by reference to an enactment or a judicial precedent or by way of analogy, it shall decide the same in the light of the principles of freedom, justice, equity, and peace of the heritage of Israel.' This law replaced the Mandatory provision that all gaps in the law should be filled in on the basis of English law and equity, which had remained on Israel's statute books, in theory if not in practice, until 1980. The scope of the 1980 law was debated by the Supreme Court in the case of *Kupat Am Bank* v. *Hendeles*, F.H. 13/80, P.D. 35(2) 785, and the majority decided that it was to be restricted to genuine gaps in the law (*lacunae*), which arise very rarely in a modern legal system. In his minority judgment, Justice Elon argued that the intention of the legislator had been to make Mishpat Ivri the primary source for judicial interpretation in difficult and complex cases in relation to which there is no clear answer in secular Israeli law. In practice, the Supreme Court in particular has always made use of Mishpat Ivri, and continues to do so, especially in cases involving serious moral and ethical issues. Defining the precise normative significance of the Foundations of Law Act is, therefore, not all that critical an issue for the future of Mishpat Ivri in Israeli law.

A striking illustration of the role played by Mishpat Ivri in secular Israeli law is the case of *Moshe Cohen* v. *State of Israel*, Cr. A 91/80, P.D. 35(3) 281, in which a husband was found guilty of raping his wife on the basis of the halakhic principles governing marital intercourse. At the time of the trial, the relevant section of the 5737-1977 Penal Code governing rape provided that a charge of rape could only be brought if the act of intercourse was an 'illegal' one. This term reflected the common-law doctrine that a husband could not be charged with the rape of his wife which was, in turn, based upon the Christian concept of the wife's obligation to pay the 'marital debt', that is, to provide her body to her husband. Under the common law, therefore, coercive intercourse with a wife could never be illegal, and the Israeli law was interpreted in this light. The prosecution in the *Cohen* case argued that the word 'illegal' should in fact be understood in accordance with Jewish law, since Moshe Cohen was an Israeli Jew and, as such, was bound by the halakhah in relation to matters of personal status. Biblical law grants a wife a right to sexual gratification from her husband (Exodus 21: 10) but not vice versa. The halakhah provides that a wife who refuses to have sex with her husband may be divorced; she is certainly not compelled to give her body to him. Indeed, the use of force is specifically forbidden in the context of marital sex (Maimonides, *Laws of Marriage*, 15: 17). The Supreme Court, in rejecting the appeal, held that the extrapolation from the realm of halakhic prohibitions to that of rape in the criminal law was perfectly legitimate, and upheld the guilty verdict.

In the *Cohen* case the application of Mishpat Ivri resulted in an unimpeachably liberal result, to the satisfaction of halakhists and secular democrats alike. The result in *Kurtam* v. *State of Israel*, Cr.A. 480/85, P.D. 40(3) 637, however, whilst not necessarily an illiberal one, would probably not be acceptable across the spectrum of contemporary liberal thought. In this case the appellant, a suspected drug-dealer, was operated on by a police surgeon against his express wishes, and two packages of pure heroin were removed from his stomach without his consent. The ostensible justification for the actions of the surgeon was the need to save Kurtam's life. Without the operation, it is likely that he would have died of an overdose. Upon his recovery Kurtam was charged with drug-dealing, and the packages of drugs removed from his stomach were entered in evidence against him. His defence was that the evidence was inadmissible since he had refused consent to the operation, and it had, therefore, been obtained by illegal means. Non-consensual life-saving medical procedures offend both against the right to privacy in Israeli law and the general principles of democracy. The Supreme Court ruled that the heroin was admissible evidence, and Justice Beiski cited Mishpat Ivri in support of the ruling. According to the halakhah, a sick person is under an obligation to accept life-saving medical treatment, and if he refuses coercion may be applied, as in the case of any refusal to perform a positive halakhic precept (R. Jacob Emden, *Mor Ukeziah, Orah Hayyim*, no. 328). This obligation is predicated upon the principle that bodies are owned by God, and divine property may not be destroyed at will. Citing the Foundations of Law Act, Justice Beiski ruled that the drugs were admissible evidence since, under Jewish law, 'the patient's wishes are of no account . . . and his lack of consent is irrelevant'. He also noted that the Jewish principle of the sanctity of human life had already been incorporated into Israeli law by the Supreme Court in 1962, in a case involving the issue of the freedom of contract. In *Zim* v. *Maziar*, C.A. 461/62, P.D. 17, 1319, the Supreme Court held that there was no freedom to include a clause in a contract for the maritime carriage of passengers absolving the company from any responsibility for damage to the health or life of those passengers as a result of the company's actions. It is noteworthy that Justice Beiski did not point out that the halakhah does recognize exceptions to the obligatory nature of medical therapy, or that coercing people to observe *mitzvot* is no longer an option in contemporary halakhah. In this particular case, however, the halakhah would have reached the same conclusion as did the Supreme Court that is, the evidence is admissible since it was not illegally obtained; Kurtam was under a legal duty to save his own life under Jewish law.

In a later Supreme Court decision Justice Elon clarified the issue of mandatory medical treatment in the halakhah, and asserted that the patient's wishes certainly do possess normative weight, especially in the case of terminally ill patients who are likely to suffer greatly as a result of any attempt to force life-sustaining treatments upon them (*Yael Sheffer* v. *State of Israel*, C.A. 560/88, P.D. 48(1) 87).

Coercive life-saving therapy is also a statutory option under Israeli law. Section 15(2) of the Patient's Rights Law, 5756-1996, provides that a hospital ethics committee is authorized to approve non-voluntary therapy if the patient is fully informed of the medical background and prognosis, all the treating doctors agree that coercive therapy is the only sure way to save the patient's life, and 'there is a reasonable possibility that the patient will consent retroactively'. Clearly, the last requirement is an attempt to combine patient autonomy with halakhic obligation, which is, after all, the hallmark of Mishpat Ivri in modern Israeli law.

FURTHER READING

Elon, M. *Jewish Law: History, Sources, Principles* (Philadelphia: Jewish Publication Society, 1994). This comprehensive four-volume work explains the methodology of Mishpat Ivri, and the role played by Jewish law in the Israeli legal system.

Freeman, M. (ed.), *Jewish Family Law in the State of Israel*, Jewish Law Association Studies, 13 (New York: State University of New York at Binghamton, 2002). A collection of articles dealing with the debate over civil marriage in Israel, the relationship between secular and religious courts in Israeli family law, temporary separation orders, the maintenance of minor children, and husbands who refuse to pay the *ketubah* or maintain their minor children.

Frimer, D. 'Israel Civil Courts and Rabbinical Courts Under One Roof', *Israel Law Review*, 24 (1990), pp. 553–9. Surveys the interaction between the two systems of law in modern Israel, that is, traditional halakhah and secular law in the context of family law, and argues for closer co-operation between them.

Hecht, N., B. Jackson, S. Passamaneck, D. Piatelli, and A. Rabello (eds.). *An Introduction to the History and Sources of Jewish Law* (Oxford: Oxford University Press, 1996). Each chapter is written by an expert in a different field of the historical development of Jewish law, including the modern period.

Jackson, B. (ed.). *Modern Research in Jewish Law* (Leiden: E. J. Brill, 1980). The Mishpat Ivri enterprise has given rise to a debate amongst Israeli legal and halakhic scholars with regard to its legitimacy. The question is whether Mishpat Ivri is an authentic expression of halakhah, or merely a secularization of the Jewish legal heritage. This collection presents the main articles in this debate, most of which were especially translated into English for the volume.

The editor's Introduction provides a theoretical framework for the differing views of the various authors.

Shifman, P. 'Family Law in Israel: The Struggle Between Religious and Secular Law', *Israel Law Review*, 24 (1990), pp. 537–52. A discussion of the tensions between the traditional halakah administered by the Israeli Rabbinical Courts, and secular family law as administered in the secular courts system. Amongst the issues raised is the introduction of civil marriage for the good of both religious law and the state.

Shilo, S. 'The Contrast Between *Mishpat Ivri* and *Halakhah*', *Tradition*, 20 (1982), pp. 91–100. A brief discussion of the major differences between traditional halakhic methodology and that of Mishpat Ivri. The article also makes a case for wider use of the Mishpat Ivri methodology.

Sinclair, D. *Jewish Biomedical Law: Legal and Extra-legal Dimensions* (Oxford: Oxford University Press, 2003). Each chapter in this book includes a description of the way in which halakhic principles in the field of biomedical law have been incorporated into Israeli jurisprudence.

29 | Contemporary issues in halakhah

Steven H. Resnicoff

Halakhah (Jewish law) applies to all facets of life: to public issues, such as whether the State of Israel can halakhically trade land for peace; and to private issues, such as whether, and under what circumstances, a person may halakhically participate in modern reproductive procedures.

Most halakhic enquiries fall into one of two categories. The first type asks what halakhah says about the propriety of a particular action (or inaction), the status of a particular thing, or the status, rights, or responsibilities of a particular person. Such questions generally enquire as to what the halakhah *is* with respect to the specific issue at hand.

The second sort of question typically arises in response to a perceived or actual social problem, and asks what, if anything, halakhah permits to be done to resolve it. While such questions attempt to ascertain what the halakhah is, they also explore whether there are authentic, halakhically recognized processes through which the halakhah may be changed.

Because questions as to what the halakhah *is* predominate, these will be examined first and will occupy most of the chapter. The chapter will conclude by considering contemporary calls for halakhic change.

An introduction to the halakhic system

To comprehend halakhah's approach to any specific contemporary problem, it is necessary to understand some basic facts about the halakhic system. Among its axioms are: (1) that biblical laws arise from teachings communicated by God to Moses; (2) that God commanded Moses to transcribe some of these teachings; (3) that these teachings were transcribed and constitute the Five Books of Moses, known either as the Written Law or the Written Torah; and (4) that God instructed Moses not to transcribe other teachings, known as the Oral Law or the Oral Torah, because they were to be transmitted orally from generation to generation. The Oral Torah resolves ostensible inconsistencies in the Written Torah, provides supplementary precepts, and articulates hermeneutic rules through which the Written Torah is interpreted and yet additional laws derived.

In a period of particularly harsh persecution against the teaching of Torah, the sages, fearing that knowledge of the Oral Torah might be forgotten, permitted it to be recorded in an abbreviated form as the *Mishnah, c.*188 CE. The teachings of the Mishnah were debated in academies in Jerusalem and Babylonia over several hundreds of years. These discussions not only addressed biblical law but also non-biblical law, such as rabbinical enactments, which were promulgated from time to time. These halakhic debates were recorded in the Jerusalem Talmud, completed *c.*350 CE, and the Babylonian Talmud, completed *c.*500 CE, which is the more authoritative.

Jewish law is not a *literalist* tradition. Where there is a conflict between the 'plain language' of a Written Torah verse and the non-literal Talmudic interpretation of the verse, Jewish law recognizes the Talmudic position as the correct one. Thus, although the words of the Written Torah (Exodus 21: 23–5 and Leviticus 24: 19–20) ostensibly posit *lex talionis* ('an eye for an eye'), tractate *Bava Kamma* (the First Gate) of the Babylonian Talmud explains that this verse is not to be construed literally but, instead, merely establishes that a tortfeasor is obligated to pay the *monetary value* of any limb the victim has lost.

To the extent that the Babylonian Talmud *definitively* resolves an issue of halakhah, later sages are generally not authorized to overrule that resolution. However, the Talmud conclusively rules on only a limited number of cases. Consequently, post-Talmudic authorities have decided untold thousands of questions not expressly or precisely addressed in the Talmud. Many of these decisions are recorded as responsa literature and become precedents which influence the judgment of subsequent authorities.

Rendering halakhic decisions involves three principal steps. First, through thorough and close examination of Talmudic and post-Talmudic texts, authorities gain a conceptual understanding of halakhic rules. Second, they carefully ascertain and scrutinize the facts of each case put to them. Finally, they apply the halakhah to the facts; they extrapolate from applicable Talmudic and post-Talmudic rulings to the case at hand.

Sociological developments exacerbate this task. As a practical matter, for instance, the increasingly global economy means that foods and goods are often grown, manufactured, or treated at great distances from their ultimate destinations, and it is therefore sometimes difficult to obtain adequate and reliable information regarding their provenance. This fact makes it difficult to determine whether such foods are permissible to be eaten in light of *kashrut* rules as well as special halakhic restrictions on products grown in Israel. Similarly, some of the halakhic rules governing the interaction between Jews and non-Jews depend on whether the non-Jews in question are halakhically regarded as idolaters. Making such a determination requires evaluation not only of their specific religious practices, which change over time, but also of the intent which accompanies those practices. As time passes, a group's members may lose sight of, or may reject, the original purposes for their practices. If so, then even if the members of a particular group were once halakhically regarded as idolaters, they may no longer bear that designation, and the halakhic rules regarding interaction with such people will change.

A number of rabbinic rules pertain to Jews who purposefully violate halakhah. Nevertheless, Rabbi Avraham Isaiah Karelitz, known as Hazon Ish (1878–1953), one of the most prominent rabbinic authorities of the twentieth century, explains that at least some of these rules are only applicable to those whose non-observance reflects a deep-seated rebelliousness against God. Halakhah requires Jews to admonish, sensitively and lovingly, a fellow Jew who violates halakhah. A person's refusal to respond appropriately to sincere rebuke reflects a defiant hostility toward God, especially during historical eras in which God manifests the divine presence openly. Kareliz, however, maintains that in the contemporary world most people lack the ability to admonish others with the proper warmth and affection. Moreover, he states that in our days God's presence is not openly revealed. Consequently, a person's failure to conform to halakhah does not necessarily reflect contumacy, rendering some of those specific rabbinic rules inapplicable.

Scientific and technological changes also complicate the halakhic decision-making process, because halakhic authorities must constantly learn about new, complex mechanisms and procedures and must place them into halakhically recognized conceptual categories. For example, permanent colouring, painting, or dyeing constitutes one of the categories of work prohibited on the Sabbath, and temporary colouring is forbidden by rabbinic decree. Does the taking of photosensitive eyeglasses into sunlight on the Sabbath, causing the lenses to darken, violate this rabbinic decree? Rabbi Ovadiah Yosef (b. 1920), a former chief Sephardic rabbi of Israel, rules that it does not.[1] The categories of work forbidden on the Sabbath are based on the performance of similar labour in the construction of the Tabernacle in the wilderness. Because the colouring used in that construction involved the use of pigments, the colouring that is biblically forbidden on the Sabbath involves the application of one material to another. For halakhic purposes, the sun's rays are not characterized as material substances. Consequently, the coloration caused by exposure of the lenses to the sun's rays is not biblically proscribed. Nor does wearing such glasses violate the rabbinic rule, because the rabbinic decree only applies to the types of coloration which, if permanent, would be biblically forbidden.

Another example involves the prohibition (Deutronomy 12: 2–4) against erasing God's name or any letter of God's name. Does this apply to 'erasing' (or overwriting) God's name from an audiocassette? The sounds produced by an audiocassette are a result of magnetic patterns created by electric charges. Rabbi Yosef and Rabbi Yosef Shalom Elyashiv (b. 1911) rule that it does not, because, at least in part, such erasing does not involve the destruction of any halakhically cognizable substance.[2] What about erasing the name from a computer? The correct answer may depend on whether it is erased from a hard disk, floppy disk, or compact disk because different technologies may be involved.[3]

Of course, sometimes it is not that the technology is difficult to understand, but that the results of the technology are difficult to interpret. Advances in medical science having the salutary effect of extending life have had the side-effect of spawning considerable controversy as to when a person is halakhically dead. Resolution of this debate in any particular case can be critically important. Not only is it relevant to the monetary rights of his or her heirs and the personal rights of his or her spouse, but it can also determine when and if scarce resources, including, possibly, the person's own organs, may be halakhically used to save the life of another.

Space constraints prevent a detailed examination of any contemporary halakhic issue. Nevertheless, it is instructive to note at least a few of the salient areas of contemporary concern.

Contemporary medical ethics problems

Medical ethics matters are among the most significant, challenging, and contentious contemporary halakhic problems. One reason is that these questions often involve enormously important stakes, including, literally, life and death. Another reason is that scientific breakthroughs have introduced choices that did not generally exist in Talmudic times. Consequently, there are few if any directly pertinent Talmudic precedents, and the relevance of the sources that are cited is often more attenuated than that of precedents in other areas. Extrapolation from such sources is therefore more difficult and more debatable. Still another explanation for such intense halakhic attention to medical practices is that, irrespective of whether they are halakhically permitted, many of them will be performed, and their halakhic consequences can be far-reaching. Modern reproductive processes, for instance, raise questions as to the halakhic status of the offspring and the familial relationships between the offspring and the various people who participated in the process.

Cloning

The successful cloning of a person would create the person's genetic twin through an asexual process using the person's cellular material, rather than the person's sperm or egg. Cloning involves the replacement of the nucleus of an egg with the nucleus of a cell of the person to be cloned. If a woman is successfully cloned using the woman's own egg, the clone will be a perfect genetic copy. If a woman is cloned using another woman's egg, or if a man is cloned, then the clone will be an extremely close, but not perfect, genetic copy, because it will still have the mitochondrial DNA of the woman whose egg is used.

Cloning was not a scientific option in Talmudic times, and there is no unambiguously relevant Talmudic precedent. Perhaps the closest ancient analogy involves golems, anthropoids created from inanimate substances through mystical means. Medieval and post-medieval rabbinic literature reports that golems were created by a number of highly reputable halakhic authorities. For example, Rabbi Zevi Ashkenazi

(1660–1718)[4] reports that his grandfather, Rabbi Elijah Ba'al Shem of Helm, created a golem. This literature provides no suggestion that such conduct was in any way wrongful. Indeed, it seems that cloning someone with cellular material taken from a living person does not violate any precise halakhic rule.

Still, some commentators argue that by cloning human beings, humanity wrongfully encroaches on a province reserved to God, the Almighty Creator. They contend that, even if no specific prohibition applies, any effort to clone human beings would contravene the proper nature of the relationship between humanity and God.

But most authorities seem to disagree, relying in part on God's direction to Adam to 'fill the earth and conquer it' (Genesis 1: 28), and on numerous midrashic sources emphasizing humankind's active role in creation. Some quote the language of Sabbath night's Kiddush, which refers to 'all of the work God created to *make*' (Genesis 2: 3; emphasis added), as referring to man's creative role. As to this role, Rabbi Yonatan Eibeschutz (c.1690–1764) and Rabbi Joseph Ber Soloveitchik (1820–92) explain that God purposely halted the process of creation before it was completed in order that humankind might contribute the missing parts. Citing these and other sources, Rabbi J. David Bleich (b. 1936) concludes:

It is abundantly clear that human intervention in the natural order is normatively interdicted only to the extent that there are explicit prohibitions limiting such intervention. Moreover, there is no evidence either from scripture or from rabbinic writings that forms of intervention or manipulation not expressly banned are contrary to the spirit of the law.[5]

Nor is the mere *possibility* that clones could be misused to contravene halakhic values relevant, absent some substantial basis for believing this would occur. After all, halakhah permits the manufacture of all sorts of items, from steak knives to weaponry, that could possibly be misused by wrongdoers.

On the other hand, most rabbinic authorities believe that, at least in the vast majority of circumstances, producing a clone certainly would not be halakhically required or even encouraged. Most authorities believe that by having oneself cloned, a person would not fulfil any applicable halakhic duty to procreate. Therefore, if cloning technology were perfected, the question whether to engage in cloning or to take actions encouraging or discouraging others from engaging in cloning would in most cases be more a question of judgement than of strict halakhah. Of course, if a person did have himself or herself successfully cloned, this would definitely raise halakhic questions regarding the status of the clone and the halakhic relationship between the clone and the person who was cloned.

There are rare instances in which having oneself cloned might enable a person to fulfil the *mitzvah* of helping to save someone's life. In such cases the person might even save his or her own life. For example, a person with leukaemia may need a bone-marrow transplant in order to survive, and there may be no compatible or willing donor available. It may be possible to clone the sick person so that a healthy and genetically compatible potential donor would be born. Some secular ethicists would object that this process would effectively treat the clone as a 'thing' or 'means to an end' rather than as a person. From a halakhic perspective, this objection, even if it were otherwise valid, would be outweighed by the opportunity to possibly save a human life. Moreover, from a halakhic perspective the objection may simply be invalid. The basis of the objection may be that the person producing the clone is doing so for some ulterior purpose. But this is arguably similar to the halakhically laudatory act of engaging in natural procreative activity for the objective of fulfilling God's commandment to procreate or fulfilling God's will that the earth be populated. Alternatively, the basis of the objection may be that, once produced, the clone is being used to provide bone marrow to serve the needs of the person with leukaemia. But the clone would not be halakhically treated differently from any naturally born person who was a compatible donor. In any event, if a genetically compatible clone were produced, there are halakhic safeguards which would limit the types of medical procedures that could be performed on the clone to ensure that the clone's health were not jeopardized.

In fact, however, the process of cloning, especially the cloning of humans, is far from perfected. Current efforts to clone human beings may result in the clones' being tragically handicapped. The possibility of causing such harm raises yet additional halakhic considerations which a rabbinic authority would have to evaluate.

Embryonic stem cell research

Another important debate focuses on the halakhic permissibility of embryonic stem cell research. The possible benefits to be derived from successful stem cell research are great. It may ultimately help to provide replacement organs, enable people with spinal injuries to walk again, or cure serious conditions or diseases such as diabetes, Alzheimer's, or Parkinson's.

According to most authorities, there are no halakhic problems with stem cell research per se. As with cloning, most authorities believe that humankind has an active role to play in the controlling of what would appear to be natural processes, especially when the purpose is to develop medical remedies. Consequently, the halakhic problem with *embryonic* stem cell research is that the stem cells are procured by destroying the embryos from which they are taken. This destruction of embryos may violate certain halakhic rules. In such cases, the question is whether, as a matter of halakhah, there is an adequate basis for excusing that possible violation.

The worst-case scenario would be if, under halakhah, the destruction of the embryo constituted some form of homicide. If so, then destroying the embryo in order to do research would not be permitted. There is considerable debate on this point. As Bleich points out, a number of prominent rabbinic authorities, including Rabbi Moshe Feinstein (1895–1986) and Rabbi Isser Yehuda Unterman (1886–1976), former chief Ashkenazic rabbi of Israel, contend that the prohibition against destroying an embryo falls within the halakhic prohibition against homicide.[6]

Even according to this position, however, it may be permissible to procure embryonic stem cells in certain situations. First, non-human stem cells could be used; there is no halakhic prohibition against killing animals for a constructive purpose such as medical research. Second, it may be halakhically permissible to destroy non-viable embryos for a constructive purpose. Destruction of an embryo might only constitute a form of homicide because it involves the destruction of the embryo's potential for life. A non-viable embryo, which cannot result in a live birth, lacks any such potential.

The question, then, is which embryos should, for halakhic purposes, be deemed non-viable? Some naturally or artificially conceived embryos may simply be unable to survive without major medical intervention and some even with such intervention. The latter, at the very least, should be halakhically considered as non-viable. In addition, there may be a halakhically permissible mechanism for creating non-viable embryos. By chemically treating the eggs of certain animals, scientists have been able, through a process called parthenogenesis, to induce these eggs to divide and develop into embryos, called parthenotes. There has been limited success in creating human parthenotes, and these human parthenotes are widely believed to be non-viable. If so, then it might be permissible to create such parthenotes for the sole purpose of destroying them and taking their stem cells. Rabbi Moshe Sternbuch (b. 1925) goes a step further, arguing that any embryo artificially created in a petri dish and still in the petri dish should be treated as a non-viable embryo because, if left in its present state, the embryo would perish. But making parthenogenesis work on humans has not been easy, and the supply of other non-viable embryos is too small and uncertain to provide an adequate source of stem cells for widespread research.

For various reasons, a number of rabbinic authorities disagree with the Feinstein and Unterman view that destroying a human embryo constitutes homicide. One position contends that destroying an embryo within the first forty days of its inception constitutes no halakhic violation at all. Another argument is that, even if the destruction of an embryo, whether during or after the first forty days, would otherwise involve some halakhic prohibition, the prohibition is much less serious than homicide and is superseded, in accordance with applicable halakhic rules, by the positive purposes served by stem cell research.

Interestingly, according to virtually all of the authorities, any halakhic problem arises at the time an embryo might be destroyed and stem cells obtained. A researcher who was not responsible for the destruction of the embryo could permissibly pursue research on the stem cells. Of course, this opens up a new, interesting line of enquiry, one which goes beyond the scope of this chapter, as to when someone may be halakhically responsible for an action that he or she has not directly done. Both the Beth Din of America and the Orthodox Union have announced, in separate statements, at least limited support for ongoing stem cell research.

Contemporary calls for halakhic change

At any given time, perceived and actual social problems give rise to calls for halakhic change to redress such matters. There are certain general rules regarding legitimate halakhic change. Biblical laws may be divided into two groups: (1) those that principally deal with monetary obligations (*dinei mamonot*) between and among people; and (2) those that primarily involve conduct that God requires, encourages, discourages, or forbids (*dinei issura*). The first group of rules can usually be changed by agreement of the parties. This agreement may be express. Alternatively, if there are established commercial customs in the relevant locality, then, unless the parties expressly agree to depart from those customs, it is as if they had specifically agreed to abide by them. This halakhic doctrine, known as *minhag ha-Soharim*, essentially treats such customs as 'default terms' for commercial contracts. This is true even if the majority of the people in the location are non-Jews and they are the ones who established the customs.

Similarly, to the extent that Jews in individual localities organize into communities, they could theoretically agree to different commercial rules through the enactment of communal legislation. This process, however, requires a broad consensus regarding the identity of authentic community leaders and an appropriate legislative process. In contemporary times, relatively few Jewish communities enjoy such a consensus.

Halakhic business law can also change through a doctrine known as *dina demalkhuta dina*, literally, 'the law of the kingdom is law'. When applicable, this doctrine provides that the non-discriminatory provisions of secular law that pertain to monetary obligations are halakhically valid. Some authorities believe that secular law has halakhic force only if there is widespread compliance with the law, because such compliance creates a binding local custom.

There are three principal views as to the scope of dina demalkhuta dina. Rabbi Yosef Caro (1488–1575), author of the *Shulhan Arukh*, the most authoritative code of Jewish law, maintains that this rule only validates laws, such as tax laws, that directly benefit the government's financial interests. By contrast, Rabbi Moshe Isserles (1530–72), whose gloss on the *Shulhan Arukh* is invariably published together with it, believes that dina demalkhuta dina also applies to laws that are enacted for the public good. Finally, Rabbi Shabsai Hakohen (1622–63) espouses a modified version of Isserles's position by stating that dina demalkhuta dina does not apply where it conflicts with an explicit halakhic rule.[7] Most Jewish law authorities follow one of the latter two approaches. As a result, modern commercial legislation designed to promote the public good, such as anti-trust, bankruptcy, and food and drug regulation laws, provide new halakhic responses to changing commercial circumstances.

Agreement, custom, and secular law, however, do not change dinei issura, even when dinei issura entail financial repercussions. Thus, even though two people's status as married or divorced has an important impact on their respective monetary rights and responsibilities, its main significance pertains to the nature of their personal status and the nature of permissible relationships with each other and with third parties. Consequently, their marital status is a matter of dinei issura, and divorce can only be accomplished through a valid Jewish divorce decree. A civil divorce decree is halakhically ineffective.

Chapter 27 describes the dilemma of the *agunah*, a woman whose marriage has failed but whose husband refuses to comply with a rabbinic court order to grant her a divorce so that she might be free to remarry. The rules regarding marriage and divorce are complex, making it infeasible to discuss them in detail. Nevertheless, it is important to summarize some contemporary developments.

Talmudic authorities recognize that a unilateral mistake by a woman about a seriously adverse, undisclosed physical condition of the man at the time of a marriage may be a ground for annulment of the marriage. This principle is known as *kiddushei ta'ut*. A rabbinic court that annulled a marriage under such circumstances would not be changing the halakhah, but simply applying it. This principle bears no obvious relevance to the plight of women who, after marrying husbands free from any unknown physical blemish, found these husbands to be emotionally or physically abusive.

In 1997 a small group of Orthodox rabbis, led by Rabbi Emanuel Rackman, formed a purported rabbinic court (*bet din*) in New York for the purpose of alleviating the agunah problem. This group, supposedly relying on the doctrine of kiddushei ta'ut, began to annul numerous marriages in which the husband did not have serious physical defects. Instead, this group held that the doctrine applied much more broadly and, for example, used it to annul marriages if it found that, at the time of the marriage, the husband had a serious, unknown character defect. To this writer's knowledge, no established Orthodox authority agrees with the positions or actions of this group.

Another possibility, while not new, has been recently re-proposed. This is that, even where kiddushei ta'ut is inapplicable, rabbinic authorities should cancel marriages retroactively where a husband who is halakhically obligated to divorce his wife refuses to do so. There is some limited Talmudic precedent for such action. Did this precedent involve *changing* the biblical halakhah? Not really. According to biblical law, one way in which a man sanctifies a woman, through *kiddushin*, to become his wife is by giving her something he owns which has at least a certain specified value. In practice, this is accomplished when the groom gives his bride a wedding ring. However, an inherent power of qualified rabbinic authorities is to deprive a person of his or her ownership of property. Therefore, the Talmudic precedent is explained as follows: the rabbis retroactively deprived the groom of ownership of the wedding ring immediately prior to the time when he gave it to his bride. Thus, the rabbis changed a *relevant legal fact*. After the fact was changed, it turned out that the groom did not give his bride anything that he owned at the time of the kiddushin. Applying the unchanged biblical rule to these facts results in a conclusion that there was no valid kiddushin, and therefore no marriage.

Jewish law recognizes that rabbinic sages possess limited authority to alter some *legal facts* or, under carefully circumscribed conditions, to affect previously promulgated rabbinic (as opposed to biblical) rules. Nevertheless, for various reasons rabbinic leaders would employ such authority with considerable restraint and only after reaching a strong consensus among recognized rabbinic authorities.

Some of the more recent 'movements' within Judaism, such as the Conservative and the Reform movements, have departed from this traditional approach to change. The Conservative movement, for instance, has established a Committee on Jewish Law and Standards which purports to determine 'Jewish law' for the Conservative movement. This committee, however, goes beyond the purview of traditional rabbinic authority by permitting practices that are largely considered violations of biblical law. Similarly, the Reform movement, through its principal rabbinical assembly, the Central Conference of American Rabbis (the CCAR), votes on issues of Jewish law without considering itself to be bound by biblical law.

Interestingly, it remains a standard of the Conservative movement that a civil divorce is insufficient to enable a married Jew to remarry.[8] By contrast, the CCAR has voted to treat civil divorces as sufficient.

Another issue involving issura regards same-sex marriage. Although advocates of such unions have been successful in some civil courts, Jewish law does not recognize the religious validity of same-sex marriages, a position the Reform movement has upheld.[9]

Many important contemporary issues have arisen relatively recently and have engendered inconsistent rabbinic rulings. One such issue involves the degree to which it is permissible for a woman to participate in the political process and hold public office, a topic debated by, among others, the first three chief rabbis of the State of Israel.[10] Another type of issue deals with the political position, if any, that Jews should take as to the legislation or enforcement of particular civil laws, from those authorizing capital punishment or same-sex civil unions on the one hand, to those banning missionary work on the other. What is halakhically desirable in such cases, however, may importantly depend on the likely pragmatic ramifications of the positions taken. These halakhic 'facts' must be determined after consultation with those whose expertise is to predict such consequences.

Conclusion

Technological and scientific innovations introduce novel halakhic questions and complicate resolution of existing ones. Displaying sophisticated technological and scientific knowledge, halakhic authorities are answering these questions. Other issues, such as the agunah problem, are socially significant and controversial. The absence of a central halakhic figure or institution whose authority is universally acknowledged and who could command a broad consensus is a major handicap in resolving these matters. Some of the sociological developments mentioned in Chapter 27 have worsened the problem by undermining the authority of rabbinic figures. Dealing with the need for, and the creation of, consensus as to the most contentious and sensitive issues remains one of the greatest halakhic challenges of contemporary Judaism.

FURTHER READING

Bleich, J. David. *Bioethical Dilemmas: A Jewish Perspective* (Hoboken, NJ: Ktav, 1998). Contains twelve chapters, each of which provides a halakhic examination of a specific medical ethics issue, such as AIDS, HIV screening for newborns, artificial procreation, surrogacy, treatment of the terminally ill, and conjoined twins.

Bleich, J. David. *Contemporary Halakhic Problems*, Vols. I–IV (Hoboken, NJ: Ktav, 1979–95). Each of these four volumes addresses diverse contemporary halakhic questions regarding commercial, professional, social, and ritual matters. Many of these topics are explored in considerable detail, while others are treated more briefly.

Breitowitz, Irving A. *Between Civil and Religious Law: The Plight of the Agunah in American Society* (Westport, Conn.: Greenwood Press, 1993). Extensively examines the halakhic and secular legal difficulties in using secular courts to resolve the agunah problem.

Broyde, Michael J. *Marriage, Divorce and the Abandoned Wife in Jewish Law* (Hoboken, NJ: Ktav, 2001). Focuses on the contemporary agunah problem in the United States, describes halakhic options, and argues that prenuptial agreements can minimize the problem. See also http://www.mucjs.org/agunahunit.htm, the website of the Agunah Research Unit established at the University of Manchester, a recent academic initiative trying to address the issue of the agunah in the United Kingdom.

Cohen, Alfred S. *Halacha and Contemporary Society* (Hoboken, NJ: Ktav, 1984). Contains an introduction and fourteen essays involving contemporary halakhic issues confronting the Jewish family, the Jewish community, and each individual Jew.

Elon, Menachem, *et al. Jewish Law (Mishpat Ivri): Cases and Materials* (New York: Matthew Bender & Co., 1999). This book, intended to be the main textbook for use in an American law-school course on Jewish law, describes the basic elements of the halakhic system. In addition, it provides English translations of excerpts from primary halakhic materials plus selected opinions of the Israel Supreme Court.

Feldman, Emanuel, and Joel B. Wolowelsky (eds.). *Jewish Law and the New Reproductive Technologies* (Hoboken, NJ: Ktav, 1997). Consists of eight essays, each of which had previously appeared in the periodical *Tradition*.

Herring, Basil F. *Jewish Ethics and Halakhah For Our Time*, Vols. I–II (New York: Ktav, 1984, 1989). Each chapter of these two books introduces a contemporary topic, poses a detailed fact pattern and related questions, provides English translations of excerpts from relevant rabbinic literature, and explores, in essay form, possible answers to the questions by reference to the excerpts and to additional authorities.

Jacob, Walter (ed.). *American Reform Responsa: Jewish Questions, Rabbinic Answers* (New York: Central Conference of American Rabbis, 1983). Contains the complete text of all 172 responsa issued by the Central Conference of American Rabbis until 1982, as well as its 'Report of the Committee on Patrilineal Descent on the Status of Children of Mixed Marriages', adopted by that body of Reform rabbis in 1983.

Jacob, Walter. *Contemporary American Reform Responsa* (New York: Central Conference of American Rabbis, 1987). Contains 202 responsa authored by Jacob, who was chairman of the Central Conference of American Rabbis' Responsa Committee from 1976 through publication of this book.

Jacob, Walter, and Moshe Zemer (eds.). *Gender Issues in Jewish Law: Essays and Responsa* (New York: Berghahn Books, 2001). Includes seven essays by Reform writers, one essay by a Conservative rabbi, and several Reform responsa which address issues regarding either gender or sexual orientation.

Kellner, Menachem Marc. *Contemporary Jewish Ethics* (Brooklyn, NY: Hebrew Publishing Co., 1978). Contains twenty-eight essays by different authors, most of which address contemporary halakhic issues regarding politics, medicine, criminal law, commerce, and gender.

Rakover, N. *Jewish Law and Current Legal Problems* (Jerusalem: Jewish Legal Heritage Society, 1984). Contains relatively short essays, many of which explore contemporary halakhic issues involving criminal law and medical ethics.

Rosner, Fred. *Biomedical Ethics and Jewish Law* (Hoboken, NJ: Ktav, 2001). Lord Immanuel Jakobovits, former chief rabbi of the United Hebrew Congregations of the British Commonwealth, wrote the Foreword for this book, which addresses thirty-nine medical ethics issues.

Sacks, Jonathan (ed). *Orthodoxy Confronts Modernity* (Hoboken, NJ: Ktav, 1991). Edited by the current chief rabbi of the United Hebrew Congregations of the British Commonwealth, this book contains essays by him and nine other leading contemporary Jewish scholars.

NOTES

1. See J. David Bleich, 'Survey of Recent Halakhic Periodical Literature', *Tradition*, 17: 2 (Spring 1978), pp. 104–5.
2. See Aryeh Brueckheimer, 'Halacha and Technology: Erasing G-d's Name from a Computer', *Journal of Halacha and Contemporary Society* (Spring 2003), pp. 50–64.
3. Ibid.
4. *Teshuvot Hakham Zevi*, 93.
5. J. David Bleich, 'Survey of Recent Halakhic Periodical Literature', *Tradition*, 32: 3 (Spring 1998), pp. 47–86, at p. 56.
6. Bleich, 'Survey of Halakhic Periodical Literature: Stem Cell Research', *Tradition*, 36: 2 (Summer 2002), pp. 56–83.
7. See Steven H. Resnicoff, 'Bankruptcy—A Viable Halachic Option?' *Journal of Halacha and Contemporary Society*, 24 (1992), pp. 5–54.
8. Elliot N. Dorff, *Conservative Judaism: Our Ancestors To Our Descendents* (New York: National Youth Commission, United Synagogue of Conservative Judaism, 1998), at p. 155.
9. Walter Jacob (ed.), *American Reform Responsa: Jewish Questions, Rabbinic Answers* (New York: Central Conference of American Rabbis, 1983), responsum no. 13. See also Moshe Zemer, 'Progressive Halakhah and Homosexual Marriage' in Walter Jacob and Moshe Zemer, *Gender Issues in Jewish Law: Essays and Responsa* (New York: Berghahn Books, 2001), pp. 151–68.
10. See David Ellenson and Michael Rosen, 'Gender, Halakhah, and Women's Suffrage: Responsa of the First Three Chief Rabbis on the Public Role of Women in the Jewish State', in Jacob and Zemer, *Gender Issues in Jewish Law*.

Gender issues

In early twentieth-century Germany, the young Franz Rosenzweig was about to convert to Christianity. Raised in an assimilated home, he was determined to enter the Church as a religious Jew, and so decided to attend Yom Kippur services in a small Orthodox synagogue rather than his parents' Reform temple. Overwhelmed by the liturgy and piety he encountered, he renounced his intention to convert, becoming instead one of the most notable twentieth-century Jewish thinkers.[1]

Franz Rosenzweig's near-conversion to Christianity is one of the best-known stories of modern Jewish thought; that the event may never have occurred in the manner described does not diminish its importance as myth. As a representation of Jews' struggles with modernity, Rosenzweig's experience is supposed to instruct us about the dangers of assimilation and the glorious return to Judaism that is possible through exposure to its pre-modern, traditional forms. Rosenzweig is invariably presented as having been 'saved' for Judaism at the very last moment by the emotional power of traditional East European Jewish religiosity that had been lost in Western Europe. His subsequent contributions to Jewish philosophy might never have occurred without that Yom Kippur experience. Implied in renditions of this tale, though never explicitly stated, is a note of triumphalism: this was not only the triumph of traditional Judaism over Reform temples, and over assimilationist Jewish identities, but also the triumph of Judaism over its old detractor and rival, Christianity. Through exposure to the traditional Judaism denigrated by Christian theologians, the great Rosenzweig could recognize Judaism's alleged superiority. He was not taken in by Christianity's victory over the centuries in mastering western civilization.

Both aspects of the implied triumphalism always bothered me, and seemed linked to a more fundamental question: What if Rosenzweig had been a woman? Would her experience in that same synagogue, but in the women's section, behind a heavily screened partition, perhaps in a separate room, have inspired her with similar Jewish commitment? Rosenzweig felt he had found his 'home' by returning to Judaism; would an assimilated Jewish woman exposed to Orthodoxy feel the same way? Why, in his desire to rejuvenate Judaism, did Rosenzweig ignore the Jewish feminist movement taking shape in Germany during his lifetime? Would the talents and fervour that brought him to a position of intellectual leadership in the Jewish community of Weimar Germany have brought a woman to a comparable position? Would her treatise on Judaism have reflected different concerns than his *Star of Redemption*? In other words, how did his male privilege affect Rosenzweig's personal experience of Judaism, his elevation to leadership by the Jewish community, and his theological formulation of Judaism's nature?—and the same questions might be asked of the other men who dominate modern Jewish thought.

Rosenzweig (1886–1929) is one of the most important figures in the collection of men who constitute the established canon of modern Jewish thought. That canon begins with Baruch (Benedict) Spinoza and Moses Mendelssohn, and extends through nineteenth-century figures such as Abraham Geiger and Samson Raphael Hirsch to the early twentieth-century thinkers, Martin Buber and Rosenzweig, generally concluding with Emmanuel Levinas, who died in 1995. Academic courses and books surveying the field have not altered the content of that canon to add any women, although many add a chapter at the end describing Jewish feminism. Unfortunately, the chapter on Jewish feminism has not transformed the presentation of the canon. For example, the revised 1995 edition of Eugene Borowitz's 1983 survey, *Choices in Modern Jewish Thought*, includes a final chapter on Jewish feminist theology, by Ellen Umansky, but gender does not play a role in the other thirteen chapters. Arnold Eisen's 1998 *Rethinking Modern Judaism* includes a positive discussion of Jewish feminist theology in its final, prescriptive chapter on the future of American Judaism, yet makes no mention of gender when analysing any of the other topics discussed in the preceding 200 pages. By contrast, Paula Hyman concludes her study of modern Jewish women by claiming that 'gendered differences in the experience of assimilation and the growing representation of women as the primary transmitters of Jewish culture shaped modern Jewish identity on the battleground of sexual politics'.[2] If she is correct, then the work of thinkers interpreting the meaning of Jewish identity should also be seen as a 'battleground of sexual politics', even when that battleground is concealed in rhetoric purportedly unaffected by gender issues.

Feminist perspectives on Jewish thought are relatively recent. Jewish feminism became a movement in the United States during the 1970s, as women began demanding equality in the synagogue. The major issues were including women in the *minyan* (basic prayer quorum); calling women to the Torah for *aliyot* (the recital of blessings over the Torah reading), during the synagogue Torah readings; and ordination as rabbis. Resistance to such changes was particularly strong from the Orthodox and Conservative movements, although Reform and Reconstructionism undertook the changes almost immediately. Still, feminists pressed new concerns: access to Torah and Talmud study, especially in Orthodox contexts. Commentaries on the Torah by women and new feminist rituals were composed. Ceremonies for naming daughters were produced to enable equal celebration as the *brit milah; Rosh Hodesh*, the New Moon, was celebrated as a women's holiday; feminist Passover Haggadot were published; the history of Jewish women began to be studied. Perhaps most importantly, revisions of Jewish laws concerning divorce, which allowed a man to withhold a divorce from his wife, leaving her 'chained' (*agunah*) to him, were implemented by non-Orthodox branches of Judaism, although Orthodox rabbis remained less tractable.

What emerged was a feminist movement that highlighted major inequalities in the central texts and teachings of the Torah, raising questions about its revelatory status. The burden fell on Jewish thinkers to explain why Judaism was permeated with the patriarchy that feminism had exposed. Why would God reveal a Torah that was unfair to female Jews? The extent of the required changes also raised theological problems: if women were granted full equality, would the result be a radically changed Judaism?

Academically, too, feminism was a challenge. The consensus of most feminist scholars was that women's history would transform the basic categories by which Jewish experience was analysed. Experiences such as modernization and assimilation would have to be reconsidered once women were studied. Did women assimilate at the same rate as men? How did modernity affect women differently? Indeed, modernization itself came to be seen as a gendered process, in which gender roles had to be reconceived. Not only prescribed roles for men and women, but even the language used to describe Jewishness were examined by feminists, to see how gender infiltrated the images and rhetorics of Jewish identity.

My goal in this chapter is to examine the discussions of women in the writings of those Jewish men whose work represents the canon of modern religious thought, with particular attention to the gendered nature of the rhetoric they employ. Feminist analysis looks for the political interests served not only by the rhetoric of modern religious thought, but also by ways historians describe it. For example, Moses Mendelssohn continues to represent the archetype of the modern Jew, primarily for his friendship with a Christian thinker, Gotthold Ephraim Lessing, yet the limitations on their relationship resulting from a male–male friendship have never been considered. Of course, no woman at that time was able to earn the status of representative of the Jewish community, or acquire the training in philosophy, that Mendelssohn had. Yet if the relationship between Jews and Christians in the modern era was modelled after the Mendelssohn–Lessing friendship, the limitations of male intimacy warrant consideration.

Abraham Geiger and Samson Raphael Hirsch

Although only limited writings of modern Jewish women of the nineteenth century have been preserved, there are indications that they were not content, a discontent evident from the defences of Jewish tradition written by both Reform and Orthodox rabbis. In one of the earliest defences of women's rights, published in 1837, Abraham Geiger (1810–74) minced no words in criticizing the position of women in Jewish law as unfair and unacceptable. Both levirate marriage, where a childless widow was obliged to marry his dead husband's brother, and the agunah were institutions that had to be abolished, he insisted. Geiger further urged that marriage and divorce be regulated by the state's secular legal apparatus, freeing women from their disabilities under halakhah.[3] Once the state declared a man dead, or proclaimed a divorce, the marriage should be regarded as fully dissolved, freeing the woman to remarry under Jewish law. Jewish marriage should be about sanctifying a relationship, not regulating it legally, Geiger insisted.

Yet an ambivalence in Geiger's attitudes toward women emerges with his calls for the subordination of wife to husband. When some Reform rabbis in the United States decided in 1869 to give brides an active role at the wedding ceremony, Geiger objected. He insisted that husband and wife would always hold different roles: the husband would 'always remain master of the house'. The husband should, therefore, speak for both, while 'the chaste bride, who has already more whispered than audibly spoken her "yes", should not have to speak and act publicly, but rather attend the words of her husband with a soulful look as she eagerly stretches out her finger so that the ring can be placed upon it. For the future as well,' Geiger concludes, 'the husband will be the one who gives, the wife the one who receives.'[4]

Geiger's main opponent on matters of Jewish law, the Orthodox leader Samson Raphael Hirsch (1808–88), disagreed with Geiger's assessment of Judaism's treatment of women. Women are placed on a pedestal, from which they exert a superior moral influence, he argued. In contrast to Geiger's critical assessment and reform of certain Jewish laws, Hirsch defended Judaism's treatment of women, not allowing the slightest reproach. Yet his views are based exclusively on aggadic statements regarding women, ignoring women's status under halakhah.

In certain ways, however, Hirsch's position reflects that of Geiger. Both argue that Judaism liberated women from the 'oriental yoke', and Hirsch's view of the marital relationship appears close to Geiger's. For Hirsch, the 'will-subordination of the wife to the husband is a necessary condition' of marriage. Clearly, both Reformers and Orthodox were able to present the secular ideology of the bourgeois marriage as expressions of Judaism. Whether Judaism's laws regarding marriage and divorce were portrayed as protecting women (Hirsch) or discriminating unfairly against them (Geiger), women's spiritual elevation was dependent upon the wife's subordination to her husband.[5] In the end, Geiger's domesticated Jewish wife is not very different from Hirsch's.

Gender and modernism

The emphasis on women's moral influence as exerted through her domesticity formed a crucial nexus in nineteenth-century Judaism, responding to a variety of concerns. The glorification of Jewish domesticity functioned to reassure male Jews of their heterosexual normalcy, and to reassure non-Jews of Jewish ethical behaviour. If sexual norms were proper, then the entire community was in good moral order.

The overdetermined insistence on Judaism's superior ethics, particularly in the realm of sexual behaviour, suggests a possible counter-tendency requiring active suppression. Modern Jewish men, since Spinoza, have expressed the feeling that Jewish religious life is emasculating. Geiger asserted that traditional Judaism undermined a masculine religious life. The Zionists insisted that piety and Diaspora had rendered Jewish men effeminate, and that Zionism would restore their masculinity. Other modern Jewish movements offered their own cures. For Geiger, scholarship was the answer. Leo Baeck defined Judaism as a masculine religion because of its emphasis on ethics, in contrast to the feminine Christianity, rooted in mysticism and ecstasy. Gershom Scholem, the twentieth-century scholar of Jewish mysticism, argued against those who viewed mysticism as feminine, insisting that Kabbalah was male in its origins and use.

Concern with the sexual impact of Judaism emerged concurrently with antisemites representing the male Jew as essentially effeminate, to be excluded from membership in the new German nation because of his lack of manliness. Meanwhile female Jews were portrayed as somewhat masculine and over-eroticized. While the Austrian thinker Otto Weininger, at the turn of the twentieth century, condemned Jewish men for being effeminate, the rabbinics scholar Daniel Boyarin, at the turn of the twenty-first century, praises Jewish men for having developed a feminine form of masculinity. Yet from the perspective of Jewish women, Jewish men, however effeminate their representation, remained patriarchal figures who held the power of Judaism firmly in their hands.

One reason why Jewish modernism is confined primarily to men is that the modernist rebellion against Judaism required religion as a foil against which to rebel. The pull of religion provided the necessary tension, and the patriarchal valorization of maleness endowed significance to men's rebellion. For them, the pull of traditional Judaism is the public sphere, the synagogue and the study house, which, in tension with the allure of the streets, engenders in men an ambivalence that is central to their Jewish identity. For women, the pull of traditional Judaism would be not engagement in the synagogue, nor the Talmud, nor other Jewish intellectual adventures, but their abdication in favour of domestic responsibilities. Hence, the creative tension between secular and religious intellectual life is missing for women. The tension could not be created, because the pull of Judaism was missing. Women's presence in—or absence from—the synagogue lacked the metaphoric drama it holds for men. In the days of Rosenzweig a man might return to the synagogue, or to Torah; a woman, at best, ventured to be present but remained marginal, an observer, not an essential figure required for the minyan or for Talmudic discussions.

The goal, for Rosenzweig and for scores of Jews throughout the twentieth century, was to enter the fantasized authentic 'Judaism'. His desire for it was all-encompassing, described in terms of love, and led him to embrace all aspects of Jewish tradition. Distinctions between law and custom were irrelevant; traditions assigning women to domesticity held the same significance as halakhah. What counted was the production of the nostalgic experience. Everything Jewish was to be accepted with joy and imparted with positive meaning. The Jewish woman as *Hausfrau*, one of the products of modern middle-class society, was sentimentalized and enshrined with emotion. The failure to follow certain Jewish practices was ascribed to personal, subjective deficiencies, rather than a moral flaw in the practice itself. Rosenzweig writes, 'for all those who eat Jewish dishes all the traditional customs of the menu as handed down from mother to daughter must be as irreplaceable as the separation of meat and milk. . . . Everywhere the custom and the original intention of the law must have the same rank of inviolability as the law itself.'[6] Everything can be transformed into a sacred moment, even the most egregious exclusions of women.

At issue is not why Rosenzweig was not a feminist, but how Jewish women today are to rationalize his work. Rosenzweig's uncritical embrace of Jewish tradition is unworkable for feminists. Whilst women might wish they could agree that 'every law can be changed back into a commandment', often that is simply not possible. Moreover, belief that Judaism is an expression of God's love, and our love of him, cannot be reconciled with the sexism that has pervaded Judaism since its inception.

Martin Buber

Rosenzweig's views concerning revelation and halakhah were taken up and criticized by his great friend, the theologian Martin Buber (1878–1965), whose attitude toward halakhah was antinomian, mixed with certain bitterness toward liberal Judaism. Unlike Rosenzweig's assimilated German Jewish home, however, Buber was raised by his observant grandparents in the more traditional Jewish environment of Galicia, surrounded by some of the piety Rosenzweig first experienced only as an adult. Perhaps as a result, Buber's feelings were more ambivalent; the nostalgia he expressed was directed less toward specific religious observances than toward what he viewed as their underlying emotional experience.

In letters between the two men, Buber wrote, 'I do not believe that revelation is ever a formulation of law . . . God is not a law-giver, and therefore the Law has no universal validity for me, but only a personal one.'[7] For Rosenzweig, too, 'revelation is certainly not law-giving . . . For me, too, God is not a Law-giver. But He commands.'[8] Yet while Buber distinguishes between revelation—belonging in the divine realm—and law—emanating from the human—Rosenzweig sees revelation and its human interpretation as inextricably intertwined. For Rosenzweig, the experience of revelation grants the right to provide interpretation, and gives that interpretation its authority. For Buber, it is precisely categories such as 'authority' that can never be reconciled with divinity. Both men agree that the experience, not the deed, is central, but while Buber insists on a qualitative distinction between deed and experience, Rosenzweig argues that they are bound together.

Although his rejection of halakhah might be viewed as potentially liberating for women, Buber's call for reviving Judaism's 'religiosity' is ultimately just as confining. His critique of modernity locates the heart of its problem in the anomie of society which impairs the sense of God. He finds religiosity and community best expressed in movements such as Hasidism, which he describes as one of the great expressions of Judaism. Yet for many women, it is precisely movements such as Hasidism, with its extreme marginalization of women, that gives rise to the sense of anomie and forlornness.

Buber's antinomianism was not inspired by feminist sympathies. His actual views on women can be reconstructed only from scattered references. The traditional Judaism Buber rejected for himself was necessary, he thought, for modern women. He believed they could also play a role in the rebirth of the Jewish people through the Zionist movement, by returning to their domestic role of mother. 'While only men can discover and establish cultural ideas, he needs Woman to realize them and create a living, continuing culture.'[9]

Buber made no published comment on the Jewish feminist movement, established in Germany in 1904, which attained a membership of 50,000 by the end of the 1920s. Nor does he mention the private rabbinical ordination in December 1935 of Regina Jonas, by Rabbi Max Dienemann, a colleague of his in Frankfurt am Main. In an exchange of letters with his friend Gustav Landauer, a Jewish socialist intellectual and advocate of women's rights, Buber writes that: 'The genuinely thinking man must live through the feminine, the genuinely thinking woman the masculine; each must find therein the counterpole to his own in order to allow the unity of the spiritual life to develop from both.'[10] Apparently, for Buber, men's need for women in order to think was strictly theoretical. Just a few years later, when Buber planned to open an adult Jewish educational institute, he expressed reluctance to admit women. Landauer refused to participate if women were excluded. Buber's comments illustrate Tania Modleski's insight that 'male subjectivity works to appropriate "femininity" while oppressing women'.[11]

Emmanuel Levinas

The work of Emmanuel Levinas (1905–95) also illustrates Modleski's point. Just as Jewish and French feminism began achieving remarkable successes during the 1970s and 1980s, Levinas was attracting enormous attention. As a soldier in the French army, Levinas was held by the Nazis for several years, but as a military prisoner of war rather than a Jew. The Shoah is a central element of his thought, presented as having universal implications for the moral obligations each person has for all humanity. His appeal is based primarily on his critique of philosophy, particularly that of Heidegger, and his demand that ethics, not ontology and epistemology, be the starting point of philosophy. His criticisms of Heidegger coincided with the revelations of Heidegger's

Nazi sympathies, and the centrality of the Shoah in Levinas's work gave him additional moral authority. Finally, Levinas's series of colloquia on the Talmud functioned to rehabilitate Jewish legal texts, frequently denigrated in Christian society over the past two millennia.

Ostensibly, Levinas's insistence on the centrality of ethical obligation might seem useful to feminists. For Levinas, the basis of moral action, of freedom, and indeed of selfhood, is to be found in the infinite responsibility for the other as other. While women have long been viewed as 'other' within patriarchy, with their own needs secondary to their service to men, Levinas's philosophy would seem to make such subservience untenable. Yet the ethical model he developed is contradicted by the highly problematic gender categories Levinas defines.

The representation of women's alterity in Levinas's philosophical writings has been subjected to various feminist critiques, starting with Simone de Beauvoir, yet little attention has been paid to his treatment of women in his Talmudic essays. For Levinas, the Talmud is the most significant element of Judaism, attested in his 1955 essay, 'Loving the Torah More Than God'.[12] While rabbinic Judaism includes some severe teachings regarding women, even at its worst it is not as bad as the misogyny Levinas constructs out of it. His assertion that Judaism is a religion of ethical superiority is an old tradition in Jewish apologetics, and a dubious claim, given the morally questionable teachings it includes, but the ethical Judaism that Levinas invents is untenable, given the misogyny he finds within it. Ultimately, his presentation of women in rabbinic literature is not only questionable as a reliable analysis of the texts, it also invalidates Levinas's own claim that Judaism is a religion of ethical superiority.

Starting in the 1960s, and continuing until 1989, Levinas delivered a series of colloquia in Paris on Talmudic texts, many of which were subsequently published. One of his most notorious focused on *Berakhot* 61a, and expressed his interpretation of rabbinic views of women. Strikingly, the colloquium was delivered in October 1972, just a few months after Hebrew Union College's first ordination of a woman rabbi, Sally Priesand. Although he makes no mention of that event, the coincidence is worth noting, since Levinas argues that men should not follow the leadership of women.

The text in *Berakhot* 61a states: 'A man does not walk behind a woman, even if it is his own wife on the road—and, even if he finds himself on a bridge with her, she should be beside him, and whoever walks behind a woman when crossing a river will have no part in the future.' The text continues by warning against a man handing money to a woman 'with the intention of looking at her', and then debates the verse in Judges 13: 11 which reports that 'Manoah rose and followed his wife'. Either, the Talmudic text explains, Manoah was ignorant of the prohibition not to walk behind a woman, or 'follow' is not meant literally, suggesting rather that he followed her advice. Levinas prefers the second interpretation, and presents it as the intention of the text, as if it were halakhah:

Answer: to follow can mean to take advice. Essential point: in the interhuman order, the perfect equality and even superiority of woman, who is capable of giving advice and direction. According to custom, it is the man who must nevertheless, regardless of the goal, indicate the direction in which to walk.[13]

Whereas the rabbinic text warns against the sexual seductiveness that might ensue if a man follows a woman who has raised her dress while crossing a river, Levinas extends the warning from the physical to the intellectual realm. 'Following' refers, he claims, to taking the advice of a woman—a prohibition that is not a standard part of Jewish law. Indeed, Levinas explicitly rejects the principle of gender equality:

Here equality would end in immobility or in the bursting apart of the human being. The Gemara opts for the priority of the masculine. A man must not walk behind a woman, for his ideas may become clouded. The first reason stems perhaps from masculine psychology. It assumes that a woman bears the erotic within herself as a matter of course.

What is striking is Levinas's need to separate the erotic from the intellectual, assigning each to one particular gender. Once again, he tries to separate the feminine/erotic from women, with the claim that '[i]t is not woman who is thus slighted. It is the relation based on sexual differences which is subordinated to the interhuman relation.'[14] The claim is slippery, reinforcing precisely what Levinas says he wants to overcome.

Conclusion

Feminists have inherited the gender stereotypes enshrined in the canon of modern Jewish thought. If Mendelssohn's friendship with Lessing stands as the archetype that inaugurates the modern era, the last years of Rosenzweig's life ought to be a parable for its demise. In February 1922 Rosenzweig was diagnosed with a terminal illness, which would afflict him with a progressive paralysis expected to kill him within months. In fact he lived nearly another eight years. By the end of 1922, however, he had lost the ability to write, and half a year later, to speak. He continued his work, nonetheless, dictating articles and, with Buber, translating the Bible into German. Soon he was no longer able to type or even speak; he could only communicate by blinking his eyes. His wife, Edith, would repeatedly recite the alphabet, and Franz would blink at the correct letter. Through that exhausting method, Edith would write his sentences, paragraphs, and articles; indeed, Rosenzweig remained extraordinarily prolific. This continued for years, until Franz's death in December 1929. Quite literally, she 'opened her mouth for the mute'(Proverbs 31: 8).

When I was in graduate school my professors always praised Rosenzweig's courage for continuing to write despite his paralysis. Moreover, given the terrible catastrophes that had beset modern Judaism—from secularism and assimilation to antisemitism and the Holocaust—he stood as an archetype of the noble Jew, struggling against the forces of paralysis that attacked not only his body, but the Judaism he loved. Yet to me Rosenzweig's 'heroism' was qualified by the glory that accompanied it; the real hero was his wife, a healthy woman who gave up seven years of her life to recite the alphabet, repeatedly, all day long. Hers was a voluntary paralysis of her life, yet that went curiously unmentioned, perhaps because hers was not considered heroism, but the expected behaviour of the woman as man's helpmeet. What Edith spoke and wrote were her husband's words and ideas, not her own, a caricature of what is traditionally expected of Jewish women: to repeat what she is told, rather than think and write for herself. Yet it is not only Edith's muteness that is inscribed in the story, but her husband's muteness that competes with her. He is heroic for being a man who is forced to assume the role of female: physically passive, inert, and mute—even while flexing his (masculine) mind on behalf of Judaism. Despite being feminized by disease, Rosenzweig found a way to continue his manly pursuits in the interpretation of Judaism, a kind of symbolic hermaphroditism. Rosenzweig, who had resisted the temptation of Christianity in his youth, came to be remembered in his paralysis as a kind of crucified Christ figure, cradled in the arms of his devoted wife, an image reminiscent of the *pietà*.

In a famous essay, 'Castration or Decapitation?', Hélène Cixous points out that, under patriarchy, women are undermined less through sexual disadvantage than by the rejection of their minds. While much of women's social and economic discrimination in a variety of societies was predicated upon claims of women's biological inferiority, myths of women's intellectual inadequacy have also produced powerful social and political barriers. Traditional Jewish culture may have had a positive, even lusty, attitude toward heterosexual relationships, but stringently maintained boundaries excluding women's intellectual participation in the shaping of Judaism. Women's sexuality has been at times demonized, and at other times respected and even valorized, both in traditional and modern Judaism, but it is her mouth, as the portal of her mind, that remains the constant problem. *Kol isha ervah*, a woman's voice is sinful (*Berakhot* 24a and *Kiddushin* 70a), the Talmud teaches, a statement that later is interpreted to prohibit men from hearing a woman sing. The inability to participate in the intellectual adventure of shaping Judaism, because a woman's mind was not attached to a body with a penis, is precisely the scenario that gives rise to male nostalgia, an emotion rooted, in Freudian terms, in the longing to return to an earlier age, when belief in the mother's penis had not yet been disappointed. Modern Jewish nostalgia expresses the desire to return to an era before the modern, that is, before it was no longer tenable to deny the existence of a woman's mind. Like Edith Rosenzweig, who became the physical mouth of her paralysed husband's mind, Jewish women have for too long repeated and followed the teachings of a patriarchal religious system that, until recently, has been paralysed and unable to change. The advent of modernity brought new opportunities for women, intellectually and culturally, and inaugurated their engagement in creating a new Judaism. Until now, Jewish men have had their modernity; now, thanks to feminism, women can begin to shape theirs.

FURTHER READING

Chanter, Tina. 'Feminism and the Other', in Robert Bernasconi and David Wood (eds.), *The Provocation of Levinas: Rethinking the Other* (London and New York: Routledge, 1988), pp. 32–56. See also Robert Bernasconi and Simon Critchley (eds.), *Re-Reading Levinas* (Bloomington, Ind.: Indiana University Press, 1991); and Robert Manning, 'Thinking the Other Without Violence? An Analysis of the Relations Between the Philosophy of Emmanuel Levinas and Feminism', *Journal of Speculative Philosophy*, 5: 2 (1991), pp. 132–43. These works provide some examples of questions and critiques directed at certain aspects of Levinas's philosophy.

Gubar, Susan. ' "The Blank Page" and the Issues of Female Creativity', in Elizabeth Abel (ed.), *Writing and Sexual Difference* (Chicago: University of Chicago Press, 1982), pp. 73–94. A consideration of ways in which Judaism has traditionally silenced women's voices.

Kaplan, Marion A. *The Jewish Feminist Movement in Germany: The Campaigns of the Jüdischer Frauenbund, 1904–1938* (Westport, Conn.: Greenwood Press, 1979). An account of the early development of a women's movement within Judaism.

Lamm, Norman. *A Hedge of Roses* (New York: Feldheim, 1966). This provides an example of Orthodox apologetics, presenting the laws of *niddah* (family purity) as possessing insight into the true nature of women's psychology.

Levitt, Laura. *Jews and Feminism: The Ambivalent Search for Home* (New York: Routledge, 1997). An excellent analysis of ways in which Jews and Judaism can make room for women.

Peskowitz, Miriam, and Laura Levitt (eds.), *Judaism Since Gender* (New York: Routledge, 1997). A collection of essays examining various ways of studying Judaism in the light of developments in Gender studies.

Plaskow, Judith. *Standing Again At Sinai: Judaism from a Feminist Perspective* (San Francisco: Harper & Row, 1990). A seminal work highlighting the traditional marginalization of women in Judaism and calling for far-reaching reforms.

Ruttenberg, Danya. *Yentl's Revenge: The Next Wave of Jewish Feminism* (Seattle: Seal Press, 2001). An anthology of essays written by a generation of Jewish women considering the broad range of options available to them as a result of feminist developments within Judaism.

NOTES

1. See e.g. *Franz Rosenzweig: His Life and Thought*, ed. Nahum Glatzer (New York: Schocken Books, 1953), pp. xvi–xx, 25–8.

2. Paula Hyman, *Gender and Assimilation in Modern Jewish History: The Roles and Representation of Women* (Seattle: University of Washington Press, 1995), p. 9.

3. His proposal was adopted and expanded in an 1843 book by Samuel Holdheim, who suggested that Judaism should lend sanctification to a marriage, but not regulate either marriage or divorce legally. Formal discussion of women's role in Judaism occurred at the 1846 Reform rabbinical synod in Breslau. This agreed that women should be obligated to Jewish religious practice equally with men, particularly in prayer, and both should be counted in the minyan. This decision was actually moot, since it applied to precisely those Jews who had long abandoned most religious practice, particularly the obligation to pray three times daily.

4. Cited in Michael A. Meyer, 'German-Jewish Identity', in Jacob Katz (ed.), *Toward Modernity: The European Jewish Model* (New Brunswick: Transaction, 1987), pp. 260–1.

5. Orthodoxy continues to follow Hirsch's method; charges of halakhic discrimination against women are often met with a similar apologetics of romantic flattery—whilst the laws remain unchanged.

6. Franz Rosenzweig, *The Builders* (originally written in 1923), tr. William Wolf, in Nahum Glatzer (ed.), *On Jewish Learning: Franz Rosenzweig* (New York: Schocken Book, 1965), p. 83.

7. Ibid., p. 85.

8. Ibid., pp. 118, 116.

9. Martin Buber, 'Das Zion der jüdischen Frau' (1901), in *Die jüdische Bewegung: Gesammelte Aufsätze und Ansprachen, 1900–1914* (Berlin: Jüdischer Verlag, 1920), p. 37.

10. In Maurice Friedman, *Martin Buber's Life and Work: The Early Years 1878–1923* (New York: E. P. Dutton, 1981), p. 170.

11. Tania Modleski, *Feminism Without Women: Culture and Criticism in a 'Postfeminist' Age* (New York and London: Routledge, 1991), p. 7.

12. In *Difficult Freedom: Essays on Judaism*, tr. Sean Hand (Baltimore: Johns Hopkins University Press, 1990), pp. 142–5.

13. Ibid., p. 175.

14. Ibid., p. 177.

31 | The changing role of the woman

Judith R. Baskin

Over the last two centuries the domestic, religious, and communal roles of Jewish women in the western world have undergone significant expansions as a result of the social, educational, economic, and technological transformations associated with modernity. This chapter explores how women's enhanced opportunities in organization formation, spiritual leadership, liturgical and ritual innovation, and Jewish feminist theology have altered significant aspects of contemporary Judaism.[1]

Traditional models

Prior to the end of the eighteenth century Jewish life and religious practice everywhere followed the norms of rabbinic Judaism, codified in the Babylonian Talmud and interpreted in ongoing legal and ethical rabbinic injunctions. Rabbinic Judaism mandated strict separations between male and female roles and domains: ideally, men functioned in the public realms of synagogue, study house, and community governance, while women were employed in domestic nurturing roles that enabled their husbands and sons to fulfil public obligations. Women who satisfied male expectations in their assigned roles as wives and mothers were revered and honoured.

Jewish women, like men, were responsible for obeying all of Judaism's negative commandments and for observing the Sabbath and holy days of the Jewish calendar. However, male and female obligations differed, since women were exempted from time-bound positive commandments, including communal synagogue worship and the three-times-daily recitation of a fixed liturgy of Hebrew prayers incumbent on men (Babylonian Talmud, *Berakhot* 20a–b). Women were certainly encouraged to pray, but their prayers could be spontaneous, private, and in a vernacular language. Compilations of vernacular prayers for women's domestic and synagogue use began to appear in the early modern period, following the invention of printing.[2] Women who chose to attend synagogue were required to sit apart from men, usually in an upstairs gallery or behind a visual barrier (*mehitzah*).

Women followed many ritual regulations within the domestic sphere, including adherence to dietary laws (*kashrut*), special holiday practices, and three observances designated specifically for women. These were the limitations on marital contact during the wife's menstrual period and for a specified span afterwards, followed by immersion in a ritual bath (*niddah*); separation and burning of a piece of dough used in making Sabbath bread (*hallah*), a reminder of ancient Temple sacrifices; and kindling of Sabbath lights (*hadlaqah*). Although rabbinic tradition generally presented these ritual obligations as punishments or atonements for Eve's role in bringing death into the world (*Genesis Rabbah* 17: 8; *Avot de-Rabbi Nathan* B 9), they constituted satisfying ways of sanctifying aspects of daily life for many women.

Religious education for girls in pre-modern Jewish societies focused on domestic responsibilities. Instruction in Hebrew and religious texts was limited to a very few women from rabbinic families, some of whom taught and led prayers for women in their communities. From the male point of view, learned Jewish women were irrelevant to Jewish scholarship and communal life; female testimony on legal or religious matters was valued only from women deemed reliable witnesses to the practices of distinguished fathers or husbands.

Glikl bas Judah Leib of Hameln (1646–1724), a rare Jewish female voice from early modern times, recorded her memories following her husband's death to inform her children of their ancestry and family ideals. Born into the prosperous Court Jew milieu of Central Europe, Glikl was well read in vernacular Jewish literature and probably knew some Hebrew and German as well. Married at 14 and the mother of fourteen children, Glikl was active in business, charitable, and pious in religious observance, attending synagogue regularly. At the threshold of modernity, both as a woman and as a Jew, Glikl's business activities reflect the growing economic participation of Jews in the non-Jewish world, while her religious and secular learning, as well as her literary efforts, speak to the broader horizons and new educational opportunities available to some seventeenth- and eighteenth-century Jews, including women.[3]

The impact of Jewish Enlightenment

Haskalah, the Jewish Enlightenment movement which began in late eighteenth-century Germany, brought enormous changes to Jewish religious, political, and social life in Central and Western Europe. Committed to modernity and interaction with European culture, Haskalah insisted that acculturation to mainstream customs of the host country could coexist with Jewish practices in the private domains of home and synagogue. While the central goals of this movement were political emancipation and achievement of full civil rights for Jews, with their accompanying social and economic benefits, some supporters also championed theological and ritual modernization within the Jewish community. Most contemporary forms of Judaism, including Reform, Liberal, Conservative/Masorti, and Modern Orthodoxy, were shaped in this milieu. Moses Mendelssohn, the founder of Haskalah in Central Europe, and others of his circle also advocated progressives changes in gender relations, including an end to arranged marriages.

Reform Judaism, which offered nineteenth-century Jews a modernized form of Jewish belief and practice that accentuated personal faith and ethical behaviour rather than traditional ritual observance, proclaimed that women were entitled to the same religious rights and subject to the same religious duties as men. This new emphasis on identical religious educations for girls and boys, with a confirmation ceremony for young people, and worship services that included prayers and a sermon in the vernacular, made the new movement attractive to many women. Pressure from young women apparently prompted the Reform rabbinate to adopt the innovation of double-ring wedding ceremonies in which women also made a statement of marital commitment.

However, European Reform Judaism made few actual changes in women's synagogue status or participation in rituals, and maintained separate seating by gender well into the twentieth century. This was not as much the case in the United States, where mixed seating was the norm in Reform synagogues and where women were afforded increasing opportunities to assume some synagogue leadership roles as the nineteenth century progressed. Yet, despite several young women who undertook rabbinic training during the first half of the twentieth century, American Reform Judaism did not ordain its first female rabbi until 1972.

As many European and American Jews entered the middle class in the course of the 1800s, Judaism's preferred positioning of women in the domestic realm, which conformed well to nineteenth-century Christian bourgeois models of female domesticity, was preserved. Jewish literature and the Jewish press of the late nineteenth century, both in Western Europe and the United States, described the Jewish woman as the 'guardian angel of the house', 'mother in Israel', and 'priestess of the Jewish ideal', and assigned her primary responsibility for the Jewish identity and education of her children. Women were encouraged to express their spirituality in domestic activities such as traditional Jewish cooking and home-based observance of the Sabbath and other holidays. However, the shift in responsibility for inculcating Jewish identity and practices in children away from men led rapidly from praise to denigration, as commentators began to blame mothers for their children's assimilation to the larger non-Jewish culture.[4]

In England a significant number of Jewish women also worked in the public domain to hasten Jewish Enlightenment and emancipation and to further religious reform. These included social activists and advocates of liberal Judaism like Lily Montagu (1873–1963), and writers of both fiction and non-fiction with Jewish themes directed to Jewish and Gentile audiences, such as Grace Aguilar (d. 1847), and Marion and Celia Moss (1840s). In her popular book *The Women of Israel* Aguilar defended the exalted position of women in Judaism, highlighting what she described as women's traditional role in hastening redemption as 'teachers of children' and through other domestic activities. Despite their uplifting messages, Jewish women's success in the world of literature was upsetting to the men of their milieu; while male Jewish reformers in

England supported a degree of female emancipation in principle, they tended to limit and undermine women's writing and influence in the public sphere.[5]

Women's organizations

Nineteenth- and early twentieth-century male leaders discouraged efforts by women to work with men for Jewish communal goals, but they did not object to women banding together for various public purposes that benefited the Jewish community. In emulation of bourgeois Christian models of female philanthropy and religious activism, middle-class Jewish women established service and social welfare organizations in Germany, England, and North America, including the Jüdischer Frauenbund in Germany (founded in 1904), the Union of Jewish Women in Great Britain (founded in 1902), and the National Council of Jewish Women in the United States (founded in 1893). For many Jewish women, whose synagogue roles remained limited, organizational involvement became a spiritual undertaking. These groups co-operated in the international campaign against coercion of poor women into prostitution, worked for female suffrage, instituted social welfare services, and argued for greater recognition of women within their respective Jewish communities. In the process, as women acquired administrative expertise and assumed authoritative and responsible public roles, their members blurred the boundaries between traditional male and female spheres of action.[6]

In North America Jewish women's organizations included synagogue sisterhoods, which devoted themselves to the domestic management of the synagogue, decorating the sanctuary for festivals, catering for synagogue events, and performing many other housekeeping functions. National organizations of sisterhoods, separated by denomination, encouraged local groups in their activities and provided a forum for public female leadership. While the Reform movement's National Federation of Temple Sisterhoods provided a platform for women to demand greater synagogue participation, including the ordination of women rabbis, the Conservative movement's Women's League emphasized the role of women in enhancing the Jewishness of their homes. Sisterhoods of all denominations, however, recognized that females had to be Jewishly educated in order to strengthen Jewish observance at home and instil Jewish values in their children, and encouraged expanded educational opportunities for women of all ages. Similarly, American Jewish women played a central role in establishing, supervising, and teaching in synagogue religious schools.

The life and achievements of Henrietta Szold (1860–1943) are particularly instructive. Born in Baltimore, Maryland, the eldest of eight daughters of a Hungarian-born rabbi, Szold was highly knowledgeable in classical Jewish texts, history, and thought, and assisted her father with his research while working full-time as a teacher. Her articles in the national Jewish press gained the attention of American Jewish leaders and she ultimately became the first paid employee of the Jewish Publication Society, where she served for twenty-two years as a meticulous editor, translator, and administrator. In 1902 Szold undertook a course of study at the Jewish Theological Seminary in New York, where she was allowed the status of special student on condition that she would not seek rabbinic ordination. (The Jewish Theological Seminary admitted women to rabbinical studies in 1983.) Ironically, it was Szold's futile infatuation with a scholar whose work she prepared for publication that propelled her, in her fifties, out of her ancillary roles supporting male endeavours and led her to take control of her own life. Szold founded Hadassah, the Women's Zionist Organization of America, in 1912. Under her leadership Hadassah, now the largest Zionist organization in the world, revolutionized health care and medical training in Palestine and saved thousands of Jewish children from Nazi-occupied Europe through the Youth Aliyah programme. Szold's devotion to building a complex, well-funded, international, and interdenominational organization in the service of women, children, and Jewish values exemplified the possibilities of personal and spiritual transformation available for women through organizational involvement and philanthropy.[7]

In the early twenty-first century women's roles in Jewish organizational life are in a period of significant transformation. In this more egalitarian era, where women are often highly educated and in professional jobs, it is not unusual to see women leaders in synagogues and other Jewish communal groups that are not limited to women. This integration of the sexes in general communal leadership has called into question the continued existence of same-sex organizations such as synagogue sisterhoods. Moreover, at a time when many women are employed outside the home, it is far more difficult for middle-class women to spare the hours they once devoted to volunteer activities, and this may also affect the continued existence of Jewish women's organizations.

Female ordination

The feminist movement that began in the late 1960s and early 1970s brought religious renewal and controversy to contemporary Judaism, as many women applied feminism's mandate for female equality to their own commitments to Jewish identification and the Jewish community and demanded full access to a tradition which had rarely considered women as central figures in its history, thought, religious practice, or communal life. Born at a time of sweeping social change, when women were facing new challenges in the areas of family formation, unprecedented opportunities in higher education and vocational choice, increased communal acceptance of homosexuality and other alternative lifestyles, and a wide range of options in religious and spiritual expression and political and civic activism, the Jewish feminist movement has had a significant impact on Jewish religious practice in a number of areas. Egalitarian participation both in worship and in ritual roles is now considered the norm in most liberal and progressive forms of Judaism. Another visible change is the opportunity offered to women outside Orthodox forms of Jewish practice to undertake rabbinic studies and to receive rabbinic ordination.

The question of female rabbis, a natural consequence of Reform Judaism's insistence on the spiritual and intellectual equality of men and women, had already been seriously pondered in the nineteenth century in both Germany and the United States, but was ultimately rejected for fear of social, communal, and interdenominational objections. While arguments for women as rabbis were always grounded in traditional sources, the actual push for female ordination was a result of Judaism's encounter with feminism and the reconfigurations of women's accustomed roles in the final third of the twentieth century.

The first woman to receive rabbinic ordination was Regina Jonas (1902–44) of Germany. Although she completed rabbinic studies at the Hochschule für die Wissenschaft des Judentums, her teachers refused her ordination to avoid conflict with the German Orthodox community. Instead, she was ordained privately in Berlin in 1935, by Max Dienemann, a liberal rabbi. Jonas did not find a congregational pulpit, but served as a teacher and chaplain in Berlin; she published articles about Judaism and her own experience, and lectured widely in Germany, taking on increasing communal responsibilities during the Nazi regime. In November 1942 Jonas was deported to the ghetto of Theresienstadt, where she continued her pastoral and pedagogical work. Like other incarcerated Jewish leaders, she delivered many lectures for her fellow prisoners; five of these focused on the history of Jewish women. Jonas was sent to Auschwitz, where she was murdered on 12 December 1944.[8]

Jonas remained unique until the last third of the twentieth century, when changing public attitudes and social realities prompted the leadership of the Reform movement to sanction the ordination of Rabbi Sally Priesand by Hebrew Union College in 1972. The first female rabbi in the United Kingdom, Jacqueline Tabick, was ordained in 1975 by Leo Baeck College, an institution under the joint sponsorship of the Reform Synagogues of Great Britain and the Union of Liberal and Progressive Synagogues. More than thirty years later several hundred women have been ordained as rabbis in North America, the United Kingdom, and Israel, and as many as half of rabbinical students in seminaries of liberal denominations of Judaism, including those of the Conservative/Masorti and Reconstructionist movements, are female. Women have also received ordination as cantors in the past three decades. The paths of female religious leaders in the Jewish world, however, have not been free of obstacles. Many female clergy hold subordinate positions in large synagogues, or work as educators or chaplains, rather than as senior leaders of congregations. These occupational patterns are a reflection not only of persistent cultural prejudices towards women as religious authority figures, but also of many women's choices of rabbinic options that allow them time for home and family.

Rabbinic ordination for women is still far from imminent in the Orthodox community, although educational opportunities for women have expanded impressively in traditional Judaism in the past hundred years. The first religiously oriented schools for Jewish girls from Orthodox families were established in 1918 under the leadership of Sarah Schenirer (1883–1935). A devout seamstress who was inspired with a vision of education for women, she found broad support from many Orthodox leaders in Central and Eastern Europe who had come to believe that traditions against educating girls should be disregarded, given the rapidly changing social conditions and widespread assimilation in the years after the First World War. While the Bais Yaakov school network Schenirer inspired emphasized modesty and humility more than rigorous study, it set a precedent of female education in Orthodox Judaism that has endured. In the present day, the opportunities that have transformed women's educational and vocational expectations in the wider world have had a decided impact on some sectors of the traditional community as well. Orthodox girls and women throughout the world now have many options for serious study of traditional Jewish texts, and many have also become authors on Jewish topics of all kinds. In the early twenty-first century halakhically knowledgeable women serve as rabbinic assistants in a number of Modern Orthodox synagogues in North America, and are trained to act as expert advocates on legal issues connected with women's status in Israel.

Liturgical and ritual innovations

Another example of the impact of women on Jewish religious life is alterations in liturgical language. The traditional *siddur*, the Jewish prayer book, portrays worship as a prerogative for men, who represent their wives and families in their communal prayers. Until recently, translations into English were couched in solely masculine terms, portraying women as beneficiaries of male prayers rather than as participating in prayer themselves. Another major area of change has been the elimination of masculine references in prayer, whether referring to humanity in general, the congregation of worshippers, or to God. Thus, 'Sovereign' or 'Ruler' might replace 'Lord' or 'King', while 'God of our Fathers' is generally replaced by 'God of our Fathers and Mothers', 'God of our ancestors', or 'God of Israel'. Changes in both the Hebrew and English liturgies reflecting some of these innovations have appeared in a number of new liturgical works in recent decades published by all of the non-Orthodox movements of Judaism. Marcia Falk, whose liturgical innovations have a strong theological foundation, believes that all personal images of God are limited; she attempts in her liturgical language to move beyond anthropomorphic images of deity to a multiplicity of divine images affirming the unity of all creation. By invoking God as 'Source of Life', 'Flow of Life', 'Breath of All Living Things', Falk underscores her vision of the divine as an immanent force or power that is neither apart from nor above creation.[9]

Along with changes in liturgical language, some women have adopted the prayer objects which are a part of men's worship in traditional settings, including wearing a head covering (*kippah*) and a prayer shawl (*tallit*) during communal worship; some women also pray with *tefillin*, the phylacteries which have traditionally been wrapped on the forehead and the left arm by Jewish men (from age 13) during weekday morning prayers as literal signs of the covenant between God and the Jewish people.

Innovative religious observances addressing particular aspects of women's experience are a central facet of women's changing roles in Judaism. The most widely practiced is the *bat mitzvah*, first introduced to North America in 1922 by Mordecai Kaplan, the founder of Reconstructionist Judaism, to celebrate his daughter Judith's religious coming of age. This ceremony for 12- or 13-year-old girls became widespread in various forms in the decades following the Second World War in Conservative/ Masorti, Reconstructionist, and Reform congregations. At the beginning of the twenty-first century such ceremonies, which require intensive training in Hebrew and Judaism, are generally fully equivalent to the *bar mitzvah* ceremony for boys in liberal forms of Judaism. Some Orthodox congregations also offer a bat mitzvah where a young woman may publicly affirm her Jewish knowledge and commitment; however, this ceremony will not share in the elements of a traditional bar mitzvah, since a woman is not permitted to lead worship or be counted in the worshiping congregation. In some instances the Orthodox ceremony is restricted to women, and in this same-sex context the bat mitzvah girl may read from the Torah scroll as part of a women's prayer group.

Ceremonies welcoming baby girls into the covenant of Israel (variously known as *simhat bat, shalom bat, b'rit banot,* or *b'ritah*) are also increasingly frequent. Unlike the ritual circumcision on the eighth day of life which initiates male infants into the covenant between God and Israel (*b'rit milah*), Judaism has not previously had a traditional way to celebrate the birth of a daughter, and a variety of contemporary rituals and liturgies have been developed. *Rosh hodesh*, the New Moon, a traditional female holiday from domestic chores, has also become popular in all sectors of the Jewish community as a day on which groups of Jewish women gather for study, prayer, and recreation.

Inclusion of women as equal entities in traditional rituals related to life-cycle events is another form of liturgical change. Alternative marriage contracts and wedding ceremonies emphasizing mutuality, and divorce rituals that allow women a role in acknowledging the final dissolution of their marriages, are examples of such innovations. In Orthodox Judaism, women are not counted as part of the *minyan*, the group of no fewer than ten individuals required for communal worship. Since female mourners have no standing in public worship, they have depended on men to recite the mourner's prayer, which can only be voiced in a communal context, on their behalf. Many contemporary Orthodox women now assume the traditional obligations of the mourner themselves, and attend daily communal prayers during the year of mourning that follows the death of a close relative.

Other forms of liturgical creativity recognize the sacred nature of a woman's biological cycle and ritualize such milestone events as menarche, menses, childbirth, miscarriage, and menopause. Similarly, rituals have been developed to sacralize passages not previously considered in Jewish tradition, including ceremonies for healing from sexual abuse or assault. A number of these innovative rituals incorporate immersion in the ritual bath (*mikveh*) as symbolic of a new beginning. Which of these rituals, and in what forms, will ultimately become part of normative Jewish practice remains unknowable at this time, but their wide variety is testimony to the creative impact of feminist spirituality on contemporary Judaism.

Innovations such as female rabbis and cantors, liturgical alterations and new rituals, and egalitarian worship have prompted hostile reactions in some sectors of the Orthodox community, where they are perceived as contrary to centuries of Jewish tradition and as undermining women's customary home-based enabling roles. However, most present-day forms of Orthodox Judaism are also profoundly affected by women's changing roles. As the dissonance between possibilities for women in the secular and traditional worlds has become more obvious, high-quality Jewish education for girls has become a central priority in a number of traditional Jewish communities. A number of Orthodox feminists are working within the modern Orthodox community to enhance opportunities for female participation in Jewish learning and worship, and some sympathetic Orthodox rabbis have given their sanction to female prayer groups in which women can worship together and read from the Torah scroll.[10] Orthodox feminist activists are also looking for ways to alleviate the halakhic disadvantages for women inherent in traditional Judaism's unilateral marriage and divorce laws, in which a woman is a passive participant in her marriage and must depend on an estranged husband to grant her a divorce.

The late twentieth century has seen a movement of Jewish women from liberal or secular backgrounds who have chosen to become Orthodox Jews; these *ba'alot teshuvah* often cite the special appreciation of female roles they believe characterizes Orthodoxy. Tamar Frankiel, a scholar of religion and herself a ba'alat teshuvah, writes that through the bearing and nurturing of children, the preparation and serving of food, the creation and preservation of *shalom bayit* (household harmony), and their special affinity to the Sabbath, New Moons, and other Jewish festivals, Orthodox women participate in a cycle of Jewish life rich in feminine themes. She speaks in exalted terms of the special benefits of family purity rituals, finding in monthly immersion an experience of renewal and in enforced marital separation a safeguard for the spirituality of sexual expression. Yet she also looks toward a future when women's Jewish education will be of the same quality as men's, and where women's spiritual impact on Jewish law, rituals, and custom will be recognized and appreciated.[11]

Alternative lifestyles

Contemporaneous, and in many ways linked with the growth and development of Jewish feminism, is the visibility of identified gay and lesbian Jews, as well as single Jews regardless of sexual orientation, as active participants within the Jewish community. While Jewish domestic life has historically been centred around family units consisting of male and female parents and their children, delayed age of marriage and growing numbers of unmarried Jews, as well as contemporary openness regarding homosexuality, have changed the demographic make-up of many Jewish communities. Most liberal approaches to Judaism agree that both Jewish ethical teachings and the future of the Jewish people require that communal institutions welcome and value formerly marginalized individuals and groups who do not conform to the traditional family model.

While all forms of Orthodox Judaism are adamant in their refusal to appear to condone homosexual activity through communal recognition of identified homosexuals or homosexual couples, attitudes and policies concerning the appropriateness of accepting homosexual couples for synagogue membership and the access of openly gay or lesbian individuals to rabbinic study continue to be discussed and negotiated in the more liberal forms of contemporary Judaism in the early twenty-first century.

Feminist theology in Judaism

Jewish feminism also has a theoretical aspect that looks beyond issues of ritual innovation and egalitarian practice and suggests that Judaism's traditional teachings are inherently incomplete since they discount or ignore female experience. Judith Plaskow, a central figure in the development of Jewish feminist theology, believes that ordination of women as rabbis and cantors is not a sufficient response to normative Judaism's inherent androcentrism. For Plaskow, the future of Judaism depends on transformations of the basic Jewish theological concepts—God, divine revelation, and the believing community—in directions that recognize the full and equal humanity of all Jews, that reflect and voice the female experience, and that reintegrate the female aspects of the divine into Jewish conceptions of the Godhead.[12] The theological writings of Rachel Adler combine a deep knowledge of Jewish law and traditional texts with a passionate commitment to justice. Unable to define herself as Orthodox, since she believes traditional understandings of halakhah address the Jewish people solely as a community of men, Adler emphasizes the need to reimagine the Divine in female and male ways, and she stresses the importance of expanding language about God to include masculine and feminine metaphors and words. Adler advocates retaining those practices that remain central to a progressive Jewish community, while adding new traditions that emerge out of female and male interpretation and insight; she believes Jewish law and practice must be a dynamic process, evolving co-operatively, communally, and covenantally, rather than being externally imposed and passively obeyed.[13]

Conclusion

At the beginning of the twenty-first century many younger Jews have grown up in environments where women are rabbis and cantors, where rituals for marking female milestones are commonplace, and where serious Jewish study and communal leadership are options for all who seek them. However, many of the battles for female integrity and equality within Judaism remain to be fought within traditional forms of Judaism, Jewish communities with roots in the Muslim world, and in Israel, where Jewish women's rights in marriage and divorce remain circumscribed by halakhic regulation.

FURTHER READING

Baskin, Judith R. (ed.). *Jewish Women in Historical Perspective*, 2nd edn. (Detroit: Wayne State University Press, 1998). Sixteen accessible scholarly essays about Jewish women in various historical and cultural contexts from biblical times to the present.

Fishman, Sylvia Barack. *A Breath of Life: Feminism in the American Jewish Community* (New York: Free Press, 1993). Broad-based and nuanced analysis of the various impacts of Jewish feminism on the social and religious life of the American Jewish community.

Halpern, Micah D., and Chana Safrai (eds.). *Jewish Legal Writings by Women* (Jerusalem: Urim Publications, 1998). Seventeen articles on aspects of Jewish law and practice relevant to women's lives, by Orthodox feminist teachers and scholars.

Nadell, Pamela. *Women Who Would Be Rabbis: A History of Women's Ordination, 1889–1985* (Boston: Beacon Press, 1998). Definitive study of the struggle for women's rabbinic ordination.

Orenstein, Debra (ed.). *Lifecycles: Jewish Women on Life Passages and Personal Milestones* (Woodstock, Vt.: Jewish Lights Publishing, 1994). Reflections and innovative rituals for various events and situations in women's lives.

Ruttenberg, Danya. *Yentl's Revenge: The Next Wave of Jewish Feminism* (Seattle: Seal Press, 2001). Eclectic and idiosyncratic personal essays from young Jewish women of diverse backgrounds who are shaping their own approaches to combining Judaism and feminism.

Sheridan, Sybil (ed.). *Hear Our Voice: Women Rabbis Tell Their Stories* (London: SCM Press, 1994). Fifteen female British rabbis address a range of issues that have affected women in Jewish life in the sixty years since the ordination of Regina Jonas in Germany in 1935.

Umansky, Ellen M., and Dianne Ashton (eds.). *Four Centuries of Jewish Women's Spirituality: A Sourcebook* (Boston: Beacon Press, 1992). Anthology of letters, prayers, rituals, sermons, poems, and personal statements by Jewish women from 1560 to the present, with emphasis on sources since 1800. Includes thorough introductory essay by Umansky and helpful editorial analyses and annotations throughout.

Zuckerman, Francine (director). *Half the Kingdom* (Los Angeles: Direct Cinema, Ltd., 1989). This moving and provocative 58-minute film documents the ongoing quests of seven prominent and diverse Jewish feminists in Israel, Canada, and the United States to find their places in contemporary Judaism.

NOTES

1. This essay discusses changes in Jewish women's lives in Europe and North America, and to a more limited extent, Israel, in response to modernity; the emphasis is on the last third of the twentieth century. The lives of women from Jewish communities with historic roots in the Muslim world are not addressed.

2. See Chava Weissler, *Voices of the Matriarchs: Listening to the Prayers of Early Modern Jewish Women* (Boston: Beacon Press, 1998).

3. Marvin Lowenthal (tr.), *The Memoirs of Glückel of Hameln* (New York: Schocken Books, 1977).

4. See Marion A. Kaplan, *The Making of the Jewish Middle Class: Women, Family, and Identity in Imperial Germany* (New York: Oxford University Press, 1991); and Paula E. Hyman, *Gender and Assimilation in Modern Jewish History: The Roles and Representation of Women* (Seattle: University of Washington Press, 1995)

5. See Michael Galchinsky, *The Origin of the Modern Jewish Woman Writer: Romance and Reform in Victorian England* (Detroit: Wayne State University Press, 1996); and Ellen M. Umansky, *Lily Montagu and the Advancement of Liberal Judaism: From Vision to Vocation* (Lewiston, NY: Edwin Mellen Press, 1983).

6. See Kaplan, *Making of the Jewish Middle Class*; Hyman, *Gender and Assimilation*; and Linda Gordon Kuzmack, *Women's Cause: The Jewish Woman's Movement in England and the United States, 1881–1933* (Columbus, Ohio: Ohio State University Press, 1990).

7. For Henrietta Szold's life and accomplishments, see the website at the Jewish Women's Archives, http://www.jwa.org/exhibits/wov/szold.

8. See Katharina von Kellenbach, ' "God Does Not Oppress Any Human Being:" The Life and Thought of Rabbi Regina Jonas', *Leo Baeck Institute Yearbook* 39 (1994), pp. 213–25.

9. Marcia Falk, *The Book of Blessings: New Jewish Prayers for Daily Life, the Sabbath, and the New Moon Festival* (San Francisco: Harper, 1996).

10. Rivka Haut, 'Women's Prayer Groups and the Orthodox Synagogue', in Susan Grossman and Rivka Haut (eds.), *Daughters of the King: Women and the Synagogue* (Philadelphia: Jewish Publication Society, 1992), pp. 159–82.

11. Tamar Frankiel, *The Voice of Sarah: Feminine Spirituality and Traditional Judaism* (San Francisco: Harper, 1990). On Jewish women joining traditional communities, see Lynn Davidman, *Tradition in a Rootless World: Women Turn to Orthodox Judaism* (Berkeley: University of California Press, 1991), and Debra R. Kaufman, *Rachel's Daughters: Newly Orthodox Jewish Women* (New Brunswick, NJ: Rutgers University Press, 1991).

12. Judith Plaskow, *Standing Again At Sinai: Judaism from a Feminist Perspective* (San Francisco: Harper, 1990), p. 106.

13. Rachel Adler, *Engendering Judaism: An Inclusive Theology and Ethics* (Philadelphia: Jewish Publication Society, 1998).

Gender has become one of the primary categories under which thinking Jews (re)eval-
uate themselves in the modern world; but there has been relatively little articulation of
change in fundamental attitudes to sexuality outside of gay, lesbian, or queer discourse.[1] Hence, this chapter considers modern developments in Jewish understandings
of sexuality, concentrating primarily on homosexuality.

Modern Jewish apologetics consistently portrays traditional Jewish teaching on sex
and sexuality as positive, balanced, and healthy, in contrast with alleged Christian
hostility to sex and promotion of celibacy. In Judaism, the sin of Adam and Eve in
the Garden of Eden was not consistently linked with sexuality, as it tended to be in
Christianity, although some medieval writers did make the connection. Rashi, the
doyen of biblical commentators, insists that Adam and Eve cohabited *before* their sin in
the Garden.[2] Although the dominant rationale for sexual relations was always the
fulfilment of the first biblical commandment, 'Be fruitful and multiply' (Genesis 1: 28;
9: 2), Judaism also recognized other legitimate reasons for sex, including mutual pleasure, companionship, and the avoidance of sin. While young men were forbidden to
marry women known to be barren, marriage between people past childbearing age was
regarded favourably, and the practice of mandatory divorce after ten years of childless
marriage has long fallen into disuse. The Talmud is replete with frank discussions of
sex, even adopting at times a bawdy tone—reflecting its male authorship and intended
audience.

The rabbis recognized the importance of sexual pleasure in creating happy marriages, and legislated the minimum frequency of sexual relations a husband owed his
wife (*Mishnah Ketubbot* 5: 6, interpreting Exodus 21: 10). Men were forbidden to force
sex on their wives, encouraged to treat them affectionately and considerately, and
advised to take time over intercourse to ensure wives reached orgasm first—ironically,
this enlightened sexual advice was offered with the patriarchal incentive that it would
lead to the birth of male children (Babylonian Talmud [hereafter BT], *Niddah* 31a, 71a).

Medieval Kabbalah saw sexual intercourse as a model of the union of masculine and
feminine aspects of the godhead, which, when performed correctly, aided the infusion
of God's creative and salvific power into the universe. In the *Zohar*'s elaboration of
these ideas, the acts of fondling and kissing became significant preludes to the
climactic genital union. Nevertheless, the Kabbalah reflects, and indeed reinforces,

patriarchal stereotypes of the masculine as higher and active, the feminine as lower and passive, both among the divine hypostases and in the human sphere. Recent study has revealed the profoundly phallocentric (and implicitly homoerotic) nature of kabbalistic symbolism.[3]

It hardly needs stating that Jewish law restricts sexual activity to married couples, and prohibits intercourse during the wife's menstrual period and for seven days afterwards. Within these limits, rabbinic sources manifest tension between permissive and puritanical views of sexual expression. The permissive voice asserts that 'a man may do whatever he wishes with his wife' (BT *Nedarim* 20b), including vaginal, anal, or oral sex. The puritanical voice, presented as the ideal, insists that intercourse be conducted in reverent silence, in the dark of night, at home in bed, and that for the woman to be on top, or even side by side, is indecent (*Shulhan Arukh, Orah Hayyim* 240 and *Even Ha-Ezer* 25).

The latter point was reinforced by the legend of Lilith, Adam's first wife, who left him because she refused to lie underneath during intercourse. The lurid fantasies associated with Lilith expressed men's fear of female sexuality, although she has been adopted by modern Jewish feminists and reread as a positive symbol of women's liberation. Hence, a popular journal of Jewish feminist writing is entitled *Lilith*.

If anything, however, the rabbis showed an even more acute awareness of the uncontrollable power of the male sexual urge. The intimate connection between sexuality and sin was captured by the use of the term *yetzer ha-ra'*, the 'evil impulse' or inclination. This tendency to sin was seen as an inherent part of the psyche, in conflict with the *yetzer ha-tov* (good inclination). That this conflict is a creative force in human life is indicated in a midrash, *Bereshit Rabbah* 9: 7, commenting on the verse 'God saw all that he had made, and behold it was very good' (Genesis 1: 31). The midrash explains that 'good' indicates the yetzer ha-tov, but '*very* good' includes the yetzer ha-ra', without which no one would build a house, marry, and have children, or work for a livelihood. The yetzer ha-ra', then, was what we might now call the libido, a psychic drive or energy of desire that is necessary for life, but tends to be wild and selfish unless kept in check. Although this 'evil impulse' was not simply identified with the sex drive, in popular parlance yetzer ha-ra' without qualification did generally refer to the sexual urge. This demanded constant vigilance, and the halakhah provided numerous safety measures, including prohibitions on looking at women (except potential marriage partners), being alone with a woman or touching one, touching one's genitals, or sleeping on one's stomach or back, for fear of arousal. The sovereign remedy, if sexual thoughts did take hold, was Torah study—displacing the eros of the flesh by the eros of the divine word (BT *Kiddushin* 30b).

It is commonly assumed that, outside strictly Orthodox communities, the traditional prescriptions about sex, the ban on masturbation, and the strong discouragement of contraception are widely ignored. Jews have among the lowest birth rates in the developed world, very few women visit the *mikveh* (ritual bath) after their period, and pre-marital sex and cohabitation are widely practised amongst young Jews. Rates of intermarriage, too, have risen sharply in recent years; but a discussion of the sexual dynamic operative between Jews and non-Jews is beyond the scope of this chapter.

Nowhere is contemporary Jewish acculturation to prevailing western liberal mores more evident than in the growing visibility of gay men and lesbians within the Jewish community. Bisexuals and transsexuals (and other sexual variations) are relatively less visible at the time of writing, and there is as yet little discussion about the questions they pose to Jewish ethics and institutions. Nevertheless, the challenge that overt homosexuality represents to the traditional homophobia and heteronormativity of the Jewish community is immense, and its implications have barely begun to be explored.

Constructions of homosexuality

Homosexuality is a nineteenth-century quasi-medical term for a distinctively modern concept, namely, that most human beings exhibit, throughout the greater part of their adult lives, a relatively fixed sexual orientation, in this case towards people of the same sex. The category of sexual orientation, it is often noted, was unknown in biblical and rabbinic literature, which speak only of permitted and forbidden behaviours. Leviticus 18: 22, 'You shall not lie with a male the lyings of a woman, it is an abhorrence', was addressed to all men without distinction, and was understood in rabbinic law to prohibit specifically anal intercourse. Leviticus 20: 13, which adds the prescription of the death penalty, clarifies that both insertive and receptive partners were condemned.

Known in rabbinic literature as *mishkav zakhar*, 'male-lying', anal intercourse was regarded as a quintessentially non-Jewish vice. When Rabbi Judah, in the second century CE, decreed that two bachelors should not sleep under the same sheet, other sages permitted it, declaring, 'Israelites are not suspected of male-lying or bestiality' (BT *Kiddushin* 82a). Whether they meant that Jews are immune from homosexual temptation, or just that they would never actually perform anal intercourse—or whether the distinction would even have occurred to them—is not clear. Rabbinic perception of Greco-Roman society as hopelessly immersed in every form of licentiousness, including same-sex relationships, meant that homosexuality was perceived as an external danger rather than an internal reality. In all the centuries of rabbinic legal responsa, only a handful refer to cases of suspected or attested male-to-male sex.[4]

If male homosexuality was marginal in Jewish consciousness, lesbianism was virtually invisible, not even warranting a prohibition in the Torah. This was probably because it did not qualify as sex at all, since the definition of a legally significant sexual act was one that involved penile penetration. Two Talmudic passages, however, do mention the case of *nashim ha-mesolelot*, an obscure term meaning something like 'women who engage in sex-play', and discuss whether such women are considered 'harlots' who are disbarred from marrying a priest, or have merely committed lewdness without any legal consequences. The latter view prevailed, confirming that lesbian sex was seen as a minor infraction (BT *Yevamot* 76a and *Shabbat* 65a).

Nevertheless, later codifiers found a scriptural basis for this prohibition, by reference to the halakhic midrash *Sifra* (*Aharey Mot* 9: 8) on Leviticus 18: 3: 'You shall not copy the practices of the land of Egypt where you dwelt, or of the land of Canaan to which I am taking you; nor shall you follow their laws.' Explaining the nature of these laws, the midrash states: 'A man would marry a man, a woman a woman, a man would marry a woman and her daughter, and a woman would be married to two men.' Interpreting this midrash, Maimonides decreed that 'women who play around', while not subject to biblical penalty, should be punished with discretionary lashes by the court (*Mishneh Torah, Issurey Bi'ah* 21: 8).

The paucity of reference to lesbianism reflects the general lack of interest, in both biblical and rabbinic literature, in the sexual and emotional lives of women where they did not impinge upon men. While lesbians may be grateful for the relative lack of condemnation, they may also feel alienated by the tradition's dismissal of their non-phallic lovemaking.

It is not surprising, in view of this, that the prohibition of homosexual activity in traditional sources focuses mostly on male-to-male sex. The Talmud's only clue to explaining the prohibition suggests that the word *to'evah*, 'abhorrence' or 'abomination' in Leviticus 18: 22 is a conflation of the words *to'eh [attah] vah*, 'you err by it' (BT *Nedarim* 51a). Traditional commentators explained this cryptic comment in three main ways: (1) you err by it, since from it you can have no offspring; (2) you err by it, for men leave their wives to seek homosexual intercourse; (3) you err from the fundamental pattern of creation by lying with a male.[5] The third of these explanations, usually understood to refer to the fact that the genital organs are configured best for heterosexual intercourse, seems to be a Jewish equivalent of the argument from Nature.[6] A variation on this comes in the Talmud's discussion of the verse: 'Therefore shall a man leave his father and mother, and shall cleave to his wife, and they shall be one flesh' (Genesis 2: 24). The Talmud comments: 'cleave—but not to a male', on which Rashi explains: 'For there is no cleaving, since the receptive partner derives no pleasure [from anal intercourse] and does not "cleave" to him' (BT *Sanhedrin* 58a). Countless men could refute Rashi's account of 'nature' and testify to the pleasure and deep attachment they derive from a relationship expressed in anal as in other forms of intercourse.

The argument that men would leave their wives (permanently or temporarily) to engage in homosexual relations has much greater validity, evident today from the marriages that break up when a spouse finds it impossible to remain in a relationship that cannot fulfil their deepest sexual and emotional needs. The effect of this on the abandoned spouse and children can be devastating, but the problem is fundamentally with the external and internalized pressure gay men and lesbians feel to get married and live a 'normal' life, and the terrible toll this takes on the individual and family affected. As homosexuality becomes more widely accepted, and gay people suffer less from internalized homophobia, the pressure to enter false heterosexual relationships may dwindle, ending such painful family break-ups. The advice given to the present writer, when he came out to an Orthodox rabbi many years ago, was to get married, and if necessary 'stray' occasionally when the urge became too great. Rabbi Chaim Rapoport, in chapter 7 of his recent book *Judaism and Homosexuality*, is the first Orthodox writer to insist publicly, against much contrary opinion, that it is positively inadvisable for many gay people to marry a member of the opposite sex.

The argument that carries greatest resonance in a Jewish context is that homosexuality is non-procreative, and therefore inimical to the letter and spirit of Judaism. In the powerful rhetoric of the British Orthodox chief rabbi, Jonathan Sacks, the family is the foundation not only of Jewish continuity but of Jewish ethics. The moral choice to have children, to take responsibility for their welfare and education, and to work for a world fit for them to live in represents the root and fount of our entire ethical enterprise. Hence: 'the ideals of heterosexuality . . . are written into the entire fabric of the biblical vision . . . something the Bible conveys dramatically by making "Be fruitful and multiply" the first of all the commands', and 'traditional sexual ethics becomes not one alternative among many in a sexually pluralistic world, but the only persuasive way of life for those who want to engage in the ethical undertaking'.[7]

Sacks's argument rests on a number of questionable premises. First, heterosexual pairing is not the only setting for raising children. If choosing to have children is the touchstone of ethical endeavour, he must reckon with the fact that an increasing number of lesbians and gay men are so choosing. Secondly, Sacks asserts that, on the question of procreation, the only ethical choice is to have children. As noted above, more recent Orthodox opinion suggests that, for many homosexuals, not getting married may be the morally correct choice, and childlessness too may be an ethically responsible decision. An underlying assumption of the argument seems to be that homosexuality is a selfish lifestyle choice, a common charge that is belied by the large body of scientific and psychological findings pointing to the unalterable nature of most sexual orientation, whether innate or formed in a child's earliest years. Above all, the suggestion that only those with children are committed to 'the ethical undertaking' is patently absurd, and ignores the obvious moral contributions of innumerable childless people.

Modern interpretations

As long as homosexuality was socially taboo, rationales like those mentioned, however spurious, adequately justified what scarcely seemed to need justifying. Dramatic changes began with the social and sexual revolution of the 1960s and 1970s. In Britain 1967 saw the legalization of male homosexual intercourse between two adults in private; 1969 brought the Stonewall Riots in Greenwich Village and the era of militant gay liberation. Change soon became noticeable even in Orthodox discussions of the gay question. The first major modern statement appeared in the *Encyclopaedia Judaica Yearbook* of 1974, in an article by Rabbi Norman Lamm, the influential president of Yeshiva University, entitled 'Judaism and the Modern Attitude to Homosexuality'. After presenting the interpretations noted above, he writes: 'It may be, however, that the very variety of interpretations of to'evah points to a far more fundamental meaning, namely, that an act characterized as an "abomination" is *prima facie* disgusting and cannot be further defined or explained . . . it is, as it were, a visceral reaction, an intuitive disqualification of the act . . .' Lamm proceeds to argue for an understanding attitude towards gay people based on a view of homosexuality as sickness, which diminishes slightly the culpability of the practitioner. He recommends that laws against 'sodomy' be kept on the statute books (in the United States), but rest unenforced, signalling society's abhorrence of the sin but compassion towards the sinner.

With hindsight, Lamm's account of to'evah reveals a breach in the fortress of traditional certainty. Instead of grounding the prohibition in objective problems with homosexuality, following the traditional authorities, he retreats into subjectivity. Facing the reality of openly gay people and their demand for acceptance, Lamm finds the ultimate ground of rejection in an intuitive, aesthetic distaste. His own visceral reaction, and that of people like him, is projected onto the text and its (for him) divine Author, in order to control the lives and loves of those unlike him. Obviously, such a position cannot command the respect of those whose viscera are differently constituted, and it is unsurprising that Orthodox rhetoric has changed in the years since his article.

An even more extreme reaction appeared in a 1976 responsum by Rabbi Moshe Feinstein, the doyen of ultra-Orthodox authorities, addressed to a young man seeking help in dealing with his homosexual impulses. Feinstein offers him three reflections to help him resist his 'evil inclination'. The first is to reflect on the seriousness of the sin, indicated by the statutory penalty of stoning which it incurred in ancient times, and the fact that it is so disgusting that even non-Jews are bidden to abstain. The second is that it is inconceivable for one to have natural desire for homosexual liaison, which is utterly contrary to the way humans were created. Even ordinary sinners do not indulge in homosexual practices, which have no root in the human sex drive, but are performed simply *because* they are forbidden, in wanton rebellion against God. That is why it is called an abomination, unlike other forbidden relationships, which at least arise from the natural heterosexual impulse. Thirdly, all people, even the wicked, despise homosexuals, and even homosexual partners find each other despicable.[8] Chaim Rapoport, in his recent book, is clearly troubled by the extreme and anti-empirical character of Feinstein's approach. It is contradicted by the lives of many conscientious Orthodox Jews struggling to remain faithful to Judaism while not denying their sexual identity, and by the growing consensus that homosexuality is a natural variation in human sexual behaviour. He concludes: 'I do not understand R. Feinstein's views on this matter.'[9]

Amongst non-Orthodox writers, since the late 1970s various strategies have been offered to understand the biblical law in its own context, and find space for lesbians and gay men in present-day Judaism. One approach draws upon modern understandings of the nature of sexual orientation to argue that homosexuals are in the category of *ones*—people compelled to a course of action, who are not seen as liable for their transgression of the law.[10] The usual Orthodox response to this is that sexual desire may be beyond conscious control, but action is not, and forbidden acts must still be avoided. Outside Orthodoxy, some argue that the halakhah must change to take account of the radically altered insight into human sexuality. The Leviticus commandment might be understood as addressing the heterosexual majority, who are admonished against situational and opportunistic indulgence in homosexual intercourse, while for gay men it does not apply. One creative approach suggested focusing on the phrase 'the lyings of a woman', so that what is forbidden is using a man as a substitute sex-object when the desire is really for a woman. The verse does not address those who desire a man *as a man*, and have no attraction to 'the lyings of a woman'.[11] Some Orthodox gay men note that the Torah prohibits only anal intercourse, and therefore allow themselves to transgress the lesser, rabbinic prohibition of other acts of gay intimacy.

Modern scholarly attempts to contextualize the Levitical prohibition are of three main kinds. The earliest and most common portrays the ban on homosexual intercourse as part of the Torah's suppression of idolatrous cults and practices. Many traditional and modern commentators interpret references to the *kadesh* (sacred prostitute) to mean male homosexual prostitutes, which are designated to'*evah*,[12] reinforcing the suggestion that it was the heathen cultic nature of homosexuality that was problematic. Modern gay people are thus relieved of religious stigma.

A second approach sees the problem, from the Torah's perspective, in the often unequal, violent, and exploitative nature of same-sex relations in the ancient world. Much research confirms that intercourse was rarely between equal, consenting adult partners, but usually between adults and youths, free men and slaves, or victorious warriors raping their defeated foes. Sexual relations (heterosexual as much as homosexual) were generally power relations between a dominant and a submissive party, and it is this violence, humiliation, and inequality in relations between men that the Torah is concerned to eliminate.[13] Modern homosexuality, emphasising loving relationships of equality and mutual respect, is entirely different, and not the subject of the Torah's ruling.

The third, and to my mind most persuasive, account focuses again on the biblical phrase *mishkevey ishah*, 'the lyings of a woman'. What is unacceptable, in the eyes of the Torah, is that a man should treat another man as a woman and penetrate him sexually. This is related to the previous argument about domination, but concentrates not on the emotional content of a particular relationship, but on the very fact of one man being penetrated by another. This act breaks down the essential distinction between men and women, and in 'womanizing' another man, challenges the whole basis of the patriarchal society envisaged by the social legislation of the Torah.[14] Gay sex is thus a revolutionary act, which should be understood as breaking down patriarchy at its heart. The gay liberation movement began as an offshoot of women's liberation, and the progress of gay rights has followed on the heels of the feminist revolution. This is as true for gay men as it is for lesbians, who have generally seen themselves explicitly as part of the larger women's movement. Feminism and gay liberation still have much to achieve, both in the West and in non-western countries, until all people are released from the bonds of heterosexist patriarchy and can explore their identity as men and women in free and equal relations within and between the sexes.

Jewish gay and lesbian life today

Shortly after Stonewall, gay and lesbian Jews began to organize themselves in groups. The Jewish Gay Group ('lesbian' was added later) was set up in London in 1972, and in the same year a gay synagogue, Beth Chayim Chadashim ('House of New Life') was established in Los Angeles, followed the next year by Congregation Beth Simchat Torah in New York. Since then, gay synagogues have emerged in all major Jewish population centres in the United States, and many have become important congregations in their cities, with flourishing religion schools and a mixture of lesbian, gay, and straight members. This tendency for gay people to self-segregate in their own synagogues was widely criticized by mainstream organizations, but several congregations have since affiliated to the Reform or Reconstructionist movements. In Britain, Jewish demography and a different communal culture has made the establishment of gay synagogues less feasible, but one inclusive congregation, Bet Klal Yisrael ('The House of All Israel') was created by lesbian rabbi Sheila Shulman, with a largely lesbian and gay membership, under the auspices of the British Reform movement. Small gay and lesbian groups exist in Europe, Israel, Australia, South America, and elsewhere. All these groups are represented in the World Congress of Gay, Lesbian, Bisexual and Transgender Jews, also known as Keshet Ga'avah ('Rainbow of Pride'), which has held regular regional and global conferences.

Gay rights have advanced rapidly in Israel, from the decriminalization of gay sex in 1988 to the granting of pension rights for gay and lesbian partners, and the open recognition of gay soldiers in the Israeli army in the mid-1990s. Gay pride parades have been held in Tel Aviv, and subsequently in Jerusalem, which also has a flourishing gay drop-in centre in the middle of the city. The victory of gay-identified transsexual singer Dana International in the 1998 Eurovision Song Contest helped galvanize the Israeli gay community and bring gay issues to public awareness. A current cutting-edge issue in Israel is the persecution of gay men in Palestinian-controlled areas, and whether Palestinians from the territories will be permitted to stay with their Jewish partners within Israel.

The AIDS epidemic, which reached its peak in gay communities in the West in the late 1980s, had an enormous effect on the Jewish gay community. Previously, Jewish lesbians had identified more closely with the feminist movement than with the struggle for gay men's liberation. In the AIDS crisis, however, with its personal tragedies and the wave of homophobia it triggered, women and men united for solidarity and mutual support, forging a new sense of community. Whilst before AIDS gay activists had focused on the untrammelled enjoyment of sexual liberation; the response to AIDS brought an emphasis on practical care, coalition building, and the creation of stable, faithful partnerships.

An important development in Jewish gay affairs, beginning in 2001, has been the widespread attention gained by the film *Trembling Before G-d*, directed by Sandi Simcha Dubowski. Concentrating on a handful of Orthodox, or ex-Orthodox, gay and lesbian Jews, and their relationship with their Orthodox Jewish communities, this feature-length documentary has achieved acclaim amongst Orthodox and wider audiences worldwide, and has been connected with a new openness and sensitivity to gay issues in Orthodox circles and beyond.

To appeal to Orthodox audiences, *Trembling Before G-d* deliberately omitted, in its portrayal of Jews anguished by their rejection at the hands of their families and communities, reference to the extraordinary progress of gay liberation within Progressive Jewish movements since the 1980s. In responsa of 1969 and 1973 the leading American Reform rabbi Solomon Freehof adhered to the traditional prohibitive stance, as did subsequent Reform halakhists.[15] As early as 1977, however, the Central Conference of American Rabbis (CCAR) passed a resolution supporting the decriminalization of homosexuality and full gay civil rights. In the 1980s the leading Progressive seminaries, Hebrew Union College (American Reform), the Reconstructionist Rabbinical College of Philadelphia, and Leo Baeck College in London all altered their policies to admit and ordain openly lesbian and gay students. There are now over a hundred openly gay and lesbian rabbis in the United States and Britain.

The ordination of gay rabbis is currently the single most divisive issue for the American Conservative movement, with the leadership of the Jewish Theological Seminary in New York maintaining its refusal to admit openly gay rabbinic students, despite widespread calls for change both amongst the student body and leading Conservative rabbis.[16]

For the Progressive movements, the focus rests upon the issue of same-sex marriage. The UAHC (Union of American Hebrew Congregations) in 1993, followed by the CCAR in 1996, passed resolutions supporting the right of gay men and lesbians to the benefits of civil marriage. A prolonged debate ensued before the American Reform Movement resolved in 2000 to support rabbinic officiation at same-sex commitment ceremonies. Some rabbis had already been officiating de facto for many years, both in America and, more quietly, in Britain. In the late 1990s the issue revealed deep divisions and residual homophobia in British Reform, which passed a resolution in 1998 refusing support for same-sex ceremonies, but conceding that rabbis would not be expelled from the movement for officiating at those which nevertheless took place. The smaller and more radical British Liberal movement endured no such struggle, and in 2003 issued a progressive set of resolutions supporting same-sex ceremonies (still not called marriages) in the synagogue, the creation of appropriate liturgy, and the full equality of gay and lesbian individuals and families within Liberal synagogues. Publication of official liturgies is imminent both in the United States and Britain, and the title of the Liberal movement's ceremony is *B'rit Ahavah—Seder Kiddushin l'Zuggot Had Miniim/ Covenant of Love—Service of Commitment for Same-Sex Couples*.

Despite setbacks and frustrations, the progress towards acceptance of divergent sexualities in the Jewish community since the late 1960s has been breathtaking. For Jewish lesbians and gay men (or queers, as some increasingly call themselves) it has been a process of communal coming out, analogous to the personal coming out which transforms the lives of gay and lesbian individuals, enabling them to be themselves, tap into their sexual, emotional, and creative energy, and discover healthy, ethical, and adult ways of living an integrated Jewish gay or lesbian life. Many questions remain. How far will liberation go, especially in the Orthodox world? Will the Jewish community fully embrace the possibility of gay marriage and parenthood? Will the current emphasis on monogamous partnership allow room for the flourishing and ethical discussion of other modes of sexual engagement that have been, and are being, explored in the gay and lesbian world . . .? For a Shabbat service at the thirteenth, 'bar-mitzvah' conference of the World Congress in 1993, I wrote a meditation, whose concluding lines echo a passage in the Pesach Haggadah that has special resonance for gay and lesbian Jews:

> Here and now we have emerged
> To claim our identity and our destiny;
> We have come of age;
> We have come out
>   From slavery to freedom,
>   From anguish to great joy,
>   From the closet to the world.

FURTHER READING

Alpert, Rebecca. *Like Bread on the Seder Plate: Jewish Lesbians and the Transformation of Tradition* (New York: Columbia University Press, 1997). Already a classic text of Jewish lesbian scholarship and cultural reflection.

Alpert, Rebecca T., Sue Levi Elwell, and Shirley Idelson (eds.). *Lesbian Rabbis: The First Generation* (New Brunswick and London: Rutgers University Press, 2001).

Balka, Christie, and Andy Rose (eds.). *Twice Blessed: On Being Lesbian or Gay and Jewish* (Boston: Beacon Press, 1989). Pioneering collection of essays, reflecting the background of the founding generation of the American Jewish gay/lesbian movement in the civil rights and anti-Vietnam War campaigns.

Boyarin, Daniel, Daniel Itzkovitz, and Ann Pellegrini (eds.). *Queer Theory and the Jewish Question*

(New York: Columbia University Press, 2003). Highly academic and self-consciously post-postmodern, and like Shneer and Aviv's *Queer Jews*, reflecting the growing use of 'queer' instead of 'gay/lesbian'.

Greenberg, Steven. *Wrestling With God and Men: Homosexuality in the Jewish Tradition* (Madison, Wisc.: University of Wisconsin Press, 2004). Highly readable and important statement by the first (and so far only) openly gay Orthodox rabbi.

Magonet, Jonathan (ed.). *Jewish Explorations of Sexuality* (Providence, RI: Bergbahn Books, 1995). An important collection of papers on sexuality and homosexuality by rabbis and psychotherapists.

Moore, Tracy (ed.). *Lesbiot: Israeli Lesbians Talk about Sexuality, Feminism, Judaism and their Lives* (New York and London: Cassell, 1995); and Sumaka'i Fink, Amir and Jacob Press. *Independence Park: The Lives of Gay Men in Israel* (Stanford, Calif.: Stanford University Press, 1999). These books reveal, through interviews, the variety of Israeli lesbian and gay lives.

Raphael, Lev. *Dancing on Tisha B'Av* (New York: St. Martin's Press, 1991); and Felman, Jyl Lynn. *Hot Chicken Wings* (San Francisco: Aunt Lute Books, 1992). Two pioneering collections of Jewish queer short stories, with sub-themes of Holocaust survival and food.

Rapoport, Chaim. *Judaism and Homosexuality: An Authentic Orthodox View* (London and Portland, Oreg.: Valentine Mitchell, 2004). The subtitle probably alluding to Steven Greenberg's book, this comprehensive statement by a British Lubavitcher rabbi breaks new ground in recognizing the reality of gay life and the struggles of Jewish gay men and lesbians, and proposes a humane and courageous modus vivendi with Orthodoxy.

Shneer, David, and Caryn Aviv (eds.). *Queer Jews* (New York and London: Routledge, 2002). A collection based consciously on Balka and Rose's *Twice Blessed*, updating its themes for the twenty-first century.

Shokeid, Moshe. *A Gay Synagogue in New York* (New York: Columbia University Press, 1995). Unique and fascinating essay in the social anthropology of a major Jewish gay institution.

Walzer, Lee. *Between Sodom and Eden: A Gay Journey Through Today's Changing Israel* (New York: Columbia University Press, 2000). A superbly written thematic account of gay life in Israel.

NOTES

1. See Judith Plaskow, *Standing Again At Sinai: Judaism From a Feminist Perspective* (San Francisco: Harper, 1991), chap. 5, 'Toward a New Theology of Sexuality'. It should be noted that writers who are driving forward Jewish thinking about sexuality, like Plaskow and Boyarin, write from an implicitly or explicitly lesbian, gay, or queer perspective even when their writings are not primarily focused on homosexuality. For discussion of the position of women and female sexuality, see Chaps. 30 and 31 in this volume.

2. Rashi (Solomon b. Isaac, France, 1040–1105), Genesis 4: 1.

3. For a kabbalistic view of marital sexuality see *The Holy Letter: A Study in Jewish Sexual Morality*, tr. Seymour J. Cohen (Northvale, NJ and London: Jason Aronson, 1993). For Zoharic passages dealing with the symbolism of kissing and intercourse, see Isaiah Tishby, *The Wisdom of the Zohar*, tr. David Goldstein (Oxford: Littman Library, 1989), vol. i, pp. 364–70. For groundbreaking studies of the phallocentric nature of kabbalistic sexual symbolism and its tendency to marginalize women by subsuming the feminine within the masculine, see Elliot R. Wolfson, *Circle in the Square: Studies in the Use of Gender in Kabbalistic Symbolism* (New York: State University of New York Press, 1995).

4. See Steven Greenberg, *Wrestling With God and Men: Homosexuality in the Jewish Tradition* (Madison, Wisc.: University of Wisconsin Press, 2004), pp. 127–34, and Chaim Rapoport, *Judaism and*

Homosexuality: An Authentic Orthodox View (London and Portland, Oreg.: Valentine Mitchell, 2004), pp. 162–3.

5. Explanation (1) derives from the midrash *Pesikta Zutrata* (*Lekach Tov*), p. 52, and the thirteenth-century *Sefer Ha-Hinnukh*, commandment 209. Explanation (2), also from the twelfth–thirteenth century, is given by *Tosafot* and *Perush Ha-Rosh* (Asher b. Yehiel) on *Nedarim* 51a. Explanation (3) is found in the early twentieth-century commentary *Torah Temimah* by Barukh Ha-Levi Epstein, to Leviticus 18: 22.

6. For a discussion of arguments from Nature, see John Boswell, *Christianity, Social Tolerance, and Homosexuality: Gay People in Western Europe from the Beginning of the Christian Era to the Fourteenth Century* (Chicago: University of Chicago Press, 1980), Introduction and chap. 11. The most recent and comprehensive Orthodox treatment of the subject, Rapoport's *Judaism and Homosexuality* (p. 147, n. 25), rather lamely invokes the principle *nishtanu ha-tivim*, that 'nature has changed', so that 'certain aspects of empirical scientific phenomena, including human biology and psychology, may have changed since the era of the Talmud and the early Codes of *halachah*'. Despite the very different social setting of homosexuality, there is ample evidence that men in ancient and medieval times derived pleasure from anal intercourse—and indeed the testimony of the *Sifra* quoted earlier, that 'a man would marry a man'.

7. Jonathan Sacks, *Tradition in an Untraditional Age: Essays on Modern Jewish Thought* (London: Valentine, Mitchell), pp. 169–70.

8. Moshe Feinstein, *Iggerot Moshe, Orah Hayyim* (New York: Moriah Offset, 1982), vol. 4, no. 115, pp. 205–6.

9. Rapoport, *Judaism and Homosexuality*, p. 29. See also pp. 10–15.

10. See Herschel Matt, 'Sin, Crime, Sickness, or Alternative Lifestyle?: A Jewish Approach to Homosexuality', *Judaism*, 27 (1978), pp. 13–24.

11. Yehudah ben Ari, *Menorah* (July/Aug. 1983), p. 1, cited in Rebecca Alpert, *Like Bread on the Seder Plate: Jewish Lesbians and the Transformation of Tradition* (New York: Columbia University Press) p. 39.

12. 1 Kings 14: 24; see also 15: 12; 22: 47; 2 Kings 23: 7; and the law in Deut. 23: 18. Some scholars understand *kadesh* to refer to male *heterosexual* prostitutes.

13. See Greenberg, *Wrestling With God and Men*, chap. 13.

14. There is not space here to demonstrate the pervasively patriarchal world-view of the Torah, but note the ban on transvestism in Deut. 22: 5 (designated as to'evah) and the insistence that men should wear beards in Lev. 19: 27. See Plaskow, *Standing Again At Sinai*, chap. 2, and for a milder version of my argument, Greenberg, *Wrestling With God and Men*, chap. 12.

15. See Solomon B. Freehof, 'Homosexuality', in *Current Reform Responsa* (Cincinnati: Hebrew Union College Press, 1969), pp. 236–8; 'Homosexual Congregations', in *Contemporary Reform Responsa* (Cincinnati: HUC Press, 1974), pp. 23–6; Walter Jacob, 'Homosexuals in Leadership Positions' (1981), in *American Reform Responsa* (New York: CCAR, 1983), pp. 52–4; and 'Homosexual Marriage' (1985), in *Contemporary American Reform Responsa* (New York: CCAR, 1987), pp. 297–8.

16. The importance of this issue in Conservative rabbinic circles is shown by the voluminous collection of conflicting responsa in *Responsa 1991–2000*, published by the Committee on Jewish Law and Standards of the Conservative Movement, ed., Kassel Abelson and David J. Fine (New York: The Rabbinical Assembly, 2002), pp. 612–729.

Judaism and the other

33 | As others see Jews

Elliott Horowitz

Introduction

When visiting Palestine in 1836 the American traveller John Lloyd Stephens, who was later to achieve fame for his *Incidents of Travel in Central America, Chiapas, and the Yucatan* (1841), entered Hebron and was brought by his guide to 'a distant and separate quarter of the city'. At first the young New Jersey native had no idea where he was being taken, but, as he later wrote, 'I had not advanced a horse's length in the narrow streets before their peculiar costume and physiognomies told me that I was among the unhappy remnant of a fallen people, the persecuted and despised Israelites'.

Later, in Jerusalem, Stephens entered a synagogue, where he saw a rabbi 'reading to a small remnant of the Israelites the same law which had been read to their fathers on the same spot ever since they came up out of the land of Egypt'. Although he saw 'sternness' in the faces of this 'feeble remnant of a mighty people', he somehow knew that in their hearts they carried 'a spirit of patient endurance and a firm and settled resolution to die and be buried under the shadow of their fallen temple'. Stephens, who was then only about 30, also paid close attention to the faces of the fairer sex. Since leaving Europe several months earlier he had not been anywhere 'where the women sat with their faces uncovered', and so during the (to him) inscrutable Saturday morning sermon 'it was not altogether unnatural' that his gaze turned 'from the rough-bearded sons of Abraham to the smooth faces of their wives and daughters'. In the women's section of the synagogue Stephens spied 'many a dark-eyed Jewess who appeared well worthy' of his gaze, and boastfully reported that 'many a Hebrew maiden turned her black orbs' upon him as well.[1]

The young American was not the only western visitor to Palestine to remark on the distinct physiognomy of the Jews or on the surprising beauty of their women. Thomas Skinner, a British military officer travelling to India overland from Egypt during the mid-1830s, passed through Tiberias, whose women he found 'very fair and exceedingly pretty', noting also (to his evident surprise) that 'there were blue eyes among them and rosy cheeks'. Skinner, who was quite well travelled for a man still in his mid-thirties, felt that there was a distinct look that characterized the Jews throughout the world, an expression that was 'so strongly marked, and so invariably fixed that, of whatever colour or in whatever costume they may be, they are still detected'.[2]

He was not the first British traveller to express such an opinion. The Scottish solicitor William Wilson commented in his *Travels in the Holy Land . . .* (1823) that:

In various circumstances, at home and abroad, all Jews may be said to appear the same. Look at their face, the dark forehead, the flashing eye, raven locks, bushy beard and eyebrow. A strong eastern character is in fact stamped on every countenance. Whether they are among their own people, or surrounded by those of other lands, Jews appear as the most extraordinary beings on the face of the earth.[3]

This chapter investigates the reactions of Anglo-American travellers and missionaries to actual Jews and Jewish communities they encountered far away from home, and the degree to which these encounters either strengthened or undermined their pre-existing prejudices regarding these 'extraordinary beings'.

Early modern encounters

Although the emphasis here is on the nineteenth and early twentieth centuries, it is important to stress that since early modern times much attention had been devoted to the 'look'—both in terms of physical features and facial expression—of the Jew. In 1608 the young Englishman Thomas Coryate, when visiting Venice as part of his Grand Tour, entered one the synagogues of its famous ghetto on a Sabbath, where he was struck by the appearances of both the men and the women he saw:

I observed some fewe of these Jewes, especially some of the Levantines, to bee such goodly and proper men, that then I said to my selfe our English proverbe: To looke like a Jewe (whereby is meant sometimes a weather beaten warp-faced fellow, sometimes a phrenticke and lunaticke person, sometimes one discontented) is not true. For indeed I noted some of them to be the most elegant and sweete featured persons, which gave me occasion the more to lament their religion.

Moreover, like Stevens and Skinner in the nineteenth century, he was particularly impressed by the Jewish women, some of whom, he later wrote, 'were as beautiful as ever I saw, and so gorgeous in their apparel, Jewels, chaines of gold, and rings adorned with precious stones, that some of our English Countesses do scarce exceed them'.[4]

Henry Blount, an Oxford graduate who travelled through the Levant during the 1630s, later reflected in his popular account of that voyage on why the Jews could never 'ciment into a temporall Government of their owne'. Among the reasons that he gave was that 'the *Jewish* complexion is so prodigiously *timide*, as cannot be capable of Armes; for this reason they are no where made Souldiers, nor slaves . . .'.[5] Four decades later another Oxford graduate, Lancelot Addison, who had served as chaplain to the British garrison in Tangier between 1662 and 1670, wrote similarly of his experience among the Jews of Morocco. Even when bullied by the Moors, he reported, 'they dare not move a finger, or wag a tongue in their own defense and vindication'. Addison stressed, however, that the 'stoical patience' with which they faced all injuries and insults 'cannot be imputed to any Heroick Temper in this People, but rather to their customary suffering, being born and Educated in this kind of Slavery. By reason whereof, they were never acquainted with the Sentiments of an ingenuous and manly Usage.' Addison also commented on the Jewish aversion to all matters military: 'The *Moor* permit not the *Jews* the possession of any warlike Weapons . . . And herein they do not so much restrain, as gratifie their disposition, for they seem generally enclined to a great averseness to everything that is Military: being as destitute of true Courage, as good Nature'.[6]

Fear, Pharisees, and physiognomy

The lack of courage that allegedly characterized the Jews was sometimes 'seen' on their faces by discerning Christians. During the early 1820s the Anglican missionary William Jowett visited Jerusalem, where he met a certain 'Rabbi Mendel', who was highly respected 'on account of his Talmudical Learning'. Jowett, a graduate of Cambridge, was quite certain that he could read the rabbi's face like a book:

In addition to a certain wild abstracted gaze, which nature and Talmudical studies have given to the countenance of Rabbi Mendel, he was further suffering from terror, the impression of which was not yet effaced from his mind; he having been, about a week before, forcibly seized in the night, and carried off to prison by order of the new [Ottoman] Governor.[7]

Jowett noted that the rabbi, who had been arrested on a flimsy charge and released only after paying 'a heavy fine', had proposed turning for assistance to the Austrian consul in Acre, since he was nominally an Austrian subject. He preferred, however, going in person to writing, since 'if it were known in Jerusalem that he had written, it would subject him to fresh insults or exactions'. Jowett then piously added: 'How truly is that threat accomplished, "Thy life shall hang in doubt before thee, and thou shalt fear day and night, and shalt have none assurance of thy life" (Deut. 28: 66).'[8]

He was not the only nineteenth-century missionary to see biblical verses reflected in contemporary Jewish countenances. Less than two decades later the Scottish missionaries A. A. Bonar and R. M. M'Cheyne travelled to Palestine and continued as far as Poland in their efforts to assess the potentials and pitfalls of Protestant conversion efforts. Of the Jews in the Galilean town of Safed they wrote: 'It was easy to read their deep anxiety in the very expression of their countenances: they were truly in the state foretold by Moses more than 3,000 years ago.' The prooftext cited by the two Presbytarians was Deuteronomy 28: 65–6: 'The Lord shall give thee a trembling heart . . . and sorrow of mind: and thy life shall hang in doubt before thee; and thou shalt fear day and night, and shalt have none assurance of thy life.' When visiting a synagogue in Tarnopol some months later the two missionaries were also quite confident about the message to be read on the countenances of the local Jews: 'Our entrance caused considerable commotion to the worshippers', whose faces, they wrote, 'assumed an aspect of terror . . . and they whispered anxiously to another'. Explaining that the Jews' alarm was based on their fear that the two Christians 'were officers of the Austrian government come to spy their doings', the authors piously added: 'How truly these words have come to pass, "I will send a faintness into their hearts in the land of their enemies; and the sound of a shaken leaf shall chase them; and they shall flee as fleeing from a sword; and they shall fall when none pursueth" (Leviticus 26: 36–7).'[9]

Later in the century William McClure Thomson, who was sent to Jerusalem from Beirut in 1834 by the American Board of Commissioners for Foreign Missions, commented in his enormously popular *The Land and the Book* (1858), on his first visit to one of the Holy City's synagogues: 'I never saw such an assemblage of old, pale, and woebegone countenances', adding that there was 'something inexpressibly sad in the features, deportment, and costume of these children of Abraham, as they grope about the ruins of their once joyous city'. Like many visitors, Thomson recognized that many of Jerusalem's elderly Jews had come there to die, and he felt that this helped to explain their generally forlorn appearance: 'Many of them', he asserted, 'have been great sinners elsewhere', and had come to Jerusalem 'to purge away their guilt by abstinence, mortification, and devotion; then to die, and be buried as near the Holy City as possible.' The Ohio-born missionary suggested, quite reasonably, that 'a community gathered for that specific purpose will not be particularly gay, nor very careful about appearances'.

Yet there were also visitors to Jerusalem who felt that its Jewish residents were more aesthetically pleasing than their co-religionists elsewhere. Bayard Taylor, one of the most prolific American travel writers of the nineteenth century, who was also a landscape artist and popular lecturer, remarked, after visiting Palestine in the 1850s, that the 'native Jewish families in Jerusalem, as well as those in other parts of Palestine, present a marked difference to the Jews of Europe and America'. Although the 'physical characteristics', Taylor claimed, were the same—'the dark, oblong eye, the prominent nose, the strongly marked cheek and jaw'—he felt that among the latter these traits had become 'harsh and coarse' as a consequence of 'centuries devoted to the lowest and most debasing forms of traffic, with the endurance of persecution and contumely'. By contrast, he asserted, 'the Jews of the Holy City still retain a noble beauty' which, to his mind, proved 'their descent from the ancient princely houses of Israel'. There were clear signs of their aristocratic provenance: 'The forehead is loftier, the eye larger and more frank in its expression, the nose more delicate in its prominence, and the face a purer oval.'

Taylor even convinced himself, early in his visit to Jerusalem, that he had seen a Jew whose face was identical with that of Jesus:

On the evening of my arrival in the city, as I set out to walk through the bazaars, I encountered a native Jew, whose face will haunt me for the rest of my life . . . It was the very face which Raphael has painted—the traditional features of the Saviour, as they are recognised and accepted by all Christendom. The waving brown hair, partly hidden by a Jewish cap, fell clustering about the ears; the face was the most perfect oval, and almost feminine in the purity of its outline; the serene, child-like mouth was shaded with a light moustache, and a silky brown beard clothed the chin; but the eyes—shall I ever look into such orbs again? Large, dark, unfathomable, they beamed with an expression of divine love and divine sorrow, such as I never saw before in a human face . . . As the dusk gathered in the deep streets, I could see nothing but the ineffable sweetness and benignity of that countenance, and my friend was not a little astonished, if not shocked, when I said to him, with the earnestness of belief, on my return: 'I have just seen Christ.'[10]

And just as Taylor thought that he saw in the faces of Jerusalem Jews evidence of 'their descent from the ancient princely houses of Israel', so some other western visitors to the Holy City stressed different aspects of the continuity between its contemporary Jewish residents and those of the distant past. The young British traveller Alexander Kinglake, a graduate of Eton and Trinity College, Cambridge, whose *Eothen* (1844) became a classic of nineteenth-century travel writing, commented that 'he could not help looking upon the Jews of Jerusalem as being in some sort the representatives, if not the actual descendants, of the men who crucified our Saviour'.[11]

Do all Jews look alike?

In contrast to Bayard Taylor, many nineteenth-century writers, as we have already seen, felt that all Jews looked basically alike. In 1828 a British traveller who had been to the Jewish ghetto of Frankfurt commented that 'the undeviating and uniform identity of the features and general character of the countenance which accompany these singular people, wherever they settle, is certainly one of the most curious phenomena in nature'. In his view, 'climate, and all those wonderful changes in the physical circumstances belonging to localities, which work such wonderful changes in the physical character of man . . . appear to have no influence upon the tribe of Israel'. As a consequence, whether Jews were by 'birth and residence German, English, Russian, Portuguese, or Polish, still the one and only set of features belonging to the race will be seen equally in all'.[12] Similarly, in his popular *Travels into Bokhara*, first published in 1834, the British soldier, traveller, writer, and diplomat Sir Alexander Burns compared the appearances of the Uzbeks, Russians, Chinese, Hindus, and Jews he had seen along the way from India to Kabul. 'No mark', he wrote, 'is so distinguishing as the well known features of the Hebrew people.'[13]

In his widely read *New York by Gaslight* (1850), the American writer George Foster described the 'Five Points' section of the city, including its Jewish population. 'However low the grade or wretched the habitation . . . of the Jew,' wrote Foster, 'the race always retains the peculiar physical conformation constituting that peculiar style of beauty for which his tribe has been celebrated from remotest antiquity.' He also felt that he could describe that peculiar physical conformation: 'The roundness and suppleness of limb, the elasticity of flesh, the glittering eye-sparkle—are as inevitable in the Jew or Jewess, in whatever rank of existence, as the hook of the nose which betrays the Israelite as a human kite, formed to be feared, hated and despised, yet to prey on mankind.'[14]

In *A Scamper in Sebastopol and Jerusalem in 1867* the Irish traveller James Creagh commented on 'that strange expression, or might I say mark, which all over the world indicates so distinctly the chosen people of God'. Whether in the East or the West, 'whether the individuals themselves are dark or fair, handsome or ugly—there is still the Jew,' he asserted, 'which nothing can conceal'. Creagh continued, with considerable pathos:

I have seen Jews in all parts of the world. I have seen them in different costumes, in different positions of society, and even of different religions . . . and I have seen them on the coast of Malabar, where they were quite black in colour, and had been separated from immemorial time from their country and kindred—yet nothing can change them, nothing can conceal the mark which, they say, was implanted on this mysterious and scattered race by the hand of the living God.

Yet, when visiting Warsaw Creagh felt that its Jews were 'very different looking people from their brethren of Holywell Street [in London], who certainly have a great advantage over the Polish Hebrews in personal appearance'. The latter, he asserted, 'among their other peculiarities, do everything they can to make themselves look repulsive'.[15] Here Creagh followed in the tradition of those who had stressed the differences in appearance between the Jews in different parts of the world. A British visitor to Prague in the 1830s commented that its Jews, like those of Poland and Russia, had 'light-blue eyes and fair complexions; which, although the features be still of the Hebrew form, give an expression to the countenance very dissimilar to that which prevails among their co-religionists of western and southern Europe'.[16] The English traveller Miss Julia Pardoe commented on the appearance of the Jews of Hungary, who in her opinion bore 'physically . . . very slight resemblance to their brethren of more southern Europe; their physiognomies are rather Italian than Hebrew, and their features much less prominent and sharply cut than we are accustomed to see them in our part of the world'. She nonetheless believed that there was one way that Jews could be detected anywhere in the world—'that peculiarity of gait of which no Jew can ever thoroughly divest himself'.[17]

Some four decades later the Harvard graduate Thomas Appleton found that the Jews of Jerusalem 'differed singularly in appearance, according as they came from different countries', but were 'a short and slender race, particularly narrow across the chest'. He contrasted them not only with the robust Arab *felaheen* of Egypt, but also with their co-religionists in England: 'The hooked nose, the heavy lips, the ruddy cheeks, and portly person of many an English Jew', wrote Appleton, who was a nephew of the poet Longfellow, 'are not to be found in the mixed crowd of those who [in Jerusalem] worship in the ancient faith.'[18]

Another writer to contrast the appearance of Jerusalem Jews with that of their English co-religionists was G. K. Chesterton (1874–1936), who commented that, although the former 'may be ugly or even horrible, they are not vulgar like the Jews of Brighton; they trail behind them too many primeval traditions and laborious loyalties'.[19]

Men and women

Just as the physical appearance of Jews in one part of the world could be contrasted with that of their co-religionists in another, so too could the relative attractiveness of Jewish men and women be contrasted. In 1856 the American novelist Nathaniel Hawthorne, when visiting London, was invited to a formal dinner at the home of the newly elected lord mayor David Salomons, the first Jew to hold that office, and found himself seated opposite the latter's brother and sister-in-law. Although neither was mentioned by name, the brother was evidently Philip, to whom we shall return, and his wife was evidently Emma Abigail Salomons, who later served as the model for the half-Jewish Miriam in Hawthorne's novel *The Marble Faun*.

'My eyes', he wrote in his *English Notebooks*, 'were mostly drawn to a young lady who sat . . . across the table. She was, I suppose, dark and yet not dark, but rather seemed to be of pure white marble, yet not white; but of the purest and finest complexion . . . that I ever beheld.' Hawthorne described both her hair and nose as being characteristically Jewish, but nonetheless attractive: 'Her hair was a wonderful deep, raven black, black as night, black as death . . . wonderful hair, Jewish hair. Her nose had a beautiful outline, though I could see that it was Jewish too.' Yet, as much as he was attracted to her, he also felt repelled: 'She was slender, and youthful, but yet had a stately and cold, though soft and womanly grace . . . I should never have thought of touching her, nor desired to touch her; for, whether owing to distinctness of race, my sense that she was a Jewess, or whatever else, I felt a sort of repugnance, simultaneously with my perception that she was an admirable creature.'

Towards the husband of this 'miraculous Jewess', however, Hawthorne's feelings were considerably less ambivalent:

But at the right hand of this miraculous Jewess, there sat the very Jew of Jews, the distilled essence of all the Jews that have been born since Jacob's time . . . he was the worst, and at the same time the truest type of his race, and contained within himself, I have no doubt, every old prophet and every old clothesman, that ever the tribes produced; and he must have been circumcised as much as ten times over. I never beheld anything so ugly and disagreeable, and preposterous, and laughable, as the outline of his profile, it was so hideously Jewish, and so cruel, and so keen . . . And yet his manners and aspect, in spite of all, were those of a man of the world, and a gentleman . . . I rejoiced exceedingly in this Shylock, this Iscariot; for the sight of him justified me in the repugnance I have always felt towards his race.[20]

The aesthetic dichotomy between the attractive Jewess and the repulsive male of the species was quite common in the nineteenth century, if rarely expressed as repugnantly as by Hawthorne. Early in the century the young British traveller Clarissa Trant, finding herself in the ghetto of Rome, noted that it was not like any other part of the city: 'the streets are narrower, the houses more wretched, and the inhabitants have a particularly squalid and miserable appearance.' The Jewish men were, in Trant's opinion, 'generally speaking, very ugly', but she 'remarked many black eyes amongst the notable Jewesses'.[21] At around the same time another British traveller, Sir Arthur de Capell Brooke, passed through Morocco, commenting afterward that 'in no part of the world, perhaps, are more beautiful women to be seen than among the Jewesses of Tangier'. Their complexions, he wrote, 'are generally rather dark, but not swarthy, and mixed frequently with the most beautiful and inviting red possible, their eyes are brilliant, black, and sparkling', and their hair was 'like shining jet'. Sir Arthur contrasted these beautiful women with the Jewish men of Tangier: 'The iron claw of despotism, however different may be the case with the other [male] sex, has passed lightly over the countenances of these captivating females.'[22] Late in the nineteenth century the American lawyer J. M. Buckley commented on the Jews of Tangier that 'they wear a peculiar dress and are despised, but have their revenge by making money constantly out of their persecutors'. The Jewish women, he wrote, 'are so handsome that now, as in the time of Esther, they are sometimes the means of protecting the men from their oppressors'.[23] This was clearly not intended entirely as a compliment.

Jewish work and Jewish normality

Just as observers sometimes noted physical differences between the Jews of various countries, so too did they sometimes observe rather different work ethics. In 1867 the young American diplomat John Hay, who later served as secretary of state (1898–1905), visited Vienna, where he was fascinated by the 'endless tide of Polish Jews' flowing through the streets around the Judenplatz, which he described as 'squalid veins and arteries of impoverished and degenerate blood', filled with 'stooping, dirty figures in long, patched and oily black gabardines', wearing 'battered soft felt' hats that crowned their 'oblique, indolent, crafty' faces. Hay was also struck by the difference between these 'slouching rascals', who were as 'idle as they are ugly', and the more industrious Jews of the United States, whose enterprising habits had given rise to the expression 'Rich as a Jew'.[24]

When visiting Jerusalem a decade earlier, the American writer Herman Melville had met his countryman Walter Dickson, 'a man of Puritanic energy' who had established an agricultural colony on the city's outskirts. Melville asked Dickson whether he had any Jews working with him on the twelve acres he had under cultivation, to which the Boston native replied: 'No, can't afford to have them . . . Besides, the Jews are lazy and don't like to work.' Melville himself later wrote in his journal: 'The idea of making farmers of the Jews is vain. In the first place, Judea is a desert with few exceptions. In the second place, the Jews hate farming. All who cultivate the soil in Palestine are Arabs.'[25]

Melville was not entirely correct. The Englishman Hanmer Dupuis, who spent two years in Palestine during the 1850s, later described his excitement at seeing 'about forty Jews engaged in clearing a field, which had been purchased or leased by some society at home'. These Jews were employed, he explained, by the English consul in Jerusalem, 'in order to afford some relief . . . to their exigencies', and 'appeared very thankful, and willing to work for the trifling wages given them'. For Dupuis, 'a more interesting sight, among the sights of Palestine, could not have been witnessed, than once more to behold these people working and tilling that land which ratified the covenant between God and man'.[26]

A different sort of amazement was experienced in Tel Aviv several decades later by Joseph Broadhurst, who had been a senior British police officer in Mandatory Palestine. 'Tel Aviv', he wrote in his candid 1936 memoir *From Vine Street to Jerusalem*, 'is the only place where you can see Jews working in large numbers by the sweat of their brows; building houses and magnificent public buildings, making roads . . . driving trains, and even sweeping streets, which is a rare occupation for a Jew, who is not usually addicted to manual labour.' Although this was clearly intended as praise, it also reflected the enduring power of the notion that most Jews were either unsuited for manual labour or unwilling to perform it.

When the British Labour MP Richard Crossman visited in 1946 as part of the Anglo-American Committee on Palestine, he was taken to see a detention camp in Latrun, where 300 accused Jewish terrorists were being held, some of whom he was allowed to interview. Crossman, a graduate of Winchester and Oxford, described them as being of 'magnificent physique, morale, intelligence, and discipline', and stressed that, although 'my antisemitic virus made me expect them to squeal', the young men 'did not cringe to me or ask for favours'. He also contrasted their appearance with that of the Jews of London and New York: 'They certainly don't look like Whitechapel or Bronx Jews, and some have the heavy clod-hopping postures of people who have worked on the land all their lives.'[27]

In 1950, two years after the foundation of the State, the Hungarian-born British journalist George Mikes visited Israel. Before departing he was assured by 'several people in Britain' that all Jews there, 'and especially the Jewish children are blond, blue-eyed, and Aryan in appearance'. In Tel Aviv, too, he often heard people proudly say that 'our Jews are not-Jewish looking at all'. Not surprisingly, Mikes discovered that this was not quite the case: 'I made very thorough inquiries,' he wrote, 'but could not find one single person who used to be short, dark, and flat-footed in Vienna and now, in Israel, looks like a prototype of the Swedish aristocracy.' He did concede, however, that there was 'one very important and noticeable change in their appearance: most of them are sunburnt, healthy-looking, and strong', which he felt was better cause for pride 'than being blond and blue-eyed'.[28]

Shortly afterwards the American writer Edmund Wilson also visited the newly founded State of Israel, and described his powerful impressions of such diverse groups as the zealots of *Neturei Karta* and the residents of Kibbutz *Degania*. He observed, in conclusion, that 'the return of the Jews to their country of origin, the reversion to their ancient language, and, with these, a certain relaxation . . . into their habits of self-sufficiency, has made it possible for them to stand alone and not to worry about pleasing some dominant "race" '. Consequently, Wilson noted, 'the Jews seem in Israel less different instead of more different from other people'. This, he added, 'has had its moral effect on Jews all over the world, and it is a great thing to grasp about Israel'.[29] Half a century later these words, by America's last great man of letters, still ring true—although perhaps in a sense somewhat different from the one he intended.

FURTHER READING

Cheyette, Bryan. *Constructions of 'the Jew' in English Literature and Society: Racial Representations, 1875–1945* (Cambridge: Cambridge University Press, 1993). A discussion, based primarily on literary sources (from Anthony Trollope to T. S. Eliot), of how the emerging cultural identity of modern England involved constructing Jews both as a force that could be transformed by a superior culture, and as a 'race' outside the 'English nation'. A similar, though more wider-ranging, work is Ragussis (below).

Cohen A. (ed.). *An Anglo-Jewish Scrapbook, 1600–1840: The Jew Through British Eyes* (Westmead: Gregg International, 1969 [1943]). An extremely useful collection of sources, some otherwise quite obscure, organized by geography and theme rather than by chronology.

Cowen, Anne, and Roger Cowen (eds.). *Victorian Jews Through Victorian Eyes* (London: Littman Library, 1998). The Cowens pick up, more or less, where Cohen left off, and rely mostly on newspaper entries (and illustrations). Unlike Cohen's book, there is much material on England itself.

Finnie, D. H. *Pioneers East: The Early American Experience in the Middle East* (Cambridge, Mass.: Harvard University Press, 1967). An important monograph dealing with such figures as Stephens and McClure.

Harap, Louis. *The Image of the Jew in American Literature*, 2nd edn. (Philadelphia: Jewish Publication Society, 1978). First published in 1974, this is an encyclopaedic literary study of the Jew's status in American society to 1917, with considerable attention devoted to little-known authors. In 2003 Harap's book was reissued by Syracuse University Press.

Horowitz, Elliott. ' "A Different Mode of Civilty": Lancelot Addison on the Jews of Barbary', *Studies in Church History*, 29 (1992), pp. 309–25.

Horowitz, Elliott. 'A "Dangerous Encounter": Thomas Coryate and the Swaggering Jews of Venice', *Journal of Jewish Studies*, 52 (2001), pp. 341–53.

Melville, Herman. *Journal of a Visit to Europe and the Levant*, ed. H. C. Horsford (Princeton: Princeton University Press, 1955). A classic and well-annotated account.

Ragussis, Michael. *Figures of Conversion: The Jewish Question and English National Identity* (Durham, NC: Duke University Press, 1995).

Ravid, Benjamin. 'Christian Travelers in the Ghetto of Venice: Some Preliminary Observations', in Stanley Nash (ed.), *Between History and Literature: Studies in Honor of Isaac Barzilay* (Hakibbutz Hameuchad: Bnei Brak, 1997), pp. 111–50.

Vogel, L. I. *To See a Promised Land: Americans and the Holy Land in the Nineteenth Century* (University Park, Pa.: Pennsylvania State University Press, 1993).

NOTES

1. See J. L. Stephens, *Incidents of Travel in Egypt, Arabia Petraea, and the Holy Land*, ed. V. W. von Hagen (Norman Okla.: University of Oklahoma Press, 1970 [1837]), p. 312.
2. Quoted from Skinner's *Adventures During a Journey Overland to India by Way of Egypt, Syria, and the Holy Land* (1836), in A. Cohen, *An Anglo-Jewish Scrapbook, 1600–1840* (Westmead: Gregg International, 1969), pp. 26, 332.
3. Quoted ibid., p. 332.
4. *Coryate's Crudities* (1611), quoted ibid., p. 154, and by Benjamin Ravid, 'Christian Travelers in the Ghetto of Venice', in Stanley Nash (ed.), *Between History and Literature: Studies in Honor of Isaac Barzilay* (Hakibbutz Hameuchad: Bnei Brak, 1997), pp. 121–2.
5. H[enry B[lount], *A Voyage into the Levant*, 2nd edn. (1636), p. 123.
6. L. Addison, *The Present State of the Jews*, 2nd edn. (1676), pp. 8–9. See also Horowitz, ' "A Different Mode of Civilty" Lancelot Addison on the Jews of Barbary', *Studies in Church History*, 29 (1992), pp. 316–17.
7. W. Jowett, *Christian Researches in Syria and the Holy Land*, 2nd edn. (London, 1826), p. 232.
8. Ibid., pp. 232–3.
9. A. A. Bonar and R. M. M'Cheyne, *Narrative of a Mission of Inquiry to the Jews . . . in 1839* (Edinburgh, 1842), pp. 365–6, 591.
10. Bayard Taylor, *The Lands of the Saracen* (repr. New York: Arno Press, 1977 [1855]), pp. 81–2.
11. A. W. Kinglake, *Eothen* (repr. Lincoln, Nebr.: University of Nebraska Press, 1970), p. 203.
12. Quoted from P. Granville, *St. Petersburgh in 1827* (1828), in Cohen, *Anglo-Jewish Scrapbook*, p. 205.
13. Ibid., p. 73.
14. Quoted in Harap, *The Image of the Jew in American Literature*, 2nd edn. (Philadelphia: Jewish Publication Society), pp. 54–5.
15. J. Creagh, *A Scamper in Sebastopol and Jerusalem in 1867* (London, 1873), pp. 37, 56.
16. Quoted from P. E. Turnbull, *Austria* (1840), in Cohen, *Anglo-Jewish Scrapbook*, p. 158.
17. Quoted from her *The City of the Magyar in 1839* (1840), in ibid., pp. 171–2.
18. Appleton, *Syrian Sunshine* (Boston, 1877), pp. 60, 64.
19. G. K. Chesterton, *The New Jerusalem* (London, 1920), p. 93. On Chesterton, see Cheyette, *Constructions of 'the Jew' in English Literature and Society: Racial Representation, 1875–1945* (Cambridge: Cambridge University Press, 1993), pp. 179–205.
20. *The English Notebooks by Nathaniel Hawthorne*, ed. R. Stewart (New York, 1941), p. 321, quoted in Harap, *The Image of the Jew*, pp. 109–10. On Mrs Salomons as the model for Miriam, see ibid., p. 112.
21. Quoted from the *Journal of Clarissa Trant*, in Cohen, *Anglo-Jewish Scrapbook*, pp. 144–5.
22. Quoted from Brooke, *Sketches in Spain and Morocco* (1831), in ibid, pp. 90–1.
23. J. M. Buckley, *Travels in Three Continents* (New York, 1895), p. 91.
24. Quoted by Harap, *The Image of the Jew*, p. 362.
25. Melville, *Journal of a Visit*, pp. 159–60.
26. H. L. Dupuis, *The Holy Places: A Narrative of Two Years' Residence in Jerusalem and Palestine*, 2 vols. (London, 1856), vol. i, pp 126–7.
27. Richard Crossman, *Palestine Mission: A Personal Record* (London: Hamish Hamilton, 1947), p. 145.
28. G. Mikes, *Milk and Honey: Israel Explored* (London: Wingate, 1950), pp. 52–4.
29. Edmund Wilson, *Red, Black, Blond, and Olive: Studies in Four Civilizations* (New York: Farrar, Straus & Young, 1956), p. 492.

34 | Jewish–Christian relations

Margie Tolstoy

For Jewish–Christian relations to have an impact, Jews and Christians must relate to each other in ways that acknowledge difference whilst affirming a shared destiny. Learning to listen to those who are 'other' is the only approach that builds trust, mutual respect, friendship, and love. But the aim is ultimately more ambitious; namely, to 'seek peace and pursue it' (Psalm 34: 15). Jonathan Magonet points out that, 'for most other commandments, we are only instructed to do them when they come our way—but when it comes to peace, we are to be actively engaged in seeking it out'.[1] Some Jewish leaders have come to recognize that there are positive benefits to be derived from the encounter with Christianity:

> It may begin in fear—fear of having our certainties challenged, overcome by the still greater fear of what may happen if we do not talk and learn to live at peace. But it ends in self-knowledge. We come to understand what, within our own heritage, makes us unique, and what makes us like others, human beings created in the image of God.[2]

Jewish–Christian relations after the Holocaust

Since the Holocaust the goalposts of Jewish–Christian relations have moved. The Holocaust occurred within the context of a mainly Christian civilization, and ever since there has been an urgent desire among discerning Christians to reassess critically the legacy of anti-Judaism in their faith tradition. Christians need to engage in learning and unlearning: learning about Judaism as a dynamic living faith, and unlearning deeply ingrained liturgical and theological habits that perpetuate anti-Judaism. It is not surprising that hostility towards Judaism as a religion—anti-Judaism—easily turns into antisemitism—racist hostility towards Jews. Without serious attention to these prejudices, there is no basis for friendship.

Christians often assume that a reference to the 'Judeo-Christian tradition' indicates sufficient recognition of the Jewish connection. This is quite misleading, as it mainly indicates the minimal awareness that the Old Testament is also the Bible of the Jews. Simultaneously it manages to absorb Judaism linguistically within Christianity.

In the immediate aftermath of the Second World War Jews and Christians met at Seelisberg in Switzerland to discuss what had gone wrong and how a future repetition could be prevented. Those discussions contributed to the establishment of the International Council of Christians and Jews, and ultimately fed into the important Roman Catholic document *Nostra Aetate* issued in 1965 by the Second Vatican Council.

Rosemary Radford Ruether was one of the first Christian theologians to engage seriously in Jewish–Christian relations *after* the Holocaust. In 1974 she published her book *Faith and Fratricide*. The title is unambiguously critical, with a pointed reference to the story of Cain and Abel. Ruether blew the whistle on the connection between the Holocaust and Christian anti-Judaism. After the Holocaust Jewish–Christian relations take on an entirely new dimension. It is no longer just a matter of replacing Christian teaching of contempt by teaching of respect, or of building bridges to bring Jews and Christians together to promote social and national cohesion. In order to make Jewish–Christian relations possible again, Christians have to go back to the beginning and engage first of all with the nature of Messianic hope, this time not with an attitude of supersessionist triumphalism, but as a voyage of discovery. An engagement with the social, historical, and theological context of rabbinic Judaism of the Second Temple period and early Christianity in the Roman world is therefore necessary.

Messianic hope

The early followers of Jesus were firmly situated within the Jewish tradition. They may well have been part of a religious and political movement among Pharisees in Galilee, who hoped that the Kingdom of God was imminent. In the Gospel of Luke, chapter 3, John the Baptist proclaims, using words from the Book of Isaiah (40: 3–5): 'a voice cries in the wilderness, prepare the way for the Lord . . . all mankind shall see God's deliverance.' He baptizes Jesus and the Holy Spirit descends upon him like a dove and a voice from heaven says: 'You are my beloved Son, in you I delight' (Luke 3: 22). After forty days in the desert, Jesus travels to Nazareth:

where he had been brought up, and went to the synagogue on the Sabbath day as he regularly did. He stood up to read the lesson and was handed the scroll of the prophet Isaiah. He opened the scroll and found the passage which says,

> The spirit of the Lord is upon me
> Because he has anointed me;
> He has sent me to announce good news to the poor,
> To proclaim release for prisoners
> And recover the sight for the blind;
> To let the broken victims go free,
> To proclaim the year of the Lord's favour.

He rolled up the scroll, gave it back to the attendant, and sat down; and all eyes in the synagogue were fixed on him. He began to address them: 'Today,' he said, 'in your hearing this text has come true'.

(Luke 4: 16–21)

The Church Father Jerome (342–420 CE) suggested that Isaiah should be identified as an evangelist rather than a prophet, because he describes the mysteries of Christ so clearly that you believe he is composing a history of what has already happened rather than prophesying about what is to come. This, of course, is deeply problematic. The prophet Isaiah in the passage quoted above (Isaiah 61: 1–3) was talking metaphorically about the restoration of divine favour and return to Jerusalem after the Babylonian exile. These themes gave comfort in times of danger and confusion; fierce admonitions could be accepted with humility. It is not fanciful to think that the Book of Isaiah inspired Jesus, as it seemed to speak with particular eloquence to the situation of Roman occupation of the Land of Israel. However, there is no agreement among theologians whether Jesus himself believed that the carefully selected texts from the Book of Isaiah indicated the history of his own journey.

The suffering servant

The most widely known description of Jesus Christ as Saviour is not from the gospels, but from the so-called 'suffering servant' passage in Isaiah 53:

. . . he was pierced for our transgressions,
crushed for our iniquities;
the chastisement he bore restored us to health
and by his wounds we are healed
We had all strayed like sheep, each of us going his own way,
But the Lord laid on him the guilt of us all.

(53: 5–7)

Yet the Lord took thought for his oppressed servant
And healed him who had given himself as a sacrifice for sin.

(53: 10)

In the history of Christian devotional practice, Isaiah's 'man of sorrows' motif has remained popular and idiosyncratic. In 1741 Charles Jennens wrote the libretto for Handel's *Messiah,* and the main body of the text revolves around Isaiah's suffering servant. It provides a biblical justification for the crucifixion and death of the Messiah and simultaneously offers Christians a theology of atonement—a specific understanding of forgiveness. Without the Book of Isaiah, the Christian story would be difficult to imagine. It has been ironically referred to as the Fifth Gospel. Christians need reminding that God supplied Jews with a different interpretative key.

Once the disciples were convinced that the Jewish messianic hope was fulfilled in Jesus, they stepped outside of Judaism. The anti-Jewish polemic found in the Christian Bible is intrinsically defensive. It is a policy that aims to discredit Jews who rejected Jesus as the Christ. To have furthermore held Jews (*the* Jews) responsible for the death of Jesus distorted the historical facts and seriously unbalanced the future relationship between Jews and Christians. This is the unfortunate beginning of the Christian story. Yvonne Sherwood summarizes the situation without frills:

The Jew stands at the origin of Christianity *and* represents the dangerous possibility of its denial; the Christian narrative of Self depends on 'him', and yet if 'he' retains his distinctiveness then that same narrative is under threat. The mythologised spectre of the Jew is both the vilified Christ-killer and the one to whom Christianity is in debt.[3]

It is important to appreciate what it is in their heritage that makes Jews and Christians unique and what makes them like others. Before that can be done with integrity, Jews and Christians need to be infused with a desire to restore justice. It is therefore imperative to understand the origin of this miserable antagonism. In trying to imagine and bring about a world where Jewish–Christian relations flourish, we need to have a sense of what has happened between then and now.

Is Christianity irredeemably anti-Judaic?

Ruether wonders whether Christianity is irredeemably anti-Judaic. This seems at first an odd question, for not only was Jesus Jewish, so too were his disciples. The different interpretations of Jewish messianism form the heart of the dispute. Jews generally believe its primary focus to be a future age of divine rule, exemplified by this-worldly social and political harmony. The first followers of Jesus must have shared this understanding. They lived with the expectation that the messianic kingdom was imminent. It failed to appear. Jesus was crucified instead.

After the meeting with the 'resurrected' Christ on the road to Emmaus, a realized, spiritualized, internalized eschatology was put in place. A second coming of Christ (Messiah) was projected to the future, thus reconnecting with Jewish expectations. Through the teaching of Paul in particular, the saving presence of the resurrected Christ, incorporated in the doctrine of the Holy Trinity, now formed the heart of the Christian faith. This was not just unacceptable, but incomprehensible in the Jewish tradition.

The followers of Jesus created a narrative history of the life of Jesus. They found the evidence for what they believed in their own Jewish sacred Scriptures. They now considered themselves to be the 'new' Israel; the covenant transferred. Augustine of Hippo wrote: 'In the Old Testament the New Testament lies hid; in the New Testament the Old Testament becomes clear.'[4] The Hebrew Bible was Christianized, an ungracious form of colonization. It has been clearly understood by serious theologians that the Christian Bible has no point of reference without the Hebrew Bible. But Judaism had become dispensable. The consequences of this attitude have been catastrophic.

Jews and Christians in the Roman Empire

The destruction of the Temple in 70 CE by the Romans was a confirmation for Christians and a disaster for Jews. After the loss of the Temple, rabbinic (Pharisaic) Judaism was able to carry on the tradition. Unlike the followers of Jesus Christ, Jews experienced this calamity as a punishment from God. Jewish communities dispersed and re-established themselves, hoping that one day they would return to what had become the Roman province of Judaea. This indeed happened in 1948, with the establishment of the State of Israel.

Jewish communities established themselves as self-governing entities in the Diaspora. Worship, teaching, and the study of Torah continued in synagogues. Scholars created the Talmud, providing detailed practical guidance and discussions of important issues. The Talmud ensures that the commandment to live a life of holiness would not be adversely affected without Jerusalem and without the Temple.

Both Jews and Christians were minorities within the Roman Empire. Early Christianity in Rome was a religion of the poor, who lived mainly in the working-class areas of Trastevere and Porta Capena. Jewish communities in Rome had already been in existence before the fall of the Temple. Apart from the belief in Jesus as the Messiah, Jewish and Christian neighbourhoods in the first two centuries, in terms of living conditions, had much in common. Christians tended to proselytize, Jews did not. Modern scholars have discovered that the parting of the ways between Christians and Jews took place over a much longer period then was first assumed. The Church Fathers warn against Christian participation in Jewish observances well into the fourth century. Neither John Chrysostom in the East (Antioch) nor Augustine in the West (Rome) advocated violence against Jews or the destruction of synagogues. Their fierce anti-Jewish rhetoric may be seen in the context of the sophistical tradition of *psogos* (rebuke). The situation changed dramatically for Christians when they started to attract the upper classes and the attention of emperors. It is fair comment that

> . . . the Christian era did not start with the birth of Jesus. It dates from the first half of the fourth century, commencing when Constantine the Great established Christianity as the state religion of the Roman Empire. The characteristic mark of the era was militancy. This was inherent in its beginnings: Christianity did not capture the Roman Empire by the power of a religious idea but by the sword of the emperor.[5]

Constantine converted to Christianity and experienced a vision of the cross. It was then that this Roman instrument of torture became the dominant Christian symbol. It caused a major shift: not the life, but the suffering of Jesus became central. Anti-Judaic legislation followed.

Jewish responses to Jesus

In the early middle ages, during the Crusades (named for the cross displayed on the tunic of the Crusaders), Jews were murdered by Christians on their way to the Holy Land. Despite remaining vulnerable to such attacks and despite discriminatory legislation, Jewish communities survived and flourished all over Europe and the Middle East.

Some of the greatest Jewish scholars during that time worked under Muslim rule; among these was the formidable scholar, philosopher, and theologian Moses Maimonides (1138–1204). He argued that it was the task of Jews to make Christians aware of their erroneous interpretation of the Hebrew Scriptures. This Jewish–Christian encounter would be conducted as a philosophical discourse. Maimonides was not interested in conversion per se, but in the truth of revelation and ultimately in bringing about the messianic reign. He issued a stern warning in his *Mishneh Torah* that Christians who proclaim Jesus as the Messiah are idolaters.

The reconquest of Spain by Christianity and the Inquisition created large numbers of so-called 'new Christians', many of whom maintained their Jewish practices and beliefs in secret. By the seventeenth century a large and dynamic community of Sephardic and Ashkenazi Jews had settled in Amsterdam. This is reflected in the paintings, drawings, and gouaches of Rembrandt. They were his neighbours and friends. It was said that while others painted the Bible, Rembrandt painted Jewish Scripture. The accuracy of the Hebrew writing in his painting of Belshazzar's Feast and in other works was the result of his friendship with the famous rabbi Menasseh Ben Israel. Menasseh's scholarship was much admired by Jews and Christians alike, and he is an important figure in the history of Jewish–Christian relations. He was teasingly called the 'apostle to the Gentiles'. He was less concerned with the figure of Jesus than with building bridges between the two faith traditions. He was the first Jewish rabbi genuinely dedicated to dialogue with the Christian world. In 1632 Menasseh published *Conciliador*, the first in a series of four volumes in which he attempted to reconcile apparent inconsistencies in the Hebrew Scriptures. He wrote in Spanish, so that those Sephardic Jews who had become Christian (*conversos*) would return to their ancestral faith. It was translated into Latin specifically so that Christian scholars could read it as well. Menasseh Ben Israel, like other Jewish commentators, also used classical and Christian sources to explain problematic passages of Hebrew Scripture.

A fascination with the historical Jesus developed in nineteenth-century Germany. Christian theologians must have been surprised that Abraham Geiger (1810–74) also had an interest in this subject. In *Das Judentum und seine Geschichte* (Judaism and its History), Geiger suggested that Jesus was a Pharisee and early Christianity a pagan misrepresentation of the Jewish message of Jesus. Geiger genuinely believed that if Jews were to be fully integrated into German society, the cultural and religious misgivings of Christians about Jews had to be exposed and shown to be misplaced. Telling the story of Christian origins from a Jewish perspective was therefore a necessary corrective. Geiger thought it was reasonable to assume that the more Jewish Jesus was shown to have been, the more Christians would want and need to know about Judaism. Today this is true, but in the time of Geiger it had the opposite effect. The rage he evoked among Christian theologians demonstrates that he had touched a raw nerve. The quest for the historical Jesus continued, as indeed did the disputes, but Christian theologians were unable to tolerate a Jewish perspective. The militancy with which Christians tried to distance themselves from the Jewish Jesus reached its peak during the Nazi period.

Franz Rosenzweig (1886–1929) almost converted to Christianity but changed his mind and resolved to remain a Jew. In his book *The Star of Redemption*, which he started writing in the trenches during the First World War, he explains why:

Before God, then, Jew and Christian both labour at the same task. He cannot dispense with either. He has set enmity between the two for all time and withal has most intimately bound each to each . . . The truth, the whole truth thus belongs to neither of them nor to us . . . And thus we both have but a part of the whole truth. But we know that it is in the nature of truth to be imparted, and that a truth in which no one had a part would be no truth.[6]

The image of the star (of redemption) illustrates for Rosenzweig the difference and interdependence between Judaism and Christianity: Judaism as the burning core, Christianity as the rays. By remaining faithful to Judaism, he also supports Christianity. Rozenzweig read the Christian Scriptures and accepted the teaching in John's Gospel (John 14: 6) that no one can reach the Father except through Jesus. For him, however, this did not apply to Jews, the people of Israel, because they are already with the Father.

Martin Buber (1878–1965) shared Rozenzweig's magnanimous attitude towards Christianity, and even went so far as to say that from an early age he considered Jesus his great brother. Buber believed Jesus to be a significant figure in the history of Israel, but qualified this by saying that Jesus cannot be described by any of the usual categories. This covers both the Christian claim of Jesus as the Messiah and the Jewish counterclaim that he is not the Messiah. For Buber, the I–Thou relationship applies, as it describes the dynamic relationship between people and between an individual and God. Addressing a Christian audience, he said: . . . 'whenever we both, Christian and Jew, care more for God himself than for our images of God, we are united in the feeling that our Father's house is differently constructed than our human models take it to be.'[7] Buber could not have known that Jewish and Christian feminist theologians years later would use this argument to deconstruct the patriarchal pattern of their respective faith traditions.

Tainted greatness: anti-Judaism in Christian theology

The vicious polemic against Jews and Judaism in the writing of famous and influential Christian theologians is deeply problematic. Among the Church Fathers there is no one who is not to a lesser or greater degree anti-Judaic. After the Holocaust, Martin Luther's 1543 treatise, written the year before he died, on 'The Jews and Their Lies' has had particularly nasty reverberations. The language used was so vicious that at the Nuremberg Trials a confessed 'killer of Jews' (*Judenfresser*) defended himself by simply saying that Martin Luther would have done likewise, given the opportunity. Scholars and Lutherans in particular have speculated as to why Luther wrote this deplorably anti-Judaic tract: why he wrote that synagogues should be burned, that Jews should be forced into manual labour, that their houses should be taken away, usury be prohibited, and rabbinic teaching stopped. There is an appalling familiarity about this rant. The only thing he did not write is that Jews should be killed.

His greatness as a theologian has been severely tainted. It seemed so out of character with what he wrote twenty years earlier, in an essay entitled 'That Jesus Was Born a Jew':

If the apostles, who were Jews, had dealt with us Gentiles as we Gentiles deal with the Jews, there would never have been a Christian among the Gentiles. Since they dealt with us Gentiles in such a brotherly fashion, we in our turn ought to treat the Jews in a brotherly manner in order that we might convert some of them . . . When we are inclined to boast of our position we should remember that we are but Gentiles, while the Jews are the lineage of Christ. We are aliens and in-laws; they are blood relatives, cousins and brothers of our Lord . . . God has also demonstrated this by his acts, for to no nation among the Gentiles has he granted so high an honour as he has to the Jews.

Luther held the doctrine of 'justification by faith alone' so dear that it became his life's work and his mission to convert everyone to this doctrine. For him, within Judaism, as indeed within Roman Catholicism, there was a piety of achievement, a works righteousness, that he militantly opposed. There is little consolation in the fact that his motivation was theological. The example of his life undermined the validity of the doctrine.

The legacy that Christians bring to Jewish–Christian relations affects the current dialogue. It is entirely justifiable to dwell on the serious historical defects of Christians in relation to Jews. The relationship is not yet symmetrical. Serious efforts are made by Christian theologians to get their house in order. Co-operation between Jewish and Christian scholars is proving to be fruitful. To read an extensive and honest study about the German Churches and the Holocaust, edited by a Jewish academic (Susannah Heschel) and a scholar who teaches at a Lutheran university (Robert Ericksen), is exciting. They move beyond the ways of the past, and the creative tension is constructive. Triumphalism and supersessionism are left behind. Yvonne Sherwood, in her imaginative study of the Book of Jonah, shows how, with a sense of humour and fine scholarship, the Jewish and Christian perspectives are given their due. Daniel Boyarin, a Jewish scholar, is immersed in Christian patristic writing.

Jewish–Christian relations are beginning to have an impact in the theological world and beyond.

Daniel Deronda

George Eliot inhabited the world of Jewish–Christian relations. She came to this by a rather curious route. In 1848 the German Christian theologian D. F. Strauss wrote a massive historical study: *The Life of Jesus Critically Examined*. His characterization of Christology in terms of mythology caused consternation among fellow theologians. George Eliot translated this controversial work from German into English. Around the same time, Ludwig Feuerbach demythologized Christianity in *The Essence of Christianity*, when he proclaimed that consciousness of God is self-consciousness, knowledge of God being self-knowledge. George Eliot translated Feuerbach as well. It left her mentally and physically exhausted, and in the process she lost her enchantment with Christianity. A study of the great Jewish scholar Leopold Zunz renewed her zest for life and brought her into contact with Emmanuel Deutsch. Deutsch was involved with Jewish settlements in Palestine and in establishing Hebrew as a spoken language. He became her teacher and the inspiration for her last novel, *Daniel Deronda* (1876). With this book, Eliot hoped to promote an appreciation and understanding of Judaism among her predominantly Christian readers.

Daniel Deronda, adopted by an English aristocrat, knowing nothing about his parents, enters the Jewish community and experiences a strong sense of kinship through his friendship with a Jewish brother and sister. In the meantime, he learns what it means to be Jewish and Zionist. When Daniel meets his mother for the first time and finds out that she is Jewish, he is overwhelmed with a sense of gratitude and homecoming. It is an extraordinary encounter, in which the mother confesses how oppressive Judaism is for her, explaining the reasons why she secured for him an upbringing as an Englishman. When Daniel expresses his delight about being Jewish, she exclaims: 'How could I know that you love what I hated.' Daniel than reassures her, and provides the reader with a sensible summary of what it is to be a Jew in the modern world

I shall call myself a Jew, said Deronda . . . but I will not say that I shall profess to believe exactly as my fathers have believed. Our fathers themselves changed the horizons of their belief and learned of other races. But I think I can maintain my grandfather's notion of separateness with communication. I hold that my first duty is to my own people, and if there is anything to be done toward restoring or perfecting the common life, I shall make that my vocation.

George Eliot learned Hebrew, visited synagogues, and retained a great affection for Judaism till the end of her life.

Feminist contributions to Jewish–Christian relations

Had Judith Plaskow, the Jewish theologian, met Daniel Deronda's mother she would have understood her very well. In her book *Standing Again At Sinai*,[8] Plaskow wants to bring women in from the margins, away from images that represent patriarchal dominance. She wants to reshape memory, to include women in the moment of entry into the covenant at Sinai and imagine what women would have heard God say.

The Christian theologian Carter Heyward rejects the patriarchal logic that produced a deity—Father or Mother—who reigns above us and seeks our submission or obedience. Instead, she is committed to the belief that right relationship with God is a communal learning process, and that relationships, even the relationship with God, are based on mutuality. For her, as for Buber, Jesus is brother rather than Lord. Jewish and Christian feminist theologians meet, talk to each other, and support each other's work. Katharina von Kellenbach showed that anti-Judaism is found even in Christian feminist religious writing. Melissa Raphael offers a post-Holocaust feminist theology of relation that affirms the redemptive presence of God even in Auschwitz; ordinary acts of kindness sanctified God's name. By means of mutual care, women summoned the Shekhinah, the divine presence. She writes that 'Nazism represented a demonic but logical conclusion of the patriarchal world-view which objectifies all things as disposable means to power'.[9] In this, as in so many other things, Jewish and Christian feminist theologians agree.

The future of Jewish–Christian relations

The major historical stumbling-block in Jewish–Christian relations, the figure of Jesus Christ, no longer generates the heat it used to. That does not mean that there is agreement, or that the issue no longer matters. Increased familiarity with the complexity of circumstances in the first few centuries of the Christian era creates a sense of perspective. Learning about Judaism lets fresh air and wisdom and humility into the Christian world. Learning about Christianity is for Jews also a voyage of discovery into a world both familiar and alien. A Jewish Statement on Christians and Christianity known as *Dabru Emet* (Speak the Truth), organized under the auspices of the Institute for Christian and Jewish Studies in Baltimore, is remarkable and instructive.[10] It affirms similarity—*Jews and Christians worship the same God*—and acknowledges difference—*the humanly irreconcilable difference between Jews and Christians will not be settled until God redeems the entire world as promised in Scripture*. Above all, it states that *Jews and Christians must work together for peace*. The statement is accompanied by a book in which Jews and Christians engage in major theological issues. The issues are approached with care and humility, the voices are strong and confident. After Auschwitz, Jews and Christians have developed a sense of responsibility for each other.

436 | Jewish–Christian relations

FURTHER READING

Boys, Mary C. *Has God Only One Blessing?—Judaism as a Source of Christian Self-Understanding* (New York: Paulist Press, 2000). Offers a comprehensive introduction to the historical and theological context of Jewish–Christian relations.

Ericksen, Robert P., and Susannah Heschel (eds.). *Betrayal: German Churches and the Holocaust* (Minneapolis: Fortress Press, 1999). An illuminating perspective is provided on the role of the Christian Church in Nazi Germany, as well as an overview of German theological responses since 1945.

Frymer-Kensky, Tikva, David Novak, Peter Ochs, David Fox Sandmel, and Michael A. Signer (eds.). *Christianity in Jewish Terms* (Boulder, Col.: Westview Press, 2000). Required reading for anyone interested in Jewish–Christian relations today.

Harrowitz, Nancy A. (ed.). *Tainted Greatness: Antisemitism and Cultural Heroes* (Philadelphia: Temple University Press, 1994). A useful and fair assessment of the different ways antisemitism has played itself out in the lives and works of some very talented and famous people.

Heschel, Susannah. *Abraham Geiger and the Jewish Jesus* (Chicago and London: University of Chicago Press, 1998). A fascinating and profoundly scholarly work, that not only provides a passionate Jewish perspective on Jesus, but also offers valuable insights into nineteenth-century German intellectual life.

von Kellenbach, K. *Anti-Judaism in Feminist Religious Writing* (Atlanta, Ga.: Scholars Press, 1994). A German feminist scholar points out that anti-Judaism is still present in the work of Christian feminist theologians.

de Lange, Nicholas (ed.). *Ignaz Maybaum: A Reader* (New York and Oxford: Bergbahn Books, 2001). Makes the writings and sermons of Maybaum available again, and it is well worth engaging with this passionate, wise rabbi.

Linafelt, Tod (ed.). *Strange Fire: Reading the Bible After the Holocaust* (Sheffield: Sheffield Academic Press, 2000). A valuable collection of essays on reading the Hebrew Bible after the Holocaust by Jewish and Christian scholars.

Linafelt, Tod (ed.). *A Shadow of Glory: Reading the New Testament After the Holocaust* (New York and London: Routledge, 2002). Contains post-Holocaust theology by Jewish and Christian scholars, with special reference to the Christian Bible.

Novak, David. *Jewish–Christian Dialogue: A Jewish Justification* (New York and Oxford: Oxford University Press, 1989). A valuable Jewish introduction to Jewish–Christian relations.

Raphael, Melissa. *The Female Face of God in Auschwitz: A Jewish Feminist Theology of the Holocaust* (London and New York: Routledge, 2003). A remarkable contribution to post-Holocaust theology, relevant for Jews and Christians.

Ruether, Rosemary. *Faith and Fratricide: The Theological Roots of Antisemitism* (New York: Seabury Press, 1979). A robust and detailed study of the early history of Jewish–Christian relations, identifying the sources of anti-Judaism.

Sawyer, John F. A. *The Fifth Gospel: Isaiah in the History of Christianity* (Cambridge: Cambridge University Press, 1996). A detailed and revealing exposition of the Christian interpretation of the Book of Isaiah.

Sherwood, Yvonne. *A Biblical Text and Its Afterlives: The Survival of Jonah in Western Culture* (Cambridge: Cambridge University Press, 2000). A brilliant and witty exposition of the extraordinary history of interpretations of the Book of Jonah.

NOTES

1. Jonathan Magonet, *Talking to the Other—Jewish Interfaith Dialogue with Christians and Muslims* (London: I. B. Tauris, 2003), p. 9.

2. Jonathan Sacks, in Helen P. Fry, (ed.), *Christian–Jewish Dialogue: A Reader* (Exeter: University of Exeter Press, 1996), p. xi.

3. Yvonne Sherwood, *A Biblical Text and Its Afterlives—The Survival of Jonah in Western Culture* (Cambridge: Cambridge University Press, 2000), p. 73.

4. '. . . quamquam et in vetere novum lateat, et in novo vetus patet.' Augustine, *Questions on the Heptateuch*, in J. P. Migne (ed.), *Patrologiae cursus completus: series latina*, vol. 34, (Paris, 1944–55).

5. Eliezer Berkovits, *Faith After the Holocaust* (New York: Ktav, 1973).

6. Franz Rosenzweig, *The Star of Redemption*, tr. from the German of the 2nd edn. of 1930 by William W. Hallo (London: Routledge & Kegan Paul, 1971), pp. 415–16.

7. David Novak, *Jewish–Christian Dialogue: A Jewish Justification* (New York and Oxford: Oxford University Press, 1989), p. 82.

8. *Standing Again At Sinai: Judaism From a Feminist Perspective* (San Francisco: HarperCollins, 1990).

9. Melissa Raphael, 'When God Beheld God: Notes Towards a Jewish Feminist Theology of the Holocaust', *Feminist Theology*, 21 (1999), p. 61.

10. See Tikva Frymer-Kensky *et al.* (eds.), *Christianity in Jewish Terms* (Boulder, Col.: Westview Press, 2000).

35 | Jewish–Muslim relations

Reuven Firestone

It is impossible to understand the complex nature of modern Jewish–Muslim relations without revisiting Arabia of the seventh century, when the new Believers (*mu'minūn*) of emerging Islam began to establish their foundational world-views. It is in this context that Muhammad and his followers came into contact with Jews, and this contact became extremely important because reactions to it were recorded for posterity in the Qur'an.

The Qur'an on the Jews

Muhammad was forced out of Mecca by his own tribe in 622, and found refuge in Medina, where he came into contact with the Jewish community living there. It was out of this contact that Islamic images of Jews—positive, negative, and neutral—were first established and then sanctified by their appearance in Islamic Scripture.

The Qur'an is ambivalent about the Jews. On the one hand, it instructs Muhammad to go to the Jews and learn from them: 'And if you [Muhammad] are uncertain about what We have sent down to you, ask those who read the Book [that was] before you. The truth has come to you from your Lord, so do not be one of those who doubt' (10: 94).[1] The Qur'an also teaches that Jews, Christians and others who believe in God and act righteously will have nothing to fear, suggesting that, like Muslim believers, they will find salvation (2: 62, 5: 69, 22: 17). On the other hand, the Qur'an repeatedly condemns the Jews for rejecting the prophetic status of Muhammad. It refers to Jews as stiff-necked and rebellious (2: 93, 105, 5: 78, 62: 5), dishonest (2: 100), violent (2: 85, 91, 4: 157), usurious and greedy (4: 161, 6: 146, 9: 34), arrogant (3: 24, 181, 5: 64, 46: 10), insidious (2: 109, 120, 3: 69), jealous (4: 54, 5: 51), liars (3: 71, 94, 5: 41, 6: 28), and unbelievers (2: 55, 103, 3: 72, 5: 41, 9: 30–1, 59: 2–4), and it accuses them of distorting their own Scripture in order to discredit the message of the Qur'an and the prophet who brought it (2: 79, 3: 78, 4: 46, 5: 13, 41).

Even among some of the negative references to Jews, however, are reminders that not all can be typed one way or the other. 'They are not all alike. Of the People of

Scripture is an upright community . . . Whatever good they do will not be denied, for God knows the pious.' (3: 113–15; see also 3: 199, 4: 55, 4: 155).

It should not be surprising that the Qur'an contains negative and angry references directed to adherents of established religions. Polemic is a common trait among the Scriptures of all three great families of monotheism, and the anger that Scriptures direct toward established religions simply denotes the difficult environments in which Scriptures always emerge. All three Scriptures direct anger against representatives of the establishment systems that opposed them, and scriptural invective is often extremely harsh (see Deuteronomy 7: 1–2; Matthew 23). The anti-Judaism of the Qur'an, therefore, is a natural, even if unfortunate, expression of an emerging religion's claim to uniqueness.

One might ask why emerging religions must disparage such an innocent community as the Jews. The answer is that, upon close inspection, communities denigrated or vilified by emerging religions tend not to have been quite so innocent. We are not trying to blame the victim, but rather to understand the dynamics of emerging religions' relations with established religions. A newly emerging religion, by definition, raises the hackles of the establishment, an observation that is apparent with the rise of sects and 'cults' in our own generation. In response, established religions characteristically attempt to prevent the success of the upstart. Most new religious movements die within a generation. The tremendous success of the Islamic movement was seen by the Muslims as divine proof that their form of monotheism was the most perfect form of religion. According to this line of thinking, history has proven the eternal superiority of Islam and the secondary status of the other monotheisms.

The Jewish communities of Medina, the only Jews that Muhammad and his followers came to know, appear to have threatened the early Muslims in both the conceptual or ideational sense and the physical sense. The first sense caused the greater crisis, but the second was also significant. Some verses portray the Jews not only as refusing to accept Muhammad's role as prophet, but also as trying to discredit him:

O you who believe, do not take as friends those who ridicule your religion, [whether] of those to whom were given Scripture previously or the unbelievers, but be pious to God if you are believers. And when you call for prayers, they take it for ridicule and jest. This is because they are a people without sense. Say: O People of Scripture, are you revengeful toward us only because we believe in God and in what has been sent down to us, and in what has been sent down previously, and because most of you are degenerate sinners?

(Q. 5: 57–9)

The organized Jewish communities of Medina are portrayed quite consistently in the religious sources as refusing to accept Muhammad as a prophet. Those verses condemning the Jews in general while noting that a few are righteous probably refer to individual Jews who left their religion and became followers of Muhammad. The aggregate, however, is portrayed consistently as remaining steadfast (or stiff-necked) in the face of the growing strength of the Muslims. References to the Jews as stiff-necked, arrogant, or jealous probably refer to their refusal to accept the new prophet and his religion; references to them as liars or as distorting their own holy book probably refer to the problem raised by the inevitable contradictions between new revelations and those previously recorded as Scripture.

All negative descriptions of Jews recorded in the Qur'an and the early literatures were a result of the friction between the early Muslim community and the organized Jewish tribes of Medina. The Qur'an represents itself as a universal teaching, however; because of its rhetorical style it appears to refer negatively to the Jews in general terms. For Muslim believers, the Qur'an is inimitable Scripture (and the inimitability of the Qur'an is an absolute dogma of Islamic theology), so its portrayal of Jews represents a level of truth that is difficult to question. As Scripture, the Qur'an is a powerful foundation for contemporary Muslim world-views all over the globe. The conflicts it reflects lasted for only a few years, but the verses of Scripture that record them are eternal.

The rules of the *dhimma*

The layer of sacred Islamic literature that follows the Qur'an is the record of the *sunna*, or behaviour and sayings of Muhammad, the prophet. These are recorded in a literature called the Hadith. Like the Qur'an, the Hadith reflects the conflicts that grew up between the Jews and early Muslims, and definitive archetypes or stereotypes of Jews were established also in this vast literature. The later juridical literature of Islam was developed primarily from the Qur'an and the Hadith, so it both reinforced these images and created law that would perpetuate them.

Islam found itself in military and political control of vast populations of nonbelievers within only a generation after its emergence. It was therefore necessary to develop policy regarding them. The details vary, and the process of creating any kind of official policy was a long one. Moreover, the laws or policies that were developed were often ignored by rulers or were enacted only when it suited them. Once established, however, they were 'on the books', meaning that they represented an authoritative articulation of expected relations with religious minorities, including the Jews.

It should be stated clearly that the Qur'an nowhere calls for the destruction of the Jews. The policies of relationship between Muslims and Jews are based upon and authorized by Qur'an 9: 29:

Fight those who do not believe in God or in the Last Day and do not make forbidden what God and His messenger have made forbidden, and do not practise the religion of truth, among those who have been given the Book, until they pay the *jizya* off hand (*'an yad*^{in}), being humbled/humiliated (*wahum sāghirīn*).

The meaning and significance of the words marked by italics in the qur'anic context are unclear and have been discussed by both traditional Muslim and modern western scholars for generations. Whatever its original intent, its canonical interpretation teaches that the Peoples of the Book (originally Jews and Christians, but also extended to include Zoroastrians and sometimes others) were to be fought until they capitulated and recognized the political and religious domination of Islam. This recognition was confirmed formally by a special poll tax and by a series of sumptuary laws that legally established inferior status for Peoples of the Book in Islamic society. Once these corporate religious communities acknowledged their secondary status by paying the tax and accepting certain social restrictions, they were protected by the state, which guaranteed their lives, their property, and the right to worship as they chose (with some limits, such as restrictions on public religious processions and ceremonies). This was the rule of the *dhimma* or 'protection', and the Peoples of the Book (*ahl al-kitāb*) were therefore also *dhimmi* peoples (*ahl al-dhimma*), protégés of the Islamic community.

The pact of ʿUmar

Societal restrictions that define the inferior status of Peoples of the Book were formulated from a letter purportedly sent by Christians to the second caliph, ʿUmar b. al-Khattab, which established the terms of surrender to the conquering Muslim armies. These restrictions include a promise not to build new places of worship or other religious establishments, hold public religious ceremonies, proselytize, or prevent people from converting to Islam. They volunteered to distinguish themselves in dress so as not to be confused with Muslims and always to defer to Muslims. They would not bear weapons of any kind, take slaves designated for Muslims, or build homes higher than those of Muslims.

This document is known as the Pact of ʿUmar, and it defined relations between Jews and Muslims in the pre-modern Muslim world. Peoples of the Book were barred from holding positions of influence in government and society, but this was sometimes observed in the breach when Jews such as Maimonides became personal physicians of governors. The most famous example is Shmuel Hanagid, who was not only vizier of the Muslim king of Granada, but also commander of his armies. He successfully broke the most sacred rules of the dhimma by commanding such power, but he also brought his kingdom great fame and influence. His son Yosef, however, fell victim to a revolt and massacre in 1066, allegedly caused by what was perceived as Yosef's pride and ambition in high office, which were completely at odds with the rules of the dhimma.

Both the interpretation and implementation of the sumptuary laws were thus flexible. Restrictions tended to be relaxed when Jews had valuable skills that were perceived as important to the governing power, especially from the tenth to twelfth centuries in such areas as Muslim Spain, Iraq, Egypt, and Ifriqiya (roughly today's Tunisia), and in the Ottoman Empire during the sixteenth century. These were 'golden ages' for Jews and their Muslim host countries. When times were economically good the rules of the dhimma tended to be implemented with less zeal, but when times were bad the situation of the Jews and other dhimmi peoples tended to decline.

When the Islamic Middle East entered its long period of decline, the position of Jews deteriorated along with it. Although the sixteenth century was good to the Jews under the firm and forward-looking policies of the Ottoman Empire, the seventeenth to nineteenth centuries became oppressive, not only for the Jews but for most of the inhabitants of the Middle East. The ruling Turkish minority tended to treat average Arab Muslims almost as disdainfully as it did the dhimmis, and as its control of the provinces waned the various religious communities tended to act out their antipathy and antagonism toward one another. The sumptuary laws that identified and discriminated against Jews and Christians were enforced more and more rigorously, and the dhimmis suffered as a result.

The native economies stagnated as the Middle East entered the modern era and became increasingly dominated by Europeans. As European powers encroached increasingly on parts of the Middle East, the influence of foreign powers and ideas became a critical factor in the evolving position of Jews and other religious minorities in the Islamic world.

Jewish views of Muslims

Jewish attitudes toward Muslims were much less public than Muslims' attitudes toward Jews in the pre-modern period. As a result of their dhimmi status, Jews were subject to punishment for any negative public statement or reflection on Islam or Muslims. We can, nevertheless, glean some sentiments, sometimes only hinted at, from the large corpus of Jewish writings from Muslim lands.

Muslims were usually designated as Ishmaelites in Jewish letters, because of the view that the Arabs originated from Ishmael, son of Abraham; Muslims acknowledged this genealogy in such authoritative sources as the official biography of Muhammad. Jews, therefore, tended to express their negative views through the code of commentary on the biblical Ishmael.

The Arab conquests put an end to Byzantine and Persian dominion over most Jews, and some Jewish texts portray these conquests in apocalyptic terms, suggesting that at least part of the Jewish world considered the quick and unprecedented scope of victory to herald the coming of the Messiah. A late midrash falsely attributed to the mystic Shim'on bar Yohai includes the following:

When he saw the kingdom of Ishmael that was coming, he began to say: 'Was it not enough, what the wicked kingdom of Edom did to us, but we must have the kingdom of Ishmael too?' At once, Metatron, the prince of the [divine] countenance, answered and said, 'Do not fear, son of man, for the Holy One only brings the kingdom of Ishmael in order to save you from this wickedness. He raises up over them a prophet according to his will and will conquer the land for them and they will come and restore it in greatness, and there will be great terror between them and the sons of Esau . . . when he, the rider on the camel, goes forth the kingdom will arise through the rider on an ass . . .'[2]

As Islam became entrenched as a religion of empire, it became clear that the messiah was not among the Arab armies. Secondary status, social restrictions, disrespect, and occasional violence laid bare the truth of Jewish status under the new Muslim rulers. As noted above, however, Muslim interpretation and implementation of the sumptuary laws was flexible, so communities at various times and in various parts of the Muslim world experienced their rulers differently. Abraham Ibn Daud, who lived in tolerant eleventh-century Spain, referred to Muslims positively in his *Book of Tradition*. He remarks that the caliphs honoured both the Babylonian Jewish Exilarch and the head of the academy, and even noted, when mentioning the massacre of the Jewish community of Granada, that it was provoked by the inappropriate behaviour of the Jewish leader, Yosef son of Shmuel HaNagid, according to the laws of the dhimma.[3]

Maimonides, on the other hand, suffered exile from Spain during a period of fundamentalist Islamic revival, but nevertheless reached the pinnacle of position and status as personal physician to the sultan of Egypt. In his now-famous letter to the Jewish community of Yemen, which was suffering under an intolerant and abusive regime, he describes the Jewish predicament in the following way: '. . . on account of the vast number of our sins, God has hurled us in the midst of this people, the Arabs, who have persecuted us severely, and passed baneful and discriminatory legislation against us. . . . Never did a nation molest, degrade, debase and hate us as much as they.'[4]

Both Ibn Daud and Maimonides wrote with specific agendas, so their sentiments need to be read with caution. Taken together, they portray the ambivalence of Jews toward their Muslim overlords throughout the Islamic world before the arrival of modernity. Life without non-Jewish masters would clearly have been preferred, but such a life seemed inconceivable prior to the coming of the messiah.

Muslims' view of Jews in the modern world

In the nineteenth century, when Europe was in expansion and the Middle East was weak, many Middle Eastern Jews (and even more so Christians) began to extricate their identity from the local cultures. European consular pressure on the Ottoman sultan forced a level of civil emancipation for Christians, and this emancipation was applied also to the Jews, who were also People of the Book. Christian missionary schools created an educated class of Arab Christians who, under the protection of European consuls, began to enter social and economic arenas that had been forbidden for centuries. The French-Jewish Alliance Israélite Universelle, and to a lesser extent British-, Austrian-, and German-Jewish organizations founded schools for Jews that accomplished parallel results. This movement among European Jews and Christians advanced the position of some of the dhimmis in their local situation, but it also tended to Europeanize them (though in some rural areas these European influences did not penetrate at all). Their legal and economic position improved, but these changes became a mixed blessing, especially for Jews living in more provincial areas. Privileging Jews violated the rules of the dhimma, and thus exposed them, when unprotected by the influence of foreign powers, to the hostility of the Muslim majority. With deterioration of local government control, law and order tended to break down and all those unprotected tended to become victims.

The emergence of Zionism and the Palestine question further added to the Muslim 'othering' of the Jews. From the Jewish perspective, the issue of a Jewish national home in Palestine was mostly one of modern nationalism and politics. The Palestinian Arab perspective was similar, in that it was primarily an issue of land and hegemony, with religion a minor issue. From the Islamic perspective, however, the issue was much larger, and the separation between religion and nationalism has always been fuzzy in the modern Middle East. The Zionists disregarded their secondary status entirely and even built and managed their own independent economy. Zionism thus represented a case of dhimmis attempting to break out of their divinely ordained status as protected but inferior by establishing an independent Jewish nation-state in the heartland of the Islamic Middle East.

This was unacceptable on its own terms, but its close association with European expansion and colonization made it all the more threatening. The Zionists were overwhelmingly European, and their views of Arabs reflected prevailing European attitudes and expectations. Whatever Zionism was to the Jews and to its British Christian supporters, it represented a reversal of the divine order to religious Muslims, and was regarded increasingly as contrary to the way of God by Islamists, those Muslims who were seeking a way out of the decline of the Islamic world through greater religious devotion.

Islamic antipathy to Zionism was apparent from the beginning, but because of the strong Christian and secular components in Arab political movements it was often underplayed. It always remained present under the surface, however, and the large compendium of anti-Jewish material in the Qur'an and the tradition made for a constant reminder of the negative attributes of 'the Jews'.

Today, therefore, the major subtext for the Islamic view of Jews is the Israel–Palestine conflict, with its own religious subtext of dhimmitude: Jews are expected to submit to Islamic domination. They rejected this role when they created the Jewish State of Israel against the vociferous protests of the Islamic world. Some Muslims have attempted to draw a distinction between those Jews who live in and support the State of Israel—the 'Zionists'—and those who do not. Such subtlety, however, seems to be lost on most Muslims.

The Egyptian Sayyid Qutb, for example, who is one of the most important ideologues of current Islamist groups, portrays the Jews in his work *Our Struggle With the Jews*, written in the early 1950s, as the ultimate source of adversity that has continuously beset Islam. He and others after him have used this antagonistic image of the Jews as a vehicle for promoting Islamic activism and reform.[5]

Despite such disturbing portrayals, Muslims' views of Jews are both complex and fluid. There is no single authoritative body or institution, such as the papacy, in the Islamic world that can speak in the name of Islam (or more precisely, in the name of a significant, unified body of Muslims). The decentralized, fragmented nature of religious organization and authority in Islam has militated against any kind of unity regarding most religious issues that does not rely simply on inertia. But there has been inertia in reference to Jews, and by the beginning of the twenty-first century that inertia has moved Islam toward an increasingly public anti-Jewish antipathy.

Modern Jewish attitudes toward Muslims

Zionists viewed the natives in Palestine as Arabs rather than Muslims, partly because the non-Jewish Arab population of Palestine included Christians, and partly because they preferred to think in terms of national rather than religious categories. In any case, they regarded them as rather primitive. In fact, the European Jews also considered their Arab-Jewish brethren as rather primitive. Although intended to be hyperbolic, Ahad Ha'Am's observation reflects the general tenor of the European Jewish view of Arabs: 'Outside Palestine, we are accustomed to believing that Arabs are all wild beasts of the desert, a people akin to jackasses who do not understand what is going on around them.' Inside Palestine, where Jews met Arabs daily, their views of Arabs were more realistic, though the Arab population was considered by most to be an impediment to the development of a Jewish state.

Early on, and before the violent Arab actions directed against the Zionist project beginning in 1920–1, antipathy towards Arabs did not approach the level directed by many Eastern European Jews toward their own countries of origin. The continuing pogroms and violence against Jews, despite promises of emancipation, prompted many to look toward the Holy Land, but the dream of a better life under the Muslims was transformed to a dream of a self-governing Jewish nation-state. Jewish power and numbers increased in Palestine, and Muslim antipathy increased in response.

Jewish pioneers discovered that the Arabs were not the simple and friendly Orientals depicted in nineteenth-century European Romantic art and literature. Many were quite willing to fight and kill those whom they considered to be threatening their social and economic position. This caused Jews to reconsider their view of Muslims. The war between Jews and Arabs over the land of Israel/Palestine has continued, both hot and cold, from 1921 to the present, and it has become the primary determiner of both Jews' and Muslims' view of the other. It should not be surprising that the overwhelming view of the other tends to be negative in both the Jewish and Muslim communities. The 'other' tends to represent the enemy. Despite important exceptions to the rule on both sides, it has been largely codified within the religious and social systems of both communities and perpetuated in the general culture.

Notwithstanding this sentiment, Jews have been deeply interested in Islam and in the literary, historical, and theological relationships between Jews and Muslims. Jews have played a disproportionate role in the scientific study of Islam from the beginning of modern western scholarship on religion. Rabbi Abraham Geiger (1810–74) is rightly considered to have ushered in the dawn of historical research on Islam; the work of Ignaz Goldziher (1850–1921) continues to be read more than a century after its publication; and the dean of this discipline in our own day is Bernard Lewis. In Jewish theology, Franz Rosenzweig compares Islam favourably to Christianity in his *Star of Redemption*. 'In a certain sense, Islam demanded and practised "tolerance" long before the concept was discovered by Christian Europe.'[6]

Jewish–Muslim relations today

At the time of writing, the issue of Jewish–Muslim relations has become of increasing concern for Jews throughout the world. Especially since the destruction of the American World Trade Center towers in 2001, Jewish fear of Islamic antisemitism has placed Jewish–Muslim relations on a nearly equal status with Jewish–Christian relations.

Antisemitism as known in Europe is not indigenous to the Islamic world. While Christian theologies tend to be predicated on the irrelevance of Judaism or active antagonism to it, Islamic theologies establish their position relative to two established monotheistic systems rather than one, and critique them less categorically. It is certainly true that tensions and hierarchies, polemics and prejudice, legal discrimination and violence directed specifically against Jews are indeed a part of the Islamic world, and have been since the emergence of Islam. But the particular pathology of European antisemitism, with its blood libels and virulent hatred, was imported to the Middle East by Christians. Increasing incrementally in response to the watershed events of 1948, 1967, the second or Al-Aqsa Intifada of the 1990s, and the American invasions of Afghanistan and Iraq in 2002–3, Muslim rage against Israel, the United States and the West has been expressed through increased dehumanization and demonizing of Jews in general. The spurious *Protocols of the Elders of Zion*, available in Arabic translation since before 1950, has been cited increasingly in newspaper editorials and strongly referenced in popular state-sponsored television series in Egypt and Syria–Lebanon.

The focus about which Jewish–Muslim tensions are concentrated continues to be the Jewish state. That Israeli and Palestinian leaders shook hands under the protective canopy of the United States, only to have relations reach their lowest historical level in the second or Al-Aqsa Intifada, had repercussions that have rocked relations between Jews and other religious and ethnic groups as well. But the State of Israel is the surface problem, and not the only cause of the pathology. The grounds for increased hostility between Jews and Muslims are far more complex, and they reflect the endemic tensions associated with what is now commonly called the postmodern era: local social and economic disruptions in an increasingly global economy; growing economic gaps between nations and populations; lack of social and economic integration of Arab and Muslim populations in Western Europe; increasing industrial dependence on oil and consequent western attempts to prop up dictatorial regimes in the Muslim world; the inability of Middle Eastern countries to bring economic and political stability to their own populations; and the self-perceived shame associated with the failure of Middle Eastern nations to compete with the West economically, technologically, politically, militarily, and socially. All these factors have increased the level of tensions between Jews and Muslims at the outset of the twenty-first century, but they reflect the tensions that affect global populations as well.

This chapter is being written during one of the most volatile periods of Jewish–Muslim relations. Because there are no authoritative bodies that represent a plurality of either Jews or Muslims, relations are steered as much by the shapers of public opinion as by authoritative religious representatives. Public expressions of antipathy are made by unauthoritative and unrepresentative 'spokespersons', who are heavily influenced by the violence and politics of the Middle East (including petty internal politics) and, in turn, exert a strong influence on co-religionists on the ground. On the other hand, many dozens, and perhaps hundreds, of Muslim–Jewish dialogue groups and other joint Jewish–Muslim initiatives have quietly been formed and are functioning in Israel, the United States, and Europe. The Maimonides Foundation in London is one better-known and public group. Another is the Institute for the Study and Enhancement of Muslim–Jewish Interrelations (ISEMJI) in Los Angeles. Dozens of others exist in Israel alone, and more span the boundaries between Israel and the areas across the Green Line dividing pre-1967 Israel and the West Bank. None but a prophet can successfully predict the future of Jewish–Muslim relations, but if history is any lesson, a modus vivendi will slowly emerge that will improve the current situation.

FURTHER READING

Bodansky, Yossef. *Islamic Antisemitism As a Political Instrument* (Houston: Freeman Center for Strategic Studies, 1999). Produced by a Jewish defence organization, this monograph is a good example of how accurate data can be presented in a biased and unbalanced manner with the goal of promoting a narrow and inaccurate picture of reality.

Cohen, Mark. *Under Crescent and Cross* (Princeton: Princeton University Press, 1994). Cohen compares the treatment of Jews in Christian Europe and the Islamic Middle East, to suggest where the Jews fared best and why.

Cohen, Mark, and Abraham Udovitch (eds.). *Jews Among Arabs: Contact and Boundaries* (Princeton: Darwin, 1989). This collection contains articles written by experts in the field of modern Jewish–Muslim history. The individual articles examine Jewish life in Iraq, Tunisia, and Morocco, and chronicle Jewish cultural interaction with and contribution to modern Arab culture.

Firestone, Reuven. *Journeys in Holy Lands: The Evolution of the Abraham–Ishmael Legends in Islamic Exegesis* (Albany: State University of New York Press, 1990). A study of the intertextual relationship between 'Biblical' and 'Qur'anic' narrative literatures through the Abraham stories.

Firestone, Reuven. *Children of Abraham: An Introduction To Judaism For Muslims* (New York: Schocken Books, 2001). An introduction to Judaism that notes the many parallels as well as differences between Judaism and Islam, treating some of the thorny questions that Muslims ask about Judaism.

Goitein, S. D. *Jews and Arabs: Their Contacts Through the Ages* (New York: Schocken Books, 1955). The classic survey of the history of Jewish–Arab relations, tracing the various intellectual and religious contributions of one to the other community.

Hary, Benjamin, John Hayes, and Fred Astren (eds.). *Judaism and Islam: Boundaries, Communication and Interaction: Essays in Honor of William M. Brinner* (Leiden: Brill, 2000). A recent collection of essays hosting some of the best contemporary scholarship on Judaism and Islam, covering history, literatures, Scriptures, law, philosophy and ethics, languages, and sectarian communities.

Kramer, Martin (ed.). *The Jewish Discovery of Islam* (Tel Aviv: Moshe Dayan Center, 1999). Examines the primary Jewish role of scholarship, literature, and exploration in the modern European quest to understand Islam.

Lewis, Bernard. *The Jews of Islam* (Princeton: Princeton University Press, 1984). This has become a classic survey of the intellectual and cultural relations between Muslims and Jews that counters the two stereotypes of the fanatical Muslim jihadist on the one hand, or the utopian Muslim pluralist on the other.

Nettler, Ronald (ed.). *Medieval and Modern Perspectives on Muslim–Jewish Relations* (Oxford: Harwood Academic Publishers, 1995). This collection of essays is a foray into the scholarly literature of Muslim–Jewish relations, treating topics from 'Judaizing' tendencies among some Muslims to the use of Muslim narrative as a commentary on Jewish tradition.

Newby, Gordon. *A History of the Jews of Arabia* (Columbia: University of South Carolina Press, 1988). This brief history examines the history of the Jewish (most likely sectarian) communities of Arabia from the earliest times to the rise of Islam.

Sacher, Howard M. *A History of Israel From the Rise of Zionism To Our Time* (New York: Knopf, 1976). A largely political history.

Stark, Rodney, and William Sims Bainbridge. *A Theory of Religion* (New York: Peter Lang, 1987). Provides a good theoretical foundation for the study of emerging religions.

Stillman, Norman. *The Jews of Arab Lands: A History and Source Book*, and *The Jews of Arab Lands in Modern Times* (Philadelphia: Jewish Publication Society, 1979 and 1991). This is an excellent two-volume sourcebook and commentary that provides a large compendium of translated documents treating the Jews of the Arab Middle East from the earliest sources to the end of the twentieth century.

NOTES

1. See also 16: 43: 'So if you do not know, then ask the people of the Reminder (*ahl al-dhikr*).' The great ninth-century scholar and collector of tradition, al-Tabari, cites the early tradition that God is referring here to *ahlul-tawrah*, the people of the Torah.
2. Adolph Jellinek, *Bet ha-Midrasch*, 3rd edn. (Jerusalem: Wahrmann Books, 1967), sec. 3, pp. 78–9.
3. Gerson D. Cohen, *The Book of Tradition by Abraham Ibn Daud* (London: Routledge & Kegan Paul; Philadelphia: Jewish Publication Society, 1967), pp. 45, 76.

4. Abraham Halkin, 'The Epistle to Yemen', in id. and David Hartman, *Epistles of Maimonides: Crisis and Leadership* (Philadelphia: Jewish Publication Society, 1993), p. 126.
5. Jeffrey Kenney, 'Enemies Near and Far: The Image of the Jews in Islamist Discourse in Egypt', *Religion*, 24 (1990), p. 255.
6. Franz Rozenzweig, *The Star of Redemption*, tr. from the 2nd edn. of 1930 by William W. Hallo (New York: Hold, Rinehart & Winston, 1970), p. 216.

Index

Lightning Source UK Ltd.
Milton Keynes UK
12 June 2010

155425UK00001B/16/P